Windows Version

MICROSOFT® EXCEL

BUSINESS SOURCEBOOK

Windows Version

MICROSOFT® EXCEL

BUSINESS SOURCEBOOK

An Essential Library of More Than 100 Practical Business Applications

Charles W. Kyd

PUBLISHED BY
Microsoft Press
A Division of Microsoft Corporation
16011 NE 36th Way, Box 97017, Redmond, Washington 98073-9717

Library of Congress Cataloging in Publication Data

Kyd, Charles W.
The Microsoft Excel business sourcebook / Charles W. Kyd.
p. cm.
Includes index.
1. Microsoft Excel (Computer program) 2. Business—Data processing.
I. Title.
HF5548.4.M523K95 1988 88-21105
658'.055369—dc19 CIP
ISBN 1-55615-133-0

Printed and bound in the United States of America.

1 2 3 4 5 6 7 8 9 FGFG 3 2 1 0 9 8

Distributed to the book trade in the United States
by Harper & Row.

Distributed to the book trade in Canada by General
Publishing Company, Ltd.

Distributed to the book trade outside the United States
and Canada by Penguin Books Ltd.

Penguin Books Ltd., Harmondsworth, Middlesex, England
Penguin Books Australia Ltd., Ringwood, Victoria, Australia
Penguin Books N.Z. Ltd., 182-190 Wairau Road, Auckland 10, New Zealand

British Cataloging in Publication Data available

This book is dedicated to my parents,

Mr. and Mrs. Charles R. Kyd,

who taught me that anything is possible.

CONTENTS

FIGURES LIST

INTRODUCTION

I wrote this book to meet the need that many business professionals have for a sourcebook of spreadsheet applications. Although we use spreadsheets to solve specific problems—forecasting, cash flow planning, budgeting, financial reporting, and so on—few books offer real help in solving these problems.

Most books about spreadsheets teach readers how to use the spreadsheet programs. They explain how to sort and copy, for example, and how to use the ROUND function. Although these books have their place, they often miss the point. In the crunch of day-to-day business, few people want to become spreadsheet experts; instead, they want to use spreadsheets to meet their immediate business needs.

Of course, some books do explain how to create business spreadsheets. But most of these, unfortunately, contain only 10 or 20 applications. And often, these are the same applications that many other books discuss as well. As a consequence, serious business professionals look in vain for books that can help with other common reporting and analytical needs.

How This Book Is Different

This book is different in several ways. In the first place, it contains 5 to 10 times more business applications than do other such books. As the list on page ix shows, this book contains more than 150 figures. These represent fewer than 150 complete applications, however, because many applications require more than one figure.

Second, each figure contains not only a spreadsheet, but the key information you need to create it. The figures include boxes that list and explain all range names and the key formats, column widths, row heights, and formulas used in the spreadsheets. With the help of these information boxes, in fact, you could probably create most of the spreadsheets without ever reading the text.

Third, the text takes a "real-world" approach to business applications. As an MBA with more than 10 years of experience as a chief financial officer and several years as a writer, speaker, and consultant, I know the concerns of business professionals. In the text, therefore, I use realistic examples and discuss both the practical and theoretical aspects of each spreadsheet application.

And finally, this book directly addresses business needs, not some arbitrary level of beginning or advanced spreadsheet knowledge. If you're new to Microsoft Excel, you'll learn much about this powerful program as you build the applications. To help you learn, Appendix B presents a reference guide to common Microsoft Excel operations. And if you're a power user, I know this book will reveal new and exciting features of Microsoft Excel.

How to Use This Book

Before you start your first application, thumb through the appendixes to learn the resources they provide. Although you'll find all of these appendixes useful, you'll probably want to insert a bookmark at the beginning of Appendix B, A Summary of Common Microsoft Excel Operations. This guide provides brief instructions and shortcuts as well as a column of page numbers directing you to more detailed information in the *Microsoft Excel Reference Guide.*

As you read through Appendix B, notice that I've used a slightly different convention for naming keystroke combinations than does the *Microsoft Excel Reference Guide.* For example, to move your pointer to the bottom-right cell of your spreadsheet, you hold down the control key and press End. The *Microsoft Excel Reference Guide* specifies this keystroke combination as CONTROL + END. In this book, however, I specify the combination as *Ctrl-End,* which seems to conform more with general usage. Similarly, I abbreviate the Insert key as *Ins,* as it appears on many keyboards.

If you're looking for a specific business application, first check the Figures List on page ix or the Index to see if it's listed. You'll find instructions in the text and information boxes that will help you adapt it to your own requirements if need be.

If you don't find the spreadsheet you want, look for a related application that you can adapt. Suppose, for example, that you want to analyze your accounts payable file, summarizing how quickly you've paid each vendor. Although this book doesn't contain such a report, it *does* contain a report of similar information from an accounts receivable file. Once you create the accounts receivable report, you can quickly apply similar methods to your accounts payable requirements.

If you *still* can't find the solution you need, write to me. I'm planning additional reference books and will consider all requests. With your letter, please include a sample of the report you need and a description of the data available to produce the report. Send your letter to Charles W. Kyd, President, CashMaster Business Systems, 12345 Lake City Way, Suite 220, Seattle, WA 98125.

If you're new to Microsoft Excel, take the time to create the spreadsheets described in Chapter 1 before you start those in other chapters. Although you'll find these spreadsheets easy to create, you'll learn several powerful techniques that you'll use frequently throughout the book.

The most important step to take after you've created a spreadsheet and entered your own data is to check your work. And don't simply check that all the formulas are correct—simple mistakes often seem to be invisible. After you've entered your own data, check your results with a calculator. Also, rely on what you know about your business to find hidden errors. To do so, find all results that look unreasonable, surprising, or even somewhat interesting—and double-check them. After many years of finding and correcting hidden errors, I've found that interesting results are often wrong results.

Additional Hardware Requirements

I assume that your computer hardware already satisfies the minimum requirements to run Microsoft Excel. However, your system should exceed the minimum requirements in certain ways.

Because you'll have approximately 150 KB of conventional memory available after loading Microsoft Excel, you won't need expanded memory to create most of the spreadsheets discussed in this book. However, as you add data to your spreadsheets, many will quickly reach the limit of conventional memory. I therefore recommend that your computer contain at least 1 MB of expanded memory. And while it's possible to use Microsoft Excel without a mouse, I recommend that you use this device as well. You'll find that using a mouse and a keyboard for moving around your spreadsheet is more convenient than using either device by itself.

Adjusting for System Differences

The resolution of screens and printers varies among manufacturers. Therefore, you might experience differences between the way your system displays or prints row heights and column widths and the way this book describes them. If so, you will need to adjust the given dimensions slightly.

If row heights are displayed differently, the differences will probably appear in two ways. First, the row heights provided in the row-height boxes might vary slightly from the heights that your display requires. Where my system uses a row height of 13 for the Helv 10-point font and 16 for the Helv 12-point font, your system might use heights of 12 and 15 or 15 and 18. Each graphics card generates unique variations.

The border commands might also create differences in the way row heights appear. For example, if I use the Format Borders command to outline a cell and then use the Format Row Height command to reduce its row height to 1 point, my computer system displays and prints a black bar in the cell. It does so because at a height of 1 point the two borders touch to create a thick border. Your system, however, might require a row height of, say, 1.4 points to achieve the same effect.

Differences in the display of column widths, if they occur, will probably appear in the display of large numbers or dates in narrow columns. When you enter a large number or date and set a column width, both as specified in this book, your spreadsheet might display only a series of number signs (####). This is the overflow symbol, which tells you that the number you've entered is too large for the width of your column. If you widen the column slightly, your spreadsheet will display the number correctly.

If differences occur in the display of either row heights or column widths, you might also have trouble getting your large spreadsheets to print on a single page. If you experience this problem, first issue the File Page Setup command and narrow the margins to provide more space for your copy. If the spreadsheet still won't print on one page after you have provided for the smallest margins possible, reduce the dimensions of the rows or columns using the Format Row Height or Format Column Width commands.

Using Microsoft Excel with This Book

The following tips will help you to use Microsoft Excel more effectively with this book:

- Using a mouse. When I first started to use Microsoft Excel, I used the mouse exclusively to choose commands from the menus. But after I became familiar with the commands, I learned that it's much faster to use the shortcut keys for frequently used commands. In fact, if you press the shortcut keys quickly enough, some menus never appear on your display at all when the command executes. (If you quickly press /FP Enter, which issues the File Print command, you'll see what I mean.) So now, for many commands, I use the shortcuts described in Appendix B. To assign Font 2, for example, I simply press Ctrl-2.

  Here's a trick you might try with your mouse: Because my numeric keypad is on the right side of my keyboard, I operate the mouse with my left hand, even though I'm right-handed. In this way, I can enter data with the keypad while positioning the data with my mouse. (My left hand stopped feeling clumsy about a week after I started using this procedure.) Now, when I'm in a hurry, both hands seem to move at once.

- Using full menus. Microsoft Excel provides two levels of menu choices: full menus and short menus. The short menus option limits your choices to those you'll probably use most often; the full menus option displays your full range of choices. I wrote this book using full menus throughout and made no special mention of menu choices that are available only in full menus. To use full menus, choose Options Full Menus. After you do so, Microsoft Excel records this selection and provides full menus whenever you boot the program.

- Entering arrays. Most figures in this book include a list of the key formulas used in the spreadsheet. Whenever I describe one of these as an array formula, be sure to enter it as an array by holding down Ctrl-Shift before pressing Enter. If you enter an array formula by merely pressing Enter, it usually returns the error value #VALUE!.

  Occasionally, however, a formula can return one answer when it's entered as a normal formula and another when it's entered as an array. For example, suppose you define the range A as the array constant ={1;2}. Entered as a normal formula, =SUM(2*A) returns 2 (2 times 1). But entered as an array, the formula returns 6 (2 times 1 plus 2 times 2). (Pages 14–16 of the *Microsoft Excel Reference Guide* explain array constants.)

- Understanding error messages. Whenever Microsoft Excel displays a dialog box with an error message, pressing the F1 (Help) key will display an explanation of the error. The explanations are rather brief at times, but they provide more information than do the bare dialog boxes.

- Saving files. Save your files often. If the electricity fails or your spreadsheet crashes, you'll be glad to have a recent copy saved on disk.

- Using file workspace. Many applications in this book consist of several spreadsheets that are open at one time. Save all open files as a workspace by using the File Save Workspace command. Then when you open a workspace file, which has the extension .XLW, it opens each individual file automatically.

  When you open a workspace, you can save many minutes of needless recalculation if you instruct Microsoft Excel to wait until all files are opened before it recalculates any of them. To do so, take two steps. First, before you open the workspace, issue the Options Calculation Manual command to turn off automatic calculation. If you don't take this step, the program loads a file, recalculates, loads another, recalculates, and so on. Second, after you choose File Open and open a workspace file, if Microsoft Excel finds a formula linked to a file that hasn't been opened yet, it asks if you want to update the references to unopened files. Answer "No." Then, after Microsoft Excel opens all files in the workspace, press the F9 (Calculate All) key to recalculate all open documents.

- Setting manual calculation. Microsoft Excel uses nifty programming devices to speed up automatic calculation. Even so, as you add formulas and data, your spreadsheet will grow more and more sluggish in the automatic calculation mode. Therefore, as soon as this slow response gets in your way, choose Options Calculations Manual. Doing so immediately improves the program's response but does cause two minor inconveniences. First, you must remember to press the F9 (Calculate All) key before you use a spreadsheet. Second, the program automatically recalculates all open documents when you save a file. This can become a problem with large spreadsheets because a full recalculation could take several minutes. In general, however, I find this technique worthwhile, despite its disadvantages.

Save Time with Disks

You might prefer to use these applications without taking the time to create each spreadsheet yourself. I therefore offer disks that contain every spreadsheet, macro, and graph explained in this book. When you order the disks, you'll also receive the most current information available about the applications. You'll find an order form for the disks on the last page of the book.

1

Basic Financial Statements

One reason spreadsheets have become so popular is that new users don't have to know much about them to use them successfully. The spreadsheets in this chapter, for example, use formulas that do no more than add, subtract, multiply, and divide. Yet these spreadsheets include the financial reports that businesses prepare most frequently.

A SIMPLE INCOME STATEMENT

Figure 1-1 on page 14 shows a simple income statement that takes only minutes to prepare by using Microsoft Excel but illustrates techniques you'll use anytime you create a spreadsheet, whatever its level of sophistication.

Formatting the Spreadsheet

When I create a spreadsheet, I generally start by turning off the gridlines. Gridlines tend to make underlines difficult to see, and most people who receive financial reports prefer crisp, uncluttered documents—documents without gridlines. I therefore remove them to show, as I build the spreadsheet, what the final report will look like. To delete the gridlines, choose the Options Display command and turn off the Gridlines option.

Also, when I format a spreadsheet, I seldom use dollar signs in the number format. Displaying dollar signs creates two problems. First, they clutter the spreadsheet, making it difficult to read. Second, they take up space I often need when I try to compress the width of a spreadsheet to fit the width of my computer paper. To format without dollar signs, create a custom format. First choose the Format Number command and select a format *with* dollar signs, as shown in the following dialog box:

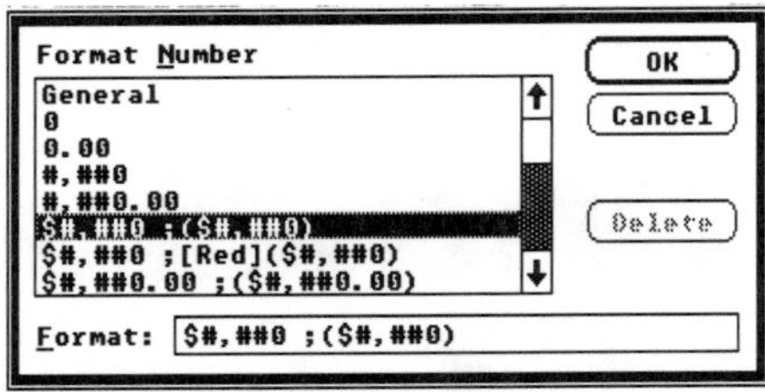

To complete the custom number format, simply edit the format displayed in the Format box by deleting the dollar signs. The format box in Figure 1-1 shows the resulting custom format for the range G7:H23.

One aspect of formatting that I seldom worry about is the column width. If a column is too narrow to contain my data, I widen it. If my spreadsheet grows too wide to print, I narrow a column. So, the rule on column widths is to use whatever works.

Entering Titles and Labels

When I began Figure 1-1, I entered the titles in cells F3 through F5 and then centered them in the column by highlighting this range, choosing the Format Alignment command, and selecting the Center option. Later, when I saw that column E had become the approximate center of the spreadsheet, I used the Edit Cut and Edit Paste commands to move the titles to cells E3 through E5, as shown in the spreadsheet. In other words, when you begin your spreadsheet, you don't have to know where all the data goes; simply get it down and then move it later.

When you label rows of data in a financial statement, you often want to indent the labels, as shown in the spreadsheet. One way to do so is to enter all labels in column A but to enter several spaces before each label you want to indent. The trouble with this approach, however, is that entering these labels is a slow process and changing them is difficult. I used a different approach for the spreadsheet in Figure 1-1.

Reduce the width of column A to a few characters, as shown in the spreadsheet, and then enter all labels in columns A or B as shown. This approach provides total flexibility. To change the width of the indention, change the width of column A. To eliminate an indention or to create an additional one, simply cut and paste labels in column B to columns A or C, depending on what you want to achieve.

Entering Data, Underlines, and Formulas

I often create financial statements in spreadsheets, even though my computerized accounting system produces perfectly accurate financial statements. I do this because the accounting package often generates financial statements that are more or less detailed than I need for a particular purpose.

When I create a spreadsheet version of an existing financial statement, however, I use all the formulas I can within the spreadsheet. I always use a SUM formula in cell H12, for example, even though I may already know the amount of total revenues. (The formula box for Figure 1-1 shows all three formulas used within this spreadsheet.)

I use these formulas for two reasons. First, they catch errors. Often, when I copy an income statement into a spreadsheet, I make data-entry errors that I can catch easily when net income according to the spreadsheet differs from net income according to my original data. Second, I often use an old spreadsheet as a template for a current statement. Having all the formulas in place reduces the time it takes to create these updated statements.

But when you enter the formulas used in column H, you touch on an issue that is key to having a flexible, error-free spreadsheet: What range should the SUM formula in cell H12 reference?

This may seem like an inconsequential question, but it's not. Several years ago a contractor made the wrong decision in a similar formula in a Lotus spreadsheet. When the dust finally settled, the contractor was several hundred thousand dollars poorer.

According to news reports at the time, the contractor used a Lotus 1-2-3 spreadsheet to calculate costs for a major bid. To add these costs, he entered a formula in his spreadsheet similar to =SUM(H8:H10) in the spreadsheet in Figure 1-1. That is, his SUM range extended from the first number to the last number in the column he was adding.

Everything went well until just before the bid was due, when the contractor realized that he had excluded a major cost from the spreadsheet. He inserted a row to contain the item, recalculated the spreadsheet, and then submitted his bid. Unfortunately, he inserted the new data at the bottom of his existing data (for example, below row 10 in Figure 1-1). Although his modified display *looked* as if the new data were added properly, it wasn't. The SUM range still referenced the original, smaller range (for example, the range H8:H10).

When the contractor realized that he'd been awarded a money-losing contract because of his miscalculation, he sued Lotus for damages. The court ruled, however, that Lotus wasn't responsible for poor design of an individual spreadsheet.

The spreadsheet in Figure 1-1 uses two techniques to reduce the chance that you'll have the contractor's problem. Cells H11 and H12 take the most flexible approach. Cell

H11 contains a bottom border created by using the Format Border command and selecting the Bottom option. This cell is 1 point high, a height assigned by using the Format Row Height command and entering *1*. The formula in cell H12 is =SUM(H7:H11); it begins in cell H11 and ends in the blank cell in row 7. Therefore, if you insert data at the top of the existing data (above row 8) or at the bottom (below row 10), you still insert data within the SUM range.

I took a slightly different approach with cells G19 and H20. The formula in cell H20 is =SUM(G14:G19). Because cell G19 contains data, using this formula would appear to be risky. Notice, however, that cell G19 also contains the bottom border. If you insert a row below row 19, therefore, the bottom border still appears in row 19. This border warns you, in other words, that you're inserting data below the SUM range.

Which method of underlining should you use? You'll probably use both. The first method is more flexible but involves several extra steps. The second method is quick and usually safe.

To complete the spreadsheet, calculate net income in cell H22. To draw the double border beneath that cell, move to cell H23; choose the Format Border command and select the Top and Bottom options; then reduce the row height to two points by choosing the Format Row Height command and entering *2*.

SINGLE-PERIOD FINANCIAL STATEMENTS

By the time you're ready to prepare an income statement and balance sheet, the tough accounting work is finished. Technically, therefore, creating these statements is easy. And yet preparing them often takes much longer than you might expect. This is because there are many ways to present the same information, and we often want to try them all.

The following sections present several financial statement formats that may help you select and create a format that fits your purposes.

A Single-Period Income Statement

Figure 1-2 on page 16 shows a single-period income-statement format that many CPAs use for small-business clients. It presents the financial performance in one report that would take several additional schedules to display for larger clients.

The biggest challenge to creating this spreadsheet is to cram all the information onto one sheet of paper while making the spreadsheet readable. This may seem like an unsophisticated concern, but it's real when you actually sit down to do the work.

Cell L10 illustrates one way to save space. If space were not a problem, the subtotal in this cell would be displayed at least one row below the data being totaled. But here,

I've saved space by putting the subtotal in the same row as the last row being totaled. Admittedly, this makes the report slightly more difficult to read, but only slightly.

If space were not a problem, you would probably skip a row in several places in this document. For example, the balance for Net Income in cell L48 generally would be highlighted by a row of blank cells above and below this figure. But because I was short of space, I increased the row height slightly to make this figure more readable.

Formatting this spreadsheet is easy. The format box shows that only three ranges have been changed from their default format settings.

A Single-Period Balance Sheet

Figure 1-3 on page 18 shows a traditional single-period balance sheet. Although it's shown for a different company than the one in Figure 1-2, the formats of both statements are similar. Both statements use several columns to calculate and display subtotals. Both indent the descriptions along the left border by entering the descriptions in columns A, B, and C. Both statements use columns I and K to adjust the space between the columns of numbers.

As Figure 1-3's format box shows, I used column F to contain all centered labels. But when I printed the spreadsheet to my screen by using the Preview option in the File Print dialog box, these labels weren't quite centered on the page. To correct this problem, therefore, I slightly widened column E and narrowed column G as shown.

A QUARTERLY REPORT

Figure 1-4 on page 20 shows a Microsoft Excel version of an actual quarterly report of the INTERMEC Corporation of Lynnwood, Washington. Unlike the previous spreadsheets, this one depends heavily on Microsoft Excel's formatting features.

To begin this spreadsheet, turn off the gridlines and set the width of column C to 3 points, F to 12 points, G to 11 points, H to 6 points, I to 10 points, and J to 1.86 points. The remaining columns use the standard width of 8.43 points.

The spreadsheet uses the four fonts illustrated by the following dialog box:

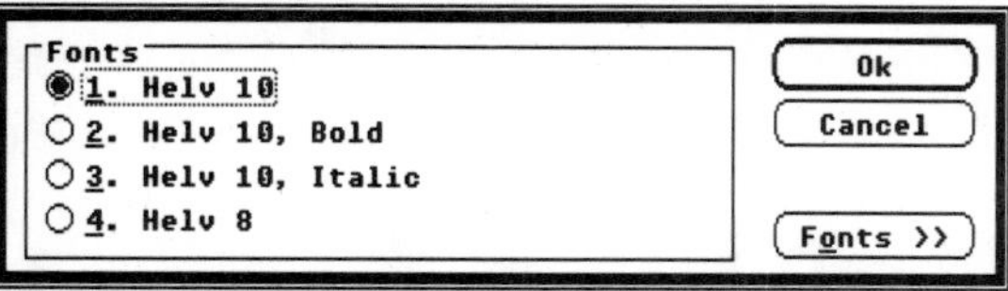

The fonts shown as numbers 1 and 2 are Microsoft Excel's default fonts for these selections. To set the other fonts, choose Format Font and then select the options shown.

Enter the label shown in cell A3 and then assign it 12-point Helv boldface by choosing Format Font and selecting font 3. Increase the height of row 3 to 22 points by choosing Format Row Height and entering *22*.

To create the horizontal bar shown below row 3, first highlight the range A4 through I7. Assign top and bottom borders to this range by choosing Format Border and selecting Top and Bottom. Then set the row height of this range to 1 point by choosing Format Row Height and entering *1*. (This procedure might require additional adjustment on certain hardware combinations to achieve the results shown, such as selecting a fractionally larger row height.)

Enter the labels shown in cells A8 and A9. Reduce the height of row 10 to 7 points. Assign bottom borders to rows 11, 13, and 15. Assign 10-point Helv boldface to cells A11 and A12 by highlighting this range, choosing Format Font, and selecting font 2. Similarly, assign the appropriate fonts as you enter the labels down the remainder of the figure. The format box for Figure 1-4 lists all formatting.

As you enter the remaining labels in this spreadsheet, create the borders or horizontal bars as shown. The thickness of each bar is determined by the number of rows used to create it. Use the row numbers at the left of the spreadsheet to guide you in determining the number of rows to use.

Because Microsoft Excel assigns one font per cell entry, you must create the label in row 23 in two separate cells. Cell A23 contains the boldface part of the label. Cell D23 contains the remainder of the label.

Enter the values shown in columns G and I, using the formulas in the formula box for Figure 1-4. Enter the dollar signs shown for column F. Right-align this column by highlighting the range F12 through F56, choosing the Format Alignment command, and selecting Right. Then copy this range to cell H12. Similarly, center the contents of the ranges G11 through I11 and G39 through I39. Then assign 10-point Helv boldface to the range F11 through G56.

COMPARATIVE FINANCIAL STATEMENTS

When most of us read financial statements, we want to know how current performance compares with previous performance. These comparisons can reveal problems and opportunities that could otherwise be missed.

A Comparative Income Statement

Figure 1-5 on page 23 shows a comparative income statement for Ben's Bargain Basement. Its format is rather unusual because most comparative financial statements exclude the last two columns of data, ending with a column similar to I. But I generally include columns similar to K and L because they help me answer many questions that come up when I read the statement.

For example, comparing cells E27 and H27 would tell Ben that net income has increased a lot. How much? Cell L27 tells him that profits increased 90 percent. But cell L10 shows that revenues increased only 15 percent. Where did all those profits come from? Cell L14 says the cost of products sold increased by only 7 percent, compared with an increase in sales of 15 percent. Because the amount in cell K14 is about half the expected increase in costs, it's reasonable to assume that improved margins have added roughly that same amount to profits. On reflection, Ben might conclude that the improved margins are reasonable. Unit volumes and costs increased by roughly 7 percent, he might conclude, and the remaining sales increase came from increased prices. But if unit volume increased by only 7 percent, why did administrative costs jump by 12 percent? And why did selling expenses fall by 4 percent? Ben had better find out.

The income statement in Figure 1-5 is easy to generate, but creating the various formulas, underlines, and formats can be time-consuming. Here's how to save time and avoid some work:

Assign the number formats shown in the format box for the ranges E9:E27 and F9:F27. To copy these formats into the remaining columns of the spreadsheet, copy the range E9:G27 to the range H9:M9. (If you've already begun to enter formulas and data in your spreadsheet, choose the Edit Paste Special command and select Formats to copy this range.)

Enter the report title in cells G3 through G5 and then center these labels by choosing the Format Alignment command and selecting Center. Reduce the widths of columns A, G, and J as shown and then enter the labels in columns A and B.

When you try to display the year between columns E and F in row 8, you discover that Microsoft Excel doesn't treat this entry as a label. Therefore, as shown in the formula box for Figure 1-5, you must enter a formula in cell E8 that forces the program to treat *1988* as a label. (Not all formulas are shown in the formula box—only key ones; but you should have no difficulty filling in the missing, simple ones.) Then, to complete the heading for columns E and F, choose the Format Border command and select Bottom to add a bottom border to cells E8 and F8.

To enter the heading for columns H and I, copy the range E8:F8 to cell H8 and then edit cell H8 to display *1987*. To enter the heading for columns K and L, enter the label shown in cell K8, preceding it with enough spaces to force it into column L, as shown. Then underline cells K8 and L8.

Enter the data and appropriate formulas in column E. To create column F, enter the formula shown for cell F12 in the formula box for Figure 1-5. Copy cell F12 to the range

F10:F27 and then delete the formulas from areas where they don't belong—from rows 16 and 17, for example. To complete columns E and F, draw the bottom borders where shown by choosing the Format Borders command and selecting Bottom.

To complete columns H and I, copy the range E10:F27 to cell H8. Then change the 1988 data in column H to the 1987 data shown.

To complete columns K and L, enter the formulas shown for cells K10 and L10 in the formula box for Figure 1-5. Copy these two cells to the range K11:K27. Then, as you did for column F, go back and delete the contents of those cells in areas where formulas don't belong—in row 13, for example. Finally, to copy the underlines into these columns, choose Edit Paste Special and select Formats to copy the formats from the range H10:I27 to cell K10.

A Comparative Balance Sheet

Figure 1-6 on page 25 shows a comparative balance sheet that is similar to the comparative income statement. Because it provides so much information on one page, this format is outstanding for internal financial reporting.

Suppose, for example, that the new president of Clandestine Manufacturing reviews her company's balance-sheet performance by using the spreadsheet in Figure 1-6. Cell L46 tells her that retained earnings have increased by 38 percent during the year, an outstanding performance. Although the overall increase in total assets seems reasonable (cell L27), the change in certain assets does not. The increase in inventory is the biggest shock—it nearly doubled. Why? And how could accounts payable fall while inventory doubled? Have Clandestine's vendors put the company on COD? And why did accumulated depreciation grow so much? A clerical mistake?

To create this statement, follow the same approach described for the income statement in Figure 1-5. The formats of these two statements differ in only three ways. First, column D was widened to provide for longer descriptions. Second, the titles were entered in column F, which centers them more closely. Third, the row heights were adjusted in several places to provide double underlines as described for the balance sheet in Figure 1-3. The formula box for Figure 1-6 illustrates the key formulas used in this spreadsheet.

CASH FLOW REPORTS

For most businesses, cash is more important than profits and losses. A profitable company with negative cash flows may not survive. But a money-losing company with positive cash flows can survive for as long as cash is positive. Unfortunately, people can't quite agree on exactly what cash flow is!

One common definition of cash flow is net profit plus depreciation. With one exception, this definition is useless, however. If your company is breaking even, your customers don't pay, your inventory has doubled, and all your vendors have put you on COD, this formula would tell you that your cash flow is positive. The formula is important for only one reason: Many people use it, particularly bankers. If the formula is important to people who are important to you, therefore, the formula should be important to you as well.

Sources and Uses of Cash

A more informative way to look at cash, however, is to look at the sources and uses of cash within a business. Figure 1-7 on page 27 shows such a report, although it is not quite finished. To finish this report, delete columns E through G, which are intermediate columns used to create the sources and uses displayed in columns H and I.

Columns H and I of the report in Figure 1-7 show that Clandestine Manufacturing used $113,547 in cash last year. Its two largest uses were to increase inventories by $58,148 and to reduce accounts payable by $26,073. The company financed these uses in two principal ways. First, it borrowed $50,000. Second, it earned $28,408.

(Notice that the report includes depreciation as a source of cash. Depreciation is *not* a true source of cash, however. Depreciation is merely a bookkeeping entry. It's listed as a "source" of cash because it's a noncash expense that was subtracted from earnings. Because we want to use cash-related earnings in our calculations, we add depreciation back into the stated profit figure.)

Compare column F of the report in Figure 1-7 with column K of the balance sheet in Figure 1-6. The values are the same, although all subtotals have been removed. In fact, I created the report in Figure 1-7 by carving up the balance sheet in Figure 1-6.

To create Figure 1-7, begin with Figure 1-6. You will delete the columns of data in rows E through I. Before you do so, however, you must change column K from a column of formulas to a column of values. To do so, highlight the range K9:K49, choose Edit Copy, choose Edit Paste Special, and select Values.

Delete column L from the balance sheet in Figure 1-6. Then, to delete the balance-sheet data for 1987 and 1988, highlight the range E8:I51, choose Edit Delete, and select Shift Cells Left. Microsoft Excel's micro-delete feature deletes the range you specify and moves the remaining cells to the left. Then widen column F as needed to display the new data it contains.

Next, delete all rows in the display that contain spaces, section descriptions, or subtotals, leaving only data and its description. When you've done so, only minor cleanup remains. To remove the surviving underlines, highlight the remaining column of data, choose Format Borders, and turn off all border selections by selecting any that are turned on. Cut and paste into column B the description *Other Assets,* which was originally in cell A25 of the balance sheet in Figure 1-6, and *Loan payable...*, originally in cell A40.

Insert a row at the top of the display and three rows in the middle, below *Other Assets.* Finally, add the labels shown in column A of the report in Figure 1-7 and the titles and borders shown for cells E8 through I9. At this point, your display looks something like the report in Figure 1-7, but with only one column of data.

Column G lists all sources of funds as positive numbers and all uses of funds as negative numbers. It uses the following reasoning:

	Increase	**Decrease**
Assets	**Use of funds** Buy inventory for cash; inventory increases and cash decreases.	**Source of funds** Collect accounts receivable; A/R decreases and cash increases.
Liabilities	**Source of funds** Borrow cash from the bank; liabilities increase and cash increases.	**Use of funds** Pay accounts payable; liabilities decrease and cash decreases.

As this table shows, an increase in an asset represents a *use* of funds, as when you buy an asset. But an increase in a liability represents a *source* of funds, as when you borrow money. A decrease in an asset represents a *source* of funds, as when you collect receivables or sell an asset. But a decrease in a liability represents a *use* of funds, as when you pay off debt.

Notice that to calculate sources and uses we look only at the results in the balance sheet, not at the process that created the results. If a vendor accepts common stock in payment of an overdue invoice, or if you trade inventory for fixed assets, no cash has changed hands. And yet *something* of value has been exchanged. Because we can't know from looking at the balance sheet whether cash was that *something* or not, we often use the more general term "funds" to describe the exchange, where funds are any means of payment, not only cash.

Column E of the report in Figure 1-7 is a column of cells containing *1* or *(1)* that you multiply by column F to obtain column G. Enter them as shown. A *(1)*, or negative 1, stands for an asset and a *1*, or positive 1, stands for a liability. Depreciation is once again the oddball, however. Depreciation isn't an asset, it's a *contra asset,* or a reducer of assets. Because it behaves in the opposite way from an asset, it requires an opposite sign in column E.

To complete columns G through I, enter the formulas for G11 through I11 that are shown in the formula box for Figure 1-7 and then copy them down the column as shown. To clean up the appearance of the spreadsheet, delete the formula from cells G20 and G21. Enter the bottom borders shown at the bottom of the report and the formulas to add the columns. The figure's formula box provides the formula for G30, which you can copy to H30 and I30.

Your spreadsheet now looks like the one in Figure 1-7. Save it under two filenames. Save it in one file as a statement of sources and uses; save it in another file as a cash flow report that you will use in the next section of this chapter.

You must take only two more steps to turn the report in Figure 1-7 into a statement of sources and uses of funds. First, change columns H and I from a column of formulas to a column of values, just as you did with column K of the balance sheet in Figure 1-6. (You need to do this, of course, because columns H and I contain formulas that depend on column G, which you are about to delete.) Second, delete columns E through G.

A Statement of Cash Flows

You can look at funds flows, or cash flows, in many different ways. Each way can reveal something new about the business in question. The statement in Figure 1-8 on page 29 is a case in point.

Suppose you were thinking of buying Clandestine Manufacturing. What would you want to know? One thing, certainly, would be the firm's ability to generate enough cash to repay the loan you must take out to buy the firm. In other words, you would be thinking of the firm as an engine that generates cash, and you would want to compare its cash-generating ability with your cash requirements. Therefore, to check Clandestine's recent performance in this regard, you would be most interested in the number shown in cell I26 of the statement in Figure 1-8.

This value, sometimes called a firm's free cash flow, is the amount of cash a firm has generated that is available for distribution to lenders and owners. In Clandestine's case, the picture looks grim at first. Why? The display shows that free cash flow is generated by two activities. Investing activities, which normally consume cash, involve the company's purchase and sale of long-term assets. Operating activities are the regular activities the firm performs to generate cash. In Clandestine's case, however, the operating activities didn't generate cash, they consumed cash.

On the other hand, new management could improve free cash flow considerably. If the firm could get inventory under control and straighten out the accounts payable problem, cash flow from operations would certainly be healthy.

Compare column H of the statement in Figure 1-8 with column G of the report in Figure 1-7. Both spreadsheets present the same information, but in a different sequence. In fact, the easiest way to create the statement in Figure 1-8 is to rearrange the report in Figure 1-7.

To do so, open the extra copy of the file that looks like the report in Figure 1-7. Change the column of formulas in column G into a column of values. Delete the unneeded columns of data. Then, by using Edit Insert, Edit Delete, Edit Copy, and Edit Paste, rearrange the rows of data in the report until they are in the same sequence as in the statement in Figure 1-8. Your first step, for example, might be to cut and paste the row for cash (row 11) to the bottom of the display; the next might be to move the row for retained earnings (row 29) to the top. (You could have accomplished the same result by starting a new spreadsheet from scratch, but copying the original statement and editing it shows you the relationship between the two statements.)

When the data is in the sequence shown in the statement in Figure 1-8, change the descriptions and headings to those in the statement. Finally, create the subtotals and totals shown in column I.

A QUICK-AND-DIRTY CASH FLOW FORECAST

Suppose you're ready to leave for the night when your president walks up to your desk. "I'm having dinner tonight with a friend who's worth $100 million or so. If the subject comes up, I'd like to be able to tell him approximately how much cash we'll need next year. Could you stick around for a couple of minutes and work up a number for me? Oh, assume that our sales will hit $300,000 next year."

There's certainly no time for a full cash flow forecast, but you've got to prepare something reasonable. What do you do?

The forecast in Figure 1-9 on page 31 presents an approach that is as close to reasonable as any. With minor exceptions, this forecast assumes that your company's balance sheet will grow as if it were printed on a balloon, with all assets and liabilities growing in proportion as next year's sales pump up the balloon. In 1988, for example, the cash balance was exactly 1 percent of yearly sales. For everything to grow in proportion, therefore, cash must increase by 1 percent of the increase in sales, or by $500, and so on for each account.

However, you *know* that some accounts won't grow so neatly. In the figure, for example, fixed assets and depreciation aren't expected to grow as quickly as sales. Notes payable, rather than growing, must be paid off within several months. Long-term debts must be amortized monthly. And you don't plan to sell any common stock.

Consequently, as things stand now in the figure, you expect assets to increase by $19,100 and liabilities to fall by $3,240. You will therefore need $22,340. You list possible solutions to your cash flow problems, but at this point you're short of ideas.

When you give this forecast to your president, you need to make him understand its weaknesses and strengths. Its weaknesses are:

- Because assets and liabilities seldom grow at exactly the same rate as sales, you know your major assumption will be wrong; but you don't know how far or in which direction.
- The forecast looks only at the end of the year; seasonal variations could cause even greater cash problems during the year.
- The forecast relies on an accurate sales estimate. The faster sales grow, the worse your cash flows will be.
- Having spent so little time with the numbers, you have no sense of the forecast's best case and worst case.

Even so, this quick-and-dirty cash flow forecast has its advantages as well:

- It's quick and easy to produce.
- Its assumptions and calculations are easy to understand and to change; there's no magic to the forecast.
- The forecast is as reasonable as you can make it on such short notice.

This forecast is similar in format to the balance sheet in Figure 1-6, with several exceptions, which are shown in the formula box for Figure 1-9. In the forecast in Figure 1-9, the percentages in columns F and K are taken with respect to sales, not with respect to total assets. The increase in sales (cell H9) is the difference between actual sales and predicted sales. With the exceptions noted in the forecast, the increase in assets and liabilities is proportionate to this increase in sales. The predicted balance sheet is equal to the actual balance sheet (column E) plus the forecasted increase (column H).

The last formula in the formula box shows that Financing Needed equals the difference between predicted assets and predicted liabilities. It is also equal, of course, to the difference between the predicted increases in assets and liabilities.

The Possible Solutions section in the bottom-right corner provides room for brainstorming. Cell J47 totals these solutions; cell J50 shows the difference between these solutions and the total financing needed.

Figure 1-1. Simple Income Statement

	A	B	C	D	E	F	G	H	I
1									
2									
3					Wee Weaver Wanda				
4					INCOME STATEMENT				
5					March, 1988				
6									
7	Revenue								
8		Sales						15,000	
9		Royalties						500	
10		Dividends and interest						300	
12	Total revenues							15,800	
13									
14	Expenses								
15		Cost of products sold					7,200		
16		Selling expenses					1,570		
17		General and administrative expenses					1,285		
18		Interest					650		
19		Income taxes					1,630		
20	Total expenses							12,335	
21									
22	Net income							3,465	
24									

COLUMN WIDTHS			
Column	***Width***	***Column***	***Width***
A	**2.71**	**F**	**8.43**
B	**8.43**	**G**	**8.43**
C	**8.43**	**H**	**8.43**
D	**8.43**	**I**	**2.43**
E	**8.43**		

ROW HEIGHTS	
Row	***Height***
11	**1**
23	**2**

(continued)

Figure 1-1. *continued*

KEY FORMULAS	
Cell	***Formula***
H12	**=SUM(H7:H11)** This formula finds total revenue.
H20	**=SUM(G14:G19)** This formula finds total expenses.
H22	**=H12–H20** This formula finds net income.

KEY CELL FORMATS			
Cell	***Number***	***Alignment***	***Font***
E3:E5	**General**	**Center**	**Helv 10**
G7:H23	**#,##0 ;(#,##0)**	**General**	**Helv 10**

Figure 1-2. Detailed Income Statement

	A	B	C	D	E	F	G	H	I	J	K	L	M
1													
2													
3					Crandall Sales Co.								
4					INCOME STATEMENT								
5					For the year ended December 31, 1988								
6													
7	Sales												
8		Sales										4,192,582	
9		Less:	Sales discounts							62,889			
10			Sales returns and allowances							41,887		104,776	
11		Net sales										4,087,806	
12													
13	Cost of goods sold												
14		Merchandise inventory, Jan. 1, 1988								638,251			
15		Purchases						2,106,259					
16		Freight and transportation in						52,557		2,158,816			
17		Total merchandise available for sale								2,797,067			
18		Less merchandise inventory, Dec. 31, 1988								584,237			
19			Cost of goods sold									2,212,830	
20		Gross profit on sales										1,874,976	
21													
22	Operating expenses												
23		Selling expenses											
24			Sales salaries and commissions					302,685					
25			Sales office salaries					68,452					
26			Travel and entertainment					52,870					
27			Advertising					42,587					
28			Office supplies					32,432					
29			Other selling expenses					29,788		528,814			
30													
31		Administrative expenses											
32			Office salaries					302,983					
33			Insurance					37,756					
34			Depreciation					8,392					
35			Office supplies					11,558					
36			Other administrative expenses					23,409		384,098		912,912	
37	Income from operations											962,064	
38													
39	Other income												
40		Dividend income								15,879			
41		Rental income								5,400		21,279	
42												983,343	
43	Other expenses												
44		Interest expenses										35,981	
45													
46	Income before taxes											947,362	
47		Income taxes										303,156	
48	Net income for the year											644,206	
49	Earnings per share											$3.64	
50													

(continued)

Figure 1-2. *continued*

COLUMN WIDTHS							
Column	*Width*	*Column*	*Width*	*Column*	*Width*	*Column*	*Width*
A	4.14	E	8.43	I	1.86	M	1.71
B	5	F	8.43	J	9		
C	8.43	G	8.43	K	1.71		
D	8.43	H	9	L	9		

ROW HEIGHTS	
Row	*Height*
11	18
20	18
37	19
48	19

KEY CELL FORMATS			
Cell	*Number*	*Alignment*	*Font*
F3:F5	General	Center	Helv 10
H7:L48	#,##0 ;(#,##0)	General	Helv 10
L49	$#,##0.00 ;($#,##0.00)	General	Helv 10

Figure 1-3. Detailed Balance Sheet

	A	B	C	D	E	F	G	H	I	J	K	L	M
1													
2													
3					Downtown Moll's Fashion Store								
4					BALANCE SHEET								
5					December 31, 1988								
6													
7					Assets								
8													
9	Current Assets												
10		Cash										2,100	
11		Accounts receivable						62,000					
12			Notes receivable					21,000					
13			Interest receivable					500		83,500			
14			Less allowance for doubtful accounts							4,200		79,300	
15													
16		Merchandise inventory on hand										49,500	
17		Unexpired insurance										600	
18		Prepaid interest expense										780	
19			Total current assets									132,280	
20													
21	Fixed assets												
22		Furniture and equipment								68,500			
23		Less accumulated depreciation								19,550			
24			Total fixed assets									88,050	
25	Total assets											220,330	
27													
28					Liabilities and stockholders' equity								
29													
30	Current liabilities												
31		Accounts payable										18,460	
32		Notes payable										25,000	
33		Property tax payable										7,500	
34			Total current liabilities									50,960	
35	Long-term Liabilities												
36		Mortgage payable										45,880	
37													
38			Total liabilities									96,840	
39	Stockholders' equity												
40		Common stock								75,000			
41		Retained earnings								48,490			
42			Total stockholders' equity									123,490	
43	Total liabilities and stockholders' equity											220,330	
45													

(continued)

Figure 1-3. *continued*

COLUMN WIDTHS							
Column	*Width*	*Column*	*Width*	*Column*	*Width*	*Column*	*Width*
A	2.43	E	10	I	2.29	M	3.57
B	2.57	F	8.43	J	8.43		
C	8.43	G	2.86	K	2.57		
D	8.43	H	8.43	L	8.43		

ROW HEIGHTS	
Row	*Height*
26	2
35	18
39	19
43	19
44	2

KEY CELL FORMATS			
Cell	*Number*	*Alignment*	*Font*
F3:F5	General	Center	Helv 10
H10:L44	#,##0 ;(#,##0)	General	Helv 10

Figure 1-4. Quarterly Statement of Operations

An actual quarterly report of the INTERMEC Corporation.

	A–F	G	H–I
1			
2			
3	**STATEMENT OF OPERATIONS**		
8	INTERMEC Corporation and Subsidiaries		
9	Comparative condensed financial statements (unaudited) are shown below.		
11	**Quarter ended June 30,**	**1987**	1986*
12	**Revenue**	**$ 17,814,710**	$ 14,427,226
13	Cost of revenue and operating expenses	**16,554,134**	13,539,337
14	Operating income	**1,260,576**	887,889
15	Net investment income	**134,869**	184,155
16	Income before taxes	**1,395,445**	1,072,044
17	Income taxes	**500,000**	414,959
20	**Net Income**	**$ 895,445**	$ 657,085
23	**Net income per share** (based on average shares		
24	outstanding during the period)	**$ .15**	$ .11
28	Average shares outstanding (includes option		
29	common stock equivalents)	**6,062,384**	5,939,870
33			
34	**BALANCE SHEET**		
39	**1987**	**June 30**	March 31*
40	**ASSETS**		
41	**Current assets**	**$ 42,453,879**	$ 39,498,729
42	Plant and equipment--net	**7,553,113**	7,269,546
43	Notes receivable	**1,375,884**	1,953,500
44	Investments in unconsolidated companies	**2,985,872**	2,468,347
45	Other assets	**839,656**	785,060
46	**Total assets**	**$ 55,208,404**	$ 51,975,182
49	**LIABILITIES & STOCKHOLDERS' EQUITY**		
50	**Current liabilities**	**$ 15,887,801**	$ 13,740,766
51	Industrial revenue bond	**1,000,000**	1,000,000
52	Deferred income tax	**134,667**	134,667
53	Other long-term liabilities	**73,555**	98,995
54	Minority interest		273,474
55	Stockholders' equity	**38,112,381**	36,727,480
56	**Total liabilities & stockholders' equity**	**$ 55,208,404**	$ 51,975,382
59	*Restated to include the financial position and results of operation of INTERMEC/MidAtlantic and INTERMEC/Metro, which		
60	were acquired in pooling of interests transactions during the quarters ended March 31 and June 30, 1987, respectively.		
61			

(continued)

Figure 1-4. *continued*

COLUMN WIDTHS			
Column	*Width*	*Column*	*Width*
A	8.43	F	12
B	8.43	G	11
C	3	H	6
D	8.43	I	10
E	8.43	J	1.86

ROW HEIGHTS							
Row	*Height*	*Row*	*Height*	*Row*	*Height*	*Row*	*Height*
3	22	20	18	34	20	47-48	1
4-7	1	21-22	1	35-38	1	49	18
10	7	25-27	1	40	18	56	19
18-19	1	30-32	1	46	18	57-58	1

KEY FORMULAS	
Cell	*Formula*
G14	=G12–G13 This formula calculates the operating income.
G16	=G14+G15 This formula calculates the income before taxes.
G20	=G16–G17 This formula calculates the net income.
G46	=SUM(G40:G45) This formula calculates the total assets.
G56	=SUM(G49:G55) This formula calculates the total liabilities and stockholders' equity.

(continued)

Figure 1-4. *continued*

KEY CELL FORMATS			
Cell	*Number*	*Alignment*	*Font*
A3	General	General	Helv 12, Bold
A11:A12	General	General	Helv 10, Bold
A20:A23	General	General	Helv 10, Bold
A34	General	General	Helv 12, Bold
A39:A41	General	General	Helv 10, Bold
A46:A50	General	General	Helv 10, Bold
A59:A60	General	General	Helv 8
F12:F56	General	Right	Helv 10, Bold
G11	General	Center	Helv 10, Bold
G12:G56	#,##0 ;(#,##0)	General	Helv 10, Bold
G24	#,###.00 ;(#,###.00)	General	Helv 10, Bold
H12:H56	General	Right	Helv 10
I11	General	Center	Helv 10
I12:I56	#,##0 ;(#,##0)	General	Helv 10
I24	#,###.00 ;(#,###.00)	General	Helv 10

Figure 1-5. Comparative Income Statement

	A B C D	E	F	G	H	I	J	K	L	M
1										
2										
3			Ben's Bargain Basement							
4			INCOME STATEMENT							
5			For the year ended December 31							
6										
7										
8		1988			1987			Increase		
9	Revenues									
10	Net sales	343,879	100%		299,175	100%		44,704	15%	
11	Other revenue	1,009	0%		1,145	0%		(136)	-12%	
12	Total revenue	344,888	100%		300,320	100%		44,568	15%	
13										
14	Cost of products sold	175,893	51%		163,674	54%		12,219	7%	
15	Gross profit margin	168,995	49%		136,646	46%		32,349	24%	
16										
17	Operating expenses									
18	Administrative expenses	41,387	12%		36,939	12%		4,448	12%	
19	Selling expenses	48,284	14%		50,153	17%		(1,869)	-4%	
20	Interest expense	13,245	4%		14,223	5%		(978)	-7%	
21	Total operating expenses	102,916	30%		101,315	34%		1,601	2%	
22										
23	Earnings before taxes	66,079	19%		35,331	12%		30,748	87%	
24										
25	Income taxes	20,484	6%		11,306	4%		9,178	81%	
26										
27	Net income	45,595	13%		24,025	8%		21,570	90%	
28										

COLUMN WIDTHS							
Column	***Width***	***Column***	***Width***	***Column***	***Width***	***Column***	***Width***
A	**1.71**	**E**	**8.43**	**I**	**5**	**M**	**4.14**
B	**5.71**	**F**	**5**	**J**	**1.86**		
C	**8.43**	**G**	**2**	**K**	**8.43**		
D	**6.71**	**H**	**8.43**	**L**	**5**		

(continued)

Figure 1-5. *continued*

KEY FORMULAS	
Cell	***Formula***
E8	**=" 1988"** The equal sign and quotes force year into next column.
F12	**=E12/E$12** The dollar sign anchors the divisor as you copy this formula down columns F and I.
K10	**=E10–H10** This formula finds the increase for the year.
L10	**=IF(H10=0,0,K10/H10)** If the last amount is 0, this formula returns 0; otherwise it returns the percentage increase for the period.

KEY CELL FORMATS			
Cell	***Number***	***Alignment***	***Font***
G3:G5	**General**	**Center**	**Helv 10**
E9:E27	**#,##0 ;(#,##0)**	**General**	**Helv 10**
F9:F27	**0%**	**General**	**Helv 10**

Figure 1-6. Comparative Balance Sheet

	A–D	E	F	H	I	K	L
1							
2							
3		Clandestine Manufacturing					
4		BALANCE SHEET					
5		For the fiscal year ended June 30					
6							
7		ASSETS					
8							
9		1988		1987		Increase	
10	Current assets						
11	Cash	15,237	5%	4,872	2%	10,365	213%
12	Accounts receivable	29,851	10%	22,015	10%	7,836	36%
13	Inventories	117,873	40%	59,725	26%	58,148	97%
14	Prepaid expenses	7,984	3%	7,281	3%	703	10%
15	Total current assets	170,945	58%	93,893	41%	77,052	82%
16							
17	Fixed assets						
18	Land	11,000	4%	11,000	5%	0	0%
19	Buildings	81,258	28%	81,258	36%	0	0%
20	Machinery and equipment	77,500	26%	74,452	33%	3,048	4%
21		169,758	58%	166,710	74%	3,048	2%
22	Less: accumulated depreciation	57,888	20%	38,972	17%	18,916	49%
23		111,870	38%	127,738	56%	(15,868)	-12%
24							
25	Other assets	9,850	3%	5,100	2%	4,750	93%
26							
27	Total assets	292,665	100%	226,731	100%	65,934	29%
29							
30							
31		LIABILITIES AND STOCKHOLDERS' EQUITY					
32							
33	Current liabilities						
34	Accounts payable	39,801	14%	65,874	29%	(26,073)	-40%
35	Income taxes	14,772	5%	2,358	1%	12,414	526%
36	Loans payable	50,000	17%	0	0%	50,000	0%
37	Other accrued liabilities	8,931	3%	5,122	2%	3,809	74%
38	Total current liabilities	113,504	39%	73,354	32%	40,150	55%
39							
40	Loan payable at 12%, due 6/30/95	45,938	16%	48,562	21%	(2,624)	-5%
41	Total liabilities	159,442	54%	121,916	54%	37,526	31%
42							
43	Stockholders' equity						
44	Common stock	12,500	4%	12,500	6%	0	0%
45	Capital in excess of par	18,000	6%	18,000	8%	0	0%
46	Retained earnings	102,723	35%	74,315	33%	28,408	38%
47	Total stockholders' equity	133,223	46%	104,815	46%	28,408	27%
48							
49	Total liabilities and equity	292,665	100%	226,731	100%	65,934	29%
51							

(continued)

Figure 1-6. *continued*

COLUMN WIDTHS							
Column	*Width*	*Column*	*Width*	*Column*	*Width*	*Column*	*Width*
A	2.57	E	8.43	I	5	M	3.71
B	3	F	5	J	2		
C	8.43	G	2.29	K	8.43		
D	17.57	H	8.43	L	5		

ROW HEIGHTS	
Row	*Height*
28	2
41	19.25
47	18
50	2

KEY FORMULAS	
Cell	*Formula*
E27	=E15+E23+E25 The total is the sum of the subtotals.
E49	=E41+E47 Total liabilities and equity is the sum of liabilities and equity.
F11	=E11/E$27 The dollar sign anchors the divisor as you copy the formula down columns F and I.
K11	=E11–H11 This formula finds the increase for the year.
L11	=IF(H11=0,0,K11/H11) If the last amount is 0, this formula returns 0; otherwise it returns the percentage increase for the period.

Figure 1-7. Sources and Uses of Funds

	A B C D	E	F	G	H	I
1						
2						
3	Clandestine Manufacturing					
4	SOURCES AND USES OF FUNDS					
5	For the fiscal year ended June 30					
6						
7						
8		(1)=A		Sources		
9		1=L	Increase	(Uses)	Sources	Uses
10	Assets					
11	Cash	(1)	10,365	(10,365)		10,365
12	Accounts receivable	(1)	7,836	(7,836)		7,836
13	Inventories	(1)	58,148	(58,148)		58,148
14	Prepaid expenses	(1)	703	(703)		703
15	Land	(1)	0	0		
16	Buildings	(1)	0	0		
17	Machinery and equipment	(1)	3,048	(3,048)		3,048
18	Depreciation	1	18,916	18,916	18,916	
19	Other assets	(1)	4,750	(4,750)		4,750
20						
21	Liabilities & stockholders' equity					
22	Accounts payable	1	(26,073)	(26,073)		26,073
23	Income taxes	1	12,414	12,414	12,414	
24	Loans payable	1	50,000	50,000	50,000	
25	Other accrued liabilities	1	3,809	3,809	3,809	
26	Loan payable at 12%, due 6/30/95	1	(2,624)	(2,624)		2,624
27	Common stock	1	0	0		
28	Capital in excess of par	1	0	0		
29	Retained earnings	1	28,408	28,408	28,408	
30	Total			0	113,547	113,547
32						

COLUMN WIDTHS			
Column	***Width***	***Column***	***Width***
A	**2.57**	**F**	**8.43**
B	**3**	**G**	**8.43**
C	**8.43**	**H**	**8.43**
D	**17.57**	**I**	**8.43**
E	**5**	**J**	**2.43**

(continued)

Figure 1-7. *continued*

ROW HEIGHT	
Row	*Height*
31	2

KEY FORMULAS	
Cell	*Formula*
G11	**=E11*F11** This formula turns the sources positive and the uses negative.
H11	**=IF(G11>0,G11,"")** If the value is a source, this formula puts it in G11; otherwise it puts a blank in G11.
I11	**=IF(G11<0,–G11,"")** If the value is a use, this formula puts it in G11; otherwise it puts a blank in G11.
G30	**=SUM(G11:G29)** The sum of all sources minus all uses equals 0.

Figure 1-8. Statement of Cash Flows

Row	A–G	H	I
1			
2			
3	Clandestine Manufacturing		
4	STATEMENT OF CASH FLOWS		
5	For the fiscal year ended June 30, 1988		
6			
7			
8	**Cash flows from operating activities**		
9	Net income	28,408	
10	Noncash expenses included in income		
11	Depreciation expense	18,916	
12	Net decrease (increase) in operating assets		
13	Accounts receivable	(7,836)	
14	Inventories	(58,148)	
15	Prepaid expenses	(703)	
16	Other assets	(4,750)	
17	Net increase (decrease) in operating liabilities		
18	Accounts payable	(26,073)	
19	Income taxes	12,414	
20	Other accrued liabilities	3,809	
21	Net cash flow from operating activities		(33,963)
22			
23	**Cash flows from investing activities**		
24	Purchase of machinery and equipment	(3,048)	
25	Net cash flows from investing activities		(3,048)
26	Net cash flows before financing (free cash flow)		(37,011)
27			
28	**Cash flows from financing activities**		
29	Increase in short-term loans payable	50,000	
30	Decrease in long-term loans payable	(2,624)	
31	Net cash flows from financing activities		47,376
32			
33	Net increase (decrease) in cash		10,365
35			
36			
37			

COLUMN WIDTHS			
Column	***Width***	***Column***	***Width***
A	2.57	F	8.43
B	3	G	10.14
C	8.43	H	6.57
D	8.43	I	8.43
E	8.43	J	2.43

(continued)

Figure 1-8. *continued*

ROW HEIGHTS	
Row	***Height***
26	18
31	19
34	2

Figure 1-9. Quick-and-Dirty Cash Flow Forecast

	A B C D	E	F	G H	I	J	K
1							
2							
3			Speedy Plumbing				
4			QUICK-AND-DIRTY CASH FLOW FORECAST				
5			-1989-				
6							
7		1988--Actual		Increase		1989--Predicted	
8							
9	Sales	250,000	100%	50,000		300,000	100%
10							
11	Assets						
12	Cash	2,500	1%	500		3,000	1%
13	Accounts receivable	40,000	16%	8,000		48,000	16%
14	Inventories	43,500	17%	8,700		52,200	17%
15	Other	1,250	1%	250		1,500	1%
16	Total current assets	87,250	35%	17,450		104,700	35%
17							
18	Fixed assets	20,000	8%	**2,000**	1	22,000	7%
19	Accumulated depreciation	6,500	3%	**350**	1	6,850	2%
20	Net fixed assets	13,500	5%	1,650		15,150	5%
21	Total assets	100,750	40%	19,100		119,850	40%
23							
24	Liabilities						
25	Accounts payable	28,800	12%	5,760		34,560	12%
26	Notes payable	10,000	4%	**(10,000)**	2	0	0%
27	Other liabilities	500	0%	100		600	0%
28	Total current liabilities	39,300	16%	(4,140)		35,160	12%
29	Long-term debt	35,000	14%	**(2,100)**	3	32,900	11%
30	Total debt	74,300	30%	(6,240)		68,060	23%
31							
32	Stockholders' equity						
33	Common stock	10,000	4%	**0**	4	10,000	3%
34	Retained earnings	16,450	7%	**3,000**	1	19,450	6%
35	Total stockholders' equity	26,450	11%	3,000		29,450	10%
36	Total liabilities and equity	100,750	40%	(3,240)		97,510	33%
38							
39				Financing needed		22,340	
41							
42							
43	**Notes**			**Possible solutions**			
44	1 Based on this year's performance			New short-term debt		15,000	
45	2 Note due, 3/31/89			Sell underused assets		1,500	
46	3 Per amortization schedule			???			
47	4 No stock sales planned			Total new sources		16,500	
49							
50				Shortfall		5,840	
52							

(continued)

Figure 1-9. *continued*

COLUMN WIDTHS			
Column	***Width***	***Column***	***Width***
A	2.57	G	4.14
B	8.43	H	8.29
C	8.43	I	4.14
D	10.14	J	8.43
E	8.43	K	5.14
F	4.86	L	2.43

ROW HEIGHTS			
Row	***Height***	***Row***	***Height***
21	19	36	19
22	2	37	2
23	27	40	2
29	18	48	2
30	17	51	2

KEY FORMULAS	
Cell	***Formula***
F9	=E9/E$9 This formula calculates the percentage increase in sales.
H9	=J9–E9 This formula calculates the dollar increase in sales.
H12	=H$9*F12 This formula calculates the dollar increase as a percentage of the sales increase.
J12	=E12+H12 The predicted value equals beginning plus increase.
J39	=J21–J36 Financing needed is the difference between assets you plan to have and the total sources of financing you've identified.

2

A Spreadsheet Accounting System

It sounds like a lot of work, I know, but from time to time I use computer spreadsheets to do my accounting, for a number of reasons:

- I was the chief financial officer (CFO) for a start-up company that changed frequently during its first few months of existence. It changed from a tiny company that wrote business plans and raised funds to a little company that developed a product to a larger company that manufactured and sold the product. I could never have produced financial statements during those changes by using an inflexible accounting software package.
- Until recently, my own little software company was too small to require a computerized accounting system. My wife, therefore, kept the books by using a spreadsheet system that I created.
- I once went to work for a company with a computerized accounting system that had never reconciled. When I realized the problem was a bug that wouldn't soon be fixed, I created a computer spreadsheet system to replace the software. We used the system for about a year, until I had time to install a "real" computerized accounting system.

- I've used several accounting systems that generate an excellent general ledger trial balance and terrible financial reports. I've therefore used spreadsheets to produce all financial reports.

This chapter discusses a computerized accounting system that consists of five sections, as illustrated in Figure 2-1.

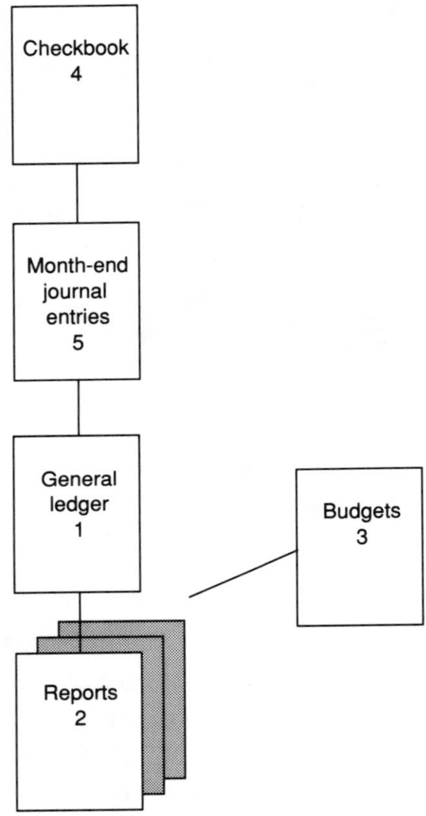

Figure 2-1. *An overview of a spreadsheet general ledger system.*

1. The general ledger file represents the heart of the system. It contains monthly financial information for each general ledger account.
2. The financial reporting system extracts information from the general ledger and reports it in financial statements.
3. The budget-reporting system reports both actual and budgeted financial performance.

4. The computerized checkbook accumulates cash receipts and payments during the month. You can easily summarize this information for entry into your accounting system.
5. Journal entries summarize all accounting activity for the month. Although the other sections of this chapter discuss templates that you create, the section titled "Transferring Monthly Data into the General Ledger" describes a process that you go through to generate the journal entries.

If you would rather begin to use these spreadsheets immediately, you can purchase a set of disks that include them. You'll find order information on the last page of this book.

A GENERAL LEDGER TRIAL BALANCE

In its simplest form, a general ledger contains the balance for every general ledger account number for every month in the fiscal year. Figure 2-2 on page 48 shows just such a spreadsheet.

Column A of the spreadsheet in Figure 2-2 contains the general ledger (GL) account number. Column H contains the ending balance from the previous fiscal year. The next 12 columns, beginning with column I, will contain the ending monthly balance for each GL account during the current fiscal year. In the version of the spreadsheet in the figure, however, August is the most recent month of activity. When you're ready to enter the September information, insert a column for September between columns L and M.

The spreadsheet in Figure 2-2 contains additional information that is convenient to store with the general ledger. Column C shows a report-line number. This number assigns each GL account to a particular line of the financial statements that follow. To summarize other financial statements in different ways, insert additional report-line columns between columns C and D.

The data in columns D through G summarizes the financial information for the month entered in cell D4. The spreadsheet in the figure, for example, summarizes the financial information for August, 1988. If you were to enter *Jul-88* in cell D4, these columns would summarize July's performance instead.

Creating a General Ledger

Open a new worksheet and turn off the gridlines. Enter the labels and borders shown in rows 3 through 9, adjusting the width of each column as necessary to contain the labels. Enter the date *8/1/88* in cell D4 and format this cell as shown in the format box. Assign the name Date to this cell.

Although you've just begun the spreadsheet, you wouldn't want to lose your work if your electricity failed. Therefore, save your spreadsheet at this point. Because this spreadsheet contains the general ledger for 1988, save it as GL_88.XLS.

Enter the formulas shown in the formula box for all cells in row 8 and format them as shown in the format box. The date in cell I8 contains the first day of the new fiscal year, which in this case is May 1, 1988. Assign the name BegDate to this cell.

Enter the GL-account numbers, descriptions, and report lines shown in columns A through C. The values in the range H10 through L20 are numbers that you enter as shown. The positive values in this range are debits, and the negative values are credits. Center the range A9 through A21 and assign the number formats shown for the remainder of the spreadsheet. Choose the Format Borders command and select Shade to shade the borders as shown.

Assign the range names shown in the figure's range-name box. Enter the formulas shown for row 10 in the formula box and then copy them down the columns as needed.

Enter the formula shown in the formula box for cell D22 and copy it across the row as shown. (Because all debits must always equal all credits, the values in this row must always equal 0.) Save your spreadsheet again.

Updating a General Ledger

To enter new account numbers in the general ledger, simply insert rows where you need them and then copy the formulas as needed from any convenient row. But keep in mind that just as column M represents the end of the data at the right side of the spreadsheet, row 21 represents the end of the data at the bottom. When you insert new rows or columns for new data, be sure to insert them to the left of or above these end markers.

If you have many GL numbers to add to your general ledger, you'll probably find that it's a slow process to find the exact place in the GL sequence to enter each number. Here's a quick way to enter the numbers, therefore, without having to worry about where they belong:

1. Insert enough rows within the general ledger to contain the new GL numbers.
2. Add the new GL numbers, descriptions, line numbers, and data within this new area, using any GL-number sequence that's convenient.
3. After you add all the new GL numbers, copy the formulas for columns D through G to these rows from any convenient row that already contains the formulas.
4. Delete any empty rows from the GL table.

5. Sort the table in GL-number sequence. To do so, highlight all rows of data from what is now cell A10 to what is now cell L20, and then choose the Data Sort command.

FINANCIAL REPORTS

Figures 2-3 through 2-5 present simple illustrations of a balance sheet, an income statement, and a statement of changes in financial position, in that order. Of course, these reports aren't detailed enough for most purposes. However, they do present the formulas you can use to create more detailed reports.

Creating a Balance Sheet

Figure 2-3 on page 51 shows a simple balance sheet that presents data contained in Figure 2-2. You would generally print columns B and C of this spreadsheet as a report.

Column A contains report-line numbers, which serve two purposes. First, they determine the values returned in column C of the balance sheet; if you change the report-line number, you change the value displayed in the report. Second, they help document your report. Suppose, for example, that the cash balance in the balance sheet in Figure 2-3 looks unreasonably high. Because Cash has a report-line number of 1 in this report, you would review the balance of all general-ledger accounts in the general ledger in Figure 2-2 that have a report-line number of 1 assigned to them; somewhere in those numbers is an explanation of the unreasonable results.

To create this balance sheet, first open a new spreadsheet and turn off its gridlines. Enter the labels and numbers shown in columns A and B of the spreadsheet in Figure 2-3, setting the column widths as necessary to contain this information. Format all cells as shown in the format box for Figure 2-3.

Notice that several rows in this spreadsheet aren't visible because their height has been reduced nearly to 0. There are several reasons for these narrow rows. In row 6, I created the heavy, dark line by assigning top and bottom borders in that row and then by setting the row height to 1. In row 12, I added a row so that the range of the SUM formula in row 13 could end below my data. In this way, I can insert a category of assets in the report between rows 11 and 12 and ensure that the SUM formula includes this new information. In row 14, I created the double underlines by assigning top and bottom borders and by setting the row height to 2. The row-height box for this figure provides all nonstandard row heights.

Enter the range names shown in the range-name box and then enter the formulas for cells C5 and C10, as shown in the figure's formula box. Copy cell C10 to cell C11.

When you do so, the formula in cell C11 returns the value shown for that cell. Add a bottom border to this cell and total the assets as shown.

Enter the remaining formulas, using the formula box to guide you. Notice that cell C24, the retained earnings for the current fiscal year, contains an amount that could come from one of two sources. The first possible source is the amount of net income from the year-to-date income statement. The second possible source is the balance sheet itself: total assets minus total liabilities and all other equity balances. Because the income statement isn't available yet, enter the formula using the second approach: C13–C20–SUM(C22:C23). Complete the formatting, as shown in the spreadsheet in the figure, and then save this general ledger report as GL_REP.XLS.

Creating an Income Statement

Figure 2-4 on page 54 shows a simple income statement. Enter the labels and values shown in columns A and B. Cell B38 contains the same date formula used in the balance sheet in Figure 2-3, but with a slightly different format. Check the formula and format boxes for specifics.

Enter the formulas shown for row 40 in the figure's formula box and then copy the range C40:F40 to cell C41. When you do so, cells C41 and E41 are displayed as negative values. This is because the formulas for Sales in these cells are preceded by a minus sign. Edit cells C41 and E41 to remove these minus signs. Add the bottom border as shown and, in cell C43, subtract Cost of Goods Sold from Sales to obtain Gross Profit.

To calculate Operating Expenses, copy the range C41:F41 to cell C45. Add the bottom border and enter a formula for Net Profit in C47. Complete columns D and F by copying the percentage calculations from any convenient cell. Finally, to complete the spreadsheet in Figure 2-4, enter the borders as shown.

Modifying a Balance-Sheet Formula

Now that you've completed the income statement, you must make one change to the balance sheet in Figure 2-3. Remember that the value in cell C24, Retained Earnings--This Year, must reconcile with the year-to-date income-statement balance. The formula in cell C24, therefore, must make this comparison and return an error message if the two values fail to reconcile. The formula box for Figure 2-3 shows this formula for cell C24. Enter it as shown.

The ROUND function in this formula eliminates minor errors created because binary computers must approximate decimal fractions. At times, therefore, a computer might store 20.79 as 20.7899997 or as 20.7900002. Without rounding of the values the formula operates on, the program could conclude that two equal values are not equal.

Creating a Funds Statement

As discussed in Chapter 1, the funds statement gives some idea of a firm's sources and uses of cash during a reporting period. Also known as a statement of changes in financial position, the funds statement provides managers with information about cash flows that is not obvious from the other statements.

The format for a funds statement varies widely, although seldom will you see one quite as condensed as the one in Figure 2-5 on page 56. However, it demonstrates the techniques you can use to create more useful funds statements.

To create Figure 2-5, enter the labels and values shown in columns A and B. Enter the formulas shown for rows 57 and 58. The formulas in row 57 pick up the profit for the month and the year to date, respectively, from the income statement; those in row 58 find the change in inventory for the periods shown. Copy the range D58:E58 to the range D59:D60.

When you copy this range, notice that you will *not* have to delete the minus signs that precede the formulas, as you have done in the past. Here's why the formulas for both the assets and the liabilities need minus signs:

Assets. An *increase* in an asset is a *use* of cash, which should appear as a negative amount in the report. Because an increase in assets (in Inventory, for example) appears as a positive amount in Figure 2-2, the formulas in Figure 2-5 need the minus signs in front of them.

Liabilities. An *increase* in a liability or an owner equity account is a *source* of cash and therefore appears as a positive amount in the report. Because increases in liabilities (in Accounts Payable, for example) appear as a negative amount in Figure 2-2, the formulas in Figure 2-5 must have minus signs in front of them as well.

Add the bottom border in row 61 and then enter the formulas shown in the formula box for row 62. These formulas are similar to the ones contained in row 24 of Figure 2-3—they compare the calculated change in cash to the actual change. If the amounts are equal, they return the amount of the change; if the amounts are not equal, they return an error message.

Debugging a Formula When You Receive an Error Value

When you create your own version of this spreadsheet, you might get quite a few error values. When I prepare to fix these errors, I generally copy the contents of cell D62 to an area below the problem cell—to cells D63 and D64, for example. To do so, select cell D63, press Ctrl-apostrophe, and then press Ctrl-Shift Enter. (Because the formula is an array formula, you enter it by using Ctrl-Shift Enter, rather than by merely pressing

Enter.) Then, to copy the formula to cell D64, select this cell and press Ctrl-apostrophe and Ctrl-Shift Enter again.

Edit cell D63, deleting everything but the part of the formula that reads =SUM(IF($A62=RptLine,MoChng)), and then press Ctrl-Shift Enter. Edit cell D64, deleting everything but the part of the formula that reads =ROUND(SUM(D56:D61),2), and then press Enter. Then, in cell D65, enter the formula =D63–D64. Cell D62, in other words, tells you only that there's an error. Cell D63 gives you one version of the truth, cell D64 gives you the other version, and cell D65 gives you the difference between them. With this information, you can more easily find and fix the error.

Entering Your Own Data

After you complete the reporting system shown in these examples, you are ready to create a similar reporting system for your own data. Your own financial reports are more complex than these simple examples, of course. But the structure of your reporting system, and your formulas, will be about the same.

Starting with a copy of the spreadsheet in Figure 2-2, erase the sample data in columns A through C and H through L. Add your own data to the rows provided and then insert enough rows into the table to allow you to enter your own general ledger account numbers, descriptions, and trial balances. Copy the formulas in columns D through G down the rows as necessary. Adjust your dates as necessary and then recalculate your spreadsheet.

Before proceeding, be sure that the totals of each column (shown in row 22 of the spreadsheet in Figure 2-2) are equal to 0. Then save this spreadsheet under a filename that's different from the one you used for Figure 2-2.

You next need to create your own financial statements, which you will substitute for the simple statements used in the preceding pages. To do so, you could open the statements you created in Chapter 1, or you could open new spreadsheets and create them now. If you create new ones, you can use any column widths, formatting, descriptions, and so on that you want. Where numeric data is needed, enter actual values. Where formulas are used to add or subtract data, enter the formulas.

After you complete the financial statements you plan to use, insert a new column at column A for each statement. In this new column A, enter a report-line number for each row of data. You will probably want to enter sequential numbers, but you can use any number scheme. When you complete your income statement, for example, it might look something like the income statement in Figure 2-6 on page 58, which is a variation of the spreadsheet in Figure 1-5.

Insert enough rows beneath the simple income statement to hold your new, detailed income statement. Highlight the new income statement, choose the Edit Cut command, and then paste your new income statement in the area you inserted beneath the simple statement. Do the same for the balance sheet and funds statements.

Next, assign each appropriate general ledger account to the report-line number that you specified in your income statement or balance sheet. For example, if you assigned report-line number 1 to Cash, enter *1* in column A of Figure 2-2 for all accounts that constitute the Cash figure. When you finish, every row of data in your version of Figure 2-2 has a report-line number assigned to it.

Check the dimensions of all range names shown in the range-name box for Figures 2-3 through 2-5, making certain that they still define the data you expect. You have two ways to do this. First, you can choose Formula Define Name, which lists the dimensions of each range you select. Second, you can press the F5 (GoTo) key and enter the range name you want to test. Doing so highlights the range name.

To complete the conversion, copy the formulas from the sample financial statements into your actual financial statements. These formulas need only minor adjustment. When you have the financials working, delete the rows containing the sample financials and save your spreadsheet.

THE BUDGET-REPORTING SECTION

There are as many ways to create and report budgets as there are accountants. Probably more. The method described in this section is quick to set up and easy to maintain, but not as flexible as others.

The spreadsheet shown in Figure 2-7 on page 59 contains the budgeted expenses for each month of the fiscal year. The spreadsheet in Figure 2-8 on page 61 contains a summary section through column H and the year-to-date budget totals for each month of the fiscal year. (The spreadsheet displays only the first six months of these totals, however.)

Lombard Associates prints only the range A15 through H23 as its budget report. For each general ledger account, the report shows the actual amount spent during the month, the amount that was budgeted, and the variance. It shows similar information for the fiscal year to date.

Creating Budgets

To create the schedule in Figure 2-7, first open a new spreadsheet and turn off the gridlines. Enter the labels and numbers shown for the range A3 through B10, adjusting the column widths as necessary to contain the labels. Enter all borders and shading shown. With the exception of BudYTD, define all range names shown in the range-name box for Figure 2-7 and Figure 2-8. Enter and format the formulas shown for cells C4 and D4 in the formula and format boxes and then copy the contents of cell D4 across the row as shown.

Enter the data shown for the range C6 through N8. To total the data, enter the SUM formula shown for cell C10 and then copy it across the row. Finally, add any remaining borders and formats and then save your spreadsheet as BUD_88.XLS.

To create the budget-variance report in Figure 2-8, enter the labels, borders, and shading shown in rows 15 through 18 and row 22. Define the range name BudYTD as shown in the figure's range-name box.

Enter and format the formulas shown in the information boxes for cells B16 and I17 and then copy the contents of cell I17 across the row as far as necessary. The figure's formula box provides all formulas for the range A19:J19; enter them and format the cells as shown in the format box. Copy the contents of cell J19 to cells K19 through T19 and then copy the contents of the range A19:T19 to the range A20:T21. Enter the formula shown for cell C25 and copy it down the row as far as necessary. Finally, add the remaining borders and save the spreadsheet again.

To add more rows of expenses to the budget, you must take two steps. First, insert rows for your data in the spreadsheet shown in Figure 2-7 and enter your data. Second, insert the same number of rows in the spreadsheet shown in Figure 2-8 and then copy the necessary formulas to these rows from any row that already contains the formulas.

AN AUTOMATED CHECKBOOK

Many small businesses have replaced manual checkbooks with computer spreadsheets. The reasons are obvious. In theory, the computer is faster, more accurate, easier to read, and more flexible than paper checkbooks. But theory breaks down unless the computerized checkbook is designed properly.

The following section of this chapter describes a computerized checkbook that consists of three spreadsheets. The first spreadsheet provides tables of special codes that many businesses use when dealing with customers and vendors. The second spreadsheet is the checkbook itself. The third spreadsheet is one that helps you extract data from the checkbook at the end of the month as part of the accounting close.

Creating Error-checking Tables

Figure 2-9 on page 63 shows the first spreadsheet, which contains three tables. Use of any or all of the tables is optional. But using them will make your data more accurate and improve your ability to analyze your income and expenses.

The first table is a list of customer and vendor codes, along with the full name of the customer or vendor. If you do not use this table, you could spell a customer's name differently each time you enter it. If your customer is RW Smith, for example, you might enter the name as *RW Smith* one time, *R.W. Smith* another time, *RWS* another, *Smith* another, *RWSmith* another, and so on. All these versions would provide the computer with an impossible task of analyzing sales by customer.

To eliminate this problem, the table provides one code per customer. The coding system that I recommend uses the first six characters of the customer or vendor name as the code. This system is the easiest one I know to learn and use quickly. A new employee, for example, can quickly guess that the code for RW Smith is RWSMIT.

At times, of course, you will have to modify the pattern. If you deal with Associated Plumbing and Associated Carpeting, for example, you cannot assign the code ASSOCI to both firms. Instead, assign a distinctive code to each; you might use something like ASPLUM and ASCARP.

The second table contains the general ledger chart of accounts. The most important table in the spreadsheet, it lets you know immediately whether the GL number you entered in the checkbook is the number you meant to enter. The easiest way to maintain this list is to copy it occasionally from columns A and B of the spreadsheet in Figure 2-2.

The final table is the least important of the three. Because the spreadsheets in Figures 2-9 through 2-11 assume that Lombard Associates acts as a property manager, this table lists each building and each apartment. Using this table lets the manager analyze costs and expenses by apartment or by building unit. Instead of tracking income and expenses by apartment, other businesses might track by product code, city code, salesperson, product category, and so on.

Because the spreadsheet in Figure 2-9 contains no formulas, it's a breeze to create. Simply enter the labels, underlines, and shading shown and create the range names shown in the range-name box. The format box shows the formats to use.

When you complete this spreadsheet, save it as CHKTBLS.XLS, which stands for "Check Tables." You might prefer to use another name, but you'll find it's easier to wait until you complete this section before changing the name.

Creating an Automated Checkbook

To create the checkbook shown in Figure 2-10 on page 65, begin with a new spreadsheet. Turn off the gridlines. Then enter all labels and underlines shown in rows 2 through 8. The range I3 through J5 contains formulas that you will enter later, however.

To mark the bottom of the spreadsheet, shade row 20 as shown. The format box for Figure 2-10 shows only those cells with formats other than the default values. Enter these formats as shown.

Enter the beginning date and cash balance shown in cells A9 and K9. The formula box for the figure shows three formulas for row 10. Enter these as shown and copy them from row 10 through row 19. Because column C contains a subtotal that is merely an intermediate calculation, you need to hide that column. To do so, move your pointer to column C, choose the Format Column Width command, and enter 0.

The range-name box for Figure 2-10 shows three range names; enter them as shown. Enter the data shown for cells A9 through J19. After you enter the range names and data, enter the formulas shown in the formula box for cells I3 through I5. When you do so, the three formulas return the data you entered in cells E16, F16, and H16, respectively. Then enter the formulas shown for cells J3 through J5.

Add any remaining borders you want and then save the spreadsheet as CHECKS.XLS. Also, save your workspace as CHKBOOK.XLW. Later, when you open the workspace, both CHECKS.XLS and CHKTBLS.XLS will be opened in one command.

Entering Your Own Data

When you enter your own data, you will need more room than the few rows provided in the spreadsheet shown in Figure 2-10. To get this room, you must take two steps. First, insert the number of rows you need into an area above the bottom of the spreadsheet in the figure and below your last row of data—in row 18, for example. Second, copy your row of formulas from any convenient row to the new rows—for example, from A17 through K17. (Doing so copies the formulas in the hidden column C as well, by the way.)

When you enter your own data, you quickly discover two additional concerns. First, when you enter data below row 19 or 20, rows 3 and 4 move off the top of your screen. To correct this problem, split the document window into two horizontal window panes and keep rows 3 through 8 in the upper pane while you scroll to and enter data in, for example, row 100 in the bottom window pane.

Second, Microsoft Excel may take longer than you would like to calculate the checkbook. To correct this problem, set manual calculation by choosing Options Calculation and selecting Manual. After you do so, recalculate your spreadsheet and check your entries each time you enter a row of data. To recalculate manually, simply press the F9 key.

Creating the Month-End Journal

At the end of each month, you'll want to summarize all cash transactions by GL-account number for entry into your general ledger. Figure 2-11 on page 67 shows a spreadsheet you can use to accomplish this task. The spreadsheet contains the accounting entry, the cash in, and the cash out for each general ledger account number.

To create this spreadsheet, first open a new spreadsheet and turn off its gridlines. Enter the labels, shading, and borders through row 11, as shown in the figure, and then enter the range names shown in the figure's range-name box.

Enter the formula shown in the figure's formula box for cell D3 and the three formulas for row 7. Because you haven't yet entered values in column A, these formulas return the value 0. Copy the formulas in the range B7:D7 to the range B8:B10.

The next step, one that you take monthly, is to summarize in column A all GL-account numbers that you referenced during the month. By creating the range names Database and Criteria, you did most of the work necessary to create this list. To complete it, do three things. First, be certain that the label in cell A5 matches the label in cell H8 of the spreadsheet in Figure 2-10. Second, select cell A5, choose the Data Extract command, and select Unique. When you choose OK, Microsoft Excel creates a list of all GL-account numbers that you entered during the month, listing each account number only once.

Be careful, however, that your spreadsheet contains no information below cell A5 that you want to save. Whenever you specify an output range that contains only one row, the Data Extract command erases all previously existing data beneath that range.

After you carry out the Data Extract command, columns A and B contain your month-end journal entry for all accounts but one: Cash. To complete the entry, you must enter the GL-account number for Cash in cell A12. The formula in cell B12 contains the amount of cash increase or decrease. Enter this and the other formula shown for row 12.

To complete this spreadsheet, add formatting and borders as needed, and then save the spreadsheet as CHK_REG.XLS.

TRANSFERRING MONTHLY DATA INTO THE GENERAL LEDGER

Most companies maintain individual journals summarizing the detailed accounting transactions that occur each month. The most common are the cash receipts journal, the sales journal, the purchase journal, the cash payments journal (check register), and the general journal. In many small businesses, however, the checkbook combines all these journals except the last, which an outside accountant prepares.

The following section of this chapter explains how to quickly summarize all your monthly journals and create a general ledger trial balance for the month. The method that you will use is both quick and easy, but it leaves a rather faint audit trail. Therefore, when you use this method, be careful to save printouts of all your work.

Figure 2-12 on page 69 shows the spreadsheet that you will use to create your general ledger trial balance. It consists of four sections. The first section contains the GL-account numbers and amounts from the previous general ledger balance. The second section contains all accounting journals. Only one journal appears in the spreadsheet in the figure, but dozens could be included. The third section is a criteria range that's used by the Data Extract command to extract a new list of GL-account numbers. The fourth section is the new general ledger trial balance, with which you can update the general ledger shown in Figure 2-2.

Creating a Summary Spreadsheet

To create the spreadsheet in Figure 2-12, open a new spreadsheet and turn off its gridlines. Copy the GL-account numbers and previous general ledger balance from the general ledger. That is, copy the contents of ranges A10:A20 and L10:L20 in the spreadsheet in Figure 2-2 to cells C7 and D7, respectively, in the spreadsheet in Figure 2-12. Enter the titles shown in cells C5 and D5. Be sure to leave an empty row between the titles and the data, as shown in row 6, columns C and D, which is shaded.

Copy your journal entries to the spreadsheet, as shown in the range C20 through D24 in Figure 2-12. Leave an empty row below each journal, as shown in the range C19 through D19. Although the system doesn't require this space, it helps remind you where one journal ends and the other begins. Be certain, however, that one column contains all GL-account numbers and another contains all GL dollar amounts.

Enter the headings for the new general ledger trial balance. Because the title in cell G5 doubles as the heading for the Criteria range, this title must match the title in cell C5 exactly (except for formatting). The safest way to enter this label is to copy it from cell C5. After you enter the headings, enter the range names shown in the range-name box for Figure 2-12.

To create the list of account numbers shown in column G, select cell G5, choose the Data Extract command, and select Unique. This command places below cell G5 all general ledger account numbers that it finds in the Database range, listing each number only once. Because this command works from top to bottom, the first "number" that it lists is the space shown in cell C4; then it lists all GL-account numbers from last month's general ledger. Finally, the command lists any new GL-account numbers at the bottom of the list, as shown in the spreadsheet in the figure.

Enter the array formula for cell H7 shown in the formula box and copy it down the column as shown. These formulas summarize the amounts entered in column D by GL-account number. Because the sum of all amounts in the beginning balance and the sum of the journal entries both equal 0, the sum of column H must equal 0 as well. Enter the formula, as shown, in cell H21.

If you haven't already done so, save this spreadsheet. Any name will be OK, but I used GL_SUM.XLS, for "GL summary."

If your journals contain new GL-account numbers, enter them in the general ledger (shown in Figure 2-2) at this point. Then sort this month's general ledger trial balance by GL-account number.

Finally, you're ready to move this data into your general ledger. To do so, insert a column for the data between columns L and M of the spreadsheet shown in Figure 2-2, copy the heading from column L to the new column M, and then copy the values of the sorted data in the range H7:H21 of the Figure 2-12 spreadsheet to the new cell M10 in the Figure 2-2 spreadsheet—that is, when you paste your copy into the Figure 2-12 spreadsheet, choose the Edit Paste Special command and select Values.

To report this new data, simply increase the date in cell D4 by one month, press the function F9 (Calculate All) key, and then print the reports you want.

Figure 2-2. General Ledger File

A general ledger spreadsheet that contains year-to-date information for each month of the fiscal year for each general ledger account. Saved as GL_88.XLS.

	A	B	C	D	E	F	G	H	I	J	K	L	M
1													
2													
3	GENERAL LEDGER FILE												
4	Month of Report			Aug-88									
5	Month Number			4									
6	G/L		Rpt	Beg	Month's	Ending	F/Y	End Bal	End	End	End	End	E
7	Acct	Description	Line#	Mo YTD	Change	Mo YTD	Change	Last FY	Bal	Bal	Bal	Bal	N
8				Jul-88		Aug-88		Apr-88	May-88	Jun-88	Jul-88	Aug-88	D
9													
10	1001	Cash in Bank	1	89	(8)	81	(19)	100	84	81	89	81	
11	1002	Petty Cash	1	25	0	25	0	25	25	25	25	25	
12	1300	Inventory	2	348	(21)	327	(128)	455	432	409	348	327	
13	2301	Accounts Payable	3	(311)	(11)	(322)	(13)	(309)	(300)	(386)	(311)	(322)	
14	2901	Common Stock	4	(200)	0	(200)	0	(200)	(200)	(200)	(200)	(200)	
15	2905	Ret Erngs, Prior Yr	5	(71)	0	(71)	(47)	(24)	(71)	(71)	(71)	(71)	
16	3101	Sales	10	(269)	(90)	(359)	472	(831)	(78)	(172)	(269)	(359)	
17	3501	Cost of Sales	11	73	24	97	(127)	224	21	46	73	97	
18	4025	Salaries	12	140	60	200	200	0	50	100	140	200	
19	4201	Supplies	12	57	15	72	(99)	171	12	49	57	72	
20	4716	Advertising	12	119	31	150	(239)	389	25	119	119	150	
21													
22	Totals			0	0	0	0	0	0	0	0	0	

COLUMN WIDTHS							
Column	***Width***	***Column***	***Width***	***Column***	***Width***	***Column***	***Width***
A	**4.14**	**E**	**6.57**	**I**	**6.29**	**M**	**2**
B	**15.71**	**F**	**6.57**	**J**	**6.29**		
C	**5**	**G**	**6.57**	**K**	**6.29**		
D	**7.57**	**H**	**6.57**	**L**	**6.29**		

(continued)

Figure 2-2. *continued*

KEY FORMULAS	
Cell	***Formula***
D4	**8/1/88** Enter the first day of the current month in this cell.
D5	**=ROUND((Date–BegDate)/30.4375,0)+1** This formula finds the number of months that have elapsed between the current month of the report and the beginning month of the fiscal year. To do so, the formula divides the number of days that have elapsed by 30.4375, the average number of days in a month. This value equals the average number of days in a year (365.25) divided by 12.
D8	**=DATE(YEAR(Date),MONTH(Date)–1,1)** This formula calculates the first day one month prior to Date.
F8	**=Date** This formula repeats the formula in cell D4.
H8	**=DATE(YEAR(I8),MONTH(I8)–1,1)** This formula finds the last month of the previous fiscal year.
I8	**5/1/88** Enter the first day of the new fiscal year in this cell.
J8	**=DATE(YEAR(I8),MONTH(I8)+1,1)** This formula adds one month to the previous month.
D10	**=INDEX(Input,ROWS(D$9:D10),Month+7)** The INDEX formula returns the value in the current row for one month prior to the current month.
E10	**=F10–D10** The change in values equals the ending minus the beginning value.
F10	**=INDEX(Input,ROWS(F$9:F10),Month+8)** Like the formula in cell D10, this formula returns the proper value from the SOURCE range.
G10	**=F10–H10** The change in values equals the ending minus the beginning value.
D22	**=SUM(D9:D21)** Because debits equal credits, this value should always equal 0.

(continued)

Figure 2-2. *continued*

RANGE NAMES	
Name	***Formula***
Date	**=$D$4** Change this date to change the dates of all reports that report from this general ledger.
Month	**=$D$5** This range contains the number of months between the beginning of the fiscal year and the date contained in the Date range.
BegDate	**=$I$8** This range contains the first day of the current fiscal year.
Input	**=$A$9:$M$21** This range contains all the data in the general ledger.
Accts	**=$A$9:$A$21**
RptLine	**=$C$9:$C$21**
BegMoYTD	**=$D$9:$D$21**
MoChng	**=$E$9:$E$21**
EndMoYTD	**=$F$9:$F$21**
FYChng	**=$G$9:$G$21**
LstFYBal	**=$H$9:$H$21**

KEY CELL FORMATS			
Cell	***Number***	***Alignment***	***Font***
A3	**General**	**General**	**Helv 10, Bold**
D4	**mmm–yy**	**General**	**Helv 10**
A6:M7	**General**	**Center**	**Helv 10**
D8:M8	**mmm–yy**	**Center**	**Helv 10**
A9:A21	**General**	**Center**	**Helv 10**
D9:M22	**#,##0 ;(#,##0)** In actual practice, however, use number format: #,##0.00 ;(#,##0.00)	**General**	**Helv 10**

Figure 2-3. Balance Sheet from the General Ledger

A simple balance sheet that reports data from the general ledger for the month shown. Saved as GL_REP.XLS.

	A	B	C	D
1				
2				
3	Sample Balance Sheet			
4	Rpt			
5	Line	Lombard Associates	Aug-88	
7				
8		ASSETS		
9				
10	1	Cash	$106.00	
11	2	Inventory	$327.00	
13		Total Assets	$433.00	
15				
16		LIABILITIES & EQUITY		
17				
18	3	Accounts Payable	$322.00	
20		Total Liabilities	$322.00	
21				
22	4	Common Stock	$200.00	
23	5	Ret Earnings--Prior Years	$71.00	
24		Ret Earnings--This Year	($160.00)	
26		Net Worth	$111.00	
27				
28		Total Liab & Equity	$433.00	
30				
31				

ROW HEIGHTS	
Row	***Height***
6	1
12	1
14	2
19	1
25	1
29	2

(continued)

Figure 2-3. *continued*

KEY FORMULAS	
Cell	***Formula***
C5	**=Date** Date, of course, refers to the Date range in GL_88.XLS.
C10	**=SUM(IF($A10=RptLine,EndMoYTD))** This array formula first creates a temporary array that contains values from EndMoYTD whenever the RptLine equals the value in column A and then returns the sum of this temporary array. Enter this, and all array formulas, by holding down Ctrl-Shift while you press Enter.
C13	**=SUM(C10:C12)** Notice that this formula includes the underline. This allows you to insert additional rows below the Inventory row while still including them in the SUM range.
C18 **C22** **C23**	**=–SUM(IF($A18=RptLine,EndMoYTD))** **=–SUM(IF($A22=RptLine,EndMoYTD))** **=–SUM(IF($A23=RptLine,EndMoYTD))** Because the GL shows credit balances as negative, you must begin formulas for liabilities with a minus sign, turning them positive for presentation in the financial statements. (These are array formulas.)
C24	**=IF(ROUND(C13–C20–SUM(C22:C23),2)=ROUND(E47,2),E47,"Error")** This formula makes sure that the balance sheet reconciles with the income statement. The formula won't work properly until you've entered cell E47.
C26	**=SUM(C22:C25)** Net worth equals the total of the equity section of the balance sheet.
C28	**=C20+C26** This formula is exactly what its label says: Liabilities plus Equity.

(continued)

Figure 2-3. *continued*

RANGE NAMES	
Name	*Formula*
Date	=GL_88.XLS!Date
RptLine	=GL_88.XLS!RptLine
BegMoYTD	=GL_88.XLS!BegMoYTD
MoChng	=GL_88.XLS!MoChng
EndMoYTD	=GL_88.XLS!EndMoYTD
FYChng	=GL_88.XLS!FYChng
LstFYBal	=GL_88.XLS!LstFYBal
	These range definitions all reference range names in the spreadsheet in Figure 2-2.

KEY CELL FORMATS			
Cell	*Number*	*Alignment*	*Font*
B5	General	Center	Helv 10
C5	mmm–yy	Center	Helv 10
A6:A29	General	Center	Helv 10
C6:C29	$#,##0.00 ;($#,##0.00)	General	Helv 10

Figure 2-4. Income Statement from the General Ledger

A simple income statement with report-line numbers that specify which data the spreadsheet reports from the general ledger in Figure 2-3. Saved as GL_REP.XLS. For range names, see Figure 2-3.

	A	B	C	D	E	F	G
34							
35							
36	Sample Income Statement						
37	Rpt	Lombard Associates					
38	Line	August 01, 1988	Month		Year to Date		
40	10	Sales	$90.00	100%	$359.00	100%	
41	11	Cost of Goods Sold	$24.00	27%	$97.00	27%	
43		Gross Profit	$66.00	73%	$262.00	73%	
44							
45	12	Operating Expenses	$106.00	118%	$422.00	118%	
47		Net Profit	($40.00)	-44%	($160.00)	-45%	
48							

KEY FORMULAS

Cell	*Formula*
C40 E40	**=–SUM(IF($A40=RptLine,MoChng))** **=–SUM(IF($A40=RptLine,EndMoYTD))** Because sales are maintained as negative numbers in the GL, the minus sign turns this value positive. (Array formulas.)
D40 F40	**=C40/C$40** **=E40/E$40** The absolute references ($) in these formulas let you copy them down columns C and F.
C41 E41	**=SUM(IF($A41=RptLine,MoChng))** **=SUM(IF($A41=RptLine,EndMoYTD))** Because the GL records expenses as positive numbers, no minus sign is needed in these array formulas.
C43 E43	**=C40–C41** **=E40–E41** Gross profit equals sales minus cost of goods sold.

(continued)

Figure 2-4. *continued*

KEY FORMULAS–continued	
Cell	***Formula***
C45 **E45**	**=SUM(IF($A45=RptLine,MoChng))** **=SUM(IF($A45=RptLine,EndMoYTD))** Copy these array formulas from row 41.
C47 **E47**	**=C43–C45** **=E43–E45** Subtract operating expenses from gross profit to calculate net profit.

KEY CELL FORMATS			
Cell	***Number***	***Alignment***	***Font***
B36:B37	**General**	**General**	**Helv 10**
B38	**mmmm dd, yyyy**	**Center**	**Helv 10**
A37:A46	**General**	**Center**	**Helv 10**
C39:C47	**$#,##0.00 ;($#,##0.00)**	**General**	**Helv 10**
D39:D47	**0%**	**General**	**Helv 10**

Figure 2-5. Statement of Changes in Financial Position

A simple statement of changes in financial condition that provides all the formulas needed to create a more detailed financial report. Saved as GL_REP.XLS. For range names, see Figure 2-3.

	A	B	C	D	E	F
51						
52						
53	Sample Changes in Financial Position					
54	Rpt	Lombard Associates				
55	Line	August 01, 1988		Month	YTD	
57		Operating Profit		($40.00)	($160.00)	
58	2	(Inc) Dec in Inventories		$21.00	$128.00	
59	3	Inc (Dec) in Accts Payable		$11.00	$13.00	
60	4	Sale (Purch) of Common Stock		$0.00	$0.00	
62	1	Inc (Dec) In Cash		($8.00)	($19.00)	
63						

KEY FORMULAS

Cell	*Formula*
D57 **E57**	**=C47** **=E47** These formulas return the profit numbers from the income statement's totals.
D58 **E58**	**=–SUM(IF($A58=RptLine,MoChng))** **=–SUM(IF($A58=RptLine,FYChng))** Minus signs precede both of these array formulas. In the GL, an increase in an asset is positive, but must be displayed as a negative because it has a negative effect on cash; an increase in a liability is negative, but must be displayed as a positive because it has a positive effect on cash.
D62 **E62**	**=IF(SUM(IF($A62=RptLine,MoChng))=ROUND(SUM(D56:D61),2), SUM(D56:D61),"Total?")** **=IF(SUM(IF($A62=RptLine,FYChng))=ROUND(SUM(E56:E61),2), SUM(E56:E61),"Total?")** If the calculated change in cash in these array formulas equals the actual change, the formulas return this value; otherwise they return *Total?*.

(continued)

Figure 2-5. *continued*

KEY CELL FORMATS			
Cell	*Number*	*Alignment*	*Font*
B53:B54	General	General	Helv 10
B55	mmmm dd, yyyy	Center	Helv 10
A54:A62	General	Center	Helv 10
D56:E62	$#,##0.00 ;($#,##0.00)	General	Helv 10

Figure 2-6. Traditional Income Statement Using the General Ledger

A more detailed income statement, an expanded form of the simple income statement shown in Figure 2-4, which reports information from the general ledger in Figure 2-2.

	A	B	C	D	E	F	G	H	I	J	K
1											
2											
3					Ben's Bargain Basement						
4					INCOME STATEMENT						
5					August 31, 1988						
6											
7											
8						Month			Year to Date		
9		Revenues									
10	20		Net Sales			28,656	100%		149,587	100%	
11	21		Other Revenue			84	0%		572	0%	
12		Total Revenue				28,740	100%		150,159	100%	
13											
14	22	Cost of Products Sold				14,657	51%		7,439	5%	
15		Gross Profit Margin				14,083	49%		142,720	95%	
16											
17		Operating Expenses									
18	23		Administrative Expenses			3,449	12%		18,469	12%	
19	24		Selling Expenses			4,024	14%		25,076	17%	
20	25		Interest Expense			1,103	4%		7,111	5%	
21		Total Operating Expenses				8,576	30%		50,656	34%	
22											
23		Earnings Before Taxes				5,507	19%		92,064	61%	
24											
25	26		Income Taxes			1,707	6%		5,653	4%	
26											
27		Net Income				3,800	13%		86,411	58%	
28											

Figure 2-7. Budgeted Expenses by Month

A schedule of budgeted expenses by month that provides data for budget-variance reports. Saved as BUD_88.XLS.

	A	B	C	D	E	F	G	H	I	J	K	L	M	N	O
1															
2															
3	**Budgeted Expenses by Month**														
4	GL#	Operating Exp	5/88	6/88	7/88	8/88	9/88	10/88	11/88	12/88	1/89	2/89	3/89	4/89	
5															
6	4025	Salaries	25	25	25	50	50	60	60	60	60	60	60	60	
7	4201	Supplies	15	15	5	20	5	20	5	20	5	20	20	20	
8	4716	Advertising	40	50	50	50	0	25	100	100	0	50	50	50	
9															
10	Total Expenses		80	90	80	120	55	105	165	180	65	130	130	130	
11															

KEY FORMULAS

Cell	*Formula*
C4	**=BegDate** This is the report date from the general ledger.
D4	**=DATE(YEAR(C4),MONTH(C4)+1,1)** This formula adds one month to the previous date. Copy it to the right as needed.
C10	**=SUM(C5:C9)** Copy this SUM formula across the row as necessary.

(continued)

Figure 2-7. *continued*

RANGE NAMES	
Name	***Formula***
BudMon	**=$A$5:$N$9** This range contains the month's budget data.
BudYTD	**=$I$18:$T$22** This range contains the year-to-date budget data.
Accts **BegDate** **Date** **EndMoYTD** **MoChng**	**=GL_88.XLS!Accts** **=GL_88.XLS!BegDate** **=GL_88.XLS!Date** **=GL_88.XLS!EndMoYTD** **=GL_88.XLS!MoChng** These range definitions all reference range names in the spreadsheet in Figure 2-2.

KEY CELL FORMATS			
Cell	***Number***	***Alignment***	***Font***
A3	**General**	**General**	**Helv 10, Bold**
C4:N4	**m/yy**	**Center**	**Helv 10**
C6:N10	**#,##0**	**General**	**Helv 10**

Figure 2-8. Budget-Variance Report

A report that combines actual spending from the general ledger with data from the budgets. Saved as BUD_88.XLS. For range names, see Figure 2-7.

	A	B	C	D	E	F	G	H	I	J	K	L	M	N
13														
14														
15	**Budget Variance Report**													
16		August 01, 1988	Current Month			Fiscal Yr To Date			Year-to-Date Budget Totals					
17	GL#	Operating Exp	Act	Bdgt	Var	Act	Bdgt	Var	5/88	6/88	7/88	8/88	9/88	10/88
18														
19	4025	Salaries	60	50	10	200	125	75	25	50	75	125	175	235
20	4201	Supplies	15	20	-5	72	55	17	15	30	35	55	60	80
21	4716	Advertising	31	50	-19	150	190	-40	40	90	140	190	190	215
22														
23	Total Operating Expense		106	120	-14	422	370	52	80	170	250	370	425	530
24														
25														

KEY FORMULAS

Cell	*Formula*
B16	**=Date** This is the report date (month).
I17	**=C4** Copy this formula as necessary across the row.
A19 **B19**	**=INDEX(BudMon,ROWS(A$17:$B19),1)** **=INDEX(BudMon,ROWS($B$17:B19),2)** These formulas return the GL accounts and descriptions entered as monthly budgets.
C19	**=INDEX(MoChng,MATCH($A19,Accts,0),1)** If the GL number exists in the GL, this formula returns its balance for the current month; otherwise the MATCH function causes it to return the #N/A error value.
D19	**=HLOOKUP(Date,BudMon,ROWS(A$17:$A19))** This formula returns the budget for this account for the current month.
E19	**=C19–D19** The variance equals the difference between Actual and Budget.
F19	**=INDEX(EndMoYTD,MATCH($A19,Accts,0),1)** If the GL number exists in the ledger, this formula returns its year-to-date balance.

(continued)

Figure 2-8. *continued*

KEY FORMULAS–continued	
Cell	*Formula*
G19	**=HLOOKUP(Date,BudYTD,ROWS(A$17:$A19))** This formula returns the year-to-date budget for this account.
H19	**=F19–G19** The variance equals the difference between Actual and Budget.
I19	**=HLOOKUP(I$17,BudMon,ROWS(A$17:$A19))** This formula finds the budgeted amount for the first month of this fiscal year.
J19	**=HLOOKUP(J$17,BudMon,ROWS($A$17:$A19))+I19** This formula adds this month's budget to last month's cumulative total. Copy this formula across the row as necessary.
C23	**=SUM(C18:C22)** As usual, the SUM range extends from the top border through the bottom border.

KEY CELL FORMATS			
Cell	*Number*	*Alignment*	*Font*
A15	General	General	Helv 10, Bold
B16	mmmm dd, yyyy	Center	Helv 10
C16:H17	General	General	Helv 10
I17:T17	m/yy	Center	Helv 10
C19:T23	#,##0	General	Helv 10

Figure 2-9. Reference Tables for the Checkbook

Tables that the computerized checkbook uses to identify data-entry errors. Saved as CHKTBLS.XLS.

	A	B	C
1			
2			
3	**Reference Tables for the Checkbook**		
4			
5	**Customer-Vendor Table**		
6			
7	ASSOCI	Associated Plumbing	
8	CREATI	Creative Arts Advertising	
9	LAPLAT	LA Platton	
10	RWSMIT	RW Smith	
11	ZZZZZZ	End of Table	
12			
13			
14	**General Ledger Chart of Accounts**		
15			
16	1001	Cash	
17	2301	Accounts Payable	
18	3102	Rental Income	
19	4201	Supplies	
20	4716	Advertising	
21	4815	Maintenance	
22	4998	Miscellaneous	
23			
24			
25	**Apartment Table**		
26			
27	1-00	Unit 1, General	
28	1-01	Unit 1, Apartment 1	
29	12-00	Unit 12, General	
30	12-04	Unit 12, Apartment 4	
31	999-99	End of Table	
32			
33			
34			

(continued)

Figure 2-9. *continued*

RANGE NAMES	
Name	***Formula***
CvTable **CvNum**	**=$A$6:$B$12** **=$A$6:$A$12** The Customer-Vendor table uses the first six letters of the customer or vendor name as the customer or vendor "number."
GLTable **GLNum**	**=$A$15:$B$23** **=$A$15:$A$23** This table of general ledger accounts and descriptions can be copied from Figure 2-2.
APTable **APNum**	**=$A$26:$B$32** **=$A$26:$A$32** In other businesses, this apartment table could become a salesperson table, route-code table, product-category table, and so on.

KEY CELL FORMATS			
Cell	***Number***	***Alignment***	***Font***
A5	**General**	**General**	**Helv 10, Bold**
A6:A12	**General**	**Center**	**Helv 10**
A14	**General**	**General**	**Helv 10, Bold**
A15:A23	**General**	**Center**	**Helv 10**
A25	**General**	**General**	**Helv 10, Bold**
A26:A32	**General**	**Center**	**Helv 10**

Figure 2-10. Checkbook

A spreadsheet that accumulates information for the GL. Saved as CHECKS.XLS.

	A	B	D	E	F	G	H	I	J	K
1										
2										
3	**Computer Checkbook--1988**						CV# :	rwsmit	RW Smith	
4	Lombard Associates						Apt# :	1-01	Unit 1, Apartment 1	
5							GL# :	3102	Rental Income	
6										
7		CHK#	CHK					CASH	CASH	CASH
8	DATE	DEP#	TOT	CV#	Apt#	INV#	GL#	IN	OUT	BALANCE
9	1-Jan									12,057.30
10	6-Jan	103		associ	1-01	1039	4201		345.00	11,712.30
11	6-Jan	103		associ		1044	4716		221.50	11,490.80
12	6-Jan	103	2,911.50	associ		1045	4815		2,345.00	9,145.80
13	8-Jan			rwsmit	1-01	86-254	3102	1,200.00		10,345.80
14	10-Jan			laplat	12-04	86-239	3102	800.00		11,145.80
15	10-Jan	104	12.03	creati		1-079	4716		12.03	11,133.77
16	10-Jan			rwsmit	1-01	86-255	3102	1,100.00		12,233.77
17										
18										
19										
20										

KEY FORMULAS	
Cell	***FORMULA***
I3 **I4** **I5**	**=INDEX(Data,COUNTA(DateCol),COLUMN(E8))** **=INDEX(Data,COUNTA(DateCol),COLUMN(F8))** **=INDEX(Data,COUNTA(DateCol),COLUMN(H8))** These formulas return the last entry in columns E, F, and H, respectively.
J3 **J4** **J5**	**=INDEX(CHKTBLS.XLS!CVTable,MATCH(I3,CHKTBLS.XLS!CVNum,0),2)** **=INDEX(CHKTBLS.XLS!APTable,MATCH(I4,CHKTBLS.XLS!APNum,0),2)** **=INDEX(CHKTBLS.XLS!GLTable,MATCH(I5,CHKTBLS.XLS!GLNum,0),2)** These formulas search the file CHKTBLS.XLS (Figure 2-9) for the data displayed here in cells I3:I5.
C10 **D10**	**=IF($B10=$B11,$C9+$J10,0)** **=IF($B10<>$B11,$C9+$J10,0)** This pair of formulas provides a subtotal by check number in column D. Column C has been hidden by setting its column width to 0. To restore column C to its standard width, press the F5 (Goto) key to go to any cell in column C and then choose Format Column Width.
K10	**=IF(AND(I10=0,J10=0),"",K9+I10–J10)** If no values exist in columns I or J, this formula returns a blank. Otherwise, it returns the cash balance.

(continued)

Figure 2-10. *continued*

RANGE NAMES	
Name	***Formula***
Data	**=$A$8:$K$20** The formulas in cells I3:I5 use this range.
DateCol	**=$A$8:$A$20** The count of this column of dates tells the formulas in cells I3:I5 which values to return.
GLNum	**=$H$8:$H$20** At month end, you will extract GL numbers from this range to create an accounting-journal entry.

KEY CELL FORMATS			
Cell	***Number***	***Alignment***	***Font***
A3	**General**	**General**	**Helv 10, Bold**
H3:I5	**General**	**Center**	**Helv 10**
A9:A20	**d–mmm**	**Center**	**Helv 10**
B9:B20	**General**	**Center**	**Helv 10**
D9:D20	**#,##0.00 ;(#,##0.00);** Because this Number format has a trailing semicolon, zeros appear as blanks.	**General**	**Helv 10**
E9:E20	**General**	**Center**	**Helv 10**
F9:F20	**##–##**	**Center**	**Helv 10**
G9:H20	**General**	**Center**	**Helv 10**
I9:K20	**#,##0.00 ;(#,##0.00)** Because this Number format lacks the trailing semicolon, zeros appear as zeros.	**General**	**Helv 10**

Figure 2-11. Check Register

A spreadsheet that creates a check register by summarizing information from the computerized checkbook. Saved as CHK_REG.XLS.

	A	B	C	D	E
1					
2					
3	Check Register			January, 1989	
4		Acct	Cash	Cash	
5	GL#	Entry	In	Out	
6					
7	4201	345.00	0.00	345.00	
8	4716	233.53	0.00	233.53	
9	4815	2,345.00	0.00	2,345.00	
10	3102	(3,100.00)	3,100.00	0.00	
11					
12	1001	176.47	3,100.00	2,923.53	
13					

KEY FORMULAS	
Cell	***Formula***
D3	**=TEXT(VALUE(Date),"mmmm, yyyy")** This formula allows the date to be displayed across several columns.
B7	**=D7–C7** The accounting entry is equal to cash out (Dr) minus cash in (Cr).
C7 **D7**	**=SUM(IF($A7=GLNum,CashIn))** **=SUM(IF($A7=GLNum,CashOut))** These array formulas summarize data from the checkbook's Cash Out and Cash In columns.
B12	**=C12–D12** The increase or decrease in Cash (GL account 1001) equals cash in minus cash out.
C12	**=SUM(C6:C11)** Copy this formula to the right.

(continued)

Figure 2-11. *continued*

RANGE NAMES	
Name	***Formula***
GLNum **CashIn** **CashOut**	**=CHECKS.XLS!GLNum** **=CHECKS.XLS!CashIn** **=CHECKS.XLS!CashOut** These range definitions all reference range names in the spreadsheet in Figure 2-10. Enter them as shown.
Date	**=MAX(CHECKS.XLS!DateCol)** This range name returns the latest date from the checkbook.
Criteria **Database**	**=$A$5:$A$6** **=CHECKS.XLS!GLNum** You will use these range names to extract GL numbers from the checkbook. Enter them as shown.

KEY CELL FORMATS			
Cell	***Number***	***Alignment***	***Font***
A3	**General**	**General**	**Helv 10, Bold**
D3	**General**	**Right**	**Helv 10, Bold**
B4:D5	**General**	**Center**	**Helv 10**
A6:A12	**General**	**Center**	**Helv 10**
B6:D12	**#,##0.00 ;(#,##0.00)**	**General**	**Helv 10**

Figure 2-12. Worksheet for Summarizing the General Ledger

An overview of the process of combining the previous month's general ledger data with the current month's accounting journals to create the current month's general ledger.

	A	B	C	D	E	F	G	H	I
1									
2									
3	**Worksheet for Summarizing the General Ledger Each Month**								
4									
5			GL#	Amt		**This Month's Year-to-date**	GL#	Amt	
6						**GL Balance.**			
7			1001	81		Create the column of general	1001	257.47	
8	**Year-to-date Balance**		1002	25		ledger numbers by choosing	1002	25	
9	**from Last Month's General**		1300	327		the Data Table command and	1300	327	
10	**Ledger**		2301	-322		selecting Extract. Use array	2301	-322	
11	Copy the data from columns A		2901	-200		formulas to generate the	2901	-200	
12	and L of Figure 2-2.		2905	-71		amounts. Add the two new	2905	-71	
13			3101	-359		account numbers at the bottom	3101	-359	
14			3501	97		of this list to the general	3501	97	
15			4025	200		ledger, and then copy the	4025	200	
16			4201	72		amounts by choosing the Edit	4201	417	
17			4716	150		Paste Special command and	4716	383.53	
18						selecting Values.The total of all	4815	2345	
19						amounts on this list equals	3102	-3100	
20	**This Month's Accounting**		4201	345		zero, as shown in cell H21.			
21	**Journals**		4716	233.53			Total	0	
22	Copy this data from columns A		4815	2345					
23	and B of Figure 2-11. (The		3102	-3100					
24	checkbook represents the		1001	176.47					
25	only journal in this illustration.)								
26									
27									

KEY FORMULAS	
Cell	***Formula***
H7	**=SUM(IF($G7=GLNum,Amt))** This array formula finds the sum of all account numbers that match the criterion.
H21	**=SUM(H6:H20)** This array formula finds the sum of all account numbers that match the criterion. Because the debits (positive values) must equal the credits (negative values), this total should always equal 0.

(continued)

Figure 2-12. *continued*

RANGE NAMES	
Name	***Formula***
GLNum **Amt**	**=$C$7:$C$24** **=$D$7:$D$24** Assign these range names as shown.
Criteria **Database**	**=$G$5:$G$6** **=$C$5:$C$24** The Data Extract command requires these two range names.

3

Financial Statements and Supporting Schedules

Long after the rest of the company has forgotten about the previous fiscal year, accountants are still translating, reconciling, analyzing, reporting, and explaining the past year's performance. This is why accountants are easy to recognize, the story goes; when accountants enter a room, they walk backward.

This chapter presents ways to speed up and simplify end-of-the-period processing. It presents techniques that you'll find useful in many spreadsheet applications.

TRANSLATING FOREIGN CURRENCY

Financial statements present information about the performance and financial status of a business. If the business consists of several individual businesses, their statements must be consolidated. If the statements of any of these businesses are maintained in a foreign currency, they must be translated into U.S. currency before consolidation.

To translate foreign financial statements into U.S. statements requires several steps. To illustrate these, suppose that Chip-Master Inc. is a U.S. manufacturer of a kitchen appliance that creates potato chips from raw potatoes. After several years of success in U.S. markets, the company decides to enter foreign markets. To do so, the company takes two steps.

First, it sets up several sales offices in Canada. Chip-Master manages these offices much as it does U.S. sales offices. Because the company records Canadian sales in the Chip-Master books and pays Canadian employees and vendors from its U.S. headquarters, the sales offices directly affect the cash flow of the U.S. company.

Second, the company establishes a British firm, Chip-Master Ltd., to import and sell the appliance in Europe. The British firm is an independent company with its own investor (Chip-Master Inc.) and its own management. This firm sets up sales offices throughout western Europe, through which it sells and distributes the appliance. The financial performance of the British firm increases or decreases the value of the U.S. firm's investment; but because the British firm is a separate entity, its financial performance does not affect the U.S. company's cash flows.

Remeasurement and Translation

To report Chip-Master's international operations, Chip-Master's controller must take several steps. First, she must adjust all foreign statements so that they conform to U.S. Generally Accepted Accounting Principles (GAAP). She must then *remeasure* the books of the European sales offices into British pounds. She uses the pound because it is the *functional currency,* the primary currency in which the European business operates. Similarly, she remeasures the books of the Canadian sales offices into their functional currency, U.S. dollars. Finally, she *translates* the consolidated books of Chip-Master Ltd. into U.S. currency.

Remeasurement

Remeasurement is used when a foreign operation is an extension of a parent company's domestic operations. This process is intended to produce the same result as if the foreign operation's books had been kept in the functional currency. Because the performance of the foreign operation directly affects the parent's income and cash flows, exchange gains and losses under remeasurement are included in net income.

The remeasuring process divides assets and liabilities into *monetary* and *nonmonetary* accounts. A monetary asset or liability is either cash or an obligation payable or collectible in a fixed amount of cash. All other assets or liabilities are nonmonetary. Remeasurement requires that monetary accounts be translated using *current exchange rates* and nonmonetary accounts be translated using *historical exchange rates.*

To understand the difference between historical and current exchange rates, suppose you purchased inventory in January, sold it in June, and reported the sale in December's financial statements. January's exchange rate is the historical rate. June's exchange rate—the rate at the time the sales transaction was recognized—is the current exchange rate for income statement accounts. December's exchange rate—the rate at the time of the report—is the current exchange rate for balance-sheet accounts.

Of course, you could spend a career tracking the exchange rates for January, for June, and for all the other dates on which your company bought or sold something. The Financial Accounting Standards Board (FASB) says this isn't necessary, however. This organization, which establishes the accounting standards that make up GAAP, explains in FAS52 paragraph 29:

"Literal application of the standards in this Statement might require a degree of detail in record keeping and computations that could be burdensome as well as unnecessary to produce reasonable approximations of the results. Accordingly, it is acceptable to use averages or other methods of approximation. For example, the propriety of using average rates to translate revenue and expense amounts is noted in paragraph 12. Likewise, the use of other time- and effort-saving methods to approximate the results of detailed calculations is permitted."

Translation

Translation is used when a foreign operation is a relatively self-contained entity. Because the foreign entity is evaluated as an investment, and because its operations don't directly affect the parent's cash flows, exchange gains and losses are excluded from net income. The translation process uses the current exchange rate to translate all but equity accounts.

Notice that the word "translation" is used in two different ways. In a specific sense, it refers to a method of converting from one currency to another. Remeasurement is another of these specific methods. But in a general sense, "translation" refers to *any* method of converting from one currency to another. You should have little trouble deciding which meaning is intended by the way the term is used in context, however.

Creating a Translated Income Statement

The report in Figure 3-1 on page 86 presents three versions of an income statement. Column E contains a statement in British pounds that has been adjusted to U.S. GAAP. Column J shows the first statement remeasured into U.S. dollars; column O shows the first statement translated into U.S. dollars.

The table at the top of the statement provides all the exchange rates used in this section of the spreadsheet file and the sections in Figure 3-3 and Figure 3-4. (These rates are provided for illustration only; they are not actual rates.) By changing the exchange rates in this table, you can change the rates used in the figures.

Both remeasurement and translation use the same rate for sales in row 20: the average exchange rate during the year. Although this rate is termed a current rate, it is also a historical rate for sales because it's an average of the rates in effect when the sales were made. The exchange rates for administrative expenses, interest, and taxes follow the same logic. Mathematically, the rate used is the average of the 12 month-end rates. This value reflects the assumption that sales and expenses were essentially equal during each month of the fiscal year.

The cost-of-sales figure for remeasurement uses historical rates. It calculates the approximate historical cost by adding the beginning inventory balance at the beginning-of-the-year rate to purchases at the average-of-the-year rate and then by subtracting the ending inventory balance at the average rate for the last three months. Translation, on the other hand, uses the average rate for the year to translate a current value for cost of goods sold.

The remeasurement of depreciation uses the weighted average rate calculated for fixed assets. The spreadsheet in Figure 3-2 on page 89 illustrates the calculation method.

As you can see from this spreadsheet, to calculate the weighted average rate, simply convert each purchase to U.S. dollars using the rate in effect when the asset was purchased and then divide the total cost in dollars by the total cost in pounds.

To create the statement in Figure 3-1, enter the numbers and labels shown in rows 3 through 19. The format box and the column-width box for Figure 3-1 will guide you in formatting this range. When you've entered the data, define the range name Rates as shown in the range-name box.

The formula box for Figure 3-1 shows all formulas in column E. Enter the data and formulas as shown. Copy the formulas, as appropriate, to columns J and O.

Columns H and M contain exchange rates that are found in the Rates table. The VLOOKUP formula in these columns looks up the adjacent note letter entered in column G or L and then returns the appropriate rate from the table. For example, cell H20 contains a formula (which is found in the formula box) that returns the rate for note *a*.

As shown in the formula box for cell J20, the formulas in columns J and O multiply the exchange rate by the number of British pounds to calculate U.S. dollars. Enter the formula as shown in the figure and copy it to the appropriate cells in columns J and O.

Cell J36 contains a formula returning an exchange rate gain or loss that will be calculated later in the spreadsheet. For now, leave this cell blank.

Creating a Translated Balance Sheet

The part of the spreadsheet shown in Figure 3-3 on page 90 shows the British company's balance sheet, along with a remeasured and a translated version. Notice that monetary assets and liabilities are remeasured using the current rate, while nonmonetary assets and liabilities are remeasured using historical rates. All assets and liabilities are translated using the current rate.

The formula box for Figure 3-3 provides all formulas used in column E. The remaining numbers in this column are entered as data. Copy each of the formulas in column E to columns J and O. Enter the formulas shown for cells H57 and J57 and then copy them as necessary to the remainder of the report.

Cell O76 contains the gain or loss from translation. Because it refers to a cell that is blank at the moment, do not enter the formula yet.

Creating a Schedule of Gains or Losses on Translation

The part of the spreadsheet in Figure 3-4 on page 92 shows the schedule of gains or losses on translation. As you can see in row 102, this gain or loss is the difference between the equity balance calculated by the assets and liabilities balance (row 94) and the assets balance calculated directly (row 100).

Because the gain or loss from remeasurement is shown on the income statement, it is also taxable. Unlike a translation adjustment, therefore, you must adjust this amount for taxes before you show it in the income statement. Rows 105 and 106 make this adjustment.

To create this section, enter the labels and borders as shown. Enter the formulas shown in the formula box and then copy the range J92:J102 to cell O92. To format this section, use formats similar to those shown for the sections in Figure 3-1 and Figure 3-3.

When you have completed this section, you must update the previous sections to reflect this data. In the section in Figure 3-1, enter the formula *=J106* in cell J36; in the section in Figure 3-3, enter the formula *=–J105* in cell J71 and *=O102* in cell O76.

CONSOLIDATING FINANCIAL STATEMENTS

The tough part about consolidating financial statements *should* be the accounting issues. The mechanical process of adding up the adjustments *should* be the easy part. But until recently, I found that both tasks were difficult.

The problem I had with adding up the adjustments was that of handling their signs correctly. For example, the spreadsheet in Figure 3-5 on page 94 shows the consolidation working papers of Tent Corporation. Cell D10 shows the value for subsidiary income to be a positive number; cell D11 shows the value for expenses to be positive as well. This is true, even though the first number is a credit and the second is a debit. But if both numbers are to be positive, what signs should the adjustments have? The adjustment in cell F10 must have an opposite sign from the entry in cell D10; should this debit therefore be negative? The adjustment in cell H11 must have the same sign as the entry in cell D11; should this debit therefore be positive? Pretty soon, things get confusing.

But there is an easy solution, which Figure 3-5 demonstrates. The solution is based on Microsoft Excel's powerful custom number formatting. The solution consists of three parts. Column C contains the first part. This column does *not* contain labels; each cell contains either *1* or *–1*. But *1* is custom formatted to be displayed as *Dr*, which stands for "debit;" *–1* is formatted to be displayed as *Cr* for "credit." The format box for Figure 3-5 shows the custom format for this column.

The columns of adjustments contain the second part of the solution. Although all values in columns F through I appear to be positive, they are not. Positive values are displayed with a *Dr*; negative values are displayed with a *Cr*.

Column K contains the third part of the solution. Each formula in this column adds the values that appear to the left, taking the positives and negatives into account. It does all this by adding the values in columns D and E to an amount that is equal to the value in column C times the sum of the adjustments. In cell K10, for example, it adds the positive value in cell D10 to the quantity –1, times the value in cell F10. (In this case, the formula returns 0, which the format displays as a blank.) And in cell K11, it adds the values in cells D11 and E11 to the quantity 1, times the value in cell H11.

The only other unusual aspect of this figure is the shading in the adjustments columns. The shading exists wherever adjustments should not be entered. You should not enter adjustments in row 13, for example, because this is merely the sum of the values or adjustments in rows 9 through 12. You should not enter adjustments in row 16 because this row merely repeats the value in row 13. Similar logic applies to the other rows that are shaded.

Creating a Consolidation Balance Sheet

To create the Consolidation Balance Sheet, enter the labels shown in rows 3 through 7 and in columns A and B, formatting them as shown in the format box for Figure 3-5. Format the range C8:C34 as shown and then enter *1* where a debit is displayed in the column and *–1* where a credit is displayed.

The column-width box in Figure 3-5 shows the width of each column used in the display. As with other figures in this book, use this information as a guide. Don't be concerned about adjusting your columns to these exact widths.

Format the range D8:E34 as shown in the format box. Enter the formulas shown for column D in the formula box and copy these formulas to columns E and K. Then enter the values shown for columns D and E.

Format the range F8:J34 as shown and then enter the adjustments and eliminations shown for columns F through I. Enter all debits as positive numbers and all credits as negative numbers. Enter the formula shown in the formula box for cell F34 and copy it to cells G34 through I34.

The explanation for each journal entry is shown at the bottom of the spreadsheet. But because this section is about spreadsheet techniques, not accounting techniques, don't be concerned if these explanations aren't particularly informative. In general, Tent Corporation has acquired 80 percent of Booth Corporation, and these journal entries consolidate Booth's income at the end of the first fiscal year.

Format the range K8:K34 as shown and then enter the formula shown for cell K9. Copy this formula down column K as necessary. Then, to complete this figure, enter the borders and underlines as shown.

Adjusting the Spreadsheet to Meet Your Needs

This spreadsheet is an easy one to adjust. If you want to add asset categories, for example, just insert the number of rows that are necessary in the assets section and then copy the formulas down column K as needed. When you update column C, enter *1* or *−1* to indicate whether Microsoft Excel should read a positive balance in column D as a debit or a credit.

To add columns for adjustments, highlight column J and then choose Edit Insert. When you do so, your spreadsheet returns a properly formatted column.

YEAR-END ADJUSTMENTS AT THE GL-ACCOUNT LEVEL

The two previous sections of this chapter demonstrated ways to adjust financial information at the summary level. Not uncommonly, however, you need to manipulate financial information at the GL-account level.

When you prepare income taxes, for example, you must assign each GL-account number to a specific income tax schedule and line number. At times you must even split a GL-account number into parts, sending the amount that's tax deductible to one line number and the amount that's not tax deductible to another. This section uses the tax problem to illustrate general techniques for adjusting and analyzing general ledger data.

As you create the spreadsheet in Figure 3-6, set your columns to any width that's convenient. The column-width box, however, shows the widths that I used.

General Ledger Tax Lines

When I last prepared a corporate tax return, I began with a general ledger trial balance. Columns A, B, and C of the spreadsheet in Figure 3-6 on page 96 illustrate a small section from just such a trial balance. Then I went through the trial balance row by row and assigned number codes for each tax schedule and line numbers to each account, as shown in columns D and E. The number codes for the tax schedules are shown at the top of the figure; the line numbers are those assigned within each schedule. (Several line numbers on the tax forms, as in row 29 of the figure, are subdivided into parts a and b. Tax line 8a, therefore, became spreadsheet tax line 8.1; line 8b on the tax form became spreadsheet tax line 8.2; and so on.)

I soon found myself dumping thousands of dollars into the "Other" category of line 26 on tax form 1120. I therefore added column F, which divides this broad category into finer detail that I could provide when I filled out the forms.

Entering a Tax-Line Summary Column

To create Figure 3-6, open your general ledger trial balance spreadsheet. If your accounting software doesn't provide a way to create a file that Microsoft Excel can open, follow the instructions provided in Appendix A for loading accounting reports into spreadsheets.

Assign the codes shown in columns D, E, and F to your data. This is the most complex step. In column G, enter the formula that combines the numbers in columns D, E, and F into one number. Represented by cell G15 in the formula box for Figure 3-6, this summary code makes your spreadsheet easier to sort and makes the formulas in the columns to the right easier to write.

The range G15:G29 in the format box shows the unusual custom number format used for column G. In cell G15, for example, this format displays the number 320000 as *3-20.0-00*. You can use a similar custom format, by the way, to add dashes or spaces to telephone numbers, social security numbers, and inventory part numbers.

After you complete column G, sort the general ledger on this column, as shown in the figure. Doing so allows you to calculate the columns of subtotals that follow. (If you've set the manual recalculation option, remember to recalculate your spreadsheet before you sort on column G. If you don't recalculate, you'll probably sort out-of-date information.)

To sort the data shown in the spreadsheet, highlight the range A15:G29, choose Data Sort, designate cell G15 as the 1st Key and cell A15 as the 2nd Key, and then press Enter. When you do so, the program sorts your spreadsheet in the sequence of column G. Where duplicate numbers exist in that column, it sorts in the sequence of column A.

Notice that I did *not* include subtotal columns in the sort range. Doing so would have hopelessly jumbled the formulas in those columns, forcing me to reenter them.

Entering Subtotal Columns

Columns H and I contain the pair of formulas that generate subtotals by using the tax-line number in column E. Columns J and K contain formulas that generate subtotals for the Tax Other column, column F. Because columns H and J contain data that is needed for the calculations but that is of no interest to humans, hide these two columns by setting their widths to 0. All four formulas are shown in the formula box for the figure.

(Be careful, however, when you use a column width of 0. Doing so creates a "black hole" that can make data seem to disappear. For example, suppose you decided to move the box of tax-schedule codes that begins in cell A5 so that it begins instead in cell G5. If you do so, the labels that now begin in cell B6 would disappear because they've been moved to the hidden column H.)

Correcting Mistakes and Entering Adjustments

After you sort and print your spreadsheet, you'll probably find mistakes in line-number assignments. However, most of these are easy to spot in two ways. First, look for subtotals that seem unreasonably large or small. Second, look at the descriptions of the accounts within each subtotal to quickly find GL-account numbers that don't belong in each grouping. When you find errors, it's easy to fix them. Simply change the appropriate number in columns D, E, or F and then sort your data again.

In addition to correcting mistakes, you need to make other adjustments. I occasionally found, for instance, that one GL-account number contained some expenses that were tax deductible and others that were not. And some accounts required more extensive adjustments. I had to change book depreciation, for example, to tax depreciation. When you document these adjustments as tax-journal entries, enter them into your spreadsheet. Rows 16 and 29 show one such entry. (I used a tilde character as the first character of the description of each of these entries, because the tilde character follows the letter *z* when it's sorted in alphabetic order. So, when I sorted on the Description field, all the entries that started with a tilde were grouped at the bottom of the database.)

Extracting the Summaries

Although you'll need to see the detailed account information when you're searching for errors, you'll eventually want to see a summary of the subtotals by line number.

Figure 3-7 on page 98 shows this summary for the data in Figure 3-6. To generate the summary, first open a new spreadsheet and turn off its gridlines. Enter the labels and borders shown in rows 3 through 8.

Next, define the range names specified in the range-name boxes for Figure 3-6 and Figure 3-7. Notice that these ranges begin with row 13, the row of labels immediately above the first shaded row in the spreadsheet in Figure 3-6. The Data Extract command will use these labels when it extracts the schedule codes and line numbers. For this reason, the labels in cells A7 and B7 of the spreadsheet in Figure 3-7 must exactly match the labels in cells D13 and E13 of the spreadsheet in Figure 3-6. The surest way to achieve this match is to copy the labels from one spreadsheet to the other.

Column C in this summary uses array formulas that return the balance from the spreadsheet in Figure 3-6 for all combinations of tax-schedule codes and tax-line numbers shown in columns A and B. To create the codes and numbers in columns A and B, highlight the range A7:B7 of the spreadsheet in Figure 3-7 and then choose the Data Extract command and select Unique.

Caution: The Data Extract command erases all data below the output range, to the bottom of your spreadsheet. Before you choose the command, therefore, be certain that you haven't entered important data beneath the output range.

To complete the spreadsheet, enter the formula shown in the formula box for Figure 3-7 and then copy it down the column as needed. Finally, save the worksheet as TAX_SUM.XLS.

CONVERTING CASH-BASIS FINANCIAL STATEMENTS TO ACCRUAL

I grew up in a part of Montana where most of the ranchers used the same CPA. At the end of every year, they'd arrive at his office carrying boxes filled with checkbooks, receipts, tally sheets, equipment inventories, and bar napkins documenting the details of contracts sealed with a handshake. I was never sure how he managed it, but within weeks he'd bring order to the chaos, generating documents accurate enough to satisfy both the banker and the IRS.

Times have changed, of course. The ranchers are more financially sophisticated; many have computers. Even so, many of the ranchers and hundreds of thousands of other small companies still run their businesses out of a checkbook. During the year, they use cash-basis accounting; at year end, their CPAs convert their financial information to an accrual basis.

Figure 3-8 on page 99 shows a simplified version of the information that one such small business might prepare for its CPA at the end of the year. The cash income statement shows that the firm produced an operating cash income of $3,000 and that it paid $2,700 for equipment and borrowed an additional $1,500.

In addition to this information, however, one needs to know the year-end balances in the major balance-sheet accounts. These are shown at the bottom of the spreadsheet in Figure 3-8. Notice in rows 31 and 32 that accounts payable has been divided into two categories: accounts payable for inventories and accounts payable for operating expenses. If A/P isn't split in this way, operating expenses tend to be reported as part of cost of goods sold.

Creating the Cash-to-Accrual Spreadsheet

Figure 3-9 on page 100 shows a spreadsheet that begins with last year's accrual-basis financial statements. In columns E through L, the spreadsheet displays journal entries used to update last year's information for the current year's activity, which generates this year's accrual-basis financial statements in column N.

This spreadsheet is similar to the one in Figure 3-5. In fact, you may find that the easiest way to create this spreadsheet is to begin with the Figure 3-5 spreadsheet and then modify it to look like the Figure 3-9 spreadsheet. When you create it, both the spreadsheet techniques and the accounting techniques may present a challenge.

Spreadsheet techniques

As with Figure 3-5, three elements make this spreadsheet work correctly. The first element is in column C, which contains either *1* or *−1*; positive values are displayed as *Dr* and negative values are displayed as *Cr.*

The second element is the way you enter and format the adjustments. Enter debits as positive values and credits as negative values; all values are displayed as positive, however, with the appropriate debit or credit notation.

The third element is the formula used in column N to properly combine the debits and credits as it totals the adjustments in each row and adds last year's balance, where appropriate, to calculate this year's balance. The formula box for Figure 3-9 shows two versions of this formula. One version is for the income statement, as represented by cell N46; the other version is for the balance sheet, as represented by cell N64.

This figure, like Figure 3-5, contains a number of shaded rows within the adjustments section. The purpose of the shading is to remind you that no adjustments are allowed within these rows. Generally, adjustments are prohibited here because these rows contain subtotals within columns D and N. You can't directly adjust the gross-profit subtotal in row 48, for example, because this amount is equal to the difference between the sales amount in row 46 and the cost-of-sales amount in row 47. Similarly, you can't adjust retained earnings in cell 84 because it is a result of the calculation of retained earnings in row 61.

Although your data will no doubt require different column widths, the column-width boxes for the figures should provide a place to start.

Accounting techniques

Columns E through L of the spreadsheet in Figure 3-9 represent a single general-journal entry each. Cell E43 provides a one-word description of the nature of the entry in that column. Cell E44 contains a code that references the specific journal entry. In this spreadsheet, however, this cell refers to a section within the formula box for Figure 3-9.

Most of the journal entries in the spreadsheet follow a pattern that we can illustrate with the entries that book sales and accounts receivable for the year in column E. In general, these two accounts have the following relationship:

```
Beginning Accounts Receivable
+Sales
-Collections
=Ending Accounts Receivable
```

In this instance, however, we want the amount of the sales. We can therefore rearrange the previous formula to read:

```
Collections
+Ending Accounts Receivable
-Beginning Accounts Receivable
=Sales
```

In cell E64, we debit cash for the $15,000 in collections. In cell E65, we debit accounts receivable for the $200 accounts receivable increase, which is equal to the ending accounts receivable minus the beginning balance. And in cell E46, we credit sales for the sum of these amounts, or $15,200. (Because sales normally has a credit balance, however, the sum is preceded by a minus sign to create that credit.)

Most of the entries in columns F through L follow a pattern similar to those in column E. The formulas and explanations in the formula box for Figure 3-9 will help you understand how the logic is applied to each of the columns.

REPORTING STOCKHOLDERS' EQUITY

When we got our first accounting test back, nearly everyone in my college class was outraged. Here we were, hotshot MBA students, and our professor had deducted points for lack of neatness!

"Many of you will be CPAs," he said. "And many of you will prepare reports for senior management. If you can't learn to present your analyses and conclusions professionally, you won't go very far in either public accounting or in private business. That's why, in this class, neatness counts."

Microsoft Excel provides the tools to generate reports neat enough to satisfy any company's professional standards. But often, the difficult and time-consuming challenge is how to arrange your data so that you can use those tools effectively.

For many companies, the Statement of Stockholders' Equity provides just such a challenge. Unlike the simple statements of retained earnings that have appeared in many figures in this chapter, the Statement of Stockholders' Equity must often report transactions that have occurred over several years in a number of different categories of equity. This section of the chapter, therefore, presents three versions of this statement, each containing successively greater detail.

Columnar Months

Figure 3-10 on page 105 presents a statement from the fictional Oak International Company. This statement, which shows few transactions in stockholders' equity, puts each year's activity in a different column.

As the formula box for Figure 3-10 shows, the formulas that generate this spreadsheet provide little food for thought. But the custom format for the range A9:D39 is another matter entirely. Although every number format can consist of four sections, this format is one of the rare ones that actually use each of the four. Here's a complete explanation of this custom number format:

Positive numbers: *#,##0 ;* Because this format contains no decimal point, it displays values rounded to the nearest whole unit. The 0, however, instructs Microsoft Excel to display positive numbers that must be rounded to 0 as 0. (If a # were to replace this 0, numbers that must be rounded to 0 would appear as blanks.) The comma, of course, separates numbers into groups of three. And notice the space following the 0; the importance of this space will become clear shortly.

Negative numbers: *(#,##0);* This format is similar to the previous format but is surrounded by parentheses. Because the right parenthesis takes up space in a column, it must be matched by a space in the custom format for positive numbers. If this space weren't included, positive and negative numbers wouldn't line up vertically.

Zeros: *----;* This format returns a dashed line followed by a blank space for a true 0 value. But because of the positive number format, a positive number that is rounded to 0 will be displayed as *0*; a negative number rounded to 0 will be displayed as *(0)*.

Labels: *@*.* This format prints a label and then fills the remainder of the cell with periods. The @ symbol instructs Microsoft Excel to print the label. The * symbol instructs the program to repeat the symbol that follows—in this case, a period. If a column isn't wide enough to contain the entire label, this formatting produces an unusual result for labels. The program fills the cell containing the label with pound signs, the overflow symbol. Generally, of course, labels overflow into adjacent cells as space is available.

Figure 3-11 on page 107 is a representation of the actual Consolidated Statement of Shareholders' Equity from Hewlett-Packard's 1986 annual report. This statement has transposed the data from Figure 3-10; that is, data for the various categories of equity is presented in columns, while data for each year is presented in rows.

This report shows how you can enhance the appearance of a document through the effective use of several font sizes and simple borders. The format box for the figure shows the specific fonts, as well as the custom number formats used in the display.

Figure 3-12 on page 109 shows the Statement of Stockholders' Equity from a fictional firm, The Gotham Companies. This statement uses the same general structure as Hewlett-Packard's statement does, but it presents a significantly greater number of transactions.

This general approach to presenting changes in stockholders' equity seems to be the most popular in annual reports. The popularity is probably a result of the significant amount of detail the format allows, as Figure 3-12 demonstrates.

You may at first have a problem fitting this statement on a single sheet of paper. When I ran into this problem, I first reduced the width of each column as far as I could. The column-width box for the figure shows the results. But the display still wouldn't fit on one printed page.

To correct this problem, I chose Format Font and redefined Font 1 as Helv 8. By reducing the size of Font 1, I reduced the width of each column, the height of most rows, and the size of characters displayed on the screen and printed on a page.

Redefining Font 1 reduced the column width because column width is defined in multiples of the width of one character in Font 1, so reducing the size of that font also reduces the column widths.

Defining a new Font 1 reduced most row heights because the size of a font determines the standard row height. Helv 10 generates a standard height of 13 points, and Helv 8 generates a height of 12 points. Therefore, the only rows that didn't change heights were those that I had set to a nonstandard height.

The format box for Figure 3-12 shows the key formats that I used in this display. The number format shown for the range A12:I50 is identical to the format shown for the range A9:D39 in the format box for Figure 3-10.

Figure 3-1. Remeasurement and Translation—Income Statement

An income statement showing both currency remeasurement and translation adjustment.

	A	B	C
1			
2			
3	**Notes for Currency Translations**		
4	*a*	1.793	Current Rate: Average of each month-end rate.
5	*b*	1.490	Current Rate: Exchange rate at year end.
6	*c*	2.118	Historical: Exchange rate at the beginning of the year.
7	*d*	1.537	Historical: Average of rates for last three months, reflecting a 90-day inventory turnover.
8	*e*	1.881	Historical: The weighted average rate for all depreciable fixed assets now on the books.
9	*f*	2.100	Historical: The exchange rate at the time the land was purchased.
10	*g*	1.913	Historical: The exchange rate at the time the capital stock was first contributed.
11	*h*	Per schedule (see Figure 3-4).	
12	*i*	Historical accumulated balance, as shown in the calculation of retained earnings for 12/31/88.	
13			

				Remeasurement into the Functional Currency			Translation into U.S. Currency		
			Local Currency	Notes	Rate	Amount	Notes	Rate	Amount
14	**Chip-Master Inc.**								
15	**Income Statement**								
16	**December 31, 1988**								
20	Sales	£	25,192	*a*	1.793	$ 45,169	*a*	1.793	$ 45,169
21	Costs and Expenses:								
22	Cost of Sales:								
23	Beginning Inventory		3,149	*c*	2.118	6,670			
24	Plus: Purchases		15,745	*a*	1.793	28,231			
25	Less: Ending Inventory		3,779	*d*	1.537	5,808			
26	Total Cost of Sales		15,115			29,092	*a*	1.793	27,101
27									
28	Depreciation		2,267	*e*	1.881	4,264	*a*	1.793	4,065
29	Selling, General, and								
30	Administrative Expenses		2,645	*a*	1.793	4,742	*a*	1.793	4,742
31	Interest Expense		1,058	*a*	1.793	1,897	*a*	1.793	1,897
32	Income Taxes		1,234	*a*	1.793	2,213	*a*	1.793	2,213
33	Total Country Expenses		22,319			42,208			40,018
34									
35	Net Income Before Trans Gain		2,873			2,961			5,151
36	Remeasurement Gain (Loss)			*h*		5,081			
37	Net Income	£	2,873			$ 8,042			$ 5,151
39									
40									
41	**Statement of Retained Earnings**								
42	Net Income--1987		2,873			8,042			5,151
43	Less: Dividends		1,486	*a*	1.793	2,664	*a*	1.793	2,664
44	Balance to Retained Earnings		1,387			5,378			2,487
45	Ret Earnings--Dec. 31, 1987		7,810	*i*		13,140	*i*		13,140
46	Ret Earnings--Dec. 31, 1988	£	9,197			$ 18,518			$ 15,627
47									

(continued)

Figure 3-1. *continued*

COLUMN WIDTHS							
Column	***Width***	***Column***	***Width***	***Column***	***Width***	***Column***	***Width***
A	3.14	E	7.86	I	3	M	6
B	6.57	F	1.14	J	7.29	N	2.57
C	12.71	G	6.14	K	2	O	6.71
D	1.86	H	5.43	L	7	P	1.86

KEY FORMULAS	
Cell	***Formula***
D20	**=CHAR(163)** To change this formula into a character, press F2 (Edit), F9 (Calc), and Enter.
H20	**=VLOOKUP(G20,Rates,2)** To change this rate, change either the note letter or the value for the note letter in the table of notes.
J20	**=H20*$E20** U.S. currency equals the conversion rate times the local currency.
E26	**=E23+E24–E25** The resulting value equals the beginning inventory plus purchases minus ending inventory.
E33	**=SUM(E26:E32)** The resulting value equals the sum of all foregoing expenses.
E35	**=E20–E33** The resulting value equals income minus expenses.
J36	**=J106** Only remeasurement shows a translation gain in the income statement.
E37	**=SUM(E35:E36)**
E42	**=E37**
E44	**=E37–E43** The resulting value equals earnings less dividends.
E46	**=E45+E44**

(continued)

Figure 3-1. *continued*

RANGE NAME	
Name	***Formula***
Rates	**=$A$4:$C$12** Putting the rates into a table allows you to modify the schedule quickly.

KEY CELL FORMATS			
Cell	***Number***	***Alignment***	***Font***
A3	**General**	**General**	**Helv 10, Bold**
A4:A12	**General**	**General**	**Helv 10, Italic**
B4:B12	**#,##0.000 ;(#,##0.000)**	**General**	**Helv 10**
A14:A15	**General**	**General**	**Helv 10, Bold**
E17:K19	**#,##0 ;(#,##0)**	**General**	**Helv 10**
D20:D79	**General**	**Right**	**Helv 10**
E20:E79	**#,##0 ;(#,##0)**	**General**	**Helv 10**
L20:L79	**General**	**Center**	**Helv 10, Italic**
M20:M79	**#,##0.000 ;(#,##0.000)**	**General**	**Helv 10**
N20:N79	**General**	**Right**	**Helv 10**
O20:O79	**#,##0 ;(#,##0)**	**General**	**Helv 10**

Figure 3-2. Calculation of Weighted Average Rate

A method of calculating the weighted average rate for translation of fixed assets.

	A	B	C	D	E	F	G	H	I
1									
2		**Calculation of Weighted Average Rate for Fixed Assets**							
3		Asset		Cost	Date	Rate		Dollar Cost	
4		Forklift	£	5,500	Oct-82	2.200	$	12,100	
5		Machinery		3,234	Feb-83	1.900		6,145	
6		Computer		9,983	Jun-85	1.700		16,971	
7		Total	£	18,717		1.881	$	35,216	
8									

KEY FORMULAS	
Cell	***Formula***
H4	**=F4*D4**
F7	**=ROUND(H7/D7,3)**

Figure 3-3. Remeasurement and Translation—Balance Sheet

A balance sheet using both remeasurement and translation adjustment. For column widths, range name, and cell formats, see Figure 3-1.

	A B C	D E	F G	H	I J	K L	M	N O P
49								
50								
51	**Chip-Master Inc.**							
52	**Balance Sheet**							
53	**December 31, 1988**							
54			Remeasurement into the					
55		Local	Functional Currency			Translation into U.S. Currency		
56	**Assets**	Currency	Notes	Rate	Amount	Notes	Rate	Amount
57	Cash	£ 1,260	*b*	1.490	$ 1,877	*b*	1.490	$ 1,877
58	Accounts Receivable	2,519	*b*	1.490	3,753	*b*	1.490	3,753
59	Inventories	3,779	*d*	1.537	5,808	*b*	1.490	5,631
60	Land	1,637	*f*	2.100	3,438	*b*	1.490	2,439
61	Machinery and Equipment	18,717	*e*	1.881	35,207	*b*	1.490	27,888
62	Total Assets	£ 27,912			$ 50,083			$ 41,589
64								
65	**Liabilities & Equity**							
66	Notes Payable--Current	1,260	*b*	1.490	1,877	*b*	1.490	1,877
67	Accounts Payable	5,038	*b*	1.490	7,507	*b*	1.490	7,507
68	Notes Payable--Long Term	6,346	*b*	1.490	9,456	*b*	1.490	9,456
69	Deferred Income Taxes							
70	Country Taxes	2,519	*b*	1.490	3,753	*b*	1.490	3,753
71	Translation Gain or (Loss)		*h*		2,178			
72	Total Liabilities	15,163			24,771			22,593
73								
74	Capital Stock	3,552	*g*	1.913	6,795	*g*	1.913	6,795
75	Retained Earnings	9,197	*i*		18,518	*i*		15,627
76	Gain or (Loss) from Translation					*h*		(3,426)
77	Total Equity	12,749			25,313			18,996
78								
79	Total Liabilities & Equity	£ 27,912			$ 50,083			$ 41,589
81								

(continued)

Figure 3-3. *continued*

KEY FORMULAS	
Cell	***Formula***
E62	**=SUM(E57:E61)**
E72	**=SUM(E66:E71)**
E75	**=E46** The Statement of Retained Earnings generates this value.
E77	**=SUM(E74:E76)**
E79	**=E77+E72**
H57 **J57**	**=VLOOKUP(G57,Rates,2)** **=H57*$E57** Copy these formulas from Figure 3-1.
J71	**=–J105** This formula references the translation income from remeasurement in the Schedule of Gains (Losses) on Translation in Figure 3-4.
O76	**=O102** This formula references the translation gain in the Schedule of Gains (Losses) on Translation.

Figure 3-4. Schedule of Gains (Losses) on Translation

A schedule of gains and losses on translation using both remeasurement and translation adjustments. For column widths and range name, see Figure 3-1.

	A	B	C	D	E	F	G	H	I	J	K	L	M	N	O	P
84																
85																
86	**Chip-Master Inc.**															
87	**Schedule of Gains (Losses) on Translation**															
88	**December 31, 1988**															
89										**Remeasurement**						
90										**Into the Functional**					**Translation**	
91										**Currency**					**Adjustments**	
92	Translated Assets								$	50,083				$	41,589	
93	Less: Translated Liabilities									22,593					22,593	
94	Translated Equity									27,491					18,996	
95																
96	Less: Actual Equity															
97		Capital Stock								6,795					6,795	
98		Beginning Retained Earnings								13,140					13,140	
99		Income Net of Dividends								297					2,487	
100	Total Actual Equity									20,232					22,422	
101																
102	Translation Gain (Loss)									7,259				$	(3,426)	
104																
105	Income Taxes on Remeasurement Gain (Loss)							30%		(2,178)						
106	Reportable Remeasurement Gain (Loss)								$	5,081						
108																

(continued)

Figure 3-4. *continued*

KEY FORMULAS	
Cell	***Formula***
J92	**=J62** This value is the total assets in the Schedule of Gains (Losses) on Translation.
J93	**=SUM(J66:J70)** This formula finds all liabilities in the Schedule of Gains (Losses) on Translation other than deferred taxes on translation gain.
J94	**=J92–J93** Equity equals Assets minus Liabilities.
J97	**=J74** This value is capital stock.
J98	**=J45** This value is the beginning retained earnings.
J99	**=J35–J43** This formula finds the local net income less dividends.
J100	**=SUM(J97:J99)** This formula finds the total of local equity in U.S. dollars.
J102	**=J94–J100** The balancing figure between the two equity values equals the gain or loss from translation.
J105	**=–H105*J102** This formula calculates taxes on the gain at the U.S. rate.
J106	**=SUM(J102:J105)** This formula reports after-tax translation income on the income statement.

Figure 3-5. Consolidation Worksheet

A spreadsheet that consolidates financial statements.

	A	B	C	D	E	F	G	H	I	J	K	L
1												
2												
3						**Tent Corporation and Subsidiary**						
4						**Consolidation Working Papers**						
5						**For the Year Ended December 31, 1988**						
6					80%	Adjustments & Eliminations					Consolidated	
7				Tent	Booth	a	b	c	d		Statements	
8	**Income Statement**											
9		Revenue	Cr	315,000	91,000						406,000	
10		Income from Subsidiary	Cr	25,980		25,980 Dr						
11		Expenses	Dr	252,000	56,000			2,020 Dr			310,020	
12		Minority Interest Net Income	Dr						7,000 Dr		7,000	
13		Net Income	Cr	88,980	35,000						88,980	
14												
15	**Retained Earnings**											
16		Net Income	Cr	88,980	35,000						88,980	
17		Retained Earnings--Jan 1	Cr	6,000	42,000		42,000 Dr				6,000	
18		Deduct Dividends	Dr	38,000	21,000	16,800 Cr			4,200 Cr		38,000	
19		Retained Earnings--Dec 31	Cr	56,980	56,000						56,980	
20												
21	**Balance Sheet**											
22		Cash	Dr	50,000	14,000						64,000	
23		Other Current Assets	Dr	113,000	70,000						183,000	
24		Investment in Booth	Dr	130,180		9,180 Cr	121,000 Cr					
25		Plant and Equipment	Dr	378,000	138,000						516,000	
26		Accumulated Depreciation	Cr	63,000	41,000						104,000	
27		Goodwill	Dr				20,200 Dr	2,020 Cr			18,180	
28			Dr	608,180	181,000						677,180	
29												
30		Liabilities	Cr	141,200	41,000						182,200	
31		Capital Stock	Cr	410,000	84,000		84,000 Dr				410,000	
32		Retained Earnings	Cr	56,980	56,000						56,980	
33		Minority Interest	Cr				25,200 Cr		2,800 Cr		28,000	
34			Cr	608,180	181,000	0	0	0	0		677,180	
35												
36	**Adjustments & Eliminations**											
37	a. To establish reciprocity as of the beginning of the period.											
38	b. To eliminate reciprocal equity and investment amounts, establish minority interest at the beginning of the											
39	period, and set up the original goodwill at acquisition.											
40	c. To adjust expenses to reflect current goodwill amortization.											
41	d. To reflect the interests of minority stockholders.											
42												

COLUMN WIDTHS							
Column	***Width***	***Column***	***Width***	***Column***	***Width***	***Column***	***Width***
A	1.43	D	7.57	G	9.29	J	0.67
B	23	E	6.86	H	8.43	K	12.29
C	2	F	8.43	I	7.57		

(continued)

Figure 3-5. *continued*

KEY FORMULAS	
Cell	***Formula***
C9	**–1** All credits in column C equal –1. All debits equal 1.
K9	**=D9+E9+C9*SUM(F9:J9)** Multiplying by cell C9 assigns the correct sign to the adjustments.
D13	**=D9+D10–D11–D12** Because cells D11 and D12 are displayed as positive values, they must be subtracted in this formula.
D19	**=D17+D16–D18**
D28	**=SUM(D22:D25)–D26+D27**
D34	**=SUM(D30:D33)**
F18 **F34**	**=0.8*E18** **=SUM(F7:F33)** The sum of all adjustments in a column must equal 0.
I18	**=0.2*E18**

KEY CELL FORMATS			
Cell	***Number***	***Alignment***	***Font***
F3:F5	**General**	**Center**	**Helv 10, Bold**
D6:K7	**General**	**Center**	**Helv 10**
C8:C34	**"*Dr*";"*Cr*"**	**Center**	**Helv 10**
D8:E34	**#,##0 ;(#,##0);**	**General**	**Helv 10**
F8:J34	**#,##0 "*Dr*";#,##0 "*Cr*";0**	**General**	**Helv 10**
K8:K34	**#,##0 ;(#,##0);**	**General**	**Helv 10**

Figure 3-6. Tax-Line Worksheet

A spreadsheet that helps you assign tax-schedule codes and line numbers to your year-end general ledger trial balance. Saved as TAX_LINE.XLS.

	A	B	C	D	E	F	G	I	K	L
1										
2										
3	Tax-Schedule Line Numbers Assigned to General-Ledger Accounts									
4										
5		Tax-Schedule Codes								
6	1	Schedule L								
7	2	Schedule A								
8	3	Schedule 1120								
9	4	Schedule M1								
10										
11	December 1988 Trial Balance, with Tax Lines									
12			Adj	Tax	Tax	Tax	Summary	Total	Other	
13	Acct	Description	Bal	Sched	Line	Other	Code	T/L	Total	
14										
15	6514	Dep'n--Mach & Equip	52,249.57	3	20		3-20.0-00			
16	6514	~TJE-1--Tax Deprn	7,352.40	3	20		3-20.0-00	59,601.97		
17	9626	Sales Promotions	6,558.02	3	23		3-23.0-00			
18	9636	Trade Shows	12,100.27	3	23		3-23.0-00			
19	9756	Co-op Advertising	98,106.00	3	23		3-23.0-00	116,764.29		
20	8205	Other Fringe Benefits	3,066.59	3	25		3-25.0-00			
21	9206	Fringe Benefits--Mkt	2,118.42	3	25		3-25.0-00			
22	9216	Med Insurance--Mktg	15,442.62	3	25		3-25.0-00	20,627.63		
23	8305	Stationery & Supplies	10,819.07	3	26	1	3-26.0-01			
24	8935	Service Charges	6,876.20	3	26	1	3-26.0-01			
25	9706	Misc Supplies--Mktg	2,291.83	3	26	1	3-26.0-01		19,987.10	
26	8325	Postage	6,465.49	3	26	2	3-26.0-02		6,465.49	
27	8146	Consulting	1,225.83	3	26	3	3-26.0-03			
28	8335	Legal & Auditing	24,077.33	3	26	3	3-26.0-03	51,755.75	25,303.16	
29	6514	~TJE-1--Tax Deprn	(7,352.40)	4	8.1		4-08.1-00	(7,352.40)		
30										
31										
32										

COLUMN WIDTHS							
Column	***Width***	***Column***	***Width***	***Column***	***Width***	***Column***	***Width***
A	**4.86**	**D**	**6**	**G**	**8.86**	**J**	**0**
B	**20.14**	**E**	**6**	**H**	**0**	**K**	**8.86**
C	**8.86**	**F**	**7.43**	**I**	**9.43**	**L**	**1.86**

(continued)

Figure 3-6. *continued*

KEY FORMULAS	
Cell	***Formula***
G15	**=100000*D15+1000*E15+F15** This formula combines three codes into one code for quicker sorting.
H15 **I15**	**=IF($E15=$E16,$H13+$C15,0)** **=IF($E15<>$E16,$H13+$C15,0)** This pair of formulas generates the subtotals shown in column I. Because column H contains scratch values needed only by the formulas in column I, column H is hidden by setting its width to 0. The quickest way to enter these is to enter H10 as shown, copy it to I10, and then change the = sign in I10 to the < and > signs.
J15 **K15**	**=IF($G15=$G16,$J13+$C15,0)** **=IF(F15>0,IF($G15<>$G16,$J13+$C15,0),0)** This pair of formulas works similarly to the preceding pair, but generates subtotals for the Tax Other category. The additional IF statement in column K forces this total to 0 where no numbers are entered in column F.

RANGE NAMES	
Name	***Formula***
Bal	**=$C$13:$C$30**
Line	**=$E$13:$E$30**
Sched	**=$D$13:$D$30**
Criteria	**=$D$13:$E$14**
Database	**=$D$13:$E$30**
	These range names let the spreadsheet in Figure 3-7 extract tax-schedule numbers and summarize them easily.

KEY CELL FORMATS			
Cell	***Number***	***Alignment***	***Font***
C15:C29	**#,##0.00 ;(#,##0.00);**	**General**	**Helv 10**
G15:G29	**##"–"##"."#"–"##**	**General**	**Helv 10**
I15:I29	**#,##0.00 ;(#,##0.00);**	**General**	**Helv 10**
K15:K29	**#,##0.00 ;(#,##0.00);**	**General**	**Helv 10**

Figure 3-7. Financial Summary by Tax Schedule Code and Line Number

A summary of a year-end general ledger trial balance by tax schedule code and line number. Saved as TAX_SUM.XLS.

	A	B	C	D
1				
2				
3	Financial Summary			
4	By Tax Schedule Code			
5	And by Line Number			
6	Tax	Tax	Total	
7	Sched	Line	Balance	
8				
9	3	20	59,601.97	
10	3	23	116,764.29	
11	3	25	20,627.63	
12	3	26	51,755.75	
13	4	8.1	(7,352.40)	
14				
15				
16				
17				

KEY FORMULA

Cell	*Formula*
C9	**=SUM(IF(Sched=A9,IF(Line=B9,Bal)))** This array formula adds all values in the Bal range that meet the criteria shown.

RANGE NAMES

Name	*Formula*
Bal	**=TAX_LINE.XLS!Bal**
Line	**=TAX_LINE.XLS!Line**
Sched	**=TAX_LINE.XLS!Sched**
Criteria	**=TAX_LINE.XLS!Criteria**
Database	**=TAX_LINE.XLS!Database** These range definitions all reference range names in the spreadsheet in Figure 3-6.

Figure 3-8. Cash Income Statement

A simple cash income financial statement and the year-end balances required to construct an accrual financial statement.

	A	B	C	D	E	F	G
1							
2							
3	**Cash Income Statement**						
4	Bill's Swap Shop				December 31, 1988		
5	**Cash Income**						
6		Cash Receipts from Sales				15,000	
7		Payments for Goods Sold				7,200	
8		Cash Profit on Sales				7,800	
9							
10		Payments for Operating Expenses				3,100	
11		Interest Payments				700	
12		Income Taxes Paid				1,000	
13		Operating Cash Income				3,000	
14							
15	**Other Cash Payments**						
16		New Equipment				2,700	
17							
18	**Other Cash Receipts**						
19		Proceeds from New Loan				1,500	
20							
21	**Year-End Balances**						
22		Cash				3,300	
23		Accounts Receivable				2,500	
24		Inventory				1,650	
25		Prepaid Interest				325	
26		Prepaid Taxes				610	
27		Fixed Assets				6,200	
28		Accumulated Depreciation					
29		(Per Depreciation Schedule)				1,675	
30							
31		Accts Payable--Inventory				825	
32		Accts Payable--Operating Expenses				500	
33		Notes Payable				1,000	
34		Loans Payable				6,500	
35							
36							

COLUMN WIDTHS							
Column	*Width*	*Column*	*Width*	*Column*	*Width*	*Column*	*Width*
A	1	E	8.14	I	7.29	M	0.67
B	18	F	6.86	J	5.43	N	6.14
C	2	G	7.14	K	7		
D	6.29	H	5.57	L	7		

Figure 3-9. Cash-to-Accrual Adjustments

A spreadsheet to convert cash-basis financial statements to accrual. For column widths, see Figure 3-8.

	A/B	C	D	E	F	G	H	I	J	K	L	N
38												
39												
40						**Bill's Swap Shop**						
41						**Cash-to-Accrual Adjustments**						
42						**For the Year Ended December 31, 1988**						
43			Accrual	Sales	COGS	OpExp	Depr	F/A	Int	Loan	Taxes	Accrual
44			1987	a	b	c	d	e	f	g	h	1988
45	**Income Statement**											
46	Sales	Cr	10,000	15,200 Cr								15,200
47	Cost of Goods Sold	Dr	5,500		7,115 Dr							7,115
48	Gross Profit	Cr	4,500									8,085
49												
50	Operating Expenses	Dr	1,700			3,050 Dr						3,050
51	Depreciation Exp	Dr	400				425 Dr					425
52	Interest Expense	Dr	600						625 Dr			625
53	Inc Before Taxes	Cr	1,800									3,985
54	Income Taxes	Dr	540								970 Dr	970
55	Net Income	Cr	1,260									3,015
56												
57	**Retained Earnings**											
58	Net Income	Cr	1,260									3,015
59	Ret Earnings--Jan 1	Cr	930									2,190
60	Deduct Dividends	Dr										
61	Ret Earnings--Dec 31	Cr	2,190									5,205
62												
63	**Balance Sheet**											
64	Cash	Dr	1,500	15,000 Dr	7,200 Cr	3,100 Cr		2,700 Cr	700 Cr	1,500 Dr	1,000 Cr	3,300
65	Accts Receivable	Dr	2,300	200 Dr								2,500
66	Inventory	Dr	1,500		150 Dr							1,650
67	Prepaid Interest	Dr	250						75 Dr			325
68	Total Current Assets	Dr	5,550									7,775
69												
70	Plant and Equipment	Dr	6,200					2,700 Dr				8,900
71	Accum Depreciation	Cr	1,250				425 Cr					1,675
72	Net Fixed Assets	Dr	4,950									7,225
73	Total Assets	Dr	10,500									15,000
74												
75	Accts Payable--Inv	Cr	760		65 Cr							825
76	Accts Pble--Op Exp	Cr	550			50 Dr						500
77	Income Taxes Pble	Cr	640								30 Dr	610
78	Notes Payable	Cr	1,000									1,000
79	Total Current Liab	Cr	2,950									2,935
80	Loans Payable	Cr	4,360							1,500 Cr		5,860
81	Total Liabilities	Cr	7,310									8,795
82												
83	Capital Stock	Cr	1,000									1,000
84	Retained Earnings	Cr	2,190									5,205
85	Net Worth	Cr	3,190									6,205
86	Total Liab & Equity	Cr	10,500									15,000
87				0	0	0	0	0	0	0	0	
88												

(continued)

Figure 3-9. *continued*

KEY FORMULAS	
Cell	***Formula***
C46	**–1** The number format for this column returns *Dr* for 1 and *Cr* for –1.
N46	**=C46*SUM(E46:M46)** The ending income statement equals the sum of all journals for the year. To display the balance properly, it is multiplied by the Dr/Cr value in column C.
N58	**=N55** This cell reference returns the net income from the income statement.
N59	**=D61** This cell reference returns the retained earnings from last year.
N60	**=C60*SUM(E60:M60)** This formula picks up any dividends that have been entered.
N64	**=D64+C64*SUM(E64:M64)** The ending balance in the balance sheet is equal to the beginning balance plus any changes.
N84	**=N61** This cell reference returns the retained earnings balance from the Retained Earnings section.
E87	**=SUM(E45:E86)** The sum of all the debits and credits should equal 0.
a. To book yearly Sales and adjust Accounts Receivable:	
E46	**=–(E64+E65)** Sales equals cash receipts from sales plus the change in A/R. (A minus sign equals a credit.)
E64	**=F6** This cell reference returns the increase in cash balance by cash receipts from sales.
E65	**=F23–D65** The increase in A/R equals ending A/R minus beginning A/R.

(continued)

Figure 3-9. *continued*

KEY FORMULAS–continued	
Cell	***Formula***
b. To book Cost of Goods Sold and to adjust Inventory and Accounts Payable:	
F47	**=–(F64+F66+F75)** Cost of goods sold equals payments for COGS plus inventory increase plus A/P increase. (A minus sign changes the credits to a debit.)
F64	**=–F7** This formula decreases the cash balance by payments for cost of goods sold.
F66	**=F24–D66** An increase in inventory equals ending inventory minus beginning inventory.
F75	**=–(F31–D75)** An increase in A/P for inventory equals ending A/P minus beginning A/P. (A minus turns a debit into a credit.)
c. To book Operating Expenses for the year:	
G50	**=–(G64+G76)** Operating expenses equal payments for operating expenses plus the change in A/P for operating expenses. (The initial minus sign changes a credit to a debit.)
G64	**=–F10** Decrease the cash balance by the amount of payments for operating expenses.
G76	**=–(F32–D76)** An increase in A/P for operating expenses equals ending A/P minus beginning A/P. (The initial minus sign turns this increase into a credit.)
d. To book depreciation for the year:	
H51	**=F29–D71** The depreciation expense equals the ending balance of accumulated depreciation minus its beginning balance.
H71	**=–H51** The change in accumulated depreciation equals the depreciation expense. (A minus sign changes the debit to a credit.)

(continued)

Figure 3-9. *continued*

KEY FORMULAS-continued	
Cell	***Formula***
e. To book the purchase of fixed assets:	
I64	**=–F16** Decrease cash by the amount of the assets purchased and paid for.
I70	**=–I64** Increase fixed assets by a like amount. (A minus sign changes a credit to a debit.)
f. To book interest expense for the year:	
J52	**=–(J64+J67)** Interest expense equals the amount paid plus the change in the prepaid balance. (A minus sign changes a credit to a debit.)
J64	**=–F11** Decrease cash by the amount of interest paid.
J67	**=F25–D67** The change in prepaid interest equals the ending balance minus the beginning balance.
g. To book the receipt of a new loan:	
K64	**=F19** Increase cash by the amount of the loan.
K80	**=–K64** Increase loans payable by a like amount. (A minus sign changes a debit to a credit.)
h. To book income taxes for the year:	
L54	**=–(L64+L77)** The income-tax expense equals the taxes paid plus the change in liability. (A minus sign turns a credit to a debit.)
L64	**=–F12** Decrease cash by the amount of taxes paid.
L77	**=–(F26–D77)** The change in tax liability equals the ending balance minus the beginning balance. (A minus sign turns the change into a credit.)

(continued)

Figure 3-9. *continued*

KEY CELL FORMATS			
Cell	***Number***	***Alignment***	***Font***
H40:H42	**General**	**Center**	**Helv 10, Bold**
D43:N44	**General**	**Center**	**Helv 10**
C46:C86	**"Dr";"Cr"**	**Center**	**Helv 10**
D45:D86	**#,##0 ;(#,##0);**	**General**	**Helv 10**
E45:M87	**#,##0 "Dr";#,##0 "Cr";0**	**General**	**Helv 10**
N45:N86	**#,##0 ;(#,##0);**	**General**	**Helv 10**

Figure 3-10. Consolidated Statement of Stockholders' Equity, Version 1

A consolidated statement of stockholders' equity that illustrates the use of ellipses and other formatting techniques (accompanying notes not shown).

	A	B	C	D	E
1					
2					
3	OAK INTERNATIONAL COMPANY				
4	Consolidated Statement of Stockholders' Equity				
5					
6		**1988**	**1987**	**1986**	
7		(In Thousands of Dollars)			
8	**Preferred Stock**				
9	Beginning of year......................................	3,581	3,581	3,581	
10	Reacquired and retained in				
11	connection with disposition				
12	of subsidiary (Notes 4 and 7)..............	(3,581)	----	----	
13	End of year...	----	3,581	3,581	
14	**Common Stock**				
15	Beginning of year......................................	5,299	5,299	5,238	
16	Issuance of shares under				
17	stock options...	91	----	61	
18	End of year...	5,390	5,299	5,299	
19	**Additional Paid-In Capital**				
20	Beginning of year......................................	716	716	658	
21	Excess of proceeds over par				
22	value of common shares				
23	issued under stock options..................	42	----	58	
24	End of year...	758	716	716	
25	**Retained Earnings**				
26	Beginning of year				
27	As previously reported..........................	23,355	25,630	24,923	
28	Adjusted to reflect				
29	capitalization of leases........................	(302)	(357)	(258)	
30	As restated..	23,657	25,987	25,181	
31	Net income (loss).....................................	2,836	(1,840)	1,296	
32	Cash dividends paid:				
33	Common...	(57)	(302)	(302)	
34	Preferred..	----	(188)	(188)	
35	Excess of redemption value				
36	of preferred stock over				
37	carrying value (Note 7)........................	(1,302)	----	----	
38	End of year...	25,134	23,657	25,987	
39	**Total Stockholders' Equity......................**	$31,282	$33,253	$35,583	
40					

(continued)

Figure 3-10. *continued*

KEY FORMULAS	
Cell	*Formula*
B9	**=C13** This year's beginning balance equals last year's ending balance.
B39	**=B38+B24+B18+B13** Total Stockholders' Equity is the sum of the four subtotals.

KEY CELL FORMATS			
Cell	*Number*	*Alignment*	*Font*
B6:D6	**General**	**Center**	**= Helv 10, Bold**
A9:D39	**#,##0 ;(#,##0);---- ;@*.** The "----" displays a 0 as a dash. The "@" prints the label; the "*." fills the remaining spaces with periods when the cell contains a label. (Where the periods aren't required in column A, as in cell A8, assign a General number format. Also, as in cell A8, assign a bold font as necessary.)	**General**	**= Helv 10**
B39:D39	**$#,##0 ;($#,##0)**	**General**	**= Helv 10**

Figure 3-11. Consolidated Statement of Stockholders' Equity, Version 2

Hewlett-Packard's statement of shareholders' equity, which illustrates attractive formatting that can serve many purposes.

	A	B	C	D	E	F	G
1							
2							
3	Hewlett-Packard Company and Subsidiaries						
4	**CONSOLIDATED STATEMENT OF SHAREHOLDERS' EQUITY**						
5							
6							
7							
8							
9		Common Stock					
10		Number of		Capital in			
11		shares	Par	excess of	Retained		
12	(Millions, except number of shares)	(Thousands)	value	par value	earnings	Total	
13	Balance October 31, 1983	254,914	$255	$478	$2,154	$2,887	
14	Employee stock plans;						
15	Shares issued	4,456	4	148	----	152	
16	Shares purchased	(3,734)	(4)	(138)	----	(142)	
17	Dividends	----	----	----	(49)	(49)	
18	Increased ownership in affiliate	842	1	31	----	32	
19	Net earnings	----	----	----	665	665	
20	Balance October 31, 1984	256,478	256	519	2,770	3,545	
21	Employee stock plans:						
22	Shares issued	7,322	8	234	----	242	
23	Shares purchased	(6,974)	(7)	(233)	----	(240)	
24	Dividends	----	----	----	(57)	(57)	
25	Other	90	----	3	----	3	
26	Net earnings	----	----	----	489	489	
27	Balance October 31, 1985	256,916	257	523	3,202	3,982	
28	Employee stock plans:						
29	Shares issued	6,238	6	213	----	219	
30	Shares purchased	(7,062)	(7)	(280)	----	(287)	
31	Dividends	----	----	----	(56)	(56)	
32	Net earnings	----	----	----	516	516	
33	Balance October 31, 1986	256,092	$256	$456	$3,662	$4,374	
35	The accompanying notes are an integral part of these financial statements.						
36							
37							
38							
39							
40							
41							
42							
43							
44							
45							
46							
47							

(continued)

Figure 3-11. *continued*

COLUMN WIDTHS			
Column	*Width*	*Column*	*Width*
A	42	E	9.43
B	10.57	F	9
C	8.43	G	0.83
D	9.57		

KEY CELL FORMATS			
Cell	*Number*	*Alignment*	*Font*
A3	General	General	Helv 8
A35	General	General	Helv 8
A4	General	General	Helv 10, Bold
B10:F12	General	Right	Helv 10
C13:F13	$#,##0 ;($#,##0)	General	Helv 10
B14:F32	#,##0 ;(#,##0);---- The "----" displays a 0 as a dash.	General	Helv 10

Figure 3-12. Consolidated Statement of Stockholders' Equity, Version 3

A statement of stockholders' equity that condenses a great deal of information onto one sheet of paper (accompanying notes not shown).

THE GOTHAM COMPANIES

Consolidated Statement of Stockholders' Equity

	5% Cumulative Preferred Stock	Common Stock	Additional Paid-In Capital	Retained Earnings	Net Unrealized Loss on Marketable Equity Securities	5% Cumulative Preferred Stock in Treasury	Common Stock in Treasury	Total
Balance--January 1, 1985	$2,145,872	$2,084,659	$7,018,568	$2,300,777	($95,463)	($239,023)	($698,375)	$12,517,015
Cash distribution paid on 5% cumulative preferred stock..............	---	---	---	(74,280)	---	---	---	(74,280)
5,888 shares of 5% cumulative preferred stock acquired for treasury..	---	---	---	---	---	(98,624)	---	(98,624)
Purchase of 5,000 shares of common stock................................	---	---	---	---	---	---	(40,000)	(40,000)
Issuance of common shares:								
6,593--employment agreement.......	---	6,593	46,954	(1,524)	---	---	---	52,023
8,934--conversion of preferred stock..	(4,857)	8,934	(5,081)	---	---	---	---	(1,004)
12,230--employee stock options.......		12,230	85,898					98,128
5% Stock dividends paid May 16, 1986 and payable Jan 14, 1986.......	---	244,111	2,681,355	(2,987,951)	---	---	---	(62,485)
Cash dividends on common stock........	---	---	---	(782,004)	---	---	---	(782,004)
Adjustment of write-down of investment in noncurrent marketable equity securities............	---	---	---	---	17,854	---	---	17,854
Other..	---	111	(4,201)	---	---	---	---	(4,090)
Net Income--1986................................	---	---	---	2,875,965	---	---	---	2,875,965
Balance--December 31, 1986	$2,141,015	$2,356,638	$9,823,493	$1,330,983	($77,609)	($337,647)	($738,375)	$14,498,498
Cash distribution paid on 5% cumulative preferred stock..............	---	---	---	(74,015)	---	---	---	(74,015)
1,250 shares of 5% cumulative preferred stock acquired for treasury..	---	---	---	---	---	(24,063)	---	(24,063)
Issue of 50,000 shares of common stock from the Treasury to acquire a business...........................	---	---	---	---	---	---	500,000	500,000
Issuance of common shares:								
4,927--employment agreement....	---	4,927	98,753	---	---	---	---	103,680
38,520--employee stock..................	---	38,520	289,725	---	---	---	---	328,245
600,000--private placement..............	---	600,000	12,088,702	---	---	---	---	12,688,702
Cash dividends on common stock........	---	---	---	(952,748)	---	---	---	(952,748)
Adjustment of write-down of investment in noncurrent marketable equity securities............	---	---	---	---	11,953	---	---	11,953
Capital transaction of a subsidiary.......	---	---	(57,896)	---	---	---	---	(57,896)
Net Income--1987................................	---	---	---	2,893,215	---	---	---	2,893,215
Balance--December 31, 1987	$2,141,015	$3,000,085	$22,242,777	$3,197,436	($65,656)	($361,710)	($238,375)	$29,915,572

The accompanying notes are an integral part of these financial statements.

(continued)

Figure 3-12. *continued*

COLUMN WIDTHS			
Column	*Width*	*Column*	*Width*
A	30.83	F	9
B	10	G	9
C	10.33	H	9.33
D	11.33	I	11
E	9.83		

KEY CELL FORMATS			
Cell	*Number*	*Alignment*	*Font*
Sheet	General Assign Font 1 as Helvetica 8. Doing so will reduce the sheet proportionately.	General	Helv 8
A4	General	General	Helv 10, Bold
A12:I50	#,##0 ;(#,##0);---- ;@*. The "----" displays a 0 as a dash. The "@" prints the label; the "*." fills the remaining spaces with periods when the cell contains a label. (Where the periods aren't required in column A, as in cell A12, assign a General number format.)	General	Helv 8
A11:I11 A32:I32 A51:I51	General Formatting the beginning and ending balances with dollar signs serves as a way to highlight the balances.	General	Helv 8
A52	General	General	Helv 8, Italic

4

Accounts Payable and Accounts Receivable

If your company is like most, nearly all of your cash flows in through accounts receivable (A/R), and much of it flows out through accounts payable (A/P). The faster you collect and the slower you pay—within limits—the better off your company is.

Unfortunately, few accounting systems provide information that managers need to monitor these important functions. For example, few of these programs can answer requests like these:

- "How do you know your data is accurate?"
- "I see that J.R.'s company hasn't been paying its bills. What have his people been telling you?"
- "We're preparing a cash flow forecast. We need collection and payment history in the same format we'll use for the forecast."

- "Our last cash flow forecast predicted specific collection and payment performance. How does actual performance compare to forecast?"
- "Based on recent activity, how much cash will we collect this month?"
- "The economy seems to be turning downward. What new trends are we seeing in collection?"
- "A slow-paying customer claims to be suffering from a seasonal cash flow crunch. Does this problem crop up every year at this time? What other customers should we watch out for?"

This chapter provides techniques to answer these and other such questions.

ACCOUNTS RECEIVABLE FORMS

In these days of high-tech solutions, it seems rather old-fashioned to talk about handwritten forms. Yet most companies swear by them, and for good reason. Well-designed forms are quick to fill out and easy to update. They're inexpensive to reproduce and easy to understand. And with Microsoft Excel, they're easy to create, as well.

Accounts Receivable Reconciliation

Figure 4-1 on page 125 shows an accounts receivable reconciliation form that I have used in various formats for about 10 years. It helps me quickly learn whether my accounts receivable balance per the aging schedule reconciles with my book balance. And when it doesn't, the form helps me find the errors.

To complete this form for one month, begin with the completed copy from the previous month. Enter the aging amount shown in row 12 of last month's form into row 7 of this month's form. Then complete the reconciliation.

If everything worked perfectly each month, this section wouldn't be needed. It simply ensures that the ending balance equals the beginning balance plus the changes—all according to the computer. When the data *doesn't* reconcile, the problem can be major. More than once, for example, I've discovered computer software that fails to adjust sales and discounts for voided invoices. Usually, however, there's a simple reason for discrepancies. The most frequent of these, I've found, is the use of an out-of-date printout for the reconciliation. (This is the reason for the request at the bottom of the form to include a copy of the last page of all printouts. These copies document which printouts from your accounting software were used for the reconciliation.)

The second section of the reconciliation form provides several lines for accruals. Generally, these adjust errors that were discovered during the close, but after the end of the month. Although these errors will be corrected by the computer during the current month, the adjustments must still be accrued into the close and then reversed in next month's close.

This form is easy to create. The various information boxes for Figure 4-1 illustrate the number formats, column widths, and row heights used in the spreadsheet. You probably will want to adjust the heights and widths to accommodate your specific data.

The command you'll use most frequently will be Format Border. This command draws the lines and produces the shading. You'll be able to draw the underlines quickly if you use the options that the dialog box provides. For example, you can draw the borders in rows 21 through 27 in three passes. First, highlight the range A21:J27, choose Format Border, and select Outline, Top, and Bottom. Second, highlight the range F21:F27, choose Format Border, and select Outline. Third, highlight J21:J27, choose Format Border, and select Outline.

Accounts Receivable Collection-Information Sheet

When cash is tight, customers can find more reasons to delay payment than children can find to avoid eating spinach. This is one of the reasons I ask a new customer the administrative questions shown on the form in Figure 4-2 on page 127 after credit is approved. Often, answers make the excuses irrelevant before they come up.

For example, some small companies use the excuse that an invoice can't be approved, or a check written, until the owner returns from a trip. But if you've already been promised that the vice president of operations can approve payment and sign checks in the owner's absence, you have another chance at immediate payment.

The answer to the first question in the form shown in Figure 4-2 can help in another way, as well. By knowing a customer's payment schedule, you know when your invoice must arrive to be paid by a particular date. Occasionally, this knowledge might justify sending an invoice by an overnight delivery service. For example, suppose you know that payment of your $10,000 invoice will be delayed two weeks unless it arrives at your customer's office tomorrow. If you're paying 12 percent interest on borrowed money, that two-week delay will cost roughly $50 in interest. (You're paying 1 percent per month for a whole month, or 0.5 percent for a half month.) Because an overnight delivery service costs less than $15, you'll make $35 by using the service.

Because companies change their policies occasionally, the form contains enough lines to update the responses. At times, however, people simply forget the promises they've made. So each answer area of the form has room for a contact's name code and the date the information was provided. This lets you say, for example, "What do you mean you aren't authorized to approve payment? Of course you are. On September 16, Mrs. Gilmore *told me* that you're authorized! I'll be by in an hour to pick up our check."

The information boxes for the figure provide the number formats, row heights, and column widths. As with other figures in this book, however, you'll want to adapt these to your own purposes. You may notice that the row heights vary slightly from the form shown in Figure 4-1. There's no science to these settings. A higher row would provide more room to write, but fewer lines to write on. The row heights that I used seemed to be a fair compromise.

Phone Log for A/R Collections

For years, as the chief financial officer for a small company, I collected overdue invoices. I kept on my desk a three-ring binder that contained phone logs similar to the one in Figure 4-3 on page 129. Whenever I made a collection call, I'd update the log. Without this record, my collection calls would have been much less successful than they were.

As with the form in Figure 4-2, I maintained a numbered list of contact names for each company. I also created codes that helped me summarize the results of a call. Without these codes, I might have had to write, for example, "Called for Mr. Hasenpfeffer. Left message." But with the codes, I would have simply entered the date, *#1* (if that was the number I'd assigned to his name), and *M* in the Codes column.

When there was something to write about, of course, I wrote as many notes as necessary. Even so, I tried to summarize what had occurred with the codes shown. This let me quickly review past collection calls. When a customer claimed to have lost an invoice, for example, I could evaluate how likely this was by adding up the number of other "lost invoices" the customer had suffered over the previous six months or so.

The information boxes for Figure 4-3 will help you to create the form.

Accounts Payable Forms

When you're managing accounts payable, you could create forms similar to those shown in Figure 4-1 through Figure 4-3. The most obvious form would be an accounts payable reconciliation form, which would be nearly identical to the one in Figure 4-1.

But if your company is having problems paying its bills, you might want to adapt the other two figures as well. Too often, companies with cash flow problems get themselves in even more trouble by forgetting what they've promised and why. Forms like these could help you minimize the damage.

ANALYZING A/R AND A/P STATEMENTS

From a manager's point of view, accounting software has changed little in the past 20 years. It's true that the software works on smaller computers today. And it's true that software prices have dropped significantly over the years. But today's accounting software provides managers about the same amount of management information today as it did 20 years ago: virtually none.

The reports provided by software publishers in their accounts payable and accounts receivable systems provide an excellent case in point. Today, as in the past, the aging schedules provide most of the information available about the performance of these critical systems. These reports provide lots of data, but not much information.

One significant improvement *has* developed, however. Today we can import data from the accounting system into spreadsheets. With this capability, we can sift the accounting data with our spreadsheets to produce much of the management information we need.

The easiest way to move accounting data into Microsoft Excel is to first save it in a file that has one of two Lotus formats: WKS or WK1. Many accounting-software packages let you save reports in this fashion, including Open Systems (Open Systems, Inc.), Solomon III (TLB, Inc.), Dac-Easy (Dac Software, Inc.), and ACCPAC (Computer Associates, Inc.).

Once you've saved an accounting report in a Lotus format, it's a simple matter to open the file in Microsoft Excel. Simply choose File Open, specify **.WK** as a filename (using the correct path), and then select the file you want.

If your accounting software doesn't save reports in a Lotus file format, you must go through an extra step, which is explained in Appendix A of this book.

Transforming an Accounting Report into a Database

Figure 4-4 on page 131 shows an open invoice report from the Harmony Accounts Receivable module, published by Open Systems, Inc. Saved as an ASCII file, it was converted to a spreadsheet file using the methods described in Appendix A. (The original report is shown in the boxed-in range B3:I45; I'll discuss the other data later in this chapter.)

Although this is now a spreadsheet file, it is nearly impossible to use in its present form. Before you can use it effectively, you must transform it into a database format.

Depending on the software and application, the term *database* can take on many different meanings, from the sophisticated to the mundane. I prefer the mundane. To me, a database is little more than many rows of data that can be sorted easily. A database therefore contains no underlines or borders within the data, no blank rows, and no rows dedicated to subtotals. To create a database from the spreadsheet in Figure 4-4, therefore, keep the 10 rows of invoice data and delete everything else.

However, you would have one problem if you tried to do this with the original report: The rows containing invoice information provide no hint as to who the customer is. Therefore, before you can delete the other data, you must create a new column for the customer number, column A. The formula box for Figure 4-4 shows the formula that generates the customer number in cell A9. After you enter the formula, copy it down the column as shown.

The easiest way to delete unwanted rows from the spreadsheet in the figure is to sort them into two groups: a group of rows that you want to save and a group that you want to delete. Columns J, K, and L provide additional assistance that will help you sort these rows easily. Column J contains a formula (shown in the formula box) that returns the value *1* if an invoice number exists in the same row as the formula; otherwise, the formula returns the value *0*. Although this particular formula is simple, you can create one as sophisticated as necessary to specify the data that you want to keep.

Column K contains sequence numbers. Often, this can be the most important column in a sort range. The reason: When you sort on the sequence column, you return your data to its original sequence. In other words, this column lets you undo the sort routine long after the Edit Undo command is no longer available. (Edit Undo lets you undo only the most recent editing action.) The ability to undo a sort after subsequent editing can be so useful, in fact, that I recommend you include a column of sequence numbers whenever your original data is not in numeric or alphabetic order.

Column L contains a short formula that returns the corresponding number in column I, if there is one; it returns the value *0* if there is no such number. The formula in cell G47 uses this data to ensure that the formulas in column J work correctly. It does this by multiplying each 1 or 0 in column J by the corresponding invoice amount in column L, and then it adds the results. If the total equals the report total in cell G44 of the report, every invoice number has a value of 1 correctly assigned.

After you complete columns J, K, and L, you can easily group together all rows with invoice data. First, however, you must turn the formulas you've created into values. Otherwise, you might get unexpected results. To do so, highlight the range A9:L45, press Ctrl-Ins, choose Edit Paste Special, and select Values. Then, to sort, choose Data Sort, designate cell J9 as the first key, and select descending order.

The spreadsheet in Figure 4-5 on page 133 is the result. The important elements of a database are in rows 9 through 18. This is data you can use to generate worthwhile management information. You can delete the remainder.

ANALYZING ACCOUNTS RECEIVABLE

Can you name the customers who represent 80 percent of your overdue invoices? (Most likely, they make up only a fraction of your total customer list.) Can you identify the customers who might create significant collection problems in a month or two? When cash is tight, can you easily set priorities for your collection efforts? On average, what are your receivables costing you in interest charges?

These are only some of the questions that you can answer from the database that began with the spreadsheet in Figure 4-5 and is shown completed in Figure 4-6 on page 134. These two spreadsheets *look* quite different at first glance. But when you compare them, you see that columns A through E of the spreadsheet in Figure 4-6 contain the important invoice data from the spreadsheet in Figure 4-5. Extensive deletion of unnecessary data combined with a little formatting has worked wonders.

The report in Figure 4-6 contains other data as well. Column F contains a subtotal by customer. When you allow for rounding, this data matches that in column G of the spreadsheet in Figure 4-4. Column G contains the total of all overdue invoices. As the percentage in cell G5 shows, this total represents 42 percent of all outstanding invoices.

Column H contains the average age of all invoices owed by each customer. The average is dollar-weighted: A $10 invoice has twice the influence on the average of a $5 invoice. The dollar-weighted age provides a measure of the true interest cost of offering credit to each customer. Suppose, for example, that you pay your bank 12 percent interest, or roughly 0.033 percent per day for the money that you borrow. And suppose that a customer has an unpaid balance of $40,000 with a dollar-weighted age of 50 days. This customer has cost you 1.65 percent (50 x 0.033 percent) of that balance in interest charges, or $660 on the $40,000.

Column I presents another point of view: the age of each customer's oldest invoice. To see how this measurement of age can be useful, compare the values in cells H11 and I11. The dollar-weighted average in cell H11 is only 19 days, which is good. But the age of the oldest invoice in cell I11 is 89 days, which is bad. Does this information suggest that the customer may wait another 70 days or so to pay the large invoice shown in cell E11? Someone in the company had better find out.

Column J reports on the interest costs associated with the credit function. In the spreadsheet, for example, cell J19 shows that the company has paid nearly $6,000 in interest charges to support the outstanding accounts receivable balance. This amount will increase as the company experiences increases in the amount of receivables, in their age, and in bank interest charges. Dividing this amount by total receivables, as in cell J5, provides the average interest cost as a percentage of outstanding receivables.

The information boxes for this figure provide all the information you need to enter the formulas and format the spreadsheet. As you enter the information, however, notice the shaded rows above and below the data that the range-name references include. Shading these rows leaves no doubt as to the borders of the range. The shaded rows are particularly important when you replace last month's data with the current month's data. To do so, you take the following steps:

1. Generate a new spreadsheet that is similar to the one in Figure 4-5.
2. Delete the unnecessary data so that the remaining data is ready to copy into the spreadsheet shown in Figure 4-6.
3. Erase all data in the range A8:F17 of the spreadsheet shown in Figure 4-6.
4. Insert more than enough rows between the shaded rows shown in the spreadsheet in Figure 4-6 to contain the new month's data. (This step, by the way, is one of the reasons shaded rows are important in the spreadsheet.)
5. Copy the new data into the spreadsheet in Figure 4-6 and then delete the extra blank rows.
6. Copy the formulas from any convenient row in columns F through J to the new rows as needed.

Preparing a Report of Major Delinquent Accounts Receivable

Although the spreadsheet in Figure 4-6 contains information not normally found in accounts receivable reports, a busy manager would hesitate to work through much of the data that still remains. The true value of the spreadsheet, however, is that it provides a convenient source from which you can extract management information, as Figure 4-7 through Figure 4-11 illustrate.

Creating a 30-day aging summary

The spreadsheet in Figure 4-7 on page 137 is a short report that can be handy for several purposes. Unlike most such summaries, this one can contain as many aging "buckets" as necessary to report accounts receivable. In other words, if you have an invoice that's 240 days overdue, this summary will display it in the 240-day bucket.

The aging summary has another convenient feature: It's not limited to 30-day buckets. By changing the value in cell M3, you can change the aging period to any length you want. You might use this ability to base a collection strategy on 10-day periods. You might ignore invoices that are 10 days overdue, send nasty letters about those at 20 days, and phone about those at 30 days.

This spreadsheet uses IF-array formulas, as described in the formula box for Figure 4-6. To create the spreadsheet, enter the formulas shown in the information boxes for Figure 4-7, format the cells containing them, and copy them down the columns as necessary.

Extracting the overdue accounts receivable

The report of major delinquent accounts receivable shows which customers account for at least 80 percent of the company's total past-due balance. To create this report, you must first extract a list of all delinquent customers, and then you must report the major ones. The spreadsheet shown in Figure 4-8 generates the initial list; Figure 4-9 contains the report itself.

To create the spreadsheet in Figure 4-8 on page 139, first enter the labels and borders shown in rows 3 through 9. Enter the formula shown for cell T8. Enter the range name *Criteria* and the formats, all of which are shown in the information boxes for Figure 4-8.

Because you've already created the range name Database, as specified in the range-name box for Figure 4-6, and because you've just created the Criteria range, you can now extract the code numbers of all customers that have an overdue balance. To do so, highlight the range P9:Q9, issue the Data Extract command, and choose OK. When you do so, data appears somewhat as shown in the range P10:Q12 of the spreadsheet in Figure 4-8.

(The Data Extract command erases all data directly beneath the output range, in columns P and Q. Therefore, be careful not to place other sections of your spreadsheet in these columns beneath row 9.)

As you compare your results of the Data Extract command with those shown in the figure, you can see that your results are in alphabetic order (following the order of the source data shown in Figure 4-6), but that the spreadsheet's data is in descending numeric order. To sort this data, highlight the range P10:Q12, specify cell Q10 as the first key, indicate that you want to sort this column in descending order, and then choose OK. When you do so, your results will resemble the range P10:Q12 in Figure 4-8.

Enter the formulas shown for cells S10 and T10 in the formula box for Figure 4-8 and copy them down their columns as shown. The formulas in column S calculate the percentage of the total balance overdue that each overdue amount represents. The formulas in column Q accumulate these totals.

As you examine the percentages in column T, you can see that the first two customers account for 98 percent of the overdue balance. These customers, therefore, are the ones that you will use for the report shown in Figure 4-9.

Creating a report of major delinquent accounts receivable

Figure 4-9 on page 141 contains the report of major delinquent accounts receivable. The customers in this report account for 41 percent of the firm's total accounts receivable, 98 percent of the amount past due, and all of the amounts in the 30-day and 90-day columns. The comments section of this report describes what action is expected on each account. (You probably will want to print this report on a wide-carriage printer, if you have one. This will leave more room both for the comment section and for the values.)

To create this report, enter the labels, numbers, and borders shown in rows 3 through 5. Copy the customer numbers of those you want to report from Figure 4-8 to Figure 4-9. (In other words, copy from the range P10:P11 to the range W6:W7.) Enter and format the formulas shown in the information boxes for cell AB3 and for row 6. Copy this row of formulas down the column as necessary.

The formula for cell X6 refers to a table in the spreadsheet CUST_CDE.XLS, which is shown in Figure 4-10 on page 143. This spreadsheet contains an alphabetic list of customer codes and customer names. Maintaining a separate spreadsheet such as this one greatly simplifies the reporting of customer names: Wherever you want to include a full customer name, simply include a formula that looks it up in the table.

To complete Figure 4-9, enter the SUM formula shown for cell AA8 and copy it across the row. Then enter the three formulas shown for row 10 and copy them across the row as instructed.

Creating a credit history log

Let's say Disco Dan's, a customer for many years, recently seems to be paying more slowly. What has its payment history been over the last year? Is the trend one of deterioration? Or let's say another customer, the New Age Building Supply and Mantra Shop, claims to be going through a seasonal slump. Is it? Or is it facing more fundamental problems? One way to evaluate the status of Disco Dan's and New Age is to compare their recent payment performance with that of other customers in similar industries.

A credit experience log can help you to quickly answer questions like these about the payment performance of your customers. Figure 4-11 on page 144 shows one such log, which contains the name of every customer sold to since the first date in the log. For each customer, you maintain the total amounts due and past due, the dollar-weighted age of the outstanding balance, and the age of the oldest invoice.

Column F contains the only formulas in this spreadsheet. These summarize information found in the spreadsheet in Figure 4-6. Once the formulas generate the credit information for a particular month, you copy them into the next column to the right and then turn column F into a column of values. Next month, the formulas in column G summarize the data for that month.

The information boxes for Figure 4-11 present the formulas, formats, and column widths. The formulas refer to the Range & Column Number References table shown near the top of the spreadsheet in Figure 4-11 when they find data in the spreadsheet in Figure 4-6. If you were to insert additional columns of data in the spreadsheet in Figure 4-6, you could adjust the formulas in the spreadsheet in Figure 4-11 by simply updating the numbers of the columns from which you want to extract data.

Creating similar A/P reports

When I work with troubled companies, I often create an accounts payable aging summary similar to the accounts receivable summary in Figure 4-7. This helps me understand where the potential accounts payable solutions are. For example, although most accounting programs place invoices that are one year overdue in the same aging bucket as those that are four months overdue, vendors generally treat these invoices quite differently. Vendors still expect to be paid in full when an invoice is four months overdue; they have no such illusions regarding a year-old invoice.

An accounts payable report similar to the one for accounts receivable in Figure 4-9 would provide greater detail about accounts payable problems. But rather than stopping the report at 120 days, as in the report in Figure 4-9, you could extend the aging schedule for as many aging periods as necessary.

A/R AGING LOG

When you forecast cash flows, you must predict how quickly you will collect accounts receivable. Unfortunately, few companies know the details of their past collection performance and therefore have no hope of correctly estimating future collection performance. The following section of this chapter shows ways to supply those details easily.

Creating an Accounts Receivable Aging Log

Figure 4-12 on page 147 presents the accounts receivable aging log, which easily tracks collection performance. Each month, enter the amount of credit sales, total receivables in the Accts Rec column, the balance from the accounts receivable aging schedule in each aging "bucket," and the amounts written off.

After you enter this data, the formulas in columns I through N calculate the ratios of sales collections and write-off. For any month's sales, these ratios tell you what percentage was collected in subsequent months. In row 7, for example, 2 percent of January's sales was collected in January (cell I7), 47 percent in February, 24 percent in March, and so on. Eventually, 0.67 percent of January's sales was written off.

The data in columns I through N applies directly to mid-term cash flow forecasts. In those forecasts, your prediction of collections from credit sales will equal projected sales multiplied by some average of these ratios. Later, when you compare the actuals to the forecast, these columns provide all the data you will need.

The formula box for Figure 4-12 shows how the ratios are calculated in columns I through N. The boldface italic numbers near the top of the spreadsheet draw attention to the source of the data for the calculations. For example, the value *2%* in cell I7 is the difference between the amount of credit sales during the month and the accounts receivable balance at the end of the month, divided by credit sales. Similarly, the amount of January sales collected in February (cell J7) is the decrease in the amount owed for January's sales (cell D7 minus cell E8), divided by January's sales.

If you prefer not to spend the time to create this spreadsheet, you can use the order blank on the last page of the book to purchase it on disk. Otherwise, to create this spreadsheet, enter the headings and borders as shown. Enter and format the date in cell A7 and the date formula in cell A8. Copy this formula down the column as necessary. Enter the formulas shown for columns I through N and copy them as well. Format the spreadsheet as shown in the other information boxes and then enter your own accounts receivable aging schedules.

Calculating Quarterly Collection Averages

Although the A/R aging log is a necessary step to forecasting future collections, it contains too much detail to use directly. The spreadsheet in Figure 4-13 on page 149 corrects this problem by summarizing collection experience by calendar quarter.

For example, consider the quarter beginning April, 1987, which is shown in rows 10 through 12. Here collections averaged 65 days (cell P11), down from the previous quarter's 68 days. Collections increased from 2 percent to 3 percent during the month of the sale, and from 46 percent to 50 percent one month after the sale. The boldface figures in this spreadsheet present similar ratios for other months.

Using the schedule for mid-term forecasts

Suppose it is now January, 1989, and you want to create a cash flow forecast for the next 12 months. Here's how you might use the spreadsheet in Figure 4-13 to estimate your collections:

First, of course, estimate your sales for each of the next 12 months. Also, record your actual sales for each of the past four months.

Second, estimate your sales-collection ratios for the following year, using Figure 4-12 and Figure 4-13 as guides. If you expect collection performance to be quite seasonal or to be greatly affected by changing economic trends, you may have to estimate a set of collection ratios for each of the next four quarters. Generally, however, one set of ratios can be used for the entire year.

Third, estimate each month's collections. Collections for any month equal the current sales times the 0–30 ratio, plus sales one month ago times the 31–60 ratio, plus sales two months ago times the 61–90 ratio, and so on.

Using the schedule for one-month cash flow forecasts

To generate a one-month cash flow forecast, you usually use receivables information from the current month. You can't use the same method for generating a one-month cash flow forecast that you use for generating a mid-term forecast because a mid-term forecast predicts what receivables will be for this month and for future months. For a one-month forecast, you already know what current receivables are; you merely want to estimate what fraction of these you will collect during the month.

Row 12 and the other rows of percentages labeled *A/R by period* in the spreadsheet in Figure 4-13 present a set of ratios used when forecasting collections one month in advance. Each number reports the percentage of that aging category that was collected during the previous quarter. Row 12, for example, shows that the company collected an average of 50 percent of its 31–60 day receivables during the previous quarter, 49 percent of its 61–90 day receivables, and so on. The spreadsheet in Figure 4-14 uses these ratios to calculate a monthly accounts receivable collections forecast.

Creating the report of quarterly collection averages

To create the spreadsheet in Figure 4-13, enter the labels shown in rows 3 through 6. Drop down to row 10 and enter the borders and labels shown. Enter the formulas shown in the formula box and format them as shown in the other information boxes. Copy the range P10:W12 to the range P7:W36 and then delete the formulas in cells Q9:W9.

You must delete the formulas in row 9 because all formulas that calculate accounts receivable collections by period look backward four months. Therefore, there isn't enough data to calculate the correct ratio for the first quarter in the schedule. Similarly, the boldface ratios for sales depend upon ratios that look forward by up to four months. This is why the quarters for July and October, 1988, contain incomplete data. As more months of data are added to the spreadsheet in Figure 4-12, the missing values appear.

Preparing an Accounts Receivable Collections Forecast

Figure 4-14 on page 151 presents a monthly forecast of A/R collections that can be generated entirely by the spreadsheet, or nearly so, from the data in Figure 4-13. The only assumption that you must enter into this forecast monthly is the amount of credit sales that you expect during the coming month.

The report is self-explanatory. Its calculations depend upon Figure 4-13 and upon the two range definitions shown in the figure's range-name box, which find the row number and date of the most recently completed month of data in Figure 4-13.

To create this forecast, enter the labels shown in column Y and all borders shown in the spreadsheet. Enter the range names and then enter and format the formulas shown in the information boxes for the figure.

Preparing an Accounts Payable Aging Log

If you pay every invoice on time, you may have no need for an accounts payable log resembling the accounts receivable log in Figure 4-12. But if you do tend to stretch payables from time to time, a similar log could help you understand your payment patterns and thus improve your cash flow forecasts.

If your accounting system can generate the information, you can generate several accounts payable logs that provide valuable information about whether you pay your bills on time or not. The information you need is a list of all checks that were written during a month—a list containing the amount paid, the invoice number, the invoice date, and the original GL-account numbers that were charged when the invoice was first entered into accounts payable.

If your accounting software can create a spreadsheet of such a list, you can use the methods described in this chapter to create logs of payments for inventory, for operating expenses, and for fixed assets. These logs may well reveal that payment patterns vary significantly among these categories. If so, you need to change your cash flow forecasts to reflect this information.

If your accounting software can't create a spreadsheet directly, you can create it indirectly. Appendix A of this book describes how to load any accounting report into Microsoft Excel as data.

Figure 4-1. Accounts Receivable Reconciliation Form

A form to use in reconciling the accounts receivable balance per detail with the balance per the financial statement.

	A	B	C	D	E	F	G	H	I	J
1										
2					**Generic Corporation**					
3					**Accounts Receivable Reconciliation**					
4										
5										Journal #
6	**This Month's Computer Aging**							Amount		This Month
7	Last month's A/R balance from the aging schedule:									
8	This month's sales from the invoice register:									
9	This month's cash receipts from the C/R register:							( )		
10	This month's cash discounts from the C/R register:							( )		
11										
12	Equals: This month's A/R balance from the aging schedule:									
13										
14										
15										
16								Journal #		Journal #
17								For Accrual		For Reversal
18	**This Month's Detail to Book**					Amount		This Month		Next Month
19	This month's A/R balance from the aging schedule:									
20	Plus accruals:									
21										
22										
23										
24										
25										
26										
27										
28										
29	Equals: This month's book balance:									
30										
31										
32	**Completed by:**							Date:		
33										
34										
35			**Attach a copy of the last page of all printouts.**							
36										
37										
38										

(continued)

Figure 4-1. *continued*

COLUMN WIDTHS			
Column	*Width*	*Column*	*Width*
A	8.43	F	14.57
B	8.43	G	1
C	8.43	H	9.29
D	8.43	I	1
E	8.43	J	11.57

ROW HEIGHTS	
Row	*Height*
2	19
3	13
5	13
6	13
7	19

KEY CELL FORMATS			
Cell	*Number*	*Alignment*	*Font*
E2:E3	General	Center	Helv 10, Bold
A6	General	General	Helv 10, Bold
A7	General	General	Helv 10

Figure 4-2. Accounts Receivable Collection-Information Form

A form to record background information about each customer to help improve collection efforts.

	A	B	C	D	E	F	G	H	I	J
1										
2					A/R Collection Info Sheet					
3	Customer							Phone		
4										
5	Address									
6										
7										
8										
9	Contacts									
10	C#	Name						Title	Ext	
11	1									
12	2									
13	3									
14	4									
15	5									
16										
17	Administrative Questions				C#	Date	Response			
18										
19	When do you write checks during the									
20	month?									
21										
22										
23	Who must approve a check before it's									
24	mailed?									
25										
26										
27	Who can sign checks?									
28										
29										
30										
31	If checks are printed by computer, will we									
32	be paid by hand if the computer breaks									
33	down?									
34										
35	How many copies of the invoice do you									
36	require?									
37										
38										
39	You will send us copies of your financial									
40	statements on the following schedule:									
41										
42										

(continued)

Figure 4-2. *continued*

COLUMN WIDTHS			
Column	*Width*	*Column*	*Width*
A	3.57	F	7.29
B	8.43	G	8.43
C	8.43	H	24.57
D	12.86	I	9.43
E	4.43		

ROW HEIGHTS	
Row	*Height*
2	17
4	13
6	17
18	13
19	17

KEY CELL FORMATS			
Cell	*Number*	*Alignment*	*Font*
F2	General	Center	= Helv 12, Bold, Underlined
A3	General	General	= Helv 10, Bold

Figure 4-3. Phone Log for Accounts Receivable Collections

A form to monitor accounts receivable collection efforts.

	A	B	C	D	E	F	G	H	I	J	K
1											
2					**Phone Log for A/R Collections**						
3	Phone:						Customer:				
4	#	Contact Name				Code	Code Description				
5	1					I	Lost invoice, send another.				
6	2					P	Promised payment.				
7	3					B	Broke a promised payment date or amount.				
8	4					M	Contact unavailable. Left message to call.				
9	5					R	Returned our call, or called without prompting.				
10											
11		**Record all facts: Dates, Contacts, Promises, Actions, Amounts, Invoice Numbers, Etc.**									
12											
13	Date		Notes							Codes	
14											
15											
16											
17											
18											
19											
20											
21											
22											
23											
24											
25											
26											
27											
28											
29											
30											
31											
32											
33											
34											
35											
36											
37											
38											
39											
40											
41											

(continued)

Figure 4-3. *continued*

COLUMN WIDTHS							
Column	*Width*	*Column*	*Width*	*Column*	*Width*	*Column*	*Width*
A	2.57	D	8.43	G	13.43	I	12.29
B	2.14	E	13.57	H	8.43	J	6
C	8.43	F	5.29				

ROW HEIGHTS	
Row	*Height*
2	17
12	13

KEY CELL FORMATS			
Cell	*Number*	*Alignment*	*Font*
F2	General	Center	Helv 12, Bold, Underlined
A11	General	General	Helv 10, Bold

Figure 4-4. Accounts Receivable Open Invoice Report, Step 1

A spreadsheet that demonstrates the first step in changing an accounting report into a database.

	A	B	C	D	E	F	G	H	I	J	K	L
1												
2												
3		3/30/87				Dome Homes, Inc.			Page: 1			
4					AR CUSTOMER OPEN INVOICE REPORT							
5										1=Yes		
6	Cust#	INV DATE	DUE DATE	AGE	INV#	DESC	AMOUNT DUE	DISC AMT	NET AMOUNT	0=No	Seq	Amt
7		-------	--------	--------	-------	------	------------	---------	----------			
8												
9	ACE001	ACE001	Ace Builders			502-555-1646				0	1	0
10	ACE001									0	2	0
11	ACE001	3/12/87	4/11/87	18	977	Invoice	12,956.04	0.00	12,956.04	1	3	12956
12	ACE001	3/18/87	4/17/87	12	995	Invoice	87,689.16	0.00	87,689.16	1	4	87689
13	ACE001						------------	---------	----------	0	5	0
14	ACE001						100,645.20	0.00	100,645.20	0	6	100645
15	ACE001						------------	---------	----------	0	7	0
16	ACE001									0	8	0
17	DAL001	DAL001	Dallas-Ft. Worth Dome Homes			214-555-2389				0	9	0
18	DAL001									0	10	0
19	DAL001	12/31/86	1/30/87	89	2	Invoice	6,179.96	0.00	6,179.96	1	11	6180
20	DAL001	3/13/87	4/12/87	17	992	Invoice	270,498.35	0.00	270,498.35	1	12	270498
21	DAL001						------------	---------	----------	0	13	0
22	DAL001						276,678.31	0.00	276,678.31	0	14	276678
23	DAL001						------------	---------	----------	0	15	0
24	DAL001									0	16	0
25	GRE001	GRE001	Greater New York Domes, Inc			212-555-0011				0	17	0
26	GRE001									0	18	0
27	GRE001	1/28/87	2/27/87	61	970	Invoice	87,662.06	0.00	87,662.06	1	19	87662
28	GRE001	2/24/87	3/26/87	34	996	Invoice	88,083.90	880.84	87,203.06	1	20	88084
29	GRE001	3/25/87	4/24/87	5	5	Invoice	150.00	0.00	150.00	1	21	150
30	GRE001						------------	---------	----------	0	22	0
31	GRE001						175,895.96	880.84	175,015.12	0	23	175896
32	GRE001						------------	---------	----------	0	24	0
33	GRE001									0	25	0
34	KAN001	KAN001	Kansas City Geodesic Homes			816-555-5333				0	26	0
35	KAN001									0	27	0
36	KAN001	12/27/86	1/26/87	93	975	Invoice	6,723.92	0.00	6,723.92	1	28	6723.9
37	KAN001	2/22/87	3/24/87	36	988	Invoice	77,031.95	0.00	77,031.95	1	29	77032
38	KAN001	3/11/87	4/10/87	19	19	Invoice	125.00	0.00	125.00	1	30	125
39	KAN001						------------	---------	----------	0	31	0
40	KAN001						83,880.87	0.00	83,880.87	0	32	83881
41	KAN001						------------	---------	----------	0	33	0
42	KAN001									0	34	0
43	KAN001						-----------	---------	----------	0	35	0
44	KAN001						637,100.34	880.84	636,219.50	0	36	637100
45	KAN001						-----------	---------	----------	0	37	0
46												
47						Test:	637,100.34					

(continued)

Figure 4-4. *continued*

KEY FORMULAS	
Cell	***Formula***
A9	**=IF(ISTEXT(B9),B9,A8)** If a new customer name exists in cell B9, the formula returns it; otherwise, it returns the old name from the cell above.
J9	**=IF(ISNUMBER(D9),1,0)** This formula determines whether the current row contains an invoice or some other type of data. As you can see in the spreadsheet, the row contains an invoice whenever a cell in column D contains a number. This formula returns a 1 when cell D9 contains a number; otherwise, it returns a 0. The formula would work just as well, by the way, if it referenced cells B9 or C9, which contain date serial numbers. In this spreadsheet, cell E9 would also work. But using invoice numbers can be risky because invoice "numbers" in many companies are really alphanumeric labels, which would return a 0 rather than a 1.
K9	**1** This column of sequence numbers lets you sort the data into its original sequence. Use the Data Series command to generate it.
L9	**=N(G9)** The column returns the numeric value of the contents of cell G9. In other words, if cell G9 contains a label or a blank, the formula returns a 0; otherwise, it returns the appropriate number.
G47	**=SUM((J9:J45)*(L9:L45))** This array formula tests that column J contains the value 1 for every invoice. It does this by multiplying each 1 or 0 in column J by the corresponding invoice amount in column L and then adding the results. If the total equals the report total, every invoice is represented. As with every array formula, you must enter it by holding down Ctrl-Shift as you press Enter.

Figure 4-5. Accounts Receivable Open Invoice Report, Step 2

The second step in converting an accounting report into a database.

	A	B	C	D	E	F	G	H	I	J	K	L
1												
2												
3		3/30/87				Dome Homes, Inc.			Page: 1			
4					AR CUSTOMER OPEN INVOICE REPORT							
5										1=Yes		
6	Cust#	INV DATE	DUE DATE	AGE	INV#	DESC	AMOUNT DUE	DISC AMT	NET AMOUNT	0=No	Seq	Amt
7		--------	---------	--------	--------	-------	-------------	----------	-----------			
8												
9	ACE001	3/12/87	4/11/87	18	977	Invoice	12,956.04	0.00	12,956.04	1	3	12956
10	ACE001	3/18/87	4/17/87	12	995	Invoice	87,689.16	0.00	87,689.16	1	4	87689
11	DAL001	12/31/86	1/30/87	89	2	Invoice	6,179.96	0.00	6,179.96	1	11	6180
12	DAL001	3/13/87	4/12/87	17	992	Invoice	270,498.35	0.00	270,498.35	1	12	270498
13	GRE001	1/28/87	2/27/87	61	970	Invoice	87,662.06	0.00	87,662.06	1	19	87662
14	GRE001	2/24/87	3/26/87	34	996	Invoice	88,083.90	880.84	87,203.06	1	20	88084
15	GRE001	3/25/87	4/24/87	5	5	Invoice	150.00	0.00	150.00	1	21	150
16	KAN001	12/27/86	1/26/87	93	975	Invoice	6,723.92	0.00	6,723.92	1	28	6723.9
17	KAN001	2/22/87	3/24/87	36	988	Invoice	77,031.95	0.00	77,031.95	1	29	77032
18	KAN001	3/11/87	4/10/87	19	19	Invoice	125.00	0.00	125.00	1	30	125
19	ACE001	ACE001	Ace Builders			502-555-1646				0	1	0
20	ACE001									0	2	0
21	ACE001						-------------	----------	-----------	0	5	0
22	ACE001						100,645.20	0.00	100,645.20	0	6	100645
23	ACE001						-------------	----------	-----------	0	7	0
24	ACE001									0	8	0
25	DAL001	DAL001	Dallas-Ft. Worth Dome Homes			214-555-2389				0	9	0
26	DAL001									0	10	0
27	DAL001						-------------	----------	-----------	0	13	0
28	DAL001						276,678.31	0.00	276,678.31	0	14	276678
29	DAL001						-------------	----------	-----------	0	15	0
30	DAL001									0	16	0
31	GRE001	GRE001	Greater New York Domes, Inc			212-555-0011				0	17	0
32	GRE001									0	18	0
33	GRE001						-------------	----------	-----------	0	22	0
34	GRE001						175,895.96	880.84	175,015.12	0	23	175896
35	GRE001						-------------	----------	-----------	0	24	0
36	GRE001									0	25	0
37	KAN001	KAN001	Kansas City Geodesic Homes			816-555-5333				0	26	0
38	KAN001									0	27	0
39	KAN001						-------------	----------	-----------	0	31	0
40	KAN001						83,880.87	0.00	83,880.87	0	32	83881
41	KAN001						-------------	----------	-----------	0	33	0
42	KAN001									0	34	0
43	KAN001						-----------	---------	----------	0	35	0
44	KAN001						637,100.34	880.84	636,219.50	0	36	637100
45	KAN001						-----------	---------	----------	0	37	0
46												
47						Test:	637,100.34					

Figure 4-6. Accounts Receivable Analysis by Customer

The final step in converting an accounting report into a database, a report that provides accounts receivable information not available in aging reports. Saved as AR_DATA.XLS.

	A	B	C	D	E	F	G	H	I	J
1										
2										
3								Date:		3/30/87
4	Accounts Receivable Analysis by Customer							Int Rate:		12%
5							42%	Inv Ages		0.94%
6	Cust#	Inv-Date	Age	Inv#	Amount	Cust-Tot	Overdue	$Wtd	Max	Interest
7										
8	ACE001	3/12/87	18	977	12,956.04					
9	ACE001	3/18/87	12	995	87,689.16	100,645		13	18	423
10	DAL001	12/31/86	89	2	6,179.96					
11	DAL001	3/13/87	17	992	270,498.35	276,678	6,180	19	89	1,693
12	GRE001	1/28/87	61	970	87,662.06					
13	GRE001	2/24/87	34	996	88,083.90					
14	GRE001	3/25/87	5	5	150.00	175,896	175,746	47	61	2,743
15	KAN001	12/27/86	93	975	6,723.92					
16	KAN001	2/22/87	36	988	77,031.95					
17	KAN001	3/11/87	19	6	125.00	83,881	83,756	41	93	1,118
18										
19					$637,100.34	$637,100	$265,682	29	65	$5,976
20										
21										

COLUMN WIDTHS							
Column	***Width***	***Column***	***Width***	***Column***	***Width***	***Column***	***Width***
A	**7.14**	**D**	**4.29**	**G**	**8.43**	**I**	**4.43**
B	**8.71**	**E**	**10.29**	**H**	**4.57**	**J**	**7.29**
C	**4.86**	**F**	**8.14**				

(continued)

Figure 4-6. *continued*

KEY FORMULAS	
Cell	***Formula***
C8	**=$J$3–B8** This formula returns the age of the invoice, in days.
F8	**=IF(A8<>A9,SUM(IF(A8=$A$7:$A$18,$E$7:$E$18,0)),0)** This array formula creates subtotals in column F by using an interesting ability of array formulas to be used with IF statements. In effect, the second IF statement begins by creating a temporary array that holds the results of its calculations, which the SUM statement adds. Specifically, the formula finds all cells in the range A7:A18 that equal cell A8. It places the corresponding values in the range E7:E18 into the temporary array. Other cells in the temporary array are filled with zeros, as the IF statement instructs. The first IF statement displays the sum of the temporary array whenever the current row contains the last Cust# in a series. To use this formula, enter it as shown, then press and hold down Ctrl-Shift while you press Enter. Use the same key combination to enter it after editing the formula. You may copy this cell like any other, however.
G8	**=IF(A8<>A9,SUM(IF(A8=$A$7:$A$18,IF($C$7:$C$18>30,$E$7:$E$18,0))),0)** This array formula uses a temporary array to subtotal all invoices that are older than 30 days.
H8	**=IF(F8=0,0,SUM(IF(A8=$A$7:$A$18,($C$7:$C$18*$E$7:$E$18),0))/F8)** This array formula finds the average dollar-weighted invoice age for each customer. It does so by loading the temporary array with the "dollar-days" (the product of each invoice and its age) for all invoices belonging to the customer in cell A8 and then by dividing the sum of these dollar-days by the customer subtotal in cell F8. To keep from dividing by 0, however, the initial IF statement returns a 0 whenever cell F8 equals 0.
I8	**=IF(A8<>A9,MAX(IF(A8=$A$7:$A$18,($C$7:$C$18),0)),0)** This array formula uses a temporary array to find the age of the oldest invoice for each customer.
J8	**=($J$4/365)*F8*H8** The total interest cost for any customer equals the average daily interest rate times the total amount due times the average age of the customer's invoices. Mathematically, this is equivalent to multiplying the daily interest rate by the total of the dollar-days for any customer.
E19	**=SUM(E6:E18)**
F19	**=SUM(F6:F18)**
G19	**=SUM(G6:G18)**

(continued)

Figure 4-6. *continued*

KEY FORMULAS–continued	
Cell	*Formula*
J19	**=SUM(J6:J18)**
J5	**=J19/$E$19** This formula finds the average interest cost, as a percentage, for uncollected receivables. It equals the total interest cost divided by total A/R balance. This is mathematically equivalent to the daily interest rate multiplied by the weighted average age of all invoices.
G5	**=$G$19/F19** The fraction of A/R that is overdue equals the total overdue divided by total A/R.
H19	**=$J$5/($J$4/365)** As explained for cell J5 above, dividing the average interest cost percentage by the daily interest rate will return the weighted average age of all invoices.
I19	**=SUM($I$7:$I$18)/COUNT(IF($I$7:$I$18>0,0))** The IF statement in this array formula generates a temporary array that contains the number of cells equal to the number of values in the range I7:I18 that are greater than 0. To find the numeric average of the cells in that range, divide their sum by a count of the values in the temporary array.

RANGE NAMES	
Name	*Formula*
Data	**=$A$7:$J$18** This range contains all data and is bounded by the shaded rows. It is used by the spreadsheet in Figure 4-9.
Database	**=$A$6:$J$18** This range is used in the spreadsheet in Figure 4-8 by the Data Extract command.

KEY CELL FORMATS			
Cell	*Number*	*Alignment*	*Font*
B7:B18	**m/d/yy**	**General**	**Helv 10**
E7:J18	**#,##0.00**	**General**	**Helv 10**
E19:G19	**$#,##0.00**	**General**	**Helv 10**

Figure 4-7. Accounts Receivable Aging Summary

An aging summary that can report outstanding receivables by any aging period. Saved as AR_DATA.XLS.

	M	N	O
1			
2			
3	30-Day		
4	Aging Summary		
5	Days	Invoice	
6	Past Due	Amount	
7	0	371,419	
8	30	165,116	
9	60	93,842	
10	90	6,724	
11	120		
12	150		
13	180		
14	210		
15	240		
16	270		
17	300		
18	330		
19	Total A/R:	637,100	
20			
21			

KEY FORMULAS	
Cell	***Formula***
M3	**30** This cell contains the value 30. Its number format generates the label.
M7 **M8**	**0** **=M7+$M$3** Copy the formula in cell M8 down the column as necessary.
N7	**=SUM(IF($C$7:$C$18>=M7,IF($C$7:$C$18<(M7+$M$3),$E$7:$E$18)))** We want each temporary array in this array formula to contain the amount of all invoices with an age greater than or equal to the age in cell M5 and less than 30 days older than this age, as specified in cell M3. Because the IF-array combination cannot use the AND function, we use this combination of IF statements to achieve the same purpose. Once these two IF statements generate the temporary array, SUM returns the desired total.

(continued)

Figure 4-7. *continued*

KEY CELL FORMATS			
Cell	*Number*	*Alignment*	*Font*
M3	#"–Day"	Left	Helv 10, Bold
M4	m/d/yy	Left	Helv 10, Bold
N7:N19	#,##0 ;(#,##0);	General	Helv 10

Figure 4-8. List of Delinquent Accounts Receivable

A spreadsheet that uses the Data Extract command to extract the code numbers of all customers with overdue accounts. Saved as AR_DATA.XLS.

	P	Q	R	S	T
1					
2					
3	**Customers with overdue accounts**				
4					
5	Criteria				
6	Overdue				
7	>0			Total	
8				Overdue	265,682
9	Cust#	Overdue		Each%	Cum%
10	GRE001	175,746		66%	66%
11	KAN001	83,756		32%	98%
12	DAL001	6,180		2%	100%
13				0%	100%
14				0%	100%

KEY FORMULAS	
Cell	***Formula***
T8	**=$G$19** This is the total overdue amount calculated by the spreadsheet in Figure 4-6.
S10	**=Q10/$T$8** This formula calculates the percentage of all overdue invoices represented by the amount in cell Q10.
T10	**=N(T9)+S10** This formula returns the running total of all percentages in column S. It should accumulate to 100 percent at the bottom of column T. The N function takes the numeric value (0) of the label in cell T9. If that function were not used, the formula would try to add the label in T9 to the value in S10, returning an error.

KEY CELL FORMATS			
Cell	***Number***	***Alignment***	***Font***
T8	**#,##0**	**General**	**Helv 10**
S10:T10	**0%**	**General**	**Helv 10**

(continued)

Figure 4-8. *continued*

RANGE NAME	
Name	***Formula***
Criteria	**=$P$6:$P$7** Defines the Data Extract command's Criteria range.

Figure 4-9. Report of Major Accounts Receivable Delinquencies

An exception report that summarizes major problems in accounts receivable. Saved as AR_DATA.XLS.

	W	X	Y	Z	AA	AB	AC	AD	AE	AF	AG	AH
1												
2												
3	Report of Major Delinquent Accounts Receivable ($1000s)											March, 1987
4							Days Past Due					Comments
5	Cust#	Customer			Due	Overdue	0	30	60	90	120	
6	GRE001	Greater New York Domes, Inc.			176	176	0	88	88			Promises $ on 10th. Now COD.
7	KAN001	Kansas City Geodesic Homes			84	84	0	77		7		Their cust just paid. Our $ mailed.
8					$260	$260	$0	$165	$88	$7	$0	
9												
10	% of Company Totals				41%	98%	0%	100%	93%	100%	0%	

KEY FORMULAS

Cell	*Formula*
AH3	**=TEXT(J3,"mmmm,yyyy")** The date from the spreadsheet in Figure 4-6.
X6	**=VLOOKUP(W6,CUST_CDE.XLS!CustName,2)** This formula looks up the customer code in the CUST_CDE.XLS spreadsheet (Figure 4-10) and returns the full customer name.
AA6	**=VLOOKUP($W6,Data,COLUMN($F6))*0.001** The formula looks up the customer code in the range Data, finds its A/R subtotal, and then multiplies it by 0.001 to display the results in thousands of dollars.
AB6	**=VLOOKUP($W6,Data,COLUMN($G6))*0.001** Finds the past-due amount in the range Data and displays it in thousands of dollars.
AC6	**=SUM(IF($A$7:$A$18=$W6,IF($C$7:$C$18>=AC$5, IF($C$7:$C$18<(30+AC$5),$E$7:$E$18,0))))*0.001** This imposing array formula isn't really very sophisticated. It adds amounts due when each of these three conditions is met: (1) The customer number in column A equals the customer number in cell W6, (2) the age in column C of Figure 4-6 is greater than or equal to the age in cell AC5, and (3) the age in column C is less than 30 plus the age in cell AC5. This sum is then multiplied by 0.001 to display the result in thousands of dollars. As with any array formula, enter it by pressing Ctrl-Shift and Enter. Copy the formula to the range AC6:AF7.
AG6	**=AB6–SUM(AC6:AF6)** Finds the remaining overdue balance. Copy it down the column as needed.

(continued)

Figure 4-9. *continued*

KEY FORMULAS—continued	
Cell	***Formula***
AA8	**=SUM(AA6:AA7)** Copy this formula to the range AB8:AG8.
AA10	**=(AA8*1000)/$E$19** This formula returns the total of all invoices owed by the Major Delinquent Accounts as a percentage of total A/R.
AB10	**=IF($G$19=0,0,(AB8*1000)/$G$19)** This formula finds overdue invoices owed by these accounts as a percentage of total overdue invoices.
AC10	**=IF(VLOOKUP(AC$5,$M$7:$N$18,2)=0,0, (AC8*1000)/VLOOKUP(AC$5,$M$7:$N$18,2))** This formula looks up the company total for this aging category in the spreadsheet in Figure 4-7. If the total equals 0, the formula returns 0. Otherwise, it calculates the percentage shown. Of course, because this display reports values in thousands of dollars, the formula must multiply cell AC8 by 1000 before performing the division. Copy this formula across the row as shown.

KEY CELL FORMATS			
Cell	***Number***	***Alignment***	***Font***
W3	**General**	**General**	**Helv 10, Bold**
AA6:AG7	**#,##0 ;(#,##0);**	**General**	**Helv 10**
AA8:AG8	**$#,##0 ;($#,##0)**	**General**	**Helv 10**
AA10:AG10	**0%**	**General**	**Helv 10**
AH6:AH7	**General**	**General**	**Helv 8**

Figure 4-10. Customer Code-Number Table

A table that lets formulas in other spreadsheets translate customer numbers into customer names. Saved as CUST_CODE.XLS.

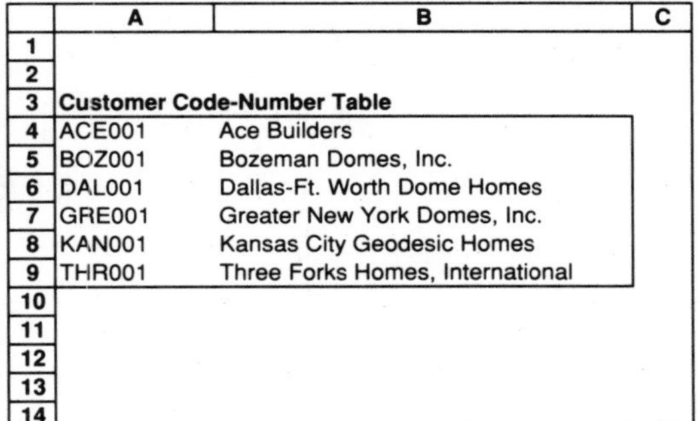

	A	B	C
1			
2			
3	**Customer Code-Number Table**		
4	ACE001	Ace Builders	
5	BOZ001	Bozeman Domes, Inc.	
6	DAL001	Dallas-Ft. Worth Dome Homes	
7	GRE001	Greater New York Domes, Inc.	
8	KAN001	Kansas City Geodesic Homes	
9	THR001	Three Forks Homes, International	
10			
11			
12			
13			
14			

RANGE NAME	
Name	***Formula***
CustName	**=$A$4:$B$9**

Figure 4-11. Credit Experience Log by Customer and Month

A quick way to review customer payment patterns.

	A	B	C	D	E	F
1						
2						
3	**Credit Experience Log by Customer and Month**					
4						
5	**Range & Column Number References**					
6	Range:	AR_DATA.XLS!Data				
7	Column Numbers:					
8	Due	6				
9	Overdue	7				
10	$Wtd Days	8				
11	Max Days	9				
12						
13						
14	**Credit Experience Log**					**Dome Homes, Inc.**
15	**Cust#**	**Customer**	**Desc**	**Jan-87**	**Feb-87**	**Mar-87**
16	ACE001	Ace Builders	Due	$43,117	$12,033	$100,645
17			Overdue	$0	$0	$0
18			$Wtd Days	14	11	13
19			Max Days	15	19	18
20	BOZ001	Bozeman Domes, Inc.	Due	$329,842	$52,888	$0
21			Overdue	$1,286	$5,236	$0
22			$Wtd Days	17	22	0
23			Max Days	32	31	0
24	DAL001	Dallas-Ft. Worth Dome Homes	Due	$78,004	$6,180	$276,678
25			Overdue	$71,824	$0	$6,180
26			$Wtd Days	35	59	19
27			Max Days	61	59	89
28	GRE001	Greater New York Domes, Inc.	Due	$178,690	$217,345	$175,896
29			Overdue	$91,028	$129,261	$175,746
30			$Wtd Days	37	42	47
31			Max Days	72	59	61
32	KAN001	Kansas City Geodesic Homes	Due	$6,724	$83,756	$83,881
33			Overdue	$6,724	$6,724	$83,756
34			$Wtd Days	34	57	41
35			Max Days	34	63	93

COLUMN WIDTHS			
Column	***Width***	***Column***	***Width***
A	10.86	D	8
B	26.71	E	8
C	9.71	F	8

(continued)

Figure 4-11. *continued*

KEY FORMULAS	
Cell	***Formula***
F15	**=DATE(YEAR(E15),MONTH(E15)+1,1)** This formula returns the date serial number of the first of the month following the date in cell E15.
F16	**=IF(VLOOKUP($A16,INDIRECT($B$6),1)=$A16, VLOOKUP($A16,INDIRECT($B$6),$B$8),0)**
F17	**=IF(VLOOKUP($A16,INDIRECT($B$6),1)=$A16, VLOOKUP($A16,INDIRECT($B$6),$B$9),0)**
F18	**=IF(VLOOKUP($A16,INDIRECT($B$6),1)=$A16, VLOOKUP($A16,INDIRECT($B$6),$B$10),0)**
F19	**=IF(VLOOKUP($A16,INDIRECT($B$6),1)=$A16, VLOOKUP($A16,INDIRECT($B$6),$B$11),0)** These formulas return the appropriate values from the spreadsheet in Figure 4-6. The range and column data in Figure 4-11 specify the file, table, and columns from which to return data. The formula in cell F16 says: Take the customer number in cell A16 and look it up in the Data range in file AR_DATA.XLS (Figure 4-6). If the table contains this customer number, look up the customer number again and return the Cust-Tot value from column 6, as specified in cell B6 of this spreadsheet. But if the customer number in cell A16 doesn't match any in the table, return a 0. (When you look up duplicate numbers in a table, as in column A of the spreadsheet in Figure 4-6, the VLOOKUP formula selects the last entry in the series of duplicates. This is why the VLOOKUP formulas return the customer totals, from row 9 of the spreadsheet in Figure 4-6, for example, rather than the 0 values from row 8.) Each month, after the month's values have been generated in this table, copy the column containing the current month's formulas into the next column to its right. Then turn the current month's column of formulas into values using the Copy and the Edit Paste Special command with the Values option selected. When you enter these formulas, enter the formula for cell F16, copy it to the range F17:F19, and then edit the remaining cells to appear as shown above. (Notice that the three references to cell $A16 do not change in each formula while the one reference to cell $B$6 in cell F16 does.) When the four formulas are correct, copy them as necessary down the column. In the spreadsheet, for example, you would copy from the range F16:F19 to the range F20:F35.

(continued)

Figure 4-11. *continued*

KEY CELL FORMATS			
Cell	***Number***	***Alignment***	***Font***
A14	General	General	Helv 10, Bold
F14	General	Right	Helv 10, Bold
D15:F15	mmm–yy	Center	Helv 10, Bold
D16:F17	$#,##0	General	Helv 10
D18:F19	#,##0	General	Helv 10

Figure 4-12. Accounts Receivable Aging Log

	A	B	C	D	E	F	G	H	I	J	K	L	M	N	O
1															
2															
3	**Accounts Receivable Aging Log**														
4	**Clem's Copper Clapper Company**														
5		Credit	Accts	Accts Receivable Balance				Write	Sales Collection Ratios					Write	
6	Date	Sales	Rec	0-30	31-60	61-90	91-120	Off	0-30	31-60	61-90	91-120	121+	Off	
7	Jan-87	***1,038***	1,932	***1,016***	509	376	31	0	***2%***	***47%***	***24%***	***25%***	***2%***	***.67%***	
8	Feb-87	861	1,721	843	***532***	294	52	0	2%	46%	25%	24%	3%	.12%	
9	Mar-87	1,086	1,829	1,060	451	***287***	31	0	2%	47%	25%	25%	0%		
10	Apr-87	1,820	2,587	1,771	548	238	***30***	1	3%	48%	25%	23%	1%	.16%	
11	May-87	1,780	2,930	1,734	892	275	29	***7***	3%	50%	25%	21%	2%		
12	Jun-87	1,929	3,171	1,878	844	444	5	1	3%	51%	25%	21%		.73%	
13	Jul-87	1,724	2,976	1,671	886	401	18	0	3%	50%	25%	19%	3%	.35%	
14	Aug-87	1,592	2,782	1,544	801	410	27	3	3%	50%	26%	20%	1%	.06%	
15	Sep-87	1,940	3,004	1,872	749	372	11	0	4%	49%	26%	20%	1%		
16	Oct-87	2,238	3,445	2,145	913	337	50	14	4%	49%	27%	17%	3%		
17	Nov-87	1,358	2,783	1,297	1,048	414	24	6	4%	50%	28%	16%	1%		
18	Dec-87	1,183	2,217	1,135	615	449	18	1	4%	51%	28%	16%	1%		
19	Jan-88	1,243	2,028	1,192	537	235	64	0	4%	51%	28%	16%	2%		
20	Feb-88	1,277	2,006	1,229	562	201	14	0	4%	48%	29%	17%	2%		
21	Mar-88	1,271	2,069	1,231	614	218	6	0	3%	48%	30%	18%	1%	.08%	
22	Apr-88	1,892	2,737	1,843	625	249	20	0	3%	48%	30%	19%	0%	.16%	
23	May-88	1,828	2,991	1,785	937	240	29	0	2%	48%	30%	19%	1%		
24	Jun-88	2,377	3,615	2,323	913	368	11	0	2%	46%	31%	20%	1%		
25	Jul-88	1,871	3,446	1,829	1,238	369	10	1	2%	44%	33%	18%	3%		
26	Aug-88	1,636	3,111	1,597	1,005	495	14	3	2%	41%	33%	23%	0%	.24%	
27	Sep-88	2,103	3,391	2,059	919	396	17	0	2%	40%	33%	24%			
28	Oct-88	2,042	3,641	1,996	1,211	380	54	0	2%	39%	33%				
29	Nov-88	1,625	3,305	1,585	1,190	523	7	0	2%	39%					
30	Dec-88	1,116	2,582	1,086	950	520	26	4	3%						
31	Jan-89														
32	Feb-89														
33	Mar-89														
34	Apr-89														
35	May-89														
36	Jun-89														
38															
39															

COLUMN WIDTHS							
Column	***Width***	***Column***	***Width***	***Column***	***Width***	***Column***	***Width***
A	**7**	**E**	**5.57**	**I**	**4.71**	**M**	**4.86**
B	**6.57**	**F**	**5**	**J**	**5.57**	**N**	**5.71**
C	**6**	**G**	**5.86**	**K**	**5.57**		
D	**6**	**H**	**4.57**	**L**	**5.57**		

(continued)

Figure 4-12. *continued*

KEY FORMULAS	
Cell	***Formula***
A7 **A8**	**01/01/87** **=DATE(YEAR(A7),MONTH(A7)+1,1)** Copy the formula in A8 down the column as necessary.
I7	**=IF($B7=0,0,(B7–D7)/$B7)** This formula calculates the percentage collected during the month of sale.
J7	**=IF(OR($B7=0,$B8=0),0,(D7–E8)/$B7)** This formula calculates the percentage collected in 31–60 days.
K7	**=IF(OR($B7=0,$B9=0),0,(E8–F9)/$B7)** This formula calculates the percentage collected in 61–90 days.
L7	**=IF(OR($B7=0,$B10=0),0,(F9–G10)/$B7)** This formula calculates the percentage collected in 91–120 days.
M7	**=IF(OR($B7=0,$B11=0),0,(G10–H11)/$B7)** This formula calculates the percentage collected after 120 days.
N7	**=IF(OR($B7=0,$B11=0),0,H11/$B7)** This formula calculates the percentage written off after 120 days.

KEY CELL FORMATS			
Cell	***Number***	***Alignment***	***Font***
A3:A4	**General**	**General**	**Helv 10, Bold**
A7:A36	**mmm–yy**	**General**	**Helv 10**
B7:H36	**#,##0**	**General**	**Helv 10**
I7:M36	**0%;–0%;**	**General**	**Helv 10**
N7:N36	**.00%;–00%;**	**General**	**Helv 10**

Figure 4-13. Modified Accounts Receivable Aging Log

A summary by quarter of two aspects of collection performance: the percentage of each month's sales collected in subsequent months (boldface) and the percentage of accounts receivable by "bucket" collected during the month (lightface).

	P	Q	R	S	T	U	V	W	X
1									
2									
3	**A/R Collection Ratios by Quarter**								
4	Collections as % of sales and as % of A/R aging category.								
5	Qtr/							Write	
6	Days		0-30	31-60	61-90	91-120	121+	Off	
7	Jan-87								
8	68	**Sales**	**2%**	**46%**	**24%**	**25%**	**2%**		
9									
10	Apr-87								
11	65	**Sales**	**3%**	**50%**	**25%**	**22%**	**1%**	**.30%**	
12		A/R, by period		50%	49%	92%	90%	10%	
13	Jul-87								
14	65	**Sales**	**3%**	**50%**	**25%**	**20%**	**2%**		
15		A/R, by period		52%	53%	96%	94%	6%	
16	Oct-87								
17	63	**Sales**	**4%**	**50%**	**28%**	**17%**	**1%**		
18		A/R, by period		52%	56%	92%	75%	25%	
19	Jan-88								
20	64	**Sales**	**4%**	**49%**	**29%**	**17%**	**2%**	**.03%**	
21		A/R, by period		52%	62%	91%	100%		
22	Apr-88								
23	66	**Sales**	**2%**	**47%**	**30%**	**19%**	**1%**		
24		A/R, by period		49%	61%	92%	100%		
25	Jul-88								
26	66	**Sales**	**2%**	**42%**	**33%**	**22%**			
27		A/R, by period		45%	60%	97%	89%	11%	
28	Oct-88								
29	0	**Sales**	**2%**						
30		A/R, by period		41%	57%	93%	95%	5%	
31	Jan-89								
32		**Sales**							
33		A/R, by period							
34	Apr-89								
35		**Sales**							
36		A/R, by period							
38									
39									

COLUMN WIDTHS			
Column	*Width*	*Column*	*Width*
P	5.71	T	5.57
Q	6	U	5.57
R	5.57	V	5.57
S	5.57	W	5.57

(continued)

Figure 4-13. *continued*

KEY FORMULAS	
Cell	***Formula***
P10	**=A10**
P11	**=15*R11+45*S11+75*T11+105*U11+135*V11** The average collection period equals the sum of the number of days at the mid-point of each period times the percentage collected in the period.
R11	**=IF(I12=0,0,AVERAGE(I10:I12))** Copy this formula to columns S through W.
S12	**=IF(D11=0,0,1–SUM(E10:E12)/SUM(D9:D11))** The percentage collected in the period equals 1 minus the ending balance divided by the beginning balance. (Because the beginning balance includes data from the previous quarter, this formula isn't used in the first quarter in the schedule.) Copy this formula to columns T through V.
W12	**=IF($D11=0,0,1–V12)** Bad debts equal accounts not collected after 120 days.

KEY CELL FORMATS			
Cell	***Number***	***Alignment***	***Font***
P3	**General**	**General**	**Helv 10, Bold**
P10	**mmm–yy**	**General**	**Helv 10**
P11	**#,##0;–#,##0;**	**Center**	**Helv 10**
R11:V11	**0%;–0%;**	**General**	**Helv 10, Bold**
W11	**.00%;–00%;**	**General**	**Helv 10, Bold**
S12:W12	**0%;–0%;** Notice that with the exception of the date, all number formats end with a semicolon. This displays 0 values as blanks.	**General**	**Helv 10**

Figure 4-14. Monthly Cash Collections Forecast

A monthly forecast of A/R collections.

	Y	Z	AA	AB	AC	AD	AE	AF
1								
2								
3	**Cash Collections Forecast for the Month of January, 1989**							
4								
5	**Expected Collections From Current Sales**							
6	Expected sales						$1,500	
7	Last quarter's average percentage collected in month of sale:						2%	
8	Expected collections from this month's sales:						$37	
9								
10	**Expected Collections From Outstanding Accounts Receivable**							
11			0-30	31-60	61-90	91-120	Total	
12	Beginning A/R balance		1,086	950	520	26	2,582	
13	Last quarter's collection ratios		41%	57%	93%	95%		
14	Expected collections by period		$441	$543	$485	$25	$1,493	
15								
16	Expected write-off:						$1	
17								
18	**Expected Collections This Month:**						**$1,530**	
19								
20								

COLUMN WIDTHS			
Column	*Width*	*Column*	*Width*
Y	10.86	AC	8.43
Z	15.71	AD	8.43
AA	8.43	AE	8.43
AB	8.43		

(continued)

Figure 4-14. *continued*

KEY FORMULAS	
Cell	***Formula***
Y3	**="Cash Collections Forecast for the Month of "& TEXT(DATE(YEAR(RcntMon),MONTH(RcntMon)+1,1),"mmmm, yyyy")** This formula combines the date of the forecast with the report title. The date is equal to the most recent month of data in the log (RcntMon) plus one month.
AE6	**1500** Enter your expected sales in this cell.
AE7	**=INDEX($1:$16384,RcntMoRow–MOD(MONTH(RcntMon),3)–1,COLUMN(R$5))** This formula returns the average percentage of sales collected during the month of the sale. This value comes from the data calculated for the most recently completed calendar quarter in Figure 4-13. To make this calculation, the formula must know which cells in the spreadsheet in Figure 4-13 contain data for the recently completed quarter. To find these cells, it depends on values returned by two range formulas: RcntMon, which returns the most recently completed month, and RcntMoRow, which returns the row number in the spreadsheet in Figure 4-12 that contains this month. The MOD function in the formula finds the number of months since the last full quarter was completed. This number is subtracted from RcntMoRow to find the row in the spreadsheet in Figure 4-12 that contains the ending month of the most recently completed quarter. This row number also represents the last row of data for the quarter in the spreadsheet in Figure 4-13. Because the sales percentage value that you want is always one row above the last row of data for the quarter in the spreadsheet in Figure 4-13, the formula reduces the row number by one. Then the INDEX function finds the correct value in this row number and in column R of the spreadsheet.
AE8	**=AE6*AE7** Expected collections equal expected sales times expected collections ratio.
AA12	**=INDEX($1:$16384,RcntMoRow,COLUMN(D$6))** This INDEX formula finds last month's A/R balance in the row number found in RcntMoRow and in column D. Copy the formula to the range AB12:AD12.
AA13	**=INDEX($1:$16384,RcntMoRow–MOD(MONTH(RcntMon),3),COLUMN(S$5))** This is similar to the formula in cell AE7. It finds the A/R collection ratios by returning to the ending month of the last full quarter and then looking in column S. Copy the formula to the range AB13:AD13.

(continued)

Figure 4-14. *continued*

KEY FORMULAS–continued	
Cell	***Formula***
AA14	**=AA12*AA13** Expected collections equal last month's A/R balance times the collection ratios. Copy this formula to the range AB14:AD14.
AE12	**=SUM(AA12:AD12)** Total A/R equals the sum of the balances owed for each period.
AE14	**=SUM(AA14:AD14)** Total collections from A/R equal the sum collected from each period.
AE16	**=AD12–AD14** Total write-offs equal the amount not collected after 120 days.
AE18	**=AE8+AE14** Total collections for the month equal the amount collected from this month's sales plus the amount collected from outstanding receivables.

RANGE NAMES	
Name	***Formula***
RcntMoRow	**=MATCH(99999,$B$1:$B$153,1)** This range-definition formula finds the last row of data in column B of the spreadsheet in Figure 4-12. By limiting its search to row 153, the formula reflects the assumption that the log will contain no more than about 12 years of monthly data.
RcntMon	**=INDEX($1:$16384,RcntMoRow,COLUMN($A$5))** This range-definition formula finds the date in column A of the last row of data in column B.

(continued)

Figure 4-14. *continued*

KEY CELL FORMATS			
Cell	*Number*	*Alignment*	*Font*
Y5	General	General	Helv 10, Bold
Y10	General	General	Helv 10, Bold
Y18	General	General	Helv 10, Bold
AE6	$#,##0 ;($#,##0)	General	Helv 10
AE7	0%	General	Helv 10
AE8	$#,##0 ;($#,##0)	General	Helv 10
AA12:AE12	#,##0 ;(#,##0)	General	Helv 10
AA13:AD13	0%	General	Helv 10
AA14:AE14	$#,##0 ;($#,##0)	General	Helv 10
AE16	$#,##0 ;($#,##0)	General	Helv 10
AE18	$#,##0 ;($#,##0)	General	Helv 10, Bold

5

Business Loans

A business might prepare for months to convince a lender to provide cash. But after they get their cash, businesses tend to forget about the lender. They concentrate, instead, on the many details necessary for using the cash profitably.

But the lender hasn't forgotten. Somewhere, someone keeps track of whether payments have arrived on time, reviews financial statements, responds to vendors' questions, confirms loan amounts with auditors, and does all those other things that lenders do in a successful lending relationship.

This chapter provides tools that can help you maintain that successful relationship with your lender: a financial calculator to help evaluate the loan, amortization tables to account for the loan properly, a mortgage analysis schedule to help choose the right terms, several other schedules to track the status of your loans, and a loan-compliance report to remind you of the things you promised your lender you would do in addition to making payments.

A FINANCIAL CALCULATOR

Your microcomputer has more power than a mainframe computer of 15 to 20 years ago. It seems silly, therefore, to reach for your hand-held financial calculator whenever you want to perform mortgage calculations.

Microsoft Excel, of course, has all the functions needed to replace a hand-held financial calculator. What these functions lack is convenience. By the time you figure out which number goes where in a PMT function, for example, you could have found several answers on your calculator. On the other hand, your calculator can become inconvenient as well. Each time your data changes, you must take the time to key it into your calculator. And after you've found your answer on a calculator, you must decide what to do with it. Do you write it down on a piece of scratch paper? Key it into a spreadsheet? Or just try to memorize it?

Figure 5-1 shows a spreadsheet that presents a convenient solution to this problem. Like a hand-held financial calculator, it lets you quickly calculate the term, interest rate, present value, payment, or future value of a loan. But because the calculator in Figure 5-1 is also a spreadsheet, it provides the resources you need for connecting your calculator to your spreadsheet, for performing side calculations, for documenting your results, and for saving your work.

Charley Kyd's			PMT = ($938.68)	
		Financial Calculator		
1	2	3	4	5
n	i	PV	PMT	FV
240	0.83%	$100,000.00	$0.00	($20,000.00)
Choice: 4				0: 0=End 1=Beg

Figure 5-1. *A financial calculator that works much like a hand-held financial calculator, displaying a loan-payment calculation.*

Using a Financial Calculator

To give you an idea of the power of this calculator, let's go through three examples.

Example 1

Your rich uncle has agreed to loan you the cash to buy a new home. He's agreed to a 20-year amortizing loan with an interest rate of 10 percent. To lower your monthly payments somewhat, he's agreed to take a balloon payment of $20,000 at the end of the 20 years. What are your monthly payments? The spreadsheet in Figure 5-1 shows the answer. Here's how to use the financial calculator to find it:

Because the term (n) is 20 years of monthly payments, enter *=20*12* for this value. Because the interest rate is 10 percent yearly, enter *=.1/12* to calculate the monthly interest rate (i). Enter the loan amount of *$100,000* as the present value (PV). Because you are receiving the cash, enter it as a positive value. Because you want to calculate the payment (PMT), skip that item. (The calculator ignores any entry for a value that it is calculating.) Enter the balloon payment in the future value (FV) cell. Because you will have to pay the amount, enter it as a negative number.

Enter *0* in the bottom-right cell of the calculator. As the label in this field explains, a 0 indicates that cash flows will occur at the end of each period. Loans typically use this calculation method, which is called an ordinary annuity. If you were to enter *1* in this field, the calculator would assume that cash flows will occur at the beginning of each period. You might use this setting, which is called a payment in advance or an annuity due, if you were calculating the balance of a savings account in which you deposited money at the beginning of each month.

Finally, to tell the calculator that you want to calculate the loan payment, enter *4* as your choice in the bottom-left cell of the calculator. This value corresponds to the value in italics immediately above the label PMT. After you enter this number, the correct payment value appears at the top of your calculator.

Example 2

At the end of the first year of your loan, you sit down to do your income taxes. When you ask your uncle for a statement of interest expenses, he tells you to type something up and he'll sign it. How much interest have you paid during the first year of the loan? The spreadsheet in Figure 5-2 shows your answer. Here's how to calculate it:

To enter the payment value, enter an equal sign in the PMT cell, cell E9; select the cell containing the result of the payment calculation from the preceding example, cell F4; press the F9 key to turn the formula in cell E9 into a value; and then press Enter. Enter *12* as the term of the loan. Then enter *5* in the Choice cell, and the calculator displays the unpaid balance.

	A	B	C	D	E	F	G	H
1								
2								
3								
4		Charley Kyd's			FV =	($98,676.26)		
5				Financial Calculator				
7		*1*	*2*	*3*	*4*	*5*		
8		n	i	PV	PMT	FV		
9		12	0.83%	$100,000.00	($938.68)	($20,000.00)		
12		Choice: 5				0: 0=End 1=Beg		
13								
14								
15		Total Payments				$11,264.16		
16		Principal Reduction						
17		Beginning Balance		$100,000.00				
18		Ending Balance		$98,676.26				
19						$1,323.74		
20		Total Interest Paid				$9,940.42		
21								
22								

Figure 5-2. *The financial calculator, modified to include a schedule that depends on results from the original calculator.*

The schedule below the calculator completes your answer. The formula for total payments is =–PMT*12. The beginning loan balance is $100,000; the formula for the ending balance is simply =–F4; and the total principal reduction is the difference between these two values. Total interest paid, therefore, is the difference between the total payments and the amount of the principal reduction.

Example 3

After your uncle signs your statement of interest paid, he explains that he needs larger monthly payments from your loan to finance his growing collection of political bumper stickers. "Tell you what," he says. "Pay me $1,200 per month for the next 10 years, and we'll call it square." What annual interest rate does this arrangement imply? The spreadsheet in Figure 5-3 shows your answer.

To get this result, enter the unpaid balance from Figure 5-2 as the present value in Figure 5-3. To do this easily, enter =– in cell D9, select cell F4 containing the answer shown in Figure 5-2, press the F9 key, and then press Enter. Enter *0* in the FV cell (cell F9), *–$1,200* in the PMT cell, and *120* months for the term in cell B9. After you enter *2* in the Choice cell, you get the answer shown in cell F4 of Figure 5-3.

	A	B	C	D	E	F	G
1							
2							
3							
4		Charley Kyd's			i = .67%		
5			Financial Calculator				
7		1	2	3	4	5	
8		n	i	PV	PMT	FV	
9		120	0.83%	$98,676.26	($1,200.00)	$0.00	
12		Choice: 2				0: 0=End 1=Beg	
13							
14							
15		Annual Interest Rate		8.04%			
16							

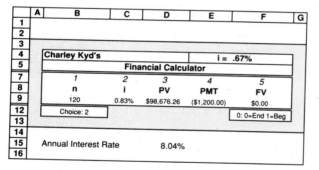

Figure 5-3. *The calculator, modified to include a formula that finds the annual interest rate.*

Finally, to convert the monthly interest rate shown to a yearly value, enter the formula *=F4*12* below the calculator as shown in Figure 5-3, and then press Enter. The results show that your uncle is offering you a good deal, if you can afford to take it.

How the Calculator Works

Figure 5-4 on page 177 shows the calculator with its hidden rows revealed. As you compare this version of the calculator with the versions in Figure 5-1 through Figure 5-3, you will notice several differences.

Notice in cell B12, for example, that the Choice number isn't shown. Instead, the cell displays a message requesting that you make a choice. The calculator displays this message whenever you enter *0* as the choice. The calculator also displays the message *Enter Data Below* in response to 0.

The values in row 10 show a difference that might at first seem disturbing: error messages. These error messages aren't a problem, however. Here's why: Each formula in row 10 generates the value described in row 8. That is, the formula in cell B10 uses the NPER function to generate the term, the formula in cell C10 uses the RATE function to generate the interest rate, and so on, with each calculation based on the values entered in row 9. When you enter a choice in cell B12, the formula in cell F4 chooses the appropriate value from row 10 and returns this value properly formatted; the other results in row 10 are ignored.

Each formula in row 10 ignores the data immediately above it in row 9. Suppose, for example, that your Choice number is 4, indicating that you want to calculate the payment. The PMT function in cell E10 looks at the other four values while ignoring whatever value may exist in cell E9. Often, this value is 0, which frequently causes the other functions to return error messages. You don't care that these values return an error, however, because row 10 will be hidden and its other values ignored.

Row 11 serves a related purpose. Each cell in the row returns the data entered in the cell above it in row 9 unless you select the result for that column, in which case the formula returns the calculated value in row 10 of the column. As a consequence, row 11 contains accurate data that you can reference from elsewhere within your spreadsheet. It will contain error messages only when there really are errors in your calculation.

Row 11 provides another value as well. The result expressed in cell F4 is rounded to the accuracy displayed on the screen. But occasionally you might want to refer to the exact result, not the rounded one. In such cases, refer to the appropriate value in row 11. In Figure 5-3, for example, cell C11 contains the value *.00671114*, while the result in cell F4 displays the rounded value *.67%*.

Because the values in row 11 are used for occasional reference, there is no need to display them in the calculator. As shown in the row-height box for Figure 5-4, the height of row 11 is 2 points. This height hides the values in this row while providing a large enough area to point to when you want to reference one of the cells in this row.

The following section explains how to create the financial calculator. However, if you would prefer to use the calculator without spending the time required to create it, you can order a set of disks that contains all models discussed in this book, including the calculator. You'll find an order form on the last page of the book.

Creating a Financial Calculator

To build this spreadsheet, first set the column widths to those shown in the column-width box and then turn off the gridlines. Outline the range A3:G13 by highlighting this area, choosing the Format Border command, and selecting Outline. Also, outline the ranges B4:D4, E4:F4, B5:F5, and B7:F9 and the cells B12 and F12.

Center-align the range B5:F12 by highlighting that range, choosing the Format Alignment command, and selecting Center. Enter the possessive form of your name in cell B4 and the label *Financial Calculator* in cell D5. In cell B6, enter the underline character (the shift position of the minus sign on your keyboard). To create a blue underline across row 6, follow the instructions in the format and formula boxes.

Enter the numbers shown in rows 7 and 9, the labels shown in row 8, and *0* in cells B12 and F12. Enter the formulas shown for row 10 in the formula box for Figure 5-4. Also, enter the formula shown for cell B11 and copy it to the range C11:F11. Then enter the formulas shown for cells E4 and F4. Notice that the formula for cell F4 is on two lines in the formula box. When you enter this formula, be sure to enter it on one line with no spaces between the characters.

Although you can't tell by the figures in this book because they're black and white, the calculator is multicolored, as you saw when you created the blue underline across row 6. In addition to the blue underline, the label *Financial Calculator* is red, the entries in rows 7 and 12 are blue, and negative values in the range D9:F9 are displayed as red. To display these colors and to display the labels shown in row 12, enter the formats shown in the format box for Figure 5-4. The number formats are particularly important; be sure to enter them exactly as shown.

When you have entered all formulas and formats, shade the areas shown in the spreadsheet by choosing the Format Border command and selecting Shade. Reduce the height of rows 6 and 11 to 2 points and the height of row 10 to 0.

To complete your calculator, eliminate your row and column headings by choosing the Options Display command and selecting the Row & Column Headings option. Reduce the size of your calculator window so that each edge of the window just touches a shaded border. Then save your calculator. It now resembles the calculator in Figure 5-1. This small spreadsheet now will be available whenever you need a financial calculator while you're working with Microsoft Excel.

Creating a Modified Version of the Calculator

While you're creating calculators, you may want to create a modified version of the one in Figure 5-4. You will notice in the range-name box that the calculator uses seven range names. While these names make the formulas easy to enter and understand, they can create problems when you copy the calculator to the same spreadsheet or other spreadsheets. When you do so, the new formulas will still refer to the old range names.

I therefore recommend that you create a second version of this calculator, a version that contains neither range names nor absolute references (the references with dollar signs in them). This will be a version that you can copy wherever you want. At times, for example, I've created a column of four or five calculators. The output from the first calculator generates part of the data for the second. The output from the second becomes part of the input for the third, and so on. By tying the calculators together in this way, I can quickly perform a multistep analysis.

When I first tried to eliminate the range names, I used the Formula Replace command, replacing each range name with its appropriate cell address. But when I did so, the command also replaced all labels and function names with cell addresses, creating something of a mess. Therefore, the easiest way to eliminate the range names is to edit each formula, manually replacing the range names with the appropriate cell addresses.

A SIMPLE AMORTIZATION TABLE

Nearly every spreadsheet program I've ever owned included a sample amortization table. Microsoft Excel is no exception. Page 21 of the Microsoft Excel Sampler illustrates just such an application. The spreadsheet, which is named AMORTIZ3.XLS, is in the LIBRARY subdirectory within the directory on your hard disk that contains your Microsoft Excel program.

Unfortunately, you can't easily modify AMORTIZ3.XLS to create your own amortization table, for reasons that will become apparent. This spreadsheet, therefore, serves no immediately useful purpose. Fortunately, however, you can easily change this spreadsheet into a general-purpose template that can create your amortization tables.

Creating an Amortization Table Template

Load the AMORTIZ3.XLS spreadsheet. Select the cell in column A that's in the row containing payment number 3, cell A17. Press the F8 key to turn on the Extend mode. Press Ctrl-End to highlight the spreadsheet from this point to the bottom-right corner. Choose Edit Delete and select All. Press Ctrl-Home, and your spreadsheet resembles the one in Figure 5-5 on page 181.

The original spreadsheet's use of range names poses two problems, one trivial, the other not. The trivial problem is that no range names are assigned to the term of the loan, cell D7, or to the date, cell D9. Although this oversight doesn't interfere with the operation of the spreadsheet, it does create a needless inconsistency. Therefore, assign the names *Term* and *Date* to the appropriate cells using the Formula Define Name command. After you do so, enter the formula for cell D11 shown in the formula box for Figure 5-5.

The other problem with the range names in AMORTIZ3.XLS is more serious. The spreadsheet contains the range name *Beginning_balance* for the range D15:D33 and *Interest* for the range E15:E33. Using these definitions, the amortization table returns error messages if you try to expand it beyond the 19 time periods for which the ranges have been defined. The easiest remedy is simply to delete these two range names. For each name, choose the Formula Define Name command, select the name, and choose the Delete button.

The formula box for Figure 5-5 provides the formulas and values that you must substitute where necessary in rows 15 and 16 of AMORTIZ3.XLS. After you make these substitutions, you can correct a minor formatting problem as well. The version of AMORTIZ3.XLS that came with my copy of Microsoft Excel had bottom cell borders for the date cells in column C. To remove these borders, highlight the range C15:C16, choose the Format Border command, deselect the Top and Bottom options in the dialog box, and then press Enter.

Finally, save this version of your spreadsheet under a new filename—AMORTIZE, for example. Then, when you want to create an amortization table, open this spreadsheet and take the steps described in the following section of this chapter.

Using the Amortization Table Template

To use this spreadsheet, first enter the information about your loan that is requested in rows 5 through 9. Press F9, if necessary, to recalculate your spreadsheet. After you've done so, remember the number of payments specified in cell D11.

Select cell B16. Press F8 to turn on the Extend mode and then press Ctrl-Down (direction key) to highlight column B from cell B16 to the bottom of the spreadsheet. Choose Data Series, enter the number of payments specified in cell D11 in the Stop Value box, and press Enter.

Column B now contains values from 1 through the number of payments specified in cell D11. You created this column so that it could serve as a guide for copying the formulas in row 16. To copy these formulas using the guide, follow these steps:

1. Highlight the range C16:H16.
2. Press Ctrl-Ins, which is a shortcut for the Edit Copy command.

3. Press the Down direction key once, moving your pointer to cell C17.
4. Press F8, turning on the Extend mode.
5. Press the Left direction key once, moving the extend range to cell B17.
6. Press Ctrl-period to highlight cell B17 within the extend range.
7. Press Ctrl-Down to extend the highlight to the last cell in column B containing a number.
8. Press Ctrl-period to highlight cell C17 again within the extend range.
9. Press the Right direction key to remove the highlight from column B.
10. Press Enter to complete the Copy and Paste command.
11. Press F9, if necessary, to calculate your new amortization schedule.

This is a long list of steps and may therefore seem to be quite complicated. But the process is really very simple, as you will see the first time you create an amortization table using this method.

Verifying Your Amortization Table

When I created my first amortization table in a spreadsheet, its long rows of numbers made it look quite impressive. But was it correct? I used two methods to verify the accuracy of the table, methods that have served me well for several years now.

The whole purpose of an amortizing loan is to bring the balance of the loan to 0 by making uniform payments over a specified number of periods. First, therefore, look at the ending balance of the loan in the last row of the table. Is it 0? (If the payment amount is rounded to the nearest penny, the ending balance may be slightly above or below 0. Nevertheless, the amount of this error should never exceed the amount of a periodic payment.)

Second, check the overall arithmetic of the loan. During the life of the loan, you paid an amount of cash equal to the periodic payment multiplied by the total number of periods. Some of this cash paid interest expenses, and the remainder repaid the loan. Therefore, if you subtract the total of all interest expenses from the total of all payments, the result should exactly equal the total amount borrowed.

A MORE USEFUL AMORTIZATION TABLE

The trouble with most amortization schedules is that they don't provide enough information. Who's the lender? What's the loan number? When is each payment due? To which general ledger accounts should you book the payments? How much of the loan is due within one year? How much interest expense should be accrued at month-end? How much interest was paid during the fiscal year? These are typical questions that people ask and that aren't answered in most amortization schedules.

Figure 5-6 presents an amortization schedule that answers these questions, a schedule that can serve as a working document in the accounting department of any business. Whenever you want to create an amortization schedule like this one, open the template shown in Figure 5-7 on page 184, enter the loan information in rows 3 through 14, open the macro shown in Figure 5-8 on page 191, press Ctrl-C to create the schedule, and press Ctrl-P to print it.

LARRY'S LAUNDRY											
The Old and Stodgy Bank, Loan #938-39474-1											
Int Rate		**Amount**		**Payment**		**# Months**		**1st Pmt**		**Lst Pmt**	
11.00%		$5,000.00		$197.13		29		10/29/88		2/28/91	
		Total Balance	Ending Bal G/L #2420	Ending Bal G/L #2720	Credit G/L #1001	Debit G/L #2420	Debit G/L #2720	Debit G/L #8201	Balance G/L #2495	Fiscal Year Totals	
Pmt#	Due Date	Remaining	S/T Liab	L/T Liab	Cash	ST Liab	LT Liab	Interest	Acrd Int	Cash	Interest
0	29-Sep-88	5,000.00	1,909.95	3,090.05					1.52		
1	29-Oct-88	4,848.70	1,927.45	2,921.25	197.13	(17.50)	168.80	45.83	1.48		
2	29-Nov-88	4,696.02	1,945.13	2,750.89	197.13	(17.68)	170.36	44.45	1.43		
3	29-Dec-88	4,541.94	1,962.96	2,578.98	197.13	(17.83)	171.91	43.05	1.38	591.39	133.33
4	29-Jan-89	4,386.44	1,980.95	2,405.49	197.13	(17.99)	173.49	41.63	1.33		
5	28-Feb-89	4,229.52	1,999.11	2,230.41	197.13	(18.16)	175.08	40.21	1.29		
6	29-Mar-89	4,071.16	2,017.43	2,053.73	197.13	(18.32)	176.68	38.77	1.24		
7	29-Apr-89	3,911.35	2,035.93	1,875.42	197.13	(18.50)	178.31	37.32	1.19		
8	29-May-89	3,750.07	2,054.59	1,695.48	197.13	(18.66)	179.94	35.85	1.14		
9	29-Jun-89	3,587.32	2,073.42	1,513.90	197.13	(18.83)	181.58	34.38	1.09		
10	29-Jul-89	3,423.07	2,092.43	1,330.64	197.13	(19.01)	183.26	32.88	1.04		
11	29-Aug-89	3,257.32	2,111.61	1,145.71	197.13	(19.18)	184.93	31.38	0.99		
12	29-Sep-89	3,090.05	2,130.97	959.08	197.13	(19.36)	186.63	29.86	0.94		
13	29-Oct-89	2,921.25	2,150.51	770.74	197.13	(19.54)	188.34	28.33	0.89		
14	29-Nov-89	2,750.89	2,170.21	580.68	197.13	(19.70)	190.06	26.77	0.84		
15	29-Dec-89	2,578.98	2,190.11	388.87	197.13	(19.90)	191.81	25.22	0.78	2,365.56	402.60
16	29-Jan-90	2,405.49	2,210.18	195.31	197.13	(20.07)	193.56	23.64	0.73		
17	28-Feb-90	2,230.41	2,230.41	0.00	197.13	(20.23)	195.31	22.05	0.68		
18	29-Mar-90	2,053.73	2,053.73	0.00	197.13	176.68	0.00	20.45	0.62		
19	29-Apr-90	1,875.42	1,875.42	0.00	197.13	178.31	0.00	18.82	0.57		
20	29-May-90	1,695.48	1,695.48	0.00	197.13	179.94	0.00	17.19	0.52		
21	29-Jun-90	1,513.90	1,513.90	0.00	197.13	181.58	0.00	15.55	0.46		
22	29-Jul-90	1,330.64	1,330.64	0.00	197.13	183.26	0.00	13.87	0.40		
23	29-Aug-90	1,145.71	1,145.71	0.00	197.13	184.93	0.00	12.20	0.35		
24	29-Sep-90	959.08	959.08	0.00	197.13	186.63	0.00	10.50	0.29		
25	29-Oct-90	770.74	770.74	0.00	197.13	188.34	0.00	8.79	0.23		
26	29-Nov-90	580.68	580.68	0.00	197.13	190.06	0.00	7.07	0.18		
27	29-Dec-90	388.87	388.87	0.00	197.13	191.81	0.00	5.32	0.12	2,365.56	175.45
28	29-Jan-91	195.31	195.31	0.00	197.13	193.56	0.00	3.57	0.06		
29	28-Feb-91	0.00	0.00	0.00	197.10	195.31	0.00	1.79	0.00	394.23	5.36
30	29-Mar-91	0.00	0.00	0.00	0.00	0.00	0.00	0.00	0.00		

Figure 5-6. *A loan-amortization schedule that includes many details not found in most amortization schedules.*

Creating the Template

Beginning with a new spreadsheet, turn off the gridlines by choosing the Options Display command and deselecting Gridlines. Change the calculation method to manual by choosing the Options Calculation command and selecting Manual. Set the column widths shown in the column-width box for Figure 5-7. (After you create your first schedule, you might have to adjust these widths. They must be wide enough to display your data but narrow enough to print on your printer.)

Creating the tables

Rows 3 through 29 of Figure 5-7 contain labels and data, but no formulas. Outline the loan and company tables, enter the labels and data shown, format this information as shown in the format box for Figure 5-7, and then complete the borders.

Notice in the spreadsheet that I formatted column G of the tables containing loan and company information as boldface. When you enter the information for your own company, the boldface format emphasizes the number that you must update. But because column G isn't wide enough to display 5,000 in 10-point Helv bold, I reduced its point size to 8.

If you have a similar problem with an even larger loan amount, you have three choices. First, you could widen column G, which might make your amortization table too wide to print on standard computer paper. Second, you could format the cell to remove the boldface. Third, you could ignore the fact that cell G8 displays the overflow symbols when you enter the value, because you won't print this section of your spreadsheet anyway.

To assign the range names in the loan table, highlight the range G8:H14, choose the Formula Create Names command, and select Right Column. Similarly, assign the range names in the company table. The range-name information box for Figure 5-7 shows additional range names to assign. Assign the first three of these as shown.

Outline the calculation box shown in rows 32 through 38. Enter the descriptions and range names shown for this box. As before, assign the range names in column H to the adjacent cells in column G. Then enter the formulas for the range G33:G38 that are shown in the formula box for Figure 5-7.

The following sections of this chapter explain how to create the amortization table and the macros that support it. But if you would prefer to use a template and macros that already exist, you can order a set of disks that contain all models discussed in this book. You will find an order blank on the last page of the book.

Creating the amortization table

Outline the range A41:N52, which will contain all of the amortization table that you will save with your template. Center-align the range A41:N48. Enter the formulas shown in the formula box for rows 41 through 45 and format them as shown in the format box. As explained in the formula box, reduce the height of row 42 to 3.

Enter the labels shown in the spreadsheet for rows 46 and 48. Enter the label shown for cells C47 and L47 and change the alignment for cell L47 to General. Then enter the formulas shown in the formula box for row 47.

Enter and format all formulas shown for rows 49 and 50. After you do, copy the formulas shown for cells D49, E49, and J49 to cells D50, E50, and J50, respectively. Copy the row of formulas in the range A50:N50 to the range A51:A52.

Next, create the borders. Highlight the range A46:K52, choose the Options Borders command, and select Outline, Left, and Right. Likewise, outline the ranges A49:N49, L48:N52, and A44:N45.

Assign the last two range names, top and source, as shown in the range-name box, and then press F9 to calculate the spreadsheet. When you do so, your spreadsheet returns the numbers shown in rows 50 through 52 of the spreadsheet in Figure 5-7. If you don't get those values, compare your results with those in the spreadsheet, beginning with the formula in cell G33. Correct any formulas or data necessary to make your formulas match those in the spreadsheet.

When your formulas work correctly, assign a width of 0 to columns K and M. These columns contain scratch values needed in the schedule by columns L and N, respectively. These columns, however, are of no interest to humans.

Finally, designate rows 41 through 48 as a print title. After you do so, Microsoft Excel will print these rows at the top of each page of your amortization schedule. To make this designation, highlight rows 41 through 48 and then choose the Options Set Print Titles command. Then save your completed template.

An Explanation of the Macros

Rows 4 through 9 of the CREATE macro in Figure 5-8 on page 191 delete the old range titled *target*, if it exists. (This is the portion of the amortization schedule that the CREATE macro creates.)

Most target ranges will be too large for Microsoft Excel to delete and still let you use the Undo command to restore them. Normally, Microsoft Excel would stop your macro and ask for permission to proceed without Undo. But the CREATE macro uses the formula =ERROR(FALSE) in row 5 to turn off error messages, including the warning about Undo. Then, after the target range is deleted in row 7, the =ERROR(TRUE) statement in row 8 turns the error messages back on. You don't want the macro to erase something at random if there is no target range. Therefore, the macro begins by selecting the empty cell E1.

Next, the macro copies the source range, A50:N52, to the remainder of the schedule as needed. Because the source range contains three rows, the target range must contain a number of rows divisible by 3. Cell B11 of the macro contains a general-purpose rounding formula that calculates this new number of rows, which the SELECT function in cell B12 uses to highlight the target range.

The text formula within the SELECT function creates cell references on which the function depends. In Figure 5-8, for example, the text formula resolves to "R[3]C:R[29]C". The complete SELECT formula therefore says: Select a range beginning three rows below the active cell (A50) and ending 29 rows below this position, staying within the current column.

After the macro names the target range *target*, in row 16 it defines the print area for the amortization table. To do so, it uses a SELECT formula similar to the one in cell B12. Finally, it calculates the spreadsheet, goes to the top of the table, and then quits.

The PRINT macro merely prints the predefined print area using the specifications shown in the macro.

Creating the Macros

Figure 5-8 shows the macros that create and print your amortization table. To build them, first open a macro sheet and turn off its gridlines.

Enter the labels shown in cells A3 and A4. When you enter the label in cell A4, be sure to enter the period shown after the *c*. If you ignore the period, Microsoft Excel thinks you are attempting to enter an invalid formula.

Using the Define Name dialog box, assign the name CREATE to cell B4. Define this name as a command macro with the command key *c*. Then enter the formulas shown in cells B4 through B19.

Similarly, enter the PRINT macro. Assign the name PRINT to cell B24 and designate the command key *p*, as the label in cell A24 specifies.

Create the borders shown on the macro sheet and add the documentation provided in column C and in cells B3 and B23. Long after you've read this book, this information will remind you of what these macros are doing.

To run this macro, activate the spreadsheet in Figure 5-7 and then press Ctrl-C. The first time you do so, however, it's a good idea to have Microsoft Excel step through the macro one command at a time. Doing so lets you see each macro command before it executes and the result of each command immediately after it executes. Viewing each command in this way lets you quickly find and fix any bugs in your macro. Then, after you step through the macro successfully, you can run it at its ordinary pace.

To step through the macro, select row 5 of the macro, insert a new row, and then add the command =STEP() in cell B5 of this new row. When you run the macro, Microsoft Excel starts single-stepping when it encounters this command. The Single Step dialog box displays each macro formula before it is executed and offers you the choice of taking the next step, halting the macro, or continuing without single-stepping. When the macro works successfully, delete the row that contains =STEP().

MORTGAGE ANALYSIS TABLES

Would you like to cut the total cost of your mortgage by at least 15 percent and perhaps by as much as 50 percent? The following section of this chapter describes a spreadsheet that suggests how to make such savings possible.

The spreadsheet in Figure 5-9 on page 192 contains four tables. Table 1 presents the monthly mortgage payments per $1,000 borrowed for various interest rates and terms. You may find this table worthwhile all by itself. Suppose, for example, that current interest rates are approximately 11.5 percent. The table shows that payments are nearly $10 per thousand for a 30-year mortgage at this interest rate. Therefore, if someone offers to sell you a building for which you must borrow $185,000, you'll know immediately that your payments will be approximately $1,850 (185 × 10) per month.

Table 2 calculates the total payments, in thousands, that will be required for each calculation in Table 1. For example, this table shows that a 9 percent, 30-year loan will require total payments of approximately $2,900 for each $1,000 borrowed. Total payments for a 14 percent, 30-year loan will require total payments of approximately $4,300.

Table 3 compares the added monthly costs of paying off a loan in less than 30 years. At a 14 percent interest rate, for example, a 10-year loan costs 31 percent more per month than a 30-year loan; a 15-year loan costs 15 percent more; a 20-year loan costs 5 percent more; and so on.

Table 4 compares the total savings from paying a loan off in less than 30 years. At a 14 percent interest rate, for example, a 10-year loan saves 56 percent; a 15-year loan saves 44 percent; a 20-year loan saves 30 percent; and so on.

Using the Mortgage Analysis Tables

Now that you understand these tables, take a closer look at what they mean. Table 4 shows that by paying off your loan more quickly, you can save 15 percent, 25 percent, or even 50 percent of the total cost of your loan. Table 3 shows that in many cases, these savings can be realized with relatively little increase in monthly payments.

Suppose, for example, that long-term interest rates are at 14 percent. Who in their right minds would agree to a 30-year mortgage when a 20-year mortgage is available? A 20-year mortgage costs only 5 percent more each month than a 30-year mortgage, but it saves 30 percent over the life of the loan. At an 11 percent interest rate, a 20-year mortgage costs 8 percent more each month, but it saves a total of 28 percent.

At the extreme, of course, a 10-year mortgage saves roughly 50 percent over the life of the loan, but it can cost from 30 percent to 60 percent more each month, depending on the interest rate. The savings are great if you can afford the payments. But you can use these tables to find the right balance between higher payments and larger savings.

After you create the spreadsheet in Figure 5-9, you can adjust Table 1 to refine the analysis. For example, to evaluate interest rates growing from 8 percent to 18 percent in increments of 1 percent, change the entry in cell A10 to *8%* and the entry in cell A11 to *=A10+.01*. Recalculate if you've set the recalculation mode to manual. To change the amount borrowed in Tables 1 and 2, change the value hidden in cell A5. (The formula and format tables for Figure 5-9 discuss this hidden value.) Finally, to change the life of the mortgage to a different selection of years, enter the terms of whatever lengths you want at the top of Table 1.

Creating the Mortgage Analysis Tables

To build the tables, open a new spreadsheet and turn off its gridlines. Adjust the column widths to those shown in the column-width box for Figure 5-9.

Enter the label shown in cell A3 and format it as shown in the format box. To create the dark line below this label, outline the range A4:M4 and then set its row height to 1 point. (Some monitors require a slightly larger row height, however. For example, if a height of 1 point doesn't work on your monitor, try 1.5 points.)

To begin Table 1, outline the range A6:F20. Assign the font Helv 10 Bold to ranges A6:F9 and A10:A20. Enter the labels shown in cells C6 and C7, and the labels and values in rows 8 and 9. Enter the value and the formulas shown for cells A10 through A12 in the formula box for Figure 5-9. Copy the formula in cell A12 to the range A13:A20.

Enter the formula shown in the formula box for cell B10 and then copy it to the range B10:F20. Format this range as shown in the format box. Finally, to complete Table 1, add the outlines as shown.

To complete Tables 2 through 4, copy Table 1 to the appropriate positions and then modify the labels and formulas as needed. The formula and format boxes provide all the information you need.

A LINE-OF-CREDIT TRACKER

Many businesses arrange lines of credit with their banks. Such an agreement, which is sometimes called a revolving line of credit, has the following general terms:

- During a period, typically one year, the bank agrees to provide a short-term loan, up to a specified amount, on demand.
- The interest rate is a certain percentage above the prime rate. The interest rate can therefore change several times during a month.
- Most banks require payment of a commitment fee at the time the agreement is signed. The amount of this fee varies from 0.25 percent to 1 percent of the total commitment. As a practical matter, businesses generally borrow the fee from the bank, reducing the amount available under the line of credit.

If your business depends on a line of credit, you probably would benefit from tracking the line daily. By doing so, you can discover the occasional bank error, you'll know the amount of credit that's available each day, you'll know the current interest expenses at the end of the month, and you'll have better information than your bank provides on your true cost of the borrowed funds.

Tracking a Line of Credit

Figure 5-10 on page 196 presents a line-of-credit tracker that provides the information you need. During the month, the tracker lists your current loan balance and available credit. At the end of the month, it provides summary statistics about the loan.

In the tracker in Figure 5-10, for example, the company began the month with a loan balance of $35,398.77 (which the number format rounds to $35,399 in cell G4) and an interest rate of 10.25 percent. During the month, the company borrowed a total of $177,000 against its line and repaid $140,000. The interest rate increased during this time to 11 percent, producing an average rate of 10.79 percent for the month. When the commitment fee is included in the interest calculations, however, the effective interest rate for the cash used is 12.89 percent.

Notice that because February contains only 28 days, the formulas in the tracker display only 28 days. And of course, the formulas at the bottom of the tracker generate statistics that are based on 28 days as well. Both sets of formulas depend on Column H, which contains a *1* for each day during the month and a blank for each row after the end of the month. When you print this tracker, you will exclude column H.

To set up the tracker in Figure 5-10 for March, you would enter February's ending loan balance into cell G4, change the date in cell A10, change the interest rate in cell D10, copy the formula in cell D11 down column D, and then erase the amounts borrowed and repaid in columns B and C. The whole process takes about a minute.

Creating a Line-of-Credit Tracker

To build the line-of-credit tracker, open a new spreadsheet, turn off its gridlines, and set its columns as shown in the column-width box for Figure 5-10. Enter the labels and values shown in rows 2 through 9 and format them as shown in the format box.

The first nine entries of the formula box include every formula required for rows 10 and 11. Enter them as shown and format them appropriately. After you do, copy the range A11:H11 to the range A12:A40. Unlike the tracker in the figure, your spreadsheet will display zeros in rows 38 through 40. To display these zeros as blanks, choose Options Display and select Zero Values.

If you want to check your results against those in the tracker in the figure, enter the values shown in the range B12:C36 and the interest rates shown in cells D16 and D30.

The formula box provides the formulas and explanations for the summary statistics shown at the bottom of the tracker. Enter and format the formulas as shown. Notice in the formula box that cell D44 contains an array formula. This formula finds the minimum value in the range D10:D40 that is not equal to 0. To achieve this, the formula finds the minimum value of a temporary array that includes only the values in column D that are greater than 0. The other formulas in row 44 contain similar formulas.

If you were to enter the formula for cell D44 by pressing Enter, the formula would return the #VALUE! error value. Try it. To correct this problem, you must tell Microsoft Excel that cell D44 contains an array formula. To do so, you hold down Ctrl and Shift while you press Enter (not simply press Enter) when you enter the formula. Therefore, to correct the #VALUE! message in cell D44, press F2 to edit the cell and then press Ctrl-Shift and Enter.

When you have entered all formulas, add the borders and shading to the display. To quickly draw the column borders, highlight the range A7:G44; choose the Options Borders command; and select Outline, Left, and Right. To draw the borders at the bottom of the schedule, highlight the range A41:G44, choose the Options Borders command, and select Top and Bottom. Now complete the other borders and shading.

A LOAN-COMPLIANCE REPORT

Debt is a fact of life for most businesses. The loan covenants that generally accompany this debt are a fact of life as well. After a loan is funded, however, many smaller businesses file the loan documents away in the back of a drawer and never look at them again. As a consequence, such a business may get a call from its not-so-friendly banker one day, demanding an immediate meeting to discuss numerous violations of the loan agreement.

Using a Loan-Compliance Report

Figure 5-11 on page 201 shows a simple loan-compliance report. Completed monthly, this report compares your actual company performance with that required by your loan documents. (The figure's formula box describes each result in the report.) Managers who prefer to see only the loan-compliance results can receive a printout of the report only through line 26. Managers who also want to see the data on which the report is based can receive a printout of the report through row 39.

This report gives you advance warning when your performance puts you in potential or actual violation of your loan agreement. (Cells H15 and H17, for example, show a technical violation.) Because you see these results before your banker does, the report gives you time to take immediate action to deal with the problem.

Creating a Loan-Compliance Report

The report shown in Figure 5-11 is only a sample, of course. Your loan agreement may require information that isn't shown in the report, may not require information that is shown, or both. Under most circumstances, however, you should have little trouble adding and deleting the information necessary to report on your own loan agreement.

To create this report, first open a new spreadsheet. Turn off the gridlines and then set the column widths to those shown in the column-width box.

Drop down to row 29 of the spreadsheet and enter the labels shown for the remainder of the report. Cell G43 contains the only formula in this Input Data section. Enter the other numbers shown for column G in this section and then enter the formula for cell G43, as shown in the formula box for Figure 5-11. Then, to complete this section, format the section as shown in the format box and add the borders shown in the report.

To complete the top section of the report, first enter and format the labels shown in rows 3 through 9. Enter and format the data shown in the range A10:B26.

Loan covenants specify the minimum values of some ratios and the maximum values of others. In the report, for example, the Debt/Worth Ratio entry cannot rise above 2.2; the Current Ratio entry, on the other hand, cannot fall below 1.5. The range E11:E26, which contains these Min and Max notations, does not contain the labels that you see. Instead, it contains the values *1* and *–1*, where 1 returns the label *Max* and –1 returns the label *Min*. The custom number format displayed in the format box for Figure 5-11 generates these labels. To display the labels, highlight the range E11:E26, enter the format shown in the format box, and then enter the value *1* or *–1*, as is appropriate.

The range F11:F26 contains the values set by the bank for the specific loan shown in the report. Enter the values shown. The range G11:G26 contains the actual values that have been calculated from the input data entered at the bottom of the report. The formula box shows each formula in this range; enter them as shown and then format them as shown in the format box.

Enter the formula shown for the variance in cell H11 and then copy the contents of this cell to the remainder of the column. To quickly copy the contents of this cell, highlight the range H11:H12, press Ctrl-Ins, highlight the range H13:H20, and then press Enter. Copy from the range H11:H15 to cell H22. Then format the cells in column H as shown in the format box.

Most spending decisions do not involve one yearly payment. Instead, a business spends varying amounts from month to month. Column I divides the amount that remains to be spent under the loan agreement by the number of months remaining in the current year. This formula therefore returns the average amount that the business can spend monthly during the remainder of the current fiscal year. Enter and format the formula shown for cell I22 and then copy this cell down the remainder of column I.

Finally, to complete this report, draw the borders shown and assign any formats that you skipped earlier.

A NOTES PAYABLE SCHEDULE

Even a small company can have dozens of amortizing loans. Trucks, trailers, factory equipment, buildings, company cars, and more can all be purchased with the help of these loans. Because each loan has its own maturity date, interest rate, loan amount, and so on, keeping track of all this data can become a full-time occupation.

The spreadsheet in Figure 5-12 on page 205 is an automated schedule that simplifies the tracking of notes payable. After you've entered the loan information into this schedule, it recalculates its totals every time you change the date in cell A5. As a consequence, this single spreadsheet provides all the information you need to keep your company books updated monthly with loan information.

How the Notes Payable Schedule Works

Notice that each loan has three lines of information. The first line begins with the lender name and then displays information that has been labeled *Adj* for *Adjusted.* The second line gives the loan number and provides information about the original loan. The third describes each loan's collateral.

The schedule presents both original and adjusted figures, for several reasons. One reason is that some lenders track the exact number of days between the receipt of each loan payment, charging daily interest on the unpaid balance. Unless every check arrives at the lender's office on exactly the same day each month, the amount that the lender says you owe may, after several years, be quite different than the amount your financial calculator says you owe.

Another reason for the adjustments line is that some amortizing loans allow for periodic adjustments in the interest rate. When the rate is adjusted, some loan agreements require that the payments be recalculated, while other loan agreements keep the payments constant and adjust the term of the loan. But whatever adjustment is made, the adjustments line for each loan allows you to update your loan information, keeping your notes payable schedule accurate.

The first loan shown in the schedule in Figure 5-12 might look slightly familiar. It is the loan in the amortization schedule in Figure 5-6. If you compare the two schedules, you see that the one in Figure 5-6 predicts that on December 31, 1989, the balance due and other loan statistics will be the same as the values shown for that date in the schedule in Figure 5-12, if you allow for rounding. The data corresponds for any other report date that you choose.

Also notice that because this loan requires no adjustment, the original and adjustments lines contain the same data, and the adjustments line performs all calculations. Only where adjustments have actually been made, as in the second and third loans, do the original and adjusted data differ.

This report has one more characteristic that you should keep in mind. Because you don't update this schedule when you make a loan payment, it assumes that you make your loan payments on the days they are due. This can create a problem if the report date falls between the date you actually paid and the date you should have paid. Suppose, for example, that you paid the Old and Stodgy Bank on January 2, rather than on December 29 when your payment was due, but you ran the report shown in Figure 5-12 on December 31. Because December 31 is after December 29, this report assumes that you made your payment on time. If this problem occurs, you might have to adjust the report totals manually before you book the results in your accounting system.

Creating a Notes Payable Schedule

To create this schedule, begin with a new spreadsheet. Turn off its gridlines and set its columns to the widths shown in the column-width box for Figure 5-12. Enter the labels and the date shown in rows 3 through 7 and format this data as shown in the format box. The shaded areas in rows 8 and 21 serve as top and bottom borders for the formulas in row 22. With row 8 as a border, for example, you can delete the first loan or insert a loan between it and the border without disturbing the formulas in row 22.

Enter the labels, dates, and values shown for the first loan in columns A through E and in columns G through I. All of this information is data provided by your lender. The formula in cell F9 calculates the number of months that remain on the loan. Enter it as shown in the formula box.

The formula in cell J9 that finds the loan's balance due calculates the future value of the loan through the last payment made. The formula box for Figure 5-12 shows the formula that calculates this value.

As an independent test of the calculation in cell J9, open the financial calculator described at the beginning of this chapter and shown again in Figure 5-13 on page 209. To enter the term of the loan, select the calculator's term cell, enter an equal sign, select cell E9 of the schedule in Figure 5-12, enter a minus sign, select cell F9 of the schedule in Figure 5-12, and then press Enter. Similarly, enter the interest rate (cell H9), present value (cell G9), and payment (cell I9). (When you enter the interest rate, remember to divide by 12 to find the monthly interest; when you enter the payment, be sure to precede the value with a minus sign to indicate a cash outflow.)

Enter *5* as your calculation choice and then recalculate your spreadsheet, if necessary. The result is shown in Figure 5-13. The future value found by the calculator exactly matches the balance due shown for December 29, 1989, in the schedule in Figure 5-6. It also matches the value shown in cell J9 of the schedule in Figure 5-12, when you allow for rounding.

Enter the remaining formulas shown in the formula box for row 9 of the schedule in Figure 5-12. Format the cells as shown in the format box. When you do so, your results match those in the schedule in Figure 5-12.

After the first loan is working properly, there is no particular reason to enter the other loans illustrated in the schedule in Figure 5-12. Instead, you enter the grand totals at the bottom of the schedule and then enter your own loan information.

The easiest way to enter the formulas for the bottom of the schedule is to first create the shaded area shown in row 21. To do so, choose Options Border and select Outline and Shade. Then enter and format the formulas for row 22 shown in the information boxes for the figure.

To complete the schedule for your own loans, first delete the loan-description data shown in the range A9:A11. Insert enough rows below row 12 and above row 21 to contain all your loans. Copy the range A9:O11 to the empty area above your bottom border and then update the spreadsheet with data for your own loans. Finally, when your spreadsheet is complete, use the financial calculator to test the values returned by the notes payable schedule.

Figure 5-4. Financial Calculator Exploded

This version of the calculator shows the hidden formulas.

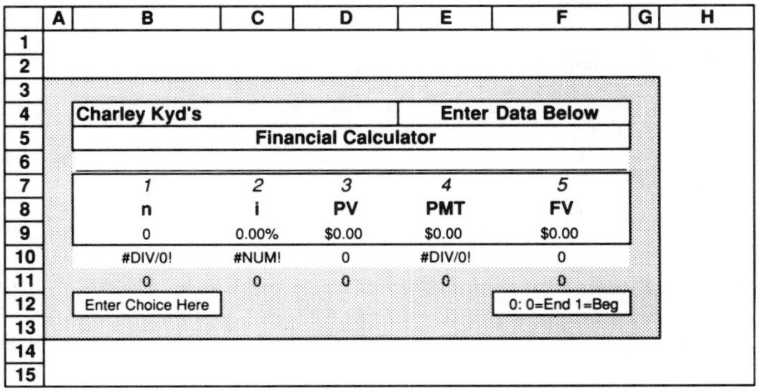

	A	B	C	D	E	F	G	H
1								
2								
3								
4		Charley Kyd's			Enter Data Below			
5				Financial Calculator				
6								
7		*1*	*2*	*3*	*4*	*5*		
8		**n**	**i**	**PV**	**PMT**	**FV**		
9		0	0.00%	$0.00	$0.00	$0.00		
10		#DIV/0!	#NUM!	0	#DIV/0!	0		
11		0	0	0	0	0		
12		Enter Choice Here				0: 0=End 1=Beg		
13								
14								
15								

COLUMN WIDTHS			
Column	***Width***	***Column***	***Width***
A	2	E	8
B	13	F	12
C	6	G	2
D	9		

ROW HEIGHTS	
Row	***Height***
6	2
10	0
11	2

(continued)

Figure 5-4. *continued*

KEY FORMULAS	
Cell	***Formula***
E4	**=IF(AND(Choice>0,Choice<6),INDEX(B8:F8,1,Choice)&" = ","Enter")** If Choice is greater than 0 and less than 6, this formula returns the appropriate label for the selection; otherwise, it returns the label *Enter*.
F4	**=IF(AND(Choice>0,Choice<6),CHOOSE(Choice,FIXED(B10,1), TEXT(C10,"#.00%"),DOLLAR(D10),DOLLAR(E10),DOLLAR(F10)),"Data Below")** If Choice is greater than 0 and less than 6, this formula returns the properly formatted result of the financial calculation; otherwise, it returns the label *Data Below*.
B6	This row contains a blue underline. The first step to creating the colored underline is to enter the underline character, as shown here. The next step is to format the cell as shown in the format table.
B9 **C9**	**=0*12** **=0/12** Generally, you will enter data in this row, not formulas. But feel free to enter formulas if you want. Here the number of months is equal to 0 years times 12 months in a year, and the monthly interest rate is equal to a 0 percent annual rate divided by 12.
B10 **C10** **D10** **E10** **F10**	**=NPER(i,PMT,PV,FV,Type)** **=RATE(n,PMT,PV,FV,Type,0.01)** **=PV(i,n,PMT,FV,Type)** **=PMT(i,n,PV,FV,Type)** **=FV(i,n,PMT,PV,Type)** After you assign the names shown in the range-name table, enter these financial functions in the cells shown. As you do so, they may return an incorrect value or an error message. Don't worry about it. When the calculator is finished, these errors will be hidden. Only the result requested by the Choice cell needs to be correct.
B11	**=IF(Choice=B7,B10,B9)** The result at the top of the calculator rounds the results to the accuracy displayed. At times, however, you will want to refer to the unrounded value. The formulas in this row generate that value. Enter this formula and copy it across the row as necessary.

(continued)

Figure 5-4. *continued*

RANGE NAMES	
Name	***Formula***
n	**=B9** The number of periods.
i	**=C9** The interest rate.
PV	**=D9** The present value.
PMT	**=E9** The periodic payments.
FV	**=F9** The future value.
Choice	**=B12** Your choice for the calculator to display a result.
Type	**=F12** Entering the value *1* in this cell tells the calculator to assume that cash flows occur at the beginning of each period; entering a *0* tells it that cash flows occur at the end of the period.

(continued)

Figure 5-4. *continued*

KEY CELL FORMATS			
Cell	***Number***	***Alignment***	***Font***
B4	**General**	**General**	**Helv 10, Bold**
E4	**General**	**Right**	**Helv 10, Bold**
F4	**General**	**General**	**Helv 10, Bold**
D5	**[Red]@** The @ symbol tells the number format to display text as entered.	**Center**	**Helv 10, Bold**
B6:F6	**[Blue]General** The Alignment Fill format repeats the underline character across the range. The number format displays the resulting line as blue.	**Fill**	**Helv 10**
B7:F7	**[Blue]General**	**Center**	**Helv 10, Italic**
B8:F8	**General**	**Center**	**Helv 10, Bold**
B9	**General**	**Center**	**Helv 8**
C9	**0.00%**	**Center**	**Helv 8**
D9:F9	**$#,##0.00 ;[Red]($#,##0.00)**	**Center**	**Helv 8**
B12	**[Blue]"Choice: "#;[Red]"Error";[Blue] "Enter Choice Here"** The custom number format displays a blue *Choice* if the choice is positive, a red *Error* if it's negative, and a blue *Enter Choice Here* if it's 0.	**Center**	**Helv 8**
F12	**[Blue]"1: 1=Beg 0=End" ;[Red]"Error"; [Blue] "0: 0=End 1=Beg"** The custom number format displays the labels shown when the Type value is entered as positive, negative, or 0.	**Center**	**Helv 8**

Figure 5-5. Simple Loan-Amortization Schedule

A modified version of the AMORTIZ3.XLS file, a sample amortization spreadsheet that comes with Microsoft Excel. Saved as AMORTIZ.XLS.

	A	B	C	D	E	F	G	H	I
1									
2		Mortgage Loan Analysis 3							
3									
4									
5		Principal		$30,000					
6		Annual interest rate		9.75%					
7		Term (years)		7					
8		Periods (per year)		12					
9		Start date		9/30/87					
10		Monthly Payment		$494.17					
11		No. of Payments		84					
12									
13		Payment	Payment	Beginning			Ending	Cumulative	
14		no.	dates	balance	Interest	Principal	balance	interest	
15		1	Sep-87	30,000.00	243.75	250.42	29,749.58	243.75	
16		2	Oct-87	29,749.58	241.72	252.45	29,497.13	485.47	
17									

COLUMN WIDTHS			
Column	***Width***	***Column***	***Width***
A	1.86	E	8.43
B	8.57	F	8.43
C	10.86	G	8.86
D	10.14	H	11.86

(continued)

Figure 5-5. *continued*

KEY FORMULAS	
Cell	***Formula***
D10	**=ABS(PMT(Rate/Period,no_of_payments,Principal))** The general form of this function is: =PMT(rate,nper,pv). If the principal is a positive value, the result will be negative, indicating a cash outflow. Therefore, taking the absolute value of the result (ABS) forces it to be positive. (I would have used a minus sign here rather than the ABS function. Doing so turns the negative payment value positive, as we want. But if an error in the formula were to generate a positive payment value, the negative sign would turn the result negative, highlighting the problem.)
D11	**=Term*Period** The number of periods equals the number of years times the number of periods per year.
B15 **B16**	**1** **2**
C15 **C16**	**=Date** **=DATE(YEAR(C15),MONTH(C15)+1,1)** This function takes the general form: =DATE(year,month,day). Because only the month and year are displayed, you can choose to calculate the day of the month that's most convenient. You therefore calculate the first day of each successive month.
D15 **D16**	**=Principal** **=G15** After the first month, each beginning balance equals the previous ending balance.
E15 **E16**	**=(Rate/Period)*D15** **=(Rate/Period)*D16** The Rate divided by the Period equals the interest rate for the period. This rate times the beginning balance equals the interest cost for the period.
F15 **F16**	**=Payment–E15** **=Payment–E16** The amount of the payment not paying interest is available to reduce the principal.
G15 **G16**	**=D15–F15** **=D16–F16** The ending balance equals the beginning balance minus the principal portion of the payment.

(continued)

Figure 5-5. *continued*

KEY FORMULAS—continued	
Cell	***Formula***
H15	**=E15**
H16	**=H15+E16**
	After the first month, cumulative interest equals the previous balance plus new interest expenses.

RANGE NAMES	
Name	***Formula***
Principal	**=$D$5**
Rate	**=$D$6**
Term	**=$D$7**
Period	**=$D$8**
Date	**=$D$9**
Payment	**=$D$10**
no_of_payments	**=$D$11**
	The italicized names have been added to the AMORTIZ3.XLS sheet. The names *Beginning_balance* and *Interest* have been deleted.

KEY CELL FORMATS			
Cell	***Number***	***Alignment***	***Font***
B5:B11	**General**	**Left**	**Helv 10, Bold**
D5	**$#,##0 ;($#,##0)**	**General**	**Helv 10**
D6	**0.00%**	**General**	**Helv 10**
D7:D8	**General**	**General**	**Helv 10**
D9	**m/d/yy**	**General**	**Helv 10**
D10	**$#,##0.00 ;($#,##0.00)**	**General**	**Helv 10**
D11	**General**	**General**	**Helv 10**
B13:H14	**General**	**Center**	**Helv 10, Bold**
B15:B19	**General**	**Center**	**Helv 10**
C15:C19	**mmm-yy**	**Center**	**Helv 10**
D15:H19	**#,##0.00 ;(#,##0.00)**	**General**	**Helv 10**

Figure 5-7. Supporting Data for the Expanded Loan-Amortization Schedule

The detailed loan-amortization schedule with supporting information visible.

ENTER THE FOLLOWING LOAN INFORMATION.

Lender: The Old and Stodgy Bank, Loan #938-39474-1

Enter the following numbers:	Number	Name
Loan amount to amortize.	5,000	loan
Yearly interest rate.	11.00%	int
Length of loan in months.	29	term
Month first payment is due.	10	month
Day first payment is due.	29	day
Year first payment is due.	88	year
Payment amount (leave blank to calculate).		epmt

ENTER THE FOLLOWING COMPANY INFORMATION.

Name: L A R R Y ' S L A U N D R Y

Enter the following numbers:	Number	Name
General ledger account numbers for:		
Cash.	1001	cash
Long-term debt due within one year.	2420	stliab
Long-term debt due in more than one year.	2720	ltliab
Interest costs.	8201	intamt
Liability for accrued interest.	2495	intliab
Our fiscal year ends on what month?	12	fyear

CALCULATIONS.

Calculation of periodic payment.	197.13	cpmt
Payment amount to use in schedule.	197.13	pmt
Calculated zero date.	9/29/88	date
End of zero date month.	9/30/88	edate
Monthly interest rate.	0.92%	mint
Interest is accrued for x% of the month.	3%	mop

L A R R Y ' S L A U N D R Y

The Old and Stodgy Bank, Loan #938-39474-1

Int Rate	Amount	Payment	# Months	1st Pmt	Lst Pmt
11.00%	$5,000.00	$197.13	29	10/29/88	2/28/91

Pmt#	Due Date	Total Balance Remaining	Ending Bal G/L #2420 S/T Liab	Ending Bal G/L #2720 L/T Liab	Credit G/L #1001 Cash	Debit G/L #2420 ST Liab	Debit G/L #2720 LT Liab	Debit G/L #8201 Interest	Balance G/L #2495 Acrd Int		Fiscal Year Totals Cash		Interest
0	29-Sep-88	5,000.00	5,000.00	0.00					1.52				
1	29-Oct-88	4,848.70	4,848.70	0.00	197.13	151.30	0.00	45.83	1.48	197.13		45.83	
2	29-Nov-88	4,696.02	4,696.02	0.00	197.13	152.68	0.00	44.45	1.43	394.26		90.28	
3	29-Dec-88	4,541.94	4,541.94	0.00	197.13	154.08	0.00	43.05	1.38	0.00	591.39	0.00	133.33

(continued)

Figure 5-7. *continued*

COLUMN WIDTHS							
Column	*Width*	*Column*	*Width*	*Column*	*Width*	*Column*	*Width*
A	4.5	E	9.17	I	8	L	8
B	10.17	F	8.17	J	8.33	M	0
C	8.83	G	9	K	0	N	7.5
D	9.67	H	8.67				

KEY FORMULAS	
Cell	*Formula*
G33	**=PMT((int/12),term,–loan)** This is the standard function to calculate a loan payment.
G34	**=IF(epmt>0,ROUND(epmt,2),ROUND(cpmt,2))** If you want to use a predefined payment value, enter that value in EPMT, cell G14. Otherwise, this formula returns the payment calculated in the previous formula.
G35	**=DATE(year,month–1,day)** This is one month before the first payment is due—generally, the date the loan was funded.
G36	**=DATE(year,month,1)–1** This is the last day of the month in which the loan was funded.
G37	**=int/12** The monthly interest equals the yearly interest divided by 12.
G38	**=1–DAY(date)/DAY(edate)** Suppose your loan is funded on the 10th. By the 30th, you will owe interest for two-thirds of a month, even though you won't pay the interest until the 10th of the following month. This formula calculates the fraction of the month for which you should accrue interest expense each month.
G41	**=company** This formula picks up the company name from the input area.
G42	**=REPT("_",LEN(company)*1.3)** This formula generates the underline shown in the schedule. While you maintain the font and style shown in the schedule, the underline adjusts itself to the length of your company name. If you change the font, adjust the multiplier value 1.3 to generate a similar underline. After you enter the formula, reduce the row height to 3.

(continued)

Figure 5-7. *continued*

KEY FORMULAS—continued	
Cell	***Formula***
G43	**=lender**
B45	**=int**
D45	**=loan**
F45	**=pmt**
H45	**=term**
J45	**=DATE(year,month,day)**
N45	**=DATE(year,month+term–1,MIN(day,DAY(DATE(year,month+term,0))))**
	These formulas display information entered in the input areas at the top of the schedule. For large loans,column D might not be wide enough to display the contents of cell D45. If so, substitute the formula =TEXT(loan,"$#,###.00") for the one shown here. This formula displays the loan amount as text, letting it extend beyond the borders of column D.
D47	**="G/L #"&stliab**
E47	**="G/L #"<liab**
F47	**="G/L #"&cash**
G47	**="G/L #"&stliab**
H47	**="G/L #"<liab**
I47	**="G/L #"&intamt**
J47	**="G/L #"&intliab**
	These formulas display the general ledger information entered at the top of the schedule. (Notice that these number values are converted to text values by the program when they are used in text formulas.)
A49	**0**
	Enter the value *0* in this cell.
B49	**=date**
C49	**=loan**
	As before, these formulas display information entered above.
D49	**=ROUND($C49,2)–ROUND($E49,2)**
	The short-term liability is equal to the total liability minus the long-term liability.
E49	**=MAX(C61,0)**
	The long-term liability is the loan amount that you will owe in 12 months. The easiest way to find this amount is to look 12 rows down the schedule.

(continued)

Figure 5-7. *continued*

KEY FORMULAS—continued

Cell	*Formula*
J49	**=C49*((1+mint)^mop–1)** This formula finds the interest expense for the fraction of the month between the payment date and the end of the month. This is equal to the amount borrowed times an interest rate. The rate is equal to 1 plus the the monthly interest rate taken to the power of MOP (MOnth's Percentage), minus 1.
A50	**=1+A49** This payment number is 1 plus the previous payment number.
B50	**=DATE(YEAR(B49),MONTH(B49)+1,MIN(day,DAY(DATE(YEAR(B49), MONTH(B49)+2,0))))** Suppose you borrowed money on January 30. When would your first monthly payment be due? Probably on February 28. This formula calculates the due date using either the last day of the month or the due day, whichever is less.
C50	**=C49*(1+mint)–F50** This month's remaining balance is equal to last month's balance plus this month's interest charges minus the amount you've paid.
F50	**=IF(A50>=term,C49*(1+mint),pmt)** Because you can't write checks for fractions of cents, the actual monthly payment seldom equals the calculated amount exactly. Therefore, the last payment is often an odd amount, which is equal to the remaining balance at the beginning of the last month, plus interest. This formula calculates that odd amount for the last payment; it returns the PMT value for all other payments.
G50	**=D49–D50** The debit for the short-term liability is simply the amount this liability has fallen during the month.
H50	**=ROUND(E49,2)–ROUND(E50,2)** The debit for the long-term liability is the amount it has fallen during the month. Rounding the values eliminates fractional errors at the end of the loan.
I50	**=F50–G50–H50** Interest expense is equal to the payment minus the total reduction in liability.

(continued)

Figure 5-7. *continued*

KEY FORMULAS—continued	
Cell	***Formula***
K50	**=IF(AND(MONTH($B50)<>fyear,$A50<>term),$K49+$F50,0)**
L50	**=IF(OR(MONTH($B50)=fyear,$A50=term),$K49+$F50,"")**
	This pair of formulas calculates the total amount of cash paid in each fiscal year and in any partial year at the end of the loan. The first formula is a scratch formula. It keeps a running total until the last month in the fiscal year or the last month of the loan; at that time, its total turns to 0. The second formula returns a blank until the last month of the fiscal year or the last month of the loan; at that time, it adds the current cash payment to the previous running total. Because column K is required only by the formula in column L, set the width of column K to 0 after you've entered its formula.
M50	**=IF(AND(MONTH($B50)<>fyear,$A50<>term),$M49+$I50,0)**
N50	**=IF(OR(MONTH($ B50)=fyear,$A50=term),$M49+$I50,"")**
	This pair of formulas works similarly to the previous pair, but this pair returns the total interest expense for each fiscal year and for any partial year at the end of the loan.

RANGE NAMES	
Name	***Formula***
In addition to those shown in column H of the figure, define the following names.	
target	**=$E$1**
	Before it creates the new amortization schedule, the macro erases the previous schedule (target), if it exists. Naming an empty cell *target* gives the macro something to erase the first time it runs.
lender	**=$C$5**
company	**=$C$20**
top	**=$A$41**
	When the macro ends, the selection returns to this cell.
source	**=$A$50:$N$52**
	The macro that creates your complete amortization table uses this range as the source of all formulas and formats.

(continued)

Figure 5-7. *continued*

KEY CELL FORMATS			
Cell	***Number***	***Alignment***	***Font***
Sheet	Set the font for the entire sheet to Helv 8.		
E3	**General**	**Center**	**Helv 10, Bold**
B5	**General**	**Left**	**Helv 10, Bold**
B7	**General**	**Left**	**Helv 10, Bold**
E18	**General**	**Center**	**Helv 10, Bold**
B20	**General**	**Left**	**Helv 10, Bold**
G22:G29	**General**	**Center**	**Helv 10, Bold**
H22	**General**	**Center**	**Helv 8**
H24:H29	**General**	**Center**	**Helv 10**
G8	**#,##0**	**Center**	**Helv 8, Bold**
G9	**0.00%**	**Center**	**Helv 10, Bold**
D32	**General**	**Center**	**Helv 10**
G33:G34	**#,##0.00**	**Center**	**Helv 10**
G35:G36	**m/d/yy**	**Center**	**Helv 10**
G37	**0.00%**	**Center**	**Helv 10**
G38	**0%**	**Center**	**Helv 10**
G41	**General**	**Center**	**Helv 10, Bold**
G42	**General**	**Center**	**Helv 8**
G43	**General**	**Center**	**Helv 8**
B44:N44	**General**	**Center**	**Helv 8, Bold**
B45	**0.00%**	**Center**	**Helv 8**
D45:F45	**$#,##0.00 ;($#,##0.00)**	**Center**	**Helv 8**
H45	**General**	**Center**	**Helv 8**
J45:N45	**m/d/yy**	**Center**	**Helv 8**
A46:N48	**General**	**Center**	**Helv 8**

(continued)

Figure 5-7. *continued*

KEY CELL FORMATS—continued			
Cell	*Number*	*Alignment*	*Font*
L47	General	General	Helv 8
A49:A52	General	Center	Helv 8
B49:B52	d–mmm–yy	Center	Helv 8
C49:N52	#,##0.00 ;(#,##0.00)	General	Helv 8

Figure 5-8. Loan-Amortization Schedule Macros

Macros that generate and print the detailed amortization schedule.

	A	B	C
1			
2			
3	CREATE	Creates an amortization table from the spreadsheet in Figure 5-7.	
4	key=c.	=SELECT("R1C5")	Highlight the blank cell E1.
5		=ERROR(FALSE)	Turn off error messages.
6		=SELECT("target")	Select the "target" range.
7		=CLEAR(1)	Delete all.
8		=ERROR(TRUE)	Turn error messages back on.
9		=SELECT("source")	Copy the first three rows of the
10		=COPY()	schedule to the remainder of the
11		=-3*INT(-!term/3)	schedule, doing so in increments
12		=SELECT("R[3]C:R["&TEXT(B11-1,"#")&"]C")	of three months.
13		=PASTE()	"
14		=DEFINE.NAME("target",SELECTION())	Name the new data "target".
15		=SELECT("R[-4]C:R["&TEXT(B11-4,"#")&"]C[13]")	Highlight the schedule.
16		=DEFINE.NAME("Print_Area",SELECTION())	Define schedule as the print range.
17		=CALCULATE.NOW()	Calculate.
18		=FORMULA.GOTO("top")	Go to the top of the schedule.
19		=RETURN()	Return.
20			
21			
22			
23	PRINT	Prints amortization schedule created by the CREATE macro.	
24	key=p.	=PAGE.SETUP("&l&d&c&f&r&t",,1,0,1,1,FALSE,FALSE)	Set up the print job.
25		=PRINT(1,,,1,FALSE,FALSE,1)	Print the schedule.
26		=RETURN()	Return.

Figure 5-9. Mortgage Loan Analysis

A mortgage loan-analysis schedule that uses simple formulas to help in choosing how quickly to pay off a mortgage.

	A	B	C	D	E	F	G	H	I	J	K	L	M	N
1														
2														
3	Mortgage Loan Analysis													
5														

(1) Monthly mortgage payments per $1,000 borrowed.

Row	Annual Rate	Life of Mortgage In Years 10	15	20	25	30
10	9.00%	12.67	10.14	9.00	8.39	8.05
11	9.50%	12.94	10.44	9.32	8.74	8.41
12	10.00%	13.22	10.75	9.65	9.09	8.78
13	10.50%	13.49	11.05	9.98	9.44	9.15
14	11.00%	13.78	11.37	10.32	9.80	9.52
15	11.50%	14.06	11.68	10.66	10.16	9.90
16	12.00%	14.35	12.00	11.01	10.53	10.29
17	12.50%	14.64	12.33	11.36	10.90	10.67
18	13.00%	14.93	12.65	11.72	11.28	11.06
19	13.50%	15.23	12.98	12.07	11.66	11.45
20	14.00%	15.53	13.32	12.44	12.04	11.85

(2) Total payments (in $1000s) during the life of the mortgage.

Annual Rate	Life of Mortgage In Years 10	15	20	25	30
9.00%	1.5	1.8	2.2	2.5	2.9
9.50%	1.6	1.9	2.2	2.6	3.0
10.00%	1.6	1.9	2.3	2.7	3.2
10.50%	1.6	2.0	2.4	2.8	3.3
11.00%	1.7	2.0	2.5	2.9	3.4
11.50%	1.7	2.1	2.6	3.0	3.6
12.00%	1.7	2.2	2.6	3.2	3.7
12.50%	1.8	2.2	2.7	3.3	3.8
13.00%	1.8	2.3	2.8	3.4	4.0
13.50%	1.8	2.3	2.9	3.5	4.1
14.00%	1.9	2.4	3.0	3.6	4.3

(3) Added costs in monthly payments as a % of payments for a 30-year mortgage.

Row	Annual Rate	Life of Mortgage In Years 10	15	20	25	30
28	9.00%	57%	26%	12%	4%	0%
29	9.50%	54%	24%	11%	4%	0%
30	10.00%	51%	22%	10%	4%	0%
31	10.50%	48%	21%	9%	3%	0%
32	11.00%	45%	19%	8%	3%	0%
33	11.50%	42%	18%	8%	3%	0%
34	12.00%	39%	17%	7%	2%	0%
35	12.50%	37%	15%	6%	2%	0%
36	13.00%	35%	14%	6%	2%	0%
37	13.50%	33%	13%	5%	2%	0%
38	14.00%	31%	12%	5%	2%	0%
39						

(4) Savings in total payments as a % of payments for a 30-year mortgage.

Annual Rate	Life of Mortgage In Years 10	15	20	25	30
9.00%	48%	37%	25%	13%	0%
9.50%	49%	38%	26%	13%	0%
10.00%	50%	39%	27%	14%	0%
10.50%	51%	40%	27%	14%	0%
11.00%	52%	40%	28%	14%	0%
11.50%	53%	41%	28%	14%	0%
12.00%	54%	42%	29%	15%	0%
12.50%	54%	42%	29%	15%	0%
13.00%	55%	43%	29%	15%	0%
13.50%	56%	43%	30%	15%	0%
14.00%	56%	44%	30%	15%	0%

COLUMN WIDTHS

Column	*Width*	*Column*	*Width*	*Column*	*Width*	*Column*	*Width*
A	8	E	6	I	6	M	6
B	6	F	6	J	6		
C	6	G	2	K	6		
D	6	H	8	L	6		

(continued)

Figure 5-9. *continued*

KEY FORMULAS	
Cell	***Formula***
A5	**1000** This value is hidden in the cell. Change it to change the values for Table 1.
C7	**=DOLLAR($A$5,0)&" borrowed."** This formula changes the label as cell A5 changes.
I9 **H10** **B27** **A28** **I27** **H28**	**=B9 (Table 2)** **=A10 (Table 2)** **=B9 (Table 3)** **=A10 (Table 3)** **=B9 (Table 4)** **=A10 (Table 4)** These formulas return the terms and rates entered into Table 1. Enter each as shown, and then copy it across the appropriate row or down the appropriate column.
A10	**0.09** Change this value to change the starting percentage.
A11	**=A10+0.005** To change the increment by which the percentages grow, change the 0.005 value in this formula. For example, =A10+0.0025 would increase the annual rates by 1/4%.
A12	**=2*A11–A10** Copy this formula to the range A13:A20.
B10	**=–PMT($A10/12,B$9*12,$A$5)** This formula takes the form: =PMT(rate,nper,pv). Because the formula would normally return a negative value (indicating a cash outflow), the minus sign turns the result positive. Pay close attention to the dollar signs. These allow the formula to be copied throughout the table while continuing to reference the correct cells.

(continued)

Figure 5-9. *continued*

KEY FORMULAS—continued	
Cell	*Formula*
H10 **A28** **H28**	**=INDEX(rates,COUNTA(H$9:H9))** **=INDEX(rates,COUNTA(A$27:A27))** **=INDEX(rates,COUNTA(H$27:H27))** After you copy Table 1 to the remaining three table positions, change these cells so that they reference the value in cell A10. Then, if you change the value in cell A10, the other tables change as well.
I10	**=B10*I$9*12/1000** This formula finds the total payments over the life of the loan and then divides by 1000 to express the result in thousands of dollars.
B28	**=B10/$F10–1** What are your additional monthly payments when you pay off your mortgage in less than 30 years? This formula returns that percentage increase.
I28	**=1–I10/$M10** What are the savings over the life of your loan when you pay it off in less than 30 years? This formula returns the savings as a percentage.

RANGE NAMES	
Name	*Formula*
terms	**=$B$9:$F$9** This range includes the lives of the mortgage at the top of Table 1.
rates	**=$A$10:$A$20** This range includes the rates of the mortgage at the side of Table 1.

(continued)

Figure 5-9. *continued*

KEY CELL FORMATS			
Cell	***Number***	***Alignment***	***Font***
A5	;; This number format hides numbers entered in cell A5.	**Left**	**Helv 10**
A3	**General**	**General**	**Helv 12, Bold**
C6:C7	**General**	**Center**	**Helv 10, Bold**
A8:A9	**General**	**Center**	**Helv 10, Bold**
D8	**General**	**Center**	**Helv 10, Bold**
B9:F9	**#,##0**	**General**	**Helv 10, Bold**
A10:A20	**0.00%**	**General**	**Helv 10, Bold**
B10:F20	**#,##0.00 ;(#,##0.00)**	**General**	**Helv 10**

Figure 5-10. Line-of-Credit Tracker

A line-of-credit tracker that keeps up-to-date information on a credit line.

	A	B	C	D	E	F	G	H	I
1									
2				Line-of-Credit Tracker					
3				Automation Northwest, Inc.					
4	Celebrity National Bank				Beginning Balance		35,399		
5	Loan #348-597245-9				Credit Limit		250,000		
6	Matures: 10/27/1989				Commitment Fee		1.0%		
7				Annual					
8		New		Interest	Interest	Loan	Available		
9	Date	Debt	Repmts	Rate	Expense	Balance	Credit	Scratch	
10	1-Feb			10.25%	9.9407505	35,409	214,591	1	
11	2-Feb			10.25%	9.9435421	35,419	214,581	1	
12	3-Feb	22,000		10.25%	16.124417	57,435	192,565	1	
13	4-Feb			10.25%	16.128945	57,451	192,549	1	
14	5-Feb			10.25%	16.133474	57,467	192,533	1	
15	6-Feb		5,000	10.25%	14.733895	52,482	197,518	1	
16	7-Feb			10.75%	15.456961	52,497	197,503	1	
17	8-Feb			10.75%	15.461514	52,513	197,487	1	
18	9-Feb			10.75%	15.466067	52,528	197,472	1	
19	10-Feb	75,000		10.75%	37.559663	127,566	122,434	1	
20	11-Feb			10.75%	37.570726	127,603	122,397	1	
21	12-Feb	80,000		10.75%	61.143435	207,664	42,336	1	
22	13-Feb			10.75%	61.161443	207,726	42,274	1	
23	14-Feb			10.75%	61.179456	207,787	42,213	1	
24	15-Feb			10.75%	61.197475	207,848	42,152	1	
25	16-Feb			10.75%	61.215499	207,909	42,091	1	
26	17-Feb			10.75%	61.233528	207,970	42,030	1	
27	18-Feb			10.75%	61.251562	208,032	41,968	1	
28	19-Feb		35,000	10.75%	50.961383	173,083	76,917	1	
29	20-Feb			10.75%	50.976392	173,134	76,866	1	
30	21-Feb			11.00%	52.177252	173,186	76,814	1	
31	22-Feb			11.00%	52.192977	173,238	76,762	1	
32	23-Feb			11.00%	52.208706	173,290	76,710	1	
33	24-Feb			11.00%	52.224441	173,342	76,658	1	
34	25-Feb			11.00%	52.240179	173,395	76,605	1	
35	26-Feb			11.00%	52.255923	173,447	76,553	1	
36	27-Feb		100,000	11.00%	22.134685	73,469	176,531	1	
37	28-Feb			11.00%	22.141356	73,491	176,509	1	
38									
39									
40									
41	Total	$177,000	$140,000		$1,092.42				
42	Average			10.79%		$132,014	$117,986		
43	Maximum			11.00%	$61.25	$208,032	$214,591		
44	Minimum			10.25%	$9.94	$35,409	$41,968		
45									
46	Effective Monthly Commitment Fee				$212				
47	Effective Annual Interest Rate				12.89%				
48									

(continued)

Figure 5-10. *continued*

COLUMN WIDTHS			
Column	*Width*	*Column*	*Width*
A	8.43	F	8.43
B	8.43	G	8.43
C	8.43	H	6.71
D	8.43	I	8.43
E	9.71		

KEY FORMULAS	
Cell	*Formula*
A10	**2/1/89**
A11	**=H11*(1+A10)** Update the value in A10 each month to change the column of dates. The remaining column of formulas will return successive dates, or 0 if the value in column H is 0.
D10 **D11**	**0.1025** **=D10*H11** The column begins with a value for an interest rate and then repeats that value throughout. If rates change, enter that value on the appropriate date, and then recalculate.
E10 **E11**	**=($G$4+B10–C10)*(D10/365)** **=(F10+B11–C11)*(D11/365)** The dollar value of the interest expense is equal to the previous balance plus new debt minus repayments, all multiplied by the daily interest rate. Cell E10 takes the previous balance from the heading. All remaining formulas take the balance from the previous day's balance.
F10 **F11**	**=($G$4+B10–C10+E10)*H10** **=(F10+B11–C11+E11)*H11** Today's balance is equal to yesterday's balance plus new debt minus repayments plus interest charges. Cell F10 takes the previous balance from the heading. As always in this spreadsheet, the value in column H forces the value to 0 after the end of the month.
G10 **G11**	**=($G$5–F10)*H10** **=($G$5–F11)*H11** Available credit equals the credit limit minus the day's outstanding balance.

(continued)

Figure 5-10. *continued*

KEY FORMULAS—continued	
Cell	***Formula***
H10 **H11**	**1** **=AND(H10=1,MONTH(A10)=MONTH(A10+1))+0** This formula returns a 1 during the current month; otherwise, it returns a 0. It returns a 1 if both of the following conditions are true: If the previous day's value in column H had a value equal to 1, and if adding one day to yesterday's date doesn't change the date to a new month. (Why look at yesterday's date rather than today's? Notice that today's date references this cell. If this cell referenced today's date, you would have a circular calculation error.) Adding 0 to this logical formula displays the results as 1 and 0 instead of TRUE and FALSE.
B41 **C41** **E41**	**=SUM(B10:B40)** **=SUM(C10:C40)** **=SUM(E10:E40)** These SUM formulas return the column totals shown.
D42	**=(($E$41/SUM($H$10:$H$40))*365)/$F$42** The average interest rate is equal to the annualized interest expense divided by the average loan balance. The annualized interest expense is equal to total interest for the month, divided by the number of days in the month (the sum of column H), multiplied by 365.
F42 **G42**	**=SUM(F10:F40)/SUM($H$10:$H$40)** **=SUM(G10:G40)/SUM($H$10:$H$40)** The average value of these columns is equal to the sums of the columns divided by the number of days in the month. (The AVERAGE function would have averaged in the 0 values occurring after the end of the month.)
D43	**=MAX(D$10:D$40)** All formulas shown in this row find the maximum values in the table. Copy this formula to columns E through G.
D44	**=MIN(IF($H$10:$H$40=1,D$10:D$40))** This array formula finds the minimum value in the column while ignoring the 0 values at the end of the month. It does so by finding the minimum value of a temporary array whose elements consist of the values in column D, but only when the comparable values in column H are equal to 1. When you enter this formula, you must tell the spreadsheet that you are entering an array formula. To do so, hold down both Ctrl and Shift while you press Enter. (After you edit an array formula, you must enter it by pressing Ctrl-Shift-Enter as well.) When the formula is working correctly, copy it to columns E through G. When you do so, the array formula will copy like any other formula.

(continued)

Figure 5-10. *continued*

KEY FORMULAS—continued	
Cell	***Formula***
E46	**=$G$5*$G$6*(1+$D$42)*(SUM($H$10:$H$40)/365)** Most lending institutions charge an up-front fee each year for a line-of-credit agreement. The fee, which can vary from 0.25 percent to 1 percent of the credit line, is charged when the line is arranged and immediately added to your loan balance. To calculate your effective interest rate for the cash you actually borrow, you must include the monthly cost of this fee with your interest charges. The yearly cost is equal to the amount of the fee plus a year's worth of interest. The monthly cost is equal to the yearly cost times the fraction that the month represents of the total calendar year.
E47	**=((($E$41+E46)/SUM($H$10:$H$40))*365)/$F$42** As in cell D42, the average interest rate is equal to the annualized interest expense divided by the average loan balance. Here the annualized interest expense is equal to the daily interest expense multiplied by 365. The daily interest expense equals the monthly interest expense plus the monthly commitment fee, divided by the number of days in the month (the sum of column H).

KEY CELL FORMATS			
Cell	***Number***	***Alignment***	***Font***
Sheet	Turn off zero values by using the Options Display command so that all zero values are displayed as blanks.		
D2:D3	**General**	**Center**	**Helv 10, Bold**
A6	**General**	**Left**	**Helv 10**
G4:G5	**#,##0 ;(#,##0)**	**General**	**Helv 10**
G6	**0.0%**	**General**	**Helv 10**
A10:A40	**d-mmm**	**Center**	**Helv 10**
B10:C40	**#,##0 ;(#,##0)**	**General**	**Helv 10**
D10:D40	**0.00%**	**General**	**Helv 10**
E10:E40	**General**	**General**	**Helv 10**
F10:G40	**#,##0 ;(#,##0)**	**General**	**Helv 10**
H10:H40	**General**	**Center**	**Helv 10**

(continued)

Figure 5-10. *continued*

KEY CELL FORMATS—continued			
Cell	*Number*	*Alignment*	*Font*
B41:C41	$#,##0 ;($#,##0)	General	Helv 10
D42:D44	0.00%	General	Helv 10
E41:E44	$#,##0.00 ;($#,##0.00)	General	Helv 10
F42:G42	$#,##0 ;($#,##0)	General	Helv 10

Figure 5-11. Loan-Compliance Report

A loan-compliance report that compares your actual business performance with the performance your lender requires.

	A	B	C	D	E	F	G	H	I
1									
2									
3					**Loan-Compliance Report**				
4					Universal Bank and Trust				
5					Loan # 3950-3290342-1				
6					Apr-88				
7									
8					Per Loan		Current		Remaining
9		Description			Covenants		Value	Variance	Variance/Mo
10	**Results**								
11	1 Debt / Worth Ratio				Max	2.2	1.4	0.8	
12									
13	2 Current Ratio				Min	1.5	1.7	0.2	
14									
15	3 Quick Ratio				Min	0.8	0.7	(0.1)	
16									
17	4 Working Capital				Min	55	51	(4)	
18									
19	5 Net Worth				Min	130	145	15	
20									
21	**Spending Decisions**								
22	6 Capital Expenditures				Max	78	57	21	10.5
23									
24	7 Dividends				Max	20	15	5	2.5
25									
26	8 Officers' Compensation				Max	125	85	40	20.0
27									
28									
29	***Input Data***								
30	**Month's Balance**								
31	Cash and Equivalents						5		
32	Accounts Receivable						48		
33	Current Assets						125		
34	Current Liabilities						74		
35	Total Debt						201		
36	Net Worth						145		
37	**Year-to-Date Data**								
38	Capital Expenditures						57		
39	Dividends						15		
40	Officers' Compensation						85		
41									
42	The fiscal year begins on this month number:						7		
43	The current fiscal year is this many months old:						10		
44									

(continued)

Figure 5-11. *continued*

COLUMN WIDTHS			
Column	*Width*	*Column*	*Width*
A	2.57	F	6
B	8.43	G	11
C	8.43	H	11
D	8.43	I	11.43
E	4.14		

KEY FORMULAS	
Cell	*Formula*
E11 E13	1 –1 This column of Min and Max labels contains the values 1 and –1, not the labels themselves. The labels are generated by the number format, which is shown in the format information box.
G11	=$G$35/$G$36 The debt/worth ratio shows the relationship between the capital contributed by creditors and capital contributed by investors. The higher the ratio, the greater the risk to creditors. This ratio is equal to total debt divided by net worth.
G13	=$G$33/$G$34 The current ratio is equal to current assets divided by current liabilities. As such, it is a rough indication of a company's ability to pay its debts when due. A current ratio of 2, for example, shows that a company has $2 of current assets for each $1 of current liabilities, and should therefore be able to pay its current liabilities.
G15	=($G$31+$G$32)/$G$34 The quick ratio, also known as the acid-test ratio, is a more conservative test of liquidity than the current ratio. It is equal to the sum of cash and accounts receivable divided by total current liabilities.
G17	=$G$33–$G$34 Working capital is equal to current assets minus current liabilities. It is, therefore, the excess amount of current assets available to work with in day-to-day operations.
G19	=$G$36 Net worth is repeated from the data entered at the bottom of the figure. Originating in the balance sheet, it's the difference between total assets and total liabilities.

(continued)

Figure 5-11. *continued*

KEY FORMULAS—continued	
Cell	***Formula***
G22	**=$G$38** Capital expenditures are calculated monthly and entered in the spreadsheet. Most accounting systems, unfortunately, don't track this number as a rule.
G24	**=$G$39** Dividends are entered from reports generated by the accounting system.
G26	**=$G$40** Officers' compensation is entered from payroll records.
H11	**=E11*(F11–G11)** This formula calculates whether the variance between the actual and required result is favorable (which returns a positive value) or unfavorable (which returns a negative value). For example, the variance for the debt/worth ratio is favorable because the actual ratio is less than the maximum limit; the current ratio is also favorable because the actual ratio is above the minimum limit. Mathematically, the first variance is positive because its formula multiplies a positive difference by the value of 1 in column E; the second variance is positive because its formula multiplies a negative value by the –1 in column E.
I22	**=IF(OR(H22<0,$G$43=12),0,H22/(12–$G$43))** This formula returns the maximum amount that can be spent monthly to stay within the spending limits set by the loan covenants. This amount equals 0 if the value in column H is negative (too much has already been spent) or if this is the last month of the current fiscal year. Otherwise, the monthly amount is equal to the variance (the amount left to be spent) divided by the number of months that remain in the current fiscal year.
G43	**=MONTH($F$6)+IF(MONTH($F$6)<G42,13,1)–G42** This formula calculates the number of months that have passed between the beginning of the current fiscal year and the current report date. The formula finds this value by subtracting the fiscal month from the report month while adding a year's worth of months if needed. That is, if the month number of the report is less than the month number of the fiscal year, the calculation adds 13 to the month number of the report (otherwise it adds 1) and then it subtracts the month number of the fiscal year.

(continued)

Figure 5-11. *continued*

KEY CELL FORMATS			
Cell	***Number***	***Alignment***	***Font***
F3	**General**	**Center**	**Helv 10, Bold**
F4:F5	**General**	**Center**	**Helv 10**
F6	**mmm–yy**	**Center**	**Helv 10**
E8:I9	**General**	**General**	**Helv 10**
A10	**General**	**General**	**Helv 10, Bold**
E11:E26	**"Max";"Min";** This number format returns *Max* if the number is positive, *Min* if it's negative, and a blank if it's 0. If the number format did not contain the semicolon after "Min", a 0 would be displayed as *Max*.	**Center**	**Helv 10**
G11:H15	**0.0 ;(0.0)**	**Center**	**Helv 10**
G17:H26	**#,##0 ;(#,##0)**	**Center**	**Helv 10**
A29	**General**	**General**	**Helv 10, Bold, Italic**
A30	**General**	**General**	**Helv 10, Bold**
G33:G43	**#,##0**	**General**	**Helv 10**

Figure 5-12. Notes Payable Schedule

A notes payable schedule that calculates monthly interest expense, balance due, and other loan statistics for the date entered in cell A5.

	A	B	C	D	E	F	G	H	I	J	K	L	M	N	O
1															
2															
3	**Notes Payable Schedule**														
4	**Pete's Potting Soil**														
5	**31-Dec-89**														
6			Loan	Maturity		Mos	Loan	Int	Monthly	Balance	L/T Liab	This Mo	This Mo	Mo-End	
7	Lender / Loan# / Collateral		Date	Date	Term	Left	Amount	Rate	Payments	Due	Due	Prin	Int	Accrual	Cur
8															
9	Old & Stodgy Bank	Adj	29-Sep-88	28-Feb-91	29	14	5,000.00	11.00%	197.13	2,579	389	172	25	1	1
10	938-39474-1	Orig	29-Sep-88	28-Feb-91	29		5,000.00	11.00%	197.13						
11	Electric Sweeper														
12	Tree-Farmers Bank	Adj	12-Oct-87	12-Apr-02	173	148	308,195.22	13.00%	3,951.40	290,713	280,494	793	3,158	1,926	1
13	1-322-482-9	Orig	12-Mar-72	12-Apr-02	360		357,902.00	13.00%	3,959.11						
14	Factory Building														
15	Rich & Associates	Adj	2-Oct-87	2-Jun-90	32	6	10,634.22	11.25%	386.20	2,243	0	362	24	20	1
16	23-359235-78	Orig	2-Jun-80	2-Jun-90	120		29,770.00	9.50%	385.22						
17	Bagging Machine														
18	Fullerton Jones, Jr.	Adj	14-Aug-86	14-Aug-91	60	20	14,750.00	12.50%	331.84	5,963	2,535	267	65	34	1
19	Per Agreement	Orig	14-Aug-86	14-Aug-91	60		14,750.00	12.50%	331.84						
20	Bobtail Truck														
21															
22	Grand Total							12.96%	4,866.57	301,499	283,418	1,594	3,273	1,981	
23															
24															

COLUMN WIDTHS							
Column	***Width***	***Column***	***Width***	***Column***	***Width***	***Column***	***Width***
A	17.5	E	4.67	I	7.83	M	6.33
B	4	F	3.67	J	7	N	6.67
C	9	G	9.5	K	7	O	2.83
D	8.67	H	6	L	6.17		

(continued)

Figure 5-12. *continued*

KEY FORMULAS	
Cell	***Formula***
F9	**=(12*YEAR(D9)+MONTH(D9)–(12*YEAR($A$5)+MONTH($A$5))+(DAY($A$5)<DAY(D9)))*O9** The number of months left on the loan is equal to the difference between the maturity date in months and the report date in months. The logical formula adds one month if a payment is not yet due in the report-date month. The number in column O sets this value to 0 when the maturity date exceeds the report date or the report date is less than the loan date.
J9	**=IF(O9=0,0,–FV(H9/12,E9–F9,–I9,G9,0))** The formula for the future value of a loan takes this form: =FV(rate,nper,pmt,pv,type). Use this formula whenever you want to find the remaining balance of the loan. However, instead of using the number of periods for which the loan is due, use the number of periods for which the loan has already been paid. Don't forget to show inflows as positive values and outflows as negative values. The IF function in this formula returns 0 if the value in column O equals zero.
K9	**=IF(F9<=12,0,–FV(H9/12,E9–F9+12,–I9,G9,0))** If the number of months left is less than or equal to 0, the full loan is short term and the long-term liability equals 0. Otherwise, this formula finds the long-term liability by finding the future value of the loan 12 months after the report date.
L9	**=IF(O9=0,0,–PPMT(H9/12,E9–F9,E9,G9))** The PPMT function returns the payment on the principal for a given period. The general form of this function is: =PPMT(rate,per,nper,pv,fv,type). (Since FV and TYPE are excluded in the formula, they are assumed to be 0.) As always, the minus sign converts the sign of the cash outflow to positive. And if the cell in column O equals 0, the formula returns 0.
M9	**=IF(O9=0,0,–IPMT(H9/12,E9–F9,E9,G9))** The IPMT function takes the same form as the PPMT function above. Alternatively, in this application, you could find the interest amount by subtracting the principal amount from the total payment. Either method returns the same result.

(continued)

Figure 5-12. *continued*

KEY FORMULAS—continued	
Cell	***Formula***
N9	**=J9*((1+H9/12)^(1–DAY(C9)/DAY(DATE(YEAR(C9),MONTH(C9)+1,0)))–1)*O9** Loans that are paid before the end of the month accrue interest expense that should be booked at month end. This formula calculates the accrual, which equals next month's interest expense compounded by the fraction of the month that remains after the monthly payment has been made. This fraction is equal to 1 minus the fraction of the month that *has* been paid. This fraction, in turn, is equal to the day of the month the payment is due divided by the number of days in the month the loan was made. To find the last day of a month, use this formula: =DAY(DATE(year,month+1,0)).
O9	**=($A$5>=C9)*($A$5<=D9)** This formula returns 1 if the loan is outstanding as of the report date; otherwise, it returns 0. The formula consists of two logical formulas, or "switches," that both must be true (equal to 1) for the formula to equal 1. The first switch is true if the report date is greater than or equal to the beginning date of the loan. The second switch is true if the report date is less than or equal to the maturity date.
H22	**=(M22/(J22+L22))*12** The average interest rate for a month is equal to the amount of interest paid in the month divided by the unpaid balance at the beginning of the month, which equals the ending balance plus the principal paid during the month. To find the annual interest rate, multiply the month rate by 12.
I22	**=L22+M22** Total payments equal the total principal payments plus the total interest payments.
J22	**=SUM(J8:J21)** Copy this formula to the range K22:N22.

(continued)

Figure 5-12. *continued*

KEY CELL FORMATS			
Cell	*Number*	*Alignment*	*Font*
Sheet	General	General	Helv 8
A3:A4	General	Left	Helv 10, Bold
A5	d–mmm–yy	General	Helv 10, Bold
A7	General	General	Helv 8
C7:O7	General	Center	Helv 8
B9	General	Center	Helv 8
C9:D9	d–mmm–yy	General	Helv 8
F9	General	Center	Helv 8
G9	#,##0.00 ;(#,##0.00)	General	Helv 8
H9	0.00%	General	Helv 8
I9	#,##0.00 ;(#,##0.00)	General	Helv 8
J9:N9	#,##0 ;(#,##0)	General	Helv 8
O9	General	Center	Helv 8

Figure 5-13. Financial Calculator Proving Notes Payable Schedule

The calculator showing the results from the notes payable schedule in Figure 5-12.

Charley Kyd's			FV = ($2,578.98)	
Financial Calculator				
1	*2*	*3*	*4*	*5*
n	**i**	**PV**	**PMT**	**FV**
15	0.92%	$5,000.00	($197.13)	$0.00
Choice: 5				0: 0=End 1=Beg

6

Sales and Marketing

As is frequently said and is generally true, selling is a numbers game. To understand which marketing strategies are working and which are failing, managers must look at the numbers. To forecast sales and set quotas, they must look at the numbers. To know quickly when the economy heads south, they must look at the numbers.

This chapter presents many different spreadsheets that help you look at the numbers. They can help you set reasonable sales goals, track daily sales, identify unprofitable products and customers, monitor the sales of new products, and so on.

CALENDARS OF WORKING DAYS

When you establish sales budgets for each month of a new year, do you pay attention to the number of working days in each month? Many people don't, to their regret.

For example, if your company in 1988 recognized the holiday schedule shown in Figure 6-1 on page 240, January would have only 19 working days, February would have 20, and March would have 23. With this schedule, in other words, January's sales would be 17 percent under March's sales if daily sales were identical for both months.

The following section of this chapter explains how to create a calendar of working days that performs several tasks. In the schedule in Figure 6-2 on page 243, the calendar creates a list of all the working days in a year. We will use this list later to help record and report daily sales. In the schedule in Figure 6-3 on page 246, it creates a planning calendar that lists on one page every working day of the year. And in the schedule in Figure 6-4 on page 249, it provides another planning calendar that redefines the months so that each has the same number of working days.

A Schedule of Holidays

The first step in creating the planning calendar is to define the holidays your company will recognize during the new year. Figure 6-1 on page 240 illustrates this schedule.

To create this schedule, begin with a new spreadsheet. Turn off the gridlines by choosing the Options Display command. Set manual calculation by choosing the Options Calculation command. Then set the column widths of the spreadsheet as shown in the column-width box for Figure 6-1 through Figure 6-4.

Enter the labels and year number in rows 4 and 5 and format them as shown in the format box. Add the bottom border in row 4 and the shaded outline in rows 7 and 17. Each column within the shaded outlines has a different format. Enter these as shown in the format box.

Choose the Formula Define Name command and assign the two range names shown in the range-name box. After you've done so, enter the hidden value shown in the formula box for cell B8 and the formulas shown for cells A8 and D8. Format these cells as shown in the format box and then copy the contents of row 8 down the columns as shown.

When you recalculate, you see two columns of dates between the shaded borders. Column A contains *1-Jan* throughout and column D contains *Friday*. Enter the description for each holiday in column C. Enter the month, a decimal point, and the day for that holiday in column B. For example, for Martin Luther King Day, enter the value *1.18* (representing Jan. 18) in cell B9, and for Independence Day, enter the value *7.04* in cell B12. Because column B is formatted to hide these numbers, you won't see them in column B. But the DATE calculation in column A displays the results in column A.

When you press the F9 (Calculate All) key, your spreadsheet recalculates and displays the holiday schedule shown in Figure 6-1. When you are satisfied with your results, save your schedule. I used the name DLY_CAL.XLS, short for "Daily Calendar."

You can quickly update the schedule at the beginning of each new year. First, enter the new year in cell D4. Second, enter in column B the month and day for holidays like Labor Day, Memorial Day, and Thanksgiving that occur on different dates from year to year. Third, add or subtract holidays. (If Christmas falls on a Tuesday, for example, you might decide to make Monday a holiday as well.) Finally, recalculate the spreadsheet. The schedule of holidays now is correct for the schedule in Figure 6-1, as well as for the calendars shown in Figure 6-2 through Figure 6-4.

A Workday List

The schedule in Figure 6-2 on page 243 contains three lists of dates. The first list, shown in column S, contains all the days in the requested year, minus the weekends. The data in cells U8 and U10 defines what constitutes a weekend. For example, if your business is open every day, cell U10 shows that your weekend has a length of 0 days. Or, if your business is open every day but Wednesday, cell U8 shows that Tuesday ends your workweek and cell U10 shows that your weekend is one day long.

Column T performs two tasks. First, it returns a 0 (formatted as 0-JAN-00) for any date that falls outside the reporting year. Second, it removes holidays. For example, cell S32 contains the date *18-Jan-88*. This date is a holiday, as defined by the schedule in Figure 6-1. Consequently, cell T32 removes this date from its list by repeating the date from the previous day.

Column U contains the final list of workdays for the reporting year. This is the list that will be used by the planning calendars shown in Figure 6-3 and Figure 6-4, and in other spreadsheets in the next section of this chapter.

Creating a workday list

To create these lists, enter into the DLY_CAL.XLS spreadsheet the labels and borders shown in rows 3 through 14 of Figure 6-2. Enter *6* in cell U8 and *2* in cell U10 and then format these cells as shown in the format box.

Create the shaded outline in row 15 and then enter *0* in cells T15 and U15. To enter the shaded outline at the bottom of the column, press the F5 (Goto) key, enter the cell range *S286:U286*, and then press Enter. Finally, use the Format Borders command to create the shading.

To format the dates in the area below the top shaded outline, first highlight the area. Select cell S286, press the F8 (Extend) key, and press Ctrl-Up. When you do so, the highlighting extends from the active cell up column S until it bumps into the label in cell S14. Press the Down direction key twice to make cell S16 the top of the highlighted area; then press the Right direction key twice to expand the highlighted area to columns T and U as well. Now, with the range highlighted, assign the formats shown in the format box for the range S16:U286.

With the range S16:U286 still highlighted, you can easily assign range names to these columns. To do so, first extend the highlighted area upward by two rows, to include the labels in row 14 of the spreadsheet in Figure 6-2. This is easy to do, but it takes some explanation.

When you select a range, the active cell turns passive for the moment, while the cell in the opposite corner from the active cell controls the size of the highlighted area. Whether you use a mouse or the direction keys, you extend a range only by controlling this cell, which I call the "opposite cell." Therefore, to extend the range S16:U286 upward to row 14, you must first move the active cell to the bottom of the range, moving the opposite cell to the top. To move the active cell press Ctrl-period, which shifts the active cell clockwise to an adjacent corner of the selected range. (Even if the active cell is already at the bottom of the selected area, press Ctrl-period simply to see what happens.) Press Ctrl-period as many times as necessary to move the active cell to the bottom row of the selected area and the opposite cell to the top row.

With the active cell in the bottom row of the range S16:U286, turn on the Extend mode by pressing the F8 key. Press the Up direction key twice, which causes two things to happen. First, it extends the top of the selected area from row 16 to row 14. Second, it moves the opposite cell, which causes Microsoft Excel to display the area of your spreadsheet that contains the opposite cell, rather than the area that contains the active cell. Finally, to assign the range names, choose Formula Create, select Top, and press Enter. Doing so assigns the labels in the top row of the selected area as the range name of each column in the area. (But because row 14 contains the actual labels, this row is excluded from the named ranges.)

Enter the formulas shown in the formula box for cells S16 and S17. Enter the formula for cell T16 and copy it to cell T17. Enter the formulas for cells U16 and U17. Copy the formulas in the range S17:U17 to the bottom of the range through row 285. To do so, highlight the range S17:U17, press Ctrl-Ins, select cell S18, press the F8 (Extend) key, press Ctrl-Down, and then press Enter.

When you press the F9 (Calculate All) key, your list of days looks like the one in Figure 6-2.

Modifying a workday list

If your workweek is six days long, you need to add approximately 55 rows to your list of days, extending the bottom to, say, row 340; if your workweek is seven days long, you need to add about 110 rows, extending the bottom to, say, row 400.

Insert the additional rows between the shaded bar at the bottom of your list and the last row of dates. To insert 60 days easily, press the F5 (Goto) key, enter the range *S286:U340*, press Enter to highlight the range, choose Edit Insert, select Down, and press Enter. After you insert space for the formulas, copy them from the last row of the list of dates to the last row above the new position of the shaded bar.

Press the F9 (Calculate All) key to recalculate your spreadsheet and then select the cell containing the last date in column S. This date should be greater than the last day in December by several days to provide a margin of safety for reporting future years, but not longer than roughly five days, which would needlessly consume memory and increase calculation time.

Finally, check the dimensions of the range names provided in the range-name box for Figure 6-2. Because these names are bounded by the shaded bar, they expanded as the bottom bar moved.

A Schedule of Working Days

Figure 6-3 on page 246 shows a schedule of working days that can serve several purposes within a company. Row 8, which shows the number of working days in each month, will help to guide your sales planning efforts. For example, you probably will want to forecast lower sales for short months than for long months.

In some companies, the accounting department issues this schedule. Often, they highlight significant days. Payroll days, for example, might be displayed in 12-point Helv boldface, and budget deadlines might be displayed in 12-Point Helv boldface italic.

To create the schedule, enter the labels and border shown in rows 4 and 5 into the spreadsheet DLY_CAL.XLS Enter the formula for cell Q4 shown in the formula box. Then format these rows as shown in the format box.

Enter and format the formulas in row 10 that generate the month names shown. Create the shaded bars in row 11 and in row 36. Enter and format the array formula shown for cell F37 and then copy it to the range G37:Q37.

Enter the formula shown for cells F12, G12, and F13. Copy cell G12 to the range H12:Q12. Copy cell F13 to the range F13:Q35. When you calculate the spreadsheet, it returns the values shown in the spreadsheet in the figure.

To complete this display, add any borders and formatting that may be missing. To draw the borders shown in the range F12:Q35, select this range, choose the Format Borders command, and select Outline, Left, and Right. To suppress the display of 0 values at the bottom of each column of months, choose the Options Display command and select Zero Values.

A Fiscal-Month Calendar

No matter how informed we might be about the varying number of working days in a calendar month, the jumbled schedule of working days can still play havoc with management planning and reporting. To deal with this problem, many companies have adopted a variation of a fiscal month.

One variation divides the year into 13 four-week months, each beginning on a Monday and ending on a Friday. While this approach does divide the year into 13 periods of equal length (ignoring holidays), it creates extra work and expense for the accounting department. The accountants, after all, must not only generate one additional set of monthly financial statements, but for each statement they must adjust some expenses, like rent, that are billed only 12 times a year.

Another variation is called the 4-4-5 year. With this variation, January and February have four weeks each, March has five, April and May have four weeks each, June has five, and so on. Each calendar quarter has fiscal months that are four, four, and five weeks long. And as in the 13-month calendar, each month begins on a Monday and ends on a Friday. Although this approach has the benefit of creating four calendar quarters with the same number of workdays (ignoring holidays), it still creates a pattern of long months and short months.

Figure 6-4 on page 249 shows a third variation that creates 12 fiscal months, each with approximately the same number of working days. The schedule shown, for example, illustrates a company that works five days a week and takes nine holidays in 1988. This policy generates a fiscal month of exactly 21 days.

Creating a schedule of fiscal months

The quickest way to create the schedule of fiscal months is to create a copy of the schedule in Figure 6-3 and then modify this copy as necessary. To do so, first copy from the range F4:Q37 in the schedule in Figure 6-3 to cell F42 in Figure 6-4 and then delete the bottom three rows of formulas that are immediately above the shaded bar. When you do so, the shaded bar at the bottom of the new schedule moves up to row 70.

Enter the formulas shown for rows 42 through 47 and cell F49 in the formula box for Figure 6-4. Enter the formula for cell F50 and copy it to the range F51:F69. Enter the formula shown for cell F71 and copy it to the range G71:Q71. Enter the formulas shown for cells F72 and G72 and then copy cell G72 to the range H72:Q72. Enter the formula shown for cell G49 and copy it to the range G49:Q69. Finally, recalculate the spreadsheet. Your schedule of fiscal months now looks like the one in Figure 6-4.

If you haven't done so, add the borders shown and set the formatting shown in the figure's format box. Finally, save this updated version of the DLY_CAL.XLS spreadsheet.

Modifying a schedule of fiscal months

If your company maintains holiday and workday schedules that are significantly different from those of the company illustrated, you can still use this schedule. Suppose, for example, that your company works six days a week but takes the holidays shown in Figure 6-1. To adapt the schedule in Figure 6-4 to this revised schedule, you must first insert enough rows of formulas at the bottom of the schedules in Figure 6-2 and Figure 6-3 to contain the additional number of working days required. Then, after you recalculate the spreadsheet, look at the value in cell Q45. This cell tells you that each fiscal month is 25.33 days long. Therefore, to allow room for every working day in your schedule, you must insert five additional rows of formulas in the fiscal-year schedule, creating a schedule that is 26 days long.

If you were to recalculate the spreadsheet at this point, your schedule would show 11 months with 26 working days each, plus December with 19 working days. Unless this is the schedule you had in mind, you must subtract working days from throughout the year so that the fiscal months are as balanced as possible. To do this, select the last row of formulas in the body of the schedule and delete formulas from the months you want to adjust. You could, for example, leave 26 days in the months of March, June, September, and December and delete the last day from each of the other fiscal months of the year. When you recalculate, the schedule adjusts to this pattern of days, producing an average fiscal month of 25.33 days.

A RECORD OF DAILY SALES INFORMATION

Few accounting systems provide the sales information many managers need. Accounting systems don't present the information frequently enough, they don't use enough graphics, and they don't do enough analysis to explain what the numbers mean.

Spreadsheets, on the other hand, do have the power to prepare many of the reports that managers need. But unfortunately, before spreadsheets can translate data into information, *someone* must enter data into the spreadsheets in the first place.

This section of this chapter describes a spreadsheet that records daily sales in a database, one that can reveal much about the general trend in sales activity. One of the strengths of this system is that someone unfamiliar with spreadsheets can learn enough in minutes to maintain the database of daily sales.

A Daily Sales Database

The spreadsheet in Figure 6-5 on page 252 shows the top and bottom several rows of a database that records one year of daily sales. The primary purpose of this spreadsheet is to capture sales data that will be used in reports explained in the following sections of this chapter. Additionally, however, the spreadsheet performs a useful analysis of weekly selling patterns.

Figure 6-6 on page 256 shows the custom dialog box you'll create to enter the daily sales information. To do so, you'll create the data-form description area shown in Figure 6-7 on page 257. Figure 6-8 on page 259 shows the analysis of weekly selling patterns.

To create the database shown in Figure 6-5, first open a new spreadsheet. Turn off the gridlines by choosing the Options Display command and selecting Gridlines. Set the column widths shown for Figure 6-5, Figure 6-7, and Figure 6-8. Enter the labels and borders shown for rows 3 through 13. Do not enter the formulas shown in the range E4:E7; you will enter these when the database has been completed.

The dates shown in column A were generated by the DLY_CAL.XLS spreadsheet, as shown in column U of the spreadsheet in Figure 6-2. To create this column, open the DLY_CAL.XLS spreadsheet, select the range U16:U267 (that is, select the range of dates from the first day of the year to the last in column U), press Ctrl-Ins to copy this range to the clipboard, select cell A14 of the new spreadsheet shown in Figure 6-5, paste the dates into the spreadsheet by choosing Edit Paste Special and selecting Values, and then, to format these serial numbers as dates, choose Format Number and specify d-mmm-yy, as shown in the format box for Figure 6-5.

Enter the formulas shown for cells B14 and D14 in the formula box and copy them to rows 15 and 16. Enter the formula shown for cell E16 and then copy the three formulas in row 16 to the bottom of the database. To do so, select the range B16:E16, press Ctrl-Ins, select cell B17, press the F8 (Extend) key, press Ctrl-End to move to the bottom-right cell of your spreadsheet (column E in the last row of dates), and then press Enter.

Enter the shaded bar shown in row 266 at the bottom of the database and then create the range names in the figure's range-name box. Enter the data shown in the range C14:C22 of the spreadsheet in Figure 6-5. Finally, to complete the spreadsheet shown in Figure 6-5, enter the formulas for the range E4:E7 shown in the formula box, and then save your spreadsheet using the name DLY_SLS.XLS.

A Custom Data Form

Figure 6-6 on page 256 shows the custom data form you use to enter daily sales into the database. Creating this form has three advantages over using the standard data form. First, the form provides instructions that allow a new or occasional operator to enter sales information with confidence. Second, the form displays only the information relevant to entering sales data. Third, by creating the data-form instructions for this database, you learn how to create similar instructions for other databases. Before you create the instructions, however, let's take a moment to see how to use this form.

Using a custom data form

When you choose the Data Form command while the DLY_SLS.XLS spreadsheet is active, the dialog box shown in Figure 6-6 appears on your screen. At this point, the form is set to enter sales data into the first database row, the shaded bar shown in row 13 of the spreadsheet in Figure 6-5. If you choose the Find Next button, the form displays the date from row 14 and pauses for you to enter sales. If you then choose the Find Prev button, the form displays the blank again from row 13. And if you choose the New button, the form is set to enter data at the bottom of the database.

The Find column of the database lets you identify the next row of the database that requires updating. This column contains a formula that returns the value 1 when sales have been entered on that row; otherwise, it returns the value 0. Therefore, the first cell in the Find column that contains a 0 is in the first row that needs updating.

To enter sales in the first empty cell in the Sales column, choose the Criteria button by clicking on it with the mouse or by pressing Alt-C. Move to the Find input box by clicking on the Find button or by pressing Alt-D; enter *0* as the value to find and then press Enter. When you do so, the date requiring data appears in the Date box, and the cursor appears in the Sales box, waiting for you to enter a value. Enter the appropriate sales amount, press Enter, and then enter data for the following days, if necessary. To end data entry, press Esc or press Alt-X.

Understanding the data-form instructions

When I first saw an example of data-form instructions in the Microsoft Excel manual, I nearly decided to forget about custom data forms. "All those little numbers in the form mean something," I told myself, "and I don't really think I have the time to learn what that is." In spite of my reservations, however, I forged ahead. And when I did so, I learned a few things that make the instructions easier to understand.

As an overview, a custom data form is a restrictive version of the custom dialog box that you can create with macros. Both versions of custom dialog boxes require specific instructions like those shown in Figure 6-7 on page 257. These instructions define everything you see within a dialog box

The five columns of numbers are the most imposing part of the instructions for a data-form dialog box. These five columns contain numbers that have three different meanings:

Data type. The numbers in the first column specify the data type for each row within the instructions. Chapter 6 of the *Microsoft Excel Functions and Macros* manual describes 20 data types that are allowed within custom dialog boxes created by macros. You will, however, use only three types within a custom data form in a spreadsheet:

Data type	*Output*	*Comment*
5	Text output	Use this type to display labels within a data form.
6	Text-input box	Use this type to enter text.
8	Number-input box	Use this type to enter a number.

The spreadsheet in Figure 6-7 uses two of these data types. With only three exceptions, it uses data type 5 throughout the form. The three times it uses data type 8 it generates the three input boxes shown in Figure 6-6: Date, Sales, and Find.

Horizontal spacing. Both the x column (for X-axis positioning) and the w column (for width of the display area) use numbers that specify horizontal spacing: Eight units in the x and w columns equal the width of one character in the System 8 font.

This fact makes both of these columns easy to manage. For example, the data-form instructions use two values in the x column (column L of the spreadsheet in Figure 6-7). The value 8 specifies a margin of one character width from the left border of the dialog box; all labels and instructions in the dialog box use this margin. The value 80 specifies a margin of 10 characters from the left border of the dialog box; the three input boxes use this margin.

Specifying eight units per character also makes the text width easy to specify (column N of the spreadsheet in Figure 6-7). As the formula box for this figure specifies, all but three cells in this column contain a formula that generates the width: =8*LEN(text). The three exceptions are the input boxes, once again. To these, I assigned a width of 10 characters, or 80 horizontal units.

Vertical spacing. Both the y column (for Y-axis positioning) and the h column (for height) use numbers that specify vertical spacing: Twelve units in the y and h columns equals the height of one character in the System 8 font. Fourteen units in these columns allows empty space between each row and approximates the spacing between rows of text in your spreadsheet.

This fact makes these columns easy to manage as well. In the h column (spreadsheet column O), for example, I set the height of all but three lines to 12 units. The three exceptions, again, were the input boxes, which I assigned a height of 18 units, or one and one-half characters.

The y column is slightly more involved, however, because of this fact: The values in the y column determine the vertical positioning of each element within the data-form dialog box, but the sequence in which these elements are listed in the spreadsheet in Figure 6-7 determines when each instruction is executed. To illustrate, compare the dialog box in Figure 6-6 and the spreadsheet in Figure 6-7. The dialog box lists the Date input box first and then the Sales input box. But even though Date is listed first, the dialog box asks for the Sales data first. It does this because its instructions specify that the Sales input row is above the Date input row on the spreadsheet.

The values within the y column now seem more reasonable: Cell M6 displays the heading six units (one-half character) down from the top of the dialog box. Cell M9 displays the Date label two characters (24 units) below the title, cell M7 displays the Sales label two characters below the Date, and cell M11 displays the Find label two characters below the Sales label. Cells M8, M10, and M12 display their input boxes three units (one-fourth of a character) above the label that precedes them. (In fact, cell M8 contains the formula *=M7–3*, a formula I copied to cells M10 and M12.)

Cell M13 displays the underline two characters below the Find label. Below the underline, where the user instructions are displayed, I worked in units of one spreadsheet line (14 vertical units) or one and one-half spreadsheet lines (21 vertical units). The *INSTRUCTIONS:* heading is 21 units below the underline, as is the first instruction below this heading. The second line of the first instruction is single-spaced (14 units); the second instruction is one and one-half spaces below that, and so on.

Now that you have a better idea what the numbers mean, you should have no problem with the remaining two columns of the data-form instructions. The column labeled *text* contains the text shown in the dialog box. The & symbol in cells P7 and P11 of the column specifies that the character that follows the symbol is the command key. In the dialog box in Figure 6-6, for example, notice that the *S* in *Sales* and the *d* in *Find* are underlined as a result of this designation.

Finally, the column labeled *field* contains the name of the field where the data is placed when entered in the data form.

Creating the custom data-form instructions

To create the data-form instructions, first enter the borders shown in the spreadsheet in Figure 6-7. Enter the headings shown in rows 3 and 4. Assign the font Helv 10 Bold to cell K3. To make the character spacing in your spreadsheet match the character spacing in your dialog box, highlight the range K4:Q20 and assign the System 10 font.

Enter the values shown for columns K, L, M, and O. Enter the formula for cell N6 shown in the formula box. Copy this formula down the column as shown and then enter *80* in cells N8, N10, and N12. Enter the labels shown in columns P and Q (including the underline label shown in cell P13.) When you have completed this step, be certain that you did not enter data in row 5.

Assign the range names Data_Form and Database, as specified in the range-name box for Figure 6-7. If the Data_Form range does not exist, Microsoft Excel uses the standard data form. And if the Database range does not exist, the program can not identify your database.

The data form now works correctly. To try it out, select Data Form and follow the user instructions displayed in the form.

After you save your spreadsheet, try experimenting with column M. Enter the formulas for this column described in the formula box and then experiment with them. Can you improve the look of the dialog box by modifying the values that generate the spacing? Also, try modifying the dialog box to display data from the Num range, column B. All values in column M are linked by formula, so you can insert the two rows this field requires and then renumber column M with little effort.

When you're ready to use this database to record your own daily sales, it's a good idea to protect the spreadsheet. First, unlock the Sales range in column C. To do so, highlight the range C13:C266 and choose the Format Cell Protection command, turn off Locked, and then press Enter. When you choose Options Protect Document, the only part of the spreadsheet that you can change is the range you've unlocked. To turn this feature off, choose Options Unprotect Document.

A Chart of Weekly Selling Patterns

Many companies find that business is usually better on certain days of the week than on others. For example, restaurants generally do well on the weekends and badly on Mondays; and many manufacturers ship more on Mondays, after weekend overtime, or on Fridays, after a push to reduce weekend overtime.

Many businesses closely monitor these weekly selling patterns. Doing so helps them arrange staffing, control expenses, and convert problems into opportunities. For example, large-screen TVs were first widely sold to bars trying to attract customers during Monday Night Football. In most cases, the added business on a normally slow night quickly repaid their investment in high-tech TV.

The table titled Weekly Selling Patterns, shown in Figure 6-8 on page 259, is easy to add to the DLY_SLS.XLS spreadsheet, shown in Figure 6-5. Column E of DLY_SLS.XLS already calculates the percentage that each day's sales represent of the nearest week. (See the explanation of the formula for cell E16 in the formula box for Figure 6-5.) The table merely presents a summary of these results.

The information boxes for Figure 6-8 present all the formulas, formats, and explanations needed to create this display. Simply enter this information as shown.

A REPORT OF DAILY SALES

"How are sales?" is a question that few managers tire of asking. Although profits are the fundamental measure of business success, profits aren't possible without sales.

Generally, when businesses compare sales to budgets, they report only simple variances. The problem with this form of analysis is that it doesn't tell managers whether variances are large enough to require management action. After all, even large dollar variances might be the result of random fluctuations in day-to-day selling activity.

The DLY_SLS.XLS spreadsheet, shown in Figure 6-5, calculates the standard deviation of daily sales. This is a measure of the average amount that sales have deviated from their daily average during the reporting period. As a general rule, 68 percent of all daily sales falls within one standard deviation above and below average daily sales, and 95 percent of all daily sales falls within two standard deviations.

Strictly speaking, this calculation requires that the record of daily sales reflects only random fluctuations. Other influences, such as seasonal variations or growth trends, should be excluded from the data. If your company is experiencing moderate growth and minor seasonal variations, the standard deviation calculated by the spreadsheet in Figure 6-5 should work fine. Otherwise, you may want to refer to Chapter 7 for guidance in adjusting your sales data for these other influences before calculating a standard deviation.

Figure 6-9 on page 261 presents a daily sales summary that uses statistical reasoning to report sales performance. As a simple measure, it shows that with 47 percent of the month complete, sales are 47 percent of the month's budget. As a statistical measure, it presents the day's control limits and a revised prediction. (Both sets of limits are based on two standard deviations.)

Because the day's month-to-date sales amount is within the control limits shown in the Limits section, no action is necessary; the company has a good chance of meeting the month's sales budget of $1,920. Even so, the Prediction section shows that sales could still be as low as $1,785 for the month, or as high as $2,006.

Figure 6-10 on page 268 presents a graph showing the path each day's prediction of monthly sales has taken during the month. The prediction changes daily, because it's based on each day's actual sales, month to date. The bell-shaped curve that surrounds the prediction path represents the upper and lower limits of the budgeted sales amount, which is represented by the horizontal line. As mentioned before, while the current prediction lies within these boundaries, the company is performing within its statistical limits; no action is required.

Figure 6-11 on page 269 presents a graph of daily sales performance. The central horizontal line represents what daily sales must average for the month's sales budget to be achieved. As in the previous graph, the upper and lower limits represent two standard deviations on either side of the daily average. While daily sales stay within these boundaries, the company's daily sales are performing about as expected.

If sales break out of the limits, your company is not performing as your sales budget assumed it would; management action is required.

A Sales Summary Spreadsheet

The sales summary in Figure 6-12 on page 270 generates the data used by the spreadsheet in Figure 6-9 and the graphs in Figures 6-10 and 6-11. Although this spreadsheet generates many numbers, it's easy to maintain. At the beginning of the year, enter the previous year's standard deviation of daily sales (cell J22), the number of working days for each month in the new year (row 65), and the sales budget for the new year (row 69). At the beginning of each month, enter the date of the first day of the month to report (cell J21). The rest of the time, simply open this spreadsheet after you update the DLY_SLS.XLS spreadsheet. Press the F9 (Calculate All) key and the data is ready to present.

Creating the sales summary spreadsheet

To create the daily sales summary, open a new spreadsheet. Turn off the gridlines by choosing the Options Display command and selecting Gridlines. Set calculation to manual by choosing Options Calculation and selecting Manual. Assign Helv 8 as the default font for the spreadsheet. To do so, choose the Format Font command, select 1 in the Fonts box, choose the Fonts button, select Helv 8, choose the Replace button, and then choose OK. Set the column widths in the column-width box for Figure 6-9.

Enter the labels, data, borders, and formats shown in the spreadsheet in Figure 6-9. Instead of entering the formulas, however, enter the numbers that you see in this spreadsheet. You'll enter the formulas after you complete the spreadsheet in Figure 6-12.

Enter the borders and labels shown for rows 20 through 28 of the spreadsheet in Figure 6-12, and format them as shown in the format box for Figure 6-9. Enter and format the data shown for cells J21 and J22. Enter the labels and borders shown in rows 31 through 35. (Row 35 contains range names for several columns. If you can't read them clearly in the spreadsheet because of the shading, use the range-name box for Figure 6-9, which lists them in order.)

Enter and format the labels, data, formulas, and borders shown in rows 59 through 69. The formula box explains how to enter row 62 easily. The data in row 65 is copied from row 8 of the spreadsheet in Figure 6-3; you may prefer to type it in. Row 66 contains the only formulas in this range; enter them as shown in the formula box.

You've already entered the range names in row 35. Now enter the rest of the range names shown in the range-name box. After you do so, enter the formulas shown in the formula box for cell I3 and for the range J25:J28.

The formula box lists formulas for rows 36 and 37, columns A through R. For any column containing formulas for rows 36 and 37, copy the formula in row 37 to the bottom of the display. For any column containing a formula for row 36 only, copy the formula to the bottom. After you format these formulas, as shown in the format box, your spreadsheet resembles Figure 6-12.

Now that you've completed the summary section, enter the formulas shown for rows 7 through 15. Notice that several of these formulas are array formulas, which you must enter by holding down Ctrl-Shift while you press Enter. When you have completed this step, save your spreadsheet using the name DLY_RPT.XLS.

Creating the charts

You create both charts in virtually the same way. The following steps explain how to create the chart in Figure 6-10, with exceptions noted for the one in Figure 6-11:

1. Highlight the ranges L36:L59 and N36:P59. (For the chart in Figure 6-11, highlight the ranges C36:C59 and E36:G59.) To do this, highlight range L36:L59 as you normally would, press Shift-F8 (Add), select cell N36, press the Extend key, and then highlight the second range as you normally would.
2. Open a new chart by choosing File New and selecting Chart.
3. The new chart probably is a bar chart. Change it to a line chart by choosing the Gallery Line command and selecting chart type 2.
4. If you have a color monitor, you might want to adjust the colors of these lines to make them more readable. To do so, press the Down direction key, which selects one of the lines. (You can also click on the line with your mouse.) Choose Format Patterns and then choose the color you want. If you want the color to apply to all the lines, choose the Apply to All box.
5. Adjust the scale of the vertical axis. To do so, first click on the axis with your mouse or use the direction keys to select the axis. Choose the Format Scale command, enter *1400* as the Minimum value, and then press Enter. (For the chart in Figure 6-11, enter *70* as the Minimum value.)
6. To delete the horizontal axis, select the Chart Axes command and then turn off the Category Axis box.
7. To draw the border around the chart, choose Chart Select Chart, choose Format Patterns, select the thickest border weight, and then press Enter.
8. The heading at the top of the graph consists of both attached text (the first two lines) and unattached text (the date).

Attached text. To enter the first two lines of text, choose the Chart Attach Text command, select Chart Title, and press Enter. When you do so, the title *Title* appears on your graph and in your command line. Type the first row of the chart title shown in the chart in Figure 6-10 (or Figure 6-11), press Ctrl-Enter to designate a new row of the title, type the second row of the title, press Ctrl-Enter to designate a third row, and then press Enter. To draw a box around this title, choose Format Patterns, select the Automatic border option, and then press Enter.

Unattached text. To enter the date, first click on an empty area of your chart to be sure that nothing in your chart is selected. Type an equal sign, which appears in the formula bar; click on the date in cell I3 of the DLY_RPT.XLS spreadsheet, shown in Figure 6-9; and then press Enter. When you do so, the selected date appears somewhere in your chart. Drag the date to the blank third line of the chart title.

Unfortunately, the text that you see in this chart is not the text that you get when you print the chart. Therefore, to properly position the date for printing, choose the File Print command and select Preview to view the printed position, return to the chart and adjust the positioning of the date, preview the printed version again, and so on, until you've positioned the date properly for printing.

9. Because adding the title leaves little room for plotting the data, expand the height of your chart by dragging the bottom of the chart downward.
10. To display the chart title in boldface text, select the attached text, choose Format Font, and select Helv 10 Bold. When you do so, the two lines of text might expand to three lines, plus a date. When you print the chart, however, the text will print as you intend. Similarly, assign the font Helv 8 Bold to the date.
11. The amount of month-to-date sales at the bottom of the chart is unattached text. Enter this as you did the date, but select cell J28 in the DLY_RPT.XLS spreadsheet. After you position the text, format it as boldface. (For the chart in Figure 6-11, skip this step.)
12. Although the chart *looks* complete, it isn't. Here's why: In four plotted lines and two titles, the chart refers to absolute cell addresses in the DLY_RPT.XLS spreadsheet. If you were to insert or delete a row in that spreadsheet, the six cell addresses in the chart would not change as the spreadsheet changes. The chart would therefore plot incorrect data. To cure this problem, you must substitute range names for each of the six cell addresses.

To make this substitution, select one of the six items in the chart that contains a formula, and edit the formula in the formula bar by substituting the appropriate range name for the cell address. Refer to the figure's range-name box for a complete cross-reference between range names and cell addresses. Do the same for the other five items. (Figure 6-11 contains one unattached text formula rather than two.)

13. Save your chart. I used the name DSR_MTD.XLS for "Daily Sales Report, Month-To-Date Sales." (For Figure 6-11, I used the name DSR_DLY.XLS for "Daily Sales Report, Daily Sales.")

MONTHLY SALES SUMMARIES

Segment! Segment! Segment! This is the advice that most marketing people seem to be offering these days. But how do you segment? How do you discover and develop profitable niches in your marketplace? And how do you discover and discard the dogs? With details. Details! Details!

This section of this chapter illustrates a simple, but powerful, reporting system. It's one that can help uncover the stars and the dogs within your product lines, your customers, your distribution channels, your sales territories, and so on. In fact, you can use it to report nearly any kind of business operating performance.

Sales Performance by Month

Figure 6-13 on page 271 presents the first three reports in a spreadsheet that contains 15 reports of sales performance. All of these reports can uncover sales trends and product relationships that aren't apparent in typical accounting reports.

Notice that the second report on the spreadsheet in this figure presents the same product information as the first report, but it is sorted in descending order of total sales dollars. The final column of the spreadsheet presents cumulative percentages, which can highlight products that are candidates for discard.

Suppose, for example, that this report presented 100 products rather than the three products shown. Many companies would find that more than 80 percent of total sales (the cumulative percentage shown in column Q) are generated by the first 15 or 20 products, and 95 percent of the sales are generated by the first 70 or 80 products. Therefore, the bottom of the list would contain all those products that contribute virtually no sales, but which probably demand a large investment in inventory, marketing expenses, and support. In other words, many (perhaps most) products at the bottom of the list do not belong in your product line. (Why not eliminate *all* the products at the bottom? Looking only at sales volumes doesn't tell the full story, as the following reports show.)

Although this report presents common information, it has a feature that is quite unusual: It sorts itself whenever you recalculate the spreadsheet. In other words, in the month in which yarn overtakes hats as the highest-selling product of the year to date, this report displays yarn in the top row, hats second, and pins a distant third.

Using the sorting formula in the report offers both an advantage and a disadvantage. The advantage is that no special action is required to generate the report; it's calculated like any other. The disadvantage is that the formula that sorts the data is more complex than others in this section. On balance, however, the long-term convenience the formula provides outweighs the additional effort required to enter it.

Gathering data for the sales summary reports

The data for all sales summary reports in this section of the chapter come from two typical accounting files. The spreadsheet in Figure 6-14 on page 276 illustrates one of these, a year-to-date sales journal. Many computerized accounting systems can print this report, or a month-to-date report, on demand. If your accounting system doesn't provide a way to save this information in a file format that Microsoft Excel can read, refer to Appendix A for ways to load the information.

The spreadsheet in Figure 6-15 on page 277 illustrates the other file that the sales summary reports depend on. This file, which is often called an item master, contains the product number, description, and cost of each product purchased or sold. Typically, this file contains dozens of categories of information about each part: quantity on hand, quantity on order, selling price, stocking location, and so on. When you load this file for the first time, you'll probably want to save computer memory by deleting the columns of information that don't apply to your current reporting requirements.

Notice in the spreadsheet in Figure 6-14 that each product is listed by product number, rather than by product description. The sales summaries work primarily with this number, but they look up the product description in the Schedule of Unit Costs spreadsheet in Figure 6-15 for presentation in each report. Similarly, most accounting systems use customer numbers in their files rather than customer names. If your accounting system uses customer numbers, you have to open a customer file to provide the customer name associated with each customer number. With the formulas in column B of the spreadsheet in Figure 6-13 as a guide, you will have little trouble making this modification.

Creating the sales summary

The first step in creating the sales summary shown in Figure 6-13 is to create the reference files shown in Figure 6-14 and Figure 6-15. To do so, enter the labels, data, and formatting shown. The most important elements of each file are the range names, shown in range-name boxes. Enter the range names as shown and then save each file. Save the spreadsheet in Figure 6-14 as SLS_JRNL.XLS and the spreadsheet in Figure 6-15 as COSTS.XLS.

To begin the summary in Figure 6-13, open a new spreadsheet. Turn the gridlines off by choosing the Options Display command and selecting Gridlines. Assign the font Helv 8 to the spreadsheet by choosing the Format Font command, selecting Font 1, choosing the Fonts button, and then selecting the Helv 8 font. Set the column widths as shown in the column-width box.

Enter the labels and date shown in rows 3 through 7. Format these as shown in the format box. Enter the labels shown in row 8 and the date formulas shown in the formula box. After you format the two formulas, copy the formula in cell D8 to the right as needed. Enter the product numbers and label shown for the range A10:A14, create the borders shown, and then adjust the row heights as shown in the row-height box.

The range-name box lists the range names used in the summary reports. Enter all of them as shown.

Enter the formulas shown for cells B10 and C10. Copy the range B10:C10 to the range B11:B12. (To copy this range without copying the borders, highlight the range B10:C10, press Ctrl-Ins to copy it to the clipboard, highlight B11:B12, choose the Edit Paste Special command, and select Formulas.) Copy the range C10:C12 to the range D10:N10. Enter the formulas shown for O10 and P10 and copy these down the columns as needed. Enter the formula shown for cell C14 and copy it to the right. To complete the summary shown in Figure 6-13, format it as shown in the format box.

To create the second report in Figure 6-13, copy the range A7:P14 to cell A17 and then modify the title and formulas as necessary to match those in the figure. Enter the date formula shown for cell C18 and copy it to the right. Enter the formulas shown for cells A20 and A21. (The formula shown for cell A21 is the most complex formula in this section. Read the explanation of this formula in the formula box and enter it as described.) When the formula in cell A21 returns the part number shown in the spreadsheet in the figure, copy it to cell A22. Modify the formula in cell O20 as shown in the formula box and then copy the revised formula down the column.

When I copy these reports and then modify them, I often forget to modify the percentage calculation in column P. Don't make the same mistake. Modify the formula in cell P20 as shown in the formula box and then copy it down the column. To quickly format column Q, copy the range P18:P23 to cell Q18. Enter the formula shown for cell Q20 and copy it down the column.

To create the third report in Figure 6-13, copy the range A17:O23 to cell A27 and then modify the titles and formulas once again. Enter the formula shown for cell A30 and copy it down the column. Enter the formula shown for cell C30 and copy it to the range C30:N32. When you recalculate, your unit totals match those in the figure.

Other Sales Summary Reports

The following section of this chapter presents 12 additional sales summary reports. You can generate many additional variations from the data provided in Figure 6-14 and Figure 6-15. Each report provides information that many businesses will find useful; few businesses, however, need all the reports.

After you create the reports shown in Figure 6-13, you'll have no problem creating the other reports. Formula boxes in Figure 6-16 through Figure 6-19 provide key formulas for each figure, with explanations; the formats are similar to the ones in the reports you've already created.

Gross profits by product by month

Merely analyzing sales volume, as the reports in Figure 6-13 do, misses one important point: The purpose of selling a product is to make a profit. A product with relatively low sales could contribute significantly to the bottom line, while a product with high sales could be a money-loser.

Figure 6-16 on page 278 presents a report that details the amount of gross profits each product contributes to the bottom line. In this report, we see that yarn represents 20 percent of the company's year-to-date gross-profit margin even though the reports in Figure 6-13 tell us that yarn represents only 10 percent of sales.

At least three variations of the report in Figure 6-16 might be useful. First, you can create a report that sorts products in descending order of gross-profit margin, just as in the second report in Figure 6-13. This would tell you which products contribute the most to the bottom line.

Second, in addition to reporting gross-profit dollars by month, you can report gross-profit margins by month. This approach would help you monitor the effects of changing selling prices, purchase prices, and product mix on each of your products and on your total company sales.

Third, you can report any of the previous information by product class, by sales territory, or by any other category for which your sales dollars are recorded.

Distribution of sales dollars by month

Some products can be very seasonal: Christmas trees, suntan lotion, lawn and garden supplies, snow shovels, and so on. But the sales of many other products can rise and fall significantly through the year, for no apparent reason. Keeping track of past variations in sales can help you plan for future variations. The two reports shown in Figure 6-17 on page 279 can help you do this.

The first report shows the monthly distribution of sales dollars by product. It shows the percentage that each product has contributed to each month's total sales. For example, cell D62 says that hats represented 96 percent of February's total sales.

The second report presents one measure of sales seasonality. For the total yearly sales of any product, it shows the distribution of those sales by month. For example, cell C74 says that of all the yarn sold in 1988, 60 percent was sold in January.

Other reports might be useful. For example, two such reports might analyze gross profits rather than sales dollars. If the company has had large price changes during the year, a similar analysis of unit volume might show results that are significantly different from the reports by sales dollars.

Sales performance by customer by month

If you converted your life savings to cash and put it in a briefcase, you wouldn't watch that briefcase any more carefully than some companies watch the distribution of their sales dollars by customer. The reason: The loss of only one of a company's major customers could ruin the company.

The spreadsheet in Figure 6-18 on page 280 contains several of many reports you can create to monitor monthly sales performance by customer. The first report, of course, tracks total sales by customer. Many companies find this to be the most important indicator of a specific customer's importance to a company.

The second report tracks gross-profit margin by customer. This report can be slightly deceptive, however, as a measure of how much your company makes from each of its customers. This is because many customers demand significant support and non-price concessions that this report doesn't include. However, if you can assemble a monthly list of these costs by customer, you can easily add them to the calculation.

The third report divides gross profits by total sales to calculate gross-profit margin by customer. Often, this can be an enlightening display. You may discover that your favorite customers are contributing your lowest profit margins. You may discover some encouraging trends in the profit margins gained from your largest customers, or you may discover some frightening trends. But whatever you learn from this report, be careful that it doesn't fall into the hands of your customers.

Sales performance by customer and product

The reports discussed so far in this section report total company sales by month. Doing so reveals both successful products and dogs. Similarly, an analysis of sales by customer by product can reveal similar successes and opportunities for improvement. The spreadsheet in Figure 6-19 on page 282 contains three pairs of reports that analyze sales performance by customer and product. Within each pair, one report analyzes performance for the year to date and the other analyzes performance for the current month.

The first pair of reports presents sales dollars by product and customer. The second pair presents unit sales. Unless prices vary significantly between customers or over time, these two pairs of reports generally reveal similar information. One reason to prepare both sets, however, is that doing so lets you easily generate the third pair, average unit prices by customer by product. These two reports allow senior management to look over the shoulder of the sales force to be certain that it is following corporate pricing policies.

By now, the variations on these reports are obvious. You might report profit margins or percentages. You might isolate sales by territory or channel of distribution. You might rank performance by customer. Nearly any combination is possible using the formulas presented for these reports. All you need is the original data on which to perform your analysis.

A Marketing-Contribution Report

Many businesses spend a significant percentage of their revenues on marketing and sales expenses. And many spend significantly more to sell through some channels of distribution than to sell through others. The marketing-contribution report shown in Figure 6-20 on page 284 will help you monitor the effect of both aspects of marketing performance.

Although this report has a different appearance from the other summary reports in this section, it has the same basic structure. The range C6:K40 contains the area of the spreadsheet that is printed and distributed. Row 4 and column A of the spreadsheet contain codes the report requires—much like column A and row 127 of Figure 6-19, which contain customer names and codes *that* report requires.

The reference data in this report serves two purposes. First, it documents the source of the data presented in the report. Second, it provides a quick way to update the report. Suppose, for instance, that the company adds a new product. To add this information to the report, the controller would insert a row within the Sales section (at row 12, perhaps), copy a row of formulas to the new row (12) from an adjacent row, enter the new product or department number in the cell in column A of the new row (cell A12), and then recalculate.

Taking a closer look at the marketing-contribution report

The Sales section of the report in Figure 6-20 divides sales by product and by channel, much like the reports in Figure 6-19. This section shows that distributors account for 90 percent of the company's sales, and the other two channels account for the remaining 10 percent (when you allow for rounding errors).

The Direct Costs section reports all costs that vary directly with the manufacture and sale of the product through each marketing channel. Additional direct costs might include certain salaries, advertising, training costs, warranty costs, and so on. In the report shown, distributors account for 95 percent of all direct costs. From another standpoint, direct costs represent 65 percent of distributor sales.

The Marketing Contribution Margin section shows the amount remaining to support company overhead. Notice that the mail-order channel is the most profitable one on a percentage basis. Although mail-order sales represent only 6 percent of total sales, they contribute 11 percent of total margin. At 65 percent, the mail-order channel's contribution margin is nearly twice that of the distributor channel's margin.

The Indirect Selling Expenses section represents all other selling expenses. Subtracting these from the Marketing Contribution Margin amount yields the Marketing Contribution to Profits amount.

Assembling data for the marketing-contribution report

To generate this report for your own company, you need two categories of data that we've not yet discussed. First, you need to open a file containing general ledger data from the month you want to report. This file must contain all marketing expenses for the period you want to report.

Second, the general ledger file and the sales file must contain codes that assign sales and expenses by channel of distribution. This requirement sounds the most challenging, but it probably is less difficult than you might think. Many microcomputer accounting systems can tag each sales transaction with a code for management analysis. Some businesses use this code to assign each sale to a geographic sales territory or to a specific sales manager. For this report, however, you use this code to specify the sales channel, as shown in column D of the report in Figure 6-14.

You have several alternatives if your general ledger doesn't categorize expenses by sales channel. Some companies assign a special department-number code to identify each sales channel. In the table in Figure 6-21 on page 288, for example, the company's marketing department uses the last digit of the department number to indicate the channel number for which an expense was incurred. Other companies create special patterns within their account numbers. As a third alternative, you might have to create a table containing three columns: an account number, a department number, and the sales channel to which the account and department numbers generally apply.

Creating the marketing-contribution report

To create the report shown in Figure 6-20, first create the table shown in Figure 6-21. To do so, open a new spreadsheet, format it as shown, and then enter all labels and borders shown. Enter the data shown in columns A through C. Enter the formula shown for cell

D7 in the figure's formula box and copy it down the column as needed. Define the range names shown in the figure's range-name box. Finally, save the spreadsheet using the name GL.XLS.

To create the report in Figure 6-20, open a new spreadsheet, turn off the gridlines, and assign the column widths shown in the column-width box. Enter the labels and values shown in columns A through C and in rows 4 through 10. Create the range names shown in the range-name box. The formula box explains the key formulas for the report; enter them as shown and copy them as appropriate. Finally, format the report as shown in the format box.

TRACKING HOURLY SALES

Debbi Fields credits hourly sales goals as a key element in the success of Mrs. Fields' Cookies, her chain of roughly 500 company-owned stores in 37 states. (Tom Richman, "Mrs. Fields' Secret Ingredient," *INC* magazine [October 1987]: 65.)

Hourly sales goals?

That's right. If the customer count at a store is OK but the average check is down, the store's computer program asks whether crew members are doing enough "suggestive selling." If the customer count is down, the computer may suggest that managers conduct mini-promotions to lure passing shoppers into the store.

Store managers also keep the computer informed about business conditions during the day. If more shoppers are out, the program expects more business; if fewer shoppers are out, the program expects less.

The need for careful inventory control provides Mrs. Fields with a major incentive for tracking hourly performance so carefully. Each store's computer tells the store manager how many batches of baking dough to mix, when to bake it, and how to minimize leftovers. If actual sales don't meet the computer's expectations, a store might have too many leftovers on the one hand, or run out of cookies on the other.

An Hourly Sales Recap Report

Although your retail business may not need to bake exactly the right number of cookies at precisely the right times during the day, it can benefit in many ways from tracking hourly retail sales. Among other things, by tracking hourly sales you can:

- More accurately set your staffing level at various hours in the day.
- Identify slow periods that you might improve through promotions.
- Evaluate the immediate effect on sales of special promotions, sales training, and changes in store layout.

- Make informed decisions about the profitability of various times for opening and closing the store.
- Determine whether you have the right number of cash registers.

Figure 6-22 on page 289 shows a form that a drugstore might use to track hourly sales by cash register. This form serves two purposes. First, with its sample data missing, it serves as a form that an office copier can reproduce for recording sales data by hand.

Second, at the end of the day, you can enter the manually gathered data into the computer version of this form. When you do so, the spreadsheet converts the information to a database format, which is shown in Figure 6-23 on page 292. This format is one that you can use to analyze and report periodic sales using the techniques described in the previous section.

To create the spreadsheet in Figure 6-22, first open a new spreadsheet, turn off the gridlines, and set the column widths to those shown in the column-width box. Enter the labels and borders shown in rows 2 through 11. Outline rows 7 and 11 and assign them a row height of 1.

Enter the checkstand numbers in row 6 and the value *1* in cell A9. Although cell A8 looks blank, it contains the hidden value 8, which is the store's starting time. Enter this value and the formulas shown for cells B8 and B10; the contents of all three cells are shown in the formula box. Format the spreadsheet to this point using the formats shown in the format box.

Copy the range A8:N11 to cell A12. Delete the hidden value 8 from cell A12 and enter the formula shown in the formula box for cell A13.

Copy the range A12:N15 down the spreadsheet to contain as many hours as needed for a working day. One way to do this is to calculate the exact number of rows you need to contain your form. I took an easier approach. I selected the range A12:N15, pressed Ctrl-Ins to copy it to the clipboard, moved my pointer to cell A16, pressed the F8 (Extend) key, and highlighted a range in column A that was slightly larger than the range I thought I needed. When I pressed Enter, my computer beeped and displayed the error message *Copy and paste areas are different shapes*. I pressed Enter, pressed the Extend key, pressed the Down direction key once to extend the range by one row, pressed Enter, and so on, until the destination range matched the source range and the Edit Paste command worked successfully. And finally, after recalculating the spreadsheet, I deleted the excess rows.

After you create a form that contains the number of working hours you need, enter any footnotes that are necessary, as shown at the bottom of the spreadsheet in Figure 6-22. Finally, define the range name Data to contain all the data you might enter into your recap. Use the dimensions shown in the range-name box to guide you. After you create this range, save the spreadsheet as HRLY_SLS.XLS.

A Database Format for an Hourly Sales Recap

The data-input form shown in Figure 6-22 was designed for data entry, not for analysis. The spreadsheet in Figure 6-23 on page 292 translates the data into a database format. Because the database contains one row of data for each hour each checkstand can be open, it contains 110 rows (11 hours multiplied by 10 checkstands.)

Creating a database format for an hourly sales recap

To create the database shown in Figure 6-23, first open the spreadsheet HRLY_SLS.XLS. Enter the labels shown for rows 61 through 63. Enter the formulas shown in the formula box, format them as shown, and then copy them down the column to row 173. To complete the database, enter the borders shown, and then save HRLY_SLS.XLS.

How to enter data into the database

To enter data into the database, open the HRLY_SLS.XLS spreadsheet and enter data into the recap shown in Figure 6-22. When you do so, it also appears in the database format shown in Figure 6-23, as the sample data illustrates.

After you enter the data, sort the database on the Row Used column in descending order. This column returns the value 1 in each row containing data that you entered; otherwise, it contains a 0. By sorting on this column, you sort all active data to the top of the database, making the data easy to copy to the monthly database.

The monthly database, which contains all hourly activity for a month, resembles the database in Figure 6-23. The monthly database, however, lacks the data shown in columns B and I of the database in Figure 6-23 and contains values rather than formulas. To copy data to this database, first open your monthly database file and then copy the active data in columns C through H to the bottom of your monthly database. When you do so, however, choose the Edit Paste Special command and select Values, copying the values contained in the HRLY_SLS.XLS database rather than its formulas.

After you copy the data you entered in HRLY_SLS.XLS, print a copy of the spreadsheet in Figure 6-22 for your records and then close the file. *Do not save this file*, because, if you do, you will have a cluttered spreadsheet when you start entering data the following day. To protect yourself against accidentally saving the cluttered spreadsheet, it's a good idea to save a copy of the correct version on a floppy disk or in a second directory on your hard disk.

TRACKING SALES HISTORY

One of the many flaws of most accounting systems is that they were designed to satisfy CPAs, not managers. CPAs want monthly, quarterly, or annual reports. Managers often want additional reports that may span mere hours at one extreme or years at the other. Therefore, until the publishers of accounting systems design these products for managers, we must make special efforts to record information in the way that we need it for management analysis.

This chapter has already covered ways to capture and analyze hourly and daily sales information. Now we'll look at the other extreme.

A New-Product Sales History

The introduction of a new product marks the end of many months or years of hard work to develop the product and the beginning of many months of uncertainty and years of hard work to sell the product. Managing uncertainty is often the biggest challenge.

"Is the product selling?" everyone asks. "Should we contract to buy more raw materials inventory," the purchasing department asks, "or should we try to liquidate the inventory we already have?" "Should we change our promotion strategy," the marketing department asks, "or should we keep on doing what we're doing?" "Is the public buying?" prospective dealers and distributors ask. "Is it going to make money?" the lenders and investors want to know.

One of the reasons these questions are difficult to answer confidently is that most manufacturers don't sell directly to the public. Instead, they sell through dealers, distributors, and other distribution channels. As a consequence, it's difficult to tell in the first few months after introduction whether sales of a new product are merely "filling the pipeline" or actually moving into customers' hands.

The uncertainty becomes even greater when a company must sell a new product through a new channel of distribution, because sales take time to build. "Are sales building as fast as they should?" everyone wants to know. "Are we selling *to* the channel or *through* the channel?"

One of the ways to answer these questions is to analyze the sales of previous new products, finding patterns that can help you evaluate the developing sales pattern of current new products. To perform this analysis, however, you must have past sales records available. The spreadsheet in Figure 6-24 on page 295 presents one simple method of tracking these sales.

This spreadsheet tracks the first 12 months of sales, in both dollars and units, for each new product. Row 9 records the month that the product was introduced. Row 44 calculates the average price during the first month. Row 45 calculates the average price during the twelfth month.

The spreadsheet illustrates several patterns that you might encounter. The first product was sold into an existing distribution channel; its first three months of sales merely filled the pipeline. By the fourth month, however, reorders started giving some indication of how the product was selling at retail.

The second product was sold into a new channel of distribution. Because dealers bought the product cautiously, a larger proportion of the early sales came from reorders. Finally, in the middle of the year, the product began to take off. This was probably caused by three trends: Existing dealers developed faith in the product and stocked larger quantities; new dealers placed larger initial orders because of the product's record of success; and customers, encouraged by enthusiastic dealers, bought the product in growing numbers.

The third product was sold into an existing channel and failed. After the first four months, credits for returned goods exceeded new sales, causing net sales to turn negative. By the seventh month, the product was abandoned.

The last product was sold into an existing channel as an accessory for an existing product. After an initial spurt to fill the pipeline, sales settled into a reliable pattern, driven by the sales of the underlying product.

To create the spreadsheet in Figure 6-24, simply format a new spreadsheet as shown and then enter your own data. The formula box lists the only formulas used in this spreadsheet; enter them as shown.

A Product-Lifetime Sales History

A sales history, such as the one shown in Figure 6-25 on page 297, can reveal much about trends in the sales of a product. The sales history in Figure 6-25, for example, shows a 10-year-old product for which sales in dollars have fallen during the past several years. Unit sales are near their historical high, on the other hand, maintained by continually eroding prices. And notice that roughly half of the product's sales have come during the Christmas season, a trend that has reliably continued through the years.

Eroding prices, high volume, seasonal sales, ten-year life—the sales history describes a product with both problems and opportunities. One opportunity might be to segment the existing market, offering both a premium and a low-end product. An additional opportunity might be to segment the market by season. People who buy the product before Christmas might have different performance needs and price requirements than do those who buy the product during the rest of the year.

To create this sales history, begin with a new spreadsheet. Turn off the gridlines and set the column widths as shown in the column-width box. Enter the headings and borders shown in the spreadsheet and the formulas shown in the formula box. Finally, to complete the sales history, format the spreadsheet as shown in the format box.

You can enter your data into the sales history in one of two ways. The easiest approach is to simply enter the data manually. Or, instead, you could enter formulas similar to those in the spreadsheet in Figure 6-13. These formulas would return the sales amount for the year and product specified. And then, at the end of a fiscal year, you would turn these formulas into values by choosing the Edit Paste Special command and selecting Values.

Figure 6-1. Schedule of Holidays

A schedule of holidays for 1988 on which Figure 6-2 through Figure 6-4 depend. Saved as DLY_CAL.XLS.

	A	B	C	D	E
1					
2					
3					
4	**Schedule of Holidays**			**1988**	
5	Mason Campbell Corp.				
6					
7					
8	1-Jan		New Year's Day	Friday	
9	18-Jan		Martin L. King Day Obs.	Monday	
10	15-Feb		Washington's Birthday Obs.	Monday	
11	30-May		Memorial Day	Monday	
12	4-Jul		Independence Day	Monday	
13	5-Sep		Labor Day	Monday	
14	24-Nov		Thanksgiving	Thursday	
15	25-Nov		Thanksgiving	Friday	
16	26-Dec		Christmas	Monday	
17					
18					
19					

COLUMN WIDTHS							
Column	*Width*	*Column*	*Width*	*Column*	*Width*	*Column*	*Width*
A	8.86	G	5	M	5	S	9
B	2.14	H	5	N	5	T	8.71
C	24.14	I	5	O	5	U	8.86
D	10.86	J	5	P	5		
E	10.14	K	5	Q	5		
F	5	L	5	R	3.71		

(continued)

Figure 6-1. *continued*

KEY FORMULAS	
Cell	***Formula***
D4	**1988** This cell is named Year. Change the entry in it to change the year the calendar reports.
A8	**=DATE(Year,INT(B8),ROUND(100*(B8–INT(B8)),0))**
B8	**1.01** The formula in column A converts the year and the value in column B to the date shown. Enter the value in column B as the month, a period, and the day. For example, January 1 is 1.01; May 30 is 5.30, and so on.
D8	**=A8** Column D repeats column A but uses a different number format, as shown in the format box for this figure.

RANGE NAMES	
Name	***Formula***
Holidays	**=$A$7:$A$17** This is the range of holiday dates.
Year	**=$D$4** Enter this value to specify the year to report.

(continued)

Figure 6-1. *continued*

KEY CELL FORMATS			
Cell	*Number*	*Alignment*	*Font*
Spread-sheet	When the spreadsheet is completed, choose the Options Display command and select Zero Values to suppress the display of 0 values.		
A4	General	General	Helv 10, Bold
D4	General	General	Helv 10, Bold
A7:A17	d–mmm	Center	Helv 10
B7:B17	;;	Center	Helv 10
C7:C17	General	General	Helv 10
D7:D17	dddd	Left	Helv 10

Figure 6-2. Workday List

A schedule for 1988 that contains only working days and on which Figure 6-3 and Figure 6-4 depend. For column widths, see Figure 6-1.

	S	T	U	V
1				
2				
3	**Workday List**			
4				
5	**Enter:**			
6	Number of last			
7	workday in week			
8	(Sunday = 1):		Friday	
9	Length of weekend			
10	in days:		2 Days	
11				
12	All Days		Calendar	
13	Minus	Holiday	Of	
14	Weekends	Removal	Workdays	
15		0	0	
16	25-Dec-87	0-Jan-00	4-Jan-88	
17	28-Dec-87	0-Jan-00	5-Jan-88	
18	29-Dec-87	0-Jan-00	6-Jan-88	
19	30-Dec-87	0-Jan-00	7-Jan-88	
20	31-Dec-87	0-Jan-00	8-Jan-88	
21	1-Jan-88	0-Jan-00	11-Jan-88	
22	4-Jan-88	4-Jan-88	12-Jan-88	
23	5-Jan-88	5-Jan-88	13-Jan-88	
24	6-Jan-88	6-Jan-88	14-Jan-88	
25	7-Jan-88	7-Jan-88	15-Jan-88	
26	8-Jan-88	8-Jan-88	19-Jan-88	
27	11-Jan-88	11-Jan-88	20-Jan-88	
28	12-Jan-88	12-Jan-88	21-Jan-88	
29	13-Jan-88	13-Jan-88	22-Jan-88	
30	14-Jan-88	14-Jan-88	25-Jan-88	
31	15-Jan-88	15-Jan-88	26-Jan-88	
32	18-Jan-88	15-Jan-88	27-Jan-88	
33	19-Jan-88	19-Jan-88	28-Jan-88	

	S	T	U	V
256	25-Nov-88	23-Nov-88	14-Dec-88	
257	28-Nov-88	28-Nov-88	15-Dec-88	
258	29-Nov-88	29-Nov-88	16-Dec-88	
259	30-Nov-88	30-Nov-88	19-Dec-88	
260	1-Dec-88	1-Dec-88	20-Dec-88	
261	2-Dec-88	2-Dec-88	21-Dec-88	
262	5-Dec-88	5-Dec-88	22-Dec-88	
263	6-Dec-88	6-Dec-88	23-Dec-88	
264	7-Dec-88	7-Dec-88	27-Dec-88	
265	8-Dec-88	8-Dec-88	28-Dec-88	
266	9-Dec-88	9-Dec-88	29-Dec-88	
267	12-Dec-88	12-Dec-88	30-Dec-88	
268	13-Dec-88	13-Dec-88	0-Jan-00	
269	14-Dec-88	14-Dec-88	0-Jan-00	
270	15-Dec-88	15-Dec-88	0-Jan-00	
271	16-Dec-88	16-Dec-88	0-Jan-00	
272	19-Dec-88	19-Dec-88	0-Jan-00	
273	20-Dec-88	20-Dec-88	0-Jan-00	
274	21-Dec-88	21-Dec-88	0-Jan-00	
275	22-Dec-88	22-Dec-88	0-Jan-00	
276	23-Dec-88	23-Dec-88	0-Jan-00	
277	26-Dec-88	23-Dec-88	0-Jan-00	
278	27-Dec-88	27-Dec-88	0-Jan-00	
279	28-Dec-88	28-Dec-88	0-Jan-00	
280	29-Dec-88	29-Dec-88	0-Jan-00	
281	30-Dec-88	30-Dec-88	0-Jan-00	
282	2-Jan-89	0-Jan-00	0-Jan-00	
283	3-Jan-89	0-Jan-00	0-Jan-00	
284	4-Jan-89	0-Jan-00	0-Jan-00	
285	5-Jan-89	0-Jan-00	0-Jan-00	
286				
287				
288				

(continued)

Figure 6-2. *continued*

KEY FORMULAS	
Cell	***Formula***
U8	**6** This cell contains the number of the last working day of the week. Enter a value from 1 through 7 in this cell, where 1 indicates Sunday and 7 indicates Saturday. Here, the value 6 indicates that Friday is the last day of the working week.
U10	**2** This value indicates the number of days the business is closed each week. Here, the business is closed for two days. If the business is open seven days a week, enter a 0 in this cell.
T15 **U15**	**0** **0** Enter *0* in each of these cells. If the 0 is missing, the formula in the schedules in Figure 6-3 and Figure 6-4 will return an error.
S16	**=DATE(Year,1,1)–7** This column eliminates weekends from the calendar year. But to ensure that it properly handles the first few days of the new year, the column must start one week prior to the new year.
S17	**=(IF(WEEKDAY(S16)=$U$8,$U$10+1,1)+S16)** If the previous day is the last day of the week, this formula adds the number of days in the weekend to calculate the first day of the new week.
T16	**=IF(ISNA(MATCH(S16,Holidays,0)),S16,T15)*(YEAR(S16)=Year)** The general form of the MATCH function is =MATCH(lookup_value, lookup_array,type_of_match). When the type_of_match equals 0, the function returns an #N/A if an exact match isn't found. Here, the function checks the holiday schedule for the day referenced in column S. If no match is found, the formula returns the date from column S. But if the date in column S is found to be a holiday, the formula returns the previous day's date. Finally, the results are multiplied by a logical switch, which equals 1 if the date in column S is in the current year and 0 if the date is not in the current year.
U16	**=INDEX(Removal,MATCH(DATE(Year,1,1),Removal,1)+1,1)** This formula searches the Removal column to find the first day after January 1 of the current year.
U17	**=INDEX(Removal,MATCH(U16,Removal,1)+1,1)*(U16<>0)** This formula searches the Removal column for the previous day and then returns the day that follows. (If the MATCH function encounters duplicate dates generated by holidays, the function identifies the last day in the sequence.) Finally, multiplying by the logical switch forces the results to be 0 if the previous day's date was 0.

(continued)

Figure 6-2. *continued*

RANGE NAMES	
Name	*Formula*
Weekends	**=$S$15:$S$286** This is the column of dates from which the weekends have been removed.
Removal	**=$T$15:$T$286** This is the column of dates, absent weekends, from which the holidays have been removed.
Workdays	**=$U$15:$U$286** This is the column of workdays: all days minus weekends minus holidays.

KEY CELL FORMATS			
Cell	*Number*	*Alignment*	*Font*
U8	**dddd**	**Center**	**Helv 10**
U10	**#"Days"**	**Center**	**Helv 10**
S16:U286	**d–mmm–yy**	**General**	**Helv 10**

Figure 6-3. Schedule of Working Days

A schedule that reflects both holidays and working days in a given week. For column widths, see Figure 6-1.

	F	G	H	I	J	K	L	M	N	O	P	Q	R
1													
2													
3													
4	**Schedule of Working Days**											**1988**	
5	Mason Campbell Corp.												
6													
7	Number of Working Days												
8	19	20	23	21	21	22	20	23	21	21	20	21	
9													
10	**Jan**	**Feb**	**Mar**	**Apr**	**May**	**Jun**	**Jul**	**Aug**	**Sep**	**Oct**	**Nov**	**Dec**	
11													
12	4	1	1	1	2	1	1	1	1	3	1	1	
13	5	2	2	4	3	2	5	2	2	4	2	2	
14	6	3	3	5	4	3	6	3	6	5	3	5	
15	7	4	4	6	5	6	7	4	7	6	4	6	
16	8	5	7	7	6	7	8	5	8	7	7	7	
17	11	8	8	8	9	8	11	8	9	10	8	8	
18	12	9	9	11	10	9	12	9	12	11	9	9	
19	13	10	10	12	11	10	13	10	13	12	10	12	
20	14	11	11	13	12	13	14	11	14	13	11	13	
21	15	12	14	14	13	14	15	12	15	14	14	14	
22	19	16	15	15	16	15	18	15	16	17	15	15	
23	20	17	16	18	17	16	19	16	19	18	16	16	
24	21	18	17	19	18	17	20	17	20	19	17	19	
25	22	19	18	20	19	20	21	18	21	20	18	20	
26	25	22	21	21	20	21	22	19	22	21	21	21	
27	26	23	22	22	23	22	25	22	23	24	22	22	
28	27	24	23	25	24	23	26	23	26	25	23	23	
29	28	25	24	26	25	24	27	24	27	26	28	27	
30	29	26	25	27	26	27	28	25	28	27	29	28	
31	0	29	28	28	27	28	29	26	29	28	30	29	
32	0	0	29	29	31	29	0	29	30	31	0	30	
33	0	0	30	0	0	30	0	30	0	0	0	0	
34	0	0	31	0	0	0	0	31	0	0	0	0	
35	0	0	0	0	0	0	0	0	0	0	0	0	
36													
37	**Jan**	**Feb**	**Mar**	**Apr**	**May**	**Jun**	**Jul**	**Aug**	**Sep**	**Oct**	**Nov**	**Dec**	
38													
39													

(continued)

Figure 6-3. *continued*

KEY FORMULAS	
Cell	***Formula***
Q4	**=Year** This formula merely repeats the year for the heading.
F8	**=SUM(IF(F11:F36>0,1))** This array formula counts the number of working days by summing the values in a temporary array that contains 1 for each value in the column that exceeds 0. Enter this formula after you complete the rest of the spreadsheet and then copy it across the row as shown.
F10	**=DATE(Year,1,1)** This cell contains the date January 1 for the year being reported.
G10	**=DATE(YEAR(F10),MONTH(F10)+1,1)** The formula adds one month to the previous date, returning the first day of the current month. Copy it across the row.
F37	**=MAX(IF(MONTH(Workdays)=MONTH(F10),Workdays))** This array formula finds the date of the last working day in the current month. It does so by creating a temporary array containing all dates within the current month and then returning the maximum value of these. As with all array formulas, you must enter it by pressing Ctrl-Shift and Enter.
F12	**=INDEX(Workdays,MATCH(F10,Workdays,1)+1,1)** This formula searches the Workdays column to find the first day after January 1 of the reporting year.
G12	**=INDEX(Workdays,MATCH(F37,Workdays,1)+1,1)** This formula searches the Workdays column to find the last day of the previous month and then returns the following day. Copy this formula across its row as necessary.
F13	**=IF(F12=F$37,0,INDEX(Workdays,MATCH(F12,Workdays,1)+1,1))*(F12<>0)** If the previous day was the last day of the current month, this formula returns a 0. Otherwise, the formula finds the previous date within the Workdays column and then returns the following day. Finally, a logical switch sets the results equal to 0 if the previous date was 0. Copy this formula to the range F13:Q35.

(continued)

Figure 6-3. *continued*

KEY CELL FORMATS			
Cell	*Number*	*Alignment*	*Font*
F4	General	General	Helv 10, Bold
F5	General	General	Helv 10
F10:Q10	mmm	Center	Helv 10, Bold
F11:Q36	d	Center	Helv 10
F37:Q37	mmm	Center	Helv 10, Bold

Figure 6-4. Schedule of Working Days in the Fiscal Month

A schedule that creates a calendar year in which each fiscal month has approximately the same number of working days. For column widths, see Figure 6-1.

	F	G	H	I	J	K	L	M	N	O	P	Q	R
40													
41													
42	**Schedule of Working Days in the Fiscal Month**											**1988**	
43	Mason Campbell Corp.												
44													
45	Total # of Working Days					252	Avg # of Working Days/Month:					21	
46													
47	**Jan**	**Feb**	**Mar**	**Apr**	**May**	**Jun**	**Jul**	**Aug**	**Sep**	**Oct**	**Nov**	**Dec**	
48													
49	4	3	4	4	3	2	1	2	31	30	31	1	
50	5	4	7	5	4	3	5	3	1	3	1	2	
51	6	5	8	6	5	6	6	4	2	4	2	5	
52	7	8	9	7	6	7	7	5	6	5	3	6	
53	8	9	10	8	9	8	8	8	7	6	4	7	
54	11	10	11	11	10	9	11	9	8	7	7	8	
55	12	11	14	12	11	10	12	10	9	10	8	9	
56	13	12	15	13	12	13	13	11	12	11	9	12	
57	14	16	16	14	13	14	14	12	13	12	10	13	
58	15	17	17	15	16	15	15	15	14	13	11	14	
59	19	18	18	18	17	16	18	16	15	14	14	15	
60	20	19	21	19	18	17	19	17	16	17	15	16	
61	21	22	22	20	19	20	20	18	19	18	16	19	
62	22	23	23	21	20	21	21	19	20	19	17	20	
63	25	24	24	22	23	22	22	22	21	20	18	21	
64	26	25	25	25	24	23	25	23	22	21	21	22	
65	27	26	28	26	25	24	26	24	23	24	22	23	
66	28	29	29	27	26	27	27	25	26	25	23	27	
67	29	1	30	28	27	28	28	26	27	26	28	28	
68	1	2	31	29	31	29	29	29	28	27	29	29	
69	2	3	1	2	1	30	1	30	29	28	30	30	
70													
71	**Jan**	**Feb**	**Mar**	**Apr**	**May**	**Jun**	**Jul**	**Aug**	**Sep**	**Oct**	**Nov**	**Dec**	
72	21	42	63	84	105	126	147	168	189	210	231	252	
73													
74													

(continued)

Figure 6-4. *continued*

KEY FORMULAS	
Cell	***Formula***
Q42	**=Year** This formula merely repeats the year for the heading.
K45	**=SUM($F$8:$Q$8)** The total number of working days equals the sum of the number of working days in each month.
Q45	**=$K$45/12** The average number of days equals the total days divided by 12.
F47	**=DATE(Year,1,1)**
G47	**=DATE(YEAR(F47),MONTH(F47)+1,1)** These formulas are copied from the schedule in Figure 6-3.
F49	**=$F$12** The first day of this schedule equals the first day of the previous one.
F50	**=INDEX(Workdays,ROWS(F$48:F49)+1,1)** In January, the number of rows that have preceded this formula directly relate to the number of workdays that have preceded the current date in the reporting year. The formula uses this number to find the current workdate in the Workdays range.
G49	**=INDEX(Workdays,F$72+ROWS(G$48:G48)+1,1)** After January, add the cumulative number of workdays prior to the current month to those in the current month to find the total number of days worked year to date. The INDEX function returns the date associated with this number of days. (This formula won't work correctly, of course, until the formula has been completed in cell F72.)
F71	**=F$37** Copy this formula across the row as shown.
F72 **G72**	**=COUNT(F48:F70)** **=COUNT(G48:G70)+F72** This row of formulas finds the cumulative number of days worked in the reporting year. Enter the two formulas and then copy the second one across the row as shown.

(continued)

Figure 6-4. *continued*

KEY CELL FORMATS			
Cell	***Number***	***Alignment***	***Font***
F42:Q42	General	General	Helv 10,Bold
F47:Q47	mmm	Center	Helv 10, Bold
F49:Q70	d	Center	Helv 10
F71:Q71	mmm	Center	Helv 10, Bold
F72:Q72	General	Center	Helv 10

Figure 6-5. Sales Statistics and Daily Sales Database

A database of daily sales that serves as the input for the management reports in Figure 6-7 and Figure 6-8. Saved as DLY_SLS.XLS.

	A	B	C	D	E	F
1						
2						
3	**Sales Statistics**					
4	#Sales Days			Days	9	
5	Total YTD Sales			Sls.Tot	$898	
6	Average Daily Sales			Avg	$100	
7	Standard Deviation			Std	$10.37	
8						
9						
10	**Daily Sales Database**					
11		Day	Daily			
12	Date	Num	Sales	Find	Day_Avg	
13						
14	4-Jan-88	1	123	1		
15	5-Jan-88	2	95	1		
16	6-Jan-88	3	95	1	18.77%	
17	7-Jan-88	4	87	1	18.47%	
18	8-Jan-88	5	106	1	22.36%	
19	11-Jan-88	6	88	1	18.14%	
20	12-Jan-88	7	98	1	19.68%	
21	13-Jan-88	8	106	1	0.00%	
22	14-Jan-88	9	100	1	0.00%	
23	15-Jan-88	0		0	0.00%	
24	19-Jan-88	0		0	0.00%	
260	22-Dec-88	0		0	0.00%	
261	23-Dec-88	0		0	0.00%	
262	27-Dec-88	0		0	0.00%	
263	28-Dec-88	0		0	0.00%	
264	29-Dec-88	0		0	0.00%	
265	30-Dec-88	0		0	0.00%	
266						
267						
268						

(continued)

Figure 6-5. *continued*

COLUMN WIDTHS							
Column	*Width*	*Column*	*Width*	*Column*	*Width*	*Column*	*Width*
A	9.71	F	8.43	K	4	P	42.29
B	5	G	11.57	L	4	Q	8.43
C	5	H	8.43	M	4.86		
D	7	I	8.43	N	5		
E	10	J	8.43	O	4		

KEY FORMULAS	
Cell	*Formula*
E4	**=MAX(Num)** The Num column counts each sales amount entered. The maximum value in this column equals the number of days for which sales have been entered.
E5	**=SUM(Sales)** The amount of year-to-date sales equals the sum of the Sales column.
E6	**=Sls.Tot/Days** Average daily sales equals total sales divided by the number of days.
E7	**=((SUM(IF(Sales>1,(Sales–Avg)^2)))/Days)^0.5** This array formula calculates the standard deviation of the sales column. (You can't use =STDEVP(Sales) because this formula would include in its calculations the 0 values for the sales not yet entered.) The array formula creates a temporary matrix that contains values only for rows in which sales have been entered. Each element of this matrix contains the square of the difference between each sales value and the average. The sum of these "squared deviations from the mean" is divided by the number of days to find the average squared deviation from the mean. Finally, the standard deviation is equal to the square root of this number. To check the accuracy of this figure, enter the STDEVP function in an empty cell, referencing only the sales values that have been entered in column C; the results should match.
A14	**1/4/88** The Date range of column A contains no formulas. Instead, it contains date values generated by the spreadsheet in Figure 6-2 and copied to column A by choosing the Edit Paste Special command and selecting Values.
B14	**=(1+B13)*D14** This column counts each successive day. It equals 0 if the value in Scratch is equal to 0.

(continued)

Figure 6-5. *continued*

KEY FORMULAS–continued	
Cell	***Formula***
C14	**123** The Sales range of column C contains no formulas. Instead, it contains the amount of each day's sales, entered daily.
D14	**=(C14<>0)+0** This logical formula returns the value 1 if the value in column C is not equal to 0; otherwise, it returns a 0. If the value 0 weren't added to this formula, it would return TRUE and FALSE instead of 1 and 0.
E16	**=IF(D18=0,0,C16/SUM(C14:C18))** Business is better on some days of the week than on others. This formula calculates the percentage of a week's sales that were contributed by the current day's sales. The formula compares each day's sale to a "centered" sum of five daily sales results. (A centered sum includes the same number of values before and after the current day. Here the calculation sums sales for the week beginning two days before the current day and ending two days after.) The previous calculation assumes a five-day working week. For a six-day working week, enter the formula =IF(D20=0,0,C17/SUM(C14/2,C15:C19,C20/2)) into cell E17. This calculation puts the current day in the center of a six-day time period that includes two half-days and five whole-days. And for a seven-day working week, enter =IF(D20=0,0,C17/SUM(C14:C20)) into cell E17. This formula divides sales for the current day by the centered sum of seven days.

(continued)

Figure 6-5. *continued*

RANGE NAMES	
Name	***Formula***
DS.Data	**=$A$13:$E$266** This range includes all data in the daily-sales database.
Date **Num** **Sales** **Find** **Day_Avg**	**=$A$13:$A$266** **=$B$13:$B$266** **=$C$13:$C$266** **=$D$13:$D$266** **=$E$13:$E$266** These columns are explained in the formula box for this figure. To create these names quickly, highlight the range A12:E266, choose the Formula Create command, and select Top.
Days **Sls.Tot** **Avg** **Std**	**=$E$4** **=$E$5** **=$E$6** **=$E$7** To create these names quickly, highlight the range D4:E7, choose the Formula Create command, and select Left.

KEY CELL FORMATS			
Cell	***Number***	***Alignment***	***Font***
A3	**General**	**General**	**Helv 10, Bold**
A10	**General**	**General**	**Helv 10, Bold**
A13:A266	**d-mmm-yy**	**General**	**Helv 10**
B13:B266	**General**	**Center**	**Helv 10**
C13:C266	**General**	**General**	**Helv 10**
D13:D266	**General**	**Center**	**Helv 10**
E13:E266	**0.00%**	**General**	**Helv 10**

Figure 6-6. Input Form for Daily Sales

A custom data form that simplifies updating the database in Figure 6-5.

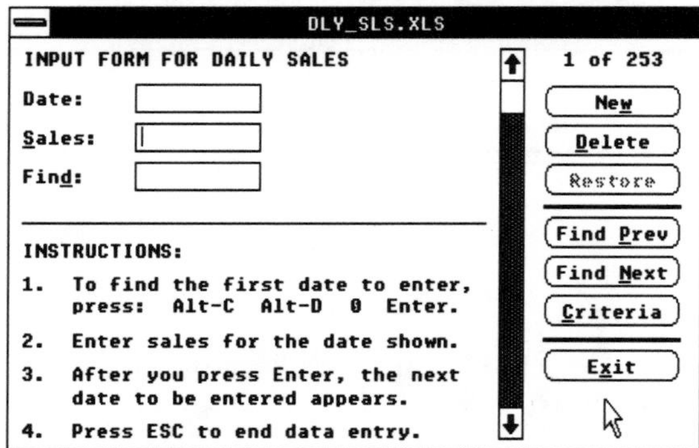

DLY_SLS.XLS
INPUT FORM FOR DAILY SALES
Date:
Sales:
Find:
INSTRUCTIONS:
1. To find the first date to enter, press: Alt-C Alt-D 0 Enter.
2. Enter sales for the date shown.
3. After you press Enter, the next date to be entered appears.
4. Press ESC to end data entry.
1 of 253
New
Delete
Restore
Find Prev
Find Next
Criteria
Exit

Figure 6-7. Description for a Custom Data Form

A spreadsheet that describes the custom dialog box for the database shown in Figure 6-5. Saved as DLY_SLS.XLS. For column widths, see Figure 6-5.

	K	L	M	N	O	P	Q	R
1								
2								
3	Description For a Custom Data Form							
4	type	x	y	w	h	text	field	
5								
6	5	8	6	208	12	INPUT FORM FOR DAILY SALES		
7	5	8	54	56	12	&Sales:		
8	8	80	51	80	18		Sales	
9	5	8	30	40	12	Date:		
10	8	80	27	80	18		Date	
11	5	8	78	48	12	Fin&d:		
12	8	80	75	80	18		Find	
13	5	8	102	296	12	______________________________________		
14	5	8	123	104	12	INSTRUCTIONS:		
15	5	8	144	296	12	1. To find the first date to enter,		
16	5	8	158	280	12	press: Alt-C Alt-D 0 Enter.		
17	5	8	179	280	12	2. Enter sales for the date shown.		
18	5	8	200	280	12	3. After you press Enter, the next		
19	5	8	214	248	12	date to be entered appears.		
20	5	8	235	256	12	4. Press Esc to end data entry.		
21								
22								

KEY FORMULAS

Cell	*Formula*
M9	**=M6+24**
M10	**=M9-3**
M15	**=M14+21**
M16	**=M15+14**

When working with a data form, entering a difference of 14 in the Y column creates vertical spacing that is approximately that of your spreadsheet. (A difference of 12 equals the height of one character.) These formulas therefore keep the lines in the input form properly spaced. (Every number in this column after the first value 6 contains similar formulas.) The labels for the input boxes are 24 units (2 characters) apart; their input boxes begin 3 units above those labels; each numbered instruction is 21 units (one and one-half lines) below the previous line; and the second line of a numbered instruction is 14 units (one line) below the first line of the instruction.

(continued)

Figure 6-7. *continued*

KEY FORMULAS—continued	
Cell	***Formula***
N6	**=8*LEN(P6)** Each 8 units in this column equals the width of one character in the System 8 font. (Notice, for example, that this data form and the illustrations provided in the Microsoft Excel documentation all begin the X position at the eighth unit, or one character to the right of the left border of the dialog box.) This formula creates the appropriate width value for text entries. It does so by multiplying the number of characters in each label by 8 units per character.

RANGE NAMES	
Name	***Formula***
Data_Form	**=$K$5:$Q$20**
Database	**=$A$12:$E$266** Both of these names must be defined as shown before you can use the data form.

KEY CELL FORMATS			
Cell	***Number***	***Alignment***	***Font***
K3	**General**	**General**	**Helv 10, Bold**
K4:Q20	**General** The dialog box created by the data form uses the monospaced System font. Using the same font in the data form itself helps visually position text used in it.	**Center**	**System 8**

Figure 6-8. Weekly Selling Patterns

A table that calculates the average percentage that each day's sales contribute to weekly sales. Saved as DLY_SLS.XLS. For column widths, see Figure 6-5.

	G	H	I	J
1				
2				
3	Weekly Selling Patterns			
4		Unadj.	Adjusted	
5	Monday	18.14%	18.62%	
6	Tuesday	19.68%	20.20%	
7	Wednesday	18.77%	19.27%	
8	Thursday	18.47%	18.96%	
9	Friday	22.36%	22.95%	
10		97.43%	100.00%	
11				
12				
13				

KEY FORMULAS	
Cell	***Formula***
G5	**2** Enter the values 2 through 6 in this and the following cells. When you format them as shown in the format box, the days of the week appear as shown in the spreadsheet.
H5	**=AVERAGE(IF(Day_Avg>0,IF(WEEKDAY(Date)=G5,Day_Avg)))** This array formula finds the average of all of Monday's percentages in column E; the cell below averages all of Tuesday's percentages; and so on. Because these averages never quite add up to one whole day's sales, column I calculates an adjusted percentage that adds to 100 percent of a week's sales.
H10	**=SUM(H5:H9)** Enter this formula before entering the formulas in column I.
I5	**=H5*(1/H$10)** This formula adjusts the percentages in column I to add to one whole day of sales. Generally, the adjustment is less than the amount shown in the spreadsheet; the unusually small amount of data accounts for the larger adjustment.
I10	**=SUM(I5:I9)** Because this is the sum of the adjusted figures, this total always equals 1.

(continued)

Figure 6-8. *continued*

KEY CELL FORMATS			
Cell	***Number***	***Alignment***	***Font***
G3	General	General	Helv 10, Bold
G5:G9	dddd	General	Helv 10
H5:I10	.00%	General	Helv 10

Figure 6-9. Daily Sales Summary

A report that compares actual and budgeted sales for the month to date and uses statistical techniques to predict sales for the month. Saved as DLY_RPT.XLS. The information boxes shown here also apply to Figure 6-12.

	A	B	C	D	E	F	G	H	I	J
1										
2										
3	Daily Sales Summary						January 14, 1988			
4	Mason Campbell Corp.									
5										
6										
7	Sales						Limits			
8	Actual Sales				$898		Low		$857	
9	Month's Budget				$1,920		High		$962	
10	% of Budget				47%					
11										
12	Sales Days						Prediction			
13	Number This Report				9		Low		$1,785	
14	Number This Month				19		Middle		$1,896	
15	% Completed				47%		High		$2,006	
16										

COLUMN WIDTHS							
Column	*Width*	*Column*	*Width*	*Column*	*Width*	*Column*	*Width*
A	6.33	F	4.83	K	5	P	7.33
B	5	G	4.67	L	5	Q	4
C	5	H	5.33	M	5.5	R	4.5
D	5.67	I	6.5	N	5		
E	6.67	J	6.17	O	6.33		

(continued)

Figure 6-9. *continued*

KEY FORMULAS	
Cell	***Formula***
I3	**=TEXT(INDEX(Data,$E$13+1,1),"mmmm d, yyyy")** Cell E13 finds the number of work days entered for the month in the daily sales database shown in Figure 6-5. The INDEX function returns the date associated with this number. The TEXT function formats the date as text so that it can be displayed in more than one cell. The cell alignment shown in the format box sends text that overflows this cell to the left of the cell, rather than to the right, as is customary.
J21	**1/1/88** This date value determines the month of the report.
J22	**11.72** This value for the historical standard deviation of daily sales is the amount that daily sales tend to vary above and below the average sale. This value comes from the standard deviation calculated in the daily sales database for the previous year—not from the current year's data that now appears in the spreadsheet shown in Figure 6-5.
J25	**=2*$J$22** Suppose that it's the middle of the month and that actual sales are less than budget. Is the shortfall the result of random variations or the result of a more fundamental problem? If the daily variation from the sales budget is caused only by random variations, sales should seldom vary by more than two standard deviations from the daily sales budget. This formula calculates the amount added to and subtracted from the budget to calculate the upper and lower sales limits. Sales performance beyond these limits, in other words, is probably the result of circumstances not anticipated by your sales budget.
J26	**=MONTH(Date)**
J27	**=$E$9/$E$14** The daily sales budget is equal to the monthly sales budget divided by the number of working days in the month.
J28	**="Month-to-Date Sales = "&TEXT(E8,"$#")** This string formula generates a label that is used by one of the graphs.

(continued)

Figure 6-9. *continued*

KEY FORMULAS–continued	
Cell	***Formula***
A36	**=INDEX(DS.Date,1+INDEX(Workdays,2,Month) –INDEX(Workdays,1,Month)+B36)*$Q36** The first INDEX formula finds the date associated with the workday number in column B. It does this first by using the second INDEX function, which finds the total number of days that will have been worked at the end of the current month, subtracting the number of workdays in the current month (found by the third INDEX function),and then adding the number of working days in the current month, found in column B.
B36 **B37**	**1** **=(1+B36)*$Q37** This column counts the number of work days possible during the month. The cell in column Q contains a 1 if the current row represents a potential workday; otherwise, it contains a 0.
C36	**=IF($R36=0,NA(),VLOOKUP($A36,DS.Data,3))** This formula looks up the sales that have been entered for the day in the daily-sales database. If no sales have been entered, the formula returns #N/A.
D36 **D37**	**=C36** **=D36+C37** Column D calculates the month-to-date amount of actual sales.
E36 **F36** **G36**	**=IF($Q36=0,NA(),(Avg–Limit))** **=IF($Q36=0,NA(),Avg)** **=IF($Q36=0,NA(),Avg+Limit)** These three formulas calculate the minimum, average, and maximum amounts expected for average daily sales. Because these columns contain a label in the shaded area of row 33, the columns are used by one or both of the graphs.
I36 **I37**	**=F36** **=(F37+I36)*$Q37** This column calculates the month-to-date amount for budgeted sales. In other words, the last value in this column equals the amount budgeted for the month.

(continued)

Figure 6-9. *continued*

KEY FORMULAS – continued	
Cell	***Formula***
H36 J36	**=IF($Q36=0,NA(),$I36–Limit*SQRT($B36)*SQRT((Days–$B36)/(Days–1)))** **=IF($Q36=0,NA(),$I36+Limit*SQRT($B36)*SQRT((Days–$B36)/(Days–1)))** These formulas calculate the lower and upper limits that month-to-date sales can total if sales are affected only by random variations. The limits are calculated by subtracting an amount from or adding an amount to the balance of the month-to-date sales budget. This amount is equal to the daily limit multiplied by the SQRT calculations that adjust the limit for the fraction of the month completed. (These calculations are based on a model of sampling from a finite population without replacement.)
K36 L36 M36	**=IF($Q36=0,NA(),(($D36–($I36–$H36))/$B36)*Days)** **=IF($Q36=0,NA(),($D36/$B36)*Days)** **=IF($Q36=0,NA(),(($D36+($I36–$H36))/$B36)*Days)** These three formulas predict total monthly sales based on actual performance to date and on the historical variation in daily sales. To illustrate, the prediction for the minimum sales for the month is equal to actual month-to-date sales, minus the adjusted limit, divided by the actual number of days in the month (which calculates the average daily sales at the minimum). This balance is multiplied by the number of days in the month to find the predicted minimum value of actual daily sales.
N36	**=IF($Q36=0,NA(),$E$9)** This formula repeats the monthly sales budget for each day during the month.
O36 P36	**=IF($Q36=0,NA(),H36*$E$14/B36)** **=IF($Q36=0,NA(),J36*$E$14/B36)** If actual sales are affected only by random variations, the middle value for predicted monthly sales should vary within the boundaries set by these two formulas. At the beginning of the month, the minimum and maximum boundaries are quite large—nearly any performance is possible. But the boundaries narrow as the month draws to a close. These limits take the shape of the bell-shaped curve shown in the graph in Figure 6-10.
Q36	**=(ROWS(A$35:A35)<=INDEX(Workdays,1,Month))+0** The formulas in this column return the value 1 for each working day during the month. They return the value 0 for all rows in excess of the number of working days in the current month.

(continued)

Figure 6-9. *continued*

KEY FORMULAS–continued	
Cell	***Formula***
R36	**=(VLOOKUP($A36,DS.Data,3)<>0)+0** The formulas in this column return the value 1 if actual sales data exists for the current working day. If actual sales data does not exist, the formula returns a 0.
A62:L62	The months in this row are labels that remain unchanged from year to year. To create them easily, enter the value *1* in cell A62, highlight the 12 cells shown, choose the Data Series command, specify Rows, Date, and Month, and then press Enter. Finally, format this row as shown in the format box for this figure.
A65:L65	This row contains the actual number of working days for each month calculated by the schedule of working days shown in Figure 6-3. Use Edit Paste Special and specify Value to copy these values from that schedule.
A66 **B66**	**=A65** **=A66+B65** This row calculates the number of working days, year to date, at the end of each month in the schedule. Copy the formula in column B to the right as needed.
A69:L69	This row contains the sales budget for each month of the year. Transfer this information from your company's budget.
E8	**=INDEX(Data,$E$13+1,COLUMNS($A$35:$D$35))** Actual sales are found in the month-to-date column of the schedule.
E9	**=INDEX(Budget,1,MONTH(Date))** This amount is extracted from the Budget range.
E10	**=E8/E9** This cell calculates the percentage of the sales budget that's been achieved, month to date.
E13	**=SUM(IF(ISNA(A.Day),0,IF(A.Day>0,1)))** This array formula counts the number of days of actual sales that appears in the schedule.
E14	**=INDEX(Workdays,1,MONTH(Date))** The number of working days this month comes from the Workdays range.
E15	**=E13/E14** At times, it's convenient to compare this percentage of the month that has passed to the percentage of the month's sales budget (above) that has been achieved.

(continued)

Figure 6-9. *continued*

KEY FORMULAS–continued

Cell	*Formula*
I8	=INDEX(Data,$E$13+1,COLUMNS($A$35:$H$35))
I9	=INDEX(Data,$E$13+1,COLUMNS($A$35:$J$35))
I13	=INDEX(Data,$E$13+1,COLUMNS($A$35:$K$35))
I14	=INDEX(Data,$E$13+1,COLUMNS($A$35:$L$35))
I15	=INDEX(Data,$E$13+1,COLUMNS($A$35:$M$35))
	These formulas all depend on the sales-day number to extract the correct information from the body of the schedule. The Limits section shows the high and low values that actual sales can be while staying within the theoretical limits of the month's budget. The Prediction section shows the range of values that sales could total for the current month.

RANGE NAMES

Name	*Formula*
Rpt.Date	=$I$3
Days	=$E$14
Date	=$J$21
Limit	=$J$25
Month	=$J$26
Avg	=$J$27
Graf.Sales	=$J$28
Data	=$A$35:$R$59
Workdays	=$A$65:$L$66
Budget	=$A$69:$L$69
	Use the Formula Define Name command to assign these range names.
A.Day	=$C$36:$C$59
D.Min	=$E$36:$E$59
D.Mid	=$F$36:$F$59
D.Max	=$G$36:$G$59
P.Mid	=$L$36:$L$59
Bud	=$N$36:$N$59
B.Min	=$O$36:$O$59
B.Max	=$P$36:$P$59
	To create these names quickly, enter the names as shown in row 35, highlight the range C35:P59, choose the Formula Create command, and select Top.

(continued)

Figure 6-9. *continued*

RANGE NAMES–continued	
Name	***Formula***
DS.Date	**=DLY_SLS.XLS!Date**
DS.Data	**=DLY_SLS.XLS!DS.Data**
	These two names refer to the worksheet containing the daily-sales database (Figure 6-5). Use the Define Name command to enter them. When you do so, remember to include the equal sign in the Refers To box.

KEY CELL FORMATS			
Cell	***Number***	***Alignment***	***Font***
Sheet	General	General	Helv 8
I3	General	Right	Helv 10, Bold
A7	General	General	Helv 10, Bold
G7	General	General	Helv 10, Bold
I8:I15	$#,##0 ;($#,##0)	General	Helv 8
A12	General	General	Helv 10, Bold
G12	General	General	Helv 10, Bold
E8:E9	$#,##0 ;($#,##0)	General	Helv 8
E10	0%	General	Helv 8
E13:E14	#,##0 ;(#,##0)	General	Helv 8
E15	0%	General	Helv 8
J21	m/d/yy	General	Helv 8
J22	$#,##0.00 ;($#,##0.00)	General	Helv 8
A35:A59	d–mmm	General	Helv 8
B35:B59	#,##0 ;(#,##0)	Center	Helv 8
C35:P59	#,##0 ;(#,##0)	General	Helv 8
Q35:R59	#,##0 ;(#,##0)	Center	Helv 8
A62:L62	mmm	Center	Helv 10, Bold
A65:L66	General	Center	Helv 8
A69:L69	#,##0	Center	Helv 8

Figure 6-10. Predicted Sales for the Month *vs* Budget

A graph that shows that while actual cumulative sales stay within the border of the bell-shaped curve, the company has a reasonable expectation of achieving its monthly sales budget.

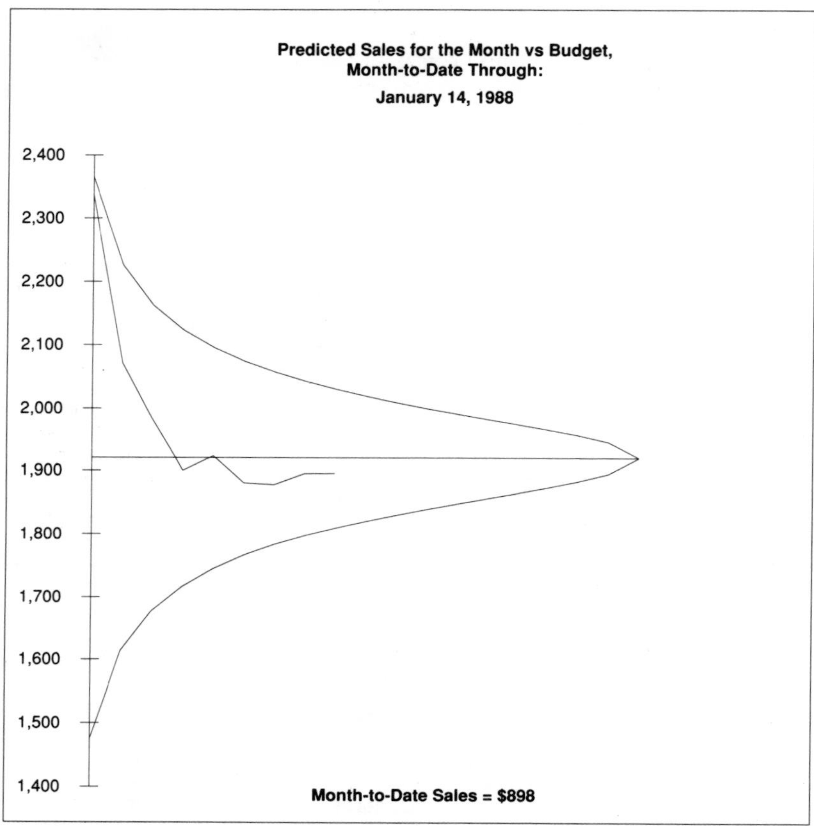

Figure 6-11. Daily Sales Performance, Actual *vs* Budget

A graph that tracks actual daily sales within upper and lower limits, letting you see immediately when sales begin to perform differently from plan.

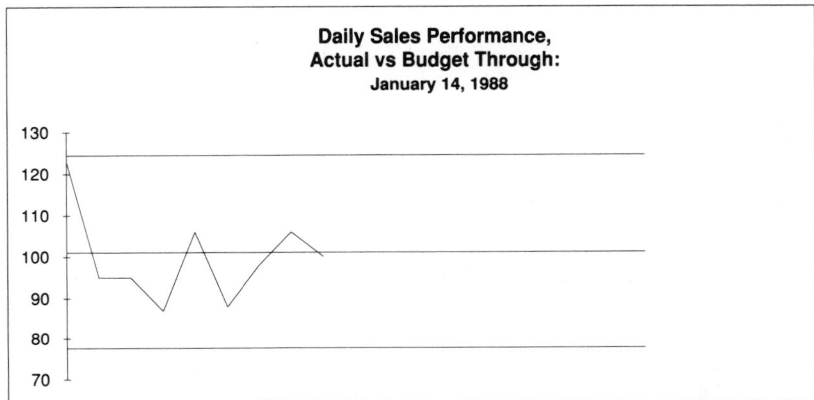

Figure 6-12. Sales Summary

A spreadsheet that generates the values plotted by the graphs in Figure 6-10 and Figure 6-11. Saved as DLY_RPT.XLS. For column widths, formulas, range names, and formats, see Figure 6-9.

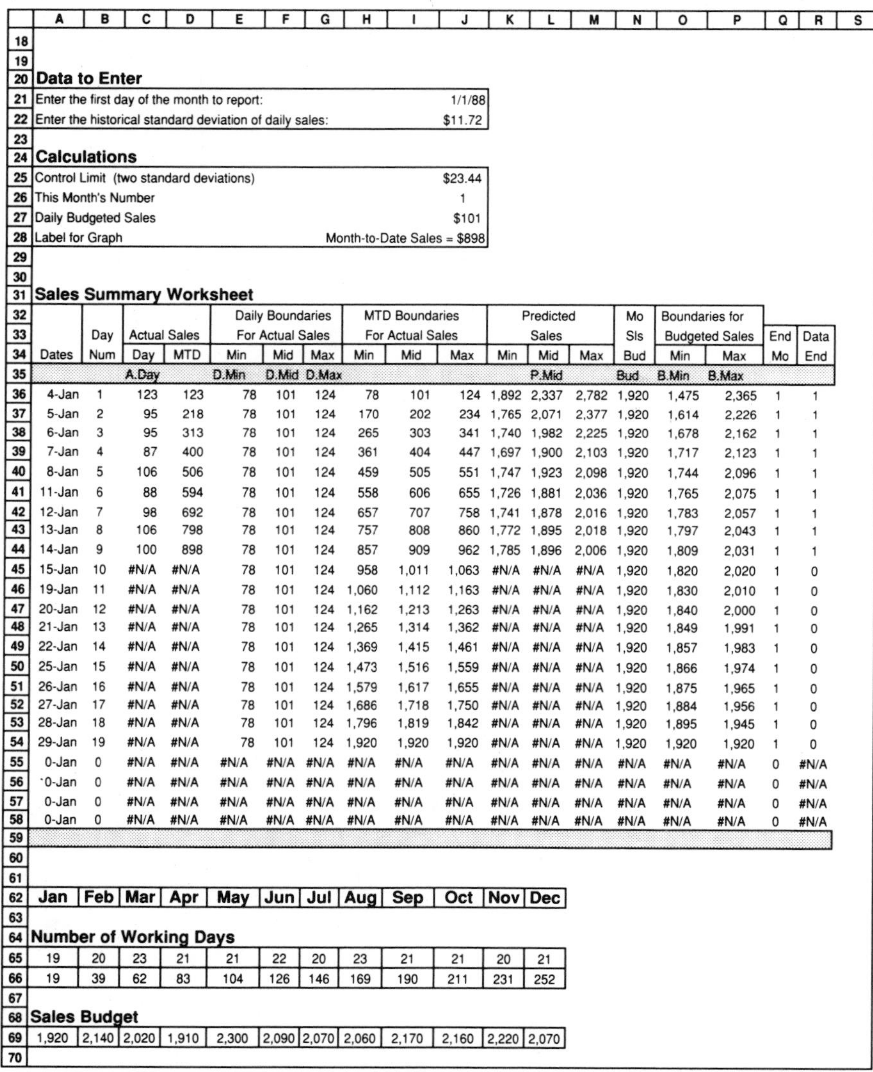

	A	B	C	D	E	F	G	H	I	J	K	L	M	N	O	P	Q	R	S
18																			
19																			
20	**Data to Enter**																		
21	Enter the first day of the month to report:									1/1/88									
22	Enter the historical standard deviation of daily sales:									$11.72									
23																			
24	**Calculations**																		
25	Control Limit (two standard deviations)									$23.44									
26	This Month's Number									1									
27	Daily Budgeted Sales									$101									
28	Label for Graph									Month-to-Date Sales = $898									
29																			
30																			
31	**Sales Summary Worksheet**																		
32					Daily Boundaries			MTD Boundaries			Predicted			Mo	Boundaries for				
33		Day	Actual Sales		For Actual Sales			For Actual Sales			Sales			Sls	Budgeted Sales		End	Data	
34	Dates	Num	Day	MTD	Min	Mid	Max	Min	Mid	Max	Min	Mid	Max	Bud	Min	Max	Mo	End	
35			A.Day		D.Min	D.Mid	D.Max					P.Mid		Bud	B.Min	B.Max			
36	4-Jan	1	123	123	78	101	124	78	101	124	1,892	2,337	2,782	1,920	1,475	2,365	1	1	
37	5-Jan	2	95	218	78	101	124	170	202	234	1,765	2,071	2,377	1,920	1,614	2,226	1	1	
38	6-Jan	3	95	313	78	101	124	265	303	341	1,740	1,982	2,225	1,920	1,678	2,162	1	1	
39	7-Jan	4	87	400	78	101	124	361	404	447	1,697	1,900	2,103	1,920	1,717	2,123	1	1	
40	8-Jan	5	106	506	78	101	124	459	505	551	1,747	1,923	2,098	1,920	1,744	2,096	1	1	
41	11-Jan	6	88	594	78	101	124	558	606	655	1,726	1,881	2,036	1,920	1,765	2,075	1	1	
42	12-Jan	7	98	692	78	101	124	657	707	758	1,741	1,878	2,016	1,920	1,783	2,057	1	1	
43	13-Jan	8	106	798	78	101	124	757	808	860	1,772	1,895	2,018	1,920	1,797	2,043	1	1	
44	14-Jan	9	100	898	78	101	124	857	909	962	1,785	1,896	2,006	1,920	1,809	2,031	1	1	
45	15-Jan	10	#N/A	#N/A	78	101	124	958	1,011	1,063	#N/A	#N/A	#N/A	1,920	1,820	2,020	1	0	
46	19-Jan	11	#N/A	#N/A	78	101	124	1,060	1,112	1,163	#N/A	#N/A	#N/A	1,920	1,830	2,010	1	0	
47	20-Jan	12	#N/A	#N/A	78	101	124	1,162	1,213	1,263	#N/A	#N/A	#N/A	1,920	1,840	2,000	1	0	
48	21-Jan	13	#N/A	#N/A	78	101	124	1,265	1,314	1,362	#N/A	#N/A	#N/A	1,920	1,849	1,991	1	0	
49	22-Jan	14	#N/A	#N/A	78	101	124	1,369	1,415	1,461	#N/A	#N/A	#N/A	1,920	1,857	1,983	1	0	
50	25-Jan	15	#N/A	#N/A	78	101	124	1,473	1,516	1,559	#N/A	#N/A	#N/A	1,920	1,866	1,974	1	0	
51	26-Jan	16	#N/A	#N/A	78	101	124	1,579	1,617	1,655	#N/A	#N/A	#N/A	1,920	1,875	1,965	1	0	
52	27-Jan	17	#N/A	#N/A	78	101	124	1,686	1,718	1,750	#N/A	#N/A	#N/A	1,920	1,884	1,956	1	0	
53	28-Jan	18	#N/A	#N/A	78	101	124	1,796	1,819	1,842	#N/A	#N/A	#N/A	1,920	1,895	1,945	1	0	
54	29-Jan	19	#N/A	#N/A	78	101	124	1,920	1,920	1,920	#N/A	#N/A	#N/A	1,920	1,920	1,920	1	0	
55	0-Jan	0	#N/A	#N/A	#N/A	#N/A	#N/A	#N/A	#N/A	#N/A	#N/A	#N/A	#N/A	#N/A	#N/A	#N/A	0	#N/A	
56	0-Jan	0	#N/A	#N/A	#N/A	#N/A	#N/A	#N/A	#N/A	#N/A	#N/A	#N/A	#N/A	#N/A	#N/A	#N/A	0	#N/A	
57	0-Jan	0	#N/A	#N/A	#N/A	#N/A	#N/A	#N/A	#N/A	#N/A	#N/A	#N/A	#N/A	#N/A	#N/A	#N/A	0	#N/A	
58	0-Jan	0	#N/A	#N/A	#N/A	#N/A	#N/A	#N/A	#N/A	#N/A	#N/A	#N/A	#N/A	#N/A	#N/A	#N/A	0	#N/A	
59																			
60																			
61																			
62	**Jan**	**Feb**	**Mar**	**Apr**	**May**	**Jun**	**Jul**	**Aug**	**Sep**	**Oct**	**Nov**	**Dec**							
63																			
64	**Number of Working Days**																		
65	19	20	23	21	21	22	20	23	21	21	20	21							
66	19	39	62	83	104	126	146	169	190	211	231	252							
67																			
68	**Sales Budget**																		
69	1,920	2,140	2,020	1,910	2,300	2,090	2,070	2,060	2,170	2,160	2,220	2,070							
70																			

Figure 6-13. Sales Dollars by Product by Month

Reports summarizing the data found in most accounting systems.

	A	B	C	D	E	F	G	H	I	J	K	L	M	N	O	P	Q
1																	
2																	
3	**Sales Summary, Page One**																
4	Janell's Fashion Supply																
5	Mar-88																
6																	
7	**Sales Dollars by Product by Month--Listed in Product Number Sequence**																
8	Product	Desc	Jan-88	Feb-88	Mar-88	Apr-88	May-88	Jun-88	Jul-88	Aug-88	Sep-88	Oct-88	Nov-88	Dec-88	Total	%	
9																	
10	5-723	Hats	12,577	13,926	14,103	0	0	0	0	0	0	0	0	0	40,606	88%	
11	6-222	Pins	700	0	92	0	0	0	0	0	0	0	0	0	792	2%	
12	8-234	Yarn	2,909	524	1,397	0	0	0	0	0	0	0	0	0	4,830	10%	
13																	
14	Total Dollars		16,186	14,450	15,592	0	0	0	0	0	0	0	0	0	46,228	100%	
15																	
16																	
17	**Sales Dollars by Product by Month--Listed in Descending Order of Total Sales Dollars**																
18	Product	Desc	Jan-88	Feb-88	Mar-88	Apr-88	May-88	Jun-88	Jul-88	Aug-88	Sep-88	Oct-88	Nov-88	Dec-88	Total	%	+%
19																	
20	5-723	Hats	12,577	13,926	14,103	0	0	0	0	0	0	0	0	0	40,606	88%	88%
21	8-234	Yarn	2,909	524	1,397	0	0	0	0	0	0	0	0	0	4,830	10%	98%
22	6-222	Pins	700	0	92	0	0	0	0	0	0	0	0	0	792	2%	100%
23																	
24	Total Dollars		16,186	14,450	15,592	0	0	0	0	0	0	0	0	0	46,228	100%	
25																	
26																	
27	**Unit Sales by Product by Month**																
28	Product	Desc	Jan-88	Feb-88	Mar-88	Apr-88	May-88	Jun-88	Jul-88	Aug-88	Sep-88	Oct-88	Nov-88	Dec-88	Total		
29																	
30	5-723	Hats	1,358	1,994	1,750	0	0	0	0	0	0	0	0	0	5,102		
31	6-222	Pins	272,176	0	27,087	0	0	0	0	0	0	0	0	0	299,263		
32	8-234	Yarn	3,892	588	1,771	0	0	0	0	0	0	0	0	0	6,251		
33																	
34																	
35																	
36																	

COLUMN WIDTHS							
Column	*Width*	*Column*	*Width*	*Column*	*Width*	*Column*	*Width*
A	8.33	F	6.5	K	6.5	P	5.17
B	8.33	G	6.5	L	6.5	Q	4.67
C	6.5	H	6.5	M	6.5		
D	6.5	I	6.5	N	6.5		
E	6.5	J	6.5	O	6.5		

ROW HEIGHTS	
Row	*Height*
9	6
13	6

(continued)

Figure 6-13. *continued*

KEY FORMULAS	
Cell	***Formula***
A5	**3/1/88** Enter the first day of the month of the report.
C8 **D8**	**1/1/88** **=DATE(YEAR(C8),MONTH(C8)+1,1)** To begin the year with the first month of your fiscal year, enter that date in column C.
B10	**=VLOOKUP(A10,C.Data,2)** This formula finds the description in the second column of the C.Data range of the COSTS file.
C10	**=SUM(IF(Prod=$A10,IF(Month=C$8,Sales)))** This array formula finds the sum of a temporary matrix that takes its values from the SLS_JRNL.XLS file. For each row in which the product number in that file is equal to the value in column A and the date is equal to the value in column C, the temporary matrix holds the amount of the sale, and the SUM function totals these individual sales values. As with any array function, you must enter it by holding down Ctrl and Shift while pressing Enter. Copy the formula to every month for every product.
O10	**=SUM(C10:N10)–ROW(O10)*0.0000001** Normally, of course, you expect to see only the SUM function here, not an additional ROW function multiplied by 0.0000001. Subtracting the small amount from the sum doesn't change the report totals by a penny, but it does ensure that the totals do not contain duplicate values. If they did contain duplicates, the formulas that sort on this column would skip over any value duplicating a previous value.
P10	**=O10/O$14**
C14	**=SUM(C9:C13)** Copy this formula across the row as shown.
C18	**=C$8** Copy this formula across the row as necessary. All date headings below this row contain the same formula.
A20	**=SUM(IF(Total=MAX(Total),Product))** The IF function creates a temporary array that contains the product number containing the largest value in the Total column. The SUM function returns this product number.

(continued)

Figure 6-13. *continued*

<table>
<tr><th colspan="2">KEY FORMULAS–continued</th></tr>
<tr><th>Cell</th><th>Formula</th></tr>
<tr><td>A21</td><td>=INDEX(Product,MATCH(MAX(IF(Total<LOOKUP(A20,Product,Total),Total)),Total,0),1)
[5] =INDEX(Product, ,1)
[4] MATCH(,Total,0)
[3] MAX( )
[2] IF(Total< ,Total)
[1] LOOKUP(A20,Product,Total)
This array formula finds the product number containing the largest value in the TOTAL column that is smaller than the total for the preceding product number. In other words, a column containing this formula returns the product numbers whose values will be sorted in descending order. The formula becomes easier to understand when it's broken into pieces. Here's what each piece means:
[1] General function: =LOOKUP(lookup_value,lookup_vector,result_vector). Find the value in the Total column belonging to the product number of the preceding product in this table.
[2] Create a temporary array containing all values in the TOTAL column that are less than the value found in [1].
[3] Find the largest value in the temporary array.
[4] General function: =MATCH(lookup_value,lookup_array,type_of_match). Find the value found in [3] in the Total column and return its row number within the array.
[5] General function: =INDEX(array,row_num,column_num). Return the product belonging in the row number found in [4].
First enter [1], which will return total sales for the product in cell A20. Then edit cell A21 and add [2], [3], and so on, getting each step to work before adding the next part of the formula. When you add [2], the formula becomes an array formula, so remember to enter it from that step on by holding down Ctrl and Shift while you press Enter. (Depending on your data, step [2] will often return the value FALSE, which may be correct for this step.) When you've entered all five steps, the formula will return the value shown in the spreadsheet in Figure 6-13.</td></tr>
<tr><td>O20</td><td>=SUM(C20:N20)</td></tr>
<tr><td>P20</td><td>=O20/O$24</td></tr>
<tr><td>Q20</td><td>=Q19+P20</td></tr>
<tr><td>A30</td><td>=A10</td></tr>
<tr><td>C30</td><td>=SUM(IF(Prod=$A30,IF(Month=C$28,Units)))
Enter this array formula by holding down Ctrl and Shift while you press Enter. Copy it as necessary.</td></tr>
<tr><td>O30</td><td>=SUM(C30:N30)</td></tr>
</table>

(continued)

Figure 6-13. *continued*

RANGE NAMES	
Name	***Formula***
Date	**=$A$5** All report headings that contain a date refer to this range name.
Product	**=$A$10:$A$12**
Total	**=$O$10:$O$12** Notice that these two ranges begin and end with cells containing data, not with the top and bottom borders. You must remember, therefore, to adjust the dimensions of the range if you insert rows of data at the very top or bottom of the table.
C.Data **C.Prod** **Cost** **Desc**	**=COSTS.XLS!C.Data** **=COSTS.XLS!C.Prod** **=COSTS.XLS!Cost** **=COSTS.XLS!Desc** These range names refer to range names within the COSTS file (Figure 6-15), which contains information about unit costs. To define the C.Data range as shown, first define the C.Data range within the COSTS spreadsheet. Next, from within this SLS_SUM.XLS spreadsheet, choose Formula Define Name, enter C.Data, press Tab, and in the Refers To box enter the formula shown in this range name box for C.Data. When you do so, be sure to enter the equal sign as well. Enter the other names similarly. (The names within the two spreadsheets don't have to match. But you will find them easier to remember if they do match.) Although each formula could refer directly to the appropriate file and range name, using the approach shown here has several advantages. First, formulas using range names in other spreadsheets are shorter, faster to write, and easier to understand. Second, when you substitute one source file for another, perhaps at the beginning of a new year, the formulas within this spreadsheet don't change; only their range-name definitions do. This allows the documentation for each formula within the spreadsheet to remain unchanged over the years.
Cust **Month** **Prod** **Sales** **Units**	**=SLS_JRNL.XLS!Cust** **=SLS_JRNL.XLS!Month** **=SLS_JRNL.XLS!Prod** **=SLS_JRNL.XLS!Sales** **=SLS_JRNL.XLS!Units** These range names refer to the file containing the sales journal for the year (Figure 6-14).

(continued)

Figure 6-13. *continued*

KEY CELL FORMATS			
Cell	***Number***	***Alignment***	***Font***
Sheet	**General**	**General**	**Helv 8**
A3	**General**	**General**	**Helv 10, Bold**
A9:A13	**#–###**	**Center**	**Helv 8**
B9:B13	**General**	**Left**	**Helv 8**
C9:O13	**#,##0**	**General**	**Helv 8**
P9:P13	**0%**	**General**	**Helv 8**
A14:O14	**#,##0**	**General**	**Helv 8**

Figure 6-14. Year-to-Date Sales Journal

A spreadsheet that supplies information for several sales summaries. Saved as SLS_JRNL.XLS.

	A	B	C	D	E	F	G
1							
2							
3	**Year-to-Date Sales Journal**					**1988**	
4	Janell's Fashion Supply						
5				Sales			
6	Month	Cust	Prod	Channel	Sales	Units	
8	Jan-88	Smith & Co	6-222	1	123	36,176	
9	Jan-88	Smith & Co	6-222	2	235	65,000	
10	Jan-88	Smith & Co	5-723	1	3,232	323	
11	Jan-88	Smith & Co	8-234	2	556	624	
12	Jan-88	Raster Ribbons	8-234	3	2,353	3,268	
13	Jan-88	Phoenix Threads	6-222	2	342	171,000	
14	Jan-88	Phoenix Threads	5-723	2	9,345	1,035	
15	Feb-88	Smith & Co	5-723	1	4,539	453	
16	Feb-88	Smith & Co	8-234	1	524	588	
17	Feb-88	Xavier's Hats	5-723	3	9,387	1,541	
18	Mar-88	Smith & Co	6-222	1	92	27,087	
19	Mar-88	Smith & Co	5-723	2	5,002	450	
20	Mar-88	Smith & Co	8-234	1	417	468	
21	Mar-88	Raster Ribbons	8-234	3	980	1,303	
22	Mar-88	Phoenix Threads	5-723	2	9,101	1,300	
24							
25							

RANGE NAMES

Name	*Formula*
Sales.Jrnl	**=$A$7:$F$23** This range refers to the entire sales-journal database.
Month	**=$A$7:$A$23**
Cust	**=$B$7:$B$23**
Prod	**=$C$7:$C$23**
Channel	**=$D$7:$D$23**
Sales	**=$E$7:$E$23**
Units	**=$F$7:$F$23** To assign these names, highlight the range A6:F23, choose the Formula Create command, and select Top.

Figure 6-15. Schedule of Unit Costs

A schedule of unit costs, also known as an item master. Saved as COSTS.XLS. For column widths and formats, see Figure 6-13.

	A	B	C	D
1				
2				
3	**Schedule of Unit Costs**			
4	Janell's Fashion Supply			
5	March, 1988			
6				
7	C.Prod	Desc	Cost	
8				
9	5723	Hats	4.92	
10	6222	Pins	0.0016	
11	8234	Yarn	0.15	
12				
13				
14				

RANGE NAMES	
Name	***Formula***
C.Data	**=$A$8:$C$12** This range references the entire costing database.
C.Prod **Desc** **Cost**	**=$A$8:$A$12** **=$B$8:$B$12** **=$C$8:$C$12** The easiest way to assign these names is to highlight the range A7:C12, choose the Formula Create command, and select Top.

Figure 6-16. Gross Profits by Product by Month

A report that helps analyze gross profits by month, a way of finding the products that are most important to the bottom line. For column widths, range names, and formats, see Figure 6-13.

	A	B	C	D	E	F	G	H	I	J	K	L	M	N	O	P	Q
37																	
38																	
39	**Sales Summary, Page Two**																
40	Janell's Fashion Supply																
41	Mar-88																
42																	
43	**Gross Profits by Product by Month**																
44	Product	Desc	Jan-88	Feb-88	Mar-88	Apr-88	May-88	Jun-88	Jul-88	Aug-88	Sep-88	Oct-88	Nov-88	Dec-88	Total	%	
46	5-723	Hats	5,896	4,116	5,493	0	0	0	0	0	0	0	0	0	15,504	79%	
47	6-222	Pins	265	0	49	0	0	0	0	0	0	0	0	0	313	2%	
48	8-234	Yarn	2,325	436	1,131	0	0	0	0	0	0	0	0	0	3,892	20%	
50	Total Dollars		8,485	4,551	6,673	0	0	0	0	0	0	0	0	0	19,710	100%	
51																	
52																	

KEY FORMULAS

Cell	*Formula*
A41	**=Date** All report headings that contain a date refer to the Date range name.
C46	**=SUM(IF(Prod=$A46,IF(Month=C$8,Sales–VLOOKUP($A46,C.Data,3)*Units)))** This formula, which calculates gross profits, demonstrates the power that array formulas can provide. The formula builds a temporary array that contains the gross profit for each sale of the product specified in column A during the month specified in row 8. After the correct rows of data are selected, the formula calculates the gross profit for each sale. It does so by finding each sale and subtracting the cost per unit multiplied by the total number of units sold. The total gross profit for all sales of the product in the month referenced is therefore equal to the sum of these individual gross profits, hence the SUM function that begins the formula. As always, enter this array formula by holding down Ctrl and Shift while you press Enter. Copy the formula to the remaining months and products as needed.

Figure 6-17. Distribution of Sales by Product

Two reports that show which products contribute the most to company sales during each month of the year. For column widths, range names, and formats, see Figure 6-13.

	A	B	C	D	E	F	G	H	I	J	K	L	M	N	O	P	Q
53																	
54																	
55	**Sales Summary, Page Three**																
56	Janell's Fashion Supply																
57	Mar-88																
58																	
59	**Distribution of Sales by Product--Product Sales as a Percentage of Total Monthly Sales**																
60	Product	Desc	Jan-88	Feb-88	Mar-88	Apr-88	May-88	Jun-88	Jul-88	Aug-88	Sep-88	Oct-88	Nov-88	Dec-88			
62	5-723	Hats	78%	96%	90%												
63	6-222	Pins	4%		1%												
64	8-234	Yarn	18%	4%	9%												
66	Total		100%	100%	100%												
67																	
68																	
69	**Distribution of Sales by Product--Monthly Sales by Product as a % of Total Sales by Product**																
70	Product	Desc	Jan-88	Feb-88	Mar-88	Apr-88	May-88	Jun-88	Jul-88	Aug-88	Sep-88	Oct-88	Nov-88	Dec-88	%		
72	5-723	Hats	31%	34%	35%										100%		
73	6-222	Pins	88%		12%										100%		
74	8-234	Yarn	60%	11%	29%										100%		
76	Total Sales		35%	31%	34%										100%		
77																	
78																	

KEY FORMULAS

Cell	*Formula*
C62	**=IF(OR(C$14=0,C10=0),"",C10/C$14)**
C72	**=IF(OR($O10=0,C10=0),"",C10/$O10)**

Both formulas return a blank under one of two conditions: First, when the percentage calculation would otherwise divide by 0, a blank keeps the formulas from returning divide-by-0 errors. Second, when the calculation would otherwise return a 0, a blank makes the remaining percentages easier to read.

Figure 6-18. Gross Profits, Gross-Profit Margins, and Sales Dollars by Customer by Month

Reports that analyze customer sales from different viewpoints, revealing which customers are most important to your bottom line. For column widths, range names, and formats, see Figure 6-13.

	A	B	C	D	E	F	G	H	I	J	K	L	M	N	O	P	Q
79																	
80																	
81	**Sales Summary, Page Four**																
82	Janell's Fashion Supply																
83	Mar-88																
84																	
85	**Sales Dollars by Customer by Month**																
86	Customer		Jan-88	Feb-88	Mar-88	Apr-88	May-88	Jun-88	Jul-88	Aug-88	Sep-88	Oct-88	Nov-88	Dec-88	Total	%	
87																	
88	Smith & Co		4,146	5,063	5,511	0	0	0	0	0	0	0	0	0	14,720	32%	
89	Raster Ribbons		2,353	0	980	0	0	0	0	0	0	0	0	0	3,333	7%	
90	Phoenix Threads		9,687	0	9,101	0	0	0	0	0	0	0	0	0	18,788	41%	
91	Xavier's Hats		0	9,387	0	0	0	0	0	0	0	0	0	0	9,387	20%	
92																	
93	Total Dollars		16,186	14,450	15,592	0	0	0	0	0	0	0	0	0	46,228	100%	
94																	
95																	
96	**Gross Profits by Customer by Month**																
97	Customer		Jan-88	Feb-88	Mar-88	Apr-88	May-88	Jun-88	Jul-88	Aug-88	Sep-88	Oct-88	Nov-88	Dec-88	Total	%	
98																	
99	Smith & Co		2,301	2,746	3,183	0	0	0	0	0	0	0	0	0	8,231	42%	
100	Raster Ribbons		1,863	0	785	0	0	0	0	0	0	0	0	0	2,647	13%	
101	Phoenix Threads		4,321	0	2,705	0	0	0	0	0	0	0	0	0	7,026	36%	
102	Xavier's Hats		0	1,805	0	0	0	0	0	0	0	0	0	0	1,805	9%	
103																	
104	Total Dollars		8,485	4,551	6,673	0	0	0	0	0	0	0	0	0	19,710	100%	
105																	
106																	
107	**Gross Profit Margins by Customer by Month**																
108	Customer		Jan-88	Feb-88	Mar-88	Apr-88	May-88	Jun-88	Jul-88	Aug-88	Sep-88	Oct-88	Nov-88	Dec-88	Avg		
109																	
110	Smith & Co		56%	54%	58%										56%		
111	Raster Ribbons		79%		80%										79%		
112	Phoenix Threads		45%		30%										37%		
113	Xavier's Hats			19%											19%		
114																	
115	All-Customer Average		52%	31%	43%										43%		
116																	
117																	

(continued)

Figure 6-18. *continued*

KEY FORMULAS	
Cell	***Formula***
C88	**=SUM(IF(Cust=$A88,IF(Month=C$86,Sales)))** This array formula is similar to previous ones. Copy it as necessary.
C99	**=SUM(IF(Cust=$A99,IF(Month=C$86,Sales–VLOOKUP(Prod,C.Data,3)*Units)))** The key formula in the report in Figure 6-16 returned gross profits by product by month. This array formula returns gross profits by customer. To create this formula easily, copy it from the previous report and then make the necessary alterations. As always, enter the formula by holding down Ctrl and Shift while pressing Enter.
C110	**=IF(C88*C99=0,"",C99/C88)** Like the percentage calculations in the report in Figure 6-17, this formula returns a blank whenever either the top or bottom number in the percentage calculation equals 0. Otherwise, the formula returns the company's gross profit margin by customer by month.

Figure 6-19. Average Unit Prices, Sales Dollars by Product, and Unit Sales by Product by Customer

Three pairs of reports that can reveal problems and opportunities in a sales organization. For column widths, range names, and formats, see Figure 6-13.

Sales Summary, Page Five
Janell's Fashion Supply
Mar-88

Year-to-Date Sales Dollars
By Product by Customer **March, 1988**

Customer	Pins 6-222	Hats 5-723	Yarn 8-234	Total	%
Smith & Co	450	12,773	1,497	14,720	32%
Raster Ribbons	0	0	3,333	3,333	7%
Phoenix Threads	342	18,446	0	18,788	41%
Xavier's Hats	0	9,387	0	9,387	20%
Total Dollars	792	40,606	4,830	46,228	100%

Monthly Sales Dollars
By Product by Customer **March, 1988**

Customer	Pins 6-222	Hats 5-723	Yarn 8-234	Total	%
Smith & Co	92	5,002	417	5,511	35%
Raster Ribbons	0	0	980	980	6%
Phoenix Threads	0	9,101	0	9,101	58%
Xavier's Hats	0	0	0	0	0%
Total Dollars	92	14,103	1,397	15,592	100%

Year-to-Date Unit Sales
By Product by Customer

Customer	Pins 6-222	Hats 5-723	Yarn 8-234
Smith & Co	128,263	1,226	1,680
Raster Ribbons	0	0	4,571
Phoenix Threads	171,000	2,335	0
Xavier's Hats	0	1,541	0
Total Dollars	299,263	5,102	6,251

Monthly Unit Sales
By Product by Customer

Customer	Pins 6-222	Hats 5-723	Yarn 8-234
Smith & Co	27,087	450	468
Raster Ribbons	0	0	1,303
Phoenix Threads	0	1,300	0
Xavier's Hats	0	0	0
Total Dollars	27,087	1,750	1,771

Average Unit Prices
By Customer--Year-to-Date

Customer	Pins 6-222	Hats 5-723	Yarn 8-234
Smith & Co	.0035	10.42	0.89
Raster Ribbons			0.73
Phoenix Threads	.0020	7.90	
Xavier's Hats		6.09	
Weighted Average	.0026	7.96	0.77

Average Unit Prices
By Customer--March, 1988

Customer	Pins 6-222	Hats 5-723	Yarn 8-234
Smith & Co	.0034	11.12	0.89
Raster Ribbons			0.75
Phoenix Threads		7.00	
Xavier's Hats			
Weighted Average	.0034	8.06	0.79

(continued)

Figure 6-19. *continued*

KEY FORMULAS	
Cell	***Formula***
G125	**=TEXT(Date,"mmmm, yyyy")** Notice that column D is about half the width necessary to display the month and year as a value. But if you change the value to text that is formatted correctly, you can display the date in more than one column. Also, notice in the format box that the cell is aligned to the right. This forces excess text to move into adjacent cells to the left.
D129	**=SUM(IF(Cust=$A129,IF(Prod=D$127,Sales)))** Because this array formula calculates year-to-date sales by customer, it doesn't select for the date as most of the previous array formulas in this chapter do.
G129	**=F129/F$134** Notice that this percentage calculation doesn't test for 0 values. If you add the names of customers that haven't yet purchased from you during the year, you must alter this formula to test for 0 values, as shown in the report in Figure 6-17.
L129	**=SUM(IF(Cust=$I129,IF(Prod=L$127,IF(Month=Date,Sales))))** This array formula tests for three conditions before summing sales. Even more conditions could be added.
O129	**=SUM(L129:N129)**
P129	**=O129/O$134** As in the formula for cell G129, this formula doesn't check for 0 values.
C142 **L142**	**=SUM(IF(Cust=$A142,IF(Prod=C$140,Units)))** **=SUM(IF(Cust=$A142,IF(Prod=L$140,IF(Month=Date,Units))))** Enter these array formulas as shown and copy them as necessary.
I151	**="By Customer--"&TEXT(Date,"mmmm, yyyy")** This formula displays text, with the current date properly formatted.
C155	**=IF(C142=0,"",C129/C142)**
C160	**=IF(C147=0,"",C134/C147)** This formula calculates the average price, weighting each sale by the number of units sold. Enter it by copying the formula from the preceding formula. To calculate the arithmetic average of the prices offered each customer, use this formula: =SUM(C141:C146)/COUNT(C141:C146).
L155	**=IF(L142=0,"",L129/L142)**
L160	**=IF(L147=0,"",L134/L147)**

Figure 6-20. Marketing Contribution by Channel of Distribution

A report that subtracts both product and marketing costs to calculate marketing contribution to profits.

	A	B	C	D	E	F	G	H	I	J	K
1											
2											
3											
4			Sales Channel Codes		1	2	3				
5											
6			**Marketing Contribution, by Channel of Distribution**								
7	Prod,		Janell's Fashion Supply								
8	Acct,		March, 1988								
9	& Dept						Mail				
10	Codes				Dealer	Distrib	Order	Total	%		
11	5-723		Sales	Hats	0	14,103	0	14,103	90%		
12	6-222			Pins	92	0	0	92	1%		
13	8-234			Yarn	417	0	980	1,397	9%		
14					509	14,103	980	15,592	100%		
15				% of sales	3%	90%	6%	100%			
16											
17											
18			Direct Costs	Cost of Sales	114	8,610	195	8,919	57%		
19	6631			Commissions	45	273	145	463	3%		
20	6635			Travel Expenses	0	291	0	291	2%		
21					159	9,174	340	9,673	62%		
22				% of total	2%	95%	4%	100%			
23				% of channel sales	31%	65%	35%	62%			
24											
25											
26			Marketing Contribution Margin		350	4,929	640	5,919	38%		
27				% of total	6%	83%	11%	100%			
28				% of channel sales	69%	35%	65%	38%			
29											
30											
31	8000		Indirect Selling Expenses					3,279	21%		
32											
33											
34											
35			Marketing Contribution to Profits					2,640	17%		
36											
37											
38											
39											
40											

COLUMN WIDTHS			
Column	*Width*	*Column*	*Width*
A	8.43	F	6.43
B	2.43	G	6.43
C	15.57	H	6.43
D	16.43	I	5
E	7.86	J	2.71

(continued)

Figure 6-20. *continued*

KEY FORMULAS	
Cell	***Formula***
C8	**3/1/88** Enter any date within the month that you want to report.
D11	**=VLOOKUP(A11,C.Data,2)** By looking up the product description, you save typing and assure yourself that you've entered the correct product code in column A.
E11	**=SUM(IF(MONTH(Month)=MONTH(Date),IF(Prod=$A11,IF(Channel=E$4,Sales))))** This array formula extracts data from the sales journal file. (You know it refers to the sales journal because the definitions for Month, Prod, Channel, and Sales all reference that spreadsheet.) The nested IF statements in this formula screen out all data in this file but the required data, which the SUM function totals. Copy this formula to the remainder of the Sales section as necessary.
H11 **I11** **E14**	**=SUM(E11:G11)** **=H11/H$14** **=SUM(E11:E13)** Enter these formulas as shown and copy them down the columns or across the row as necessary.
E18	**=SUM(IF(MONTH(Month)=MONTH(Date), IF(Channel=E$4,VLOOKUP(Prod,C.Data,3)*Units)))** This array formula selects sales from the correct month and product channel, looks up the cost of each product sold, and multiplies its cost by the number of units sold. Finally, the SUM function totals all appropriate costs. Copy the formula to the right as needed.
E19	**=SUM(IF($A19=GL.Acct,IF(E$4=GL.Chnl,GL.Amt)))** This array formula selects all expenses with the combined GL-account number and product channel required and then returns the sum of the amounts listed in the GL. (Selecting the proper month isn't necessary here because the GL spreadsheet contains only March expenses.) Copy this formula down and to the right as necessary.
H18	**=SUM(E18:G18)** Copy this formula down the column as needed.

(continued)

Figure 6-20. *continued*

KEY FORMULAS–continued	
Cell	***Formula***
E21	**=SUM(E18:E20)**
E22	**=E21/$H$21**
E23	**=E21/E14**
E26	**=E14–E21**
E27	**=E26/$H$26**
E28	**=E26/E14**
	Copy these formulas to the right as necessary.
A31	**8000**
	This company, like many, assigns department numbers to major departments in blocks of 1000. Numbers for the Marketing and Sales Department fall in the range 8000–8999.
H31	**=SUM(IF(GL.Dept>=A31,IF(GL.Dept<1000+A31,GL.Amt)))–H21+H18**
	Indirect selling expenses are equal to all selling expenses minus direct selling expenses. This array formula first finds all selling expenses by summing all expenses in the range 8000–8999. And then, to calculate indirect selling expenses, it subtracts all direct expenses and adds back the cost of goods sold, which is not a selling expense.
H35	**=H26–H31**

(continued)

Figure 6-20. *continued*

RANGE NAMES		
Name	***Formula***	
Date	**=$C$8**	
C.Data	**=COSTS.XLS!C.Data**	**Figure 6-15**
C.Prod	**=COSTS.XLS!C.Prod**	"
Cost	**=COSTS.XLS!Cost**	"
GL.Acct	**=GL.XLS!GL.Acct**	**Figure 6-21**
GL.Amt	**=GL.XLS!GL.Amt**	"
GL.Chnl	**=GL.XLS!GL.Chnl**	"
GL.Data	**=GL.XLS!GL.Data**	"
Channel	**=SLS_JRNL.XLS!Month**	**Figure 6-14**
Month	**=SLS_JRNL.XLS!Month**	"
Prod	**=SLS_JRNL.XLS!Prod**	"
Sales	**=SLS_JRNL.XLS!Sales**	"
Units	**=SLS_JRNL.XLS!Units**	"
	These range names link three other spreadsheets to this report. To create these names, enter them as shown. But when you do so, use lowercase letters. Here's why: If Microsoft Excel recognizes the files you specify, your dialog box displays their names in uppercase when you choose the Formula Define command and then select the name you've just defined.	

KEY CELL FORMATS			
Cell	***Number***	***Alignment***	***Font***
C6	**General**	**General**	**Helv 10, Bold**
C8	**mmmm, yyyy**	**Left**	**Helv 10**
A11:A13	**#-###**	**Center**	**Helv 10**
E11:H35	**#,##0**	**General**	**Helv 10**
I11:I35	**0%**	**General**	**Helv 10**

Figure 6-21. Partial General Ledger

A general ledger table that provides information for the marketing-contribution report shown in Figure 6-20. Saved as GL.XLS.

	A	B	C	D	E
1					
2					
3	**Partial General Ledger--March, 1988.**				
4					
5	GL.Acct	GL.Dept	GL.Amt	GL.Chnl	
6					
7	6101	8000	1,200	0	
8	6105	8120	975	0	
9	6120	8120	153	0	
10	6342	8120	382	0	
11	6631	8131	45	1	
12	6631	8132	273	2	
13	6631	8133	145	3	
14	6635	8202	56	2	
15	6635	8312	235	2	
16	6711	8121	19	1	
17	6722	8350	550	0	
18					
19					
20					

KEY FORMULA

Cell	*Formula*
D7	**=IF(INT(0.001*B7)<>8,0,B7–10*INT(0.1*B7))** This company's marketing department uses the last digit of each of their department numbers (those beginning with 8) to specify the marketing channel to which an expense belongs. They use a 0 in the last digit for other expenses. This formula returns a 0 for all departments not beginning with 8; otherwise, it returns the last digit of each department number.

RANGE NAMES

Name	*Formula*
GL.Data	**=$A$6:$D$18** Use the Formula Define Name command to create this name.
GL.Acct	**=$A$6:$A$18**
GL.Dept	**=$B$6:$B$18**
GL.Amt	**=$C$6:$C$18**
GL.Chnl	**=$D$6:$D$18** To create these names, highlight the range A5:D18, choose the Formula Create command, select Top, and then press Enter.

Figure 6-22. Hourly Sales Recap by Checkstand

A form that tracks hourly sales by checkstand and serves as both a manual-input form and a computer-entry form. Saved as HRLY_SLS.XLS.

	A	B	C	D	E	F	G	H	I	J	K	L	M	N	O
1															
2								**Hourly Sales Recap**							
3								Johnson's Drugstore							
4															
5	Date:		9/1/88	Checkstand Numbers											
6	Store:		23	1	2	3	4	5	6	7	8	9	10	Total	
8		8:00 AM	Customers	20	7	19								46	
9	1	to	Sales $	123	27	129								279	
10		8:59 AM	Staffing*	3	3	3								9	
12		9:00 AM	Customers	10	8	2								20	
13	2	to	Sales $	40	56	3								99	
14		9:59 AM	Staffing*	2	2	0								4	
16		10:00 AM	Customers	23	42	18	5							88	
17	3	to	Sales $	125	173	80	8							386	
18		10:59 AM	Staffing*	3	3	3	0							9	
20		11:00 AM	Customers												
21	4	to	Sales $												
22		11:59 AM	Staffing*												
24		12:00 PM	Customers												
25	5	to	Sales $												
26		12:59 PM	Staffing*												
28		1:00 PM	Customers												
29	6	to	Sales $												
30		1:59 PM	Staffing*												
32		2:00 PM	Customers												
33	7	to	Sales $												
34		2:59 PM	Staffing*												
36		3:00 PM	Customers												
37	8	to	Sales $												
38		3:59 PM	Staffing*												
40		4:00 PM	Customers												
41	9	to	Sales $												
42		4:59 PM	Staffing*												
44		5:00 PM	Customers												
45	10	to	Sales $												
46		5:59 PM	Staffing*												
48		6:00 PM	Customers												
49	11	to	Sales $												
50		6:59 PM	Staffing*												
52															
53	***Staffing Codes--Cashier checking with:**														
54		0--No clerk helpers bagging.													
55		1--One clerk helper bagging one checkstand.													
56		2--A clerk helper bagging two checkstands.													
57		3--A clerk helper bagging three checkstands.													

(continued)

Figure 6-22. *continued*

COLUMN WIDTHS							
Column	*Width*	*Column*	*Width*	*Column*	*Width*	*Column*	*Width*
A	2.43	E	5	I	5	M	5
B	8.43	F	5	J	5	N	8.43
C	9.57	G	5	K	5		
D	5	H	5	L	5		

ROW HEIGHTS	
Row	*Height*
7	1
11	1

KEY FORMULAS	
Cell	*Formula*
A8	8 This value determines the starting time in column B. To open at 10 AM, for example, enter 10 in this cell. To hide this value, as is shown in the spreadsheet, format the cell as shown in the format box.
A9 A13	1 =1+A9 This column labels successive hours the store is open.
B8	=TIME($A$8–1+A9,0,0)
B10	=TIME($A$8+A9,–1,0) The general format for these functions is =TIME(hour,minute,second). The hour is determined by the value in column A.
N8	=SUM(D8:M8) This formula totals each row of data in the input form. If you manually calculate a similar total before entering the handwritten input forms, the computer total provides a check figure that can catch data-input errors. Notice that the number format for this column returns a blank when this formula equals 0. Therefore, when the form contains no data, a printout of this spreadsheet can serve as an input form for manual data entry.

(continued)

Figure 6-22. *continued*

RANGE NAME	
Name	*Formula*
Data	=$A$8:$M$51 After you enter the day's information into the spreadsheet in Figure 6-22, the formulas in the spreadsheet in Figure 6-23 extract information from this range.

KEY CELL FORMATS			
Cell	*Number*	*Alignment*	*Font*
H2	General	Center	Helv 10, Bold
A8	;;	Center	Helv 10
A9:A51	General	Center	Helv 10
B8:B51	h:mm AM/PM	Center	Helv 10
C8:C51	General	Center	Helv 10
D8:M51	#,##0 ;(#,##0)	General	Helv 10
N8:N51	#,##0 ;(#,##0);	General	Helv 10
C64	m/d/yy	Center	Helv 10

Figure 6-23. Hourly Sales Recap in Database Format

A form that converts the hourly sales information generated by the form in Figure 6-22 into a database format. For column widths, range name, and formats, see Figure 6-22.

	A	B	C	D	E	F	G	H	I	J
59										
60										
61		**Hourly Sales Recap in Database Format**								
62					Check				Row	
63		Seq	Date	Hour	Stand	Cust	Sales	Staff	Used	
64		1	9/1/88	8	1	20	123	0.333	1	
65		2	9/1/88	8	2	7	27	0.333	1	
66		3	9/1/88	8	3	19	129	0.333	1	
67		4	9/1/88	8	4	0	0	0	0	
68		5	9/1/88	8	5	0	0	0	0	
69		6	9/1/88	8	6	0	0	0	0	
70		7	9/1/88	8	7	0	0	0	0	
71		8	9/1/88	8	8	0	0	0	0	
72		9	9/1/88	8	9	0	0	0	0	
73		10	9/1/88	8	10	0	0	0	0	
74		11	9/1/88	9	1	10	40	0.5	1	
75		12	9/1/88	9	2	8	56	0.5	1	
76		13	9/1/88	9	3	2	3	0	1	
77		14	9/1/88	9	4	0	0	0	0	
169		106	9/1/88	18	6	0	0	0	0	
170		107	9/1/88	18	7	0	0	0	0	
171		108	9/1/88	18	8	0	0	0	0	
172		109	9/1/88	18	9	0	0	0	0	
173		110	9/1/88	18	10	0	0	0	0	
174										
175										
176										

(continued)

Figure 6-23. *continued*

KEY FORMULAS	
Cell	***Formula***
B64 **B65**	**1** **=1+B64** This sequence number guides the remaining formulas in this spreadsheet to find the proper values. It counts from 1 to the product of hours open and the number of checkstands. In the spreadsheet, for example, it counts from 1 to 110 (11 x 10).
C64	**=$C$5** Each date value repeats the date entered in the spreadsheet in Figure 6-22.
D64	**=HOUR(INDEX(Data,INT(($B64–1)/10)*4+1,2))** This formula converts each hour's beginning time into an integer value. The general format of the INDEX formula is =INDEX(array,row_num,column_num). Finding the row number is the most complex part of this formula. To do so, the INT (integer) function finds the number of times that 10 (the number of checkstands) divides completely into the sequence number. Then, to find the number of rows from the top of the Data range, this value is multiplied by 4 and increased by 1. The first hour, for example, contains sequence numbers 1 through 10. Any of these values, minus 1, divided by 10, and taking the integer of the result, equals 0. Adding 1 assigns the first row of the Data range. The second hour uses sequence numbers 11 through 20. Any of these values, minus 1, divided by 10, and taking the integer of the result, equals 1. Multiplying by 4 and adding 1 yields the fifth row of the Data range, where the second time value can be found.
E64	**=MOD($B64–1,10)+1** The modulus function finds the remainder after dividing by a value. Here, the function divides the sequence number, –1, by the number of checkstands, returning the checkstand number. For example, sequence number 1, minus 1, divided by 10 has a remainder of 0; adding 1 yields checkstand 1. Sequence number 2, minus 1, divided by 10, has a remainder of 1; adding 1 returns checkstand number 2. Similarly, sequence number 12, minus 1, divided by 10, leaves a remainder of 1; adding 1 returns checkstand number 2.
F64 **G64**	**=INDEX(Data,INT(($B64–1)/10)*4+1,3+$E64)** **=INDEX(Data,INT(($B64–1)/10)*4+2,3+$E64)** These formulas perform much like the INDEX function in column D to return the appropriate values.

(continued)

Figure 6-23. *continued*

KEY FORMULAS–continued	
Cell	***Formula***
H64	**=IF(INDEX(Data,INT(($B64–1)/10)*4+3,3+$E64)=0,0, 1/INDEX(Data,INT(($B64–1)/10)*4+3,3+$E64))** This formula divides each staff code into the value 1 to find the approximate number of clerk helpers that were used during the hour. Because dividing by 0 would produce an error, the formula returns a 0 if that is the value found; otherwise, it returns the result of the division.
I64	**=(SUM(F64:H64)>0)+0** This formula converts the data to a format that can be copied to a database. There is no need, however, to copy data for checkstands that weren't used in the hour. This column of formulas returns the value 1 if the checkstand has been used; otherwise, it returns a 0. To do so, it uses a logical formula that checks to see if the sum of the sales data is greater than 0. If so, it returns the value 1; otherwise, it returns 0. (If the value 0 weren't added in the formula, it would return the values TRUE and FALSE instead of 1 and 0.) After all data is entered and this column is calculated, you can sort the data for all active checkstands to the top of the spreadsheet. To do so, simply sort this column in descending order. After the data is sorted, copy the values of the active data to a separate database spreadsheet.

Figure 6-24. New Product Sales History

A spreadsheet that helps you predict how new products will sell, based on how past products have sold immediately after introduction.

	A	B	C	D	E	F
1						
2						
3	**New Product Sales History by Model Number**					
4	For the First 12 Months After Introduction					
5						
6	**Dollar Sales**					
7	**Prod**	**8220A**	**85F**	**64-40**	**1620**	
9	**Month**	Feb-82	Aug-84	Jun-86	Nov-87	
11	1	286	3,656	29,123	21,265	
12	2	14,533	9,183	109,435	15,574	
13	3	6,879	28,826	62,833	11,275	
14	4	2,911	10,992	7,846	9,039	
15	5	3,955	50,219	(4,522)	10,741	
16	6	4,765	75,078	(24,853)	13,166	
17	7	5,571	112,581	(1,287)	11,790	
18	8	7,325	104,878		15,236	
19	9	9,767	121,738	(453)	17,043	
20	10	10,829	84,453		12,238	
21	11	20,355	149,849	(89)	12,261	
22	12	37,484	175,129		14,776	
23	Total	124,660	926,582	178,033	164,404	
24						
25						
26	**Unit Sales**					
27	**Prod**	**8220A**	**85F**	**64-40**	**1620**	
29	1	8	42	1,533	1,772	
30	2	415	106	5,760	1,298	
31	3	197	331	3,307	940	
32	4	83	126	413	753	
33	5	113	577	(238)	895	
34	6	136	863	(1,308)	1,097	
35	7	159	1,294	(68)	983	
36	8	209	1,205	0	1,270	
37	9	279	1,194	(24)	1,420	
38	10	309	828	0	1,020	
39	11	485	1,469	(5)	1,022	
40	12	892	1,717	0	1,231	
41	Total	3,285	9,752	9,370	13,701	
42						
43	**Average Prices**					
44	Mo 1	35.75	87.05	19.00	12.00	
45	Mo 12	42.02	102.00	0.00	12.00	
46						
47						

(continued)

Figure 6-24. *continued*

KEY FORMULAS	
Cell	***Formula***
B23	**=SUM(B11:B22)**
B41	**=SUM(B29:B40)**
B44	**=IF(B29=0,0,B11/B29)**
B45	**=IF(B40=0,0,B22/B40)**
Copy these formulas across the row as needed.	

Figure 6-25. Sales History by Product

A sales history of a product, revealing problems and opportunities that standard financial statements might hide.

	A	B	C	D	E	F	G	H	I	J	K	L
1												
2												
3	**SALES HISTORY ($1000)**									**Model X295 Table Saw**		
4		1981	1982	1983	1984	1985	1986	1987	1988	1989	1990	
5	July		959	1,217	1,636	2,016	2,223	2,264	2,039	1,836	1,653	
6	August		1,478	1,991	2,368	3,088	3,357	3,551	3,065	2,904	2,721	
7	September		1,785	2,425	3,381	3,741	4,279	4,791	4,096	3,483	3,191	
8	October		2,517	3,300	4,259	5,527	5,671	5,910	5,119	5,020		
9	November		2,722	3,702	5,183	5,679	7,019	6,224	5,645	5,045		
10	December		2,747	3,971	4,941	6,091	6,951	6,513	6,379	5,304		
11	January		437	568	863	1,084	1,097	1,179	1,114	997		
12	February	1,029	963	1,295	1,610	1,871	2,140	2,080	1,957	1,898		
13	March	882	1,456	1,675	2,697	3,071	3,534	3,714	3,295	2,941		
14	April	822	845	1,311	1,609	2,079	2,243	2,273	2,107	1,758		
15	May	1,058	474	629	894	1,084	1,136	1,121	943	891		
16	June	851	467	566	797	1,043	1,106	1,163	952	980		
17	Total	4,642	16,850	22,650	30,238	36,374	40,756	40,783	36,711	33,057	7,565	
18												
19	**SALES HISTORY (Units)**									**Model X295 Table Saw**		
20		1981	1982	1983	1984	1985	1986	1987	1988	1989	1990	
21	July		2,863	3,409	3,868	3,984	4,680	5,241	4,973	5,216	5,182	
22	August		4,412	5,577	5,598	6,103	7,067	8,220	7,476	8,250	8,530	
23	September		5,328	6,793	7,993	7,393	9,008	11,090	9,990	9,895	10,003	
24	October		7,513	9,244	10,069	10,923	11,939	13,681	12,485	14,261		
25	November		8,125	10,370	12,253	11,223	14,777	14,407	13,768	14,332		
26	December		8,200	11,123	11,681	12,038	14,634	15,076	15,559	15,068		
27	January		1,304	1,591	2,040	2,142	2,309	2,729	2,717	2,832		
28	February	3,430	2,875	3,627	3,806	3,698	4,505	4,815	4,773	5,392		
29	March	2,940	4,346	4,692	6,376	6,069	7,440	8,597	8,037	8,355		
30	April	2,740	2,522	3,672	3,804	4,109	4,722	5,262	5,139	4,994		
31	May	3,527	1,415	1,762	2,113	2,142	2,392	2,595	2,300	2,531		
32	June	2,837	1,394	1,585	1,884	2,061	2,328	2,692	2,322	2,784		
33	Total	15,474	50,297	63,445	71,485	71,885	85,801	94,405	89,539	93,910	23,715	
34												
35	Avg Price	300	335	357	423	506	475	432	410	352	319	
36												
37												

COLUMN WIDTHS			
Column	*Width*	*Column*	*Width*
A	11.14	G	7.57
B	6.14	H	7.57
C	7	I	7.57
D	7	J	7.57
E	7	K	8.29
F	7		

(continued)

Figure 6-25. *continued*

KEY FORMULAS	
Cell	*Formula*
B4	7/1/81
C4	=DATE(YEAR(B4)+1,1,1)
A5	=$B$4
A6	=DATE(YEAR(A5),MONTH(A5)+1,1)
B17	=SUM(B5:B16)
B20	=B$4
A21	=A5
B33	=SUM(B21:B32)
B35	=ROUND(1000*(B17/B33),0)
Enter these formulas as shown and copy them as necessary across the rows or columns.	

KEY CELL FORMATS			
Cell	*Number*	*Alignment*	*Font*
A3	General	General	Helv 10, Bold
K3	General	Right	Helv 10, Bold
B4:K4	yyyy	Center	Helv 10
A5:A16	mmmm	Left	Helv 10
B5:K17	#,##0 ;(#,##0)	General	Helv 10

7

Sales and Expense Forecasting

This chapter combines sophisticated spreadsheet and statistical techniques to present several different approaches to sales and expense forecasting. Many readers will find it to be the most exciting and challenging chapter in this book.

One of the most common theories in business is that of fixed and variable costs. Unfortunately, the theory often falls apart when businesses try to apply it to the reality of their actual expenses. After all, to determine the fixed and variable components of each of hundreds of cost categories in the general ledger, businesses must perform a regression analysis on each expense. Performing such an analysis simply wasn't practical—until now. This chapter shows you how to create a spreadsheet that can simultaneously analyze each of your expenses by using simple regression analysis, and it shows you how to create a similar spreadsheet for multiple regression analysis.

Sales forecasting offers another common application of multiple regression analysis. In the past, however, only businesses that had access to statistical software programs could generate the full set of statistics that most analysts need. This chapter shows you how to create a spreadsheet that generates these statistics.

Time-series analysis is another common method of sales forecasting. To use it, you analyze past sales to determine the seasonal variations, a trend, and an economic cycle, and then use these facts to forecast future sales. This chapter presents a system of spreadsheets that generates exactly such an analysis and forecast.

On the other hand, the first application in this chapter uses no statistics at all. Even so, it presents surprising challenges.

LINKING PRICES, UNITS, AND SALES DOLLAR FORECASTS

The task sounds simple. You have one spreadsheet that contains your unit-sales forecast for each month of the next year. You have a second spreadsheet that contains the unit prices you expect to charge during each month of the year. All you want is a third spreadsheet that contains dollar sales by product by month.

If the two spreadsheets have exactly the same format, the task *is* simple: Copy one of the spreadsheets to the other using the Multiply option in the Paste Special dialog box. Unfortunately, this seldom is a feasible solution.

In the real world, there isn't only one set of prices and one unit forecast; there might be dozens. There might be at least one forecast for each sales region, and forecasts for each what-if scenario. Often, many of these forecasts include products the others lack. There might be different price lists and discount schedules. In the last-minute madness to get forecasts done, the products in each schedule usually are in the most convenient order, without reference to products in other schedules. Forecasting isn't pretty.

The spreadsheet in Figure 7-1 on page 324 contains a price list for each month of a forecast; the spreadsheet in Figure 7-2 on page 325 contains the unit forecast for a new year; and the spreadsheet in Figure 7-3 on page 326 multiplies the appropriate prices and quantities to return the sales dollar forecast for each product during the year. Notice that these schedules are in no particular order and that the schedule of prices contains a product missing from the other two schedules.

The formula that returns the dollar sales forecast in each cell of the spreadsheet in Figure 7-3 is simply =Prices*Units. The range definitions in the three spreadsheets do all the work of finding the right prices and the right units for each of these cells.

Creating Pricing and Units Schedules

To create the schedules of prices and units, open two new spreadsheets. Save one of these as PRICES.XLS and the other as UNITS.XLS. In each, turn off the gridlines and set the recalculation mode to manual. Enter the labels, values, and formats shown in the spreadsheet in Figure 7-1 and Figure 7-2. Cell D6 of the spreadsheet in Figure 7-2 contains the formula =SUM(B6:C6). Enter this formula and copy it down the column as necessary.

Define the names shown in the range-name box for each figure. Notice that each of these names is anchored to a range that expands as your data expands. As you insert rows to add products, the shaded borders still define the top and bottom of the range names. As you add months to the right of February, column D moves to the right in both spreadsheets, expanding the range definitions as needed.

Creating a Sales Forecast

To create the sales forecast, open a new spreadsheet and save it as SALES_A.XLS. Turn off its gridlines and then enter the labels and borders shown in rows 7 through 14.

The range-name box for Figure 7-3 defines the range names used in this spreadsheet. Enter the first six of these using the Formula Define Name command.

The definitions of the Prices and Units names are actually formulas. The easiest way to enter these is to first enter them as formulas in the spreadsheet and then to copy the formulas to the Formula Define Name dialog box. To do so, begin with the Prices formula. Select cell B10 of the spreadsheet in Figure 7-3 and enter the formula shown for the Prices range definition. When you do so, the formula returns the value 2, which is January's price for Washers shown in the spreadsheet in Figure 7-1. Copy this formula to cell C11, and it returns the value 5, which is February's price for Nuts.

Define the name Prices using a copy of the formula as a range definition. Here's how to do this:

1. Select cell B10, which displays in the formula bar the formula you want to copy.
2. Highlight the entire formula in the bar.
3. Press Ctrl-Ins, which copies this formula to the clipboard. When you do so, a marquee does not appear; there is no indication that a copy has been made. But it has.
4. Press Esc to return to the Ready mode.
5. Choose Formula Define Name and enter the range name *Prices.*
6. Press Tab to highlight the Refers To box.
7. With your mouse, choose the Edit Paste command. (Yes, you can access this menu sequence while the Formula Define Name dialog box is active.) When you do so, the program pastes the Prices formula from the clipboard into the Refers To box. Press Enter.

After you define the name Prices, use cell B10 to develop the Units formula. If you compare the two formula definitions in the range-name box for Figure 7-3, you can see that you can create the Units formula simply by substituting U for P in the range names used by the Prices formula. After you create the Units formula, define the range name Units just as you did the range name Prices.

To complete the spreadsheet in Figure 7-3, enter the formula =Prices*Units in cell B10. When you do so, the program returns the value shown in the spreadsheet. Choose the Edit Paste Special command and select Formulas to copy this formula to the range B10:C12. Enter the SUM formulas shown for cells D10 and B14 in the formulas box and copy them down the column and across the row as needed.

Adding File-Selection Capability to the Sales Forecast

Figure 7-4 on page 328 shows a modified version of the sales forecast. This version lets you enter names in cells C4 and C5 to specify which units and pricing files the forecast should use. Suppose, for example, that the file UNITS2 contained an alternative units forecast. To have the spreadsheet in Figure 7-4 report the dollar values for these shipments, enter the label *Units2* in cell C4 and recalculate.

To change the forecast in Figure 7-3 into the forecast in Figure 7-4, first save your SALES_A.XLS file as SALES_B.XLS. Enter the labels and borders shown in rows 3 through 5 of the forecast in Figure 7-4.

The Scratch Formulas section of the forecast in Figure 7-4 contains new formulas used to define the six range names shown in columns A and C of this section. Enter the labels shown in these two columns and the border surrounding the section.

The range-name box for Figure 7-4 shows all formula definitions used in this spreadsheet. The definitions for FileP and FileU are new; enter them as shown. The six definitions that follow these names represent the major change to the spreadsheet. The range-name box explains the formulas and describes how to enter them quickly.

Using the Sales-Forecast Spreadsheet for Real Data

To expand the spreadsheet in Figure 7-1 through Figure 7-4 to hold 12 months of data, simply insert the appropriate number of columns in each, adding column headings and data as needed. When you do so, all range names expand as necessary. However, you have to modify the SUM formulas in the three Total columns. Without modification, these formulas continue to return the totals for only the first two columns of data.

In actual use, the spreadsheet in Figure 7-4 may take several minutes to recalculate when you press the F9 (Calculate All) key while you're in the manual calculation mode. In some applications, you will find that the spreadsheet calculates more quickly if you switch to the automatic calculation mode, let it recalculate, and then switch back to the manual mode. Or you may find that the automatic mode works just fine in your application. Experiment with all three approaches.

FORECASTING EXPENSES WITH LINEAR REGRESSION

Often during the year, you need to know how expenses tend to vary in response to the major activities within your firm:

- You want to perform a break-even analysis and therefore need an estimate of fixed and variable costs.
- You are budgeting for the new year and need a set of baseline-expense figures. These are the expenses you probably will incur if past spending trends continue. Managers will alter these baseline numbers in response to the operating changes they expect in the new year.
- Actual expenses have begun to behave differently than you expected at the first of the year. You decide to analyze all expenses to see where the major changes in behavior have occurred and what actions you must take to correct the problems you find.

Linear and multiple regression techniques are excellent tools for analyzing expenses. By regressing expenses against sales and other major cost drivers in your company, you can identify cost relationships that will probably continue in the future. (If you need to brush up on regression, you can turn to the short bibliography on the subject at the end of this chapter.)

A regression equation can be an early warning device. "If current trends continue," the regression equation may imply, "here's the mess you're going to be in next year at this time." And at times, it can pinpoint the results of management action. "Because you reorganized the shipping and receiving departments," it might reveal, "your costs are rising faster with respect to sales."

In the past, most software has treated each set of regression calculations as a major event requiring much thought and analysis. In the past, therefore, you could spend a career analyzing the several hundred expense accounts that a typical business has in its general ledger. But today, Microsoft Excel provides an easy way to analyze all your expense accounts at one time in one spreadsheet.

Regression Statistics

Figure 7-5 on page 330 shows a spreadsheet that contains a linear regression analysis of each expense account in the company's general ledger. The analysis provides the following information:

The constant and slope of the regression equation. In row 7, for example, the regression equation says that janitorial expenses in any month should equal $888 plus 0.00002 times sales for the month; in row 8, freight equals $1,550 plus 0.03871 times sales for the month.

The R-squared. The coefficient of determination, or R-squared, shows the percentage of the total squared deviations from the mean that are explained by the regression equation. For example, only 1 percent of the squared deviations in the janitorial expenses are explained by the regression equation, but 95 percent of the squared deviations in freight costs are explained by sales.

The F statistic. This statistic tests the overall significance of a regression model. In simple linear regression, F equals $t^2$2, where t is the t statistic that appears in column G. But unlike the t statistic, the F statistic has two numbers for its degrees of freedom (df). The degrees of freedom for the numerator (the first number in cell F5) equals the number of independent variables. In simple linear regression, this value is always equal to 1. The degrees of freedom for the denominator equals the number of observations (in this example, months) minus the total number of dependent and independent variables, including the constant term. In Figure 7-5, therefore, this value is equal to 3 (5 months minus 2).

The importance of knowing the degrees of freedom is that this information allows you to test the significance of a model by looking up the critical values for the F distribution in a table found in most introductory statistics books. Such a table, for example, will tell you that at the 95 percent confidence level and with degrees of freedom of 1 and 3, F must equal at least 10.128 for the model to be significant.

(Yes, it *does* seem primitive these days to have to look up the critical value of F in a table. But unfortunately, calculating the value is no easy task.)

The t statistic. Student's t statistic was developed by William S. Gosset, a brewmaster, who first published it in 1908, using the pen name "Student." Used for very small samples, it provides a measure of the confidence you should have that the coefficient belongs in the regression equation.

The critical value of the t statistic depends on the degrees of freedom and the level of confidence required. The degrees of freedom for a t statistic equals the number of observations minus the total number of variables. In the spreadsheet in Figure 7-5, each regression equation uses five observations (months) in the analysis. Linear regression uses two variables, the X and the Y. Therefore, the t calculation for the spreadsheet in Figure 7-5 has 3 (5 minus 2) degrees of freedom.

As a rule of thumb, the t statistic must be greater than 2 for the coefficient to be significant. To be more exact, you can find the critical value in a table in most introductory statistics books. For example, because each calculation in the spreadsheet in Figure 7-5 has 3 degrees of freedom, this table will tell you that for the coefficient to be significant, the t value should exceed 2.353 at a 95 percent confidence level.

In the example spreadsheet, only the equations for freight, travel, and training have t values greater than 2.353 and F values greater than 10.1. You can say with confidence, therefore, that you've identified a significant relationship between variations in sales and the variations in these expenses. The other expenses do not show this relationship; factors other than sales must influence their behavior.

Errors in the Regression Statistics

The regression statistics display error values in row 13 and a 0 in each cell in row 14. The causes of both problems are common within a business:

- Array formulas return #VALUE! error values when they try to work with cells containing blanks, as in the range C13:F13. To correct this problem, simply enter a 0 in each of the blank cells, J13 and M13.
- Each cell in the range I14:M14 contains the same value, which often causes problems for regression formulas. Because the variance is 0 in these circumstances, several of the calculations return #DIV/0 (division by 0) error values. To solve this problem, the formulas in columns E through G return a 0 whenever all values in Y are equal.

How to Use the Linear Regression Spreadsheet

To use the spreadsheet shown in Figure 7-5, first sort it in descending order by the F value and then insert a row at the dividing line between the significant and insignificant F statistics. The spreadsheet in Figure 7-6 on page 332 shows the result.

As a means of analysis, this spreadsheet can help you to better understand the behavior of your costs. In Figure 7-6, for example, notice that training costs are negatively correlated with sales. As sales increase, in other words, training costs go down. The reason for this phenomenon is obvious: The busier people become, the less time they take for training.

As a forecasting tool, this spreadsheet can help you forecast many of your costs. You can forecast those costs found above the blank row by using the regression equation shown in columns C and D. In the future, for example, travel costs for the month can be estimated at $1,031 plus 0.01886 times the expected sales for the month. You must use other methods, however, to forecast those costs below the blank row. You might, for example, try multiple regression analysis, which is described later in this chapter.

This spreadsheet can also help you identify fixed and variable costs. Variable costs, those that vary with sales, are equal to the sum of the slope values above the blank row. Fixed costs are equal to the sum of the constant values above the blank row plus an estimate of the average monthly expenses below the blank row. Total costs, therefore, will be equal to fixed costs plus the quantity of variable costs times sales.

Creating a Variable-Expense Analysis

To create the spreadsheet in Figure 7-5, open a new spreadsheet, turn off the gridlines, and set the calculation mode to manual. Enter the entire spreadsheet as shown, with the exception of cells F5 and G5 and the range C7:G14; these are the only cells that contain formulas.

Before you enter the range definitions shown in the range-name box for Figure 7-5, you might want to read Appendix C on defining dynamic ranges. Appendix C explains why you frequently use index formulas to define range names.

Define the range names as shown in the range-name box for Figure 7-5, and then enter the formulas shown in the formula box. The formulas calculate only four of many statistics that are commonly calculated when doing linear regression analysis. Appendix D of this book presents a general summary of the formulas you can use to calculate these statistics. Most introductory statistics books include a chapter on linear regression that explains the theory behind these formulas.

Entering Your Own Data

To enter your own data, first open a spreadsheet that contains your general ledger trial balance. (If you don't have such a spreadsheet, you probably won't need to enter it by hand. Appendix A describes how to transfer this information from your accounting system into a spreadsheet.)

Copy the expense descriptions and account numbers from your general ledger trial balance to your version of the spreadsheet in Figure 7-5. Insert the number of columns necessary between columns H and N and then enter the appropriate date titles in row 5 of the spreadsheet.

Copy the monthly expenses from your trial balance to the appropriate columns of your version of the spreadsheet in Figure 7-5. Then, when all columns of data are in place, copy the statistics formulas from any convenient row down columns C through G as necessary. Clean up the borders and shading and then save your spreadsheet.

After you create a spreadsheet containing your own data, try speeding its recalculation time by moving the definition for the range name Sxx into the spreadsheet. Appendix E of this book discusses the reason for this change. If this change markedly improves your spreadsheet's recalculation time, leave the definition in your spreadsheet. Otherwise, your spreadsheet will be less cluttered if you copy the formula definition for this variable back into the Formula Define Name dialog box.

FORECASTING SALES WITH MULTIPLE REGRESSION

Many companies find that their sales are strongly affected by economic conditions. For example, the sales of machine tools are greatly affected by the opinions of corporate officers about the future direction of the economy—there's little reason to tool up if you expect sales to fall. And if you sell electronic controls for machine tools, a drop in capital-goods orders means a drop in your orders as well.

Seldom, however, does only one economic statistic dominate the fate of an industry. Even if capital-goods orders plummet, customers might continue to buy, either to replace older controls or to automate existing manual equipment. Additional economic indicators might, therefore, help forecast this business. For example, the real supply of money—M2 divided by the price index—might indicate customers' ability to pay for your controls in the first place. (M2 is a measure of the money supply that includes currency, checking deposits, savings accounts, and mutual funds.)

Multiple regression analysis can help define the relationship between your sales and the economic indicators important to your business. Establishing this relationship can provide several benefits:

- By forecasting sales as a function of the economic forecasts of outside experts, you can check the validity of the forecasts of your marketing department, which can often be wildly optimistic.
- You can immediately evaluate the effect that changes in the economy imply for changes in your own sales. Used this way, the regression equation acts as an early warning device.
- By understanding the relationship between your sales and economic trends, you can discover potential changes in corporate strategy that can ease the pain

of recessions. For example, suppose the controls manufacturer discovers that sales of a low-end product tend to increase as the economy declines. On further research, the manufacturer learns that businesses buy these inexpensive controls to marginally improve product quality and labor productivity during bad times. Expanding the low-end business might, therefore, help the controls manufacturer maintain sales during a recession while developing a customer base that might move up to more expensive controls during good times.

To illustrate, suppose the controls manufacturer takes a closer look at its low-end product, a printed circuit board that plugs into business and home computers to switch electrical equipment on and off. The spreadsheet in Figure 7-7 on page 333 presents the data the manufacturer might assemble in preparation for a multiple regression analysis of this product's sales. The company controller might speculate that sales are affected most strongly by corporate profits, disposable consumer income, and the sales of personal computers. She therefore assembles the data shown.

Notice that column B in this spreadsheet contains only the value 1. The matrix formulas that follow cannot work if this column is missing. If you want to hide this column after you've entered it, do so by assigning the number format *;;*.

Interpreting the Multiple Regression Spreadsheet

The spreadsheet in Figure 7-8 on page 334 contains the statistics that are commonly produced by software specifically designed for multiple regression analysis. The information boxes for the figure explain how each value was calculated.

How might the corporate controller interpret these results? Overall, the analysis shows a strong association between changes in sales and changes in the economic indicators that she's selected. The R-squared value, which is the easiest value to interpret, tells the controller that 90.1 percent of the variations in sales can be explained by variations in the independent variables. When she looks up the F value in a table at the back of her statistics book, she learns that she's identified a statistically significant relationship in her analysis. And the standard error of the estimate tells her that actual sales generally fall within $0.922 of their estimated value. This value represents a relatively accurate estimate, considering that her sales range is from $10 to $17.

Row 19 of the spreadsheet in Figure 7-8 shows the regression formula, which estimates that monthly sales equal $–48.646 plus 0.704 times corporate profits in the month plus 0.318 times disposable income plus 0.714 times computer sales. Rows 20 and 21 help her evaluate the significance of these coefficients. Row 20 contains a measure of variability of each coefficient, and row 21 contains a ratio that shows how many times greater each coefficient is than its measure of variability. When she looks up each of these t-statistic ratios in her statistics book, she finds that each coefficient is significant at the 95 percent confidence level.

Rows 28 and 29 help the controller to estimate future sales. She enters economic forecasts of corporate profits, disposable income, and computer sales in row 28. When she recalculates the spreadsheet, it combines the coefficients in row 19 and the estimates in row 28 to predict in cell B29 the sales of her own printed circuit boards.

The spreadsheet includes an ANOVA table for two reasons. First, it generates certain values required by other formulas in the spreadsheet. Second, it summarizes the regression results from yet another viewpoint. You can see that the sum of the squares due to regression (SSR) is almost as large as the total sum of squares (SST). In fact, as the R-squared value tells you, the SSR represents 90.1 percent of the SST. Similarly, the mean sum of squares due to regression (MSR) is significantly greater than the mean sum of squares due to error (MSE). In fact, as the F value tells you, the MSR value is 24.28 times the MSE value.

The correlation matrix at the bottom of the spreadsheet in Figure 7-8 displays the correlation coefficients for each pair of variables. This coefficient is a measure of the linear association between each pair of variables. If the variables have a perfect linear relationship, the correlation coefficient equals either 1 or –1, depending on whether the variables both rise and fall together or whether one rises as the other falls. (Of course, each variable in the matrix is perfectly correlated with itself.) The correlation coefficient equals 0 if there is no linear relationship between the variables.

This correlation matrix helps the controller uncover a potential problem with her regression analysis: Her forecast may be unreliable if two or more independent variables are closely correlated, a condition that statisticians call multicolinearity. In the spreadsheet, however, the correlation matrix shows that none of the independent variables has a correlation coefficient greater than 0.1461. Therefore, multicolinearity is definitely not a problem for her because, as a rule of thumb, multicolinearity problems arise only when correlation coefficients are greater than 0.70 or less than –0.70.

Suppose, however, that the controller had included two additional independent variables in her analysis: sales of monitors for personal computers and corporate bankruptcies. If she had, she probably would have found that sales of personal computers show a high and positive correlation with the sales of monitors and that business profits show a high and negative correlation with corporate bankruptcies (as profits go up, bankruptcies go down). She would therefore eliminate these variables for two reasons. From a statistical standpoint, they create multicolinearity problems. From a practical standpoint, these two variables add little to the analysis, and there is no need to go to the work and expense of including them.

Creating the Multiple Regression Spreadsheet

To create the spreadsheet shown in Figure 7-7, first open a new spreadsheet file. Turn off its gridlines and set the manual calculation mode.

The spreadsheet in Figure 7-7 contains no formulas. Enter the labels, data, and formatting as shown. The range-name box presents the one name to define for this spreadsheet. When you have assigned the range name, save your spreadsheet, using the name MR_DATA.XLS.

To create the spreadsheet in Figure 7-8, first open a new spreadsheet file and turn off its gridlines. Enter all labels and borders shown and then enter the names and formulas. Enter all range-name definitions shown in the range-name box. Many of these names have no values associated with them yet, but this will not cause any problems.

The spreadsheet in Figure 7-8 has been arranged in a logical sequence that's convenient for reading the results of a regression analysis, not in a sequence that's convenient for entering the formulas. Therefore, the formula box includes numbers that indicate the sequence to follow when you enter the formulas. When you follow this sequence, each formula you enter builds on formulas entered previously.

When you have completed the spreadsheet in Figure 7-8, save it using the name MR_3.XLS. This name stands for multiple regression using three independent variables.

Entering Your Own Data

To enter your own data into the spreadsheet in Figure 7-7, you probably will need to modify its size.

To insert or delete rows of data in the spreadsheet, do so in any row between the shaded borders. When you insert data, be sure to copy the value 1 to every new cell added to column B.

To insert or delete columns of independent variables, you must adjust the spreadsheets in both Figure 7-7 and Figure 7-8. To adjust the spreadsheet in Figure 7-7, column B (containing the value 1) and column F (containing the dependent variable) act as borders; you can insert or delete columns between them.

To use the spreadsheet in Figure 7-7 to analyze additional independent variables, you must use a version of the spreadsheet in Figure 7-8 that contains an equivalent number of independent variables. To add these variables to or delete them from the spreadsheet in Figure 7-8, treat column C (containing variable X1) and column E (now containing variable X3) as borders; insert or delete columns of variables between these.

Specifically, here's how to insert one additional column of variables:

1. Highlight the range E12:E30, choose Edit Insert, and select Right.
2. Copy the formulas in the range D14:D28 to the range E14:F14.
3. If you try to insert rows in the correlation matrix, you get an error message that says, *Can't change part of an array*. (To read an explanation of any error message, press the F1 (Help) key when the message is displayed on your screen.) To work around this problem, highlight the correlation matrix (cells B41:E44 in the section in Figure 7-8), press the F2 (Edit) key, and then press Ctrl-Enter (*not* Ctrl-Shift and Enter). When you do so, the correlation matrix returns the #VALUE! error value.
4. Insert a row in the matrix between its first and last row—between rows 42 and 43, for example. Insert a column between the first and last column of the matrix. When you do so, do not insert an entire spreadsheet column, but only a column in the area of the correlation matrix. You might, for example, highlight the range D39:D46, choose Edit Insert, and select Right.
5. To adjust the headings of the matrix, adjust the headings that were originally in the ranges A41:A43 and B40:D40.
6. Highlight the correlation matrix that now contains five rows and columns. Press the F2 (Edit) key and then press Ctrl-Shift and Enter. When you do so, the matrix might continue to display the #VALUE! error value because it depends on the recalculation of other values in your spreadsheet. If so, don't worry about it. When you recalculate your spreadsheet, the correlation matrix should return the correct values. If your spreadsheet still returns a #VALUE! error value, check your version of the spreadsheet against the spreadsheet in Figure 7-7. Your version must have five columns of data for your revised multiple regression analysis to work correctly.
7. When the new spreadsheet is working properly, save it using the name MR_4.XLS. From now on, whenever you want to analyze data with four independent variables, simply arrange your data to resemble the spreadsheet in Figure 7-7 with four X variables, properly assign the Input range, open the MR_4 spreadsheet, choose File Links to change existing links to the name of the file containing your new data, and then recalculate.

EXPENSE ANALYSIS WITH MULTIPLE REGRESSION

You can adapt the multiple regression formulas used in the spreadsheet in Figure 7-8 to many other spreadsheet formats and uses. Figure 7-9 on page 340, for example, presents a spreadsheet that applies multiple regression analysis to a modified version of the spreadsheet in Figure 7-5.

This spreadsheet tests the theory that two factors cause monthly expenses to vary. One of these is sales; the other is time, which is represented by the values 1 through 5 in the range L7:P7. It's a fact of business life that expenses rise over time. In companies that are out of control, however, expenses often rise more quickly than they do in businesses that are not.

If you compare the spreadsheet in Figure 7-5 and Figure 7-9, you can see that adding time to the model has improved your knowledge of some of the expenses:

Janitorial. Nothing seems to tell you much about this account. This doesn't seem to be a job for statistics.

Freight. The F statistic in the spreadsheet in Figure 7-5 is roughly twice that of the spreadsheet in Figure 7-9. Adding time to the model has therefore hurt the model's predictive power. Notice in the spreadsheet in Figure 7-9 that the t statistic for the time coefficient is significantly less than 2, confirming the conclusion that time hasn't helped this model.

Travel. As with freight, adding time has hurt the model.

Telephone. Bingo! The F statistic has skyrocketed! The spreadsheet in Figure 7-9 tells you that telephone expenses are rising by $488.33 per month, no matter what sales do. To refine this calculation, run a third analysis, using only time as the independent variable.

Office Supplies. You nearly have a paradox. Because the F statistic isn't near its critical value of 19.0, you know that the model isn't significant. But because the t values approach their critical values of 2.92, you know they may well be significant. How can the model be wrong and each of its elements right? In fact, this conflict often crops up when two independent variables are correlated, as sales and time tend to be. A statistician would suggest that you substitute more refined independent variables and try the analysis again. But because you might have hundreds of expense accounts to analyze and because the dollars aren't large, I would suggest that you lump Office Supplies in with Janitorial as accounts to analyze when time permits.

Training. Adding a time variable seems to have improved the Training model. Training expenses appear to fall monthly and to fall as sales increase. Soon training expenses will disappear entirely. (Notice that the t statistic for Time in cell I14 is negative. This indicates that Training expenses are negatively correlated with time. When you look up the t statistic in the tables, however, look up its absolute value.)

Legal Fees. Nothing has helped to predict these expenses. Talk to your lawyer.

Building Rent. With constant expenses across the board, building rent is easy to predict, although this statistical model doesn't reveal that fact.

To create the spreadsheet in Figure 7-9, begin with the spreadsheet shown in Figure 7-5. Insert two rows between rows 5 and 6 and add the values to these new rows (now rows 6 and 7), shown above the monthly observations in the spreadsheet in Figure 7-9. Insert the extra columns needed for the spreadsheet in Figure 7-9 and change the column titles as needed.

The range-name and formula boxes provide all the information you need to create the names and formulas for this spreadsheet. After you enter this information and the figure is working properly, set the height of row 6 to 0.

SALES FORECASTING WITH TIME-SERIES ANALYSIS

Time-series analysis is one of the most powerful tools available for forecasting monthly sales during a 12-month period. It's based on the realization that four factors affect the month-to-month sales of most businesses:

Seasonal variations. Toys sell well at Christmas. Lawn and garden products sell well in late winter and early spring. School products sell well in late summer. And nothing sells well in Europe during the summer, when the entire continent takes a vacation. Whatever business you're in, seasonal variations probably affect your sales as well.

Trends. The sales of most companies follow one of three trends: up, down, or sideways. Good years and bad years can distort the picture, but when you look back over several years, a distinct trend is apparent in the sales of most companies.

Economic Cycles. Economic cycles affect most businesses, just as the tides affect boats. When the economic tide is high, it's business as usual. When the tide starts to fall, you really don't notice the change at first; business seems normal but challenging. But soon, almost without warning, the tide is out, and if you anchored in shallow financial water, you're high and dry with low sales, high costs, and no cash.

Random Events. Random events continually affect monthly sales: You schedule a large shipment for the 30th, but unexpected problems delay it until the 2nd. Your supplier's warehouse burns down, slowing sales for several weeks until you can arrange alternate sources of supply. A quality problem creates unusual customer returns. Your new product takes off unexpectedly. Your new clerk files a large purchase order in your accounts payable file. Everything simply goes *right* some month. Random events.

The category called random events also includes the errors you make by failing to identify your true seasonal index, trend, and economic cycle exactly. As a consequence, the term "Errors" and the term "Random Events" tend to be used interchangeably in time-series forecasting.

Time-series analysis decomposes historical sales into these four factors and then uses this information to predict future sales. Your sales forecast will reflect a continuation of the trend, which is modified by your seasonal index, which is further modified by your prediction of future economic cycles. You can ignore random events and errors; by definition, these are impossible to forecast.

Time-Series Data

One limitation of time-series analysis is that it requires three to four years of data. The reason it needs at least three years of data is obvious when you think about it. A seasonal index describes how well your business will perform each month in comparison to average monthly sales over a period of a year. You can't even begin to calculate an index, therefore, until you've acquired 12 months of sales.

But to eliminate the effects of the trend from the calculations, you compare each month's sales to a centered moving average. That is, you compare July's sales to an average of the 12-month period of which July is the center. You must add a month to calculate August's average, another to calculate September's, and so on. In other words, you must have two years of data before you can calculate a seasonal index for one year. (The averaging process is slightly more involved than this, as the formula box for Figure 7-10 on page 344 explains.)

To use the seasonal index with any assurance at all, you really should take an average of the indices for two years. Therefore, you must have at least three years of data to use the seasonal index.

While you need at least three years of data for time-series forecasting, you probably should use no more than four. If your earliest data is too old, it will overpower more recent data, hiding changes that may have occurred in your seasonal index and trend.

Using a Time-Series Spreadsheet

Figure 7-10 on page 342 shows a time-series spreadsheet that contains 48 months of actual performance and 12 months of forecasted performance. Each column is numbered, and most columns are assigned at least one range name. Row 15 contains the range names that include both actual and forecasted performance. In row 16, the range names include actual performance only; these, you will notice, begin with an A.

The range names specified in rows 15 and 16 are dynamic; they adjust themselves in response to your data in two ways. First, the named ranges expand as your data expands, as described in Appendix C. Second, the ranges expand as you substitute actual performance for forecasted performance. In other words, if you change the date in cell E7 to 1/1/89, all ranges named in row 16 expand by one row to include the new month as part of the database of actual performance.

At first glance, the 12 numbered columns in the spreadsheet in Figure 7-10 probably look rather gray and meaningless. Let's take a closer look at each of them:

1. The sequence numbers in column A serve as counters. They help the other formulas find specific months within the database.

2. The column of months serves to label each row of data. It also provides a date serial number that several formulas use to extract data for specific months from other spreadsheets. Notice that the data in columns A and B extends to row 86 while all other data ends in row 85. The partial row is for the benefit of two graphs that follow. If it were missing, the graphs would not properly display the dates in the Y-axis label.

3. This column contains a formula that returns actual sales from the Sales History table in the spreadsheet in Figure 7-11 on page 349. In the bottom part of the schedule, which returns forecasts rather than actual performance, the same formula returns a forecast of future sales.

4. The first step in calculating a seasonal index is to find the ratio of actual sales to a moving average. This column performs that calculation. Because the average is centered, formulas don't begin in this column until the seventh month of data.

5. The Average Seasonal Index table in the spreadsheet in Figure 7-12 on page 351 averages each month's ratios in column 4 and calculates an average seasonal index. Column 5 (column E in Figure 7-10) returns this seasonal index value. (Column E contains the first of the four factors needed to prepare the forecast. The other three factors are the trend in sales, the economic cycle, and the error values.)

6. If there had been more room in the title section of column F, this column would have been titled Deseasonalized Sales. It contains a column of the sales for each month adjusted to remove the effect of seasonality.

7. The Miscellaneous Data & Calculations section in the range F7:I9 calculates a least-squares trendline through the data in column F. Column G uses that information to calculate the dollar amount of the sales trend. (This is the second of the four factors.)

8. Column H contains a ratio that reflects the effect of economic cycles and random events on previous sales. Our next step, therefore, is to strip away the economic cycles, leaving only the random events.

9. The lighter of the two lines of the graph in Figure 7-13 on page 353 shows the data in column H, which somewhat resembles the course that a drunken statistician might make in a snow-covered alley. Running through the middle of this uncertain track is our rough estimate of the path the old sot intended to follow, which we calculate with a centered average over a seven-month period. This path is called the economic cycle. (This is the third of the four factors.)

10. Understanding past economic cycles can provide some help in forecasting new ones. One way to gain this understanding is to perform a multiple regression analysis using the data in column I as the dependent variable and economic indicators important to your industry as the independent variables. Figure 7-7 and Figure 7-8 provide spreadsheets you can adapt to this purpose.

Alternatively, you can examine past turning points in the cycle and then use this information in combination with current economic forecasts to predict future trends in the cycle. The formulas in column J mark the turning points in each cycle. The table titled Turning Points of Past Economic Cycles in the spreadsheet in Figure 7-14 on page 354 summarizes these events and calculates the average amount that each half cycle rose or fell monthly. The table titled Economic Cycle Forecast in the spreadsheet in Figure 7-15 on page 357 helps you use this information to predict the cycle index for each month over the next 12.

Column I returns this information in its forecast at the bottom of the database. So the bottom of column I contains the third of the four factors required to forecast sales.

11. Because we've identified three of the factors that affect sales, the fourth is easy to find. It equals the original sales value minus the combined effect of the other three factors. Column K contains this amount.

12. The chart in Figure 7-16 on page 358 graphs three columns of sales data. The straight line marks the trend over four years and the trend that we expect in the next 12 months (column G). The wavy line shows the combined effect of the trend and the economic cycle. Column L contains the data for this line. The remaining jagged line shows four years of actual sales and the fifth year of forecasted sales (column C).

You can easily see the effect of the economic cycle when you compare the December values in this graph with the economic cycle. December 1985, the lowest point in the graph, is near the middle of a cycle. December 1986, near the high point of a cycle, shows a considerable improvement over the previous December. December 1987, which is near the bottom of a cycle, shows sales nearly as bad as those two years before. In December 1988, only minor cyclical effects have been experienced, which is also the predicted effect in December 1989.

Beginning the Time-Series Spreadsheet

To create the time-series spreadsheet, begin by opening a new spreadsheet. Turn off its gridlines, set manual calculation, and then save the spreadsheet as TIME_SER.XLS. Enter all labels and borders shown through row 25 of Figure 7-10 on page 342. Format these as shown in the figure. Enter the shaded and outlined border shown in row 87.

The dynamic range definitions depend on the column numbers in row 14. The formula box for Figure 7-10 shows the formula that returns the number for cell A14; copy this formula to the right as needed.

The range-name box for Figure 7-10 lists all range names used in this figure. Enter the names *Now* through *AMonth.* To assure yourself that you're entering the dynamic range names properly, press the F5 (Goto) key and type the name *ASeq.* When you do so, the program highlights the range A26:A73. (Dynamic range names don't appear in the Goto dialog box, however.)

Enter and format the data shown in cells E7 and E8. Enter the formula shown for cell E9 in the figure's formula box. Beginning with the value shown for cell A26, the formula box shows values and formulas for each column of formulas in the schedule. Enter the values and formulas shown for columns A and B and then copy the formulas shown for row 27 down their columns to row 86.

Column C returns the value of actual sales entered in the spreadsheet in Figure 7-11. Therefore, before you continue with the time-series spreadsheet, you must complete the spreadsheet in Figure 7-11, which contains the actual sales values.

Creating the Table of Sales History

Figure 7-11 on page 349 shows the table of sales history. Each month, you update this table with the current month's sales. To create this table, first open a new spreadsheet, turn off the gridlines, and save it, using the name SLSHIST.XLS.

Enter the labels and borders shown for rows 3 and 4. The information boxes for Figure 7-11 show the formulas, formats, and range names for the spreadsheet. Enter the value and formula shown for row 4 and copy the formula across the row as shown. Enter the value and formula shown for column A, format them as shown, and then copy the contents of cell A6 down the column. Enter and format the formula shown for cell B17 and copy it across the row. Finally, enter and format the data shown.

After you enter all the formulas and data, enter the remaining text and borders as needed. Define the range name Sales as shown and then save the spreadsheet.

Generating the Seasonal Index

Activate the spreadsheet TIME_SER.XLS, shown in Figure 7-10. Define the name SlsHist as shown in the range-name box. Enter the formulas shown for cells C26 and D32 in the formula box for Figure 7-10. Copy these down the column to row 85 of the spreadsheet in Figure 7-10. Define the range names Sales and ASales, which apply to column C of the spreadsheet in Figure 7-10, and the name AStageA, which applies to column D.

Column E returns the seasonal index calculated by the spreadsheet in Figure 7-12. Therefore, before you can continue with the time-series spreadsheet, you must create the spreadsheet in Figure 7-12 on page 351. To do so, first open a new spreadsheet, turn off its gridlines, and save the spreadsheet, using the name SEAS_NDX.XLS.

Enter the labels and borders shown for rows 3 and 4 of the spreadsheet in Figure 7-12 and the month numbers shown for column A. Enter the definitions for the range names AMonth and AStageA, as provided in the range-name box for Figure 7-12. After you do so, enter the array formula shown for cell B5, copy it down the column as shown, and then enter the SUM formula shown for cell B17.

Enter the formula for the seasonal index shown for cell C5, copy it down the column, and then enter the SUM formula shown for cell C17. Finally, to complete the spreadsheet, define the name Index and save your spreadsheet.

Finding the Actual Economic Cycle

Activate the TIME_SER.XLS spreadsheet, shown in Figure 7-10. Define the names Seas through Index, as shown in the figure's range-name box. You can test these range names by pressing the F5 (Goto) key and then selecting the name you want to test.

Enter the formulas shown in the formula box for cells E26 and F26 and then copy these formulas down their columns to row 85. Now that column F contains data, return to the top of the spreadsheet and enter the formulas that calculate the regression statistics. The formula box shows the formulas for cells I7, I8, and I9; enter them as shown.

After the formulas in the range I7:I9 return values, enter the formulas shown for cells G26 and H26 and copy them down their columns to row 85. The formula box shows a separate formula for each cell in the range I26:I29. Enter each and then copy the contents of cell I29 down the column. Because you've not yet defined the range name CycFcst, the last 12 rows of column I return error values when you recalculate. This fact should cause no problem.

Enter the formula shown for cells J26 and J27 and then copy the contents of cell J27 down the column to row 85. Before you can complete this spreadsheet, you must complete the two displays that help you estimate the future economic cycle.

Estimating the Economic Cycle

The spreadsheet in Figure 7-14 on page 354 lists the turning points of past economic cycles that your business has experienced. For each turning point, it calculates the cycle index at the turning point, the elapsed time in months from the previous turning point, and the average rise or fall per month.

To create this section, first open a new spreadsheet, turn off its gridlines, and save it as CYCL_NDX.XLS. Enter all but the last range name specified in the figure's range-name box.

Enter the labels shown through row 6 of the spreadsheet in Figure 7-14 and then enter the formulas shown in the figure's formula box. Copy the last formula entered in each column down the column to row 14 and then format the display as specified in the figure's format box and as shown in the spreadsheet.

Figure 7-15 on page 357 shows a spreadsheet that helps you forecast the cycle index for each of the next 12 months. You do so by entering into column B the expected amount of the cycle's rise or fall for each month. You base your estimate for each month's rise or fall on the amounts shown in columns D and H of the spreadsheet in Figure 7-14. An alternative approach would be to base the index on the results of a multiple-regression equation you've generated using the methods illustrated in the spreadsheets in Figure 7-7 and Figure 7-8.

To create this forecast, enter into your CYCL_NDX.XLS spreadsheet the labels shown in rows 20 through 22. Enter the formulas shown for cells A23 and A24, format them as shown, and then copy the contents of cell A24 down the column to cell A35.

Enter the data shown in column B. Enter the formulas for cells C23 and C24 and then copy the contents of cell C24 down its column to row 35. Format the spreadsheet as shown and then assign the range name CycFcst, as shown in the range-name box for Figure 7-14 and Figure 7-15. Finally, save your spreadsheet.

Completing the Time-Series Spreadsheet

Activate the TIME_SER.XLS spreadsheet. Define the range CycFcst, as shown in the range-name box for Figure 7-10. All range names are now defined.

Recalculate your spreadsheet. When you do so, the last 12 cells in column I return values from CYCL_NDX.XLS. To complete the spreadsheet, enter the formulas shown for cells K26 and L26 and copy these down their columns to row 85.

Your sales forecast for the next 12 months is in the range C74:C85 of the spreadsheet in Figure 7-10. A graph will help you evaluate whether this forecast makes sense.

Graphing Your Forecasting Data

Figure 7-13 on page 353 shows a chart that graphs the economic cycle as it weaves its way through the deseasonalized and de-trended sales data. The chart in Figure 7-16 on page 358 shows past and future trends, cycles, and sales. To generate either graph, you follow nearly the same procedure. The following instructions explain how to create the chart in Figure 7-13; special instructions for creating the chart in Figure 7-16 appear in parentheses:

1. Activate the TIME_SER.XLS spreadsheet. Highlight the ranges StageC and Cycle. To do so quickly, press the F5 (Goto) key, type *StageC*, press Shift and F8 (the Add key), press the Goto key again, and then select Cycle. (For the chart in Figure 7-16, select the ranges Trend, GraphA, and Sales.)
2. Press the F11 (New Chart) key. (Press Alt-F1 if your keyboard doesn't have an F11 key.)
3. To change the graph from a bar chart to a line chart, choose Gallery Line and select chart type 2.
4. To label the horizontal axis with dates, copy the Month column into the chart. To do so, activate the TIME_SER.XLS spreadsheet; press the Goto key; select Month; press Ctrl-Ins to copy this range to the clipboard; activate your chart; choose Edit Paste Special; turn on the Columns, Categories in First Column, and Replace Existing Categories options; and then press Enter.
5. To adjust the scale of the vertical axis, select that axis, choose Format Scale, and then set the minimum value to 0.9, the maximum value to 1.1, and the major unit to 0.1. (For the chart in Figure 7-16, set the minimum value to 10,000, the maximum value to 18,000, and the major unit to 2,000.)

6. To adjust the scale of the horizontal axis, select that axis, choose Format Scale, and enter the value *12* for both the Number of Categories Between Tick Labels and the Number of Categories Between Tick Marks options.

7. Notice in your graph of Figure 7-16 that the Cycle line contains 13 more months of data than your StageC line does. If the horizontal labels of your graph stop at Jan-88, the SERIES formula of the shorter line is assigned a plot order argument of 1. To display labels for the complete horizontal axis, you must rearrange the plot orders. This is easy to do. First, select the line displaying the economic cycle in the graph (the longer line). When you do so, the formula bar displays a SERIES formula. The last number in this formula is the plot order, which no doubt contains the value 2. To rearrange the order, edit the SERIES formula, changing the value 2 to 1. When you press Enter, the plot order of the other graph line switches to 2, and the graph displays the complete set of labels for the horizontal axis.

8. If you have a color monitor, you might want to change the colors of the lines in the graph. To do so, select one of the lines, choose Format Patterns, and then select the colors you want. To make one color apply to all lines, turn on the box labeled Apply to All.

9. Notice that the SERIES formula references cell addresses rather than range names in the TIME_SER.XLS spreadsheet. This is dangerous. If you change the position of any data in the spreadsheet, the cell address in the chart *will not change,* and the chart will reference incorrect cell addresses. To correct this problem, you must edit each SERIES formula, changing the cell addresses into range names. Change the following cell addresses to the range names shown:

   For Figure 7-13

Range	***Name***
$B$26:$B$86	Month
$H$26:$H$73	StageC
$I$26:$I$86	Cycle

   For Figure 7-16

Range	***Name***
$B$26:$B$86	Month
$C$26:$C$86	Sales
$G$26:$G$86	Trend
$L$26:$L$86	GraphA

10. To draw the gridlines, choose Chart Gridlines and turn on the Major Gridlines option for both the Category Axis and the Value Axis.

11. To draw the border around the chart, choose Chart Select Chart, choose Format Patterns, select the thickest border weight, and then press Enter.

12. To enter the graph title, first choose Chart Attach Text and select Chart Title. When the word *Title* appears in your graph, type the title, pressing Ctrl-Enter to begin the second line of the title. To change the title's font to 14-point Helv bold, as shown in the chart in the figure, choose Format Font and then select the font you want.
13. To enter the vertical-axis title, choose Chart Attach Text and select Value Axis. When the letter *Y* appears in your graph, type the Y-axis title shown in the chart in the figure. After you press Enter, the label is displayed horizontally rather than vertically. To display it vertically, choose Format Text and then turn on the Vertical Text box, leaving the other boxes at their default selections. After you press Enter, the title is displayed vertically, as in the chart in the figure. If you want to, change the title's font to boldface by using the Format Font command.
14. Finally, save your chart, using any name you want.

Entering Your Own Data in the Time-Series Spreadsheet

To enter your own data in the Time-Series spreadsheet, first enter your past sales into the Sales History spreadsheet and the correct dates into cells E7 and E8 as shown in the spreadsheet in Figure 7-10.

If you have less than three years of sales data, the spreadsheet returns a forecast for more than 12 months. The additional months of forecast mean little, however, because the cycle value for these months equals the cycle value calculated for the twelfth month.

To eliminate these extra months, first delete the necessary number of rows from near the bottom of the database in TIME_SER.XLS. (Don't delete the last row; the graph depends on it.) After you delete these rows, many of the remaining rows return error values because they refer to data that is no longer in the spreadsheet. To correct this problem, copy a row of formulas from near the top of the spreadsheet (row 32 of the spreadsheet in Figure 7-10 is a safe row) to the remainder of the schedule. Be careful, however, that the last row of your schedule resembles row 86 of the spreadsheet in Figure 7-10; that is, be sure that it contains data only in columns A and B.

If you have more than four years of sales data, insert additional rows of formulas near the bottom of your schedule and then copy the formulas contained in row 32 to the remainder of your schedule. As before, leave the bottom row in its modified form.

Update your forecast of the economic cycle and then recalculate. After you do so, the graph of your forecast looks reasonable in view of past forecasts. Finally, when the spreadsheets display reasonable information, save your workspace. I used the workspace name TIME_SER.XLW.

References on Statistics

Draper, Norman and Smith, Harry. *Applied Regression Analysis, 2d ed.* Wiley-Interscience, 1981. This graduate-level textbook provides an excellent reference for nearly any aspect of regression analysis.

Neter, John and Wasserman, William. *Applied Linear Statistical Models*. Richard D. Irwin, Inc., 1974. This textbook provides explanations of regression analysis using both traditional and array formulas. Its introductory chapter on matrix algebra is particularly helpful for those new to the subject.

Makridakis, Spyros; Wheelwright, Steven C.; and McGee, Victor E. *Forecasting: Methods and Applications, 2d ed.* John Wiley & Sons, 1983. This 926-page book was written for people who want to generate forecasts, not merely to teach the subject. It covers the full range of forecasting methods and outlines the steps needed to apply them, without getting bogged down in theory.

Searle, Shayle R. *Matrix Algebra Useful for Statistics*. John Wiley & Sons, 1982. Intended primarily for statisticians, this book provides a detailed explanation of statistical uses of matrix algebra.

Searle, S.R. and Hausman, W.H. *Matrix Algebra for Business and Economics*. Wiley-Interscience, 1970. Although this book is nearly 20 years old, I've found it to be a useful reference for matrix calculations in Microsoft Excel. Its chapter on regression analysis is particularly helpful.

Siegel, Andrew F. *Statistics and Data Analysis, An Introduction*. John Wiley & Sons, 1988. This book, written by a good friend and an outstanding statistician, contrasts sharply with most other statistics textbooks. Written as an introductory undergraduate text for nontechnical students, it provides lucid explanations, dozens of examples, and few formulas.

Figure 7-1. Schedule of Prices

A spreadsheet that provides expected unit prices each month for the coming year. Saved as PRICES.XLS.

	A	B	C	D	E
1					
2					
3	**Product Pricing Assumptions**				
4	**Prices**	Jan	Feb		
5					
6	Bolts	3.00	3.50		
7	Nails	1.50	1.50		
8	Nuts	4.00	5.00		
9	Washers	2.00	2.00		
10					
11					

COLUMN WIDTHS

Column	*Width*	*Column*	*Width*
A	8.43	C	8.43
B	8.43	D	3.29

RANGE NAMES

Name	*Formula*
Prods	=$A$4:$A$10
Dates	=$A$4:$D$4
Data	=$A$4:$D$10

These ranges are all anchored in cells that will retain their integrity as you add data. As you add products, the bottom border will remain at the bottom; as you add months, the shaded column will remain at the right.

KEY CELL FORMATS

Cell	*Number*	*Alignment*	*Font*
A3	General	General	Helv 10, Bold
A4:D4	General	Center	Helv 10
B5:C10	#,##0.00	General	Helv 10

Figure 7-2. Schedule of Units

Provides forecasted unit sales each month for the coming year. Saved as UNITS.XLS.

	A	B	C	D	E
1					
2					
3	**Unit Forecast**				
4	**Units**	Jan	Feb	Total	
5					
6	Bolts	1,000	1,100	2,100	
7	Washers	500	600	1,100	
8	Nuts	100	200	300	
9					
10					

COLUMN WIDTHS

Column	*Width*	*Column*	*Width*
A	8.43	C	8.43
B	8.43	D	8.43

KEY FORMULA

Cell	*Formula*
D6	=SUM(B6:C6) Copy this formula down the column as needed.

RANGE NAMES

Name	*Formula*
Prods	=$A$4:$A$9
Dates	=$A$4:$D$4
Data	=$A$4:$D$9

KEY CELL FORMATS

Cell	*Number*	*Alignment*	*Font*
A3	General	General	Helv 10, Bold
A4:D4	General	Center	Helv 10
B5:D9	#,##0	General	Helv 10

Figure 7-3. Sales Forecast in Dollars, Version 1

A sales forecast in dollars in which the forecast amounts equal unit sales times unit prices. Saved as SALES_A.XLS.

	A	B	C	D	E
1					
2					
3					
4					
5					
6					
7	**Sales Forecast (Dollars)**				
8		Jan	Feb	Total	
9					
10	Washers	1,000	1,200	2,200	
11	Nuts	400	1,000	1,400	
12	Bolts	3,000	3,850	6,850	
13					
14	Total	4,400	6,050	10,450	
15					
16					

KEY FORMULAS

Cell	*Formula*
B10	**=Prices*Units** Although this simple formula appears first in the list, it is among the last to be entered. After you properly define all range names, the spreadsheet knows which file contains the prices you want, and it knows which specific price to use from that list for each product in each month. The same is true of the Units information.
D10	**=SUM(B10:C10)** When you expand the spreadsheet to include all 12 months of your forecast, remember to redefine the SUM range to include those months.
B14	**=SUM(B9:B13)** Notice that the SUM range includes the top and bottom borders.

(continued)

Figure 7-3. *continued*

RANGE NAMES	
Name	***Formula***
Pdata **Pdates** **Pprods**	**=PRICES.XLS!Data** **=PRICES.XLS!Dates** **=PRICES.XLS!Prods** These refer to the range names described in Figure 7-1.
Udata **Udates** **Uprods**	**=UNITS.XLS!Data** **=UNITS.XLS!Dates** **=UNITS.XLS!Prods** These refer to the range names described in Figure 7-2.
Prices	**=IF(ISNA(MATCH($A10,Pprods,0)),0,INDEX(Pdata,MATCH($A10,Pprods,0), MATCH(B$8,Pdates,0)))** The first MATCH function checks to see if the product in cell A10 exists in the PRICES file. If it doesn't, the formula returns a 0. The second MATCH function finds the number of the row within the Pprods (Price products) range that contains the product shown in cell A10. The third MATCH function finds the number of the column within the Pdates range that contains the date found in row 8. The INDEX function uses these row and column numbers to find the appropriate sales amount for the product and month specified.
Units	**=IF(ISNA(MATCH($A10,Uprods,0)),0,INDEX(Udata,MATCH($A10,Uprods,0), MATCH(B$8,Udates,0)))** To enter this name easily, copy it from the Prices range definition and substitute U's for P's in the range names like Pprods.
Enter the Prices definition as a formula in cell B10 of the spreadsheet. When it correctly returns the prices for the file you specify, copy the formula to the definition for the range name Prices. Edit the formula in cell B10 to look for units, and then copy that formula to the definition for the range name Units.	

Figure 7-4. Sales Forecast in Dollars, Version 2

A sales forecast with file-selection capabilities in cells C4 and C5. Saved as SALES_B.XLS.

	A	B	C	D	E
1					
2					
3	Files used for this forecast:				
4	for units sold:		Units		
5	for selling prices:		Prices		
6					
7	**Sales Forecast (Dollars)**				
8		Jan	Feb	Total	
9					
10	Washers	1,000	1,200	2,200	
11	Nuts	400	1,000	1,400	
12	Bolts	3,000	3,850	6,850	
13					
14	Total	4,400	6,050	10,450	
15					
16	Scratch Formulas				
17	Pprods	Prices	Uprods	Units	
18	Pdates	Prices	Udates	Units	
19	Pdata	Prices	Udata	Units	
20					
21					

RANGE NAMES	
Name	*Formula*
FileP **FileU**	**=$C$5** **=$C$4** Enter the filenames shown in these cells and then name the cells as shown.
Pprods	**=INDEX(INDIRECT(FileP&".xls!prods"),1,1):INDEX(INDIRECT(FileP&".xls!prods"),ROWS(INDIRECT(FileP&".xls!prods")),1)**
Pdates	**=INDEX(INDIRECT(FileP&".xls!dates"),1,1):INDEX(INDIRECT(FileP&".xls!dates"),1,COLUMNS(INDIRECT(FileP&".xls!dates")))**
Pdata	**=INDEX(INDIRECT(FileP&".xls!data"),1,1):INDEX(INDIRECT(FileP&".xls!data"),ROWS(INDIRECT(FileP&".xls!data")),COLUMNS(INDIRECT(FileP&".xls!data")))**
Uprods	**=INDEX(INDIRECT(FileU&".xls!prods"),1,1):INDEX(INDIRECT(FileU&".xls!prods"),ROWS(INDIRECT(FileU&".xls!prods")),1)**
Udates	**=INDEX(INDIRECT(FileU&".xls!dates"),1,1):INDEX(INDIRECT(FileU&".xls!dates"),1,COLUMNS(INDIRECT(FileU&".xls!dates")))**

(continued)

Figure 7-4. *continued*

RANGE NAMES–continued

Name	*Formula*
Udata	**=INDEX(INDIRECT(FileU&".xls!data"),1,1):INDEX(INDIRECT(FileU&".xls!data"), ROWS(INDIRECT(FileU&".xls!data")),COLUMNS(INDIRECT(FileU&".xls!data")))**

Believe it or not, the previous six range-definition formulas aren't nearly as difficult to understand or to enter as they might appear. Each formula defines a range in a spreadsheet by specifying the range's top-left and bottom-right cells. Each formula takes the general form:

=INDEX(array,top_row_num,left_column_num)
:INDEX(array,bottom_row_num,right_column_num)

In all cases, the top row and left column numbers are equal to 1. An array's bottom-row number equals the number of rows in the array; an array's right column number equals the number of columns in the array; for arrays one column wide or one row deep, there is no need to count the column or row number; each equals 1.

The INDIRECT function gives this spreadsheet its ability to refer to the filenames you enter at the top of the sheet. This function returns as a reference the range defined as a text string within its boundaries. Therefore, when you enter a new filename and then recalculate, the text formulas create new range descriptions, which the INDIRECT functions convert to references, which the INDEX functions use to specify the end points of each array, which the range formulas use to define the array itself.

To enter these arrays quickly, first enter them as array formulas in the Scratch Formulas section of the spreadsheet. Enter the Pprods formula in cell B17 (using Ctrl-Shift Enter), copy this formula to the Pdates cell, edit the Pdates formula as necessary, copy it to the Pdata cell, and then edit that cell as necessary. Copy these three formulas to the cells for the Units formulas in column D. Edit the Units formulas as needed, or if you prefer, use the Formula Replace command to replace FileP with FileU in the three Units formulas in column D.

After you enter the scratch formulas, replace the definitions of these six names that you created in Figure 7-3. To do so, simply copy each formula from its formula bar to the appropriate Refers To box in the Formula Define Name dialog box. Finally, when all range definitions are working correctly, erase the scratch formulas from your spreadsheet.

Prices	**=IF(ISNA(MATCH($A10,Pprods,0)),0,INDEX(Pdata,MATCH($A10,Pprods,0), MATCH(B$8,Pdates,0)))**
Units	**=IF(ISNA(MATCH($A10,Uprods,0)),0,INDEX(Udata,MATCH($A10,Uprods,0), MATCH(B$8,Udates,0)))**
	These definitions remain unchanged from Figure 7-3.

Figure 7-5. Expense Analysis with Linear Regression

A spreadsheet that uses linear regression to analyze expenses, letting you determine a fixed and a variable component for each expense.

	A	B	C	D	E	F	G	H	I	J	K	L	M	N	O
1															
2															
3	**Expense Analysis with Linear Regression**														
4						**F**	**t**		**Performance for the Month**						
5	**Description**	**Acct**	**Const**	**Slope**	**r.^2**	(df=1,3)	(df=3)		**Jan**	**Feb**	**Mar**	**Apr**	**May**		
6	Sales (X-value)	3050							123,423	161,098	149,093	224,293	186,244		
7	Janitorial	4762	$888	.00002	1%	0.02	.155		882	902	893	888	890		
8	Freight	4833	$1,550	.03871	95%	56.45	7.513		6,201	7,926	7,645	10,432	8,222		
9	Travel	5983	$1,031	.01886	79%	11.59	3.405		2,883	4,503	4,106	5,020	4,562		
10	Telephone	6234	$147	.01437	56%	3.80	1.949		1,730	2,055	2,502	2,995	3,580		
11	Office Supplies	6341	$1,165	.00120	9%	0.29	.536		1,305	1,523	1,334	1,520	1,156		
12	Training	6734	$1,350	-.00410	92%	33.45	5.783		866	711	733	474	509		
13	Legal Fees	6819	#VALUE!	#VALUE!	#VALUE!	#VALUE!	#VALUE!		3,750		138	1,900			
14	Bldg Rent	6901	$6,250	.00000	0%	0.00	.000		6250	6250	6250	6250	6250		
15															
16															

KEY FORMULAS

Cell	*Formula*
F5 G5	**="(df="&1&","&COUNTA($H$5:$N$5)–2&")"** **="(df="&COUNTA($H$5:$N$5)–2&")"** These text formulas calculate the degrees of freedom (df) for the F and t statistics, respectively. Where n is the number of observations and k is the number of independent variables, the df for F equals k and n–k–1; the df for t equals n–k–1.
C7 D7	**=INDEX(LINEST(Y,X),1,2)** **=INDEX(LINEST(Y,X),1,1)** For linear regression, the LINEST function returns an array that contains the regression constant in its second column and the regression coefficient in its first column. The INDEX functions return the proper values.
E7	**=IF(MAX(Y)=MIN(Y),0,(Sxy/(Sxx*Syy)^0.5)^2)** If all values of Y are equal, this formula returns a 0; otherwise, it uses a common formula in statistics that finds the correlation coefficient, r, and then squares its value to find the coefficient of determination, r^2.
F7	**=G7^2** In linear regression, F equals the t statistic squared.
G7	**=IF(E7=0,0,((Sxy^2*(n–2))/(Sxx*Syy–Sxy^2))^0.5)** A common way to calculate the t statistic is to divide the regression coefficient by its standard deviation (also known as its standard error of estimate). Solving for the t statistic in terms of the available information produces this formula.

(continued)

Figure 7-5. *continued*

RANGE NAMES	
Name	***Formula***
XX	**=$H$6:$N$6** Enter this range definition as you enter most such definitions.
YY	**=RC8:RC14** This name is easier to understand when defined using the R1C1 format. The formula defines YY as the range between the eighth column (H) and the fourteenth column (N) on any row that uses this range name. To enter this definition, first switch to the R1C1 format by choosing Options Workspace and turning on the R1C1 option. After you define the name, switch back to the A1 format.
X **Y**	**=INDEX(XX,1,2):INDEX(XX,1,COLUMNS(XX)–1)** **=INDEX(YY,1,2):INDEX(YY,1,COLUMNS(YY)–1)** These range formulas define the ranges X and Y in terms of XX and YY. As described in Figure 7-6, defining X and Y this way allows these ranges to expand and contract as the data expands and contracts between the shaded borders.
n	**=COUNT (Y)** The variable "n" contains the number of observations (months) for each regression.
Sxx	**=VARP(X)*n** This range definition uses the calculation of the variance of a population to calculate the sum of the squared deviations from the mean of X. In other words, subtract the average (mean) of the X row from the first value of X to find the deviation from the X mean and then square the result to find the squared deviation. Do the same for the next value of X, and so on. The sum of all these squared deviations equals the result of this calculation.
Syy	**=VARP(Y)*n** This range definition formula finds the sum of the squared deviations from the mean of Y.
Sxy	**=Sxx*LINEST(Y,X)** This range definition formula sums the quantities of the X deviations multiplied by the Y deviations.

Figure 7-6. Expense Analysis with Linear Regression, Sorted by F Statistic

The linear regression spreadsheet from Figure 7-5 sorted by the F statistic, showing which expenses can be explained by variations in sales.

	A	B	C	D	E	F	G	H	I	J	K	L	M	N	O
1															
2															
3	**Expense Analysis with Linear Regression**														
4						F	t		**Performance for the Month**						
5	**Description**	**Acct**	**Const**	**Slope**	**r.^2**	(df=1,3)	(df=3)		**Jan**	**Feb**	**Mar**	**Apr**	**May**		
6	Sales (X-value)	3050							123,423	161,098	149,093	224,293	186,244		
7	Freight	4833	$1,550	.03871	95%	56.45	7.513		6,201	7,926	7,645	10,432	8,222		
8	Training	6734	$1,350	-.00410	92%	33.45	5.783		866	711	733	474	509		
9	Travel	5983	$1,031	.01886	79%	11.59	3.405		2,883	4,503	4,106	5,020	4,562		
10															
11	Telephone	6234	$147	.01437	56%	3.80	1.949		1,730	2,055	2,502	2,995	3,580		
12	Office Supplies	6341	$1,165	.00120	9%	0.29	.536		1,305	1,523	1,334	1,520	1,156		
13	Legal Fees	6819	$3,096	-.01148	7%	0.23	.477		3,750	0	138	1,900	0		
14	Janitorial	4762	$888	.00002	1%	0.02	.155		882	902	893	888	890		
15	Bldg Rent	6901	$6,250	.00000	0%	0.00	.000		6250	6250	6250	6250	6250		
16															
17															

Figure 7-7. Data for Multiple Regression Analysis

Economic data for the multiple regression analysis of printed circuit board sales in Figure 7-8. Saved as MR_DATA.XLS.

	A	B	C	D	E	F	G
1							
2							
3	**Data for Multiple Regression Analysis**						
4			Corp	Disposable	Computer	Board	
5			Profits	Income	Sales	Sales	
6	**Month**		**1**	**2**	**3**	**Y**	
7							
8	January	1	35	49	33	17	
9	February	1	30	48	30	10	
10	March	1	34	50	32	14	
11	April	1	35	50	28	12	
12	May	1	34	51	29	12	
13	June	1	39	49	30	16	
14	July	1	34	55	33	16	
15	August	1	36	47	33	14	
16	September	1	35	50	31	14	
17	October	1	34	47	31	12	
18	November	1	36	50	34	17	
19	December	1	31	49	31	10	
20							
21							
22							

RANGE NAME	
Name	***Formula***
Input	**=$B$7:$F$20** This matrix extends from the borders above and below the data and from the column of ones to the last column of data. Definitions for several arrays in the spreadsheet in Figure 7-8 depend on this array.

Figure 7-8. Multiple Regression Analysis

A multiple regression analysis that can help determine whether sales of the company's circuit cards can be explained by the economic data in column D through column E of Figure 7-7.

	A	B	C	D	E	F	G
1							
2							
3	**Multiple Regression Analysis**						
4							
5							
6	**Regression Results**						
7	Number of Observations (n)		12				
8	Number of Ind. Variables (k)		3				
9	Std Error of Estimate		.922				
10	R-Squared		90.10%				
11	F Value (df= 3,8)		24.28				
12							
13							
14	**Variable Number**		1	2	3	Y	
15							
16							
17	**Individual Variables**						
18		Constant					
19	Coefficients	-48.646	.704	.318	.714		
20	Std Error of Coef.	8.471	.121	.132	.156		
21	t Statistic (df= 8)	-5.742	5.803	2.398	4.594		
22							
23	Average Value		34.417	49.583	31.250	13.667	
24	Standard Deviation		2.314	2.109	1.815	2.498	
25							
26							
27	**Point Estimate**						
28	Enter Values:		35	49	33		
29	Est. Y Value	15.142					
30							
31							
32	**Analysis of Variance (ANOVA)**						
33		SS		df	MS		
34	Regression	SSR	61.87	3	20.62	MSR	
35	Error	SSE	6.80	8	0.85	MSE	
36	Total	SST	68.67	11			
37							
38							
39	**Correlation Matrix**						
40			1	2	3	Y	
41		1	1.0000	.0202	.1461	.7337	
42		2	.0202	1.0000	.1009	.3336	
43		3	.1461	.1009	1.0000	.6414	
44		Y	.7337	.3336	.6414	1.0000	
45							
46							

(continued)

Figure 7-8. *continued*

KEY FORMULAS	
Cell	***Formula***
C7	**=COUNT(Y)** The number of Y values equals the total number of observations.
C8	**=COLUMNS(X)** The number of X columns equals the number of independent variables, range name k.
C9	**=(SSE/(n–k–1))^0.5** The standard error of the estimate equals the standard deviation of the error values. To find the standard deviation, divide the sum of the squares of the error terms by (n–k–1) and then take the square root of the result.
C10	**=SSR/SST** The R-squared represents the proportion of all squared deviations that have been explained by the regression equation. That is, it's the simple ratio shown.
A11	**="F Value (df= "&k&","&n–k–1&")"** This formula returns both the label and F's degrees of freedom.
C11	**=MSR/MSE** The F value compares the mean sum from regression to the mean sum from errors.
C14 **D14**	**1** **=1+C14** Copy this formula to the right as needed.
B19	**=INDEX(LINEST(Y,X),1,k–B14+1)** The LINEST function returns an array that contains the coefficients of the regression equation in the order of X3, X2, X1, and the constant. The INDEX function displays the appropriate value from the array. Copy this formula to the right as needed.
B20	**=SQRT(INDEX(MINVERSE(MMULT(TRANSPOSE(Xi),Xi)),B$14+1B$14+1)*$C^2)** Multiplying the MINVERSE portion of this array formula by the square of the Standard Error of the Estimate ("sigma squared") returns the variance-covariance matrix. Taking the square roots of the diagonal elements of this matrix returns the standard deviations of each of the coefficients of the regression equation, which are more commonly referred to as the Standard Errors of the Coefficients. When you've entered this formula in the one cell shown, copy it to the right as necessary.

Note: The numbers next to the column of cell addresses indicate the sequence to follow when entering formulas in Figure 7-8. Enter all the 1's, then all the 2's, and so on.

(continued)

Figure 7-8. *continued*

	KEY FORMULAS–continued	
	Cell	***Formula***
3	**A21**	**="t statistic (df= "&n–k–1&")"** This formula returns both the label and t's degrees of freedom.
13	**C21**	**=C19/C20** The t statistic equals each coefficient divided by its standard error.
4	**C23** **C24**	**=AVERAGE(INDEX(Data,1,C$14):INDEX(Data,ROWS(Data),C$14))** **=STDEV(INDEX(Data,1,C$14):INDEX(Data,ROWS(Data),C$14))** Copy these formulas to the right as needed. However, because the Y column contains a "Y" in row 14 rather than a number, this formula won't work for the Y values.
4	**F23** **F24**	**=AVERAGE(INDEX(Data,1,COLUMNS(Data)):INDEX(Data,ROWS(Data), COLUMNS(Data)))** **=STDEV(INDEX(Data,1,COLUMNS(Data)):INDEX(Data,ROWS(Data), COLUMNS(Data)))** Use these two formulas to calculate the average and standard deviation of the Y value in the Data range.
5	**B28**	**1** This cell contains the value 1, which is hidden by its number format.
5	**C28**	**35** The remaining cells in this row contain your forecast values for the independent variables (the X values).
6	**B29**	**=MMULT(Est,TRANSPOSE(b))** This array formula calculates the Y value by multiplying the estimated values of the independent variables by the coefficients of the regression equation.
7	**C34**	**=SUM((AvgY–MMULT(Xi,TRANSPOSE(b)))^2)** To find the sum of the squared deviations due to Regression in this array formula, subtract the column of predicted Ys (generated here by the MMULT section of this array formula) from the mean of the Ys (AvgY), square the results, and then sum the squares.
7	**C35**	**=SUM((Y–MMULT(Xi,TRANSPOSE(b)))^2)** To find the sum of the squared deviations caused by Errors in this array formula, subtract the column of predicted Ys (generated here by the MMULT section of this array formula) from each value of Y, square the results, and then sum the squares.

(continued)

Figure 7-8. *continued*

KEY FORMULAS–continued	
Cell	***Formula***
C36	**=SUM((Y–AvgY)^2)** To find the total sum of the squared deviations in this array formula, subtract the average Y from each value of Y, square the results, and then sum the squares.
D34	**=k** The SSR degrees of freedom equals the number of independent variables.
D35	**=n–k–1** The SSE degrees of freedom equals the total number of observations less the number of both the dependent and independent variables.
D36	**=n–1** The SST degrees of freedom equals the total number of observations less the number of dependent variables. It also equals the sum of the previous two degrees of freedom.
E34	**=SSR/D34** The mean squared deviation due to regression equals the sum of the squares due to regression divided by the SSR degrees of freedom.
E35	**=SSE/D35** The mean squared deviation caused by the error equals the sum of the squares caused by the error divided by the SSE degrees of freedom.
A42 **C40**	**=1+A41** **=1+B40** Copy these formulas down or to the right as needed.
B41	**=(MMULT(TRANSPOSE(Data–Avg),Data–Avg)/(TRANSPOSE(Std)*Std))/(n–1)** If we let U and W be any variables in the Data range and we let u and w equal the values of the deviations from their means, their correlation coefficient is equal to Sum(u*w)/Sqrt(Sum(u^2)*Sum(w^2)). This formula generates an array that contains all such combinations of correlations. To enter this formula, first highlight the range B63:E66, enter the formula as shown, and then enter the formula by holding down Ctrl-Shift while pressing Enter.

(continued)

Figure 7-8. *continued*

RANGE NAMES	
Name	***Formula***
Input	**=MR_DATA.XLS!Input** This range name refers to the spreadsheet in Figure 7-7.
Data	**=INDEX(Input,2,2):INDEX(Input,ROWS(Input)–1,COLUMNS(Input))** The Data matrix contains all the data and only the data. It excludes both the borders and the column of ones from the Input matrix.
Xi **X**	**=INDEX(Input,2,1):INDEX(Input,ROWS(Input)–1,COLUMNS(Input)–1)** **=INDEX(Input,2,2):INDEX(Input,ROWS(Input)–1,COLUMNS(Input)–1)** These two arrays of X data differ in only one way. The Xi matrix includes the column of ones; the X matrix excludes this column.
Y	**=INDEX(Input,2,COLUMNS(Input)):INDEX(Input,ROWS(Input)–1, COLUMNS(Input))** The Y column contains the data in the rightmost column of the Data matrix.
The previous four range names use dynamic range definitions as described in Appendix C of this book.	
n	**=$C$7** This name defines the cell that contains the number of observations (in this example, the number of months of data).
k	**=$C$8** Authorities are divided between whether k should represent the number of independent variables--the Xs--or the number of all variables--the Xs and the Y. Here k represents the number of X variables.
b	**=$B$19:$E$19** This name contains all coefficients of the regression equation.
Avg **AvgY**	**=$C$23:$F$23** **=$F$23** The Avg name contains the averages of both the X and the Y variables. The AvgY name contains only the average for the Y variable.
Std	**=$C$24:$F$24** This name contains the standard deviation of each of the X and Y variables.
Est	**=$B$28:$E$28** The Point Estimate section of the spreadsheet forecasts a value of Y when you enter values of X. This range contains the estimate values of X. Notice, however, that the range includes cell B28, which contains the hidden value 1.

(continued)

Figure 7-8. *continued*

RANGE NAMES–continued	
Name	***Formula***
SSR	**=$C$34**
SSE	**=$C$35**
SST	**=$C$36**
	These names contain the respective values for the sum of the squares due to regression (SSR), attributed to errors(SSE), and adding to the total(SST).
MSR	**=$E$34**
MSE	**=$E$35**
	These two names label values from the ANOVA table. MSR represents the regression mean square. MSE represents the error mean square.

KEY CELL FORMATS			
Cell	***Number***	***Alignment***	***Font***
B28	;;	**General**	**Helv 10**
	This cell contains the value 1, hidden by this number format. Format the other numbers in the spreadsheet as shown.		

Figure 7-9. Expense Analysis with Multiple Regression Analysis

A spreadsheet that regresses each expense on both time and company sales.

	A	B	C	D	E	F	G	H	I	J	K	L	M	N	O	P	Q	R
1																		
2																		
3	**Expense Analysis with Multiple Regression**																	
4				**Slope**			**F**	**t-Statistic (df=2)**				**Performance for the Month**						
5	**Description**	**Acct**	**Const**	**Time**	**Sales**	**r.^2**	**(2,2)**	**Const**	**Time**	**Sales**		**Jan**	**Feb**	**Mar**	**Apr**	**May**		
6	**(When you complete this spreadsheet, assign this row a height of 0.)**											1	1	1	1	1		
7	Time (X1-value)											1	2	3	4	5		
8	Sales (X2-value)	3050										123,423	161,098	149,093	224,293	186,244		
9	Janitorial	4762	$887	-0.31	.0000	1%	0.01	33.620	-.059	.125		882	902	893	888	890		
10	Freight	4833	$1,084	-193.03	.0449	97%	27.86	1.059	-.956	5.394		6,201	7,926	7,645	10,432	8,222		
11	Travel	5983	$1,222	79.44	.0163	80%	4.10	.942	.310	1.547		2,883	4,503	4,106	5,020	4,562		
12	Telephone	6234	$1,325	488.33	-.0013	99%	111.59	5.281	9.868	-.632		1,730	2,055	2,502	2,995	3,580		
13	Office Supplies	6341	$842	-133.72	.0055	81%	4.36	3.465	-2.789	2.778		1,305	1,523	1,334	1,520	1,156		
14	Training	6734	$1,242	-44.93	-.0027	99%	118.27	22.896	-4.199	-6.027		866	711	733	474	509		
15	Legal Fees	6819	$998	-869.73	.0164	34%	0.52	.206	-.909	.416		3,750	0	138	1,900	0		
16	Bldg Rent	6901	$6,250	0.00	.0000	0%	0.00	.000	.000	.000		6250	6250	6250	6250	6250		
17																		
18																		

KEY FORMULAS

Cell	*Formula*
G5 I4	**="("&2&","&COUNTA($K$5:$Q$5)–3&")"** **="t Statistic (df="&COUNTA($K$5:$Q$5)–3&")"** These two formulas return the degrees of freedom for the two statistics as labels.
L6	**1** The Xi range in this spreadsheet needs a column containing the value 1 at its left, just as it did in the spreadsheet in Figure 7-7. Copy this value to the range L6:P6. The definition of the Xi range transposes this row so that it becomes a column at the left of the Xi range.
L7 M7	**1** **=1+L7** Copy the formula to the right as needed.
C9 D9 E9	**=INDEX(LINEST(Y,X),1,3)** **=INDEX(LINEST(Y,X),1,2)** **=INDEX(LINEST(Y,X),1,1)** For multiple regression, the LINEST function returns an array that contains the regression constant in its last column, the first regression coefficient in the column before that, and so on. The INDEX function returns the proper values.

(continued)

Figure 7-9. *continued*

KEY FORMULAS–continued	
Cell	***Formula***
F9	=IF(MAX(Y)=MIN(Y),0,SSR/SST)
G9	=IF(F9=0,0,(SSR/(COUNT(X)/n))/((SSE/(n–(COUNT(X)/n)–1))))
H9	=C9/SQRT(INDEX(MINVERSE(MMULT(TRANSPOSE(Xi),Xi)),1,1)*s^2)
I9	=D9/SQRT(INDEX(MINVERSE(MMULT(TRANSPOSE(Xi),Xi)),2,2)*s^2)
J9	=E9/SQRT(INDEX(MINVERSE(MMULT(TRANSPOSE(Xi),Xi)),3,3)*s^2)
	These formulas for the R-squared, F, and t statistics are based on those in the spreadsheet in Figure 7-8. Enter the formulas in H9, I9, and J9 as array formulas.

RANGE NAMES	
Name	***Formula***
XX	=$K$6:$Q$8
YY	=RC11:RC17
X	=INDEX(XX,2,2):INDEX(XX,3,COLUMNS(XX)–1)
Y	=INDEX(YY,1,2):INDEX(YY,1,COLUMNS(YY)–1)
	These range definitions are similar to those in the spreadsheet in Figure 7-5.
Xi	=TRANSPOSE(INDEX(XX,1,2):INDEX(XX,3,COLUMNS(XX)–1))
	This definition of the Xi range creates a range in memory that contains three columns of data: a column containing the value 1, the data 1–5, and the sales data.
b	=RC3:RC5
SST	=SUM((Y–AVERAGE(Y))^2)
SSE	=SUM((TRANSPOSE(Y)–MMULT(Xi,TRANSPOSE(b)))^2)
SSR	=SST–SSE
	These range definitions are similar to those in the multiple regression spreadsheet in Figure 7-8.
n	=COUNT(Y)
s	=(SSE/(n–3))^0.5
	This formula defines the standard error of the estimate, as shown in the spreadsheet in Figure 7-8.

Figure 7-10. Time-Series Analysis of Sales

A time-series spreadsheet, which helps identify the influence that seasonality, long-term trends, and economic cycles have on monthly sales—information it uses to forecast future sales by month. Saved as TIME_SER.XLS.

	A	B	C	D	E	F	G	H	I	J	K	L	M
1													
2													
3	**Time-Series Analysis of Sales**												
4													
5													
6	**Miscellaneous Data & Calculations**												
7	Enter last date of actual data			12/1/88	Sales Constant				12,624				
8	Enter beg year of actual data			1985	Sales Growth / Month				51				
9	Cur Month's # in Database			48	R-Squared				63%				
10													
11													
12	**Dynamic Range Names**												
13	(The first row of names includes both actual and forecasted performance; the second row includes only actual performance.)												
14	1	2	3	4	5	6	7	8	9	10	11	12	
15	Seq	Month	Sales		Seas		Trend	StageC	Cycle			GraphA	
16	ASeq	AMonth	ASales	AStageA		AStageB			ACycle	APoints			
17													
18													
19	**Time-Series Decomposition Calculations**												
20–24	Seq #	Month	Actual and Fcstd Sales	Ratio: Sales to Moving Average	Seas Index	Sales w/out Seas Index	Sales Trend	Ratio of Econ Cycle and Random	Econ Cycle	Econ Cycle Turning Points	Random Sales $ Variance	Sales Trend w/ Cycle	
25													
26	1	Jan-85	11,905		0.873	13,636	12,675	1.076	1.080	1	(48)	13,691	
27	2	Feb-85	12,783		0.926	13,801	12,726	1.084	1.071		164	13,625	
28	3	Mar-85	13,078		0.973	13,435	12,778	1.051	1.051		9	13,426	
29	4	Apr-85	13,857		1.037	13,368	12,829	1.042	1.042		(3)	13,371	
30	5	May-85	14,331		1.113	12,878	12,880	1.000	1.033		(474)	13,303	
31	6	Jun-85	14,943		1.134	13,182	12,932	1.019	1.021		(22)	13,201	
32	7	Jul-85	13,516	0.959	1.028	13,145	12,983	1.012	1.011		21	13,125	
72	47	Nov-88	14,935	0.000	0.960	15,551	15,037	1.034	1.013		310	15,228	
73	48	Dec-88	12,026	0.000	0.807	14,895	15,089	0.987	1.014	1	(330)	15,304	
74	49	Jan-89	13,420	0.000	0.873	15,372	15,140	1.015	1.015		0	15,372	
75	50	Feb-89	14,300	0.000	0.926	15,439	15,191	1.016	1.016		0	15,439	
76	51	Mar-89	15,094	0.000	0.973	15,506	15,243	1.017	1.017		0	15,506	
77	52	Apr-89	16,144	0.000	1.037	15,574	15,294	1.018	1.018		0	15,574	
78	53	May-89	17,407	0.000	1.113	15,642	15,346	1.019	1.019		0	15,642	
79	54	Jun-89	17,756	0.000	1.134	15,663	15,397	1.017	1.017		0	15,663	
80	55	Jul-89	16,127	0.000	1.028	15,685	15,448	1.015	1.015		0	15,685	
81	56	Aug-89	16,679	0.000	1.062	15,706	15,500	1.013	1.013		0	15,706	
82	57	Sep-89	17,101	0.000	1.087	15,727	15,551	1.011	1.011		0	15,727	
83	58	Oct-89	15,730	0.000	0.999	15,747	15,602	1.009	1.009		0	15,747	
84	59	Nov-89	15,143	0.000	0.960	15,768	15,654	1.007	1.007		0	15,768	
85	60	Dec-89	12,747	0.000	0.807	15,788	15,705	1.005	1.005		0	15,788	
86	61	Jan-90											
87													
88													

(continued)

Figure 7-10. *continued*

COLUMN WIDTHS							
Column	*Width*	*Column*	*Width*	*Column*	*Width*	*Column*	*Width*
A	4.86	E	7	I	6.14	M	2
B	6.57	F	7.57	J	7		
C	6.86	G	7	K	7.57		
D	7.57	H	7.43	L	7.57		

KEY FORMULAS	
Cell	*Formula*
E9	**=LOOKUP(Now,Month,Seq)** This formula looks up the current data in the list of months and returns the sequence number corresponding to the number of actual months of data in the database.
I7 I8	**=INDEX(LINEST(AStageB),1,2)** **=INDEX(LINEST(AStageB),1,1)** These formulas fit a straight line to the deseasonalized sales data.
I9	**=I8^2*VAR(ASeq)/VAR(AStageB)** The R-squared presents the total of the squared deviations that can be explained by the regression equation.
A14	**=CELL("col",A14)** Copy this formula to the right as needed.
A26 A27	**1** **=1+A26**
B26 B27	**1/1/85** **=DATE(YEAR(B26),MONTH(B26)+1,1)** The formula returns the first day of each successive month.
C26	**=IF(A26>End,E26*G26*I26,VLOOKUP(DATE(1900,MONTH(B26),1), SlsHist,YEAR(B26)–BYear+2))** If the sequence number in column A exceeds the value of End, this formula returns a sales forecast; otherwise, it returns the actual sales value. The sales forecast equals the seasonal index times the trend times the economic cycle.

(continued)

Figure 7-10. *continued*

KEY FORMULAS–continued	
Cell	***Formula***
D32	**=IF(A32<End–6,C32/(SUM(C26:C38,C27:C39)/24),0)** This formula finds the ratio of the current month's sales to a "centered moving average" of actual sales data over a one-year period. The center of average sales from January through December is the period June 15–July 15; the center of average sales from February through the following January is the period July 15–August 15. By averaging the two periods in this cell, we obtain the required center for the month of July, which we compare to actual July sales. Begin this formula seven months below the first month of data. Copy this formula downward as needed.
E26	**=VLOOKUP(MONTH(B26),Index,3)** This formula looks up the calculated seasonal index in the Index range.
F26	**=C26/E26** By dividing Sales by the seasonal index, we "deseasonalize" the sales.
G26	**=Constant+A26*Growth** The trend calculation for any period is equal to the constant from the linear regression plus the sequence number for the period times the amount of periodic growth.
H26	**=F26/G26** Deseasonalized sales divided by the sales trend leaves a ratio that combines the economic cycle and random fluctuations.
I26 **I27** **I28**	**=AVERAGE(H$26:H27)** **=AVERAGE(H$26:H28)** **=AVERAGE(H$26:H30)** The averaging formula in cell I29 looks forward and backward three periods. These first three formulas start the averaging process.
I29	**=IF(A29>End,VLOOKUP(B29,CycFcst,3),** **AVERAGE(H26:INDEX(StageC,MIN(A28+2,End)),1))** If the current row contains forecasted data, this formula looks up the cycle forecast; otherwise, it calculates the seven-month moving average. As the average approaches the end of the actual data, however, be careful not to include forecasted data in the average. (Doing so generates circular-calculation errors.) The MIN expression therefore limits the average to actual data.
J26	**=IF(I26>I27,1,–1)** This formula sets a turning point value of 1 or –1 (respectively), depending on whether the cycle is decreasing or increasing.

(continued)

Figure 7-10. *continued*

KEY FORMULAS–continued	
Cell	***Formula***
J27	**=IF($A27<End,($I27=MAX($I26:$I28))–($I27=MIN($I26:$I28)),0)+ IF($A27=End,IF(I27>I26,1,–1),0)** If the current period is less than the last month of actual performance, this formula returns a 1 if both the preceding and following values in column I are less than the current value (a peak), and –1 if they are both greater than the current value (a trough). Otherwise, they return the value 0. If the current period is the last one showing actual performance, this formula returns a 1 if the cycle is rising and a –1 if it's falling.
K26	**=C26–E26*G26*I26** This column shows random, or unexplained, variations in sales. It equals actual sales less sales predicted from the seasonal index, trend, and economic cycle.
L26	**=G26*I26** This column, which generates one of the graph values, combines the sales trend with the economic cycle.

RANGE NAMES	
Name	***Formula***
Now	**=$E$7** Enter the most recent month of actual data in this cell.
Constant **Growth**	**=$I$7** **=$I$8** The growth trend is a straight line drawn through actual sales data. These names contain the description of that line.
BYear	**=$E$8** This cell contains the first year for which actual sales data exists.
End	**=$E$9** This cell contains the number of months of actual sales data on file.
Data	**=$A$25:$L$87** This range, which extends from the top border to the bottom border of the data, serves as a guide for naming most of the remaining ranges.

(continued)

Figure 7-10. *continued*

RANGE NAMES–continued	
Name	***Formula***
Seq **ASeq**	**=INDEX(Data,2,$A$14):INDEX(Data,ROWS(Data)–1,$A$14)** **=INDEX(Data,2,$A$14):INDEX(Data,End+1,$A$14)** These range formulas define the sequence number in column A. Seq defines all numbers in the schedule. ASeq defines only the numbers for actual performance.
Month **AMonth**	**=INDEX(Data,2,$B$14):INDEX(Data,ROWS(Data)–1,$B$14)** **=INDEX(Data,2,$B$14):INDEX(Data,End+1,$B$14)** These range formulas define the month for each row of data. The Month range defines all months; the AMonth range defines months associated with actual performance.
SlsHist	**=SLSHIST.XLS!Sales** This name references the Sales History table in the spreadsheet in Figure 7-11.
Sales **ASales**	**=INDEX(Data,2,$C$14):INDEX(Data,ROWS(Data)–1,$C$14)** **=INDEX(Data,2,$C$14):INDEX(Data,End+1,$C$14)** All sales data is in Sales. Actual sales performance is in ASales.
AStageA	**=INDEX(Data,2,$D$14):INDEX(Data,End+1,$D$14)** When performing time-series analysis, you strip patterns from actual sales data to understand what forces affect sales. In doing so, you go through several stages of intermediate calculations. Each stage has little independent meaning, except that each represents subtotals from which you can extract meaning. This first stage represents a ratio of actual sales to a 12-month moving average. Each month's seasonal index is equal to an average of these ratios for each month over several years.
Seas	**=INDEX(Data,2,$E$14):INDEX(Data,ROWS(Data)–1,$E$14)** This range contains the seasonal index calculated from AStageA.
AStageB	**=INDEX(Data,2,$F$14):INDEX(Data,End+1,$F$14)** This stage contains actual sales with the seasonal effects removed.
Trend	**=INDEX(Data,2,$G$14):INDEX(Data,ROWS(Data)–1,$G$14)** The trend column is the result of a linear-regression calculation performed on AStageB. A graph of the data in this column would produce a straight line.
StageC	**=INDEX(Data,2,$H$14):INDEX(Data,End+1,$H$14)** This range contains actual sales with the seasonal index and the trend removed. What remains is a ratio representing both the economic cycle and random events.

(continued)

Figure 7-10. *continued*

RANGE NAMES–continued	
Name	*Formula*
Cycle	**=INDEX(Data,2,$I$14):INDEX(Data,ROWS(Data)–1,$I$14)** This range contains data representing both the past economic cycle and the projected cycle.
ACycle	**=INDEX(Data,2,$I$14):INDEX(Data,End+1,$I$14)** Only the actual economic cycle is represented in this range.
APoints	**=INDEX(Data,2,$J$14):INDEX(Data,End+1,$J$14)** The turning points of the economic cycle are represented in this range. The top of each cycle is represented by a 1. The bottom is represented by a –1.
GraphA	**=INDEX(Data,2,$L$14):INDEX(Data,ROWS(Data)–1,$L$14)** The data in this column is used by the graph shown in Figure 7-16. It contains the actual and projected values of the sales trend combined with the economic cycle.
Index	**=SEAS_NDX.XLS!Index** This name references the forecast of the economic cycle in the spreadsheet in Figure 7-12.
CycFcst	**=CYCL_NDX.XLS!CycFcst** This name references the Seasonality Index in the spreadsheet in Figure 7-15.

KEY CELL FORMATS			
Cell	*Number*	*Alignment*	*Font*
A3	General	General	Helv 10, Bold
A6	General	General	Helv 10, Bold
E7	m/d/yy	General	Helv 10
I9	0%	General	Helv 10
A12	General	General	Helv 10, Bold
A13	General	General	Helv 8
A14:L14	General	Center	Helv 10, Bold
A15:L16	General	Center	Helv 10
A19	General	General	Helv 10, Bold
A20:L24	General	Center	Helv 10

(continued)

Figure 7-10. *continued*

KEY CELL FORMATS—continued			
Cell	*Number*	*Alignment*	*Font*
A25:A87	General	Center	Helv 10
B25:B87	mmm-yy	Center	Helv 10
C25:C87	#,##0 ;(#,##0)	General	Helv 10
D25:E87	General	General	Helv 10
F25:G87	#,##0 ;(#,##0)	General	Helv 10
H25:I87	0.000	General	Helv 10
J25:J87	#;(#);	Center	Helv 10
K25:L87	#,##0 ;(#,##0)	General	Helv 10

Figure 7-11. Sales History for Time-Series Analysis

A sales history that provides the raw data for the time-series analysis in Figure 7-10. Saved as SLSHIST.XLS.

	A	B	C	D	E	F	G
1							
2							
3	**Sales History**						
4	Month	1985	1986	1987	1988	1989	
5	Jan	$11,905	$10,874	$12,780	$12,547		
6	Feb	$12,783	$11,150	$13,602	$13,977		
7	Mar	$13,078	$11,980	$14,084	$14,725		
8	Apr	$13,857	$12,744	$15,194	$15,496		
9	May	$14,331	$14,310	$15,467	$16,614		
10	Jun	$14,943	$14,885	$15,680	$16,639		
11	Jul	$13,516	$13,225	$14,622	$14,731		
12	Aug	$13,729	$14,075	$15,180	$15,879		
13	Sep	$14,134	$14,622	$15,558	$16,341		
14	Oct	$12,939	$14,009	$14,088	$15,627		
15	Nov	$12,907	$13,477	$13,308	$14,935		
16	Dec	$10,529	$11,774	$11,090	$12,026		
17	Total	$158,651	$157,125	$170,653	$179,537	$0	

KEY FORMULAS	
Cell	***Formula***
B4	**1985**
C4	**=1+B4**
A5	**1**
A6	**=DATE(1900,1+MONTH(A5),1)**
B17	**=SUM(B5:B16)**
Copy all formulas down or to the right as needed.	

RANGE NAME	
Name	***Formula***
Sales	**=$A$5:$G$16** Formulas and range definitions in the spreadsheet in Figure 7-10 refer to this range name.

(continued)

Figure 7-11. *continued*

KEY CELL FORMATS			
Cell	***Number***	***Alignment***	***Font***
A4:G4	General	Center	Helv 10
A5:A16	mmm	Left	Helv 10
B5:G17	=$#,##0 ;($#,##0)	General	Helv 10

Figure 7-12. Average Seasonal Index

An average seasonal index that provides data for the time-series analysis in Figure 7-10. Saved as SEAS_NDX.XLS.

	A	B	C	D
1				
2				
3	Average Seasonal Index			
4	Month	Average	Index	
5	1	0.804	0.873	
6	2	0.853	0.926	
7	3	0.896	0.973	
8	4	0.954	1.037	
9	5	1.025	1.113	
10	6	1.044	1.134	
11	7	0.947	1.028	
12	8	0.978	1.062	
13	9	1.001	1.087	
14	10	0.920	0.999	
15	11	0.884	0.960	
16	12	0.743	0.807	
17	Totals	11.049	12.000	
18				
19				

KEY FORMULAS	
Cell	***Formula***
B5	**=AVERAGE(IF(MONTH(AMonth)=$A5,IF(AStageA>0,AStageA)))** This array formula returns the average of a temporary array. The array contains the values from AStageA in the spreadsheet in Figure 7-10 for the current month, but only if these are greater than 0. (The last seven values in AStageA equal 0.)
C5	**=(12/$B$17)*B5** This formula adjusts the averages in column B so that their total equals 12. Using this formula ensures that all seasonal indices total exactly 12 during the course of a year.
B17 **C17**	**=SUM(B5:B16)** **=SUM(C5:C16)**

(continued)

Figure 7-12. *continued*

RANGE NAMES	
Name	***Formula***
AMonth **AStageA**	**=TIME_SER.XLS!AMonth** **=TIME_SER!AStageA** When you define these file linkages to Figure 7-10 in range definitions, formulas in this spreadsheet become shorter and easier to create.
Index	**=$A$5:$C$16** Range definitions and formulas in the spreadsheet in Figure 7-10 refer to this range name.

KEY CELL FORMATS			
Cell	***Number***	***Alignment***	***Font***
A3	**General**	**Center**	**Helv 10**
A4:C4	**General**	**Center**	**Helv 10**
A5:C17	**General**	**Center**	**Helv 10**
B5:C17	**0.000**	**General**	**Helv 10**

Figure 7-13. Economic Cycle and Unexplained Sales

A chart of the economic cycle (the heavy line) and the unexplained sales variations (the light line).

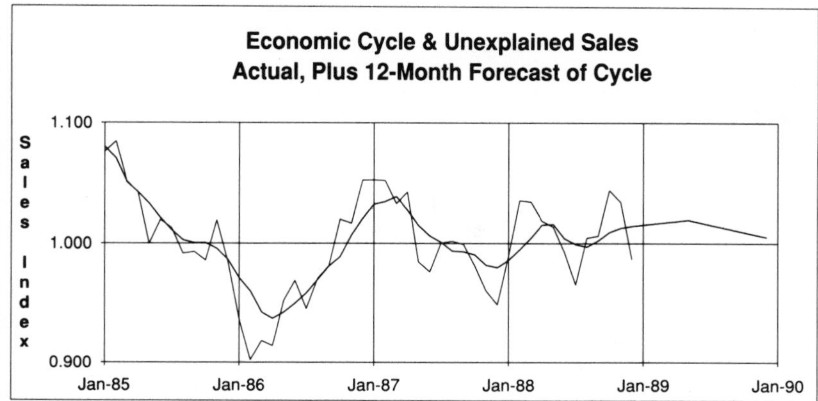

Figure 7-14. Turning Points of Past Economic Cycles

An analysis of turning points of economic cycles, based on data from the time-series analysis in Figure 7-10. Saved as CYCL_NDX.XLS.

	A	B	C	D	E	F	G	H	I
1									
2									
3	Turning Points of Past Economic Cycles								
4	Low Points				High Points				
5		Cycle	Elapsed	Index		Cycle	Elapsed	Index	
6	Date	Index	Months	Fall/Mo	Date	Index	Months	Rise/Mo	
7					Jan-85	1.08			
8	Apr-86	.94	14	-.010	Mar-87	1.04	11	.009	
9	Dec-87	.98	9	-.007	May-88	1.02	5	.007	
10	Aug-88	1.00	3	-.006	Dec-88	1.01	4	.004	
11									
12									
13									
14									
15									
16									

KEY FORMULAS	
Cell	***Formula***
A7	**=IF(INDEX(APoints,1,1)=–1,INDEX(DATE,1,1),0)** If the beginning value in the turning point column of the spreadsheet in Figure 7-10 is negative, this formula returns the beginning date; otherwise, it returns a 0.
A8	**=IF(E7=0,0,MIN(IF(AMonth>E7,IF(APoints=–1,AMonth))))** This array formula returns the next turning point on record at the trough of an economic cycle. The formula first checks to see if the last turning point in the schedule has already been displayed; if so, it returns a 0. If the last turning point has not been reached, it returns the date of the next negative turning point.
B7	**=IF(A7=0,0,LOOKUP(A7,DATE,Cycle))** If the first turning point is positive, this formula returns a 0; otherwise, it returns the cycle value.
B8	**=IF(A8=0,0,LOOKUP(A8,AMonth,Cycle))** If the last turning point has been listed, this formula returns a 0; otherwise, it returns the cycle value.
C7 **C8**	**(blank)** **=IF(A8=0,0,ROUND((A8–E7)/31.4375,0))** If the last turning point has been listed, this formula returns a 0; otherwise, it returns the number of months in the last cycle. This value equals the number of days in the cycle divided by the average number of days in a month (31.4375 = 365.25/12).

(continued)

Figure 7-14. *continued*

KEY FORMULAS–continued	
Cell	*Formula*
D7	(blank)
D8	=IF(C8=0,0,(B8–F7)/C8) If the last turning point has been listed, this formula returns a 0; otherwise, it returns the average monthly change in the index.
E7	=IF(A7=0,INDEX(AMonth,1,1),MIN(IF(AMonth>A7,IF(APoints=1,AMonth)))) If this cell begins the list of turning points, this array formula finds the first date in the AMonth column; otherwise, it returns the next positive turning point.
E8	=IF(A8=0,0,MIN(IF(AMonth>A8,IF(APoints=1,AMonth)))) If the last turning point has been listed, this array formula returns a 0; otherwise, it returns the date for the next positive turning point.
F7	=IF(E7=0,0,LOOKUP(E7,AMonth,Cycle)) If the last turning point has been listed, this formula returns a 0; otherwise, it returns the cycle index value for this turning point.
G7	=IF(A7=0,0,ROUND((E7–A7)/31.4375,0)) If the last turning point has been listed, this formula returns a 0; otherwise, it returns the elapsed time in months of the current turning point.
H7	=IF(G7=0,0,(F7–B7)/G7) If the last turning point has been listed, this formula returns a 0; otherwise, it returns the average monthly change in the cycle index since the last turning point.

RANGE NAMES	
Name	*Formula*
AMonth	=TIME_SER.XLS!AMonth
APoints	=TIME_SER.XLS!APoints
Cycle	=TIME_SER.XLS!Cycle
Now	=TIME_SER.XLS!Now These range names refer to the spreadsheet in Figure 7-10.
CycFcst	=$A$24:$C$35 The spreadsheet in Figure 7-10 refers to this name.

(continued)

Figure 7-14. *continued*

KEY CELL FORMATS			
Cell	***Number***	***Alignment***	***Font***
A7:A14	**mmm–yy;;**	**General**	**Helv 10**
B7:B14	**#.00;;**	**General**	**Helv 10**
C7:C14	**#;;**	**General**	**Helv 10**
D7:D14	**#.000;–#.000;**	**General**	**Helv 10**
E7:E14	**mmm–yy;;**	**General**	**Helv 10**
F7:F14	**#.00;;**	**General**	**Helv 10**
G7:G14	**#;;**	**General**	**Helv 10**
H7:H14	**#.000;–#.000;**	**General**	**Helv 10**

Figure 7-15. Economic Cycle Forecast

A forecast of economic cycles, which the time-series analysis in Figure 7-10 uses to forecast for the coming year. Saved as CYCL_NDX.XLS. For range names, see Figure 7-14.

	A	B	C	D
18				
19				
20	Economic Cycle Forecast			
21		Rise (Fall)	Cycle	
22	Date	/Month	Index	
23	Dec-88		1.014	
24	Jan-89	.001	1.015	
25	Feb-89	.001	1.016	
26	Mar-89	.001	1.017	
27	Apr-89	.001	1.018	
28	May-89	.001	1.019	
29	Jun-89	-.002	1.017	
30	Jul-89	-.002	1.015	
31	Aug-89	-.002	1.013	
32	Sep-89	-.002	1.011	
33	Oct-89	-.002	1.009	
34	Nov-89	-.002	1.007	
35	Dec-89	-.002	1.005	
36				
37				

KEY FORMULAS

Cell	*Formula*
A23	**=Now** This formula returns the last date in the spreadsheet in Figure 7-10 containing actual performance.
A24	**=DATE(YEAR(A23),MONTH(A23)+1,1)** The actual schedule begins with the first month after the date in cell A23.
B24	**0.001** Using the schedule in the spreadsheet in Figure 7-14 as a guide, enter the amount you expect the economy to rise or fall monthly during the next 12 months.
C23	**=LOOKUP(A23,AMonth,Cycle)** This formula returns the last index value based on actual sales performance.
C24	**=C23+B24** This formula calculates the new cycle index based on the previous cycle value plus the forecasted change during the current month.

Figure 7-16. Sales, Trend, and Economic Cycle

A chart of the first four years of actual sales, trends, and economic cycles and the fifth-year prediction generated by the time-series analysis in Figure 7-10.

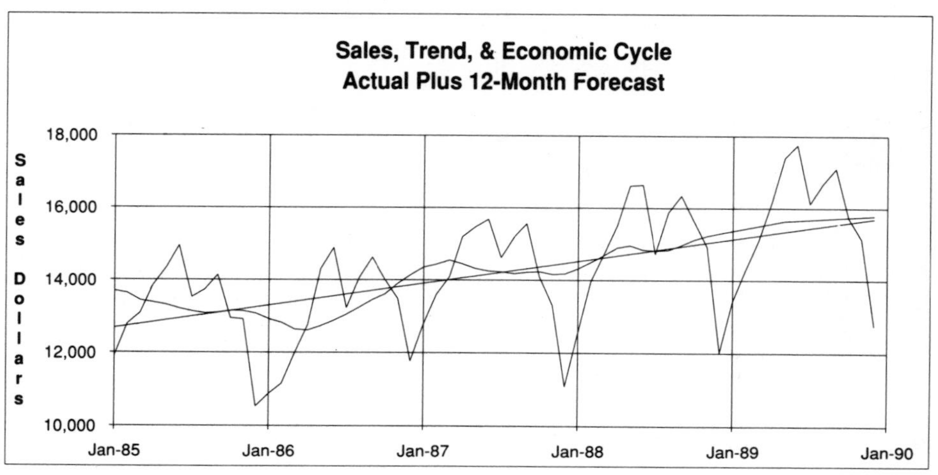

8

Budgets and Budget Reports

If your company is like most, your computer spreadsheet is the only tool you use for generating budgets. Even if you own a computerized accounting system that generates budget reports, you still might prefer to use spreadsheets for this purpose. This chapter presents spreadsheets that can help you simplify and improve both tasks.

The first series of spreadsheets represents a system that lets you group expenses in the general ledger by budget code, a procedure that simplifies budgeting for everyone involved. The second series of spreadsheets provides ways to budget direct material, direct-labor hours and wages, and overtime hours and wages. The final series shows you how to budget asset purchases and depreciation.

DEPARTMENTAL EXPENSES

Computerized accounting systems often do a great job of accumulating expenses, but a bad job of reporting them.

- Most of these systems require that you create a budget for each general ledger account number, which creates problems. The accounting department must often use many account numbers to track expenses in fine detail; but department managers, when they budget, think in broad categories. "I know how much we'll spend in advertising and promotion next year," a marketing manager might say, "but I can't tell you right now the amount we'll spend for direct mail, print advertising, trade shows, and so on."

- Many accounting systems provide no way to load budgets from spreadsheets into the budget fields of the accounting system. Instead, they require that clerks spend days manually entering and correcting budgets for hundreds, often thousands, of expense accounts.
- Many companies work with two or three sets of budgets: annual, quarterly, and revised. But most accounting systems can contain only one set of budgets. As a consequence, the accounting system cannot compare actual spending with more than one budget or compare one budget with another.
- Every dollar a business spends can be placed in many different categories that accounting systems don't report, but that managers often need. For example, a business might classify a dollar as having been spent: by the Manufacturing department, in February, for hand tools, to improve product quality, for products produced by a welding jig, for the camp stove product, and as part of the Outdoors product line.

  Also, the president might need a schedule of quality-improvement costs by product line by month. Or the manufacturing manager might want to see a schedule of welding-jig expenses by product by expense item. It's the rare accounting system that could produce these reports.

Because spreadsheets can easily report and analyze expenses in so many different ways, it makes sense to use spreadsheets for this purpose.

Generating Data for Budget Reporting

The spreadsheet that reports budget performance must refer to several different files. Figure 8-1 on page 375 presents one of these, a general ledger chart of accounts. Like most charts of accounts, this spreadsheet contains the general ledger account number and its description. Unlike most charts of accounts, however, this spreadsheet also contains a column of budget codes.

Many large companies use budget codes to provide both accountants and managers the flexibility they need when reporting and budgeting expenses. The GL-account numbers provide the detail that accountants need for both legal and internal reporting. The budget codes group these numbers into more general categories that managers can use for budgeting. The spreadsheet in Figure 8-1, for example, assigns the six GL-account numbers to three budget codes, which the spreadsheet in Figure 8-2 on page 376 defines.

Some managers, in fact, would say that even the three budget categories shown in the spreadsheet in Figure 8-2 are too many, that travel and entertainment should be one budget category. One of the advantages of using budget codes is that you can change their definitions when you want. If it makes sense, for example, to budget travel and entertainment as a single category, you are perfectly free to do so; the categories are for your benefit, after all.

To create the spreadsheets shown in Figure 8-1 and Figure 8-2, open a new spreadsheet for each, turn off their gridlines, and enter the labels, borders, and values shown. Information boxes for each spreadsheet provide all range definitions and formulas. Save the spreadsheet in Figure 8-1 as GL_CODE.XLS and the spreadsheet in Figure 8-2 as BUD_CODE.XLS.

The spreadsheet in Figure 8-3 on page 377 contains the department codes used in the budget reports that follow. This spreadsheet resembles the previous two. Enter it as shown, using the information boxes provided, and save it using the name DPT_CODE.XLS.

Creating a Trial Balance

The spreadsheet in Figure 8-4 contains data that most accounting systems print as part of the general ledger trial balance. In most systems, this monthly report presents last month's balance by account and department, the total change for each combination, and the new balance by account and department. The spreadsheet in Figure 8-4 on page 378 contains only the changes for the departmental expenses for the month. For simplicity, I'll refer to this spreadsheet as the trial balance.

Column E of this spreadsheet contains a formula that returns *New* if the account and department combination cannot be found in the spreadsheets that follow. At times, this message might uncover a data-entry error in your accounting system. It can alert you, for example, that someone charged sales commissions to the manufacturing department. Generally, however, the message merely tells you to make room in the two spreadsheets that follow for a new category of expenses.

To create this spreadsheet, enter the labels, data, and numbers shown, and then enter the formulas and define the range names specified in the information boxes for Figure 8-4. Save the figure as TRIALBAL.XLS. To substitute your own data in this file, begin with the spreadsheet shown, erase the data in columns A through D, insert enough rows between the shaded bar (row 18) and the description row (row 5) to contain your own data, copy your data into the spreadsheet, and then copy the formula from any convenient cell in column E down the expanded column.

Creating a Budget Containing Budget-Code Numbers by Department

The spreadsheet in Figure 8-5 on page 380 contains all departmental budgets, by budget code, for the 1989 fiscal year. Each department manager creates his or her own budgets using actual spending from the previous fiscal year, knowledge of the fixed-cost and variable-cost relationships discussed in Chapter 7, and, most likely, instinct sharpened by experience. This spreadsheet combines all of these individual budgets into one budget database.

Columns C and D in the budget in Figure 8-5 contain the only formulas in the range A6:P17. Enter the entire budget in a new spreadsheet, but leave the ranges C4:D4 and C7:D16 blank for now. The figure's range-name box shows the range names Data, Bcode, Dept, Month, and Year in one group. Enter these range names as shown; you will enter the remaining name in a moment. Save this spreadsheet as BUD_89.XLS.

Creating a Summary of Actual Expenses

The spreadsheet in Figure 8-6 on page 383 resembles the one in Figure 8-5. But while the one in Figure 8-5 contains budget information, the one in Figure 8-6 contains a summary of actual expenses. This spreadsheet takes more effort to maintain than most in this chapter, for two reasons:

- If you add a new combination of department and budget code to your actual spending, you must add this data to Figure 8-6. To do so, insert a row between the shaded borders, enter the new budget and department codes, and then copy the appropriate formulas from an adjacent row. Afterwards, sort the data, using the department as the first key and the budget code as the second key.
- The formulas in this spreadsheet summarize information from the current trial balance, which is shown in Figure 8-4. But before you can replace last month's trial balance with the new one, you must turn last month's data, now in the spreadsheet in Figure 8-6, into values. In the spreadsheet in Figure 8-6, for example, I changed January's formulas into values by highlighting the range E6:E17, pressing Ctrl-Ins, choosing Edit Paste Special, and selecting Values.

The easiest way to create this spreadsheet is to begin with a working copy of the BUD_89.XLS spreadsheet, shown in Figure 8-5. However, that budget spreadsheet isn't yet completed. Therefore, we'll move on to the spreadsheet in Figure 8-7, and then return to the spreadsheets in Figure 8-5 and Figure 8-6 a little later. The reason for this delay will become clear shortly.

Figure 8-7 on page 386 contains the first of six reports in one spreadsheet file, a report of monthly spending by budget code. This part provides an overview of how actual spending behaved during the past month. To begin this report, open a new spreadsheet, turn off the gridlines, and set the column widths specified in the column-width box. Enter the labels, dates, and underlines shown in rows 3 through 7 and then format them as shown in the figure's format box.

Define the first three range names shown in the range-name box for Figure 8-7. You will define the remaining range names shortly.

After you complete the first seven rows of the report in Figure 8-7, you can complete the spreadsheet in Figure 8-5 by defining the remaining range name for that figure and by entering the formulas shown in the figure's formula box. When you do so, you can see that the spreadsheet in Figure 8-7 contains the current date, which the spreadsheet in Figure 8-5 must reference to calculate the budgets for the month and for the year to date. This is why you had to wait to complete this spreadsheet until the one in Figure 8-7 was started.

Now it's time to create the spreadsheet in Figure 8-6. Save the spreadsheet shown in Figure 8-5, BUD_89.XLS. Save it again as ACT_89.XLS. Then, open the BUD_89.XLS spreadsheet. You now have two identical spreadsheets saved under two different names.

Activate the spreadsheet ACT_89.XLS, which will become the spreadsheet in Figure 8-6. The range-name box for this figure contains two groups of names. You defined all the names in the first group and RepMonths in the second group when you created the spreadsheet in Figure 8-5. Define the remaining range names shown in the range-name box for Figure 8-6.

With one exception, all the formulas in the formula box for Figure 8-6 have already been entered as well. Enter the exception—the formula in cell F7—and copy it to the range F7:P16. To complete this spreadsheet, enter the values shown in the range E7:E16 and then save the spreadsheet ACT_89.XLS.

Completing the Report of Actual Monthly Spending by Budget Code

You can now complete the report in Figure 8-7. To do so, first define the remaining range names shown in the figure's range-name box. This might appear to be an unreasonable number of range names to define. But if it's any consolation, remember that six reports in this one spreadsheet file will use these names.

Enter the labels, underlines, values, and shading shown in rows 10 through 13, the range A14:A16, and rows 17 and 18. After you do so, fill in the formulas shown in the formula box and then complete the borders and formats.

Creating a Year-to-Date Report of Departmental Spending by Budget Code

Figure 8-8 on page 390 presents a year-to-date report of departmental spending by budget code, a report that is quite similar to the one in Figure 8-7. The easiest way to create this report is to copy the report in Figure 8-7 to the range shown and then modify the formulas as necessary. As always, the figure's formula box presents the key formulas.

Creating a Monthly Departmental Budget Report

Figure 8-9 on page 391 presents a report that provides more specific details about departmental spending. This typical budget report compares actual spending by the accounting department with its budget, for both the month and for the year to date. To report instead on, say, the manufacturing department, you enter the department code *16* in cell C36 and then recalculate.

To create this report, enter the labels, underlines, and so on, just as you did for previous reports. After you do so, fill in the formulas shown in the figure's formula box.

Creating a Departmental Spending Summary by Budget Code by Month

One problem with the report shown in Figure 8-9 is that you get no hint of spending trends. The report in Figure 8-10 on page 393 presents this information. This report summarizes the sales department's spending by budget code by month for the current fiscal year. As before, you can change the department shown in this report by changing the department code in cell C52. Create this report as shown, entering the formulas described in the figure's formula box.

Figure 8-11 shows a report that tracks spending trends by department, a report that can reveal which departments have kept their spending under control and which have not. To create this report, copy the report in Figure 8-10 to the range shown and then enter the formulas described in the formula box for Figure 8-11 on page 395.

The problem with the report in Figure 8-11 is that it includes no budget information. The marketing department, for instance, might have doubled its spending in recent months, but it might have been budgeted to do exactly that. Figure 8-12 on page 396, therefore, presents budget variances by department by month. The totals in row 92 present total budget variances by month and year to date. To create this display easily, copy the report in Figure 8-11 to the area shown and then enter the formulas shown in the formula box for Figure 8-12.

Finally, when you've completed the report in Figure 8-12, save your spreadsheet using the name BUD_RPT.XLS.

How to Adapt These Reports to Your Own Data

After you have entered the preceding reports, you can easily adapt them to your own data. To do so, modify them in the order of their appearance in this chapter.

To modify the reports in Figure 8-1 through Figure 8-3, erase the sample data and insert enough rows in the areas that contained the data to copy in your own general ledger account numbers, descriptions, budget codes, and department numbers.

If you've not yet assigned budget codes for your own business, do so now. As you do, remember that they are easy to change. Don't be too concerned about getting them right the first time. When you're finished, you probably will have between 10 and 25 budget codes.

After you assign the codes, sort the spreadsheet shown in Figure 8-1 in budget-code sequence, print the list, and then discuss the assignments with your department managers. Because they'll have to use these codes the next time they budget, they'll need to modify the account numbers you've assigned to each code so that they make sense for their own departments.

When you create the budget shown in Figure 8-5 for your own business, you probably will begin with the same number of spreadsheets as you have departments. Copy these departmental spreadsheets to a single spreadsheet. Move this data left or right as needed until all the budget-code numbers are in one column, January's budgets are all in another column, and so on. Add a column of department numbers, if necessary; delete unneeded rows of column descriptions; and then sort the entire database by department number and budget code. Finally, delete the sample data from the budget in Figure 8-5, insert the number of rows needed between the shaded borders, copy your own data to this spreadsheet, and then copy the formulas in columns C and D down the columns as needed.

Now that you've entered all the data, you can easily expand the remaining spreadsheets to report this information. As you do so, be certain that all data reconciles. For example, the total of all expenses in cell D19 of the spreadsheet in Figure 8-4 should equal the total of all expenses for the same month in row 18 of the spreadsheet in Figure 8-6, in cell G18 of the spreadsheet in Figure 8-7, and in row 77 of the spreadsheet in Figure 8-11.

FORECASTING THE COSTS OF DIRECT LABOR AND MATERIALS

From a distance, there's nothing difficult about forecasting the costs of direct labor and materials. You simply figure out the labor and material costs per product and then multiply these values by the number of products you plan to ship monthly. It's easy.

Unfortunately, it's *not* so easy. Many real-life complexities can make the task quite time-consuming:

- Because different manufacturing operations require different levels of skill and education, most manufacturers vary wage rates among their operations. And because each product usually requires a unique combination of operations and time per operation, each generally has a unique average-wage rate.
- Some changes in the unit shipment forecast can send planned overtime costs through the roof; others can virtually eliminate planned overtime. As a consequence, labor costs for any one product seldom are constant when the unit shipment forecast changes.
- Unit material costs, as well, can change frequently while you prepare the forecast. Therefore, you must be able to update your materials forecast easily.
- Unit sales forecasts tend to change frequently during a forecasting cycle. Each time they change, you must recalculate your costs of regular labor, overtime labor, and material. This is no simple task, given the preceding complications.

The spreadsheets in this section of this chapter provide a system that can help you overcome these problems quickly and easily as you forecast your costs of labor and materials.

A Unit Shipment Forecast

Figure 8-13 on page 397 presents a unit shipment forecast by product by month. Although a great deal of work is required to generate this forecast, the schedule itself is rather mundane—with one exception. Row 4 of the schedule contains the number of working hours available each month to produce the units forecasted in this schedule. The calculation of these hours reflects three facts about your business:

Your own workweek schedule. Whether your company works Monday through Friday eight hours a day plus a half day on Saturday, Monday through Thursday ten hours a day, or some other schedule, this row reflects your workweek in its calculations.

Your own holiday schedule. You must update this schedule for holidays at the beginning of each year, of course. But that takes less than a minute.

The number of hours you work daily. Because most manufacturing companies work eight hours a day, the formula in row 4 uses this value. But if you work multiple shifts or extended hours, you can easily modify this formula to reflect that work pattern.

To create this forecast, first open a new spreadsheet, turn off the gridlines, and set its columns to a convenient width; columns B through M of the sample forecast in Figure 8-13, for example, use a width of about 6.

Skipping the hour formulas in row 4 for the moment, enter the labels, values, borders, dates, and so on shown in the sample forecast. Its formula box shows the date formula and its format box defines the formatting.

Define the range names shown in the figure's range-name box. When you do so, you define three types of range names:

Common range names. The range names Input and Hours are garden-variety range names. To define these, highlight the ranges shown and then choose the Formula Define Name command.

Dynamic range-name formula. The formula that defines the range name Units causes this range to expand or contract as the range name Input expands or contracts. Many spreadsheets in this book use this approach.

Range-name constants. The range names Workweek, Holidays, and Days contain constant values that define the schedule for your workweek, your holidays, and a range that contains the numbers of the days of the week, from 1 for Sunday through 7 for Saturday.

After you define the range names, enter the formula shown in the formula box for cell B4. This formula, which the formula box explains in detail, processes the schedules you enter as range constants to calculate your working hours per month.

When you've completed the forecast, save the spreadsheet as UNITS.XLS.

Creating the Labor-Routing Schedule

The schedule in Figure 8-14 on page 401 contains your average labor-utilization rate, pay rates by operation, and manufacturing time required by product by operation. From this information, the spreadsheet calculates the labor hours used (by product), the worker hours used, and the labor cost per unit of product.

Most manufacturing companies experience two inefficiencies that force them to pay for more labor than they actually use to produce their product. The labor-utilization rate, shown in cell A6, calculates the effective use you get from your direct-labor employees, after allowing for these inefficiencies.

One of these inefficiencies is measured by the efficiency rate, which reflects the average percentage of worker time available to the company after coffee and bathroom breaks, personal phone calls, late lunches, and so on. The other is measured by the effectiveness rate, which reflects the average percentage of the available time that management actually uses employees for productive work. Time used for housekeeping, waiting for parts, searching for tools, and so on reduces this rate. In combination, they reflect the percentage of labor used to produce products.

The report in Figure 8-14 reflects the assumption that each labor operation specified in row 11 uses the same labor skills for all products and therefore requires the same hourly rate. Suppose, for example, that the company in the report has assigned the operation number 70 to the packaging operation. This report reflects the assumption that packaging labor earns $8.50 per hour, no matter which product an employee packs. If this assumption doesn't apply to your company, you may prefer to use the operation numbers to specify specific ranges of pay and the hours by product by operation to reflect the number of hours at each pay rate required for each product.

Column K, which shows labor hours used per product, simply totals the time shown for each product. Column L, which shows total worker hours needed, divides labor hours used by the labor-utilization rate. Column M, which calculates the labor cost per unit, multiplies the time required for each operation by its wage rate, sums the results, and then divides by the utilization rate.

To create this report, first open a new spreadsheet, turn off the gridlines, and set the column widths as shown in the column-width box. The only formulas in this report are in cell A6 and in columns K, L, and M. Skipping these formulas for the moment, enter the remainder of the schedule as shown. The figure's format box provides the key formats used.

Enter the range names shown in the range-name box and then enter the formulas shown in the formula box. After you do so, save the spreadsheet, using the name ROUTINGS.XLS.

Creating Schedules of Workers and Dollars Required, by Operation by Month

The schedule in Figure 8-15 on page 404, the first of five schedules in one spreadsheet file, multiplies the shipping schedule by the labor-routing schedule and then adjusts for the labor-utilization rate and the number of hours available in each month to calculate the number of full-time workers required by operation by month.

This schedule probably does not describe your worker budget for the new year. To see why, look at the workers required for operation 10 in the first three months of the new year. In January, the company requires 38 workers for this operation. In February, this number grows by four workers, perhaps influenced both by an increased shipping schedule and by a decrease in the number of working hours available in the month. In March, the number of workers required falls to 36, perhaps caused by a decrease in the shipping schedule and an increase in the number of hours available. Therefore, if you managed the company in this example, unless you planned to hire workers one month and fire them several weeks later, you would budget for the valleys and schedule overtime for the peaks.

The formulas in the body of the schedule in Figure 8-16 on page 407 suggest a worker budget, one that reflects more stability in the labor force than the requirements specified in the schedule in Figure 8-15. But these formulas represent only an initial estimate. You, of course, must adjust these numbers to reflect your own knowledge of your business, your prospects, and your labor market. To adjust the numbers, simply enter values in the range C23:N29, replacing the formulas that generate the initial numbers.

After you generate your budget, as shown in Figure 8-16, the schedule in Figure 8-17 on page 408 calculates the total regular wages that the budget implies by operation by month. It does so by multiplying each worker in an operation by the number of working hours in a month by the wage rate for the operation, and then it totals the cost for each operation in the month to calculate monthly regular pay.

To create the schedule in Figure 8-15, first open a new spreadsheet, turn off its gridlines, and then set the column widths shown in the column-width box in Figure 8-15. The range-name box in Figure 8-15 contains range names used by most formulas in the spreadsheet. Enter them as shown.

Using the formula and format boxes as a guide, create the schedule in Figure 8-15 as shown. After you do so, save your spreadsheet as LABOR.XLS.

To create the schedules in Figure 8-16 and Figure 8-17, copy the schedule in Figure 8-15 to the ranges shown, assign the range name shown in the range-name box for Figure 8-17, and then modify the formulas and formats as shown in the information boxes. Save your spreadsheet again.

Creating the Overtime Schedules

The schedule in Figure 8-18 on page 410 shows, as a percentage of the regular workweek, the additional time each worker must work to satisfy planned overtime requirements. Negative values in this schedule indicate a planned excess of direct-labor workers. This information alerts you to circumstances in which more overtime is planned than workers can reasonably be expected to work or in which the budget calls for an unreasonable number of excess workers.

Figure 8-19 on page 411 calculates overtime pay by multiplying non-negative percentages by regular pay in the schedule in Figure 8-17 times 1.5. The value of 1.5, of course, represents time and a half for overtime. If your company pays double time for overtime, change 1.5 to 2 in the formulas shown in Figure 8-17.

To create the schedules in Figure 8-18 and Figure 8-19, copy the schedule in Figure 8-15 to the ranges shown and then modify the spreadsheet as needed. The information boxes for these two figures provide plenty of guidance.

Creating the Material Cost of Sales Forecast

The spreadsheet in Figure 8-20 on page 412 forecasts the material cost of sales by product for the new fiscal year. The forecast depends on the spreadsheet in Figure 8-13, which contains the unit shipment forecast. To keep the forecast simple, formulas in the spreadsheet in Figure 8-20 reflect the assumption that products shown in the shipment forecast are in exactly the same sequence as those in the materials forecast.

To create this schedule quickly, first open a new spreadsheet and turn off the gridlines. Then, copy the forecast in Figure 8-13 to the new spreadsheet and modify the copy as needed. The information boxes for Figure 8-20 provide all the help you need. After you complete this schedule, save it as MATLS.XLS.

BUDGETING AND TRACKING FIXED ASSETS

At this writing, businesses must apply three tax depreciation systems:

- The "useful life" system for property placed into service prior to 1981.
- The accelerated-cost-recovery system (ACRS) for property placed into service from 1981 through 1986.
- The modified accelerated-cost-recovery system (MACRS) for property placed into service after 1986.

Most businesses also apply a fourth system, straight-line depreciation, which they use for reporting financial information to everyone but the IRS. This method has two virtues. First, it's easy to calculate. Second, it produces lower depreciation expenses in the early years of an asset's life than do the other methods. Straight-line depreciation, therefore, is better suited for reporting to bankers, stockholders, and others whom we want to impress with our financial statements.

All these depreciation methods make it difficult to calculate depreciation, both for existing assets and for planned purchases. This section presents spreadsheets that help you track and forecast depreciation for all but the first method. The useful life method requires fractional-year depreciation, which the other tax methods don't. Because including this method would vastly increase the complexity of the following spreadsheets and because you've applied this method to your older assets for at least the past eight years, I've left this method out of this chapter.

Creating the Depreciation-Reference Spreadsheet

The spreadsheet in Figure 8-21 on page 414 creates a database of the depreciation ratios for most of the depreciation methods you will use. In the spreadsheet, for example, the Depreciation-Ratios Calculator finds the yearly depreciation ratios for a five-year recovery period, using double-declining balance with a half-year convention. Formulas repeat this information in the Depreciation-Ratios Database so that you can easily convert the ratios to values for easy reference.

To create this spreadsheet, first open a new spreadsheet, turn off the gridlines, set the calculation mode to manual, and set the widths specified in the column-width box. Then enter the labels and borders shown for the entire spreadsheet.

The Calculation Assumptions section contains three assumptions. With the help of the figure's format box, enter and format them as shown. For most businesses, the Recovery Period under MACRS is either five years or seven years. Five-year property includes computers, light trucks, cars, typewriters, duplicating equipment, and so on. Seven-year property includes office furniture and fixtures and property not otherwise classified.

Exceptions to these recovery periods abound, however. Dozens of specific industries have been awarded their own recovery periods. Manufacturers of leather products, for example, use different recovery periods for their equipment than, say, publishers or manufacturers of rubber products. Check with your CPA.

The Depreciation Method under MACRS depends on the recovery period. For three-year through ten-year property, use 200 percent declining balance. For 15-year and 20-year property, use 150 percent declining balance. For recovery periods in excess of 20 years, use straight-line depreciation. Under ACRS, the depreciation method was approximately 150 percent. (This percentage wasn't exact, however, which is why you must copy the ACRS tables into the ratio database.) Both methods generally use the half-year convention.

Under the half-year convention, every asset is assumed to be placed into service in the middle of the year, eliminating the need to calculate fractional-year depreciation. To illustrate, suppose you're a calendar-year taxpayer. Whether you place five-year property into service in January or December, you apply half-year depreciation in the first year and then depreciate the remaining balance over the next five and one-half years. As a consequence, you'll depreciate five-year property over six years, seven-year property over eight years, and so on.

However, there's one more twist, as there always seems to be with taxes. If more than 40 percent of your aggregate bases were placed in service during the last three months of the tax year, you must use the mid-quarter convention, specifying which quarter of the tax year each property was placed in service. As the spreadsheet notes, enter the convention code *0* if no convention is used; enter the values *1* through *4* for the first through the fourth quarter; and enter the value *5* to use the half-year convention. (There are more exceptions, of course, which your CPA can explain.)

Assign the range names shown in the range-name box and then enter the formulas shown in the figure's formula box. When you do so, you can use the Depreciation Ratios Calculator to calculate any of the depreciation methods in current use.

The Depreciation Check Sum calculates the sum of all values in row 11. Because all depreciation ratios must add up to 0 over the life of the property, this calculation assures you that the depreciation is correct in this regard. Enter the formula for cell N15 shown in the figure's formula box.

The Depreciation Reference spreadsheet contains a small database of each set of depreciation ratios that apply to your business. You can update this database in two ways. First, you can enter ratios directly into the database. In the spreadsheet shown, for example, I entered the three-year and five-year ACRS ratios (A.03 and A.05) directly into the database. Second, you can use the Depreciation Ratios Calculator to calculate the ratios for you.

To complete this database, first enter the formulas for cells C23 and E29 shown on page two of the formula box for Figure 8-21. Copy cell C23 down its column and cell E29 to the range E26:N30. Finally, convert the rows of formulas in this section to rows of depreciation-ratio values, as explained in the formula box for Figure 8-21, and then save the spreadsheet as DEP_REF.XLS.

Creating the Depreciation Schedule

The depreciation schedule shown in Figure 8-22 on page 419 lists every asset, its cost, its age, and its depreciation using both straight-line and accelerated depreciation methods. For each method, the schedule shows depreciation both for prior years and for the most recent 12 months.

You can use this schedule in two ways. First, by entering the date of the last month of the current fiscal year, you can calculate year-end depreciation. This helps you calculate monthly depreciation expenses for your company's books. Second, by entering the date of the last month of the coming fiscal year, you can calculate depreciation expenses for that year, as well. When you add this information to the depreciation for the new assets you intend to purchase, you have calculated the depreciation expenses for your forecast of the coming fiscal year.

To create the depreciation-schedule section, first open a new spreadsheet, turn off the gridlines, and set the column widths as shown in the column-width box for Figure 8-22. Enter the column labels, borders, and shading shown in the spreadsheet, and then enter the data shown in columns A, B, C, D, and K.

Enter the range names shown in the figure's range-name box and then enter the formulas from the formula box. The figure's format box shows how to format the formulas correctly. Save the spreadsheet as DEP_SCHED.XLS.

Creating the Assets-Planning Spreadsheet

Figure 8-23 on page 422 presents the first part of a spreadsheet that can help you prepare a fixed-assets plan. The first column shows the month in which each purchase is planned, and the second column shows the number of the responsible department. The next several columns provide categories in which you can distribute the asset purchases. These categories serve two purposes. First, they help you better understand the assets plan by providing subtotals of asset groups that are relevant to your business. Second, the groups provide a simple way to specify depreciation methods, as the following spreadsheets in this chapter demonstrate. The final column in the spreadsheet in Figure 8-23 contains a short description of each planned asset purchase.

Because this spreadsheet contains no formulas, it's easy to create. First open a new spreadsheet, turn off the gridlines, and then set the column widths as shown in the column-width box for the figure. Then enter the labels, values, borders, and shading as shown. Finally, to complete the spreadsheet, enter the range names shown in the range-name box for Figure 8-23 through Figure 8-26, and save it as FXD_ASTS.XLS.

The portion of the spreadsheet shown in Figure 8-24 on page 424 distributes the data from the portion in Figure 8-23 by months. This information serves two purposes. First, by providing a schedule of asset purchases by month, it provides information that you can use when you create the cash flow forecast described in Chapter 9. Second, it provides a starting point for calculating monthly depreciation.

To create this portion of the spreadsheet, enter the labels, borders, and shading as shown. Enter the month numbers shown in row 25 and the formulas shown in the formula box; copy the formulas as needed.

The part of the fixed-assets plan shown in Figure 8-25 on page 425 calculates the monthly book-depreciation expense by the asset classes you first specified in the portion of the spreadsheet in Figure 8-23. To calculate the monthly depreciation expense you will need for your forecast of the coming fiscal year, add the depreciation calculated in this part of the spreadsheet to the monthly depreciation calculated with the help of the portion in Figure 8-22.

The easiest way to create this part of the spreadsheet is to copy the portion in Figure 8-24 to the area shown in Figure 8-25 and then modify the new portion as necessary. Refer to the figure's formula box for the formulas you need.

The part of the spreadsheet in Figure 8-26 on page 426 presents the calculation of tax depreciation by class for the planned purchases in the new fiscal year. You will use this information to adjust book income to tax income for calculating income taxes in your forecast. To create this part of the spreadsheet, first enter the labels, borders, and shading as shown and then enter the formulas shown in the figure's formula box. Finally, to complete this spreadsheet, save it once again as FXD_ASTS.XLS.

Figure 8-1. General Ledger Chart of Accounts with Budget Codes

A general ledger chart of accounts that lets you specify budget codes to group general ledger account numbers for budget purposes. Saved as GL_CODE.XLS.

	A	B	C	D
1				
2				
3	GL Chart of Accounts			
4	1	2	3	
5	Acct	Bcode	Description	
6	6103	101	Clerical Labor	
7	6105	101	Managerial Labor	
8	6234	229	Air Travel Expense	
9	6237	230	Entertainment Expense	
10	6245	229	Auto Expense--Employee Mileage Reimb.	
11	6359	229	Auto Expense--Rented & Leased	
12				
13				
14				

KEY FORMULAS

Cell	*Formula*
A4	**1**
B4	**=1+A4**
	Copy this formula to the right as needed.

RANGE NAMES

Name	*Formula*
Input	**=$A$5:$C$12**
	The Input range provides the reference dimensions for the following dynamic range names.
Acct	**=INDEX(Input,2,$A$4):INDEX(Input,ROWS(Input)–1,$A$4)**
Bcode	**=INDEX(Input,2,$B$4):INDEX(Input,ROWS(Input)–1,$B$4)**
Desc	**=INDEX(Input,2,$C$4):INDEX(Input,ROWS(Input)–1,$C$4)**
	These range definitions reference data for the accounts, budget codes, and descriptions. Because these formulas define the names dynamically, the names adjust themselves as the data expands and contracts.

Figure 8-2. Budget-Code Definitions

A table of the budget codes used in the general ledger chart of accounts in Figure 8-1. Saved as BUD_CODE.XLS.

	A	B	C
1			
2			
3	**Budget Codes**		
4	1	2	
5	**Bcode**	**Description**	
6			
7	101	Labor	
8	229	Entertainment Expense	
9	230	Travel Expense	
10			
11			
12			

KEY FORMULAS

Cell	*Formula*
A4	**1**
B4	**=1+A4**

RANGE NAMES

Name	*Formula*
Input	**=$A$6:$B$10**
Bcode	**=INDEX(Input,2,$A$4):INDEX(Input,ROWS(Input)–1,$A$4)**
Desc	**=INDEX(Input,2,$B$4):INDEX(Input,ROWS(Input)–1,$B$4)**
	As in the previous figure, these definitions let you define the last two ranges dynamically.

Figure 8-3. Department-Code Definitions

A table of department codes used in the general ledger chart of accounts in Figure 8-1. Saved as DPT_CODE.XLS.

	A	B	C
1			
2			
3	Department Codes		
4	1	2	
5	Dept	Description	
6	10	Executive Department	
7	12	Accounting Department	
8	15	Sales Department	
9	16	Manufacturing Department	
10			
11			
12			

KEY FORMULAS	
Cell	*Formula*
A4	**1**
B4	**=1+A4**

RANGE NAMES	
Name	*Formula*
Input	**=$A$5:$B$10** Input serves as a guidepost for the dynamic range definitions.
Dept **Desc**	**=INDEX(Input,2,$A$4):INDEX(Input,ROWS(Input)–1,$A$4)** **=INDEX(Input,2,$B$4):INDEX(Input,ROWS(Input)–1,$B$4)** These dynamic range definitions allow the range of department codes to expand and contract, allowing the ranges to reference the proper data.

Figure 8-4. GL Trial Balance

A trial balance containing actual spending for February. Saved as TRIALBAL.XLS.

	A	B	C	D	E	F
1						
2						
3	GL Trial Balance--February, 1989					
4	1	2	3	4	5	
5	Acct	Dept	Date	Amt	New?	
6	6103	12	Feb-89	5	OK	
7	6103	15	Feb-89	40	OK	
8	6103	16	Feb-89	9	OK	
9	6105	10	Feb-89	47	OK	
10	6234	10	Feb-89	4	OK	
11	6234	15	Feb-89	51	OK	
12	6237	10	Feb-89	63	OK	
13	6237	15	Feb-89	20	OK	
14	6245	12	Feb-89	9	OK	
15	6359	10	Feb-89	5	OK	
16	6359	12	Feb-89	27	OK	
17	6359	16	Feb-89	13	OK	
18						
19	Total Dept Expenses			293		
20						
21						

KEY FORMULAS	
Cell	***Formula***
A4 **B4**	**1** **=1+A4** Copy this formula to the right as needed.
C6	**2/1/89** Enter the dates as shown.
E6	**=IF(SUM(IF(ActDept=$B6,IF(VLOOKUP($A6,GAcct,1)=$A6, IF(ActBcode=LOOKUP($A6,GAcct,GBcode),1)))),"OK","New")** This array formula converts each combination of department number and account to department number and budget code and then it checks to see if the ACT_89.XLS spreadsheet contains the latter combination. If the formula finds the proper combination, it returns *OK;* otherwise, it returns *New.*
D19	**=SUM(D5:D18);** Be sure this total of monthly department expenses equals the appropriate totals in the reports that follow.

(continued)

Figure 8-4. *continued*

RANGE NAMES		
Name	***Formula***	
Input	**=$A$5:$D$18**	
Acct	**=INDEX(Input,2,$A$4):INDEX(Input,ROWS(Input)–1,$A$4)**	
Dept	**=INDEX(Input,2,$B$4):INDEX(Input,ROWS(Input)–1,$B$4)**	
Date	**=INDEX(Input,2,$C$4):INDEX(Input,ROWS(Input)–1,$C$4)**	
Amt	**=INDEX(Input,2,$D$4):INDEX(Input,ROWS(Input)–1,$D$4)**	
	Enter these dynamic range definitions as shown.	
ActDept	**=ACT_89.XLS!Dept**	**Figure 8-6**
GAcct	**=GL_CODE.XLS!Acct**	**Figure 8-1**
GBcode	**=GL_CODE.XLS!Bcode**	"
	Enter these range definitions as shown.	

Figure 8-5. Budget by Budget-Code Number by Month

A fiscal-year budget for 1989, containing budget-code numbers by department. Saved as BUD_89.XLS.

	A	B	C	D	E	F	G	H	I	J	K	L	M	N	O	P	Q	R
1																		
2																		
3	1989 Budget, with Subtotals for the Periods Shown																	
4			February, 1989															
5	Bcode	Dept	Month	FYTD	Jan	Feb	Mar	Apr	May	Jun	Jul	Aug	Sep	Oct	Nov	Dec	Total	
6																		
7	101	10	51	103	52	51	53	52	49	45	42	42	47	50	54	60	597	
8	229	10	8	16	8	8	8	9	10	11	12	12	13	15	16	15	137	
9	230	10	58	112	54	58	63	65	68	72	79	84	79	76	83	89	870	
10	101	12	5	10	5	5	5	5	5	5	5	5	5	5	5	6	61	
11	229	12	35	69	34	35	39	42	43	42	42	45	43	41	44	41	491	
12	101	15	43	84	41	43	46	43	42	39	41	38	42	45	46	47	513	
13	229	15	49	101	52	49	47	52	48	53	57	64	65	70	67	63	687	
14	230	15	27	53	26	27	29	32	32	31	33	34	36	38	35	34	387	
15	101	16	10	19	9	10	9	9	10	10	10	11	11	11	12	13	125	
16	229	16	14	28	14	14	16	16	15	16	16	15	17	16	16	16	187	
17																		
18					295	300	315	325	322	324	337	350	358	367	378	384	4,055	
19																		
20																		
21																		

COLUMN WIDTHS							
Column	*Width*	*Column*	*Width*	*Column*	*Width*	*Column*	*Width*
A	6.29	F	4	K	4	P	4
B	4.43	G	4	L	4	Q	4.43
C	6.29	H	4	M	4		
D	5.71	I	4	N	4		
E	4	J	4	O	4		

(continued)

Figure 8-5. *continued*

KEY FORMULAS

Cell	*Formula*
C4	**=TEXT(INDEX($E$5:$P$5,1,RepMonths),"mmmm,yyyy")** If you try to display this date as a value, it returns ####, the familar overflow symbol. To cure this problem, convert the date value to formatted text, letting you display it across two columns.
E5 **F5**	**1/1/89** **=DATE(YEAR(E5),MONTH(E5)+1,1)** Copy the formula to the right as needed.
C7	**=INDEX(Data,ROWS(C$6:C7),RepMonths)** This formula returns the budget for the current month, as specified by the value in the RepMonths reference.
D7	**=SUM(INDEX(Data,ROWS(D$6:D7),1):INDEX(Data,ROWS(D$6:D7),RepMonths))** The first INDEX function marks the first month of the current fiscal year; the second one marks the current month. The SUM function returns the fiscal year-to-date budget. Remember to enter this array formula by holding down Ctrl-Shift and then pressing Enter.
Q7 **E18**	**=SUM(E7:P7)** **=SUM(E6:E17)** Copy these formulas down or to the right as needed.

RANGE NAMES

Name	*Formula*
Data **Bcode** **Dept** **Month** **Year**	**=$E$6:$P$17** **=$A$6:$A$17** **=$B$6:$B$17** **=$C$6:$C$17** **=$D$6:$D$17** Because the formulas that refer to these names can accept blanks above and below the actual data, the names don't need to be defined by using dynamic formulas. Instead, the names are tied to the top and bottom borders.
RepMonths	**=BUD_RPT.XLS!Months** When you specifiy a date to report in the BUD_RPT.XLS spreadsheet that follows (Figure 8-7), this range name reflects the number of months that have passed during the current fiscal year. Formulas within this spreadsheet use this information to summarize the budgets for the month and for the fiscal year to date (FYTD).

(continued)

Figure 8-5. *continued*

KEY CELL FORMATS			
Cell	***Number***	***Alignment***	***Font***
A4:Q5	mmm	Center	Helv 8, Bold
A6:Q18	#,##0	Center	Helv 10

Figure 8-6. Actual Spending Performance by Budget-Code Number

A summary of actual performance by budget-code number. Saved as ACT_89.XLS.

	A	B	C	D	E	F	G	H	I	J	K	L	M	N	O	P	Q	R
1																		
2																		
3	1989 Actual Performance, with Subtotals for the Periods Shown																	
4			February, 1989															
5	Bcode	Dept	Month	FYTD	Jan	Feb	Mar	Apr	May	Jun	Jul	Aug	Sep	Oct	Nov	Dec	Total	
6																		
7	101	10	47	88	41	47	0	0	0	0	0	0	0	0	0	0	88	
8	229	10	9	18	9	9	0	0	0	0	0	0	0	0	0	0	18	
9	230	10	63	119	56	63	0	0	0	0	0	0	0	0	0	0	119	
10	101	12	5	10	5	5	0	0	0	0	0	0	0	0	0	0	10	
11	229	12	36	71	35	36	0	0	0	0	0	0	0	0	0	0	71	
12	101	15	40	83	43	40	0	0	0	0	0	0	0	0	0	0	83	
13	229	15	51	99	48	51	0	0	0	0	0	0	0	0	0	0	99	
14	230	15	20	44	24	20	0	0	0	0	0	0	0	0	0	0	44	
15	101	16	9	9	10	9	0	0	0	0	0	0	0	0	0	0	19	
16	229	16	13	13	13	13	0	0	0	0	0	0	0	0	0	0	26	
17																		
18	Totals		293	554	284	293	0	0	0	0	0	0	0	0	0	0	577	
19																		
20																		
21																		

COLUMN WIDTHS							
Column	*Width*	*Column*	*Width*	*Column*	*Width*	*Column*	*Width*
A	6.29	F	4	K	4	P	4
B	4.43	G	4	L	4	Q	4.43
C	5.86	H	4	M	4		
D	5.71	I	4	N	4		
E	4	J	4	O	4		

(continued)

Figure 8-6. *continued*

KEY FORMULAS	
Cell	***<Formula***
C4	**=TEXT(INDEX($E$5:$P$5,1,RepMonths),"mmmm,yyyy")** If you try to display this date as a value, it returns ####, the familar overflow symbol. To cure this problem, convert the date value to formatted text, letting you display it across two columns.
E5 **F5**	**1/1/89** **=DATE(YEAR(E5),MONTH(E5)+1,1)** Copy the formula to the right as needed.
C7	**=INDEX(Data,ROWS(C$6:C7),RepMonths)** This formula returns the amount spent for the current month, as specified by the value in the RepMonths reference.
D7	**=SUM(INDEX(Data,ROWS(D$6:D7),1):INDEX(Data,ROWS(D$6:D7),RepMonths))** The first INDEX function in this array formula marks the first month of the current fiscal year; the second one marks the current month. The SUM function returns the fiscal year-to-date amount spent. Remember to enter this array formula by holding down Ctrl-Shift and then pressing Enter.
E7 **F7**	**41** **=IF(F$5<>Date,0,SUM(IF(TDate=F$5,IF(TDept=$B7, IF(LOOKUP(TAcct,GAcct,GBcode)=$A7,TAmt)))))** This array formula first selects all records from the trial balance for the current month and department. From these, it selects all records with accounts that translate into the current budget code. Finally, it returns the sum of all transaction amounts that pass this three-stage selection criteria. Notice that column E contains January's expenses as values rather than formulas. After you've summarized each month's expenses, turn its column of formulas into a column of values by choosing the Edit Paste Special command and selecting Values. Of course, when you first create this spreadsheet, copy cell F7 to the complete schedule, from January through December.
Q7 **C18**	**=SUM(E7:P7)** **=SUM(C6:C17)** Copy these formulas down or to the right as needed.

(continued)

Figure 8-6. *continued*

RANGE NAMES		
Name	***Formula***	
Data	**=$E$6:$Q$17**	
Bcode	**=$A$6:$A$17**	
Dept	**=$B$6:$B$17**	
Month	**=$C$6:$C$17**	
Year	**=$D$6:$D$17**	
	Because the formulas that refer to these names can accept blanks above and below the actual data, the names don't need to be defined using dynamic formulas. Instead, the names are tied to the top and bottom borders.	
Date	**=BUD_RPT.XLS!Date**	**Figure 8-7**
RepMonths	**=BUD_RPT.XLS!Months**	"
GAcct	**=GL_CODE.XLS!Acct**	**Figure 8-1**
GBcode	**=GL_CODE.XLS!Bcode**	"
TAcct	**=TRIALBAL.XLS!Acct**	**Figure 8-4**
TAmt	**=TRIALBAL.XLS!Amt**	"
TDate	**=TRIALBAL.XLS!Date**	"
TDept	**=TRIALBAL.XLS!Dept**	"
	Enter these range definitions as shown.	

KEY CELL FORMATS			
Cell	***Number***	***Alignment***	***Font***
A3	**General**	**General**	**Helv 10, Bold**
A4:Q5	**mmm**	**Center**	**Helv 8, Bold**
A6:B18	**General**	**Center**	**Helv 10**
C6:Q18	**#,##0**	**General**	**Helv 10**

Figure 8-7. Actual Monthly Spending by Budget Code by Department

A report that summarizes actual monthly spending by budget code by department. Saved as BUD_RPT.XLS.

	A	B	C	D	E	F	G	H
1								
2								
3	**Enter Reporting Month:**		2/89					
4								
5	**Miscellaneous Information**							
6	First Month of Fiscal Year:		1/89					
7	Number of Months to Report:		2					
8								
9								
10	**Monthly Spending by Budget Code**				**February, 1989**			
11	**Budget**		**Exec**	**Actg**	**Sls**	**Mfg**		
12	**Code**	**Description**	**10**	**12**	**15**	**16**	**Tot**	
13								
14	101	Labor	47	5	40	9	101	
15	229	Entertainment Expense	9	36	51	13	109	
16	230	Travel Expense	63	0	20	0	83	
17								
18	Total Spending		119	41	111	22	293	
19								
20								

COLUMN WIDTHS

Column	*Width*	*Column*	*Width*	*Column*	*Width*	*Column*	*Width*
A	11	E	4	I	3.43	M	3.43
B	22.43	F	3.43	J	5	N	3.43
C	4	G	3.71	K	3.43	O	3.43
D	4	H	3.43	L	3.43		

(continued)

Figure 8-7. *continued*

KEY FORMULAS	
Cell	***Formula***
C3 **C6**	**2/1/89** **1/1/89** When you enter these dates, be sure to specify the first day of the month.
C7	**=ROUND((C3-FirstMo)/30.4375+1,0)** This formula finds the number of months that have elapsed between the two dates. The value 30.4375 is the average number of days in a month. It equals 365.25 divided by 12.
G10	**=TEXT(Date,"mmmm,yyyy")** This formula returns the formated text of Date. Unlike a date value, the text version can be displayed across several cells, as shown.
B14	**=LOOKUP(A14,BBcode,BDesc)** This formula looks up the budget-code description from the BUD_CODE.XLS file.
C14	**=SUM(IF(ActBcode=$A14,IF(ActDept=C$12,ActMonth,0)))** This array formula returns the sum of all values in the ACT_89.XLS file (Figure 8-6) whose records meet the criteria shown. Copy this formula down and to the right as needed.
G14 **C18**	**=SUM(C14:F14)** **=SUM(C13:C17)** Copy these formulas down or to the right as needed.
G18	**=IF(ABS(SUM(ActMonth)–SUM($G$13:$G$17))<0.001, SUM($G$13:$G$17),"Total?")** This array formula compares spending for the month in the ACT_89.XLS spreadsheet with the sum of the column totals for the budget report. If the totals match, it returns the total; otherwise, it returns *Total?* The formula does not compare the two totals by testing to see if they are equal; they probably won't be. This is because binary computers often can't store decimal fractions (cents) that are accurate to the smallest decimal place. Therefore, when computers compare totals of accounting data, the totals often differ around the twelth decimal place. This difference isn't important to humans, but it's enough to make a computer decide that two totals aren't equal. Therefore, instead, you evaluate the absolute difference between the two totals. If the difference is less than an insignificant amount—0.001 in this formula—you can conclude that the totals are equal.

(continued)

Figure 8-7. *continued*

RANGE NAMES

Name	*Formula*	
Date	**=$C$3** When you enter a date in this cell, be sure to specify the first day of the month.	
FirstMo	**=$C$6** This range contains the first day of the first month of the new fiscal year.	
Months	**=$C$7** The value in this range reflects the number of months between the two previous dates.	
ActBcode	**=ACT_89.XLS!Bcode**	**Figure 8-6**
ActData	**=ACT_89.XLS!Data**	"
ActDept	**=ACT_89.XLS!Dept**	"
ActMonth	**=ACT_89.XLS!Month**	"
ActTop	**=ACT_89.XLS!Top**	"
ActYear	**=ACT_89.XLS!Year**	"
BudBcode	**=BUD_89.XLS!Bcode**	**Figure 8-5**
BudData	**=BUD_89.XLS!Data**	"
BudDept	**=BUD_89.XLS!Dept**	"
BudYear	**=BUD_89.XLS!Year**	"
BBcode	**=BUD_CODE.XLS!Bcode**	**Figure 8-2**
BDesc	**=BUD_CODE.XLS!Desc**	"
DDept	**=DPT_CODE.XLS!Dept**	**Figure 8-3**
DDesc	**=DPT_CODE.XLS!Desc**	"
GAcct	**=GL_CODE.XLS!Acct**	**Figure 8-1**
GBcode	**=GL_CODE.XLS!Bcode**	"
	By defining linking range names as shown, you can keep the formulas within this spreadsheet as short and as easy to understand as possible. Notice that the first letters of each name refer to the file that generates it: Act=Actual performance, Bud=Budget, B=Budget Code, D=Department Code, and G=GL Chart of Accounts Code.	

(continued)

Figure 8-7. *continued*

KEY CELL FORMATS			
Cell	*Number*	*Alignment*	*Font*
A3	General	General	Helv 10, Bold
C3	m/yy	General	Helv 10
A5	General	General	Helv 10, Bold
C6	m/yy	General	Helv 10
A10	General	General	Helv 10, Bold
G10	General	Right	Helv 10, Bold
A11:G12	General	Center	Helv 10, Bold
A13:A17	General	Center	Helv 10
B13:G18	#,##0	General	Helv 10

Figure 8-8. Actual Year-to-Date Spending by Budget Code by Department

A summary of actual spending for the year to date by budget code by department. Saved as BUD_RPT.XLS. For column widths and range names, see Figure 8-7.

	A	B	C	D	E	F	G	H
21								
22								
23	YTD Spending by Budget Code					February, 1989		
24	Budget		Exec	Actg	Sls	Mfg		
25	Code	Description	10	12	15	16	Tot	
26								
27	101	Labor	88	10	83	9	190	
28	229	Entertainment Expense	18	71	99	13	201	
29	230	Travel Expense	119	0	44	0	163	
30								
31			225	81	226	22	554	
32								

KEY FORMULAS

Cell	*Formula*
G23	**=TEXT(Date,"mmmm, yyyy")**
B27	**=LOOKUP(A27,BBcode,BDesc)** The formula finds the budget-code description in the budget-code file.
C27	**=SUM(IF(ActBcode=$A27,IF(ActDept=C$12,ActYear,0)))** This array formula returns the sum of all values in the ACT_89.XLS file records that meet the criteria shown. Copy this formula down and to the right as needed.
G27 C31	**=SUM(C27:F27)** **=SUM(C26:C30)** Copy these formulas down or to the right as needed.
G31	**=IF(ABS(SUM(ActYear)–SUM($G$26:$G$30))<0.001,SUM($G$26:$G$30),"Total?")** As in the previous report, this array formula returns the totals only if two comparable totals match.

Figure 8-9. Monthly Budget Report by Department

A monthly budget report by department that reports on a different department when you change the department number in cell C36. Saved as BUD_RPT.XLS. For column widths and range names, see Figure 8-7.

	A	B	C	D	E	F	G	H	I	J	K
34											
35											
36	Enter Department Number to Report:		12								
37											
38	**Accounting Department**										
39	**Monthly Budget Report**									**February, 1989**	
40	**Budget**		**Month**				**Year**				
41	**Code**	**Description**	Act	Bud	Var	%	Act	Bud	Var	%	
42											
43	101	Labor	5	5	0	0%	10	10	0	0%	
44	229	Entertainment Expense	36	35	1	3%	71	69	2	3%	
45	230	Travel Expense	0	0	0	0%	0	0	0	0%	
46											
47			41	40	1	3%	81	79	2	3%	
48											
49											

KEY FORMULAS

Cell	*Formula*
C36	**12** Enter the department number you want to report into this cell.
A38	**=LOOKUP(C36,DDept,DDesc)** This formula finds the description for the department number in the department file.
J39	**=TEXT(Date,"mmmm,yyyy")**
B43	**=LOOKUP(A43,BBcode,BDesc)** This formula finds the budget-code description in the budget-code file.
C43	**=SUM(IF(ActBcode=$A43,IF(ActDept=$C$36,ActMonth,0)))** This array formula returns the sum of the amounts from the ACT_89.XLS file for all records with the department number, month, and budget code shown.
D43	**=SUM(IF(BudBcode=$A43,IF(BudDept=$C$36,BudMonth,0)))** This array formula returns budget information to compare with the result of the previous formula.

(continued)

Figure 8-9. *continued*

KEY FORMULAS–continued	
Cell	*Formula*
E43 **F43**	**=C43–D43** **=IF(D43=0,0,E43/D43)** These formulas find the dollar and percentage variance between the budget and actual amounts.
G43 **H43** **I43** **J43**	**=SUM(IF(ActBcode=$A43,IF(ActDept=$C$36,ActYear,0)))** **=SUM(IF(BudBcode=$A43,IF(BudDept=$C$36,BudYear,0)))** **=G43–H43** **=IF(H43=0,0,I43/H43)** These four formulas return information for the fiscal year to date that is similar to the information returned in the four previous formulas for the month. Of course, the first two of these formulas are array formulas and must be entered by holding down Ctrl-Shift and pressing Enter.
C47	**=SUM(C42:C46)** Copy this formula to the right as needed.
F47 **J47**	**=E47/D47** **=I47/H47** These formulas calculate the total variance for the month and year to date.

KEY CELL FORMATS			
Cell	*Number*	*Alignment*	*Font*
A38:A39	General	General	Helv 10, Bold
J39	General	Right	Helv 10, Bold
A40:J41	General	Center	Helv 10, Bold
A42:A46	General	Center	Helv 10
B42:E47	#,##0	General	Helv 10
F42:F47	0%	General	Helv 10
G42:I47	#,##0	General	Helv 10
J42:J47	0%	General	Helv 10

Figure 8-10. Spending Summary by Budget Code by Month

A report of spending by budget code by month, which can alert you to trends in labor and other expenses that might not be apparent from a report by department. Saved as BUD_RPT.XLS. For column widths and range names, see Figure 8-7.

	A	B	C	D	E	F	G	H	I	J	K	L	M	N	O	P
50																
51																
52	Enter Department Number to Report:		15													
53																
54	**Sales Department**															
55	**Spending Summary by Budget Code by Month**														**February, 1989**	
56			1	2	3	4	5	6	7	8	9	10	11	12		
57	Bcode	Description	Jan	Feb	Mar	Apr	May	Jun	Jul	Aug	Sep	Oct	Nov	Dec	Tot	
58																
59	101	Labor	43	40	0	0	0	0	0	0	0	0	0	0	83	
60	229	Entertainment Expense	48	51	0	0	0	0	0	0	0	0	0	0	99	
61	230	Travel Expense	24	20	0	0	0	0	0	0	0	0	0	0	44	
62																
63			115	111	0	0	0	0	0	0	0	0	0	0	226	
64																
65																

KEY FORMULAS

Cell	*Formula*
C52	**15** Enter the number of the department to report.
A54	**=LOOKUP(C52,DDept,DDesc)** This formula looks up the description of the department to report.
O55	**=TEXT(Date,"mmmm,yyyy")** This formula returns the formated text of Date.
C57 **D57**	**=FirstMo** **=DATE(YEAR(C57),MONTH(C57)+1,1)** Copy the formula to the right as needed.
B59	**=LOOKUP(A59,BBcode,BDesc)** To save time, you might want to copy this formula from previous reports.
C59	**=SUM(IF(ActBcode=$A59,IF(ActDept=$C$52,INDEX(ActData,1,C$56):INDEX(ActData,ROWS(ActData),C$56))))** This array formula first finds all rows of the ACT_89.XLS spreadsheet that match the budget-code and department selection criteria. Then, from these rows, it returns the sum of the current month's expenses.

(continued)

Figure 8-10. *continued*

KEY FORMULAS–continued	
Cell	***Formula***
O59 **C63**	**=SUM(C59:N59)** **=SUM(C58:C62)** Copy these formulas down or to the right as needed.
O63	**=IF(ABS(SUM(C63:N63)–SUM(O58:O62))<0.001,SUM(O58:O62),"Total?")** This formula "foots and cross-foots" the table.

KEY CELL FORMATS			
Cell	***Number***	***Alignment***	***Font***
C56:N56	**General**	**Center**	**Helv 10, Bold**
A57:B57	**General**	**Center**	**Helv 10, Bold**
C57:N57	**mmm**	**Center**	**Helv 8, Bold**
A58:A62	**General**	**Center**	**Helv 10**
C58:O63	**#,##0 ;(#,##0)**	**General**	**Helv 10**

Figure 8-11. Spending Summary by Department by Month

A report of spending by department by month. Saved as BUD_RPT.XLS. For column widths and range names, see Figure 8-7.

	A	B	C	D	E	F	G	H	I	J	K	L	M	N	O	P
66																
67																
68	Spending Summary by Department by Month													February, 1989		
69			1	2	3	4	5	6	7	8	9	10	11	12		
70	Dept	Description	Jan	Feb	Mar	Apr	May	Jun	Jul	Aug	Sep	Oct	Nov	Dec	Tot	
71																
72	10	Executive Department	106	119	0	0	0	0	0	0	0	0	0	0	225	
73	12	Accounting Department	40	41	0	0	0	0	0	0	0	0	0	0	81	
74	15	Sales Department	115	111	0	0	0	0	0	0	0	0	0	0	226	
75	16	Manufacturing Department	23	22	0	0	0	0	0	0	0	0	0	0	45	
76																
77			284	293	0	0	0	0	0	0	0	0	0	0	577	
78																
79																

KEY FORMULAS

Cell	*Formula*
O68	**=TEXT(Date,"mmmm,yyyy")**
C70 **D70**	**=FirstMo** **=DATE(YEAR(C70),MONTH(C70)+1,1)** Copy the formula across the row as needed.
B72	**=LOOKUP(A72,DDept,DDesc)** This formula looks up the proper description.
C72	**=SUM(IF(ActDept=$A72,INDEX(ActData,1,C$69):INDEX(ActData,ROWS(ActData),C$69)))** This array formula returns total spending for each department for each month.
O72 **C77**	**=SUM(C72:N72)** **=SUM(C71:C76)** Copy these formulas as needed.
O77	**=IF(ABS(SUM(C77:N77)–SUM(O71:O76))<0.001,SUM(O71:O76),"Total?")**

Figure 8-12. Budget Variances by Department by Month

A report that presents a company's total budget variance by department by month. Saved as BUD_RPT.XLS. For column widths and range names, see Figure 8-7.

	A	B	C	D	E	F	G	H	I	J	K	L	M	N	O	P
80																
81																
82																
83	Budget Variances by Department by Month														February, 1989	
84			1	2	3	4	5	6	7	8	9	10	11	12		
85	Dept	Description	Jan	Feb	Mar	Apr	May	Jun	Jul	Aug	Sep	Oct	Nov	Dec	Tot	
86																
87	10	Executive Department	(8)	2	0	0	0	0	0	0	0	0	0	0	(6)	
88	12	Accounting Department	1	1	0	0	0	0	0	0	0	0	0	0	2	
89	15	Sales Department	(4)	(8)	0	0	0	0	0	0	0	0	0	0	(12)	
90	16	Manufacturing Department	0	(2)	0	0	0	0	0	0	0	0	0	0	(2)	
91																
92			(11)	(7)	0	0	0	0	0	0	0	0	0	0	(18)	
93																
94																

KEY FORMULAS

Cell	*Formula*
O83	**=TEXT(Date,"mmmm,yyyy")**
C85	**=FirstMo**
D85	**=DATE(YEAR(C85),MONTH(C85)+1,1)** Copy the formula to the right as needed.
B87	**=LOOKUP(A87,DDept,DDesc)**
C87	**=IF(C$85>Date,0,SUM(IF(ActDept=$A87,INDEX(ActData,1,C$84):INDEX(ActData,ROWS(ActData),C$84)))–SUM(IF(BudDept=$A87,INDEX(BudData,1,C$84):INDEX(BudData,ROWS(BudData),C$84))))** This array formula finds actual department spending for each month and then subtracts the comparable budgets to calculate the variance.
O87	**=SUM(C87:N87)**
C92	**=SUM(C86:C91)**
O92	**=IF(ABS(SUM(C92:N92)–SUM(O86:O91))<0.001,SUM(O86:O91),"Total?")**

Figure 8-13. Unit Shipment Forecast

A unit shipment forecast, which serves as the source of reference data for a forecast of direct-labor and material costs. Saved as UNIT.XLS.

	A	B	C	D	E	F	G	H	I	J	K	L	M	N
1														
2														
3	Unit Shipment Forecast											1989 Budget		
4	Hours:	168	160	184	160	176	176	160	184	160	176	160	152	
5	Product	Jan-89	Feb-89	Mar-89	Apr-89	May-89	Jun-89	Jul-89	Aug-89	Sep-89	Oct-89	Nov-89	Dec-89	
6														
7	10-106	296	317	305	316	305	292	331	330	336	376	382	431	
8	23-574	18	19	18	20	22	23	24	26	27	28	28	32	
9	27-958	503	507	511	526	527	604	602	687	663	724	818	903	
10	38-342	851	867	869	826	907	934	958	1,038	986	1,095	1,205	1,208	
11	50-505	38	42	48	47	46	49	49	47	45	48	51	52	
12	53-410	19	22	23	26	29	29	31	33	38	37	41	47	
13	67-280	566	628	621	703	698	717	811	906	943	985	947	933	
14	70-969	114	111	108	104	110	124	119	125	126	139	132	133	
15	85-697	19	18	20	21	23	24	23	22	22	25	26	29	
16														
17														
18														

COLUMN WIDTHS							
Column	***Width***	***Column***	***Width***	***Column***	***Width***	***Column***	***Width***
A	8.43	E	6	I	6	M	6
B	6	F	6.43	J	6	N	2
C	6	G	6	K	6		
D	6	H	6	L	6		

(continued)

Figure 8-13. *continued*

KEY FORMULAS

Cell	Formula
B5	1/1/89
C5	=DATE(YEAR(B5),MONTH(B5)+1,1)
	Copy the formula to the right as necessary.
B4	=8*(4*SUM(Workweek)–INDEX(Holidays,1,MONTH(B$5)) +SUM(((MOD(Days–WEEKDAY(B$5),7)) <MOD(DATE(YEAR(B$5),MONTH(B$5)+1,1)–B$5,7))*Workweek))

Using your own holiday schedule and workweek, this array formula calculates the number of working hours per month. It does so by multiplying 8 working hours per day by the number of working days calculated for each month. The number of working days is equal to the result of three operations.

- Four weeks times the number of working days in each week. This section of the formula recognizes that even the shortest month contains four full workweeks.
- Minus the number of holidays scheduled for the month.
- Plus the number of workdays in the fraction of the fifth week that exceeds the first four weeks. The portion of the formula that calculates this value begins in the second row above. (When you enter the formula, of course, enter it on one line with no spaces.)

To see how this operation works, suppose that January 1 falls on Friday, which means that the first day of the fractional week (January 29) begins on Friday as well. Beginning with the Days range name, the first MOD function creates a temporary array of seven cells, the first cell representing Sunday, the last cell Saturday. In each of these cells the MOD function enters a number. It enters 0 in the cell representing Friday (the first day of the fractional week), 1 in the cell representing Saturday, and so on, creating the result: ={2;3;4;5;6;0;1}.

The second MOD function finds the number of days in the fractional fifth week (3 days). Then, the formula compares the results of these two MOD functions with a < (less than) operator, returning a 1 in each cell of the temporary array that contains a value less than 3, and a 0 in each cell containing a 3 or a value greater than 3. The temporary array now contains 1 in each cell that represents a day falling within the fractional fifth week; otherwise it contains 0. In the example, the temporary array contains: ={1;0;0;0;0;1;1}.

Next, the formula multiplies each day in the temporary array by the appropriate Workweek value. (This range contains a 1 for each workday in the week and a 0 for each nonworkday.) As a result of the multiplication, only those days that fall in the fractional month and that are also workdays contain the value 1; all others contain 0: ={0;0;0;0;0;1;0}. To complete the operation, the SUM function at the beginning of the second row of the formula sums the values in the final temporary array

(continued)

Figure 8-13. *continued*

KEY FORMULAS–continued	
Cell	***Formula***
	to find the number of working days in the fractional fifth week. Finally, the formula adds this number to the results of the other two operations to generate the number of working days in the month, which it multiplies by 8 to calculate the number of working hours in the month. When you enter this array formula, be sure to enter it using Ctrl-Shift and pressing Enter. Copy it to the right as needed.

RANGE NAMES	
Name	***Formula***
Input	**=$A$6:$M$16** This range, which begins and ends with the shaded borders, contains the unit shipments forecast.
Hours	**=$B$4:$M$4** This range contains the number of regular-time hours scheduled for the new year.
Units	**=INDEX(Input,2,2):INDEX(Input,ROWS(Input)–1,COLUMNS(Input))** This dynamic definition contains only the actual data; it excludes the borders.
Days	**={1;2;3;4;5;6;7}** This array constant provides a count of the numbers 1 though 7, which stand for the days Sunday through Saturday. Because semicolons separate the numbers, the program treats this array as a column of numbers. (Using commas specifies a row array.)
Workweek	**={0;1;1;1;1;1;0}** This array constant presents the weekly schedule of working days, where 0 represents the weekend and 1 represents workdays. This particular schedule represents the traditional workweek, showing Sunday and Saturday as the weekend.
Holidays	**={1,0,0,0,1,0,1,0,1,0,2,2}** Each of the 12 cells in the Holidays schedule contains the number of holidays your business expects to recognize in the month. The business represented here plans to take eight holidays: one each in January, May, July, and September, and two each in November and December.

(continued)

Figure 8-13. *continued*

KEY CELL FORMATS			
Cell	*Number*	*Alignment*	*Font*
A3	General	General	Helv 10, Bold
M3	General	Right	Helv 10, Bold
A4	General	Right	Helv 8
B4:M4	General	Center	Helv 10
A5	General	Center	Helv 10, Bold
B5:M5	mmm–yy	Center	Helv 8, Bold
A6:A16	##–###	Center	Helv 10
B6:M16	#,##0	General	Helv 10

Figure 8-14. Direct-Labor Spreadsheet with Hours by Product by Operation

A labor-routing report, which contains an estimate of the amount of direct-labor time required by operation for each product. Saved as ROUTINGS.XLS.

	A	B	C	D	E	F	G	H	I	J	K	L	M	N
1														
2														
3	**Labor Utilization Rates**													
4	85%		Efficiency											
5	90%		Effectiveness											
6	77%		Total Utilization											
7														
8	**Direct-Labor Spreadsheet, with Hours by Product by Operation**												**1989 Budget**	
9			**Manufacturing Operations**								**Labor**	**Worker**	**Labor**	
10	Rates:		8.25	8.10	9.00	15.00	20.00	10.00	8.50		**Hours**	**Hours**	**Cost**	
11	**Product**		**10**	**20**	**30**	**40**	**50**	**60**	**70**		**Used**	**Needed**	**Per Unit**	
12														
13	10-106		.5	.0	1.2	.0	.0	.0	3.6		5.3	6.9	45.53	
14	23-574		2.3	3.9	1.2	4.0	1.7	.6	2.7		16.4	21.4	184.32	
15	27-958		2.5	2.4	.0	.6	3.4	.0	4.0		12.9	16.9	151.07	
16	38-342		.7	.6	2.0	3.6	4.2	1.3	4.1		16.5	21.6	214.49	
17	50-505		.0	2.9	1.9	.0	.0	1.3	4.0		10.1	13.2	87.59	
18	53-410		3.2	2.9	1.3	1.2	1.4	1.9	1.8		13.7	17.9	141.89	
19	67-280		4.0	2.7	3.2	.0	3.6	2.0	1.6		17.1	22.4	189.27	
20	70-969		4.1	1.7	.0	.0	.0	.0	.8		6.6	8.6	54.40	
21	85-697		.0	.0	.0	1.4	.0	.0	1.9		3.3	4.3	37.15	
22														
23														
24														

COLUMN WIDTHS							
Column	*Width*	*Column*	*Width*	*Column*	*Width*	*Column*	*Width*
A	8.29	E	6	I	6	M	7.71
B	2	F	6	J	1.14		
C	6	G	6	K	6		
D	6	H	6	L	8.43		

(continued)

Figure 8-14. *continued*

KEY FORMULAS

Cell	*Formula*
A4	**0.85**
A5	**0.9**
A6	**=A5*A4** Accountants refer to the labor-efficiency variance as the loss due to inefficient use of direct labor. Many manufacturing managers, however, refer to labor-utilization rates. Every employee, they say, wastes a certain amount of time; the percentage of time they *don't* waste is their labor-efficiency rate. Managers also waste direct-labor time; the time they *don't* waste is the labor-effectiveness rate. Total labor utilization is the product of the two rates. Here, for example, managers make effective use of only 90 percent of the 85 percent of the direct labor available, for a total utilization rate of 77 percent.
K13	**=SUM(B13:J13)** Total labor hours used equals the sum of each operation.
L13	**=K13/Usage** The total number of worker hours needed is equal to the labor hours used divided by the labor-utilization rate.
M13	**=SUM(Rates*B13:J13)** This array formula multiplies each labor rate by the amount of time expected to be used at that rate and then sums the results.

RANGE NAMES

Name	*Formula*
Usage	**=$A$6** As most employers realize, an employee on the job isn't always working at the job. This range name contains the average fraction of time that employees are actually producing useful goods and services. This utilization rate combines paid breaks (such as coffee breaks and bathroom time) with the waiting-around time caused by inefficient management.
Rates	**=$B$10:$J$10** This range contains the average labor rates for each operation, as well as the beginning and ending borders—columns B and J.
Input	**=$A$12:$J$22** The Input range contains both the data and the top and bottom borders.

(continued)

Figure 8-14. *continued*

RANGE NAMES–continued	
Name	***Formula***
Routings	**=INDEX(Input,2,3):INDEX(Input,ROWS(Input)–1,COLUMNS(Input)–1)** Manufacturing routings describe each operation necessary to produce a product. Often, this term also applies to the schedules that estimate the manufacturing time required for each operation. This dynamic range definition contains this schedule of labor times.

KEY CELL FORMATS

Cell	*Number*	*Alignment*	*Font*
A3	General	General	Helv 10, Bold
A4:A6	0%	General	Helv 10
A8	General	General	Helv 10, Bold
M8	General	Right	Helv 10, Bold
F9	General	Center	Helv 10, Bold
K9:M11	General	General	Helv 10, Bold
A10	General	Right	Helv 8
C10:I10	0.00	Center	Helv 10
A11:I11	General	Center	Helv 10, Bold
A12:A22	##–###	Center	Helv 10
C12:L22	.0	General	Helv 10
M12:M22	#,##0.00	General	Helv 10

Figure 8-15. Total Workers Required by Operation by Month

A schedule of the number of workers required by operation by month to meet the production schedule in Figure 8-13. Saved as LABOR.XLS.

	B	C	D	E	F	G	H	I	J	K	L	M	N	O
1														
2														
3	Total Workers Required by Operation by Month										1989 Budget			
4	Operation	Jan	Feb	Mar	Apr	May	Jun	Jul	Aug	Sep	Oct	Nov	Dec	
5														
6	10	38	42	36	44	41	43	51	49	57	55	62	67	
7	20	29	32	28	34	31	33	39	37	43	42	48	52	
8	30	31	35	30	36	34	35	41	39	45	44	50	53	
9	40	27	29	25	28	28	29	32	31	34	34	41	44	
10	50	57	63	55	64	61	64	74	71	81	80	93	100	
11	60	18	20	18	21	20	21	25	23	27	26	30	31	
12	70	61	66	58	67	63	66	76	72	81	80	95	104	
13														
14	Total Workers	261	287	249	294	277	291	338	323	368	362	418	451	
15														
16														

COLUMN WIDTHS							
Column	*Width*	*Column*	*Width*	*Column*	*Width*	*Column*	*Width*
A	11	E	4	I	4	M	4
B	9.86	F	4	J	4	N	4
C	4	G	4	K	4	O	3.14
D	4	H	4	L	4		

(continued)

Figure 8-15. *continued*

KEY FORMULAS

Cell	*Formula*
C4	01/01/89
D4	=DATE(YEAR(C4),MONTH(C4)+1,1) Copy this formula to the right as necessary.
C6	=MMULT(TRANSPOSE(Routings),Units)/(Hours*Usage) This short array formula, which calculates the number of workers required per operation per month, is really quite sophisticated. First, it performs a TRANSPOSE operation on the Routings range, producing an array of labor times by operation, with labor operations in each row and part numbers in each column. The Units array contains the unit shipment forecast, with part numbers in each row and months in each column. When you matrix-multiply these arrays as shown, you create an array containing forecasted labor hours for each operation by month, with the operations by row and the months by column. But at this point, you don't have the number of workers you need by operation. You haven't factored in the labor-utilization rate, and you don't know the number of hours each month that a worker can spend on the job. Dividing each cell in the array by the product of these two factors gives the results you need. To illustrate, suppose the array tells you that an operation requires 8,000 hours of direct labor applied to a manufacturing operation in a specific month. If the factory has a utilization rate of 80 percent, it will need to pay for 10,000 hours of direct labor monthly. If each worker can work 200 hours per month, 50 workers will be required. That is: 8000/(0.80 * 200) = 50 workers. When you enter this formula, first enter it in cell C6, using Ctrl-Shift Enter. After you get the value shown, highlight the range C6:N12, press the Edit (F2) key, and then use Ctrl-Shift Enter. When you do so, the entire array is displayed as shown. Later, if you must add your own labor operations, the program won't allow you to insert rows in this range. Therefore, highlight the range, press the Edit key, and press Ctrl-Enter (*not* Ctrl-Shift Enter.) When you do so, the array displays error values. Insert the rows you need and enter the operation numbers. Then highlight the new range, press the Edit key, and press Ctrl-Shift Enter. When you do so, new labor values fill your array. If this array returns incorrect numbers, check for these problems: • Neither the Routings nor the Units ranges can contain blank cells; if they do, enter *0* instead. • The Routings and Units ranges must contain exactly the same part numbers in exactly the same order; the two arrays must therefore contain exactly the same number of rows. • The Hours and Usage files must contain the same number of columns.
C14	=SUM(C5:C13) Copy this formula to the right as needed.

(continued)

Figure 8-15. *continued*

RANGE NAMES		
Name	***Formula***	
Rates	=ROUTINGS.XLS!Rates	Figure 8-14
Routings	=ROUTINGS.XLS!Routings	"
Usage	=ROUTINGS.XLS!Usage	"
Hours	=UNITS.XLS!Hours	Figure 8-13
Units	=UNITS.XLS!Units	"
	Enter these range names as shown.	

KEY CELL FORMATS			
Cell	***Number***	***Alignment***	***Font***
N3	General	Right	Helv 10, Bold
B4:N4	General	Center	Helv 8, Bold
C5:N13	#,##0	General	Helv 10
B14	General	Center	Helv 8

Figure 8-16. Worker Budget by Operation by Month

A schedule that shows the number of workers the company actually intends to use. Saved as LABOR.XLS. For column widths and range names see Figure 8-15.

	B	C	D	E	F	G	H	I	J	K	L	M	N	O
17														
18														
19														
20	Worker Budget by Operation by Month												1989 Budget	
21	Operation	Jan	Feb	Mar	Apr	May	Jun	Jul	Aug	Sep	Oct	Nov	Dec	
22														
23	10	36	36	36	41	41	43	49	49	55	55	62	67	
24	20	28	28	28	31	31	33	37	37	42	42	48	52	
25	30	30	30	30	34	34	35	39	39	44	44	50	53	
26	40	25	25	25	28	28	29	31	31	34	34	41	44	
27	50	55	55	55	61	61	64	71	71	80	80	93	100	
28	60	18	18	18	20	20	21	23	23	26	26	30	31	
29	70	58	58	58	63	63	66	72	72	80	80	95	104	
30														
31														
32														

KEY FORMULAS

Cell	*Formula*
C21	**01/01/89**
D21	**=DATE(YEAR(C21),MONTH(C21)+1,1)**
	Copy this formula to the right as needed.
C23	**=MIN(IF(C6:F6>0,C6:F6))**

The schedule in Figure 8-14 calculates the number of workers needed for each operation during the fiscal year. But this isn't necessarily the number of workers you should plan to have on the payroll, for at least two reasons. First, you may not trust your forecast; you don't want to be stuck with a factory full of people you don't need. Second, the schedule shows that you will need more people in some months than in others; you can't raise and lower your staffing levels like a flag on a flagpole.

Therefore, this array formula looks at the worker requirements forecasted for each month and for the next three months and then returns the minimum number of workers required during that four-month period. This is merely a first estimate, however. You need to apply your own experience to setting the actual values in this schedule.

Enter this array formula as shown and then copy it to the range C23:N29. When you use this schedule for your own forecast, enter values in place of the formulas where appropriate.

Figure 8-17. Total Direct-Labor Wages by Operation by Month

A schedule that combines elements of several of the previous schedules to calculate monthly direct-labor costs for the workers you actually intend to use. Saved as LABOR.XLS. For column widths and other range names, see Figure 8-15.

	A	B	C	D	E	F	G	H	I	J	K	L	M	N	O
33															
34															
35	Total Direct-Labor Wages by Operation ($1000s)											1989 Budget			
36		Hours:	168	160	184	160	176	176	160	184	160	176	160	152	
37	**Operation**	**Rates**	**Jan**	**Feb**	**Mar**	**Apr**	**May**	**Jun**	**Jul**	**Aug**	**Sep**	**Oct**	**Nov**	**Dec**	
38															
39	10	$8.25	50	48	55	54	59	63	65	75	73	80	82	84	
40	20	$8.10	38	36	41	40	44	47	48	56	54	60	62	64	
41	30	$9.00	45	43	50	49	54	55	57	65	64	70	72	72	
42	40	$15.00	64	61	70	67	73	76	74	85	81	90	99	100	
43	50	$20.00	183	175	201	195	214	226	228	263	254	280	297	304	
44	60	$10.00	30	28	33	32	35	36	38	43	42	46	47	47	
45	70	$8.50	82	78	90	86	94	99	98	112	109	120	129	135	
46															
47	Total Wages ($1000s)		492	469	539	522	574	602	607	698	678	746	787	807	
48															
49															

KEY FORMULAS

Cell	*Formula*
C37 D37	**01/01/89** **=DATE(YEAR(C37),MONTH(C37)+1,1)** Copy the formula to the right as needed.
B39	**=INDEX(Rates,1,ROWS(B$38:B39))** This formula returns the labor rates from the Rates range. Copy it down the row as needed.
C39	**=C23*C$36*$B39*0.001** This formula calculates the planned regular-pay labor dollars by operation. To do so, it multiplies the number of people forecasted by the number of hours they are expected to work monthly by their hourly pay by 0.001, to convert the result to thousands of dollars. Copy this formula to the remainder of the schedule as needed.
C47	**=SUM(C38:C46)** The sum of each column calculates the direct-labor wages forecasted for each month of the budget period. Copy the formula to the right as needed.

(continued)

Figure 8-17. *continued*

RANGE NAME	
Name	***Formula***
Wages	**=$C$47:$N$47** This range name contains projected regular-time wages for each month of the new year.

Figure 8-18. Planned Overtime as a Percentage of the Monthly Labor Base

A schedule that shows the percentage of workers you intend to hire that is more or less than is apparently needed. Saved as LABOR.XLS. For column widths and range names, see Figure 8-15.

	B	C	D	E	F	G	H	I	J	K	L	M	N	O
51														
52														
53	Planned O/T as Percentage of Monthly Labor Base												1989 Budget	
54	Operation	Jan	Feb	Mar	Apr	May	Jun	Jul	Aug	Sep	Oct	Nov	Dec	
55														
56	10	4%	16%		9%			4%		3%				
57	20	4%	15%		8%			3%		3%				
58	30	3%	16%		7%			5%		3%				
59	40	7%	15%		1%			6%						
60	50	5%	15%		6%			4%		2%				
61	60	3%	15%		6%			5%		3%				
62	70	6%	15%		6%			6%		1%				
63														
64														
65														

KEY FORMULAS

Cell	*Formula*
C54	01/01/89
D54	=DATE(YEAR(C54),MONTH(C54)+1,1)
C56	=ROUND(C6/C23–1,2) Dividing the workers required by the number you plan to hire and then subtracting 1 tells you the percentage of overtime you are planning for each operation for each month. Copy this formula to the remainder of the schedule as needed.

KEY CELL FORMAT

Cell	*Number*	*Alignment*	*Font*
C55:N63	0%;–0%;	General	Helv 10

Figure 8-19. Scheduled Overtime at 150 Percent of Regular Pay

A schedule that calculates the cost of overtime at 150 percent of normal wage rates. Saved as LABOR.XLS. For column widths and other range names, see Figure 8-15.

	B	C	D	E	F	G	H	I	J	K	L	M	N	O
66														
67														
68	Scheduled Overtime at 150% of Regular Pay ($1000s)											1989 Budget		
69	Operation	Jan	Feb	Mar	Apr	May	Jun	Jul	Aug	Sep	Oct	Nov	Dec	
70														
71	10	3	11		7			4		3				
72	20	2	8		5			2		2				
73	30	2	10		5			4		3				
74	40	7	14		1			7						
75	50	14	39		18			14		8				
76	60	1	6		3			3		2				
77	70	7	18		8			9		2				
78														
79	Sched O/T	36	107		46			42		20				
80														

KEY FORMULAS

Cell	*Formula*
C69 D69	01/01/89 =DATE(YEAR(C69),MONTH(C69)+1,1)
C71	=MAX(C56,0)*C39*1.5 Overtime for each operation equals the percentage of overtime worked times regular pay times the overtime multiplier of 150 percent.
C79	=SUM(C70:C78) Total overtime per month equals the column totals. Copy this formula to the right as needed.

RANGE NAME

Name	*Formula*
OverTime	=$C$79:$N$79 This range contains scheduled overtime for each month of the new year.

KEY CELL FORMAT

Cell	*Number*	*Alignment*	*Font*
C70:N78	#,###;–#,###;	General	Helv 10

Figure 8-20. Total Projected Material Cost of Sales

A schedule that multiplies the costs shown in column B by the unit shipment forecast in Figure 8-13 to calculate the total material cost by product. Saved as MATLS.XLS.

	A	B	C	D	E	F	G	H	I	J	K	L	M	N	O	P
1																
2																
3	**Total Projected Material Cost of Sales ($1000s)**														**1989 Budget**	
4	**Prod#**	**Cost**	**Jan**	**Feb**	**Mar**	**Apr**	**May**	**Jun**	**Jul**	**Aug**	**Sep**	**Oct**	**Nov**	**Dec**	**Total**	
5																
6	10-106	66.53	20	21	20	21	20	19	22	22	22	25	25	29	267	
7	23-574	264.18	5	5	5	5	6	6	6	7	7	7	7	8	75	
8	27-958	263.88	133	134	135	139	139	159	159	181	175	191	216	238	1,999	
9	38-342	216.22	184	187	188	179	196	202	207	224	213	237	261	261	2,539	
10	50-505	150.06	6	6	7	7	7	7	7	7	7	7	8	8	84	
11	53-410	186.44	4	4	4	5	5	5	6	6	7	7	8	9	70	
12	67-280	195.22	110	123	121	137	136	140	158	177	184	192	185	182	1,846	
13	70-969	68.51	8	8	7	7	8	8	8	9	9	10	9	9	99	
14	85-697	58.48	1	1	1	1	1	1	1	1	1	1	2	2	16	
15																
16	Total Materials		470	489	489	501	519	549	575	634	625	678	720	746	6,996	
17																
18																

COLUMN WIDTHS							
Column	*Width*	*Column*	*Width*	*Column*	*Width*	*Column*	*Width*
A	7	E	4	I	4	M	4
B	7	F	4	J	4	N	4
C	4	G	4	K	4	O	5.71
D	4	H	4	L	4	P	5

(continued)

Figure 8-20. *continued*

KEY FORMULAS	
Cell	***Formula***
C4 D4	01/01/89 =DATE(YEAR(C4),MONTH(C4)+1,1)
C6	=INDEX(Units,ROWS($C$6:C6),COLUMNS($C$6:C6))*$B6*0.001 This formula finds total material costs by multiplying the units to be shipped each month by the appropriate material cost and then by 0.001 to display the results in thousands of dollars. The formula that finds the unit shipments reflects the assumption that the products shown in the shipment forecast are in exactly the same sequence as in this schedule. Copy the formula to the schedule as needed.
O6 C16	=SUM(C6:N6) =SUM(C5:C15) Copy these formulas down or across as needed.

RANGE NAMES	
Name	***Formula***
Matls	=$C$16:$N$16 This range contains total material costs by month.
Units	=UNITS.XLS!Units This range refers to the spreadsheet in Figure 8-13.

KEY CELL FORMATS			
Cell	***Number***	***Alignment***	***Font***
A3	General	General	Helv 10, Bold
O3	General	Right	Helv 10, Bold
A4:O4	mmm	Center	Helv 8, Bold
A5:A15	##-###	Center	Helv 10
B5:B15	#,##0.00	General	Helv 10
C5:O16	#,##0	General	Helv 10

Figure 8-21. Depreciation Reference

A spreadsheet that creates a database of depreciation methods that subsequent schedules in this chapter use to calculate depreciation expense. Saved as DEP_REF.XLS.

Row											
1											
2											
3	**Depreciation Reference Spreadsheet**										
4											
5											
6	**Depreciation Ratios Calculator**										
7		1	2	3	4	5	6	7	8	9	10
8	Beginning Undepreciated Balance	1.000	.800	.480	.288	.173	.058				
9	Residual Straight Line Depreciation	.182	.178	.137	.115	.115	.115				
10	Declining Balance Depreciation	.400	.320	.192	.115	.069	.023				
11	Depreciation, This Year	.200	.320	.192	.115	.115	.058				
12											
13											

Row	Calculation Assumptions		Depreciation Check Sum	
14	**Calculation Assumptions**		**Depreciation Check Sum**	
15	Recovery Period	5	Total should equal 1.0000:	1.0000
16	Depreciation Method (150%, 100%, etc.)	200%		
17	Mid-Pd Code: (0=None, 1-4 = Qtr, 5=Hlf-Yr)	5		
18				
19				

Depreciation Ratios Database (row 20)

Row	Check Sum	Dep Code	Depreciation Year 1	2	3	4	5	6	7	8	9	10
23	Okay	A.03	.250	.380	.370							
24	Okay	A.05	.150	.220	.210	.210	.210					
25	Total?	Land	0	0	0	0	0	0	0	0	0	0
26	Okay	M.05	.200	.320	.192	.115	.115	.058				
27	Okay	M.07	.143	.245	.175	.125	.089	.089	.089	.045		
28	Total?	M.315	.016	.032	.032	.032	.032	.032	.032	.032	.032	.032
29	#REF!		.200	.320	.192	.115	.115	.058				
30	#REF!		.200	.320	.192	.115	.115	.058				
31												
32												

COLUMN WIDTHS

Column	*Width*	*Column*	*Width*	*Column*	*Width*	*Column*	*Width*
A	8.43	E	4.43	I	3.86	M	3.86
B	8.43	F	4.43	J	3.86	N	3.86
C	8.43	G	3.86	K	3.86	O	3.86
D	8.43	H	3.86	L	3.86		

(continued)

Figure 8-21. *continued*

KEY FORMULAS	
Cell	***Formula***
E7	**1**
E8	**1** All property begins with an undepreciated balance of 100 percent.
E9	**=E8/(RecovPd–E7+1+(1–INDEX(MP.Rates,1,Conv+1)))** The residual straight-line depreciation is equal to the undepreciated balance divided by the number of recovery periods remaining. This number of periods is equal to the recovery period, minus the number of the current period, plus the portion of the year remaining from the mid-period convention.
E10	**=E8*Method/RecovPd** By definition, the declining-balance depreciation is equal to the undepreciated balance times the depreciation method (200 percent, say), divided by the recovery period.
E11	**=MAX(E9,E10)*INDEX(MP.Rates,1,Conv+1,1)** The actual depreciation used depends on two factors. First, you can switch to straight-line depreciation if that would produce a larger amount. Second, in the initial year, depreciation is reduced by the mid-period convention amount.
F7	**=1+E7**
F8	**=E8–E11** The undepreciated balance is equal to the previous balance minus the depreciation actually used in the previous period.
F9	**=IF(F$7>RecovPd+(Conv>0),0, F8/(RecovPd–F7+1+(1–INDEX(MP.Rates,1,Conv+1))))** If the current period is greater than the recovery period (plus 1 if a mid-period convention is used), this formula returns 0. Otherwise, it calculates the residual straight-line depreciation.
F10	**=F8*Method/RecovPd** Copy this formula from cell E10.
F11	**=IF(RecovPd+(Conv>0)=F$7,F$8,MAX(F9,F10))** If this is the last year of depreciation, this formula returns the undepreciated balance as the year's depreciation. Otherwise, it returns the larger of the straight-line and the declining-balance amounts.
Copy the formulas in column F to the right as needed.	

(continued)

Figure 8-21. *continued*

KEY FORMULAS–continued	
Cell	***Formula***
E15	**5** Enter the recovery period you want to calculate into this cell.
E16	**2** Enter the depreciation method.
E17	**5** Enter the mid-period convention code.
N15	**=TEXT(SUM($11:$11),".0000")** If the depreciation schedule is working properly, the sum of all depreciation should equal 100 percent. By summing all values in row 11, this formula doesn't need to know the number of years of depreciation to include in its range. And by displaying this value as text and then right-aligning the text, you allow the display to intrude on column D. Of course, numeric values display #### when they are too large to display a full value in a cell.
E22 **F22**	**1** **=1+E22**
C23	**=IF(ROUND(SUM(INDIRECT($D23)),4)=1,"Okay","Total?")** This column of formulas ensures that the depreciation ratios that you actually use all correctly add up to 1. Land, of course, does not add up to 1; its formula therefore returns the error message shown in the spreadsheet. Because the spreadsheet contains only 10 of the 32 years that the 31.5-year depreciation method requires, it returns that message, as well. The #REF error values arise because they are searching for range names that don't exist in column D. When you add more depreciation methods, the errors disappear.
E29	**=E$11** When you first create the schedule, enter the two ACRS depreciation rates shown in rows 23 and 24. These rates were specified by the IRS and can't be calculated directly. Enter *0* for land depreciation and then enter the depreciation codes for all three rows. Enter the formula shown here, copy it to the range E26:N30, and then calculate the values for the depreciation method shown in row 26. When you do so, the remaining schedule returns the same results throughout. Enter the depreciation code in cell D26 and then turn the row of formulas into a row of values by copying the row onto itself by choosing the Edit Paste Special command and selecting Values. Repeat the process for each MACRS depreciation method you want to calculate.

(continued)

Figure 8-21. *continued*

RANGE NAMES

Name	*Formula*
RecovPd	**=$E$15** This range contains the number of years over which the property will be depreciated.
Method	**=$E$16** This range contains the declining-balance depreciation method to use in the calculations. The most common methods are 100 percent (straight line), 150 percent (one and a half declining balance), and 200 percent (double declining balance).
Conv	**=$E$17** MACRS uses several conventions to simplify depreciation calculations for the first year that property is placed in service. Generally, it uses the half-year convention, which treats all property as if it were purchased in the middle of the year. Using this convention for five-year property, for example, you would take half the normal depreciation in the first year and then five more years of depreciation. Using the half-year convention, in other words, generates a depreciation schedule that is one year longer than the recovery period. If more than 40 percent of the aggregate bases of your property is placed in service during the last three months of the year, you must use the mid-quarter convention. This requires that all property placed in service during any quarter of a tax year be treated as placed in service at the midpoint of the quarter. The IRS has assigned specific depreciation percentages to be applied to each quarter. These are reflected in the following array constant and used in the calculations when needed.
MP.Rates	**={1,0.875,0.625,0.375,0.125,0.5}** This array constant contains the fraction of the first year's depreciation that is used under various MACRS mid-period depreciation conventions—hence *MP.Rates*. Specifically, 1 = No mid-period convention, 0.875 = 1st Quarter, 0.625 = 2nd Quarter, 0.375 = 3rd Quarter, 0.125 = 4th Quarter, and 0.5 = Half-year convention.

(continued)

Figure 8-21. *continued*

RANGE NAMES–continued	
Name	***Formula***
A.03	=$E$23:$N$23
A.05	=$E$24:$N$24
Land	=$E$25:$N$25
M.05	=$E$26:$N$26
M.07	=$E$27:$N$27
M.315	=$E$28:$N$28
	Assign a depreciation code to each depreciation method. By doing so, you can easily refer to any method you want. Here, the code A.03 stands for ACRS depreciation with a 3-year recovery period; M.07 stands for MACRS with a 7-year recovery period. For consistency, land has its own method, which contains depreciation ratios of 0. Although the spreadsheet shows only 10 years of depreciation, you will probably create a schedule with more years. If you do so, redefine all these ranges to have the larger dimension. In this way, you won't generate error values in formulas that refer to the 15th year, say, of a 3-year depreciation schedule, which would contain a value of 0, of course. To quickly redefine the range-name dimensions, select the range D23 through the bottom right side of your schedule, choose Formula Create Names, specify Left, and then choose OK.

KEY CELL FORMATS			
Cell	***Number***	***Alignment***	***Font***
A3	0%	General	Helv 8
A6	0%	General	Helv 8
E7:N7	0%	General	Helv 8
E8:N11	0%	General	Helv 8
N15	0%	General	Helv 8
E16	General	Right	Helv 10
C20	General	Right	Helv 10
E21:N22	General	Right	Helv 10
D23:D30	General	Center	Helv 10
E22:N22	General	Center	Helv 10, Bold
E23:N30	.000;–.000;	General	Helv 10
E25:N25	General	Center	Helv 10

Figure 8-22. Depreciation Schedule

A schedule that calculates book depreciation and tax depreciation both for past years and for the most recent 12 months. Saved as DEP_SCHED.XLS.

	A	B	C	D	E	F	G	H	I	J	K	L	M	N
1														
2														
3	**Depreciation Schedule for:**			**Dec-89**										
4					Age			Book Dep--SL			Tax Depreciation			
5	Asset#	Description	Date	Cost	Yrs	Mos	Life	SV	Prior	Cur	Method	Prior	Cur	
6														
7	3001	Personal Computer	Apr-86	4,516.89	3	9	5	452	2,236	813	M.05	3,216	520	
8	3011	Copier	Jul-88	1,895.00	1	6	5	190	171	341	M.05	379	606	
9	6003	Sales Mgr's Car	Nov-87	12,895.00	2	2	5	1,290	2,708	2,321	M.05	6,705	2,476	
10	7002	Chair	Feb-84	57.50	5	11	5	6	51	10	A.05	58	0	
11	7010	Desk	Jan-89	235.50	1	0	7	24	0	30	M.07	0	34	
12	9001	Unimproved Lot	Sep-87	250,000.00	2	4	0	0	0	0	Land	0	0	
13														
14	Total Depreciation			269,599.89					5,165	3,516		10,358	3,636	
15														
16														

COLUMN WIDTHS							
Column	***Width***	***Column***	***Width***	***Column***	***Width***	***Column***	***Width***
A	**11.14**	**E**	**3.57**	**I**	**4.71**	**M**	**4.86**
B	**16.43**	**F**	**3.86**	**J**	**4.86**	**N**	**3**
C	**6.71**	**G**	**4.86**	**K**	**8.14**		
D	**9.29**	**H**	**4.57**	**L**	**5.43**		

(continued)

Figure 8-22. *continued*

KEY FORMULAS	
Cell	***Formula***
D3	**12/01/89** Enter this value as shown here.
E7	**=MAX(0,INT((12*(YEAR(Date)–YEAR($C7))+MONTH(Date)–MONTH($C7)+1)/12))** This formula finds the age of the asset in complete years. For example, if an asset were 1 year and 11 months old, this formula would return 1 year. The MAX function ensures that this age is never less than 0.
F7	**=MAX(0,12*(YEAR(Date)–YEAR($C7))+MONTH(Date)–MONTH($C7)+1–12*E7)** This formula finds the age of the asset in months and then subtracts 12 times the value in column E to find the age, in months, in excess of the years shown. For example, if an asset were 1 year and 11 months old, this formula would return 11 months. As in the previous formula, the MAX function keeps this value from falling below 0.
G7	**5** Enter the depreciable life of the asset in this column.
H7	**=ROUND(D7*0.1,2)** Salvage value has been estimated at 10 percent of the asset's purchase price.
I7	**=IF($G7*$E7=0,0,($E7–1+$F7/12)*(($D7-$H7)/$G7))** If either the number of elapsed years or the life is equal to 0, this formula returns 0; otherwise, it returns the depreciation for one year less than its age.
J7	**=IF(OR($G7=0,($E7+$F7)=0),0,IF($E7>0,12,$F7)/(12*$G7))*($D7–$H7)** If the asset life equals 0 or its age equals 0, this formula returns 0; otherwise, it returns depreciation for either 12 months or for the life of the asset, whichever is less.
K7	**M.05** Enter the depreciation-method code in this column.

(continued)

Figure 8-22. *continued*

KEY FORMULAS–continued	
Cell	***Formula***
L7	**=IF(($E7+$F7/12)<=1,0,SUM(INDEX(INDIRECT(File&"!"&$K7),1,1):INDEX(INDIRECT(File&"!"&$K7),1,–INT(–$E7–$F7/12)-1))*$D7)** Enter this formula on one line with no spaces.
M7	**=$D7*IF((E7+F7)=0,0,INDEX(INDIRECT(File&"!"&$K7),1,$E7+($F7>0)))**
The two tax depreciation formulas above calculate depreciation in whole years only. The first formula calculates the prior year's depreciation by adding the depreciation ratios for one year fewer than the age of the asset and then multiplying by its cost. The second formula calculates the current year's depreciation by using the ratio for the current year.	
D14	**=SUM(D6:D13)** Copy this formula to the right as needed.

RANGE NAMES	
Name	***Formula***
Date	**=$D$3** This range contains the date for which you want the spreadsheet to calculate depreciation.
File	**="DEP_REF.XLS"** The definition for the File range displays the text of the filename containing your table of depreciation ratios, shown in Figure 8-21. When you enter this definition, be sure to enter the quotes shown; otherwise, formulas that use this range return error values.

Figure 8-23. Fixed-Assets Plan

The first part of a fixed-assets plan for the new year that provides plenty of room for describing each asset purchase. Saved as FXD_ASTS.XLS.

	A	B	C	D	E	F	G	H	I	J	K	L
1												
2												
3	Fixed Assets Plan									1989 Budget		
4	Purch		Furn		EDP	Plant						
5	Month	Dept	& Fixt	Vehic	Equip	Equip	Description					
6												
7	1	10	1,200				New VP's Furniture					
8	1	12	750				Two Desks					
9	2	10		22,000			New VP's Car					
10	2	15				37,000	Fixtures for New Robot					
11	3	16			3,500		286 PC for Production Sched					
12	5	15			7,500		386 PC System--Direct Mail					
13	7	10			1,250		PC for President					
14	9	16				2,495	Welding Fixture					
15	9	16		17,500			Utility Tractor					
16	11	16		11,200			Delivery Van					
17	12	15		12,500			New Sales Rep's Car					
18												
19												
20												

COLUMN WIDTHS

Column	*Width*	*Column*	*Width*	*Column*	*Width*	*Column*	*Width*
A	5.29	E	5.86	I	4.71	M	4.71
B	4.86	F	5.86	J	4.71	N	4.71
C	4.71	G	5.86	K	4.71	O	5.86
D	6	H	4.71	L	4.71		

(continued)

Figure 8-23. *continued*

RANGE NAMES	
Name	***Formula***
File	="DEP_REF.XLS" This name definition refers to Figure 8-21. Enter it as text, as shown.
Month	=$A$6:$A$18
Furn	=$C$6:$C$18
Vehic	=$D$6:$D$18
EDP	=$E$6:$E$18
Equip	=$F$6:$F$18 These range definitions, which include top and bottom borders, refer to columns of data in the part of the fixed-assets plan, shown in Figure 8-23.

KEY CELL FORMATS			
Cell	***Number***	***Alignment***	***Font***
A3	General	General	Helv 10, Bold
K3	General	Right	Helv 10, Bold
A6:B18	General	Center	Helv 10
C6:F18	#,##0	General	Helv 10
C26:O31	#,##0	General	Helv 10

Figure 8-24. Planned Fixed-Asset Purchases by Asset Class by Month

A portion of the fixed-assets plan that arranges the fixed assets shown in Figure 8-23 by asset class by month. Saved as FXD_ASTS.XLS. For column widths and range names, see Figure 8-23.

	A	B	C	D	E	F	G	H	I	J	K	L	M	N	O	P
22																
23																
24	**Planned Fixed Asset Purchases in 1989 by Asset Class by Month**														**1989 Budget**	
25	**Class**		**1**	**2**	**3**	**4**	**5**	**6**	**7**	**8**	**9**	**10**	**11**	**12**	**Total**	
26																
27	Furn		1,950	0	0	0	0	0	0	0	0	0	0	0	1,950	
28	Vehic		0	22,000	0	0	0	0	0	0	17,500	0	11,200	12,500	63,200	
29	EDP		0	0	3,500	0	7,500	0	1,250	0	0	0	0	0	12,250	
30	Equip		0	37,000	0	0	0	0	0	0	2,495	0	0	0	39,495	
31																
32	Total Assets		1,950	59,000	3,500	0	7,500	0	1,250	0	19,995	0	11,200	12,500	116,895	
33																
34																
35																

KEY FORMULAS

Cell	*Formula*
C27	**=SUM(IF(Month=C$25,INDIRECT($A27)))** This array formula sums all purchases planned in the current month for the class of asset defined by the range name entered in column A. These range names, of course, refer to columns in the part of the fixed-assets plan, shown in Figure 8-23. Copy the formula to the range C27:N31.
O27 **C32**	**=SUM(C27:N27)** **=SUM(C26:C31)** Copy these formulas down or to the right as needed.

Figure 8-25. Book Depreciation by Asset Class by Month for Planned Fixed-Asset Purchases

A portion of the fixed-assets plan that calculates book depreciation for the assets you intend to buy during the coming year. Saved as FXD_ASTS.XLS. For column widths and range names, see Figure 8-23.

	A	B	C	D	E	F	G	H	I	J	K	L	M	N	O	P
36																
37																
38	**Book Depreciation by Asset Class by Month for Planned 1989 Purchases**														**1989 Budget**	
39	**Class**	**Life**	**1**	**2**	**3**	**4**	**5**	**6**	**7**	**8**	**9**	**10**	**11**	**12**	**Total**	
40																
41	Furn	7	23	23	23	23	23	23	23	23	23	23	23	23	279	
42	Vehic	5	0	367	367	367	367	367	367	367	658	658	845	1,053	5,782	
43	EDP	5	0	0	58	58	183	183	204	204	204	204	204	204	1,708	
44	Equip	5	0	617	617	617	617	617	617	617	658	658	658	658	6,950	
45																
46	Total		23	1,007	1,065	1,065	1,190	1,190	1,211	1,211	1,544	1,544	1,731	1,939	14,718	
47																
48																

KEY FORMULAS

Cell	*Formula*
C41	**=C27/($B41*12)** Because book depreciation is always assumed to be straight line, the calculation is easy. It's simply the asset value divided by its life in months. Copy this formula down the column.
D41	**=C41+D27/($B41*12)** In succeeding months, depreciation for the month is equal to depreciation from previous months plus additional depreciation for assets purchased in the current month. Copy this formula to the remainder of the schedule.
O41 **C46**	**=SUM(C41:N41)** **=SUM(C40:C45)** Copy these formulas down or to the right as needed.

Figure 8-26. Tax Depreciation by Asset Class by Month for Planned Fixed-Asset Purchases

A portion of the fixed-assets plan that calculates tax depreciation for the assets you intend to buy during the coming year. Saved as FXD_ASTS.XLS. For column widths and range names, see Figure 8-23.

	A	B	C	D	E	F	G
50							
51							
52	**1989 Budget**						
53	**Tax Depreciation by Asset Class**						
54	**for Planned 1989 Asset Purchases**						
55			**Depreciation**		**Total**	**Total**	
56	**Class**		**Code**		**Purch**	**Dep**	
57							
58	Furn		M.07		1,950	279	
59	Vehic		M.05		63,200	12,640	
60	EDP		M.05		12,250	2,450	
61	Equip		M.05		39,495	7,899	
62							
63	Total Tax Dep for 1989 Purch				116,895	23,268	
64							
65							

KEY FORMULAS

Cell	*Formula*
A58	**=A27** This formula repeats the row descriptions found in column A of the part of the spreadsheet shown in Figure 8-24. Copy the formula down the column.
E58	**=O27** Total purchases are equal to the values calculated in column O of the part of the spreadsheet shown in Figure 8-24. Copy the formula down the column.
F58	**=($O27*INDEX(INDIRECT(File&"!"&$C58),1,1))** Tax depreciation for the first year equals total purchases times the tax depreciation ratio found in the first year of the appropriate range of the depreciation-reference file. Copy the formula down the column as needed.
E63	**=SUM(E57:E62)** Copy this formula to the right as needed.

9

Cash Flow Reports and Forecasts

I was just out of the service, on my first civilian job, and flying several hundred miles on my first business trip. As the plane took off, I struck up a conversation (executive-to-executive, you understand) with a man twice my age who was sitting across the aisle. He owned companies, he told me, many of them. I wish I could remember his name.

During the short flight, he tried to read his *Wall Street Journal,* and I tried to pump him for his business knowledge. He apparently won that battle because I don't remember that he told me a thing during the flight. But at our destination, as we shuffled down the aisle to the door, he turned to me and said, "Remember this: Cash is time."

At the time, I had no idea what he meant. But since then I've seen many cases for which his words hold true. Cash gives a business at least a little time to survive and grow. This is why cash flow forecasts are so important—they tell managers how much time remains in which to find more time.

This chapter presents three types of cash flow forecasting systems. One of these, which is in the largest spreadsheet in this book, generates the traditional monthly forecast of the income statement, balance sheet, and cash flows. Another system presents a format for weekly cash flow forecasts, a database to track them, and a variance analysis that can help improve them. But first, this chapter presents a spreadsheet that solves a problem that many businesses have: tracking periodic cash requirements.

A SCHEDULED PAYMENTS CALENDAR

Most accounting systems offer only one report of future cash requirements: the accounts payable aging schedule. This report does a satisfactory job of telling you when you must pay your 30-day invoices. Generally, however, it does a poor job of telling you when you must pay your rent, loan payments, taxes, lease payments, and other periodic payments.

Figure 9-1 on page 445 shows a calendar of scheduled payments that tracks these periodic payments for you. The calendar schedules each cash requirement that it contains, based on the dates in rows 8 and 34 and on the scheduling information in columns A, D, and E. To update this calandar, simply enter in cell H8 the date for Monday of the first week you want to schedule and then recalculate and print the spreadsheet.

As you use this schedule, you will find that it offers at least three benefits. First, it serves as a checklist that keeps you from forgetting to pay a bill when it is due. Second, it serves as a vital ingredient in the cash flow forecast that follows. Third, it summarizes the fixed cash requirements your company must satisfy monthly, an amount that is surprisingly large in most companies.

Let's take a closer look at the calendar.

Using a Scheduled Payments Calendar

The calendar shows the payee in column B and the reason for payment in column C. In column D, the monthly schedule of payments shows the day of the month to pay, while the schedule of weekly payments shows the day of the week to pay.

Because many payments aren't due every month or week, column E specifies the payment schedule. In the monthly schedule, entering a *1* in this column instructs the spreadsheet to schedule payment monthly, entering *3* instructs it to schedule payment every three months, and so on. In the weekly schedule, entering *2* in column E specifies payment every other week, and so on.

To calculate payment dates, the spreadsheet depends on the beginning date in column A. This can be any payment anniversary date that you want to use as a reference; it need not be the initial contract date. Because column A is of little interest to people who normally use this calendar, you will generally skip it when you print the calendar. This is the reason that titles for the sample calendar are in column B.

Column F contains a notation of the general ledger account number your accounts payable department uses when making payments. Enter *Misc* for requirements such as amortizing loans that require more than one debit. Column G, of course, contains the amount (often estimated) that you owe periodically. The remaining columns schedule the payment appropriately.

Creating a Scheduled Payments Calendar

To create the calendar, first open a new spreadsheet, turn off its gridlines, and then set the column widths shown in the column-width box. Enter the labels, underlines, and shading shown throughout the schedule.

Enter the date shown in the formula box for cell H8 and then enter the date formulas shown for cell M3 and for rows 7, 8, and 34. Format these dates as shown in the figure's format box.

You need to enter some of the data shown in the calendar in Figure 9-1 to test the formulas, but not the descriptions in columns B, C, and F. Therefore, enter the date shown in cell A10, the formula shown in the formula box for cell D10, and the values in cells E10 and G10. Format the range G9:M29 as shown in the format box.

The range-name box explains the three range definitions that the formula in cell H10 requires. Enter these range definitions and then enter the formula shown in the formula box for cell H10. Copy this formula to the range I10:M10.

Copy the range A10:M10 to the range A11:A27 and then enter the dates, as shown in column A, and the values for the *Sched Every* column, as shown in column E. As you do so, the schedule begins to appear as shown in the range H10:M27.

Using the formula and format boxes to guide you, complete the calendar in Figure 9-1. When the complete calendar works correctly, add any borders and formatting that may be missing, and then save your spreadsheet. I used the name CALENDAR.XLS.

When you add your own data, simply insert or delete the rows between the two sets of shaded bars and then copy formulas as needed. If your company has little need for a schedule of weekly payments, simply end your spreadsheet at row 29 and then delete rows 4 through 6.

CREATING AND IMPROVING WEEKLY CASH FLOW FORECASTS

Preparing a cash flow forecast each week is much like using dim headlights on a dangerous mountain road. Neither action provides much warning of danger ahead; but any warning is far better than none at all.

Many managers would object to this analogy, however, because their cash flow forecasts aren't nearly as useful as dim headlights. Their forecasts, these managers would say, often warn them of nonexistent dangers on the one hand but fail to alert them to mortal dangers on the other.

Although no forecast can predict cash flows with absolute precision, you can create a cash flow forecast accurate enough to serve as a useful management tool. Here's the process:

1. Divide your cash income and expenses into prediction categories that make sense for your business. For example, if you offer customers both cash and credit, create categories for both cash sales and collections. If you receive COD shipments, create a cash expense category for CODs. If an officer of your company occasionally says, "By the way, tomorrow I'll need a check made payable to the Smith Co. for..." and then names a large amount, establish that individual as a category of cash expense when you prepare your cash flow forecast.
2. Prepare a cash flow forecast weekly. To improve your forecasts, you must generate them consistently. Skipping a weekly forecast will throw weeks of analysis out the window.
3. Record actual cash flows in the same format you use for predicting them. This might turn out to be the most challenging step, because accounting systems aren't designed to report cash spending by prediction category. Therefore, you may need to develop special systems to track COD payments, say, or all the checks requested by Mr. Jones. But if you decide that you cannot possibly identify actual spending for a specific prediction category, eliminate that category from your forecast—a prediction category serves no purpose if you can't compare actual and predicted values for the category.
4. Compare your forecasts with actual cash flows, finding the categories that create the most trouble when you try to predict them. You may discover, for example, that CODs and the collection of accounts receivable create the greatest uncertainty in your cash flow forecast. Simply by identifying this fact, you have come a long way. You've turned a general problem of inaccurate cash flow forecasts into two specific problems, each having specific causes and solutions.
5. Work to improve the troublesome categories. After you identify the major problems, many of the solutions become obvious. In one company, for example, the president complained bitterly about inaccurate cash flow forecasts. I discovered that his own special requests for cash, brought on by his love for wheeling and dealing, caused much of the problem. I therefore insisted that

each week he forecast his own cash requirements for each of the coming six weeks. At a smaller company, large numbers of CODs created significant uncertainty. By establishing credit, changing vendors, and forecasting COD delivery dates, the company virtually eliminated the uncertainty for this prediction category.

Creating and Updating the Weekly Cash Flow Report and Forecast

Figure 9-2 on page 449 presents a weekly cash flow report and forecast that's typical of the kind used by many companies. In column D, the spreadsheet reports actual cash flows for the past week. Then, for each of the next six weeks, it predicts cash receipts and expenses.

The date in cell K3 specifies the Monday of the week for which the actual cash flows are shown. This is true even when the report is prepared late the following Friday or early the following Monday for the preceding week. The dates in row 5 specify the Monday for each week shown.

This spreadsheet is easy to create. First open a new spreadsheet, turn off its gridlines, and set the column widths as shown in the column-width box. Enter the labels, borders, and shading. Formulas in several spreadsheets that follow reference the numbers in column A; enter the numbers as shown. Then use the information provided by the range-name, formula, and format boxes to complete the spreadsheet. Save your version as WK_FCST.XLS.

When it's time to create your weekly forecast using the spreadsheet in Figure 9-2, you can easily modify last week's forecast with updated information. Here's how:

1. Last week's columns E and F become this week's columns D and E. Therefore, enter the label *Actual* in cell E4 and the value *1* in cell F4. Then convert the formula in cell E5 into a date value. To convert this cell quickly, edit cell E5, press the F9 (Calculate All) key, and then choose OK.

2. Delete column D from last week's schedule by selecting the range DeleteCol, choosing the Edit Delete command, and selecting Left. To select this range quickly, press the F5 (Goto) key, enter the range name DeleteCol, and then choose OK.

3. To contain the new sixth week in the forecast, insert a new column. To do so quickly, select the range InsertCol, choose the Edit Insert command, and select Right. After doing so, copy column I of the schedule into this new column.

4. Before you deleted the old column D, cell E24 contained the only formula in the spreadsheet that referenced this column. That cell, which is now cell D24, therefore contains a #REF! error value. To fix this problem, enter the actual value of the beginning cash balance in cell D24.
5. Finally, modify the revised spreadsheet as necessary to reflect your actual cash flows and new assumptions about the weeks ahead. Then save and print your new cash flow report and forecast.

Notice that each time you set up your spreadsheet for the new week, you enter exactly the same keystrokes. You should have no problem, therefore, using the Macro Record command to create a macro that automates this set-up process.

Creating the Cash Flow History

When you use the cash flow report and forecast in Figure 9-2 regularly, you will generate six weeks of forecasts before you report actual cash flows on the seventh week. This is why many companies don't compare weekly cash flow forecasts to actual—there's simply too much data to compare.

The cash flow history in Figure 9-3 on page 452 takes the first step toward automating the summary and analysis of all that cash flow data. This history is a database that contains past reports of actual and forecasted cash flows. The analysis in Figure 9-4 uses this information to report your forecast variances.

To create the history in Figure 9-3, first open a new spreadsheet and turn off its gridlines. Enter the labels, borders, and shading shown for rows 51 through 53. (You'll enter the analysis in Figure 9-4 at the top of this spreadsheet.)

In actual practice, you'll use the macro shown in Figure 9-5 to update this schedule weekly. But to set up this spreadsheet, enter the data shown in the spreadsheet in Figure 9-3 and format it as shown. Use the figure's format box to guide you. (If you would rather not enter this data, you can purchase a disk that contains all the spreadsheets discussed in this chapter. You will find an order form on the last page of this book.)

Enter the borders and shading shown for row 86. To do so, highlight the shaded range, choose the Format Borders command, and select Outline, Left, Right, and Shade.

Enter the range names specified in the figure's range-name box. Enter the labels, borders, and values shown for rows 88 through 94. Cell C89 contains the only formula in this range; enter it as shown in the formula box. Finally, to complete this part of the spreadsheet, save it, using the name WK_HIST.XLS.

Creating the Analysis of the Weekly Cash Flow Forecasts

Figure 9-4 on page 456 shows an analysis of the cash flow forecasts contained in the cash flow history in Figure 9-3. For each category used in the forecast in Figure 9-2 and for each week of the forecast, this report presents information that will help you improve future forecasts.

Columns F through I are blank in this forecast because the history in Figure 9-3 does not contain enough data for these columns to analyze. To display a complete analysis, you must take two steps. First, enter four more weeks of cash flow reports. Second, adjust the date contained in the definition for the range name BegDate, as explained in the figure's range-name box. This date specifies the date in the schedule on which the analysis of actual cash flows begins. Because the analysis in the figure contains forecasts that are six weeks in advance of the actual cash flows, this beginning date should be at least seven weeks after the first date in your schedule. Otherwise, the analysis displays blank columns as shown.

The figure contains four sections:

Average Cash Flow Activity. On average, what do you collect weekly from accounts receivable? How much do you pay in CODs? What's your total cash flow? This report provides that information in column C. Additionally, the report tells you the average amounts that you predicted these categories would be, from one to six weeks in advance of the actual cash flows.

Standard Deviations of Activity. How much do cash flows for each category tend to vary each week from their average level of activity? The standard deviation provides this information. For example, cell C18 shows that actual collections tend to vary above and below the average by about $800. Cell E18 shows that forecasts of collections two weeks in advance tend to vary by $1,800. (Theoretically, roughly 65 percent of your future cash flows and predictions should fall within one standard deviation on either side of the average; roughly 95 percent will fall within two standard deviations.)

Average Forecast Variance. How accurate do your forecasts tend to be? The average forecast variance tells you. For example, cell D35 shows that weekly cash flows tend to average $3,900 below the amounts predicted only one week in advance; cell E35 shows they average $5,800 below the amounts predicted two weeks in advance. Where are the biggest problems with the forecast? Rows 28 and 33 show that collections and CODs produce the largest average variance.

Average Forecast Variance as a Percentage of Total Variance. This section displays the previous information as a percentage of the total variance. For example, cell D38 shows that the shortfall in actual collections explains 88 percent of the total variance in the cash flow forecast one week in advance. Similarly, cell E40 shows that you tend to pay fewer accounts payable than you forecast, creating a favorable effect on cash. This shortfall in payments explains roughly 12 percent of the variance in total cash flows predicted two weeks in advance.

To create this analysis, first open the WK_HIST.XLS spreadsheet and set the calculation option to manual. Enter the labels, borders, and values shown in rows 3 through 5. Enter the range definitions shown in the figure's range-name box and then enter the formula shown for cell I3.

Using the figure's formula and format boxes to assist you, create the first analysis section shown in rows 7 through 15. When you have this section working properly, copy it to the remaining three sections shown in Figure 9-4 and then modify each section as necessary, using the figure's information boxes to guide you. Finally, to complete the analysis, save it as WK_HIST.XLS.

Creating a Macro That Updates the Cash Flow Analysis

The macro in Figure 9-5 on page 461 inserts enough rows at the bottom of the history in Figure 9-3 to contain the values from the new week's cash flow report and then copies data from that report into the history.

Cell B16 contains the key formula in the macro. The MATCH function in this formula finds the row number in the forecast in Figure 9-2 that contains the appropriate category code; the INDEX function uses this row number as well as the column number from the Weeks range in the history shown in Figure 9-3 to return the appropriate value from the report.

To create this macro, first open a macro sheet, turn off its gridlines, and enter the macro statements shown. Assign the range name Update to cell B3, specifying the command key combination Ctrl-u, and then save the macro sheet as WK_UPDT.XLM.

To use this macro, first open the spreadsheets WK_HIST.XLS, WK_FCST.XLS, and WK_UPDT.XLM and then activate the WK_HIST.XLS spreadsheet. When you press Ctrl-u, the macro summarizes data from the WK_FCST.XLS spreadsheet at the bottom of your version of the history, shown in Figure 9-3.

When you run the macro the first time, a horizontal border might appear above your new category codes. The macro has copied this border from the analysis in Figure 9-4. To eliminate the border from future copies, highlight the range B8:B15 in your version of the analysis, choose Format Border, and then be sure both the Top and Bottom options are turned off. Then, if necessary, draw a bottom border in cell B7 and a top border in cell B16. These steps leave the appearance of your spreadsheet unchanged, but keep the macro from copying unwanted borders into your cash flow history.

Entering Your Own Cash Flow Data

To enter your own cash flow data, begin with the forecast in Figure 9-2. Modify this report to display the categories of income and expense that make sense for your business. Assign category codes to each category, including the Weekly Cash Flow category. Do not assign category codes to subtotals, such as Total Cash Expenses and Beginning Cash Balance.

Enter short descriptions and category codes in the first section of the analysis, shown in Figure 9-4, inserting or deleting rows as needed to accommodate your cash flow categories. Add or delete rows as needed in the other three sections of the analysis, and then copy your descriptions and codes to those sections. Finally, to complete the analysis, copy formulas as needed into any rows that you've inserted in each section.

Delete all but one row of data from the cash flow history in Figure 9-2; delete all formulas from this one row. When you've done so, the two shaded rows are separated by one unshaded row.

(Why leave the unshaded row? If the two shaded rows touch and you insert rows between them for your data, the new rows will be shaded and will contain top and bottom borders. That would look messy. By temporarily leaving the unshaded row, you eliminate this formatting problem.)

Update the Category Signs section shown in rows 91 through 94 of the analysis in Figure 9-3. To do so, enter the categories and signs in the appropriate rows, being sure that you enter *+1* for sources of cash and for the value of Total Cash Flow and *–1* for cash expenses. And if you add or delete categories, be sure to adjust the dimensions of the Signs range name.

Enter data into your version of the forecast in Figure 9-2, being sure that the dates in row 5 specify successive Mondays. Activate your version of the schedule in Figure 9-3 and then press Ctrl-u to update the history with your first cash flow report and forecast. After doing so, delete the empty row that you left at the top of your history spreadsheet.

Prepare a new cash flow report and forecast each week for four weeks, using your version of the forecast in Figure 9-2 and using the macro to update your cash flow history. At the end of this period, modify the range name BegDate in the WK_HIST.XLS file to contain the date one week prior to the most recent date. When you recalculate your spreadsheet, your analysis resembles the one in Figure 9-4.

Until all columns of the analysis return values, add a week to the BegDate range definition when you update your history each week. Then, after you accumulate a total of eight weeks of cash flow history, you can ignore the BegDate value when you update your history and print your analysis. Each week, your version of the analysis will analyze actual and forecasted cash flows from the BegDate through the most recent date.

Ideas for Extending the Analysis

The cash flow analysis in Figure 9-4 provides only an introduction to the analysis that you can perform on the cash flow data in the history in Figure 9-3. Here are some ideas for more detailed analysis:

- Create a spreadsheet that reports actual cash flows by week by category, using array formulas similar to those that generate the spreadsheet in Figure 6-13. In this report, however, put your dates in a column down the left side of your spreadsheet and the category numbers in a row across the top. Then graph this display. At a glance, you can see trends in your actual cash flows that could help you to predict future cash flows with greater accuracy.
- After you use the cash flow history for, say, six months, create a second page of analysis below the analysis in Figure 9-4 that reports on the most recent 12 weeks of cash flow activity. Comparing six-month averages with three-month averages can reveal trends in your cash flow activity that may not be apparent by using your graph. To create this new analysis, insert 60 rows at the bottom of your version of the analysis in Figure 9-4; copy the analysis to this new area; define a second version of the BegDate name (call it, say, BegDateTwo) that contains a date 12 weeks in the past; and then use the Formula Replace command to substitute BegDateTwo for BegDate in the second page of analysis.
- Add a new section to your version of the analysis that divides each cash flow variance either by the amount of the actual cash flow for that category or by the amount of the prediction. Doing so can reveal which cash flow categories are the most difficult to forecast. This section will resemble the last section of the original analysis; this section, however, will show the percentage by which each category tends to vary from either forecast or actual, while the existing section shows the percentage that each variance represents of the weekly variance in total cash flows.

A ONE-YEAR FORECAST

If a six-week forecast is like dim lights on a dark mountain road, a one-year forecast is like daylight on the desert. You can see nearly forever. But watch out for mirages.

The following section of this chapter presents a forecast that reduces mirages by grounding itself in reality. The forecast of sales is based on the time-series analysis discussed in Chapter 7. The forecast of accounts receivable collections is based on the analysis explained in Chapter 4. Labor and materials come from the spreadsheets presented in Chapter 8. Operating expenses come from the spreadsheets in Chapter 7 and Chapter 8. And so on.

After you complete all the pieces of your forecast, you will summarize them in the large spreadsheet presented in the following section. As the range-name box for the spreadsheet illustrates, this spreadsheet consists of many sections. First, it contains sections for each major financial activity in your company: sales and collections, material cost of sales and purchases, labor and overhead expenses, and so on. Second, it contains forecasts of the income statement, balance sheet, and cash flow for each month of the coming year. And third, it contains a section that helps you to find and correct errors in this large spreadsheet.

Creating a Sales and Collections Section

Figure 9-6 on page 462 contains the first section of the forecast, the sales and collections section. This section contains your total sales forecast in row 7 and an area for adjustments to the forecast in row 8. The adjustments section lets you pose what-if questions of your sales forecast without having to adjust the detail that generated row 7. Row 9 contains the sales forecast used by this spreadsheet; it is equal to values in row 7 plus (or minus) the percentage increase (or decrease) you specify in row 8.

Note that row 7 contains values copied from sales forecasts developed in other spreadsheets. You could link this spreadsheet to the six or eight supporting spreadsheets that provide data for it, but you probably will decide not to do so, for at least three reasons. First, establishing all those file links would slow calculation time considerably. Second, your supporting schedules will probably change little at this stage of the forecast. There is little point, therefore, in linking up with static schedules. Third, this spreadsheet and all supporting schedules probably would consume more computer memory than you have available.

Instead, copy the values for sales, cost of sales, operating costs, and so on from your supporting schedules. If you must change a supporting schedule, do so and then copy the new information to the forecast. If you find you must continually copy this data, you can reassess whether you want to link this forecast to the schedules that change frequently and whether your hardware can support the links.

When you begin the forecasting period, you will have existing accounts receivable, which you must collect. Rows 11 through 18 use past collection experience to estimate these collections. Ratios in the range G13:G17 tell you that, historically, you collect 49 percent of all receivables up to 30 days old in the following month, 61 percent of the remainder in the month after that, 92 percent of the remainder in the month after that, and so on. You write off anything not collected after 120 days. (Figure 4-13 contains a spreadsheet that can generate these ratios for your company.)

Rows 20 through 25 contain ratios that you apply to sales each month to estimate when you'll collect them. The ratios in the spreadsheet reflect the estimate that you'll collect 2 percent in the month of the sale, 44 percent in 30 days, 33 percent in 60 days, and so on. The forecast allows you to change these ratios monthly; but in all cases, they must add up to 100 percent.

Rows 27 through 29 summarize the two sources of cash, collections of current receivables and collections of new sales. Row 31 calculates your bad debts.

Notice in this spreadsheet that columns M through P have column widths of 0.5. I assigned these widths so that the forecast would fit on one page of this book. Although you can't see what these columns contain, you aren't missing anything. Throughout this spreadsheet, the hidden columns contain copies of columns you can see.

To create this spreadsheet, open a new spreadsheet, turn off the gridlines, and then set the column widths as shown in the column-width box. Using the figure's formula and format boxes to guide you, create the portion of the spreadsheet shown in Figure 9-6. After you complete the portion shown, save the spreadsheet as FORECAST.XLS.

As you add more sections to this spreadsheet, it will take longer and longer to recalculate. At some point, therefore, you probably will decide to switch from automatic to manual recalculation. After you do so, remember to press the F9 (Calculate All) key when you need to view the results of your formulas.

Creating a Material Costs and Purchases Section

Row 40 of the section of the spreadsheet shown in Figure 9-7 on page 466 contains the material cost of sales corresponding to the sales figures in row 7 of the portion in Figure 9-6. (Figure 8-20 presents a spreadsheet that helps you calculate these values.) The sales adjustment in row 41 repeats the percentage you entered in row 8 of the portion of the spreadsheet in Figure 9-6.

Row 43 contains your estimate of the material waste and scrap you will generate, as a percentage of material cost of sales. Row 45 contains the total material costs that you expect to generate monthly.

The inventory-purchasing schedule in rows 47 through 53 uses reasoning similar to that used in the collections schedule. But while the collections schedule depended on past performance, the purchasing schedule depends on future performance. In other words, it requires that you estimate what percentage of this month's cost of sales you will purchase this month, what percentage of this month's cost of sales you normally purchase 30 days in advance, 60 days in advance, and so on. Row 53 uses this information to calculate total purchases for each month.

Notice that in November and December you will purchase goods you expect to ship in the following year. You must therefore estimate what those costs of sales will be and when you will purchase the goods. The range T36:V51 contains these estimates.

Rows 55 through 61 contain your estimate of how quickly you expect to pay your current accounts payable. Rows 63 through 67 contain similar estimates for your new purchases. Both sets of schedules follow the same reasoning as the two collections schedules. Finally, rows 69 through 71 summarize the two payment schedules.

Use the figure's formula box for guidance as you add this portion to your FORECAST.XLS spreadsheet. After you complete it, save your spreadsheet again.

Creating a Labor and Overhead Section

The portion of the spreadsheet in Figure 9-8 on page 469 presents labor and overhead expenses from your detailed schedules. Figure 8-17 presents a spreadsheet that helps you calculate labor expenses, Figure 8-19 presents overtime expenses, and the spreadsheets in Figure 8-1 through Figure 8-12 provide information for calculating overhead expenses.

Sales commissions and co-op advertising are both directly related to the amount of sales. This spreadsheet calculates those expenses, rather than depending on an estimate in a supporting schedule. Cells E87 and E88 contain the percentages that are applied to sales when you calculate these expenses.

Because the expenses in this portion of the spreadsheet tend to be paid more quickly than do inventory costs, the payment schedule contains fewer rows. You can easily expand this schedule if you want, however.

Create this portion of the spreadsheet as you did the others. Use its formula box to guide you. After you finish, save the spreadsheet again as FORECAST.XLS.

Creating a Capital Budget Section

Row 106 of the capital budget section, shown in Figure 9-9 on page 471, contains the amount of your planned purchases of fixed assets in the coming year, which you can copy from your supporting schedule. Figure 8-24 presents a spreadsheet that can help you to calculate these values.

Paying for fixed assets often involves the payment of cash when you place the order, when you take delivery, and when, after several months of use, you agree to final acceptance. The payment schedule in rows 108 through 113 provides for this type of payment schedule. And because you might have to pay for assets in November and December that you won't take delivery of until the following year, columns T and U of the forecast provide for asset purchases into the following year.

Row 117 contains book depreciation for the new year. (Figure 8-22 and Figure 8-25 provide the resources you need to complete this row.) Row 119 contains tax depreciation. (To calculate the monthly amount in this row, refer to Figure 8-22 and Figure 8-26.)

Create this portion of the spreadsheet as you did the others, using its formula box to guide you. As before, save your spreadsheet after you've added this portion.

Creating a Financing Section

Row 129 of the financing section of the spreadsheet, shown in Figure 9-10 on page 472, contains the annual interest rate that you expect to pay during each month of the coming year. This row allows you to adjust rates monthly, to reflect the trend you expect interest rates to follow during the coming year.

The forecast borrows cash at the current interest rate if the cash balance falls below the amount entered in cell F130. (That is, it increases the amount of the loan outstanding in the spreadsheet.) And the forecast "repays" this loan, in part or in full, using cash in excess of the amount entered in cell F131.

Rows 134 through 136 contain information about your long-term loan. Cell F135 contains the outstanding balance at the beginning of the forecast. Cell F134 contains its annual interest rate and cell F136 contains its payment amount. The remaining columns in this section provide an amortization schedule for the loan during the coming year, calculating the monthly interest expense and the amount of the loan reduction.

Although this section of the spreadsheet shows only one amortizing loan, you can easily add as many as you want. To do so, insert the number of rows that you want just above the current long-term loan section. Copy the long-term loan section to this new area and then adjust each copy's values and formulas to calculate your various amortization schedules. After you have the new amortization schedules working properly, add all interest expenses into the Interest Payment row of the existing schedule, all principal payments into the Principal Payment row, and the total payments into the Total Loan Payment row. By turning the existing schedule into a summary of several other amortization schedules, you won't need to adjust any other formulas in the spreadsheet that refer to the existing schedule.

Rows 139 and 140 contain your planned equity transactions during the coming year. If yours is a private company with no equity transactions, enter *0* in each cell in these rows, but leave the rows in place. Doing so produces two benefits. First, leaving the schedule in the forecast is easier than removing it. Second, presenting the schedule with equity transactions equal to 0 reminds outsiders who may review your forecast what your plans are in this regard.

Create this schedule, using the formula box for Figure 9-10 as guidance. Save the spreadsheet after you complete this portion.

Creating an Income Tax Section

You will probably want to expand the simple section, shown in Figure 9-11 on page 474, which calculates taxable income. Here the only difference between book and tax income is the difference between the two methods of depreciation. In many companies, of course, the differences can run on for pages.

Row 153 presents your quarterly tax payments. If you want to change the months in which you make these payments, simply copy the formulas shown in the figure's formula box to the appropriate cells in this row. Also, change the income tax rate to reflect both the state and federal tax rates for your own company.

Enter this portion of the spreadsheet and then save the spreadsheet.

Creating a Pro Forma Income Statement

All rows of the pro forma income statement, shown in Figure 9-12 on page 475, refer to formulas and data you've already entered in this spreadsheet. All you need to do is reference the correct data as you create this portion of the spreadsheet.

To create this portion, enter rows 158 through 160 as shown, enter the labels in columns A and B, and then enter the formulas shown in the figure's formula box. After you enter all formulas, add the borders as shown and then save the spreadsheet.

Creating a Pro Forma Balance Sheet

Column G of the pro forma balance sheet, shown in Figure 9-13 on page 477, contains ending balance-sheet data for the period immediately prior to the beginning of the forecast; it contains values rather than formulas. The existing balances of accounts payable, accounts receivable, and loans outstanding must equal the data used in previous sections of this spreadsheet.

This schedule calculates the remaining columns by adding the changes that have transpired during the month to the ending balance of the previous month. In so doing, it performs exactly like your own accounting system.

Unlike in your own accounting system, the assets and liabilities probably won't be equal the first time you create this schedule. Because this schedule can be quite difficult to debug, the spreadsheet contains a reconciliation section, as shown in Figure 9-15. Therefore, if row 220 doesn't return a 0 in each cell when you create this portion of the forecast spreadsheet, don't worry about it for now. Continue building the spreadsheet and then use the reconciliation section to find your problem.

As always, use the formulas shown in the figure's formula boxes to help you to create this section. And after you do so, save it once again.

Creating a Cash Flow Forecast

Fundamentally, a cash flow forecast calculates the changes that will occur in each asset and liability during a period of time and then reports these changes in a sequence that makes sense to the reader. The portion of the spreadsheet shown in Figure 9-14 on page 482 divides these changes into three categories:

Operating Cash Flows. Day-to-day operations of a company are much like an engine that generates cash. Operating cash flows represent the cash that this engine generates.

Investing Cash Flows. In most companies, the purchase and sale of capital assets represent the firm's only investing activity. Even so, it makes sense to separate these activities from operating activities. Often, the purchase or sale of equipment can significantly distort the ability that a company has to generate cash. Excessive purchases can make a company look worse than it should; excessive sales can make it look better.

Financing Activities. Over the life of a company, the sum of operating and investing cash flows must be large enough to pay all creditors and provide investors with an adequate return on their investments. This section of the cash flow statement reflects your company's plans for compensating your creditors and investors during the coming year or for obtaining more cash from them.

Row 255 contains the ending cash balance, which must equal the Cash line of the pro forma balance sheet. Row 260 tests this relationship by subtracting one of these balances from the other; the result, of course, must be equal to 0.

Row 245 contains your predicted cash balance before financing, which is also called your operating cash flow. If this row is positive, you can reduce debt and pay dividends while growing as planned. If this row is negative, you must borrow cash, sell stock, or both to finance your plans for the new year. Row 257 contains the cumulative amount of this important calculation.

Now that you've gotten this far, this part of the spreadsheet should be a breeze to create. Enter the headings and descriptions as shown and then enter the formulas as described in the figure's formula boxes. As always, save the spreadsheet after entering this portion of it.

Creating a Reconciliation Section

Figure 9-15 on pages 486 and 487 presents two halves of one wide reconciliation schedule that allows you to select any pair of columns to reconcile. Suppose, for example, that your assets equal your liabilities in the balance sheet of column K but not in column L. To find the problem, you enter the letter *K* in cell G270, as shown, and then recalculate. When you do so, column G returns the balance sheet from column K; column H calculates the balance sheet for column L by adding column K's ending balance to the sum of the changes specified in columns I through Z.

If you create the reconciliation section correctly, the new total in column H reconciles. That is, cell H308, which subtracts the reconciliation assets from its liabilities, equals 0. You now have two balance sheets that should be identical but aren't. Simply compare the balance sheet in column H of the part of the spreadsheet in Figure 9-15 to the balance-sheet figures in column L of the part of the spreadsheet in Figure 9-13. When you find a difference, decide which schedule is correct, make the necessary change, recalculate, and start the process over.

Note: Always research the cash and notes payable accounts last. The formulas that generate notes payable in the balance sheet attempt to compensate for problems in other accounts, which the formula for the cash account recognizes. When you correct other accounts that don't reconcile, notes payable and cash often correct themselves.

The reason that the balance sheet in Figure 9-15 always reconciles easily is that each accounting entry that affects the balance sheet has been placed in plain view in the schedule. All calculations are easy to understand and correct, if necessary.

For example, Column I shows the entry for sales. Cell I268 specifies that when the forecast calculates the balance sheet in column L it uses sales data from cell L9. This sales figure increases accounts receivable, as illustrated in cell I276, and increases retained earnings, as illustrated in cell I301. (With the exception of dividend payments, all entries to retained earnings also appear in the pro forma income statement.) Every other transaction that affects the balance sheet is in plain view as well.

Spreading each entry across the columns also helps you add new transactions to your forecast. Suppose, for example, that you ship goods on consignment and that you must add this fact to the forecast. To do so, add an account titled *Consignments* to the assets section of the balance sheets in Figure 9-13 and Figure 9-15. Insert a column between columns Z and AA to hold the consignment transactions and then temporarily add values in this column to signify the transactions. You might, for example, increase Consignments and decrease Inventory by $100.

Now that you've worked out which accounts will be affected by your change to the forecast, add the necessary detail to the early part of your forecast, perhaps in the Sales and Collections section. When you've worked out your Consignments assumptions, incorporate them into the balance sheet in Figure 9-13 by modifying the Inventory formula and adding a formula for Consignments. Finally, return to the part of the spreadsheet in Figure 9-15 and turn the sample values in the Consignments column into formulas, exactly as columns I through Z contain formulas.

To create the part of the spreadsheet in Figure 9-15, first set the column widths as shown in the column-width box. Enter the labels, borders, and shading shown in rows 265 through 267 of both figures, and the label in cell F270. Copy the balance-sheet descriptions, formulas, and data from the range A187:H217 of the part of the spreadsheet in Figure 9-13 to cell A274.

Enter the label shown for cell G270 and the formula shown in the figure's formula box for cell H270. Enter the formula shown for cell I268, copy it to the right as needed, and then modify the formulas as shown in the formula box.

Enter the labels and borders shown in rows 271 through 273. Enter the formulas shown for cells G275 and H275 and then copy them down their columns as shown in the formula box. When you calculate the sheet, column G returns the values shown and column H returns amounts equal to those in column G.

The formula boxes for Figure 9-15 explain each formula contained in the range I275:Z304. Enter them as shown. When you do so, pay particular attention to the sign of each formula; if you enter a plus sign or a minus sign in error, your reconciliation balance sheet won't balance.

After you enter all formulas in columns I through Z, enter the labels in the range A306:A310 and then enter the formulas shown for the range G308:H310. After you recalculate, all formulas return a value of 0 if your balance sheet balances. If it doesn't balance, use the values provided in the sample spreadsheet in the figure to help you find the error. Finally, save your spreadsheet once again as FORECAST.XLS.

As shown here, the reconciliation and the forecast are inconvenient in one regard: They require different column widths. This could become a problem if you intended to leave columns M through P with a width of 0.5. In actual practice, however, this will not be the case. Even so, you might want to adjust the column widths. Figure 9-16 on page 491 presents two simple macros that adjust column widths as shown in the sample spreadsheet. The WIDTH1 macro sets the widths used in the forecast displays; the WIDTH2 macro sets the widths used in the reconciliation displays.

Figure 9-1. Calendar of Scheduled Payments by Week

A scheduled payments calendar that calculates the cash required to satisfy recurring needs for each of the next six weeks. Saved as CALENDAR.XLS.

	A	B	C	D	E	F	G	H	I	J	K	L	M	N
1														
2														
3		**Calendar of Scheduled Payments**									**December 19, 1988**			
4														
5														
6		**Scheduled for Monthly Payments**												
7	Beginning			Pay	Sched	GL		Monday	Monday	Monday	Monday	Monday	Monday	
8	Date	Payee	Reason	Date	Every	Acct	Amount	19-Dec	26-Dec	2-Jan	9-Jan	16-Jan	23-Jan	
9														
10	15-Oct-84	Farmer's Bank	Loan	15	1	Misc	3,087.50				3,087.50			
11	10-Oct-81	Lanyard Jones	S/H Loan	10	1	Misc	1,905.40				1,905.40			
12	29-Apr-79	Pacific Realty	Trailer Loan	29	1	Misc	570.00		570.00				570.00	
13	28-Feb-83	Ranier Electric	555-3823	28	1	6589	1,400.00		1,400.00				1,400.00	
14	30-Nov-85	Pac Tel	800-555-2352	30	1	7839	960.04		960.04					
15	8-May-82	Vino's Leasing	Car--Sls Mgr's	8	1	7847	1,300.00			1,300.00				
16	9-Oct-84	McElway Leasing	Car--President's	9	1	6495	881.60				881.60			
17	25-Oct-86	City Electronics	Forklift	25	1	5997	2,587.00	2,587.00					2,587.00	
18	1-Oct-84	WT Door & Co.	Factory Lease	1	1	5374	1,995.87		1,995.87					
19	1-May-80	LA Partners	Warehouse Rent	1	1	7987	776.00		776.00					
20	20-Nov-85	Susan Prig	Royalties	20	3	2464	2,800.00							
21	10-Dec-83	Handy Hauling	Trash	10	2	2405	2,393.02							
22	10-Aug-85	Union Plastics	AP Paydown	10	1	7138	2,133.98				2,133.98			
23	1-Aug-83	Bob's Trucking	AP Paydown	1	1	7054	1,324.00		1,324.00					
24	9-May-88	Larson's 'Lectric	Electricity, W/H	9	2	4515	575.80				575.80			
25	25-Jan-80	King County	Property Taxes	25	12	7044	1,238.31						1,238.31	
26	7-Sep-82	Farmer's	Car Insurance	7	3	4656	1,040.00							
27	1-Apr-79	Western Ins.	General Liab	1	12	4457	1,000.00							
28														
29		Total Amount Scheduled for Monthly Payments					27,968.52	2,587.00	7,025.91	1,300.00	8,584.28		5,795.31	
30														
31														
32		**Scheduled for Weekly Payments**												
33	Beginning			Pay	Sched	GL								
34	Date	Payee	Reason	Day	Every	Acct	Amount	19-Dec	26-Dec	2-Jan	9-Jan	16-Jan	23-Jan	
35														
36	19-Mar-85	Sander's Elect.	AP Paydown	Tue	2	2201	100.00		100.00		100.00		100.00	
37	18-Dec-84	Janson's Supplies	AP Paydown	Tue	1	2201	225.00	225.00	225.00	225.00	225.00	225.00	225.00	
38	1-Mar-82	John Jones	Royalty Payment	Mon	5	2318	500.00	500.00					500.00	
39														
40		Total Amount Scheduled for Weekly Payments					825.00	725.00	325.00	225.00	325.00	225.00	825.00	
41														
42														
43		**Grand Total**												
44		Total Cash Requirements Per Week:						3,312.00	7,350.91	1,525.00	8,909.28	225.00	6,620.31	
45														
46														

COLUMN WIDTHS							
Column	*Width*	*Column*	*Width*	*Column*	*Width*	*Column*	*Width*
A	9	E	6	I	7.5	M	7.5
B	15.5	F	5	J	7.5		
C	13.67	G	9.83	K	7.5		
D	4.33	H	7.5	L	7.5		

(continued)

Figure 9-1. *continued*

KEY FORMULAS	
Cell	***Formula***
M3	**=TEXT($H$8,"mmmm dd, yyyy")** Turning the date into text lets you display it in more than one cell.
H7	**=WEEKDAY(H8)** Displaying the weekday assures you that the dates you've chosen really are Mondays.
H8	**12/19/88** To change all dates in the schedule, enter the new beginning date in this cell.
I8	**=7+H8** Copy this formula to the right as needed.
D10	**=DAY(A10)** This formula returns the day of the month specified in column A.
H10	**=(–INT(–(1+Date–H$8)/7)=1)*(MOD(Months,$E10)=0)*$G10** A bill is due to be paid when two facts are true: • The due date falls between this Monday and next Sunday. To understand how the INT function makes this determination, suppose that today is the 15th and that the due date is the 21st. The INT function returns 1. (That is, –INT(–(1+21–15)/7)=1.) And if the bill is due on the 15th, the INT function still returns 1. (That is, –INT(–(1+15–15)/7)=1.) But if the bill is due on the 14th, the INT function returns 0. (That is, –INT(–(1+14–15)/7)=0.) If the bill is due on the 22nd, the INT function returns 2. (–INT(–(1+22–15)/7)=2.) Therefore, only those dates falling between this Monday and next Sunday return the value 1 for the INT function shown. When the complete expression (–INT(etc)=1) is stated as a "logical formula," as shown, it returns the value 1 when the relationship is true and the value 0 when it's false. • The payment schedule lets the bill be paid this month. Suppose the bill should be paid every five months and that 60 months have passed since you first agreed to this arrangement. You know that you must pay again this month because 5 divides evenly into 60. In other words, 60 divided by 5 leaves a remainder of 0. Or, using the mathematical function, MOD(60,5)=0. As before, if the logical formula (MOD(etc)=0) is true, it returns the value 1; otherwise, it returns 0. The product of the two logical statements equals 1 only if both statements are true (that is, only if both values equal 1); otherwise, the product equals 0. Therefore, multiplying these results by the payment amount will return the amount itself when both tests succeed; otherwise, the formula will return 0.

(continued)

Figure 9-1. *continued*

KEY FORMULAS–continued	
Cell	***Formula***
G29	**=SUM(G9:G28)** Copy this formula to the right as needed.
H34 **D36**	**=H$8** **=WEEKDAY(A36)** Copy these formulas to the right or downward as needed.
H36	**=(MOD(INT((H$34–$A36)/7),$E36)=0)*$G36** The INT function determines the number of weeks that have passed since the beginning date of the payment plan. The logical formula (MOD(etc)=0) returns 1 if the value in column E divides evenly into the number of weeks that have passed; otherwise, it returns 0. Multiplying by the amount returns the payment amount when it's time to pay; otherwise, it returns 0.
H40 **H44**	**=SUM(H35:H39)** **=H$29+H$40** Copy these to the right as needed.

RANGE NAMES	
Name	***Formula***
Each formula in the monthly schedule decides whether it's time to pay the amount in column G. To do so, the formulas must calculate several intermediate results. You will find these easier to manipulate if you define them as the range names that follow. *You will find these definitions easier to enter if you use R1C1 references rather than A1 references. To use R1C1 references, choose Options Workspace, turn on the R1C1 box, and then choose OK. After you do so, choose Formula Define Name and then enter the range definitions shown below.*	
Day	**=MIN(DAY(DATE(YEAR(R8C),MONTH(R8C)+1,1)–1),RC4)** If payment is due on the 31st of the month, it is also due on February 28, on September 30, and so on. This formula defines the name Day to be equal either to the Due Day in the schedule or to the last day of the month, whichever is less. Suppose your pointer is in cell H10 of the spreadsheet. This formula finds the last day of the month in cell H8 (row 8, same column), finds the day shown in cell D10 (same row, column 4), and then returns the lesser of the two.

(continued)

Figure 9-1. *continued*

RANGE NAMES–continued	
Name	***Formula***
Date	**=DATE(YEAR(R8C),MONTH(R8C)+(Day<DAY(R8C)),Day)** This formula defines Date to contain the date serial number for the next date that payment is due for the day of the month specified by Day. For example, if today is June 29, the next pay date for an invoice due on the 30th is June 30; for an invoice due on the 28th, it's July 28; and for an invoice due on the 2nd, it's July 2. Suppose your pointer is in cell H10. This formula finds the date serial number for the year of the date in cell H8 and for the day specified by Day. If Day is less than DAY(H8), this formula adds one month to the month of cell H8; otherwise, it adds 0 to the month in cell H8.
Months	**=MONTH(Date)–MONTH(RC1)+12*(YEAR(Date)–YEAR(RC1))** Column A contains the beginning date by which to measure the passing of time. This formula defines the range name Months to contain the number of months that have passed since that date. Suppose, for example, that since August 3, 1987, an insurance payment has been due every three months. This range contains the number of months that have passed since that date.

KEY CELL FORMATS			
Cell	***Number***	***Alignment***	***Font***
Sheet	**Set Font 1 to Helv 8**		
B3	**General**	**Left**	**Helv 10, Bold**
M3	**General**	**Right**	**Helv 10, Bold**
B6	**General**	**Left**	**Helv 10, Bold**
H7:M7	**dddd**	**Center**	**Helv 8**
H8:M8	**d-mmm**	**Center**	**Helv 8**
G9:M29	**#,##0.00 ;(#,##0.00);**	**General**	**Helv 8**
A9:A28	**d-mmm-yy**	**Center**	**Helv 8**
B32	**General**	**Left**	**Helv 10, Bold**
A33:G34	**General**	**Center**	**Helv 8**
H34:M34	**d-mmm**	**Center**	**Helv 8**
D35:D39	**ddd**	**Center**	**Helv 8**
B43	**General**	**General**	**Helv 10, Bold**

Figure 9-2. Weekly Cash Flow Report and Forecast

A weekly cash flow report and forecast that you generate at the beginning of each week. Saved as WK_FCST.XLS.

	A	B	C	D	E	F	G	H	I	J	K
1											
2											
3	**Weekly Cash Flow Report and Forecast**								**August 21, 1989**		
4				**Actual**	**1**	**2**	**3**	**4**	**5**	**6**	
5	**Cash Receipts**			**21-Aug**	**28-Aug**	**4-Sep**	**11-Sep**	**18-Sep**	**25-Sep**	**2-Oct**	
6											
7	10	A/R Collections		10,840	14,660	13,370	11,500	11,800	14,000	12,000	
8	20	Other Cash Receipts				1,000					
9											
10	Total Cash Receipts			10,840	14,660	14,370	11,500	11,800	14,000	12,000	
11											
12	**Cash Expenses**										
13											
14	30	Payment of Accounts Payable		4,707	6,352	8,080	6,300	6,900	7,000	6,000	
15	40	Scheduled Payments		1,331	176	3,248	2,936	616	5,655	316	
16	50	Payroll		3,228	3,084		3,100		3,200		
17	60	CODs		3,415	200	200	200	200	200	200	
18	70	Special Payments		500	3,000			5,000			
19											
20	Total Cash Expenses			13,181	12,812	11,528	12,536	12,716	16,055	6,516	
21											
22	**Cash Flow**										
23											
24		Beginning Cash Balance		10,619	8,278	10,126	12,968	11,932	11,016	8,961	
25	100	Weekly Cash Flow		-2,341	1,848	2,842	-1,036	-916	-2,055	5,484	
26											
27	Ending Cash Balance			8,278	10,126	12,968	11,932	11,016	8,961	14,445	
28											
29											

COLUMN WIDTHS			
Column	*Width*	*Column*	*Width*
A	3	G	6
B	11.43	H	6
C	13.86	I	6
D	6	J	6
E	6	K	2
F	6		

(continued)

Figure 9-2. *continued*

KEY FORMULAS	
Cell	***Formula***
D5	**08/21/89**
F5	**=7+E5**
	Copy the formula to the right as needed.
K3	**=TEXT(Date,"mmmm d, yyyy")**
	By displaying the date as formatted text, you can let it extend as far as necessary to the left.
E10	**=SUM(E6:E9)**
E20	**=SUM(E13:E19)**
E24	**=D27**
E25	**=E10–E20**
E27	**=SUM(E23:E26)**
	Copy these formulas to the right as needed.

RANGE NAMES	
Name	***Formula***
Codes	**=$A$4:$A$27**
	This range contains the codes for each prediction category.
Input	**=$C$4:$K$27**
	The Input range begins one column to the left of the data and ends one column to the right. Notice that Codes and Input begin and end in the same rows.
Date	**=INDEX(Input,2,2):INDEX(Input,2,2)**
	This date is the Monday of the current report.
InsertCol	**=INDEX(Input,1,COLUMNS(Input)):INDEX(Input,ROWS(Input),COLUMNS(Input))**
DeleteCol	**=INDEX(Input,1,2):INDEX(Input,ROWS(Input),2)**
	The easiest way to create this week's forecast is to modify last week's forecast. To do so, you insert a column at the InsertCol range and delete a column at the DeleteCol range.

(continued)

Figure 9-2. *continued*

KEY CELL FORMATS			
Cell	*Number*	*Alignment*	*Font*
K3	General	Right	Helv 10, Bold
D5:K5	d-mmm	Center	Helv 8, Bold
E6:K27	#,##0	General	Helv 10

Figure 9-3. Cash Flow History, Actual and Forecasts by Category by Week

A cash flow history that helps you improve cash flow forecasts by comparing actual cash flows to forecasted. Saved as WK_HIST.XLS.

	A	B	C	D	E	F	G	H	I	J
48										
49										
50										
51	**Cash Flow History--Actual and Forecasts by Category by Week**									
52	**Date**	**Codes**	**Actual**	**1**	**2**	**3**	**4**	**5**	**6**	
53										
54	7/31/89	10	11,982	15,051	13,342	16,007	13,501	10,747	12,873	
55	7/31/89	20	100	0	0	0	943	0	0	
56	7/31/89	30	-4,958	-6,902	-4,494	-6,056	-8,070	-7,080	-6,481	
57	7/31/89	40	-5,000	0	-1,396	-150	-3,045	-2,944	-539	
58	7/31/89	50	-3,259	0	-3,605	-3,041	0	-3,489	0	
59	7/31/89	60	-200	-3,445	-4,343	-206	-189	-227	-202	
60	7/31/89	70	0	-4,486	0	0	0	0	-5,085	
61	7/31/89	100	-1,335	218	-496	6,554	3,140	-2,993	566	
62	8/7/89	10	14,987	11,206	15,927	12,877	10,537	12,909	13,281	
63	8/7/89	20	0	50	0	974	0	0	0	
64	8/7/89	30	-6,888	-4,274	-5,932	-8,587	-6,774	-6,660	-7,682	
65	8/7/89	40	0	-1,384	-159	-3,250	-3,137	-583	-5,142	
66	8/7/89	50	0	-3,544	-2,957	0	-3,376	0	-3,027	
67	8/7/89	60	-3,598	-4,155	-202	-192	-215	-215	-215	
68	8/7/89	70	-4,200	0	0	0	0	-5,263	0	
69	8/7/89	100	301	-2,101	6,677	1,822	-2,965	188	-2,785	
70	8/14/89	10	9,695	13,111	11,950	10,280	10,500	12,500	11,000	
71	8/14/89	20	250	0	894	0	0	0	0	
72	8/14/89	30	-4,210	-5,681	-7,226	-5,634	-6,171	-6,260	-5,366	
73	8/14/89	40	-1,190	-157	-2,905	-2,626	-551	-5,057	-283	
74	8/14/89	50	-2,887	-2,758	0	-2,772	0	-2,862	0	
75	8/14/89	60	-4,827	-200	-200	-200	-200	-200	-200	
76	8/14/89	70	0	0	0	0	-4,472	0	0	
77	8/14/89	100	-3,169	4,315	2,513	-952	-894	-1,879	5,151	
78	8/21/89	10	10,840	14,660	13,370	11,500	11,800	14,000	12,000	
79	8/21/89	20	0	0	1,000	0	0	0	0	
80	8/21/89	30	-4,707	-6,352	-8,080	-6,300	-6,900	-7,000	-6,000	
81	8/21/89	40	-1,331	-176	-3,248	-2,936	-616	-5,655	-316	
82	8/21/89	50	-3,228	-3,084	0	-3,100	0	-3,200	0	
83	8/21/89	60	-3,415	-200	-200	-200	-200	-200	-200	
84	8/21/89	70	-500	-3,000	0	0	-5,000	0	0	
85	8/21/89	100	-2,341	1,848	2,842	-1,036	-916	-2,055	5,484	
86										
87										
88	**Side Calculation**									
89	Skip Value		2							
90										
91	**Category Signs**									
92	Enter +1 for Collections and for Total Cash Flow. Enter -1 for cash expenses:									
93	Category	10	20	30	40	50	60	70	100	
94	Sign	1	1	-1	-1	-1	-1	-1	1	
95										

(continued)

Figure 9-3. *continued*

COLUMN WIDTHS			
Column	*Width*	*Column*	*Width*
A	13.57	F	8.43
B	8	G	8.43
C	8.43	H	8.43
D	8.43	I	8.43
E	8.43	J	5.57

KEY FORMULAS	
Cell	*Formula*
C52	**0** Notice that this cell contains a 0 although it displays the label *Actual* in the spreadsheet. The number format generates the label. (This figure's format box shows the custom format, and the explanation for *Weeks* in the range-name box provides additional information.)
C89	**=(BegDate–MinDate)/7** This formula returns the number of weeks of actual cash flow history that the analysis must skip before it can calculate its statistics. For example, the history must skip at least one week of actual cash flows to compare actual data to the forecast one week earlier (column D). Similarly, it must skip six weeks of actual data before it can compare the first forecast in column I to the actual results that occurred six weeks later. To calculate this value, the formula first finds the number of days to skip by subtracting the earliest date in the cash flow history from the beginning date you've specified in the BegDate range definition. Then, to find the number of weeks, it divides by 7.

(continued)

Figure 9-3. *continued*

<table>
<tr><th colspan="2">RANGE NAMES</th></tr>
<tr><th>Name</th><th>Formula</th></tr>
<tr><td>Weeks</td><td>=$C$52:$I$52
This range contains the week numbers 0, for actual cash flows, through 6. The macro statement in row 16 of the macro in Figure 9-5 uses this range to update the cash flow history spreadsheet in Figure 9-3.</td></tr>
<tr><td>Input</td><td>=$A$53:$I$86
This range surrounds the data, providing a reference for other range formulas.</td></tr>
<tr><td>Top
Bottom</td><td>=$A$53
=$A$86
Enter these range definitions as shown.</td></tr>
<tr><td>MaxDate
MinDate</td><td>=MAX($A$53:$A$86)
=MIN(IF($A$53:$A$86>0,$A$53:$A$86))
These range-definition formulas return the latest and earliest report dates in the schedule.</td></tr>
<tr><td>Skip</td><td>=$C$89
This range contains the number of weeks of actual cash flow history the analysis must skip before it can calculate its statistics. See the formula box for a more complete definition.
Notice that you could enter the formula in cell C89 as the definition of the range name Skip. Doing so would let you erase rows 88 and 89, reducing clutter in your spreadsheet. Unfortunately, doing so can also lengthen calculation time considerably. As Appendix E shows, range definitions recalculate every time they're referenced during a single recalculation, while formulas recalculate only once. Because most formulas in this spreadsheet reference Skip and because Skip references two other range definitions that must recalculate as well, you eliminate many calculations by accepting a slight increase in spreadsheet clutter.</td></tr>
<tr><td>Signs</td><td>=$B$94:$I$94
This range contains either a +1 or a –1 for each category, depending on whether the category represents a source or a use of funds, respectively. Enter a +1 for the Total Cash Flows category.</td></tr>
</table>

(continued)

Figure 9-3. *continued*

KEY CELL FORMATS			
Cell	***Number***	***Alignment***	***Font***
A51	**General**	**General**	**Helv 10, Bold**
C52	**"Actual"** Notice that the number format generates the label in this cell.	**Center**	**Helv 10, Bold**
A54:I54	**m/d/yy**	**Center**	**Helv 10**
A53:A86	**m/d/yy**	**Center**	**Helv 10**
B53:B86	**General**	**Center**	**Helv 10**
C53:I86	**#,##0**	**General**	**Helv 10**
A88	**General**	**General**	**Helv 10, Bold**
A91	**General**	**General**	**Helv 10, Bold**
B93:I94	**General**	**Center**	**Helv 10**

Figure 9-4. Analysis of the Weekly Cash Flow Forecast

An analysis of actual cash flows by week. Saved as WK_HIST.XLS. For column widths, see Figure 9-3.

	A	B	C	D	E	F	G	H	I	J
1										
2										
3	**Analysis of the Weekly Cash Flow Forecasts**							**8/14/89 thru 8/21/89**		
4	**Category**	**Category**	**Actual**	**# of Weeks the Forecast Precedes Actual Cash Flows**						
5	**Description**	**Codes**	**Flows**	**1**	**2**	**3**	**4**	**5**	**6**	
6										
7	**Average Cash Flow Activity**							($1000s, + = Collections)		
8	A/R Collections	10	10.3	12.2	14.6					
9	Other Rcpts	20	.1	.0						
10	A/P Payments	30	-4.5	-5.0	-5.2					
11	Sched Pmts	40	-1.3	-.8	-.8					
12	Payroll	50	-3.1	-3.2	-3.3					
13	CODs	60	-4.1	-2.2	-2.3					
14	Special Pmts	70	-.3							
15	Tot Cash Flow	100	-2.8	1.1	3.1					
16										
17	**Standard Deviations of Activity**								($1000s)	
18	A/R Collections	10	.8	1.3	1.8					
19	Other Rcpts	20	.2	.0						
20	A/P Payments	30	.4	1.0	1.0					
21	Sched Pmts	40	.1	.9	.9					
22	Payroll	50	.2	.6	.5					
23	CODs	60	1.0	2.8	2.9					
24	Special Pmts	70	.4							
25	Tot Cash Flow	100	.6	4.5	5.1					
26										
27	**Average Forecast Variance**						($1000s, + = Favorable Variance)			
28	A/R Collections	10		-1.9	-4.4					
29	Other Rcpts	20		.1	.1					
30	A/P Payments	30		.5	.8					
31	Sched Pmts	40		-.5	-.5					
32	Payroll	50		.1	.2					
33	CODs	60		-1.9	-1.8					
34	Special Pmts	70		-.3	-.3					
35	Tot Cash Flow	100		-3.9	-5.8					
36										
37	**Average Forecast Variance as a Percentage of Total Variance**							(+% = Favorable Variance)		
38	A/R Collections	10		-88%	-96%					
39	Other Rcpts	20		9%	5%					
40	A/P Payments	30		10%	12%					
41	Sched Pmts	40		0%	-3%					
42	Payroll	50		27%	12%					
43	CODs	60		-56%	-27%					
44	Special Pmts	70		-4%	-3%					
45	Tot Cash Flow	100		-100%	-100%					
46										
47										

(continued)

Figure 9-4. *continued*

KEY FORMULAS	
Cell	***Formula***
I3	**=TEXT(BegDate,"m/d/yy")&" thru "&TEXT(MaxDate,"m/d/yy")** This formula displays the reporting dates as shown in the spreadsheet.
I7	**="($"&TEXT(Round,"#")&"s, + = Collections)"** When you change the value in the Round range name, this label changes as well.
C8	**=AVERAGE(IF(Codes=$B8,Actual))/Round** This array formula returns the average of all data in the Actual range name containing category codes that match the one in cell B8. Copy this formula down the column as needed.
D8	**=AVERAGE(IF(Codes=$B8,IF(Skip>=E$5,Predicted,0)))/Round** This array formula returns the average of the predicted cash flows that compare to the actual cash flows. Copy this formula down and to the right as needed.
I17	**="($"&TEXT(Round,"#")&"s)"**
C18	**=STDEV(IF(Codes=$B18,Actual))/Round** To assess the variability of the actual cash flows over time, this formula returns their standard deviation. This array formula returns an error when applied to only one week of data.
D18	**=STDEV(IF(Codes=$B18,IF(Skip>=D$5,Predicted,0)))/Round** This array formula returns the standard deviation of the predicted cash flows over time. It returns an error value when applied to one week's data. Copy it down and to the right.
I27	**="($"&TEXT(Round,"#")&"s,+=Favorable Variance)"**
D28	**=AVERAGE(IF(Codes=$B28,IF(Skip>=D$5,Actual–Predicted,0)))/Round** This array formula returns the average variance. Copy it down and to the right.
I37	**(+%=Favorable Variance)**

(continued)

Figure 9-4. *continued*

KEY FORMULAS–continued	
Cell	***Formula***
D38	**=AVERAGE(IF(Codes=$B38,IF(Skip>=D$5,(Actual–Predicted)/ ABS(VLOOKUP(ActDate,Input,3)–VLOOKUP(PredDate,Input,3+D$5)),0)))** For each week in the forecast, this array formula calculates the percentage that each category's variance has contributed to the total variance in the cash flows for the week, stores these percentages in a temporary array, and then returns the average of all these percentages. In other words, these formulas show you which categories create the greatest problems in the accuracy of your cash flow forecast. By checking Codes, the formula loads the array with data for only the category code specified in column B. By checking Skip, it suppresses the reporting of columns that contain too little data to analyze—as in columns F through I. After the data passes the Codes and Skip tests, the formula finds the variance between Actual and Predicted cash flows for the category and then divides this value by the variance in Total Cash Flows for the appropriate week. To find this variance, the formula depends on the fact that when the VLOOKUP function looks up duplicate values, it returns data for the last occurrence in the series. Here the first LOOKUP function looks up the date of the actual cash flow data and returns the amount of the total cash flow, which is the last category in any week. Similarly, it looks up the date for the prediction and returns the value of the total predicted cash flow. Finally, the formula divides the variance in total cash flows into the variance for the category and then returns the average for all such calculations. As with any array formula, enter it by pressing Ctrl-Shift and then Enter. Copy it down and to the right as needed.

RANGE NAMES	
Name	***Formula***
Round	**=1000** To round the values in the spreadsheet to, say, the nearest one hundred dollars, change this range definition to 100.
Categories	**=8** The schedule contains this number of categories of cash flow activity, from A/R Collections through Total Cash Flow.
BegDate	**=DATE(89,8,14)** This name specifies the date in the schedule on which the analysis begins. Because the schedule forecasts cash flow six weeks in advance, this date should be at least seven weeks after the first date in the schedule, when the data is available.

(continued)

Figure 9-4. *continued*

RANGE NAMES–continued	
Name	***Formula***
ActDate **Codes** **Actual**	**=INDEX(Input,2+Skip*Categories,1):INDEX(Input,ROWS(Input)–1,1)** **=INDEX(Input,2+Skip*Categories,2):INDEX(Input,ROWS(Input)–1,2)** **=INDEX(Input,2+Skip*Categories,3):INDEX(Input,ROWS(Input)–1,3)** These range definitions specify the data in columns A, B, and C of the history in Figure 9-3, which begins in the first row specified by BegDate and ends with the last row of data. The ranges refer to the date, category codes, and values associated with the actual cash flow data in the history in Figure 9-3.
Predicted	**=INDEX(Input,2+Categories*(Skip–R52C),COLUMN(RC)):** **INDEX(Input,ROWS(Input)–1–Categories*R52C,COLUMN(RC))** This name specifies the range of predictions in the history in Figure 9-3 that corresponds to the actual cash flows in that history. In column D, for example, this range begins and ends one week, or eight rows, before the Actual range; in column E, it begins and ends two weeks before the Actual range; and so on. To enter this definition, first choose Options Workspace and select R1C1 to display the spreadsheet in R1C1 format, enter the range definition with no spaces, and then return your spreadsheet to the A1 display format.
PredDate	**=INDEX(Input,2+Categories*(Skip–O$52),1):** **INDEX(Input,ROWS(Input)–1–Categories*O$52,1)** This range definition returns dates that correspond to the Predicted range name.
FcstCodes **Date** **FcstInput**	**=WK_FCST.XLS!Codes** **=WK_FCST.XLS!Date** **=WK_FCST.XLS!Input** These range names refer to ranges in the forecast in Figure 9-2.
OldCode	**=$B$8:$B$15** The Update macro uses this range as a source of category codes for the new week.
NewDate **NewCode** **NewData**	**=INDEX(Input,ROWS(Input)–Categories,1):INDEX(Input,ROWS(Input)–1,1)** **=INDEX(Input,ROWS(Input)–Categories,2):INDEX(Input,ROWS(Input)–1,2)** **=INDEX(Input,ROWS(Input)–Categories,3):** **INDEX(Input,ROWS(Input)–1,COLUMNS(Input))** These dynamic ranges define sections at the bottom of the history in Figure 9-3 where the macro in Figure 9-5 updates the cash flow history.
The Update macro in Figure 9-5 depends on the last seven range names to update the cash flow history.	

(continued)

Figure 9-4. *continued*

KEY CELL FORMATS			
Cell	*Number*	*Alignment*	*Font*
A3	General	General	Helv 10, Bold
I3	General	Right	Helv 10, Bold
A4:I5	General	Center	Helv 10, Bold
B4:B5	General	Center	Helv 8, Bold
A7	General	General	Helv 10, Bold
I7	General	Right	Helv 10
C8:I15	#,###.0;–#,###.0;	General	Helv 10
A17	General	General	Helv 10, Bold
C18:I25	#,###.0;–#,###.0;	General	Helv 10
A27	General	General	Helv 10, Bold
C28:I35	#,###.0;–#,###.0;	General	Helv 10
C38:I45	0%;–0%;	General	Helv 10

Figure 9-5. Macro to Update the Cash Flow History

A macro that updates the cash flow history each week by using the new version of the cash flow forecast, shown in Figure 9-2. Saved as WK_UPDT.XLM.

	A	B	C
1			
2			
3	Update	Macro to update cash flow history sheet.	Explanation
4	key=u	=FORMULA.GOTO("Bottom")	Go to bottom of the cash flow
5		=SELECT("R:R["&!categories-1&"]")	history and insert the number of
6		=INSERT(2)	rows that will contain one report.
7		=SELECT("Signs")	Copy the signs of the categories
8		=COPY()	into the NewDate range, trans-
9		=SELECT("NewDate")	posing the data. (Dates replace
10		=PASTE.SPECIAL(3,1,FALSE,TRUE)	the signs later in this macro.)
11		=SELECT("OldCode")	Copy the category code numbers
12		=COPY()	from the previous week into the
13		=SELECT("NewCode")	current week.
14		=PASTE()	
15		=SELECT("NewData")	Fill the formula in the NewData
16		="=INDEX(FcstInput,MATCH(RC2,FcstCodes,0),Weeks+2)*RC1"	range (a process that calculates
17		=FORMULA.FILL(B16)	each value as it's entered) and then
18		=COPY()	turn formulas into values with the
19		=PASTE.SPECIAL(3,1,FALSE,FALSE)	PASTE.SPECIAL macro function.
20		=SELECT("NewDate")	Fill the formula in the NewDate
21		=FORMULA.FILL("=Date")	range and then turn the formula
22		=COPY()	into its value with the
23		=PASTE.SPECIAL(3,1,FALSE,FALSE)	PASTE.SPECIAL macro function.
24		=CANCEL.COPY()	Cancel the Copy macro function.
25		=RETURN()	Return.
26			
27			

Figure 9-6. Sales and Collections Forecast

The top section of a spreadsheet that forecasts the income statement, the balance sheet, and cash flows for the next 12 months. Saved as FORECAST.XLS.

	A B C	D E	F	G	H	I	J	K	L	MNOP	Q	R	S	T	U	V W
1																
2																
3	**Projected Financial Performance, 1990**							**Thursday, Feb 11, 03:00 PM**								
4																
5	**Sales & Collections**				Jan	Feb	Mar	Apr	May		Oct	Nov	Dec	Jan	Feb	Mar
6																
7	Detailed Sales Forecast				200	200	200	200	200		200	200	200			
8	Adjustment to Sales Forecast				0%	0%	0%	0%	0%		0%	0%	0%			
9	Total Sales Forecasted				200	200	200	200	200		200	200	200			
10																
11		Existing A/R Aging		Std	Expected Collections											
12	**Collections**	Aging Category	Amt	Col%	30	60	90	120								
13	**Schedule:**	0-30	1,086	49%	532											
14	**Existing**	30-60	950	61%	580	338										
15	**Accounts**	60-90	520	92%	478	341	199									
16	**Receivable**	90-120	26	98%	25	41	29	17								
17		Write Off	5	100%	5	1	1	1								
18		Total A/R	2,587		1,621	720	229	18								
19																
20		Cash			2%	2%	2%	2%	2%		2%	2%	2%			
21	**Collections**	30 Days			44%	44%	44%	44%	44%		44%	44%	44%			
22	**Schedule:**	60 Days			33%	33%	33%	33%	33%		33%	33%	33%			
23	**New Sales**	90 Days			21%	21%	21%	21%	21%		21%	21%	21%			
24		120 Days--Write Off			.10%	.10%	.10%	.10%	.10%		.10%	.10%	.10%			
25		Total Collections			100%	100%	100%	100%	100%		100%	100%	100%			
26																
27	Collections of Current Receivables				1,616	719	228	17								
28	Collections of New Sales				4	92	158	200	200		200	200	200			
29	Total Collections				1,620	811	386	217	200		200	200	200			
30																
31	Bad Debts				5	1	1	1	0		0	0	0			
32																
33																

COLUMN WIDTHS

Column	Width	Column	Width	Column	Width	Column	Width
A	1.43	H	4	O	0.5	V	4
B	4.14	I	4	P	0.5	W	0.92
C	4.14	J	4	Q	4	X	5
D	5	K	4	R	4	Y	5
E	5	L	4	S	4	Z	5
F	4	M	0.5	T	4	AA	2
G	4	N	0.5	U	4	AB	3

(continued)

Figure 9-6. *continued*

KEY FORMULAS	
Cell	***Formula***
S3	**=TEXT(NOW(),"dddd")&","&TEXT(NOW(),"mmm dd")&","&TEXT(NOW(),"hh:mm AM/PM")** Formatting the NOW function in these three ways provides full information about when the projection was printed.
H5 **I5**	**01/01/90** **=DATE(YEAR(H5),MONTH(H5)+1,1)** Copy the formula to the right as needed.
H7	**200** Copy this data from your detailed sales-analysis spreadsheet.
H8	**0** Often, you'll want to increase or decrease your forecasted sales by some percentage without going through the work of changing your detailed forecast. Use the numbers in this row to make this adjustment. For example, to increase sales by 10 percent, enter 0.1; to decrease sales by 10 percent, enter −0.1.
H9	**=H7*(1+H8)** The total sales forecast is the product of the detailed forecast and 1 plus the adjustment.
H13 **I14** **J15** **K16** **K17**	**=F13*G13** **=(F13–H13)*G14** **=(F13–H13–I14)*G15** **=(F13–H13–I14–J15)*G16** **=F18–SUM(H18:J18,K16)** Chapter 4 discusses two methods of forecasting the collection of A/R, depending on the information available. If the A/R aging is available, as it is here, you can use past collection history to estimate the percentage of each aged amount that you will collect during the month. In the spreadsheet, for example, the company collects 49 percent of its A/R between 0 and 30 days old during the month; 61 percent of its 30–60 day A/R balance; and so on. The formula in column H forecasts collections for each category in the first month of the forecast. Copy the formula shown for the column downward as needed. The formula shown for column I estimates how much of the amounts not paid in the first month will be paid in the second. Enter it and copy it downward. The formula in column J estimates collections in the third month. Copy it as well. The first formula for column K estimates collections for the fourth month after the forecast. The second formula for column K writes off all of the beginning A/R not collected after four months.

(continued)

Figure 9-6. *continued*

KEY FORMULAS–continued	
Cell	***Formula***
F18	**=SUM(F13:F17)** This total must match the beginning A/R balance used in column G of the spreadsheet in Figure 9-13.
H18	**=SUM(H13:H17)** Copy this formula to the right as needed.
H23	**=1–H20–H21–H22–H24** On average, you probably will write off some small percentage of sales as uncollectable. Row 24 shows this estimated percentage. To simplify entering the schedule, this formula calculates the collections for the 90-day period to equal 1 minus the previous collection percentages, minus the estimated write-off percentage.
H25	**=SUM(H20:H24)** Copy this formula to the right as needed.
H27	**=SUM(H13:H16)** Total collections for the beginning A/R balance equal the sum of the estimates shown. Copy this formula to the right.
H28 **I28** **J28** **K28**	**=H20*H9** **=I20*I9+H21*H9** **=J20*J9+I21*I9+H22*H9** **=K20*K9+J21*J9+I22*I9+H23*H9** In the first month of the forecast, the only amount of forecasted sales that will be collected will be from cash sales. In the second month, collections from forecasted sales will arise from two months' sales. In the third month, collections will come from three months of sales, and so on. Copy the last formula to the right as needed.
H29	**=SUM(H27:H28)** Total collections equal the sum of the two rows. Copy this formula to the right.
H31 **L31**	**=H17** **=H24*H9** Here bad debts are defined as those sales that remain uncollected after four months. In the first four months of the forecast, these debts arise from receivables existing at the beginning of the forecast. After that, they arise from new sales. Copy the formula shown for cell H31 to the range I31:K31; copy the formula shown for cell L31 to the right as needed.

(continued)

Figure 9-6. *continued*

RANGE NAMES		
Name	***Formula***	
Sales_Collections	=$A$5	Figure 9-6
Material_Costs	=$A$37	Figure 9-7
Labor_Overhead_Exp	=$A$77	Figure 9-8
Capital_Budget	=$A$103	Figure 9-9
Financing	=$A$125	Figure 9-10
Income_Taxes	=$A$146	Figure 9-11
Income_Statement	=$A$159	Figure 9-12
Balance_Sheet	=$A$185	Figure 9-13
Cash_Flow_Summary	=$A$226	Figure 9-14
Reconciliation	=$A$266	Figure 9-15

These range names help you navigate. For example, to go to the cash flow summary, press the F5 (Goto) key and then select Cash_Flow_Summary from the names in the dialog box.

KEY CELL FORMATS			
Cell	***Number***	***Alignment***	***Font***
A3	General	Left	Helv 10, Bold
S3	General	Right	Helv 10, Bold
A5	General	Right	Helv 10, Bold
T5:V5	mmm	Center	Helv 8
A7:A9	General	General	Helv 10
H5:S5	mmm	Center	Helv 8, Bold
H7:S7	#,##0 ;(#,##0)	General	Helv 8
H8:S8	0%	General	Helv 8
D11	General	General	Helv 8
A12:A23	General	General	Helv 10, Bold
F13:F18	#,###	General	Helv 8
G13:G18	0%	General	Helv 8
H13:K18	#,##0	General	Helv 8
H20:S23	0%	General	Helv 8
H24:S24	.00%	General	Helv 8
H27:S31	#,##0	General	Helv 8

Figure 9-7. Material Costs and Purchases Forecast

A portion of the forecast spreadsheet that forecasts material costs and purchases for the coming year. Saved as FORECAST.XLS. For column widths and range names, see Figure 9-6.

	A–C	D–E	F	G	H	I	J	K	L	Q	R	S	T	U	V
34															
35															
36															
37	**Material Costs & Purchases**				Jan	Feb	Mar	Apr	May	Oct	Nov	Dec	Jan	Feb	Mar
38															
39	**Material Cost of Goods Sold**														
40	Per Bill of Materials				62	62	62	62	62	62	62	62			
41	Sales Adjustment				0%	0%	0%	0%	0%	0%	0%	0%			
42	Material Cost of Sales				62	62	62	62	62	62	62	62	62	62	62
43	Material Waste & Scrap				8%	8%	8%	8%	8%	8%	8%	8%	8%	8%	8%
44															
45	Net Material Cost of Sales				67	67	67	67	67	67	67	67	67	67	67
46															
47	**Inventory**	Current			25%	25%	25%	25%	25%	25%	25%	25%	25%	25%	25%
48	**Purchasing**	30 Days in Advance			50%	50%	50%	50%	50%	50%	50%	50%	50%	50%	50%
49	**Schedule**	60 Days in Advance			15%	15%	15%	15%	15%	15%	15%	15%	15%	15%	15%
50		90 Days in Advance			10%	10%	10%	10%	10%	10%	10%	10%	10%	10%	10%
51		Total COS Purchased			100%	100%	100%	100%	100%	100%	100%	100%	100%	100%	100%
52															
53	**Total Inventory Purchases**				67	67	67	67	67	67	67	67			
54															
55		Existing A/P Aging		Std	Expected Payments										
56	**Payment**	Aging Category	Amt	Pmt%	30	60	90	120							
57	**Schedule:**	0-30	759	63%	478										
58	**Existing**	30-60	459	52%	238	146									
59	**Accounts**	60-90	172	88%	151	194	119								
60	**Payable**	90-120	43	100%	43	21	26	16							
61		Total	1,433		911	360	145	16							
62															
63		Cash			17%	17%	17%	17%	17%	17%	17%	17%			
64	**Payment**	30 Days			58%	58%	58%	58%	58%	58%	58%	58%			
65	**Schedule**	60 Days			17%	17%	17%	17%	17%	17%	17%	17%			
66	**New A/P**	90 Days			8%	8%	8%	8%	8%	8%	8%	8%			
67		Total Payments			100%	100%	100%	100%	100%	100%	100%	100%			
68															
69	Payment of Current Payables				911	360	145	16							
70	Payment of New Purchases				11	50	62	67	67	67	67	67			
71	Total Payment of Accounts Payable				923	411	207	83	67	67	67	67			
72															
73															

(continued)

Figure 9-7. *continued*

KEY FORMULAS	
Cell	***Formula***
H37	**=H$5** Copy this formula to the right as needed.
H40	**62** Copy this value from your spreadsheet that details material cost of goods sold.
H41	**=H$8** This row of formulas adjusts cost of sales by the same percentage as the sales adjustment.
H42	**=H40*(1+H41)** Material cost is the product of the detail costs and 1 plus the adjustment percentage. Copy this formula through column S.
T42	**=S42** Because most companies purchase some raw materials several months in advance of shipment, you must forecast cost of sales for several months after the "end" of your forecast. This formula predicts that January's cost of sales a year hence will equal December's cost of sales, which is probably as good an estimate as any. Copy this formula to cells U42 and V42.
H43	**0.08** Most detailed estimates of material costs do not include an estimate for the scrap and waste that most companies experience. This row contains your estimate for the additional material you must buy to replace that scrap.
H45	**=H42*(1+H$43)** Net material cost of sales equals the detailed cost times 1 plus the scrap estimate.
H51	**=SUM(H47:H50)**
H53	**=H47*H45+I48*I45+J49*J45+K50*K45** This month's inventory purchases equals this month's cost of sales (COS) times the percentage of these costs you buy during the month of sale, plus next month's COS times next month's percentage, and so on. Copy this formula to the right as needed.

(continued)

Figure 9-7. *continued*

KEY FORMULAS–continued	
Cell	***Formula***
H57 **I58** **J59** **K60**	**=F57*G57** **=(F57–H57)*G58** **=(F57–H57–I58)*G59** **=(F57–H57–I58–J59)** This method of estimating when you will pay existing A/P is similar to the method of estimating when you will collect existing A/R. Enter each formula shown and copy it down its column as needed.
F61	**=G203** This formula refers to the beginning Accounts Payable balance in the Balance Sheet, Figure 9-13. If you prefer, enter the actual balance instead.
H61	**=SUM(H57:H60)**
H67	**=SUM(H63:H66)**
H69	**=H$61** Copy this formula to the right as needed.
H70 **I70** **J70** **K70**	**=H63*H53** **=I63*I53+H64*H53** **=J63*J53+I64*I53+H65*H53** **=K63*K53+J64*J53+I65*I53+H66*H53** In the first month of the forecast, payment for new purchases equals the percentage you pay in less than 30 days times this month's purchases. In the second month, payment equals current purchases times the 0–30 day factor, plus the 30–60 day factor times last month's purchases. In the third and fourth month, payments follow a similar, but growing, pattern. Copy the final formula across the row as needed.
H71	**=SUM(H69:H70)**

Figure 9-8. Labor and Overhead Expense Forecast

A portion of the forecast spreadsheet in which you enter your forecasts of labor and overhead expenses. Saved as FORECAST.XLS. For column widths and range names, see Figure 9-6.

	A–G		H	I	J	K	L	M–P	Q	R	S
74											
75											
76											
77	**Labor & Overhead Expenses**		Jan	Feb	Mar	Apr	May		Oct	Nov	Dec
78											
79	Direct Labor		10	10	10	10	10		10	10	10
80	Planned Overtime		1	1	1	1	1		1	1	1
81	Sales Adjustment		0%	0%	0%	0%	0%		0%	0%	0%
82	Total Direct Labor & Overtime		11	11	11	11	11		11	11	11
83	Manufacturing Overhead		20	20	20	20	20		20	20	20
84	Research & Development		30	30	30	30	30		30	30	30
85	General & Administrative		40	40	40	40	40		40	40	40
86	Marketing & Sales--Fixed		50	50	50	50	50		50	50	50
87	Sales Commission	7%	14	14	14	14	14		14	14	14
88	Advertising Co-op	3%	6	6	6	6	6		6	6	6
89											
90	Total Expenses		171	171	171	171	171		171	171	171
91											
92	**Payment**	Cash	70%	70%	70%	70%	70%		70%	70%	70%
93	**Schedule**	30 Days	28%	28%	28%	28%	28%		28%	28%	28%
94		60 Days	2%	2%	2%	2%	2%		2%	2%	2%
95			100%	100%	100%	100%	100%		100%	100%	100%
96											
97	Total Payment of Expenses		120	168	171	171	171		171	171	171
98											
99											

(continued)

Figure 9-8. *continued*

KEY FORMULAS	
Cell	***Formula***
H77	**=H$5** Copy this row of formulas from row H37.
H79 **H80**	**10** **1** Copy these labor expenses from your detailed spreadsheets.
H81	**=H$8** Copy this formula for the sales-adjustment percentage from row 41.
H82	**=(H79+H80)*(1+H81)** This formula adjusts labor and overtime by the sales-adjustment percentage.
H83:S86	**20** Copy these overhead expenses from your detailed spreadsheets.
E87 **E88**	**0.07** **0.03** Enter actual commission rates in these cells.
H87	**=$E87*H$9** Sales commissions equal the commission percentage times the sales amount.
H88	**=$E88*H$9** The amount of advertising co-op equals the percentage times sales.
H90 **H95**	**=SUM(H82:H89)** **=SUM(H92:H94)** Copy these formulas to the right as needed.
H97 **I97** **J97**	**=H92*H90** **=I92*I90+H93*H90** **=J92*J90+I93*I90+H94*H90** These formulas resemble those for calculating the payment of new accounts payable. Copy the formula in column J to the right as needed.

Figure 9-9. Capital Budget Forecast

A portion of the forecast spreadsheet in which you enter your capital budget forecast. Saved as FORECAST.XLS. For column widths and range names, see Figure 9-6.

	A–C	D–G	H	I	J	K	L	MNOP	Q	R	S	T	U	V
100														
101														
102														
103	**Capital Budget**		Jan	Feb	Mar	Apr	May		Oct	Nov	Dec	Jan	Feb	Mar
104														
105														
106	Purchase of Fixed Assets		100	100	100	100	100		100	100	100	100	100	
107														
108		60 Days in Advance	10%	10%	10%	10%	10%		10%	10%	10%			
109	**Payments**	30 Days in Advance	23%	23%	23%	23%	23%		23%	23%	23%			
110	**Schedule**	On Receipt	33%	33%	33%	33%	33%		33%	33%	33%			
111		30 Days After Receipt	24%	24%	24%	24%	24%		24%	24%	24%			
112		60 Days After Receipt	10%	10%	10%	10%	10%		10%	10%	10%			
113			100%	100%	100%	100%	100%		100%	100%	100%			
114														
115	Payments for Fixed Assets		66	90	100	100	100		100	100	100			
116														
117	Depreciation--Book		33	33	33	33	33		33	33	33			
118														
119	Depreciation--Tax		45	45	45	45	45		45	45	45			
120														
121														

KEY FORMULAS

Cell	*Formula*
H103	=H$5
H113	=SUM(H108:H112)
H115	=H110*H106+H109*I106+H108*J106
I115	=I110*I106+I109*J106+I108*K106+H111*H106
J115	=J110*J106+J109*K106+J108*L106+I111*I106+H112*H106
	Often, companies pay for fixed assets in a series of partial payments: at the time of order, on delivery, and after an acceptance period. These formulas provide this flexibility. Copy the formula in column J to the right as needed.
H117	33
H119	45
	Enter the values in these rows from the spreadsheets in Figure 8-22, Figure 8-25, and Figure 8-26, or from similar analysis.

Figure 9-10. Forecast of Financing Needs

A portion of the forecast spreadsheet in which you enter your current debt and which forecasts your interest expense. Saved as FORECAST.XLS. For column widths and range names, see Figure 9-6.

	A–E	F	G	H	I	J	K	L	M–P	Q	R	S	T	U	V	W
122																
123																
124																
125	**Financing**			Jan	Feb	Mar	Apr	May		Oct	Nov	Dec				
126																
127																
128	**Short-Term Loan**															
129	Interest Rate			14%	14%	14%	14%	14%		14%	14%	14%				
130	Borrow If Cash Is Below	50														
131	Repay If Cash Exceeds	125														
132																
133	**Long-Term Loan**															
134	Interest Payment	10%		18	17	17	17	17		17	16	16				
135	Principal Payment	2,101		12	12	12	13	13		13	13	13				
136	Total Loan Payment	30		30	30	30	30	30		30	30	30				
137																
138	**Equity Transactions**															
139	Stock Sales (Purchase)			100		300										
140	Dividend Payments			20	20	20	20	20		20	20	20				
141																
142																

(continued)

Figure 9-10. *continued*

KEY FORMULAS	
Cell	***Formula***
F135	**=G210** This formula references the beginning Loans Payable amount in the balance sheet, shown in Figure 9-13. If you prefer, simply enter the outstanding loan balance in this cell.
H125	**=H$5**
H134 **I134**	**=($F$134/12)*$F$135** **=$F$136–I135** For the first payment, interest is equal to the monthly rate of interest times the amount of the principal. From that point on, interest equals the payment minus the principal amount.
H135 **I135**	**=$F$136–H134** **=H135*(1+$F$134/12)** In the first period, the principal portion of the loan payment equals the total loan payment minus interest for the first month. In the following months, the calculation for the principal amount depends on a little-known fact: Each month, the principal payment grows by the monthly interest rate. To confirm these calculations, test the principal payment for the final period in the schedule using: =PPMT(rate,per,nper,pv), where rate = .10/12, per = 12, nper = 107, and pv = 2101. Copy the formula in column I to the right as needed.
H136	**=SUM(H134:H135)**

Figure 9-11. Income Tax Forecast

A portion of the forecast spreadsheet in which you enter simple income tax information. Saved as FORECAST.XLS. For column widths and range names, see Figure 9-6.

	A–G		H	I	J	K	L	Q	R	S
143										
144										
145										
146	**Income Taxes**		Jan	Feb	Mar	Apr	May	Oct	Nov	Dec
147										
148	Income Before Taxes, Per Books		(98)	(89)	(89)	(89)	(88)	(94)	(95)	(97)
149	Plus: Book Depreciation		33	33	33	33	33	33	33	33
150	Less: Tax Depreciation		(45)	(45)	(45)	(45)	(45)	(45)	(45)	(45)
151	Taxable Income		(110)	(101)	(101)	(101)	(100)	(106)	(107)	(109)
152										
153	Quarterly Income Tax Pmts at:	35%				(24)		(107)		
154										
155										

KEY FORMULAS	
Cell	***Formula***
H146	**=H$5**
H148	**=H$176** This formula looks forward in the schedule, picking up the amount of pretax income. Enter the formula as shown, but later, after you complete the income statement, remember to return to this row and be certain that this formula references the correct data.
H149 **H150**	**=H117** **=–H119** These formulas reference depreciation in the Capital Budget section, shown in Figure 9-9.
H151	**=SUM(H148:H150)**
K153 **N153** **Q153**	**=J205** **=M205** **=P205** These formulas reference Income Taxes Payable in the Income Statement. Enter them as shown, but after you create the spreadsheet that contains the Income Statement, be certain that these formulas still reference the correct data.

Figure 9-12. Pro Forma Income Statement

A portion of the forecast spreadsheet that combines information from preceding figures to generate a pro forma income statement. Saved as FORECAST.XLS. For column widths and range names, see Figure 9-6.

	A–G	H	I	J	K	L	Q	R	S
156									
157									
158									
159	**Income Statement**	Jan	Feb	Mar	Apr	May	Oct	Nov	Dec
160									
161	Sales	200	200	200	200	200	200	200	200
162	Cost of Sales	98	98	98	98	98	98	98	98
163	Gross Profit	102	102	102	102	102	102	102	102
164									
165	Operating Expenses								
166	Research & Development	30	30	30	30	30	30	30	30
167	General & Administrative	40	40	40	40	40	40	40	40
168	Bad Debts	5	1	1	1	0	0	0	0
169	Depreciation	33	33	33	33	33	33	33	33
170	Marketing & Sales	70	70	70	70	70	70	70	70
171	Total Operating Expenses	178	174	174	174	173	173	173	173
172									
173	Operating Profit	(76)	(71)	(72)	(72)	(71)	(71)	(71)	(71)
174									
175	Interest Expenses	22	17	17	17	17	23	24	26
176	Profits Before Taxes	(98)	(89)	(89)	(89)	(88)	(94)	(95)	(97)
177									
178	Provision for Income Taxes	(39)	(35)	(35)	(35)	(35)	(37)	(37)	(38)
179	Net Profit After Taxes	(60)	(54)	(54)	(54)	(53)	(57)	(57)	(59)
180									
181									

KEY FORMULAS

Cell	*Formula*
H159	**=H$5**
H161	**=H$9** This formula references the sales figures from the portion of the spreadsheet in Figure 9-6.
H162	**=H$82+H$83+H$45** The cost of sales equals direct labor plus manufacturing overhead plus the material cost of goods sold.
H163	**=H$161–H$162** Gross profits equal sales minus cost of goods sold.

(continued)

Figure 9-12. *continued*

KEY FORMULAS–continued	
Cell	***Formula***
H166	**=H$84** R&D expenses come from the value in the portion of the spreadsheet in Figure 9-8.
H167	**=H$85** G&A expenses also come from the value in the portion of the spreadsheet in Figure 9-8.
H168	**=H$31** Bad-debt expenses come from the value in the portion of the spreadsheet in Figure 9-6.
H169	**=H$117** Book-depreciation expenses come from the value in the portion of the spreadsheet in Figure 9-9.
H170	**=SUM(H$86:H$88)** Marketing expenses come from the values in the portion of the spreadsheet in Figure 9-8.
H171 **H173**	**=SUM(H$166:H$170)** **=H$163–H$171**
H175	**=(H$129/12)*G$204+H$134** Interest expense is equal to the short-term interest rate, shown in the portion of the spreadsheet in Figure 9-10, divided by 12, times the amount of short-term loans, shown in the portion in Figure 9-13, plus the amount of long-term interest, shown in the portion in Figure 9-10.
H176	**=H$173–H$175**
H178	**=$G$153*H$151** Income tax expense is equal to the tax rate times taxable income shown in the portion of the spreadsheet in Figure 9-11.
H179	**=H$176–H$178**

Figure 9-13. Pro Forma Balance Sheet

A portion of the forecast spreadsheet that generates a balance sheet based on the preceding figures. Saved as FORECAST.XLS. For column widths and range names, see Figure 9-6.

	A–F	G	H	I	J	K	L	M–P	Q	R	S
182											
183											
184											
185	**Balance Sheet**	Dec	Jan	Feb	Mar	Apr	May		Oct	Nov	Dec
186											
187	**Assets**										
188	Cash	118	275	368	527	364	176		50	50	50
189	Accounts Receivable	2,587	1,162	550	364	346	346		346	346	346
190	Inventory	2,214	2,214	2,214	2,214	2,214	2,214		2,214	2,214	2,214
191	Other Current Assets	209	209	209	209	209	209		209	209	209
192	Total Current Assets	5,128	3,860	3,342	3,313	3,133	2,945		2,819	2,819	2,819
193											
194	Fixed Assets	1,432	1,532	1,632	1,732	1,832	1,932		2,432	2,532	2,632
195	Accumulated Depreciation	573	606	639	672	705	738		903	936	969
196	Net Fixed Assets	859	926	993	1,060	1,127	1,194		1,529	1,596	1,663
197											
198	Other Non-Current Assets	129	129	129	129	129	129		129	129	129
199											
200	Total Assets	6,116	4,915	4,464	4,502	4,389	4,268		4,477	4,544	4,611
201											
202	**Liabilities & Equity**										
203	Accounts Payable	1,433	629	288	149	132	132		132	132	132
204	Notes Payable	400	0	0	0	0	0		614	809	1,006
205	Income Taxes Payable	85	46	11	(24)	(35)	(70)		(37)	(74)	(113)
206	Fixed Assets Payable	22	56	66	66	66	66		66	66	66
207	Other Current Liabilities	19	19	19	19	19	19		19	19	19
208	Total Current Liabilities	1,959	750	384	209	182	147		794	952	1,111
209											
210	Loans Payable	2,101	2,089	2,076	2,064	2,051	2,039		1,974	1,961	1,947
211	Total Liabilities	4,060	2,839	2,461	2,273	2,233	2,186		2,768	2,912	3,058
212											
213	Common Stock	932	1,032	1,032	1,332	1,332	1,332		1,332	1,332	1,332
214	Retained Earnings	1,124	1,044	971	897	823	750		377	300	221
215	Net Worth	2,056	2,076	2,003	2,229	2,155	2,082		1,709	1,632	1,553
216											
217	Total Liabilities & Equity	6,116	4,915	4,464	4,502	4,389	4,268		4,477	4,544	4,611
218											
219											
220	Error (Assets Less Liab & Equity)	0	0	0	0	0	0		0	0	0
221											
222											

(continued)

Figure 9-13. *continued*

KEY FORMULAS	
Cell	***Formula***
G185	**=DATE(YEAR(H185),MONTH(H185)–1,1)** The balance-sheet forecast requires a beginning balance sheet, which is the ending balance sheet one month before the beginning of the forecast. This formula calculates the date of the beginning values.
H185	**=H$5**
G189	**=$F$18** With the exception of this cell, column G contains values entered from the December balance sheet. This cell contains the sum of the A/R aging schedule, which is shown in Figure 9-6.
G192 G196 G200 G208 G211 G215 G217	**=SUM(G188:G191)** **=G194–G195** **=SUM(G196:G198,G192)** **=SUM(G203:G207)** **=SUM(G208:G210)** **=SUM(G213:G214)** **=G215+G211** When you enter financial statement data, it's usually a good idea to use formulas to calculate all subtotals and totals. First, doing so helps you find data-entry errors. (If the bottom line of your source data doesn't match the bottom line of your spreadsheet, there's obviously something wrong.) Also, when you create a new forecast by updating an old one, having the formulas in place reduces the amount of new data that you must enter.
G220	**=ROUND(G200–G217,4)** This formula finds the difference between the total assets and the quantity of the total liabilities plus equity. If the balance sheet is in balance, this difference should equal 0, of course. (Rounding the difference eliminates insignificant errors generated by the computer.)

(continued)

Figure 9-13. *continued*

KEY FORMULAS–continued			
Cell	***Formula***		
H188	**=G188+H29–H71–H97–H115–H153–H136–(H129/12)*G204+H254–H140+H139**		
	As in real life, Cash is the result of everything else that goes on in this forecast. Here's what each cell in this formula refers to:		
	G188	Figure 9-13	Last Month's Cash Balance
	H29	Figure 9-6	Total Collections
	H71	Figure 9-7	Total Payment of Accounts Payable
	H97	Figure 9-8	Total Payment of Expenses
	H115	Figure 9-9	Payments for Fixed Assets
	H153	Figure 9-11	Quarterly Income Tax Payments
	H136	Figure 9-10	Total Loan Payment
	H129	Figure 9-10	Interest Rate
	G204	Figure 9-13	Last Month's Notes Payable
	H254	Figure 9-14	Amounts That Borrow Against (Repay) the Line of Credit
	H140	Figure 9-10	Dividend Payments
	H139	Figure 9-10	Stock Sales (Purchase)
H189	**=G189–H29+H9–H31**		
	Accounts Receivable Variables:		
	G189	Figure 9-13	Last Month's Accounts Receivable
	H29	Figure 9-6	Total Collections
	H9	Figure 9-6	Total Sales Forecasted
	H31	Figure 9-6	Bad Debts
H190	**=G190+H53–H45**		
	Inventory Variables:		
	G190	Figure 9-13	Last Month's Inventory
	H53	Figure 9-7	Total Inventory Purchases
	H45	Figure 9-7	Net Material Cost of Sales
H191	**=G191**		
	Other Current Assets Variables:		
	G191	Figure 9-13	Last Month's Other Current Assets
I191	**=(I9/H9)*H191**		
	Other Current Assets Variables:		
	I9	Figure 9-6	Total Sales Forecasted
	H9	Figure 9-6	Last Month's Total Sales Forecasted
	H191	Figure 9-13	Last Month's Other Current Assets

(continued)

Figure 9-13. *continued*

KEY FORMULAS–continued			
Cell	***Formula***		
H194	**=G194+H106**		
	Fixed Assets Variables:		
	G194	Figure 9-13	Last Month's Fixed Assets
	H106	Figure 9-9	Purchase of Fixed Assets
H195	**=G195+H169**		
	Accumulated Depreciation Variables:		
	G195	Figure 9-13	Last Month's Fixed Assets
	H169	Figure 9-12	Depreciation
H198	**=G198**		
	Other Non-Current Assets Variables:		
	G198	Figure 9-13	Other Non-Current Assets
H203	**=G203+H53–H71+H90–H97**		
	Accounts Payable Variables:		
	G203	Figure 9-13	Last Month's Accounts Payable
	H53	Figure 9-7	Total Inventory Purchases
	H71	Figure 9-7	Total Payment of Accounts Payable
	H90	Figure 9-8	Total Expenses
	H97	Figure 9-8	Total Payment of Expenses
H204	**=G204+H254**		
	Notes Payable Variables:		
	G204	Figure 9-13	Last Month's Notes Payable
	H254	Figure 9-14	Amounts That Borrow Against (Repay) the Line of Credit
H205	**=G205+H178–H153**		
	Income Taxes Payable Variables:		
	G205	Figure 9-13	Last Month's Income Taxes Payable
	H178	Figure 9-12	Provision for Income Taxes
	H153	Figure 9-11	Quarterly Income Tax Payments
H206	**=G206+H106–H115**		
	Fixed Assets Payable Variables:		
	G206	Figure 9-13	Last Month's Fixed Assets Payable
	H106	Figure 9-9	Purchase of Fixed Assets
	H115	Figure 9-9	Payments for Fixed Assets

(continued)

Figure 9-13. *continued*

KEY FORMULAS–continued			
Cell	***Formula***		
H207	**=H191–G191+G207**		
	Other Current Liabilities Variables:		
	H191	Figure 9-13	This Month's Other Current Assets
	G191	Figure 9-13	Last Month's Other Current Assets
	G207	Figure 9-13	Last Month's Other Current Liabilities Because Other Current Assets and Other Current Liabilities have little effect on most financial statements, the forecast forces these two items to grow by the same amounts monthly.
H210	**=G210–H135**		
	Loans Payable Variables:		
	G210	Figure 9-13	Last Month's Loans Payable
	H135	Figure 9-10	Principal Payment
H213	**=G213+H139**		
	Common Stock Variables:		
	G213	Figure 9-13	Last Month's Common Stock
	H139	Figure 9-10	Stock Sales (Purchase)
H214	**=G214+H179–H140**		
	Retained Earnings Variables:		
	G214	Figure 9-13	Last Month's Retained Earnings
	H179	Figure 9-12	Net Profit After Taxes
	H140	Figure 9-10	Dividend Payments

Figure 9-14. Cash Flow Forecast for Each of the Next 12 Months

A portion of the forecast spreadsheet that depends on changes in the pro forma balance sheet to calculate a cash flow forecast. Saved as FORECAST.XLS. For column widths and range names, see Figure 9-6.

	A B C D E F G	H	I	J	K	L	M N O P	Q	R	S	T	U	V	W
223														
224														
225														
226	**Cash Flow Forecast**	Jan	Feb	Mar	Apr	May		Oct	Nov	Dec				
227														
228														
229	**Operating Cash Flows**													
230	Collection of Receivables	1,620	811	386	217	200		200	200	200				
231														
232	Cash Disbursements													
233	Payment of Inventory Purchases	923	411	207	83	67		67	67	67				
234	Payment of Operating Expenses	120	168	171	171	171		171	171	171				
235	Short-Term Debt Service	5	0	0	0	0		6	7	9				
236	Income Tax Payments	0	0	0	(24)	0		(107)	0	0				
237	Total Operating Cash Disbursements	1,047	578	378	230	238		137	245	247				
238														
239	Total Cash Generated by Operations	573	233	8	(13)	(38)		63	(45)	(48)				
240														
241	**Investing Cash Flows**													
242	Sale of (Payment for) Capital Assets	(66)	(90)	(100)	(100)	(100)		(100)	(100)	(100)				
243														
244	Beginning Cash Balance	118	275	368	527	364		50	50	50				
245	Cash Balance Before Financing	625	418	276	413	225		13	(95)	(98)				
246														
247	**Financing Activities**													
248	Stock Sales (Purchases)	100	0	300	0	0		0	0	0				
249	Long-Term Debt Service	(30)	(30)	(30)	(30)	(30)		(30)	(30)	(30)				
250	Dividend Payments	(20)	(20)	(20)	(20)	(20)		(20)	(20)	(20)				
251	Total Financing Before Line of Credit	50	(50)	250	(50)	(50)		(50)	(50)	(50)				
252	Cash Balance Before Line of Credit	675	368	527	364	176		(37)	(145)	(147)				
253														
254	Borrow (Repay)--Line of Credit	(400)	0	0	0	0		87	195	197				
255	Ending Cash Balance	275	368	527	364	176		50	50	50				
256														
257	Cumulative Cash Before Financing	507	650	558	445	306		(184)	(329)	(477)				
258														
259														
260	Error: Ending Cash Bal Minus Cash	0	0	0	0	0		0	0	0				
261														
262														

(continued)

Figure 9-14. *continued*

KEY FORMULAS			
Cell	***Formula***		
H226	**=H$5**		
H230	**=H29**		
	Collection of Receivables:		
	H29	Figure 9-6	Total Collections
H233	**=H71**		
	Payment of Inventory Purchases:		
	H71	Figure 9-7	Total Payment of Accounts Payable
H234	**=H97**		
	Payment of Operating Expenses:		
	H97	Figure 9-8	Total Payment of Expenses
H235	**=(H129/12)*G204**		
	Short Term Debt Service Variables:		
	H129	Figure 9-10	Interest Rate
	G204	Figure 9-13	Last Month's Notes Payable
H236	**=H153**		
	Income Tax Payments:		
	H153	Figure 9-11	Quarterly Income Tax Payments
H237	**=SUM(F231:H236)**		
H239	**=H230–H237**		
H242	**=–H115**		
	Sale of (Payment for) Capital Assets:		
	H115	Figure 9-9	Payments for Fixed Assets
H244	**=G188**		
	Beginning Cash Balance:		
	G188	Figure 9-13	Last Month's Cash
H245	**=H239+H242+H244**		
	Variables for Cash Balance Before Financing:		
	H239	Figure 9-14	Total Cash Generated By Operations
	H242	Figure 9-14	Sale of (Payment for) Capital Assets
	H244	Figure 9-14	Beginning Cash Balance
H248	**=H139**		
	Stock Sales (Purchases):		
	H139	Figure 9-10	Stock Sales (Purchase)

(continued)

Figure 9-14. *continued*

KEY FORMULAS–continued	
Cell	***Formula***
H249	**=–H136** Long-Term Debt Service: H136 Figure 9-10 Total Loan Payment
H250	**=–H140** Dividend Payments: H140 Figure 9-10 Dividend Payments
H251	**=SUM(H248:H250)**
H252	**=H245+H251** Cash Balance Before Line of Credit: H245 Figure 9-14 Cash Balance Before Financing H251 Figure 9-14 Total Financing Before Line of Credit
H254	**=–MIN(G204,IF(H252>$F$131,MAX(H252–$F$131,0),MIN(H252–$F$130,0)))** Borrow (Repay)—Line of Credit: G204 Figure 9-13 Notes Payable H252 Figure 9-14 Cash Balance Before Line of Credit F131 Figure 9-10 Repay If Cash Exceeds F130 Figure 9-10 Borrow If Cash Is Below This formula calculates whether the company should borrow or repay against its line of credit, and how much. It does so by returning the minimum value of three calculations, and then by changing its sign. The first calculation merely returns the current amount of the unpaid loan. If this amount is the smallest value of the three, enough cash is on hand to pay off the loan. Changing its sign shows that this repayment will have a negative effect on cash. The second calculation, which is represented by the IF function, determines the amount of cash available to repay the loan. If the cash balance is greater than the repayment limit, this formula returns that excess; otherwise, it returns 0. If this value is the smallest amount of the three, the initial minus sign indicates that this loan repayment will have a negative effect on cash. The third calculation, which is represented by the final MIN function in the formula, determines whether the cash balance shows that you should borrow cash. It does so by subtracting the borrowing limit from the cash balance. If the cash balance is less than the borrowing limit, the result of this calculation will be negative and therefore less than 0. If so, this value will be the least of the three calculations. The initial minus sign will change this value to positive, indicating that the amount borrowed will have a positive effect on cash.

(continued)

Figure 9-14. *continued*

KEY FORMULAS–continued	
Cell	***Formula***
H255	=H252+H254
H257	=H239+H242
I257	=I239+I242+H257
H260	=H255–H188
	Enter these formulas as shown and copy them to the right as needed.

Figure 9-15. Reconciliation of Changes to the Projected Balance Sheet

A two-page reconciliation portion of the forecast spreadsheet that helps identify errors. Saved as FORECAST.XLS. For range names, see Figure 9-6.

	A B C D E F	G	H	I	J	K	L	M	N
263									
264									
265									
266	**Reconciliation Of Changes To The Projected Balance Sheet**								
267									
268		Cells Used:		L9	L45	L90	L53	L29	L71
269									L97
270	**Beginning Col To Reconcile:**	K	L						
271					Cost				
272					of	Optg	Inv	Collect	Pay
273		Begin	End	Sales	Sales	Exp	Purch	A/R	A/P
274	**Assets**								
275	Cash	364	176					200	(238)
276	Accounts Receivable	346	346	200				(200)	
277	Inventory	2,214	2,214		(67)		67		
278	Other Current Assets	209	209						
279	Total Current Assets	3,133	2,945						
280									
281	Fixed Assets	1,832	1,932						
282	Accumulated Dep	705	738						
283	Net Fixed Assets	1,127	1,194						
284									
285	Other Non-Cur Assets	129	129						
286									
287	Total Assets	4,389	4,268						
288									
289	**Liabilities & Equity**								
290	Accounts Payable	132	132			171	67		(238)
291	Notes Payable	0	0						
292	Income Taxes Payable	-35	-70						
293	Fixed Assets Payable	66	66						
294	Other Current Liabilities	19	19						
295	Total Current Liabilities	182	147						
296									
297	Loans Payable	2,051	2,039						
298	Total Liabilities	2,233	2,186						
299									
300	Common Stock	1,332	1,332						
301	Retained Earnings	823	750	200	(67)	(171)			
302	Net Worth	2,155	2,082						
303									
304	Total Liabilities & Assets	4,389	4,268						
305									
306	**Error Checking**								
307	All values should equal 0:								
308	Recon assets minus liab & equity	0	0						
309	Bal sheet assets minus reconciliation	0	0						
310	Bal sheet liab minus reconciliation	0	0						
311									
312									

(continued)

Figure 9-15. *continued*

	O	P	Q	R	S	T	U	V	W	X	Y	Z	AA	AB
263														
264														
265														
266	**Reconciliation Of Changes To The Projected Bal Sheet--Continued**													
267														
268	L115	L117	L106	L153	L178	L139	L140	L254	L134	L129	K191	L31		
269									L135	K204	L191			
270									L136					
271	Pay		Purch		Book			Borrow	Make	Pay	Other	Book		
272	for	Book	Cap	Pay	Tax	Sell	Pay	ST	Pmt, LT	Int, ST	Cur	Bad		
273	Assets	Dep	Equip	Taxes	Liab	Stock	Div	Loan	Loan	Loan	A&L	Debts		
274														
275	(100)			0		0	(20)	0	(30)	0				
276												0		
277														
278											0			
279														
280														
281			100											
282		33												
283														
284														
285														
286														
287														
288														
289														
290														
291								0						
292				0	(35)									
293	(100)		100											
294											0			
295														
296														
297									(13)					
298														
299														
300						0								
301		(33)			35		(20)		(17)	0		0		
302														
303														
304														
305														
306														
307														
308														
309														
310														
311														
312														

(continued)

Figure 9-15. *continued*

COLUMN WIDTHS							
Column	***Width***	***Column***	***Width***	***Column***	***Width***	***Column***	***Width***
A	1	H	5	O	5	V	5
B	4.5	I	5	P	5	W	5
C	4.5	J	5	Q	5	X	5
D	4.5	K	5	R	5	Y	5
E	4.5	L	5	S	5	Z	5
F	4.5	M	5	T	5	AA	2
G	5	N	5	U	5	AB	3

Figure 9-15. *continued*

KEY FORMULAS	
Cell	***Formula***
H270	**=CHAR(CODE($G$270)+1)** This formula increases by one the column letter you enter into cell G270.
I268	**=$H$270&TEXT(ROW($A9),"#")** The formulas in rows 268:270 provide the cells used for the reconciliation. The formulas are somewhat slow to enter, but after you do so, you will seldom need to adjust them. To enter these formulas, copy the formula shown to the right as needed into the three rows, and then edit each formula (usually only the cell address within each ROW function) to return the cell address shown. To illustrate, the two formulas in column X will appear as follows after you've edited them:
X268	**=$H$270&TEXT(ROW($A$129),"#")**
X269	**=$G$270&TEXT(ROW($A$204),"#")**
G275	**=INDIRECT($G$270&TEXT(ROW(G188),"#"))**
H275	**=G275+SUM(I275:AA275)** Enter these two formulas as shown, and then copy them down their respective columns to every row that contains a balance-sheet account. Notice that these are only the rows containing labels in column B. (Labels in column A describe totals and subtotals.) When you recalculate, the values in column G equal the values in column K in the portion of the spreadsheet in Figure 9-13. (If you've entered a letter other than K in cell G270, column G should return values from that column of the portion in Figure 9-13 instead.)

(continued)

Figure 9-15. *continued*

KEY FORMULAS–continued		
Cell	***Formula***	
Enter all of the following formulas as shown. The notes to the right of these explain the accounting entries that each represents.		
I276	**=INDIRECT(I$268)**	Sales: Dr (Increase) Accounts Receivable
I301	**=INDIRECT(I$268)**	Sales: Cr (Increase) Income—Retained Earnings
J277	**=–INDIRECT(J$268)**	Cost of Sales: Cr (Decrease) Inventory
J301	**=–INDIRECT(J$268)**	Cost of Sales: Dr (Decrease) Income—Retained Earnings
K290	**=INDIRECT(K$268)**	Operating Expenses: Cr (Increase) Accounts Payable
K301	**=–INDIRECT(K$268)**	Operating Expenses: Dr (Decrease) Income—Retained Earnings
L277	**=INDIRECT(L$268)**	Inventory Purchases: Dr (Increase) Inventory
L290	**=INDIRECT(L$268)**	Inventory Purchases: Cr (Increase) Accounts Payable
M275	**=INDIRECT(M$268)**	A/R Collections: Dr (Increase) Cash
M276	**=–INDIRECT(M$268)**	A/R Collections: Cr (Decrease) Accounts Receivable
N275	**=–INDIRECT(N$268)–INDIRECT($N$269)**	A/P Payments: Cr (Decrease) Cash
N290	**=–INDIRECT(N$268)–INDIRECT($N$269)**	A/P Payments: Dr (Decrease) Accounts Payable
O275	**=–INDIRECT(O$268)**	Pay For Assets: Cr (Decrease) Cash
O293	**=–INDIRECT(O$268)**	Pay For Assets: Dr (Decrease) Fixed Assets Payable
P282	**=INDIRECT(P$268)**	Depreciation: Cr (Increase) Accumulated Depreciation
P301	**=–INDIRECT(P$268)**	Depreciation: Dr (Decrease) Income—Retained Earnings
Q281	**=INDIRECT(Q$268)**	Capital Purchases: Dr (Increase) Fixed Assets
Q293	**=INDIRECT(Q$268)**	Capital Purchases: Cr (Increase) Fixed Assets Payable
R275	**=–INDIRECT(R$268)**	Tax Payment: Cr (Decrease) Cash
R292	**=–INDIRECT(R$268)**	Tax Payment: Dr (Decrease) Income Taxes Payable
S292	**=INDIRECT(S$268)**	Book Tax Liability: Cr (Increase) Income Taxes Payable
S301	**=INDIRECT(S$268)**	Book Tax Liability: Dr (Decrease) Income—Retained Earnings
T275	**=INDIRECT(T$268)**	Stock Sale: Dr (Increase) Cash
T300	**=INDIRECT(T$268)**	Stock Sale: Cr (Increase) Common Stock

(continued)

Figure 9-15. *continued*

KEY FORMULAS–continued		
Cell	***Formula***	
U275	**=–INDIRECT(U$268)**	Dividend Payments: Cr (Decrease) Cash
U301	**=–INDIRECT(U$268)**	Dividend Payments: Dr (Decrease) Retained Earnings
V275	**=INDIRECT(V$268)**	Borrow Short Term: Dr (Increase) Cash
V291	**=INDIRECT(V$268)**	Borrow Short Term: Cr (Increase) Notes Payable
W275	**=–INDIRECT(W$270)**	LT Loan Payment: Cr (Decrease) Cash
W297	**=–INDIRECT(W$269)**	LT Loan Pmt: Dr (Decrease) Loans Payable (Principal Amt)
W301	**=–INDIRECT(W$268)**	LT Loan Pmt: Dr (Decrease) Income—Retained Earnings (Interest Amount)
X275	**=(–INDIRECT(X$268)/12)*INDIRECT(X$269)**	ST Loan Int: Cr (Decrease) Cash
X301	**=(–INDIRECT(X$268)/12)*INDIRECT(X$269)**	ST Loan Int: Dr (Decrease) Income
Y278	**=INDIRECT($Y$269)–INDIRECT($Y$268)**	Other Cur A&L: Dr (Increase) Other Assets
Y294	**=INDIRECT($Y$269)–INDIRECT($Y$268)**	Other Cur A&L: Cr (Increase) Other Liabilities
Z276	**=–INDIRECT(Z$268)**	Bad Debts: Cr (Decrease) Accounts Receivable
Z301	**=–INDIRECT(Z$268)**	Bad Debts: Dr (Decrease) Income—Retained Earnings
G308	**=G287–G304** The assets in the reconciliation minus its liabilities and equity should equal 0.	
G309	**=INDIRECT(G$270&TEXT(ROW(G200),"#"))–G287** The total assets in the reconciliation should match those in the balance sheet.	
G310	**=INDIRECT(G$270&TEXT(ROW(G217),"#"))–G304** The total liabilities in the reconciliation should match those in the balance sheet.	
Copy the last three formulas to column H, as shown in the spreadsheet.		

Figure 9-16. Macros to Set Column Widths for the Forecast and Reconciliation

Two macros that adjust column widths for the forecast and reconciliation sections.

	A	B	C	D
1				
2				
3		Sets the width for the forecast displays.	Columns:	
4	WIDTH1	=SELECT("R1C1")	A	
5	key=c	=COLUMN.WIDTH(1.43)		
6		=SELECT("R1C2:R1C3")	B & C	
7		=COLUMN.WIDTH(4.2)		
8		=SELECT("R1C4:R1C5")	D & E	
9		=COLUMN.WIDTH(5)		
10		=SELECT("R1C6:R1C12")	F - L	
11		=COLUMN.WIDTH(4)		
12		=SELECT("R1C13:R1C16")	M - P	
13		=COLUMN.WIDTH(0.5)		
14		=SELECT("R1C17:R1C19")	Q - S	
15		=COLUMN.WIDTH(4)		
16		=SELECT("R1C20:R1C22")	T - V	
17		=COLUMN.WIDTH(2.57)		
18		=SELECT("R1C23")	W	
19		=COLUMN.WIDTH(0.92)		
20		=SELECT("R1C1")		
21		=RETURN()		
22				
23				
24		Sets the width for the reconciliation	Columns:	
25	WIDTH2	=SELECT("R1C1")	A	
26	key=g	=COLUMN.WIDTH(1)		
27		=SELECT("R1C2:R1C6")	B - F	
28		=COLUMN.WIDTH(4.5)		
29		=SELECT("R1C7:R1C26")	G - Z	
30		=COLUMN.WIDTH(5)		
31		=SELECT("R1C27")	AA	
32		=COLUMN.WIDTH(2)		
33		=SELECT("R1C28")	AB	
34		=COLUMN.WIDTH(3)		
35		=SELECT("R1C1")		
36		=RETURN()		
37				
38				

10

Management Reporting

From time to time, when I worked as a CFO, I saved copies of all the reports that crossed my desk during a month. I did so for two reasons. First, honestly, I wondered how high the stack of paper—a stack that I was expected to read, understand, and respond to—would reach after 30 days. But second, by flipping through a month's supply of reports and memos, I could more easily identify the ruts that we'd worn in our thinking process. With luck, this quick survey would help me find nontraditional approaches to the traditional problems we faced.

This chapter presents traditional management information in nontraditional ways. The first section presents nontraditional reporting formats. Some of these, perhaps, will generate new insights on old problems that you face. But even those that don't provide insights will at least bring a fresh appearance to old reports, often a beneficial contribution itself.

The last section of this chapter offers several new ways of thinking about traditional break-even analysis. The traditional approach requires that gross margins and product mix remain constant during the term of the analysis. But in real life, of course, the one constant is *change*. Although the spreadsheets in this section still depend in part on constant mix and margins, they do let you vary your assumptions about these factors easily and thus let you calculate the limits of your break-even sales using best-case and worst-case assumptions about these factors.

NONTRADITIONAL REPORTING FORMATS

Unlike most spreadsheets, Microsoft Excel displays and prints graphics information rather than character information. This graphics orientation allows the program to display many fonts, draw borders, shade cells, and create other effects that simply aren't possible with programs that must print specific ASCII characters.

Many people, however, have spent years creating and using character-based reports. Therefore, it isn't clear to them how these new features can improve on traditional reporting formats.

The first section of this chapter presents six common reports formatted in uncommon ways. Although I've tried to make these reports useful as presented, their real purpose is to expand your thinking about ways to use this graphics-based spreadsheet to improve your own business reporting.

Those Microsoft Ads

At the time I was writing this book, many business and computer magazines featured a Microsoft advertisement with the headline "No other spreadsheet can make this statement...." Positioned below the headline were three financial statements that were produced by Microsoft Excel.

The ad was intended to appeal to managers who must present financial reports to bankers, stockholders, investors, the financial community, and so on. Not only must these reports contain favorable information, but they must appear professionally prepared. The ad's message was that Microsoft Excel can help you generate these attractive financial statements.

The problem is that if you are like most managers, neither you nor your employees have the time or skill to create the works of art the advertisement features. And even if you happen to create a spreadsheet that would look great when produced by a laser printer, you might not recognize success when you have achieved it because it looks rather primitive on your monitor.

Therefore, I talked the folks at Microsoft into sending me, on disk, the spreadsheets they used in those ads. Perhaps you can use these spreadsheets to give your own financial statements a similar look.

Figure 10-1 on page 508 presents the income statement featured in the ad. Both the fonts and the line spacing combine to make the report look as if a graphic artist prepared it, rather than some accountant in the back room. For example, the report uses 12-point Helv rather than the smaller 8-point or 10-point Helv used throughout this book. And unlike most financial reports, this one double-spaces most lines.

The row-height box for Figure 10-1 illustrates other aspects of the spreadsheet. Because the person who created the income statement assigned font 1 to 12-point Helv, the default row height increased to 16 points. The spreadsheet's creator generated the horizontal bar in rows 5 through 11 by assigning top and bottom borders to the rows shown and reducing their row height to 1 point. He or she adjusted the height of other rows to provide a double border or to make spacing more attractive.

To create this income statement, open a new spreadsheet, turn off the gridlines, and set the column widths as shown in the column-width box for Figure 10-1. Assign font 1 as Helv 12, font 2 as Helv 12 Bold, font 3 as Helv 8, and font 4 as Helv 14 Bold.

As you enter the labels in the spreadsheet, you might want to use two hyphens instead of the single hyphen shown in the description contained in line 30. Two hyphens are a better approximation of what typographers call an em dash, which signals a pause, similar to the way a comma signals a pause in reading. A hyphen causes us to wonder briefly what an *item-provision* is.

Figure 10-2 on page 511 and Figure 10-3 on page 513 contain the complete statements of assets and liabilities that the ad displays in part. With the help of the information boxes for both figures and with your experience in creating the income statement in Figure 10-1, you should have no trouble creating these statements.

A Corporate Overview

Many public and private companies distribute company fact sheets to the business press and to both current and potential employees, creditors, stockholders, and customers. Figure 10-4 on page 515 presents one such fact sheet that a publicly traded company might provide.

If your company is private, of course, this fact sheet provides information that you would never agree to reveal. But it also lacks information that you might want to publicize. Instead of the section on executive compensation, for example, you might substitute a list of your most prestigious customers or the details of the favorable effect your company has on your local community (annual payroll in dollars and people, taxes paid, dollars of goods purchased locally, and so on). Of course, in a more general sense, you could use a fact sheet such as this for many different purposes, because it gives any short list a more professional appearance.

The display is easy to create. Simply create your lists in the spreadsheet; draw a border around them; assign titles; stack the separate lists; and then create a shaded border around all the displays. The information boxes for the figure provide guidance for the line and column spacing and for formatting.

Reporting Financial Performance Using the Du Pont Method

Between the early 1920s and the early 1980s, the Du Pont Corporation measured internal performance by using a return-on-investment formula chart similar to the one illustrated in Figure 10-5 on page 518. During that time, the Du Pont formula that the chart describes gained worldwide recognition as an effective management tool. Today, most introductory textbooks on financial management discuss some variation of the formula by name. All discuss the concepts underlying the formula.

(On the other hand, few textbooks can agree on how the Du Pont name should be spelled. The corporation itself uses *Du Pont,* which I use as well.)

Notice in the chart that Du Pont uses gross investment (assets prior to the deduction of the depreciation reserve) to measure the return on investment. Although this is one aspect of the Du Pont formula that most companies have not adapted, Du Pont takes this approach for two reasons, the company explains.

First, with escalating construction costs and conscientious maintenance, they feel that gross investments tend to be more representative of the economic value of their assets than do net investments.

Second, using gross investments tends to produce returns that allow comparisons over a period of years for a single business, or comparisons between a young business and a mature one. Other methods, which reduce assets by the amount of the depreciation reserve, tend to increase returns as the asset base becomes fully depreciated.

The spreadsheet in Figure 10-6 on page 521 provides data for the chart. The income section of this spreadsheet contains an annual income statement or a report of the most recent 12 months of monthly income, which is often called a rolling 12-month income statement. The assets section represents the balance sheet at the end of the period. If you design your chart to reference standard financial spreadsheets like these, the chart becomes virtually maintenance free.

If you prefer not to spend the time to create these spreadsheets, you can use the order information on the last page of this book to purchase a set of disks that contains them. Otherwise, to create the chart in Figure 10-5, first open a new spreadsheet and turn off the gridlines. Set the widths of column A and column B as shown in the figure's column-width box. Select any cell in column B, choose Macro Record, and then choose Macro Relative Record. Enter the column widths shown for columns C, D, E, and F. Select column F and choose Macro Stop Recorder.

When you press the Ctrl key combination specified in the Record Macro dialog box, your macro assigns the column widths of the next four columns. Press this key combination three times. Column S is now selected. Set the widths of columns S, T, and U as shown.

Save your macro sheet, at least temporarily. If you decide to change the column widths that I suggest, simply alter the macro as necessary and use the revised macro to quickly change your spreadsheet's column widths.

The range C5:E9 contains a pattern of borders and symbols that you can use to quickly generate the remainder of the chart. Enter the borders and formats in this range, but do not enter labels, values, or formulas at this point. When you do so, center-align the range and assign the number format shown. To create the arrow in cell F7, enter a space, four dashes, and the greater-than symbol.

To enter the outlines and borders in the remainder of the chart, copy the range you've just created (or only the sections of it you need) to the ranges shown. Enter the remaining borders, the labels, and all signs for addition, subtraction, multiplication, and division. As the figure's formula box shows, the formula =CHAR(247) displays the division sign, the character corresponding to ASCII code 247. If your printer can't display this sign properly, you might want to leave the two cells that contain this sign blank and then mark up your printouts by hand. Alternatively, you may decide to substitute the / character as the symbol for division.

(To create a cross-reference chart of ASCII codes and their corresponding characters, first open a new spreadsheet, enter *1* in cell A1, highlight column A, choose Data Series, enter a Stop Value of 255, and then choose OK. Doing so creates a column of the numbers 1 through 255 in column A. Next, enter the formula *=CHAR(A1)* in cell B1 and copy it to the range B2:B255. Doing so generates in column B the characters generated by the Helv font. In this chart, you can find the character for the division symbol returned for the number 247 in cell B247.)

When you complete all of the chart in Figure 10-5 except the numbers, enter the spreadsheet in Figure 10-6 as shown. Then, to reference this data in your chart, first open a new window. To do so, choose Window New Window and then turn off its gridlines. To arrange these windows side by side, choose Windows Arrange All.

You now have two views of the same spreadsheet. In one window, display the first cells in the chart that you want to load; in the other window, display the part of the spreadsheet in Figure 10-6 that contains the data for those cells. Then, to enter sales in the chart, simply select cell C5 in the window containing the chart, enter an equal sign, select cell K58 in the other window, press the F4 (Abs/Rel) key to assign an absolute reference to the formula, and then press Enter. Follow a similar approach for all other cells of the chart that directly reference data.

The formula box for Figure 10-5 shows the formulas for all cells that don't directly reference data in the spreadsheet in Figure 10-6. Enter these formulas as needed. When you complete your chart, save it using any name you want. I used the name DUPONT.XLS.

Budget Variance by Department

Face it. Most budget variance reports are boring—important, but boring. Most of them contain page after page with column after column of figures. As a manager, you must understand those figures, isolate the ones that are important, and then act on them.

Figure 10-7 on page 522 presents a budget report that doesn't require careful study. This report graphs each $50,000 of a department's unfavorable variance in its shaded section and each $50,000 of its favorable variance in its unshaded section. Therefore, at a glance, you can see which departments are holding to their budgets and which aren't.

In the spreadsheet in the figure, for example, you can see that the manufacturing department is in trouble. For some reason, its final assembly area is $483,000 over budget and its Coconut assembly line is $321,000 over budget. But most of engineering has saved money; in total, this department is $289,000 under budget. Finance, which spends little money anyway, has virtually no effect on the total budget variance.

Of course, you could use this format to report almost any performance within a company. It could, for example, report profit by product line, actual sales booked as compared to quota, the percentage of increase or decrease in sales, inventory, employees, or profits, and other factors important to your business.

As the figure's formula box explains, the REPT function makes these graphs work. This function, which repeats any symbol a certain number of times, draws a bar graph by repeating the bar-graph symbol once for each $50,000 of variance. And when you left-align the unfavorable variance and right-align the favorable variance, both bar graphs appear to originate at the boundary between the two graph areas.

To create this report, open a new spreadsheet, turn off its gridlines, and then set its column widths as shown in the column-width box. Notice that the widths of columns C through G are the same as those of H through L, M through Q, and R through V, exactly as the spreadsheet in Figure 10-5 repeats the widths of columns C through F. To set the width of these columns quickly, therefore, create a macro similar to the one I described for Figure 10-5.

Enter the label and underline shown in row 3 and the formula shown for cell V3. Enter the labels in cells E5 and O5 and format these labels as shown in the format box. Then enter the outlines and shading shown in the ranges C5:F7 and J5:T7.

Enter the range definitions in the range-name box and then enter the values shown for cells C6 and J6. (You will later replace the value in cell J6 with a formula.) Enter the formulas shown for cells E6, F6, O6, and P6 and then format these four cells as shown in the format box.

With this set-up completed, you will find that completing the remainder of the spreadsheet is a breeze. To create the department reports in rows 10 through 12, simply copy the range C5:G7 to the range H10:V10 and then change the titles as needed.

To create the skeleton for the remainder of the report, first copy the range C6:F6 to cell C15. Enter and format the title shown in cell E14 and then copy the range C14:F16 to the range C17:F34. Finally, copy the range C14:G33 to the range H14:V14.

After you complete the skeleton of this report, you can quickly flesh it out. Enter the formulas shown for cells J6 and C11 and then copy the latter formula to cells H11, M11, and R11. Draw the borders and shading shown in the spreadsheet in the figure and then enter the labels shown for each work area within each major department.

To complete the report, you must do something about the values shown for the variances below row 14 and in cell C6. You have at least three alternatives. First, you can enter the values shown in the spreadsheet in Figure 10-7. This approach lets you complete and save the report quickly. Unfortunately, this approach takes special effort to update monthly.

Second, you can create a report of variances similar in concept to the one in Figure 10-6, and then enter formulas in cells C15, C18, and so on, referencing the data in your report exactly as you did for the chart in Figure 10-5. You must also update the report, of course. But you'll find it easier to update the values in a simple report than to update values in a report like the one in Figure 10-7.

Third, you can create a budget report similar to the one in Figure 8-12 and then enter a formula in cell C15 of the report in Figure 10-7 that extracts the correct information from this budget report. (When you do so, enter the department number you want to report in cell D15 and then hide it by using the *;;* format.) The following is the general format of the formula you use to extract this data:

```
=INDEX(Input,MATCH(D15,Dept,0),2+Month)
```

You define Input as the range A86:O91 of the report in Figure 8-12 and Dept as the range A86:A91 of that figure. You also define Month as the range in the report in Figure 10-7. This range contains the number of the month you want to report, a number that corresponds to those shown in row 84 of the report in Figure 8-12. The INDEX formula therefore returns a value from the Input range that is found in the row and column specified. The row is determined by the MATCH function, which finds the department number you specified in the Dept range; the column number equals the value 2 plus the number of the month you want to report.

NEW IDEAS IN BREAK-EVEN ANALYSIS

The idea of break-even sales is fundamental in most businesses. Even people who aren't quite sure what the break-even point is or how to calculate it use the term intuitively. "We're not going to make a profit," they tell their salespeople, "until we get our sales above the break-even point!"

Traditional break-even analysis uses the break-even chart extensively. For example, the *Microsoft Excel Sampler* that came with your copy of Microsoft Excel presents a traditional break-even chart. But often, other types of displays provide more value than do these traditional charts.

Creating a Schedule of Monthly Profits

Figure 10-8 on page 525 presents a schedule that doesn't mention the break-even point at all, even though it depends entirely on break-even arithmetic. This schedule shows the monthly profits you can expect under various combinations of sales, contribution margins, and the fixed costs (shown in cell G22).

The terms "fixed costs" and "contribution margin" should tip you off that this table uses break-even arithmetic. The term "fixed cost" is an unfortunate one, because no cost is truly fixed. If business gets bad enough or good enough or if enough time passes, "fixed" costs become unfixed. Fixed costs are fixed, therefore, in this one regard: They tend not to vary in the short term as sales volume varies within existing plant capacity.

Contribution margin is much like gross profit margin. But where the gross profit margin equals sales minus cost of goods sold, the contribution margin equals sales minus variable costs. The terms are similar in another regard as well; they refer both to dollars of profit and to percentage of profit on sales. Therefore, when someone refers to either a gross profit margin or a contribution margin, you must depend on the context to determine whether the reference is to dollars or to a percentage.

Figure 10-8 presents monthly profits by sales dollar and by contribution margin (as a percentage). Column A contains a range of sales dollars, beginning with the value entered in cell B23 and growing by the amount in cell C23. Row 7 contains a range of contribution margins, beginning with the value entered in cell B24 and growing by the value in cell C24.

To illustrate the table calculations, cell H19 contains the most profitable combination of sales and contribution margins. Profits equal the amount that sales contributed to fixed costs and profit ($210,000 × 60% = $126,000), minus fixed costs ($60,000 in cell G22), for a total profit of $66,000.

Notice that the upper-left half of the table shows losses and the lower-right half shows profits. Running diagonally through the table from the upper-right corner to the lower-left corner is a line of break-even points. Each of these points depends on a particular contribution margin.

For example, cell H8 shows that sales of $100,000 represents a break-even point with a 60 percent contribution margin and fixed costs of $60,000 ($100,000 × 60% – $60,000 = $0). Notice that you can easily rearrange this formula to calculate the break-even point directly. The break-even sales of $100,000 in this formula equals $60,000 divided by 60 percent.

In other words, to calculate break-even sales, divide fixed costs by the contribution margin. Confirm this fact by calculating break-even sales when contribution margins are 30 percent, 40 percent, and 50 percent. The answers are shown in cells B18, D13, and F10.

To create this schedule, first open a new spreadsheet and turn off its gridlines. Enter the labels, values, and borders shown in rows 21 through 24, and format them as shown in the format box.

Enter the labels and borders shown in rows 3 through 7 and the formulas for these rows shown in the figure's formula box. Enter and format the formulas shown for column A. Finally, enter the formula shown for cell B8, format it as shown, and then copy it to the range B8:H19.

To complete the schedule, enter any missing borders or formats and then save your spreadsheet. I used the name MO_PROF.XLS.

Break-Even Analysis with Regression

The spreadsheet in Figure 7-5 presented one way to calculate fixed and variable costs with regression analysis; the one in Figure 10-9 on page 527 presents another. The two spreadsheets look at the same data from opposite points of view. The spreadsheet in Figure 7-5 looks at each individual expense, calculating its fixed and variable component. The spreadsheet in Figure 10-9 looks at the sum of all costs for each of several months. Both methods yield the same results.

The chart in Figure 10-10 on page 530 presents the results of the spreadsheet in Figure 10-9 as a graph with three lines. The horizontal line, of course, represents fixed costs, costs that don't vary as sales vary. The line that starts at 0 in the bottom left and extends to the upper right of the graph represents sales. The third line, which begins at the fixed-cost value, is the least-squares line drawn through your total costs, which appear in the graph as Xs.

When you graph your own costs, the results will make perfect sense at times; your fixed costs will seem about right, and your individual costs will fall near the total-cost line. But at other times, this graph will seem to make no sense at all. Generally, you will find three reasons for this problem:

- Companies that grow quickly add fixed costs quickly. As a consequence, the regression formula identifies those rapidly rising fixed costs as variable costs. In extreme cases, the equation identifies so many variable costs that fixed costs appear to be negative. This occurs when all costs rise more quickly than do sales.

  To deal with this problem, subtract the categories of new fixed costs that you added from your total costs, regress the remaining costs, and then add back the current level of your fixed costs. For example, suppose that as your sales have increased during the past year, you've rented more and more factory space, but that you've also managed to keep other fixed costs constant. Subtract factory rent from total costs and then perform the regression analysis shown in the spreadsheet in Figure 10-9. To calculate your actual fixed costs, add your current factory rent to the amount of fixed costs estimated by the regression equation. Finally, graph your results.

- Companies and accounting departments that are out of control often recognize costs and profits that have no relationship to sales volume. For example, in one month they might write off a large amount of obsolete inventory, in the month following they might recognize the receipt of a large royalty payment as income, in the next month they might purchase and expense a year's worth of copy supplies, and so on. Under these circumstances, there's no way that a regression formula can work its way through the confusion and discover the underlying fixed and variable costs.

  The solution to this problem is much like the solution to the previous one. Subtract the unusual costs from total costs before you apply the regression formulas and then adjust your regression results by the amount of the unusual costs. In this case, however, you might have to adjust variable costs as well as fixed costs. Suppose, for example, that you write off $100,000 of obsolete inventory. You need to estimate the percentage this amount represents of the total sales you incurred while these obsolete goods accumulated. This percentage, then, represents an additional variable cost that you need to add to your calculations.

- Companies with multiple product lines have a more difficult problem. Break-even analysis is based on the assumption that your company-wide contribution margin will remain constant over time. But if your sales mix varies from month to month, your average contribution margin will probably vary as well. As a consequence, a break-even chart might show no relationship between sales volume and total costs.

  One way to deal with this problem is to prepare break-even charts by product line, treating each as an independent business. Of course, this approach requires that you assign fixed costs to each product line on some reasonable basis. Although this can be a challenging task, it can create a significant side benefit: You might uncover hidden winners and losers in your product lines.

  Another way to deal with multiple product lines is to forget about the idea of a break-even chart and to use other methods of analysis. The spreadsheets in Figures 10-11 through 10-13 illustrate this approach.

Creating the Basic Break-Even Chart

To create the spreadsheet in Figure 10-9, first open a new spreadsheet and turn off the gridlines. Enter the labels, borders, and shading shown. Enter the values shown for columns B and C as well as the formulas shown in the formula box for cell F3 and for columns A and D.

Enter all range names shown in the figure's range-name box and then enter the remaining formulas shown in the formula box. Copy all formulas down their columns as needed. To complete the spreadsheet, clean up the formats and borders as needed and then save it as BE_REGR.XLS.

Take the following steps to create the graph shown in Figure 10-10:

1. Activate the BE_REGR.XLS spreadsheet, highlight the range B7:F14, and then press the F11 (New Chart) key. (Press Alt-F1 if your keyboard has no F11 key.)
2. To change the graph from a bar chart to a scatter chart with lines, choose Gallery Scatter and select 2.
3. To label the horizontal axis with sales values, copy the Sales column into the chart. To do so, activate the BE_REGR.XLS spreadsheet; choose GoTo Sales; press Ctrl-Ins to copy this range to the clipboard; activate your chart; choose Edit Paste Special; turn on the Columns, Categories in First Column, and Replace Existing Categories options; and then choose OK.

4. For convenience, you graphed one more column of data than you needed, so erase it now. The graph of this column of profits appears between the fixed-cost line and the horizontal axis. Click on this line, highlight its SERIES formula in the formula bar, and then press Delete and Enter.

5. To eliminate the markers from the graph lines, click on any of them, choose Format Patterns, turn on the Invisible markers selection, turn on Apply To All, and then choose OK.

6. If you have a color monitor, you might want to change the color of the lines in the graph. To do so, select one of the lines, choose Format Patterns, and then choose the colors you want. To apply one color to all lines, turn on the box labeled Apply To All before you choose OK.

7. With one exception, all lines in your graph appear as straight lines. This one exception is the graph of total actual costs. To display each month's actual cost as an X, rather than as a line, click on this line, choose Format Patterns, assign an invisible line, assign the X marker style, and then choose OK.

8. If you click on any of the lines in the chart, you'll notice that the SERIES formulas reference cell addresses rather than range names in the BE_REGR.XLS spreadsheet. This is dangerous. If you change the position of any data in the spreadsheet, the cell address in the chart *will not change,* and the chart will reference incorrect cell addresses. To correct this problem, you must edit each SERIES formula, changing the cell addresses into range names. To do so, change the following cell addresses to the range names shown:

$B$7:$B$14	Sales
$D$7:$D$14	ActCosts
$E$7:$E$14	Fixed
$F$7:$F$14	RegCosts

9. To draw a border around the graph, choose Chart Select Chart, choose Format Patterns, choose the heaviest border weight, and then choose OK.

10. To enter the graph title, first choose Chart Attach Text and select Chart Title. When the word *Title* appears in your graph, enter the title *Break-Even Chart.* To change the title's font to 14-point Helv boldface, as shown in the chart in the figure, choose Format Font and then select that font.

11. To enter the vertical-axis title, choose Chart Attach Text and select Value Axis. When the letter *Y* appears in your graph, type the Y-axis title shown in the chart in the figure. When you press Enter, the label is displayed horizontally rather than vertically. To display it vertically, choose Format Text and then turn on the Vertical Text box, leaving the other boxes at their default selections. When you press Enter, the title is displayed vertically, as shown in the figure. To change the title's font to 12-point Helv boldface, use the Format Font command again.
12. To enter the horizontal-axis title, choose Chart Attach Text, select Category Axis, and enter the title shown. Choose the Format Font command to adjust the title's font.
13. To enter the date shown in the title, first click on a blank area of your graph so that no graph element is selected. Type an equal sign, which appears in the graph's formula bar, and then enter the range name BE_REGR.XLS!Date. When you press Enter, the graph returns the contents of the range name Date from the BE_REGR.XLS spreadsheet, which happens to be the date you want. Drag this date to the top of the graph and position it beneath the graph title.
14. To enter the title below the date, first click on a blank area; type the text you want, which appears in the formula bar; press Enter; and then drag the text into position beneath the graph title.
15. Although you aren't quite finished with your chart, save it and any other open documents in your workspace. When I was designing the chart in this chapter, my own computer locked up on me whenever I previewed a previous version of my chart, forcing me to turn off my computer and reboot each time. To avoid losing data in case this chart creates the same problem on your computer, be sure to save all your data before you preview the chart.
16. The second and third lines of the title of your chart are called unattached text. Unfortunately, when you print unattached text, it doesn't align itself in the same way that attached text (such as the first line of the graph title) does. In other words, to center unattached text below the title of a printed document, you must position it somewhere to the right of the attached title. Therefore, to position unattached text accurately, choose File Print, turn on Preview, observe the positioning of the unattached text, adjust the position as needed in the Ready mode, and then preview your document again.

Break-Even Analysis with Multiple Product Lines

Figure 10-11 on page 531 presents a planning tool that helps you project what your break-even point will be under specific assumptions about unit sales, prices, and costs. Although this report is similar to the one in Figure 10-8, it has the advantage of letting you be much more specific about your assumptions.

For example, the report in the figure presents a small company struggling to break even. With the sales and costs shown, for example, the company is losing roughly $500 per month. ($67,000 × 53% – $36,000, rounded to the nearest $250, equals a $500 loss.) The schedule at the bottom displays this amount in cell E43, which is outlined.

The report shows that the company has many alternatives for breaking even. It could decrease fixed costs by $1,000, increase contribution margins by 2 percent, or increase sales. To decrease fixed costs, it must adjust the costs shown in the range D6:D10. To increase margins, it must decrease its variable costs, increase prices, or both. To increase sales, it must increase prices, increase unit sales, or both. The report lets this company quickly test each alternative and combination of alternatives.

The report in Figure 10-12 on page 534 lets the company look at its finances from a slightly different point of view. This report presents the break-even point for each combination of fixed cost and contribution margin shown in the report in Figure 10-11. Cell E61, which is outlined, shows that the company's current break-even point is roughly $68,000. It shows that if the company did lower its fixed costs by $1,000, its break-even point would fall to roughly $66,000; or if the company could increase its average contribution margin to 55 percent, its break-even point would fall to about $65,500.

To create the reports in Figure 10-11 and Figure 10-12, open a new spreadsheet, turn off the gridlines, and then complete the reports by using the information boxes to guide you.

Break-Even Rules of Thumb

Suppose your marketing manager wants to upgrade the packaging of all your products. The new packaging will reduce your contribution margin by only 1 percent per month, she explains, but will greatly add to your company's image. Should you change your packaging?

Or suppose your administrative manager wants to install a new telephone system, which will cost an additional $1,000 per month. This telecommunication computer will bring wonderful capabilities to your outmoded telephone system, he explains, and at a very reasonable cost. Should you change your telephones?

Though you'll consider other factors as well, you should certainly weigh the effect these new costs will have on your monthly profits and break-even point. Figure 10-13 on page 535 presents a spreadsheet that helps you make these calculations quickly.

If your company's income statement resembled the one shown at the bottom of this spreadsheet, a 1 percent decrease in your total contribution margin would raise your break-even point by $1,750 per month (cell F13). Your sales would have to increase by $4,720 per month (cell F17) to maintain current profits. (I call these your "stay-even" sales.) If your sales stayed constant after the change, your profits would decrease by $2,500 per month (cell F20). Finally, if you purchased the new phone system, your profits would fall by $1,000 per month and both your break-even and stay-even sales would increase by $1,850 per month (rows 24 and 25).

The spreadsheet in Figure 10-13, in other words, presents rules of thumb that you can quickly use to calculate the effect that prospective changes in costs will have on your profits and break-even point.

This is an easy figure to create. Simply open a new spreadsheet, turn off the gridlines, and then enter the data, formulas, and so on as shown. Use the information boxes to assist you.

Figure 10-1. Statement of Income, Microsoft Ad

An income statement used in Microsoft advertisements that demonstrates the formatting powers of Microsoft Excel.

	A	B	C	D	E	F	G	H	I	J	K
1											
2											
3		**Statement of Income**						(In thousands, except per share amounts)			
12		**Two years ended September 30, 1988**						**1988**		**1987**	
13											
14		**Net sales**						**1,918,265**		**1,515,861**	
15											
16		Costs and expenses:									
17											
18			Cost of sales				$	1,057,849	$	878,571	
19											
20			Research and development					72,511		71,121	
21											
22			Marketing and distribution					470,573		392,851	
23											
24			General and administrative					110,062		81,825	
25											
26								**1,710,995**		**1,424,368**	
27											
28		Operating income before unusual item						207,270		91,493	
29											
30		Unusual item-provision for consolidation of operations						(36,981)			
31											
32		Interest and other income, net						9,771		17,722	
33											
34		Income before taxes						180,060		109,215	
35											
36		Provision for income taxes						58,807		45,115	
37											
38		**Net income**					**$**	**121,253**	**$**	**64,100**	
39											
40		Common and common equivalent shares used in the									
41			calculations of earnings per share					61,880		60,872	
42											
43		**Earnings per common share**					**$**	**1.96**	**$**	**1.05**	
45		See accompanying notes									
46											

(continued)

Figure 10-1. *continued*

COLUMN WIDTHS			
Column	*Width*	*Column*	*Width*
A	4.22	G	3
B	8.33	H	9.44
C	8.33	I	2.11
D	8.33	J	9.44
E	8.33	K	3
F	4.56		

ROW HEIGHTS							
Row	*Height*	*Row*	*Height*	*Row*	*Height*	*Row*	*Height*
1	20	13	16	25	16	37	16
2	16	14	16	26	16	38	16
3	21	15	16	27	16	39	16
4	5	16	16	28	16	40	16
5	1	17	16	29	16	41	16
6	1	18	16	30	16	42	16
7	1	19	16	31	16	43	16
8	1	20	16	32	16	44	3
9	1	21	16	33	16	45	16
10	1	22	16	34	16	46	16
11	1	23	16	35	16		
12	16	24	16	36	16		

(continued)

Figure 10-1. *continued*

KEY CELL FORMATS			
Cell	***Number***	***Alignment***	***Font***
Spread-sheet	**Set Font 1 to Helv 12.**		
B3	**General**	**General**	**Helv 14, Bold**
J3	**General**	**Right**	**Helv 8**
B12:G14	**General**	**General**	**Helv 12, Bold**
H12:J12	**General**	**General**	**Helv 12, Bold**
H14:J14	**#,##0 ;(#,##0)**	**Right**	**Helv 12, Bold**
B16:G36	**General**	**General**	**Helv 12**
H18:J24	**#,##0 ;(#,##0)**	**Right**	**Helv 12**
H26:J26	**#,##0 ;(#,##0)**	**Right**	**Helv 12, Bold**
B28:G36	**General**	**General**	**Helv 12**
H28:J36	**#,##0 ;(#,##0)**	**Right**	**Helv 12**
B38:G38	**General**	**General**	**Helv 12, Bold**
H38:J38	**#,##0 ;(#,##0)**	**Right**	**Helv 12, Bold**
B40:G42	**General**	**General**	**Helv 12**
H41:J41	**#,##0**	**Right**	**Helv 12**
B43:G43	**General**	**General**	**Helv 12, Bold**
H43:J43	**#,##0.00**	**Right**	**Helv 12, Bold**
B45	**General**	**General**	**Helv 8**

Figure 10-2. Statement of Assets, Microsoft Ad

A statement of assets used in Microsoft advertisements.

	A–G	H	I	J	K
1					
2					
3	**Assets**				(Dollars in thousands)
12	**September 30, 1988 and September 30, 1987**		**1988**		**1987**
13					
14	Current assets:				
15					
16	Cash and temporary cash investments	$	427,248	$	183,910
17					
18	Accounts receivable				
19	net of allowance for doubtful accounts of $16,209 ($10,831 in 1984)		220,142		258,223
20					
21	Inventories		166,936		264,604
22					
23	Prepaid income taxes		70,360		26,736
24					
25	Other current assets		27,554		23,040
26					
27	**Total current assets**		**912,240**		**756,513**
28					
29	Property, plant and equipment				
30					
31	Land and buildings		23,606		24,877
32					
33	Machinery and equipment		78,710		68,084
34					
35	Office furniture and equipment		38,536		30,560
36					
37	Leasehold improvements		34,723		25,993
38					
39			**175,575**		**149,514**
40					
41	Accumulated depreciation and amortization		(84,204)		(73,721)
42					
43	**Net property, plant and equipment**		**91,371**		**75,793**
44					
45	Other Assets		23,651		25,352
46					
47		**$**	**1,027,262**	**$**	**857,658**
49					
50					

(continued)

Figure 10-2. *continued*

COLUMN WIDTHS			
Column	*Width*	*Column*	*Width*
A	4.22	G	8.33
B	4	H	1.78
C	4.11	I	10
D	8.33	J	1.33
E	8.33	K	10
F	7.67	L	3

ROW HEIGHTS							
Row	*Height*	*Row*	*Height*	*Row*	*Height*	*Row*	*Height*
1	20	14	16	27	16	40	16
2	16	15	16	28	16	41	16
3	20	16	16	29	16	42	16
4	5	17	16	30	16	43	16
5	1	18	16	31	16	44	16
6	1	19	16	32	16	45	16
7	1	20	16	33	16	46	16
8	1	21	16	34	16	47	16
9	1	22	16	35	16	48	3
10	1	23	16	36	16	49	16
11	1	24	16	37	16	50	16
12	16	25	16	38	16		
13	16	26	16	39	16		

Figure 10-3. Statement of Liabilities, Microsoft Ad

A statement of liabilities used in Microsoft advertisements.

	A–H		I	J	K
1					
2					
3	**Liabilities and Shareholders' Equity**				(Dollars in Thousands)
12	**September 30, 1988 and September 30, 1987**		**1988**		**1987**
13					
14	Current liabilities:				
15	Accounts payable	$	74,729	$	109,023
16	Accrued compensation and employee benefits		25,580		20,441
17	Income taxes payable		27,785		11,253
18	Accrued marketing and distribution		75,919		50,623
19	Accrued cost of consolidation of operations		20,158		
20	Other current liabilities		71,164		63,769
21					
22	**Total current liabilities**		**295,335**		**255,109**
23					
24	Deferred income taxes		90,250		69,022
25	Commitments and contingencies				
26	Shareholders' equity:		234,610		208,933
27	Common stock, no par value, 160,000,000 shares authorized; 61,849,802				
28	shares issued and outstanding in 1985. (60,535,146 shares in 1984.)				
29					
30	**Retained earnings**		**320,309**		**259,086**
31					
32	Accumulated translation adjustment		399		(648)
33					
34			**645,568**		**536,393**
35					
36	Notes receivable from shareholders		(3,891)		(2,866)
37					
38	**Total shareholders' equity**		**641,677**		**533,527**
39		**$**	**1,027,262**	**$**	**857,658**
41					
42					

(continued)

Figure 10-3. *continued*

COLUMN WIDTHS			
Column	*Width*	*Column*	*Width*
A	4.22	G	1.22
B	4.22	H	4.33
C	3.89	I	10.11
D	8.33	J	4.67
E	8.33	K	10.11
F	8.33	L	3.71

ROW HEIGHTS							
Row	*Height*	*Row*	*Height*	*Row*	*Height*	*Row*	*Height*
1	20	12	16	23	25	34	16
2	20	13	13	24	25	35	25
3	20	14	25	25	25	36	25
4	5	15	25	26	25	37	16
5	1	16	25	27	11	38	16
6	1	17	25	28	11	39	16
7	1	18	25	29	16	40	2
8	1	19	25	30	16	41	16
9	1	20	25	31	16	42	16
10	1	21	16	32	16		
11	1	22	16	33	16		

Figure 10-4. Corporate Overview

A company fact sheet that you can adapt for many purposes.

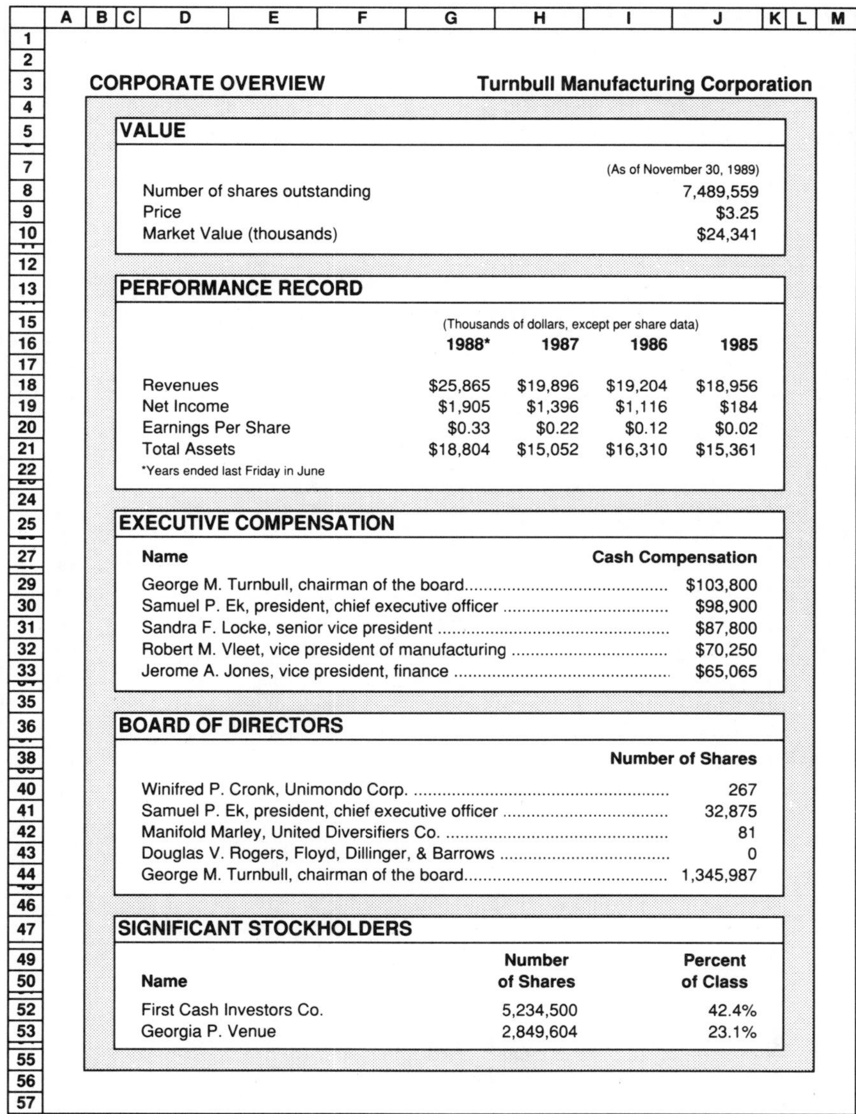

CORPORATE OVERVIEW — Turnbull Manufacturing Corporation

VALUE

	(As of November 30, 1989)
Number of shares outstanding	7,489,559
Price	$3.25
Market Value (thousands)	$24,341

PERFORMANCE RECORD

(Thousands of dollars, except per share data)

	1988*	1987	1986	1985
Revenues	$25,865	$19,896	$19,204	$18,956
Net Income	$1,905	$1,396	$1,116	$184
Earnings Per Share	$0.33	$0.22	$0.12	$0.02
Total Assets	$18,804	$15,052	$16,310	$15,361

*Years ended last Friday in June

EXECUTIVE COMPENSATION

Name	Cash Compensation
George M. Turnbull, chairman of the board	$103,800
Samuel P. Ek, president, chief executive officer	$98,900
Sandra F. Locke, senior vice president	$87,800
Robert M. Vleet, vice president of manufacturing	$70,250
Jerome A. Jones, vice president, finance	$65,065

BOARD OF DIRECTORS

	Number of Shares
Winifred P. Cronk, Unimondo Corp.	267
Samuel P. Ek, president, chief executive officer	32,875
Manifold Marley, United Diversifiers Co.	81
Douglas V. Rogers, Floyd, Dillinger, & Barrows	0
George M. Turnbull, chairman of the board	1,345,987

SIGNIFICANT STOCKHOLDERS

Name	Number of Shares	Percent of Class
First Cash Investors Co.	5,234,500	42.4%
Georgia P. Venue	2,849,604	23.1%

(continued)

Figure 10-4. *continued*

COLUMN WIDTHS			
Column	*Width*	*Column*	*Width*
A	3.57	G	8.43
B	2.43	H	8.43
C	1.71	I	8.43
D	8.43	J	8.57
E	8.43	K	1.71
F	8.43	L	2.43

ROW HEIGHTS							
Row	*Height*	*Row*	*Height*	*Row*	*Height*	*Row*	*Height*
1	13	15	13	29	13	43	13
2	13	16	13	30	13	44	13
3	16	17	13	31	13	45	6
4	13	18	13	32	13	46	13
5	16	19	13	33	13	47	16
6	6	20	13	34	6	48	4
7	16	21	13	35	13	49	13
8	13	22	13	36	16	50	13
9	13	23	6	37	5	51	4
10	13	24	13	38	13	52	13
11	6	25	16	39	6	53	13
12	13	26	6	40	13	54	4
13	16	27	13	41	13	55	13
14	6	28	4	42	13	56	13

(continued)

Figure 10-4. *continued*

KEY CELL FORMATS			
Cell	***Number***	***Alignment***	***Font***
B3	General	General	Helv 12, Bold
L3	General	Right	Helv 12, Bold
C5	General	General	Helv 12, Bold
J8	#,##0	General	Helv 10
J9	$#,##0.00	General	Helv 10
J10	$#,##0	General	Helv 10
G16:J16	General	Right	Helv 10, Bold
G15	General	General	Helv 8
J27	General	Right	Helv 10, Bold
J52	0.0%	General	Helv 10

Figure 10-5. Return-on-Investment Analysis Using the Du Pont Chart

A chart using the well-known Du Pont formula to illustrate return on investment. Saved as DUPONT.XLS.

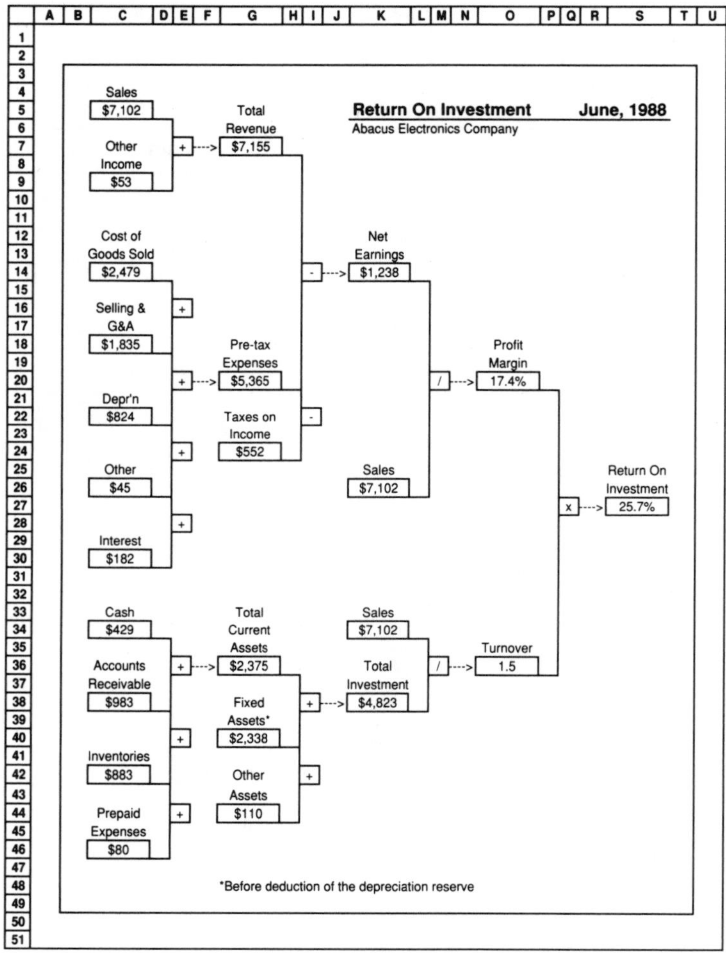

(continued)

Figure 10-5. *continued*

COLUMN WIDTHS							
Column	***Width***	***Column***	***Width***	***Column***	***Width***	***Column***	***Width***
A	3.33	G	8	M	2	S	8
B	3	H	2	N	3	T	3
C	8	I	2	O	8	U	3.33
D	2	J	3	P	2		
E	2	K	7.83	Q	2		
F	3	L	2	R	3		

KEY FORMULAS	
Cell	***Formula***
S5	=TEXT(DATE(88,6,30),"mmmm, yyyy") This text formula allows the date to extend across several columns.
F7	----> This arrow contains a space, four dashes, and a greater-than symbol.
M20	="/" The / character indicates division. I used this character because most printers won't print the standard division symbol (÷). As an alternative, you can leave this cell blank and enter the standard division symbol by hand.
G7	=C5+C9
C18	=$K$66+$K$65
G20	=SUM(C14:C30)
G36	=SUM(C34:C46)
K14	=$G$7–$G$20–$G$24
O20	=$K$14/$K$26
O36	=$K$34/$K$38
S27	=$O$20*$O$36 Enter these formulas as shown.

(continued)

Figure 10-5. *continued*

KEY CELL FORMATS			
Cell	*Number*	*Alignment*	*Font*
C5:E9	$#,##0	Center	Helv 8
C13	General	Center	Helv 8
C14	$#,##0	Center	Helv 8
E16	$#,##0	Center	Helv 8
O20	0.0%	Center	Helv 8
K5	$#,##0	General	Helv 10, Bold
S5	General	Right	Helv 10, Bold
K6	$#,##0	General	Helv 8

Figure 10-6. Data for the Du Pont Return-on-Investment Chart

A spreadsheet containing data for creating the Du Pont chart shown in Figure 10-5.

Row	Income	Oct-86	Assets	Oct-85
53				
54				
55	**Data for Du Pont Return-On-Investment Chart**			**FY, 1986**
56				
57	**Income**	**Oct-86**	**Assets**	**Oct-85**
58	Sales	7,102	Cash	429
59	Other Income	53	Accounts Receivable	983
60	Total Revenue	7,155	Inventories	883
61			Prepaid Expenses	80
62	Cost of Goods Sold	2,479	Total Current Assets	2,375
63	Gross Profit	4,676		
64			Fixed Assets	2,338
65	General & Admin	798	Less Accumulated Depreciation	876
66	Marketing & Sales	1,037	Net Fixed Assets	1,462
67	Depreciation Expense	824		
68	Other Operating Expenses	45		
69	Total Operating Expenses	2,704	Other Assets	110
70				
71	Interest Expense	182	Total Assets	3,947
72	Taxes On Income	552		
73				
74	Net Earnings	1,238		
75				
76				

Figure 10-7. Budget Variances by Department in a Bar Graph

A budget variance report by department that uses text formulas to generate bar graphs.

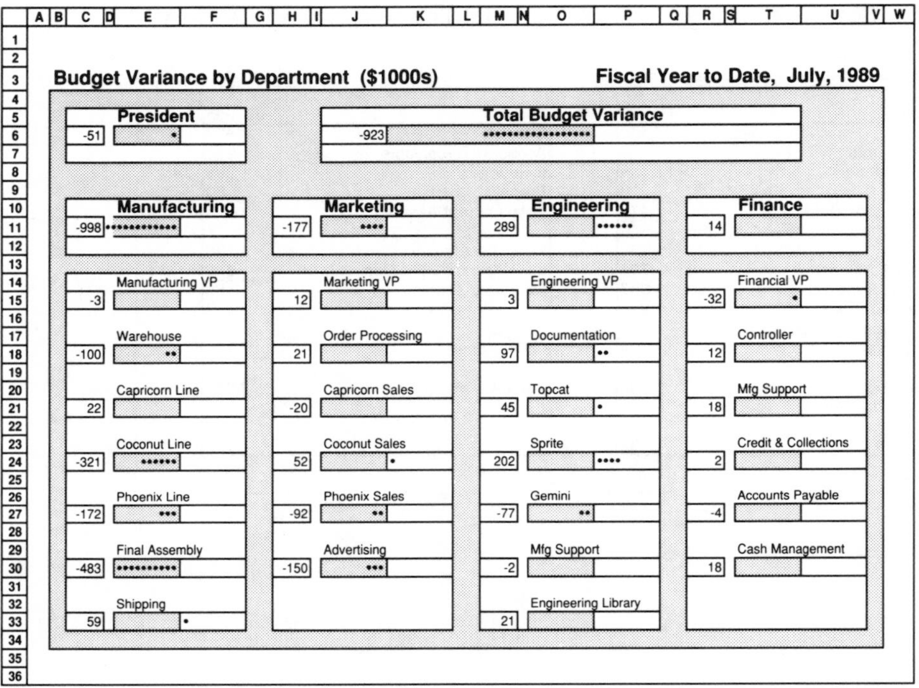

COLUMN WIDTHS							
Column	***Width***	***Column***	***Width***	***Column***	***Width***	***Column***	***Width***
A	2.33	G	3	M	4.5	S	0.82
B	1.5	H	4.5	N	0.82	T	8.5
C	4.5	I	0.82	O	8.5	U	8.5
D	0.82	J	8.5	P	8.5	V	1.5
E	8.5	K	8.5	Q	3		
F	8.5	L	3	R	4.5		

(continued)

Figure 10-7. *continued*

KEY FORMULAS

Cell	*Formula*
V3	**="Fiscal Year to Date, "&TEXT(DATE(89,7,1),"mmmm, yyyy")** Enter the date of the report in this formula.
E6 F6	**=IF(C6>=0,"",REPT(Symbol,ROUND(ABS(C6)/Scale,0)))** **=IF(C6<=0,"",REPT(Symbol,ROUND(ABS(C6)/Scale,0)))** These formulas are virtually identical. The first returns a certain number of graph symbols when the value in cell C6 is negative; the other returns the symbols for a positive value. To draw a graph, the REPT function returns the character defined by Symbol a certain number of times. This number is defined by the absolute value of cell C6 divided by the scaling value and rounded to the nearest whole number. To change the graph symbol to, say, a dollar sign, simply change the range definition for the name Symbol to ="$". To make all the graphs proportionally larger or smaller, simply decrease or increase the scaling value. This value specifies the amount that each graph symbol represents. For example, because the figure uses a scaling value of 50, each symbol represents a variance of $50,000. After you enter these formulas, copy them to all departments shown.
O6 P6	**=IF(J6>=0,"",REPT(Symbol,ROUND(ABS(J6)/Scale,0)))** **=IF(J6<=0,"",REPT(Symbol,ROUND(ABS(J6)/Scale,0)))** Because the total budget variance requires more room for its graph, you enter these formulas farther from the value you are graphing.
J6	**=$C$6+$C$11+$H$11+$M$11+$R$11** Total budget variance is equal to the variances incurred by the president and by each department.
C11	**=SUM(C13:C34)** The total manufacturing variance equals the sum of all manufacturing departments. Copy this formula to the right as needed.

(continued)

Figure 10-7. *continued*

RANGE NAMES	
Name	***Formula***
Scale	**=50** This scaling number determines the value that each bar in the graph represents. Here, each bar represents a variance of $50,000.
Symbol	**=CHAR(128)** This range specifies the symbol printed in the graph. Here, I've specified ASCII character 128, which appears as a dot when printed on my printer in the Helv font.

KEY CELL FORMATS			
Cell	***Number***	***Alignment***	***Font***
Spread-sheet	**Assign Font 1 as Helv 8.**		
B3	**General**	**General**	**Helv 12, Bold**
V3	**General**	**Right**	**Helv 12, Bold**
E5	**General**	**General**	**Helv 10, Bold**
C6	**#,##0**	**General**	**Helv 8**
E6	**General**	**Right**	**Helv 10, Bold**
F6	**General**	**Left**	**Helv 10, Bold**
O6	**General**	**Right**	**Helv 10, Bold**
P6	**General**	**Left**	**Helv 10, Bold**
E14	**General**	**General**	**Helv 8**

Figure 10-8. Monthly Profits by Sales Dollar and Contribution Margin

A spreadsheet that provides quick estimates of the profits or losses your company would sustain under various combinations of sales volume, contribution margin, and fixed costs. Saved as MO_PROF.XLS.

	A	B	C	D	E	F	G	H	I
1									
2									
3	**Monthly Profits by Sales Dollar**								
4	**And Contribution Margin**								
5	**With Fixed Costs Equal to $60,000**							**July 31, 1989**	
6		**Contribution Margin**							
7	**Sales**	**30%**	**35%**	**40%**	**45%**	**50%**	**55%**	**60%**	
8	$100,000	(30,000)	(25,000)	(20,000)	(15,000)	(10,000)	(5,000)	0	
9	$110,000	(27,000)	(21,500)	(16,000)	(10,500)	(5,000)	500	6,000	
10	$120,000	(24,000)	(18,000)	(12,000)	(6,000)	0	6,000	12,000	
11	$130,000	(21,000)	(14,500)	(8,000)	(1,500)	5,000	11,500	18,000	
12	$140,000	(18,000)	(11,000)	(4,000)	3,000	10,000	17,000	24,000	
13	$150,000	(15,000)	(7,500)	0	7,500	15,000	22,500	30,000	
14	$160,000	(12,000)	(4,000)	4,000	12,000	20,000	28,000	36,000	
15	$170,000	(9,000)	(500)	8,000	16,500	25,000	33,500	42,000	
16	$180,000	(6,000)	3,000	12,000	21,000	30,000	39,000	48,000	
17	$190,000	(3,000)	6,500	16,000	25,500	35,000	44,500	54,000	
18	$200,000	0	10,000	20,000	30,000	40,000	50,000	60,000	
19	$210,000	3,000	13,500	24,000	34,500	45,000	55,500	66,000	
20									
21	**Display Control**				**Assumption**				
22		Beginning	Growth		Fixed Costs		$60,000		
23	Sales	$100,000	$10,000						
24	Margin	30%	5%						
25									
26									

(continued)

Figure 10-8. *continued*

KEY FORMULAS	
Cell	***Formula***
A5	**="With Fixed Costs Equal to "&TEXT($G$22,"$#,###")** This text formula displays the amount of fixed costs as part of the label.
H5	**=TEXT(DATE(89,7,31),"mmmm d, yyyy")** This text formula displays the date across several columns.
B7 **C7**	**=$B$24** **=B7+$C$24** Copy the second formula to the right as needed.
A8 **A9**	**=$B$23** **=A8+$C$23** Copy the second formula down its column.
B8	**=B$7*$A8–$G$22** Profits equal the contribution margin times sales minus fixed costs. Copy this formula to the schedule as needed.

KEY CELL FORMATS			
Cell	***Number***	***Alignment***	***Font***
A3:A5	**General**	**Left**	**Helv 10, Bold**
H5	**General**	**Right**	**Helv 10, Bold**
E6	**0%**	**Center**	**Helv 10, Bold**
B7:H7	**0%**	**Center**	**Helv 10, Bold**
A8:A19	**$#,##0 ;($#,##0)**	**General**	**Helv 10**
B8	**#,##0 ;[Red](#,##0)**	**General**	**Helv 10**
B23:C23	**$#,##0**	**General**	**Helv 10**
B24:C24	**0%**	**General**	**Helv 10**

Figure 10-9. Break-Even Analysis with Regression

A spreadsheet that generates the data plotted by the break-even chart in Figure 10-10. Saved as BE_REGR.XLS.

	A	B	C	D	E	F	G
1							
2							
3	**Break-Even Analysis with Regression**					**June, 1990**	
4				Total	Fixed	Regr	
5	Date	Sales	Profits	Costs	Costs	Tot Csts	
6							
7		0			38	38	
8	Jan-90	91	(6)	97	38	98	
9	Feb-90	118	0	118	38	116	
10	Mar-90	132	12	120	38	125	
11	Apr-90	142	6	136	38	131	
12	May-90	168	21	147	38	148	
13	Jun-90	178	23	155	38	155	
14		200			38	169	
15							
16	Variable Cost as a Percentage of Sales					66%	
17							
18							

KEY FORMULAS

Cell	*Formula*
F3	**=TEXT(MAX(A6:A15),"mmmm, yyyy")** This formula returns, as date text, the most recent date entered into column A.
A8 A9	**01/01/90** **=DATE(YEAR(A8),MONTH(A8)+1,1)** Copy the formula down the column as needed. When you update this schedule monthly, insert a row beneath the last month's values, copy the last month's formulas into the new row, and then enter your new values in the remaining columns.
D8	**=B8–C8** Total costs for the month equal sales minus profits.
E7 E8	**=A** **=E7** The formula in cell E7 references the range name A, which contains the calculation of fixed costs. The other formula repeats this value. Copy the formula in cell E8 down the column as needed.

(continued)

Figure 10-9. *continued*

KEY FORMULAS–continued	
Cell	*Formula*
F7	**=A+B*B7** The total cost line estimated by the regression formula equals the fixed costs estimated by the formula (A) plus the variable costs (B) times sales. Copy the formula down the column as needed.
F16	**=B** The range name B defines the variable costs.

RANGE NAMES	
Name	*Formula*
Date	**=$F$3** The chart refers to this date.
Input	**=$A$6:$F$15** This range serves as a reference for the following dynamic range definitions.
Sales **ActCosts** **Fixed** **RegCosts**	**=INDEX(Input,2,2):INDEX(Input,ROWS(Input)–1,2)** **=INDEX(Input,2,4):INDEX(Input,ROWS(Input)–1,4)** **=INDEX(Input,2,5):INDEX(Input,ROWS(Input)–1,5)** **=INDEX(Input,2,6):INDEX(Input,ROWS(Input)–1,6)** Here's how to enter these definitions quickly: 1. Enter the first definition into any cell as an array formula. (Remember to use Ctrl-Shift Enter.) By entering the formula in a cell, you can view the entire formula definition in your formula bar, something that isn't otherwise possible. 2. Copy the formula to the clipboard. To do so, highlight the entire formula in the formula bar, press Ctrl-Ins to copy the formula to the clipboard, and press Esc to return to the Ready mode. 3. To define the range name Sales, first choose Formula Define Name, specify Sales, press Tab to highlight the Refers To box, choose Edit Paste with your mouse to copy the array formula into the Refers To box, and then press Enter. 4. To define the remaining names, first choose Formula Define Name and select the name Sales from the list in the dialog box. Then change the Sales range name to the name of another range you want to define, edit the range-definition formula as needed, and press Enter to accept the definition of the new range name. This process sounds complex, but after you go through it once, it goes quickly.

(continued)

Figure 10-9. *continued*

RANGE NAMES—continued	
Name	*Formula*
X Y	=INDEX(Input,3,2):INDEX(Input,ROWS(Input)–2,2) =INDEX(Input,3,4):INDEX(Input,ROWS(Input)–2,4) You can use a variation of the previous process to define the Y range name. First, enter the X range name as shown. But before you press Enter, highlight the complete definition in the Refers To box and press Ctrl-Ins to copy the range definition to the clipboard. Press Enter. Define the range name Y as you normally would, but when you click on the Refers To box, choose Edit Paste to copy the X definition from the clipboard. Edit this formula as needed and then press Enter.
A B	=INDEX(LINEST(Y,X),2) =INDEX(LINEST(Y,X),1) These formulas use the standard definition of LINEST to calculate the intercept (A) and the slope (B) for the regression line. In the graph, the intercept equals fixed costs and the slope equals the variable cost per dollar of sales.

KEY CELL FORMATS			
Cell	*Number*	*Alignment*	*Font*
A3	General	Left	Helv 10, Bold
F3	General	Right	Helv 10, Bold
A4:F5	General	Center	Helv 10
A6:A15	mmm-yy	Center	Helv 10
B6:F15	#,##0 ;(#,##0)	General	Helv 10

Figure 10-10. Break-Even Chart

A chart that plots break-even data from the spreadsheet in Figure 10-9.

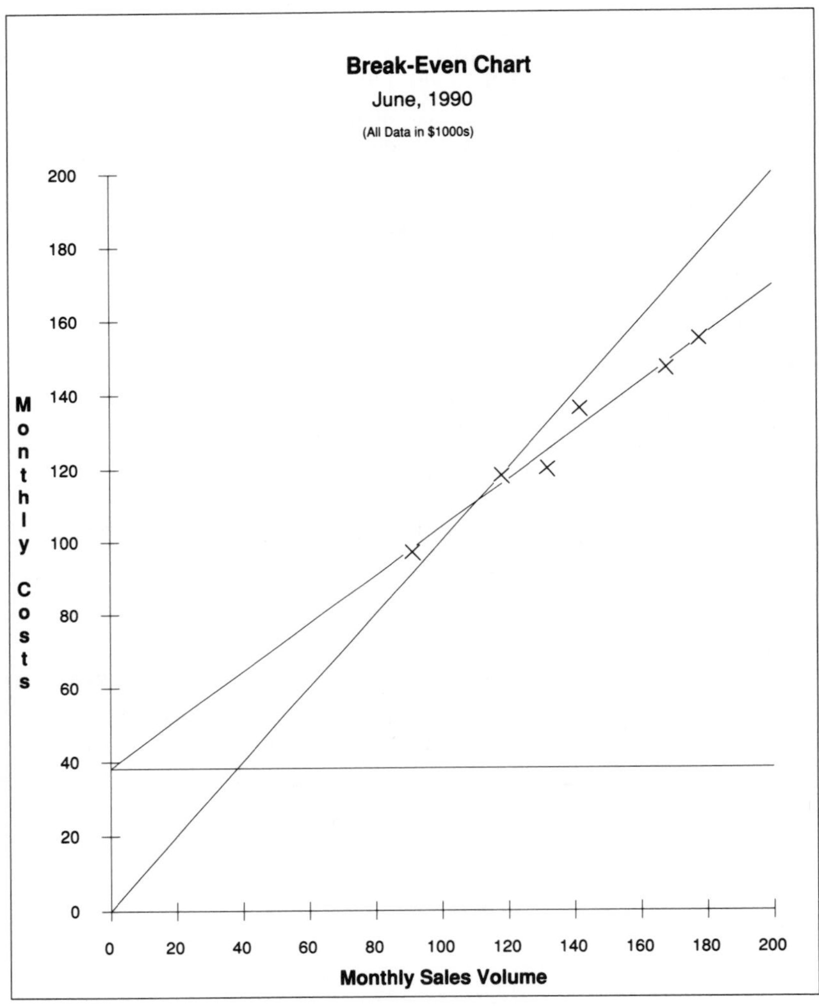

Figure 10-11. Break-Even Analysis with Multiple Product Lines

A report that offers detailed assumptions that you can adjust to calculate monthly profits.

	A	B	C	D	E	F	G	H	I
1									
2									
3	**Break-Even Analysis with Multiple Product Lines**						**November, 1989**		
4									
5	**Monthly Fixed Costs**								
6	Fixed Manufacturing			$11,250		**Display Control**			
7	General & Administrative			$9,000		Fixed-Cost Growth		$1,000	
8	Marketing & Sales			$8,500		Cont Mrgn Change		2%	
9	Product Development			$4,300		Round to nearest		$250	
10	Interest			$2,950					
11									
12	Total			$36,000					
13									
14									
15	**Sales Assumptions by Product Line**								
16	Products:		**Bolts**	**Nails**	**Clamps**	**Hinges**	**Total**		
17	Unit Sales--Pounds		300,000	425,000	60,000	25,000			
18	Price Per Pound		$0.10	$0.05	$0.20	$0.15			
19	Total Sales		$30,000	$21,250	$12,000	$3,750	$67,000		
20	Sales Mix		45%	32%	18%	6%	100%		
21									
22									
23	**Variable Cost Percentages by Product Line**								
24									
25	Variable Mfg		33%	23%	55%	45%	34%		
26	Mfg Variances		8%	3%	1%	7%	5%		
27	Freight		5%	2%	5%	3%	4%		
28	Sales Commissions		3%	2%	5%	3%	3%		
29	Advertising Co-op		2%	0%	0%	1%	1%		
30									
31	Total Variable Costs		51%	30%	66%	59%	47%		
32	Contribution Margin		49%	70%	34%	41%	53%		
33									
34									
35	**Profits With Selected Costs & Margins When Sales Equal $67,000**								
36	**Fixed**	**Contribution Margins**							
37	**Costs**	**47%**	**49%**	**51%**	**53%**	**55%**	**57%**	**59%**	
38	$31,000	500	1,750	3,250	4,500	5,750	7,250	8,500	
39	$32,000	(500)	750	2,250	3,500	4,750	6,250	7,500	
40	$33,000	(1,500)	(250)	1,250	2,500	3,750	5,250	6,500	
41	$34,000	(2,500)	(1,250)	250	1,500	2,750	4,250	5,500	
42	$35,000	(3,500)	(2,250)	(750)	500	1,750	3,250	4,500	
43	$36,000	(4,500)	(3,250)	(1,750)	(500)	750	2,250	3,500	
44	$37,000	(5,500)	(4,250)	(2,750)	(1,500)	(250)	1,250	2,500	
45	$38,000	(6,500)	(5,250)	(3,750)	(2,500)	(1,250)	250	1,500	
46	$39,000	(7,500)	(6,250)	(4,750)	(3,500)	(2,250)	(750)	500	
47	$40,000	(8,500)	(7,250)	(5,750)	(4,500)	(3,250)	(1,750)	(500)	
48	$41,000	(9,500)	(8,250)	(6,750)	(5,500)	(4,250)	(2,750)	(1,500)	
49									
50									

(continued)

Figure 10-11. *continued*

KEY FORMULAS	
Cell	***Formula***
H3	**=TEXT(DATE(89,11,1),"mmmm, yyyy")** This formula displays the date across several columns.
D12	**=SUM(D6:D11)**
C19 C20	**=C18*C17** **=C19/$G$19** Copy these formulas to the right as needed.
G25	**=SUM(C25:F25*$C$20:$F$20)** The Variable Manufacturing cost percentage for the company as a whole is equal to the sum of the cost percentage for each product line times that product line's sales mix. Enter this array formula and copy it down the column as needed.
C31	**=SUM(C24:C30)** Copy this formula to the right as needed.
C32	**=1–C31** The contribution margin is the complement of the variable cost percentage. Copy it to the right.
A35	**="Profits With Selected Costs & Margins When Sales Equal "& TEXT($G$19,"$#,###")** This text formula displays the assumed selling price.
B37 C37	**=$G$32–3*$H$8** **=B37+$H$8** The first formula calculates the beginning margin value that displays the current margin in the center of the schedule. Copy the second formula to the right.
A38 A39	**=$D$12–5*$H$7** **=A38+$H$7** The first formula calculates the fixed cost value that displays current fixed costs in the center of the schedule. Copy the second formula downward.
B38	**=$H$9*ROUND((B$37*$G$19–$A38)/$H$9,0)** To calculate profit, multiply the contribution margin by the sales value and subtract fixed costs. To round this amount to the nearest value in cell H9, divide the profit by H9, round the result, and then multiply by H9. Copy this formula to the remainder of the schedule as needed.

(continued)

Figure 10-11. *continued*

KEY CELL FORMATS			
Cell	*Number*	*Alignment*	*Font*
A3	General	General	Helv 10, Bold
H3	General	Right	Helv 10, Bold
D6:D12	$#,##0 ;($#,##0)	General	Helv 10
C17:G17	#,##0	General	Helv 10
C18:G18	$#,##0.00 ;($#,##0.00)	General	Helv 10
C19:G19	$#,##0	General	Helv 10
C20:G20	0%	Center	Helv 10
C24:G30	0%	General	Helv 10
C37:H37	0%	Center	Helv 10, Bold
A38:A48	$#,##0 ;($#,##0)	General	Helv 10
B38:H48	#,##0 ;[Red](#,##0) This format displays negative values in red, which makes the division between profit and loss easier to see when viewed on your monitor.	General	Helv 10

Figure 10-12. Break-Even Sales with Selected Costs and Margins

A report that calculates the break-even points for each combination of fixed costs and contribution margins.

	A	B	C	D	E	F	G	H	I
51									
52									
53	Break-Even Sales with Selected Costs and Margins								
54	Fixed	Contribution Margins							
55	Costs	47%	49%	51%	53%	55%	57%	59%	
56	$31,000	66,000	63,250	60,750	58,500	56,250	54,500	52,500	
57	$32,000	68,000	65,250	62,750	60,500	58,250	56,250	54,250	
58	$33,000	70,250	67,250	64,750	62,250	60,000	58,000	56,000	
59	$34,000	72,250	69,500	66,750	64,250	61,750	59,750	57,750	
60	$35,000	74,500	71,500	68,750	66,000	63,750	61,500	59,250	
61	$36,000	76,500	73,500	70,500	68,000	65,500	63,250	61,000	
62	$37,000	78,750	75,500	72,500	69,750	67,250	65,000	62,750	
63	$38,000	80,750	77,500	74,500	71,750	69,000	66,750	64,500	
64	$39,000	83,000	79,500	76,500	73,500	71,000	68,500	66,000	
65	$40,000	85,000	81,750	78,500	75,500	72,750	70,250	67,750	
66	$41,000	87,250	83,750	80,500	77,250	74,500	72,000	69,500	
67									
68									

KEY FORMULAS

Cell	*Formula*
B55	**=$G$32–3*$H$8**
C55	**=B55+$H$8**
	Copy these formulas from row 37 of the report in Figure 10-11.
A56	**=$D$12–5*$H$7**
A57	**=A56+$H$7**
	Copy these formulas from the report in Figure 10-11.
B56	**=$H$9*ROUND(($A56/B$55)/$H$9,0)**
	Break-even sales equal those sales necessary to cover fixed costs. They are therefore equal to fixed costs divided by the contribution margin. This formula rounds the result to the nearest value in cell H9. Copy it to the remainder of the schedule.

Figure 10-13. Break-Even Rules of Thumb

A spreadsheet that provides rules of thumb that you can use to estimate the effect that a change in fixed or variable costs will have on your profits and break-even point.

	A	B	C	D	E	F	G
1							
2							
3	**Break-Even Rules of Thumb**					**August, 1989**	
4							
5							
6	**Changes in Contribution Margins**						
7							
8	With a change of 1% in the contribution margin of the following products. . .						
9	Product	**Shoes**	**Socks**	**Hats**	**Coats**	**Total**	
10							
11	. . . Our company-wide break-even point changes by:						
12	With a 1% increase:	($510)	($340)	($680)	($170)	($1,680)	
13	With a 1% decrease:	$520	$340	$690	$170	$1,750	
14							
15	. . . Our level of sales needed to maintain current profits changes by:						
16	With a 1% increase:	($1,380)	($920)	($1,840)	($460)	($4,550)	
17	With a 1% decrease:	$1,400	$930	$1,870	$460	$4,720	
18							
19	. . . And our profits increase or decrease by:						
20	With any change in margin:	$750	$500	$1,000	$250	$2,500	
21							
22							
23	**Changes in Fixed Costs**						
24	Each $1.00 increase or decrease in fixed costs changes our profits by $1.00						
25	and changes both our break-even point and stay-even sales level by $1.85.						
26							
27							
28	**Assumptions**						
29	Mix	30%	20%	40%	10%	100%	
30	Product	**Shoes**	**Socks**	**Hats**	**Coats**	**Total**	
31	Sales	$75,000	$50,000	$100,000	$25,000	$250,000	
32	Variable Cost of Sales	$15,000	$20,000	$60,000	$20,000	$115,000	
33	Contribution to Fixed Costs	$60,000	$30,000	$40,000	$5,000	$135,000	
34	Contribution Margin	80%	60%	40%	20%	54%	
35	Fixed Costs					$50,000	
36							
37	**Calculations**						
38	Total Profit					$85,000	
39	Break-Even Point					$92,593	
40							
41	**Display Control**						
42	Round results to nearest	$10					
43							
44							

(continued)

Figure 10-13. *continued*

KEY FORMULAS	
Cell	***Formula***
F3	**=TEXT(DATE(89,8,1),"mmmm, yyyy")** Displaying the date as next allows it to cover several columns.
F6	**0.01** Occasionally, you might want to report on a change in the contribution margin in excess of 1 percent. The value of the change therefore appears as a parameter in this cell. Hiding a value like this isn't usually a good idea because it makes the spreadsheet more difficult to support. However, this spreadsheet contains only one hidden cell and all formulas that use this cell refer to it directly. Therefore, the hidden cell is easy to find and understand.
A8	**="With a change of "&TEXT($F$6,"#%")&" in the contribution margin of the following products. . ."** This label adjusts as you change the percentage in cell F6.
A12 **A13**	**="With a "&TEXT($F$6,"#%")&" increase:"** **="With a "&TEXT($F$6,"#%")&" decrease:"** Copy these formulas to cells A16 and A17.
B12 **B13**	**=RoundAmt*ROUND((Fixed/($F$34+$F$6*B$29)–BreakEven)/RoundAmt,0)** **=RoundAmt*ROUND((Fixed/($F$34–$F$6*B$29)–BreakEven)/RoundAmt,0)** To calculate the break-even point, divide fixed costs by the contribution margin. To calculate the change in the break-even point from a change in the contribution margin, calculate the new break-even point and subtract the old break-even point. Here, you divide fixed costs by the old contribution margin, plus or minus the change in the margin. This change in the margin equals the assumed change in the product's margin times the fraction of total sales represented by this product (the sales mix percentage). Finally, you round the result to the nearest value in the RoundAmt range. Copy this formula to the right as needed.
B16 **B17**	**=RoundAmt*ROUND(((Fixed+TotProfit)/($F$34+B$29*$F$6)–$F$31)/RoundAmt,0)** **=RoundAmt*ROUND(((Fixed+TotProfit)/($F$34–B$29*$F$6)–$F$31)/RoundAmt,0)** These formulas follow the same reasoning as the previous pair. Here, however, the formulas calculate the change in sales necessary to cover both fixed costs and the current amount of profits. Copy the formulas to the right as needed.
B20	**=$F$6*B31** The change in profits from a change in margin is equal to the amount of the change times the amount of the sales. Copy this formula to the right as needed.

(continued)

Figure 10-13. *continued*

KEY FORMULAS–continued	
Cell	***Formula***
A25	**="and changes both our break-even point and stay-even sales level by "& TEXT(1/$F$34,"$#.00")&"."** The break-even point equals fixed costs divided by the contribution margin. The change in break-even sales is equal to the change in fixed costs divided by the margin. Here, within the TEXT function, you divide the $1 change by the margin. The same reasoning applies to the stay-even sales level, which is the amount of sales necessary to maintain current profits.
B29 **B33** **B34**	**=B31/$F$31** **=B31–B32** **=B33/B31** Copy these formulas to the right as needed.
F38	**=F33–F35** Profit equals the contribution margin minus fixed costs.
F39	**=F35/F34** The break-even point in sales equals fixed costs divided by the contribution margin.

RANGE NAMES	
Name	***Formula***
Fixed **TotProfit** **BreakEven** **RoundAmt**	**=$F$35** **=$F$38** **=$F$39** **=$B$42** Define these names as shown.

(continued)

Figure 10-13. *continued*

KEY CELL FORMATS			
Cell	***Number***	***Alignment***	***Font***
A3	General	General	Helv 10, Bold
F3	General	Right	Helv 10, Bold
F6	;;	Center	Helv 10
B9:F9	General	Center	Helv 10, Bold
B12:F20	$#,##0 ;($#,##0)	General	Helv 10
B29:F29	0%	Center	Helv 10

Appendix A

Converting Text Files to Data

For several years I worked for a company that owned one XT clone, which we used for running accounting software and spreadsheets. Unfortunately, our accounting software couldn't create files the spreadsheet program could read. So, every month, we printed reports from the accounting system and then rekeyed them into the spreadsheet. Today that extra work isn't necessary. You can load any report into Microsoft Excel.

Of course, you may never have thought about entering accounting reports into spreadsheets. If not, consider the possibility. Microsoft Excel is certainly more flexible than any report generator you might have for your accounting system. In most ways, it's more powerful, and you probably know it better. If your computer has enough memory, the spreadsheet is large enough as well. With its 16,384 rows, Microsoft Excel can hold a document of more than 270 pages. (Hard to believe? Well, consider that 16,384 divided by 60 lines per page equals 273.07 pages.)

The easiest way to enter an accounting report into Microsoft Excel is to first save it as a WKS or WK1 file. You can save reports in this fashion with many accounting software packages. After you save the file, it's easy to open it in Microsoft Excel. Simply choose File Open, specify *.WK* as the filename (using the correct path), and then select the file you want to open from the list of files in the dialog box. When you choose OK, Microsoft Excel opens the file, converting the WKS or WK1 file to an XLS format.

If your accounting software won't save a report as a WKS or WK1 file, you must take two steps to load accounting reports into your spreadsheet. First, you must save your report as a text file. Second, within the spreadsheet, you must *parse* the text file—that is, change it back into numeric data.

STEP ONE: SAVE YOUR ACCOUNTING REPORTS AS TEXT

Many accounting software packages let you save reports as text. The terminology your program's documentation uses to describe this process might not be the same as the terms I use, however. Some programs might refer to ASCII files. Others might describe how to print a report to disk. But no matter what terminology your documentation uses to describe this process, the result is the same: a text file.

If your accounting software can't create a text file, you still have an option: Buy PrintQ, published by Software Directions, Inc., of Randolph, NJ. This inexpensive program ($89 in mid-1988) not only spools reports to your hard disk for printing at a more convenient time, it also lets you print any spooled report to disk in a text-file format. It is the only program I have found that can do this.

STEP TWO: PARSE THE TEXT FILE

Figure A-1 shows the first few lines of a general ledger trial balance that was printed to disk and then opened as a text file. Although this spreadsheet appears to contain labels, dates, and values, it doesn't. It consists entirely of text in column A. Before you can use this spreadsheet for analysis, therefore, you must parse the data.

	A	B	C	D	E	F	G	H
1								
2								
3			Steamy Springs Water Co.					
4			Trial Balance					
5			03-01-88					
6								
7					12-31-87	03-01-88	Net	
8	AccountAccount Title				Balance	Balance	Change	
9								
10	1001 Cash in Bank				12635.22	10555.21	-2080.01	
11	1002 Petty Cash				500.00	500.00	0.00	
12	1201 Accounts Receivable				402332.98	410879.54	8546.56	
13	1202 Allowance for Dbtfl Accts				-8921.57	-7921.57	1000.00	
14	1310 Raw Materials Inventory				235008.08	244223.89	9215.81	

Figure A-1. *The first few lines of a general ledger trial balance that was printed to disk and opened as a text file. The spreadsheet's gridlines are turned off and its Font 1 is set to a monospaced font.*

The *Microsoft Excel Reference Guide* makes parsing sound deceptively easy. All you must do, it says, is highlight the column of text you want to parse, choose Data Parse, select Guess, modify the guess to fit your data, and then choose OK. But in practice, the guess can be far wrong and the necessary modifications won't be obvious.

There *is* a simple method, however—one that requires no guessing or trial and error. To parse a spreadsheet, simply take the steps listed at the top of page 541.

1. Open the text file.
2. Assign a monospaced font.
3. Create a parsing gauge.
4. Parse the document.
5. Clean up the report.
6. Save and document the parsing gauge. (Optional.)

Let's take a look at each of these steps in more detail.

1. Open the Text File

After you create a text file of a report, you can open the file in Microsoft Excel. To do so, use the same approach you would use to open any other file. Take care, however, to specify the proper extension for the filename. For example, if the file is MYFILE.PRN, choose the File Open command, enter the filename **.PRN* (preceded by the correct path), choose OK, and then select *MYFILE.PRN* from the list of files shown.

2. Assign a Monospaced Font

When you first open this spreadsheet, you might wonder if something went wrong. Although the data looks complete, it also looks jumbled, as in Figure A-2.

	A	B	C	D	E	F	G	H
1								
2								
3	Steamy Springs Water Co.							
4	Trial Balance							
5	03-01-88							
6								
7	12-31-87 03-01-88 Net							
8	AccountAccount Title Balance Balance Change							
9								
10	1001 Cash in Bank 12635.22 10555.21 -2080.01							
11	1002 Petty Cash 500.00 500.00 0.00							
12	1201 Accounts Receivable 402332.98 410879.54 8546.56							
13	1202 Allowance for Dbtfl Accts -8921.57 -7921.57 1000.00							
14	1310 Raw Materials Inventory 235008.08 244223.89 9215.81							

Figure A-2. *A spreadsheet that demonstrates how proportional spacing jumbles text files opened as spreadsheets. The only difference between this spreadsheet and the one in Figure A-1 is that Font 1 in this spreadsheet is assigned Helv 10.*

The reason for this appearance is that Microsoft Excel's default font is Helv, which uses proportional spacing. Thus, the data does not line up properly when the report is opened as a text file. Proper alignment of the report depends on use of a monospaced font, one in which all characters are the same width. To make the report look the way you expect, select one of the four monospaced fonts in Microsoft Excel: Courier, Pica, System, and Terminal. Choose the Format Font command, choose the Fonts button, and select any one of these four fonts. Assign your selection as font number 1, which is the default font for the entire spreadsheet. After you make your selection and choose OK, the spreadsheet displays the appropriate font. Figure A-1, for example, shows a general ledger trial balance that has been imported as text into Microsoft Excel and is displayed in a monospaced font.

3. Create a Parsing Gauge

When you specify the column of data to parse, choose Data Parse, and then select Guess, Microsoft Excel uses the first row to guess at how it should divide the text in the entire range into columns. Then the program provides you an opportunity to improve on this guess. But if you provide the correct information in the first row, the initial "guess" will be entirely accurate. I call this information the parsing gauge.

In the spreadsheet in Figure A-3, row 6 contains the actual parsing gauge. The range to parse is in row 14 through row 18. The parsing gauge is a string of text, contained entirely in column A, that displays an *x* wherever a new column begins. Although you can enter this text manually, generating it by using the formulas in rows 3 through 6 is easier.

First, adjust the width of each column in the spreadsheet to the widths required by the document. Notice column A in the spreadsheet in Figure A-3. Often, text files contain spaces for the left margin in the document. To eliminate these spaces, parse them into a column established for this purpose and then delete this column after you parse the document.

Next, insert six rows at the top of the document, as shown in the spreadsheet in the figure. Enter the formulas shown in the formula box for cells A3 and A4. Copy these formulas to the right side of your report, plus one column. (The additional column tells the Guess command where the data ends. Under some circumstances you will lose data in your rightmost column if you exclude this additional column.)

Enter a formula similar to the one shown for cell A5 in the formula box. The formula shown for this cell references each cell in row 4 that contains a formula. Enter the formula *=A5* into cell A6, as shown in the formula box, and then format the formulas as shown in the format box.

You must make minor adjustments to the parsing gauge in row 6 before you can use it. The formulas in rows 3 and 4 return numbers equal to the "width" of each column. However, the actual width is slightly wider than that returned by the formulas. Microsoft Excel uses this extra space to contain its vertical borders and gridlines. You must therefore compensate by increasing the numbers in row 3 where necessary to

	A	B	C	D	E	F	G	H
1								
2								
3	4	7	25	11	11	10	8	
4	x	x	x	x	x	x	x	
5	x x x x x x x							
6	x x x x x x x							
7	Steamy Springs Water Co.							
8	Trial Balance							
9	03-01-87							
10								
11	12-31-87 03-01-88 Net							
12	AccountAccount Title Balance Balance Change							
13								
14	1001 Cash in Bank 12635.22 10555.21 -2080.01							
15	1002 Petty Cash 500.00 500.00 0.00							
16	1201 Accounts Receivable 402332.98 410879.54 8546.56							
17	1202 Allowance for Dbtfl Accts -8921.57 -7921.57 1000.00							
18	1310 Raw Materials Inventory 235008.08 244223.89 9215.81							

KEY FORMULAS

Cell	*Formula*
A3	**=CELL("width",A4)** The formula calculates the approximate width of the column. Copy this formula to the right so that the last formula is one column beyond the rightmost of the report.
A4	**="x"&REPT(" ",A3–1)** This formula creates a text string equal in length to the cell width specified in cell A3. Copy the formula as you did the one in cell A3.
A5	**=A4&B4&C4&D4&E4&F4&G4** By concatenating the strings this way, the formula creates a single string in cell A5 that resembles the series of strings in row 4.
A6	**=A5** When the formula in this cell returns a parsing gauge that looks correct, turn this formula into a string value by pressing F2 (Edit), F9 (Calculate All), and Enter. Then choose the Data Parse command.

KEY CELL FORMATS

Cell	*Number*	*Alignment*	*Font*
A3:G6	**General**	**Left**	**Monospaced**
A7:A18	**General**	**General**	**Monospaced**

Figure A-3. *Rows 3 through 6 in the spreadsheet contain the formulas used to create the parsing gauge in cell A6. This gauge contains an* x *wherever a new column should begin.*

properly position the x's in rows 5 and 6. In the spreadsheet in Figure A-3, for example, the x's in columns E, F, and G are slightly to the left of the column border. Changing the value of cell D3 to 11 places the x's where they belong.

When the x's in rows 5 and 6 are positioned where you want each new spreadsheet column to begin, change the formula in cell A6 to its value. To do so, select cell A6, press F2 (Edit) and F9 (Calculate All), and then press Enter. You can generate the same result by changing the formula in cell A5 into its value. But because creating that formula took some effort, I hesitated to destroy my work so quickly. By using the formula in cell A6 as the parsing gauge, I can easily change the text back into a formula by entering the formula in cell A6 again.

4. Parse the Document

Before you choose the Data Parse command, highlight the column of data you want to parse, beginning with the parsing gauge in cell A6. To do so, select cell A6, press F8, which toggles on the Extend mode, and then select a cell in the last row in column A that you want to parse. If this is also the last row in your spreadsheet, here's a quick way to get there: Press Ctrl-End to extend the highlight to the bottom-right corner of the spreadsheet and then press Home to move the highlight to column A. Then, if you want to view the top of the range you've highlighted, hold down the Ctrl key and press the period key twice.

Now choose Data Parse. When you do so, you can see the left side of the parsing gauge displayed in the Parse Line dialog box. When you select Guess, brackets appear around the x's, as follows:

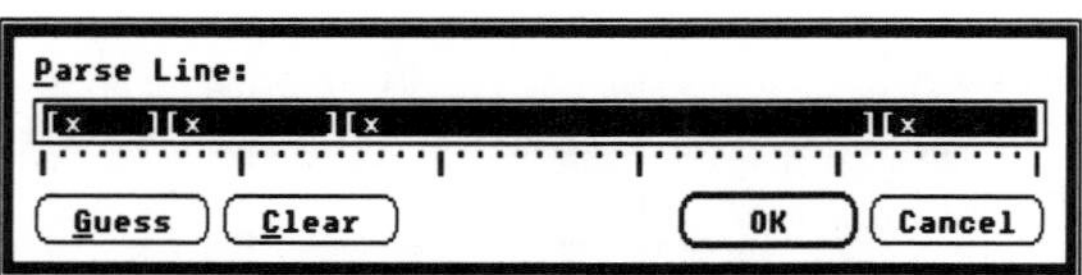

Then, when you choose OK, Microsoft Excel parses your data.

5. Clean Up the Report

Save your spreadsheet after Microsoft Excel has parsed your data. Then take a few minutes to clean up the following elements:

Excess rows and columns. Delete all rows at the top of the spreadsheet used by the parsing gauge. If you parsed the left margin of your report into column A, as shown in the spreadsheet in Figure A-3, delete this empty column.

Report titles. In most documents, the report titles extend across several columns. When the document is parsed, however, the title is parsed into each column it touches. For example, after parsing, cell C7 of the spreadsheet in Figure A-3 contained the label *Steamy Springs Wat* and cell D7 contained *er Co.*. You might need to edit report titles extensively. If this work is too extensive, you might want to create and use a parsing gauge for the heading as well as for the body of a document.

Number formats. Microsoft Excel properly formats percentages and currency values in a document. It formats other values as General. Therefore, to display these numbers properly, highlight the range you want to format, choose Format Number, and then choose the format that you want from the list.

Date formats. The parsing routine creates and formats dates, but only if no spaces exist between the date text and its left border. If spaces do exist, the date is displayed as text. In the spreadsheet in Figure A-3, for example, the dates in cells C9, D11, and E11 will remain as text. To convert cell C9 to a date serial number, enter *=DATEVALUE(TRIM(C7))* into cell C10 (which returns a date serial number), copy the value of cell C10 to cell C9 by choosing Edit Paste Special and selecting Values, format the date serial number as desired, and then erase cell C10.

Formulas. The Data Parse command converts text to values and text, but it doesn't create formulas. All numbers that appear to be the result of calculations in your document are therefore merely values. Where practical, substitute the appropriate formulas for these values. Doing so tests the accuracy of your report. In this way, you'll know you have problems with your data if the formulas return different numbers than the report originally displayed.

Fonts. After you parse a document, retaining the monospaced font is not particularly necessary. You can choose Format Font, choose the Fonts button, and select any font from the list.

Other. You may also need to adjust column widths, align column headings, change the way underlines are represented, or make other stylistic changes to your document. None of these tasks requires much work, however.

6. Save and Document the Parsing Gauge

After you turn an accounting report into a spreadsheet, you'll probably want to create a similar spreadsheet again. You can save yourself some time if you save each parsing gauge that you create. Then, when you want to parse the same report again, you need only copy the gauge into the spreadsheet that contains the data you want to parse.

One easy way to save the gauges is to save all of them in one spreadsheet, as shown in the spreadsheet in Figure A-4. Notice that because this spreadsheet uses proportional spacing, the *x*'s are much closer together than in the spreadsheet in Figure A-3. If you copy the gauge to a spreadsheet with a monospaced font, the *x*'s are positioned properly.

	A	B	C	D	E	F	G	H	I	J
1										
2										
3	**Parsing Gauges**									
4	**Steamy Springs Water Co.**									
5	Person	Report								
6	Resp	Name			Gauge					
7	Jeff	AR103	x x x x x x x x x x x							
8	Sue	GL101	x x x x x x							
9	Sue	GL102	x x x x x x x x x x							
10	Bob	GL103	x x x x x x x x xx x							
11	Jeff	Inv101	x x x x x x x x x							

Figure A-4. *A spreadsheet that stores parsing gauges used by several different people in an accounting department. After you create a parsing gauge for a specific report, you can use it for each new version of the report.*

PARSING COMPLEX REPORTS

The spreadsheet in Figure A-5 illustrates a complex report from an accounting system for attorneys. Like many accounting reports, this one alternates data of various types and overlapping lengths, making it impossible to say where column divisions for the entire spreadsheet should lie. As a consequence, this report appears to be nearly impossible to parse successfully.

Fortunately, one simple trick makes this report almost as easy to parse as the one in Figure A-1: Sort the text before you parse. When you do so, you generally find that the textual data sorts itself into uniform blocks of text that you can easily parse. Then, after you parse each block, simply sort the data back into its original sequence.

Here are the steps to take:

1. Insert a new column A. To do so, select a cell in column A and press Ctrl-Spacebar to highlight all of column A. Choose Edit Insert to insert a column.
2. Enter a data series in column A. After you sort your data, you need some method of sorting it back into its original order. To do so, you must first have created a column of sequence numbers. To create this column of numbers, enter the value *1* in cell A5, highlight column A from this cell to the bottom of the active area of your spreadsheet, and choose Data Series. The spreadsheet in Figure A-6 shows the top-left corner of the spreadsheet after this step.

	A	B	C	D	E	F	G	H	I
1									
2									
3	DATE: 07/31/87 DETAIL RECEIPT ALLOCATION REPORT PAGE: 1								
4	Steiner & Assoc TABS 3.3 Demo								
5	PRIMARY TIMEKEEPER: 1 TO 10 CATEGORY 1 TO 20								
6	------ MTD ----- ------ YTD ----- ------ TD ------ AMOUNT								
7	TIMEKEEPER BILLED PAID BILLED PAID BILLED PAID DUE								
8	---------- ------ ---- ------ ---- ------ ---- ------								
9	100.00M McBride/John RE: Miscellaneous work								
10	1 SRK 0.00 0.00 0.00 0.00 507.00 0.00 507.00								
11	---- ---- ---- ---- ------ ---- ------								
12	FEES 0.00 0.00 0.00 0.00 507.00 0.00 507.00								
13	COSTS 7.55 0.00 7.55 0.00 120.87 0.00 120.87								
14	FCHRG 154.79 0.00 154.79 0.00 154.79 0.00 154.79								
15	TOTAL 162.34 0.00 162.34 0.00 782.66 0.00 782.66								
16	BILLED WIP: 75.00								
17									
18	101.00M Barrett/Karen RE: Apartment management								
19	1 SRK 25.00 2.14 25.00 2.14 25.00 2.14 22.86								
20	2 SJM 559.00 47.86 559.00 47.86 559.00 47.86 511.14								
21	------ ----- ------ ----- ------ ----- ------								
22	FEES 584.00 50.00 584.00 50.00 584.00 50.00 534.00								
23	COSTS 134.75 0.00 134.75 0.00 134.75 0.00 134.75								
24	TOTAL 718.75 50.00 718.75 50.00 718.75 50.00 668.75								
25									
26	102.00M Richardson/Harold RE: Manage personal finances								
27	DATE: 07/31/87 DETAIL RECEIPT ALLOCATION REPORT PAGE: 2								
28	Steiner & Assoc TABS 3.3 Demo								
29	PRIMARY TIMEKEEPER: 1 TO 10 CATEGORY 1 TO 20								
30	------ MTD ----- ------ YTD ----- ------ TD ------ AMOUNT								
31	TIMEKEEPER BILLED PAID BILLED PAID BILLED PAID DUE								
32	---------- ------ ---- ------ ---- ------ ---- ------								
33	1 SRK 175.00 0.00 175.00 0.00 175.00 0.00 175.00								
34	------ ---- ------ ---- ------ ---- ------								
35	FEES 175.00 0.00 175.00 0.00 175.00 0.00 175.00								
36	COSTS 17.75 0.00 17.75 0.00 17.75 0.00 17.75								
37	TOTAL 192.75 0.00 192.75 0.00 192.75 0.00 192.75								

Figure A-5. *A complex report after it was printed as text, opened as a spreadsheet, and assigned a monospaced font. As it's shown here, this spreadsheet cannot be parsed satisfactorily.*

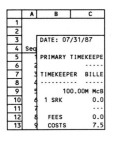

	A	B	C
1			
2			
3		DATE: 07/31/87	
4	Seq		
5	1	PRIMARY TIMEKEEPE	
6	2	-----	
7	3	TIMEKEEPER BILLE	
8	4	---------- -----	
9	5	100.00M McB	
10	6	1 SRK 0.0	
11	7	---	
12	8	FEES 0.0	
13	9	COSTS 7.5	

Figure A-6. *To parse the spreadsheet in Figure A-5, insert a new column A and create a data series in the column through the last row of data, as shown here at the top of the spreadsheet. After you sort the spreadsheet, this series lets you sort it back into its original sequence.*

3. Sort your data. First highlight the range from cell A5 to the bottom-right cell of the data to be sorted. Choose Data Sort, specify cell B5 as the first key, and then choose OK. Afterwards, your spreadsheet resembles the one in Figure A-7.

4. Parse the data. The spreadsheet in Figure A-7 shows that the data is sorted into large blocks with common dimensions. You can now parse each block as described earlier in this appendix. Rather than sorting some of the data, however, you might decide to delete it. In the spreadsheet in Figure A-7, for example, you probably would want to delete the rows of underlines shown in rows 7 through 9 and 29 through 30, the spaces shown in rows 36 through 38, and the page header shown in row 31.

5. Sort the data into its original sequence. To do so, highlight the range A5:J38 and then choose Data Sort. After you complete this step, your data is in its original sequence as a fully parsed and usable spreadsheet.

	A	B	C	D	E	F	G	H	I	J
1										
2										
3		DATE: 07/31/87		DETAIL RECEIPT ALLOCATION REPORT					PAGE: 1	
4	Seq				Steiner & Assoc TABS 3.3 Demo					
5	12						BILLED WIP:		75.00	
6	24				Steiner & Assoc TABS 3.3 Demo					
7	7		----	----	----	----	------		----	------
8	30		------	----	------	----	------		----	------
9	17		------	-----	------	-----	------		-----	------
10	2		------ MTD -----		------ YTD -----		------ TD ------			AMOUNT
11	26		------ MTD -----		------ YTD -----		------ TD ------			AMOUNT
12	5	100.00M McBride/John				RE: Miscellaneous work				
13	14	101.00M Barrett/Karen				RE: Apartment management				
14	22	102.00M Richardson/Harold				RE: Manage personal finances				
15	9	COSTS	7.55	0.00	7.55	0.00	120.87		0.00	120.87
16	32	COSTS	17.75	0.00	17.75	0.00	17.75		0.00	17.75
17	19	COSTS	134.75	0.00	134.75	0.00	134.75		0.00	134.75
18	10	FCHRG	154.79	0.00	154.79	0.00	154.79		0.00	154.79
19	8	FEES	0.00	0.00	0.00	0.00	507.00		0.00	507.00
20	31	FEES	175.00	0.00	175.00	0.00	175.00		0.00	175.00
21	18	FEES	584.00	50.00	584.00	50.00	584.00		50.00	534.00
22	11	TOTAL	162.34	0.00	162.34	0.00	782.66		0.00	782.66
23	33	TOTAL	192.75	0.00	192.75	0.00	192.75		0.00	192.75
24	20	TOTAL	718.75	50.00	718.75	50.00	718.75		50.00	668.75
25	6	1 SRK	0.00	0.00	0.00	0.00	507.00		0.00	507.00
26	15	1 SRK	25.00	2.14	25.00	2.14	25.00		2.14	22.86
27	29	1 SRK	175.00	0.00	175.00	0.00	175.00		0.00	175.00
28	16	2 SJM	559.00	47.86	559.00	47.86	559.00		47.86	511.14
29	4	----------	------	----	------	----	------		----	------
30	28	----------	------	----	------	----	------		----	------
31	23	DATE: 07/31/87		DETAIL RECEIPT ALLOCATION REPORT					PAGE: 2	
32	1	PRIMARY TIMEKEEPER:	1 TO 10					CATEGORY 1 TO 20		
33	25	PRIMARY TIMEKEEPER:	1 TO 10					CATEGORY 1 TO 20		
34	3	TIMEKEEPER	BILLED	PAID	BILLED	PAID	BILLED		PAID	DUE
35	27	TIMEKEEPER	BILLED	PAID	BILLED	PAID	BILLED		PAID	DUE
36	13									
37	21									
38	34									

Figure A-7. *The spreadsheet in Figure A-5 after adding column A and sorting the text using column B as the first key. Sorting tends to group the text into blocks of similar data that can be parsed easily. After you parse each block, use the numbers in column A to sort it back into its original sequence.*

Appendix B

A Summary of Common Microsoft Excel Operations

Operation	*Action and Explanation*
Aligning data	**Choose Format Alignment.** Aligns data in a cell or selected area. Your choices are: General, Left, Center, Right, and Fill.
Arranging documents	**Choose Window Arrange All.** Arranges all open documents so that they are visible on the screen. (If many documents are open, however, each document will be too small to use conveniently. When this is so, refer to Maximize.)
Array, entering	**Hold down Ctrl-Shift and press Enter.** Enters a formula as an array.
Borders	**Choose Format Border.** Draws borders in selected area. Your choices are Outline, Left, Right, Top, Bottom, and Shade.
Calculate All	**Press F9.** Recalculates all documents.
Calculate Cell	**Press F2 and then press Enter.** Recalculates a selected cell.
Calculate Document	**Press Shift-F9.** Recalculates the active document.

Operation	*Action and Explanation*
Calculate Range	**1. Select a range.** **2. Choose Formula Replace.** **3. Enter = in the Replace box, press Tab to move to the With box, enter =, and choose Replace All.** Recalculates a selected range. Because Microsoft Excel recalculates every cell in which Formula Replace makes a change and because all formulas begin with an equal sign, this approach recalculates the selected range by replacing an equal sign with an equal sign. (This method works only if you've selected more than one cell.)
Calculation modes	**Choose Options Calculation.** Lets you switch between manual and automatic calculation.
Center justification	(See: Aligning data.)
Closing spreadsheets	**Choose File Close.** Clears the document from memory, letting you save any changes before doing so.
Closing spreadsheets (shortcut)	**Press Ctrl-F4.** A shortcut for choosing File Close.
Colors, data	**1. Choose Format Number and then select a format.** **2. In the text box, type the color you want in square brackets in the space before the format characters for each data type, and then choose OK.** Specifies the color of data in cells. For example, the following format displays positive numbers as green, negative numbers as red, zeros as blue, and text as magenta: [Green]0.00;[Red]–0.00;[Blue]0.00;[Magenta]@
Colors, heading	**Choose Options Display and then select the color you want.** Specifies the color of gridlines and row-and-column headings.
Colors, screen	**1. Choose Run from the System menu and select Control Panel.** **2. Choose Preferences Screen Colors.** Lets you modify the colors of your menus, text, borders, scroll bar, title bar, and so on.
Column headings	(See: Headings, displayed; Headings, printed.)

Operation	*Action and Explanation*
Column width, changing	**Choose Format Column Width.** Sets the width of selected columns, using as a measurement the width of an unformatted numeric character.
Column, deleting	(See: Deleting cells.)
Column, hiding	(See: Hiding rows or columns.)
Column, selecting	(See: Moving the selection.)
Copy	**1. Select the source area and choose Edit Copy to copy the selected area to the clipboard.** **2. Select the top-left position of the destination area and select Edit Paste to copy the area from the clipboard.** Copies selected area from spreadsheet, formula bar, or dialog box to a spreadsheet, formula bar, or dialog box.
Copy (shortcut)	**1. Select the source area and press Ctrl-Ins to copy the selected area to the clipboard.** **2. Press Enter to paste the data and clear the clipboard.** Use this approach when copying from one spreadsheet to another. Because it clears the clipboard and cancels the marquee, it can make only one copy. Or: **2. Press Shift-Ins to paste the data and save the clipboard.** Use this approach when copying from a spreadsheet, formula bar, or dialog box to a spreadsheet, formula bar, or dialog box. Because it doesn't clear the clipboard, this approach can make multiple copies.
Copy duplicate formula	**Press Ctrl-' (apostrophe).** Copies an exact duplicate of the value or formula from the cell above into the formula bar. Or: **1. Highlight all or part of the contents of the formula bar.** **2. Press Ctrl-Ins to copy the selection to the clipboard.** **3. Move the pointer to where you want the copy.** **4. Press Shift-Ins to copy the selection from the clipboard.** Copies an exact duplicate of a value or formula to a cell, the formula bar, or a dialog box.

Operation	*Action and Explanation*
Copy while entering	**1. Highlight an area.** **2. Type in a formula or value.** **3. Press Ctrl-Enter.** Copies a formula or value to all cells in the highlighted area.
Cut and paste	(See: Move.)
Deleting cells	**Choose Edit Delete.** Deletes selected rows, columns, or cells from the spreadsheet. If you select entire rows or columns, this command deletes them directly. If you select any other type of area, it gives you the choice of moving cells up or left.
Deleting cells (shortcut)	**Press Ctrl-– (minus sign).** The shortcut alternative to Edit Delete.
Deleting data	**Press Del.** Erases the selected area of the spreadsheet.
Deleting documents	(See: Closing spreadsheets.)
Deleting files	(See: File, deleting.)
Directory, changing	(See: File, opening.)
Documents, closing all	(See: Files, closing all.)
Editing the formula bar	**Press Backspace.** Deletes the character to the left of the insertion point. **Press Del.** Deletes the selected area. **Press Shift-Del.** Moves the selection to the Clipboard. **Press Ctrl-Del.** Deletes from the insertion point or from the beginning of the selection to the end of the line. **Press Shift-Ins.** Pastes the clipboard data at the insertion point or over the selection. **Press Ctrl-Ins.** Copies the selection to the clipboard.

Operation	*Action and Explanation*
Erase	(See: Deleting data.)
Extracting data	**Choose Data Extract.** Extracts from a Database range to an Extract range the data specified by a Criteria range.
File, deleting	**Choose File Delete.** Deletes selected files from your disk.
File, naming	**Choose File Save As.** Saves the spreadsheet by the name you specify.
File, naming (shortcut)	**Press F12 (or Alt-F2).** A shortcut to choosing File Save As.
File, new	**Choose File New.** The standard command for creating a new spreadsheet.
File, new (shortcut)	**Press F11 (or Alt-F1).** Creates a new chart. **Press Shift-F11 (or Alt-Shift-F1).** Creates a new spreadsheet. **Press Ctrl-F11 (or Ctrl-Alt-F1).** Creates a new macro sheet.
File, opening	**Choose File Open.** The standard command for retrieving a saved file. Also, because Microsoft Excel always suggests the path used by the last File Open command, use this command to specify your file directory.
File, opening (shortcut)	**Press Ctrl-F12 (or Ctrl-Alt-F2).** A shortcut to choosing File Open.
File, saving	**Choose File Save.** Saves a file using the current name.
File, saving (shortcut)	**Press Shift-F12 (or Alt-Shift-F2).** A shortcut to choosing File Save.
Files, closing all	**While holding down Shift, choose File Close All with the mouse. With the keyboard, press the slash (/) key or Alt key and hold down Shift while you choose File Close All.** Closes all open documents.

Operation	*Action and Explanation*
Font selection	**Choose Format Font.** Offers a selection of four font options.
Font selection (shortcut)	**Press Ctrl-1.** **Press Ctrl-2.** **Press Ctrl-3.** **Press Ctrl-4.** Directly selects font option 1, 2, 3, or 4.
Fonts, changing	**Choose Format Font and select Fonts.** Lets you assign a new font to one of the four font options.
Formats, number	**Choose Format Number.** Assigns commas, colors, decimal values, etc. to numbers and text.
Formats, number (shortcut)	**Press Ctrl-~ (tilde).** Assigns the General format. **Press Ctrl-! (exclamation point).** Assigns the 0.00 format. **Press Ctrl-@ (at sign).** Assigns the h:mm AM/PM format. **Press Ctrl-# (pound sign).** Assigns the d-mmm-yy format. **Press Ctrl-$ (dollar sign).** Assigns the $#,##0.00 ;($#,##0.00) format. **Press Ctrl-% (percent sign).** Assigns the 0% format. **Press Ctrl-^ (caret).** Assigns the 0.00E+00 format.
Gridlines, displayed	**Choose Options Display and select Gridlines.** Removes or sets gridlines on the screen.
Gridlines, printed	**Choose File Page Setup and select Gridlines.** Removes or sets gridlines when printing.
Headings, displayed	**Choose Options Display and select Row & Column Headings.** Removes or sets row and column headings on the screen.

Operation	*Action and Explanation*
Headings, printed	**Choose File Page Setup and select Row & Column Headings.** Removes or sets row and column headings when printing.
Hiding cells	**1. Choose Format Number.** **2. Press Alt-F to highlight the input box.** **3. Enter: *;;;* (three semicolons).** Creates a custom format that hides all data entered in a cell. Use two semicolons in the format to hide numbers but display text. See "Zeros, hiding locally" to hide 0 values. Also, see pages 310 and 311 of the *Microsoft Excel Reference Guide* for a discussion of the Hidden option of the Formula Cell Protection command.
Hiding documents	**1. Activate the document you want to hide.** **2. Choose Window Hide.** **3. To unhide the document, choose Window Unhide.** Hides or unhides open documents.
Hiding rows or columns	**1. Select the rows or columns you want to hide.** **2. Choose Format Row Height or Format Column Width and then enter 0.** **3. To unhide, first select the hidden rows or columns. To do so, press the F5 (Goto) key, and either specify any area within the hidden rows or columns or select an area that spans the hidden rows or columns. Then press Enter. Next, choose Format Row Height or Format Column Width and specify a number greater than 0.** Hides or unhides rows or columns.
Inserting cells	**Choose Edit Insert.** Inserts selected rows, columns, or cells in the spreadsheet. If you select entire rows or columns, this command inserts them directly. If you select any other type of area, it gives you a choice of moving cells right or down.
Inserting cells (shortcut)	**Press Ctrl-+ (plus sign).** Shortcut alternative to Edit Insert for inserting rows, columns, or cells.
Left justification	(See: Aligning data.)
Maximize	**Press Ctrl-F10.** Enlarges the active document to the full size of your display. Press Ctrl-F10 again to restore the document to its previous size.

Operation	*Action and Explanation*
Memory, checking	**Choose Help About.** Reports on the amount of computer memory available.
Move	**1. Choose Edit Cut to move the selected area to the clipboard.** **2. Choose Edit Paste to copy the selection to its new position.** The standard command for moving data or formulas within or between spreadsheets.
Move (shortcut)	**1. Press Shift-Delete to move the selection to the clipboard.** **2. Press Shift-Ins to copy the selection to the new position.**
Moving in a spreadsheet	**Press Home.** Moves the pointer to the start of the row containing the active cell. **Press Ctrl-Home.** Moves to the top-left cell of the spreadsheet. **Press End.** Moves to the end of the data in the row with the active cell. **Press Ctrl-End.** Moves to the bottom-right cell. **Press Ctrl-direction key.** Moves by one block of data left, right, top, or down. **Press the F5 (Goto) key and then select a range name, type a cell address, or type the name of a dynamically defined range name. (See Appendix C.)** Selects the cell or range specified.
Moving the selection	**Press F8.** Turns the Extend mode on or off. **Press Ctrl-Spacebar.** Selects the entire column of those in the selected range. **Press Shift-Spacebar.** Selects the entire row of those in the selected range. **Press Ctrl-Shift-Spacebar.** Selects the entire spreadsheet.

Operation	*Action and Explanation*
Moving the selection *(continued)*	**Hold down the Shift key while you press a direction key.** When combined with keys for moving around the spreadsheet, the Shift key extends the selection rather than moving the pointer. For example, Ctrl-End moves the pointer to the bottom-right cell of the spreadsheet, but Ctrl-Shift-End extends the selection to that cell. Similarly, Shift-Home extends the selection to the left of the spreadsheet. In other words, when combined with these other keys, pressing the Shift key is equivalent to activating the Extend mode with the F8 key, extending the selection, and then deactivating the Extend mode.
Moving within a selection	**Press Enter.** Moves down one cell in a selection. **Press Shift-Enter.** Moves up one cell in a selection. **Press Tab.** Moves right one cell in a selection. **Press Shift-Tab.** Moves left one cell in a selection. **Press Ctrl-. (period).** Moves clockwise to the next corner of the selected area. **Press Ctrl-Tab.** In a multiple selection, moves to next area. **Press Ctrl-Shift-Tab.** In a multiple selection, moves to previous area.
Naming a spreadsheet	(See: File, naming.)
New spreadsheet	(See: File, new.)
Panes	(See: Window panes.)
Paste	**Choose Edit Paste.** Copies contents of clipboard to a specified location.

Operation	*Action and Explanation*
Paste (shortcut)	**Press Shift-Ins.** A shortcut to choosing Edit Paste.
Path, file	(See: File, opening.)
Print range, resetting	**1. Select the entire spreadsheet.** **2. Choose Options Set Print Area.** Or: **1. Choose Formula Define Name.** **2. Delete the range Print_Area.** Use either of these methods to reset the print area.
Print range, specifying	**Choose Options Set Print Area.** Specifies the selected area as the print area and assigns the range name Print_Area.
Printing	**Choose File Print.** The standard command for printing a document.
Printing (shortcut)	**Press Ctrl-Shift-F12 (or Ctrl-Alt-Shift-F2).** A shortcut to choosing File Print.
Printing gridlines	(See: Gridlines, printed.)
Printing page breaks	**1. Select the cell below or to the right of the cell where you want the page break. (That is, for horizontal page breaks, always select a cell in column A.)** **2. Choose Options Set Page Break.** **3. To remove a page break, select the cell used to set it and then choose Options Remove Page Break.** Sets manual page breaks for printing documents.
Printing titles	**1. Select the entire rows, columns, or both containing the text you want to use for titles.** **2. Choose Options Set Print Titles. (When you do so, Microsoft Excel names the selection Print_Titles.)** **3. Do not include the print titles as part of your print area.** **4. To reset print titles, delete the range Print_Titles.** Specifies titles that appear at the top, left side, or both of each printed page.

Operation	*Action and Explanation*
Quit	**Press Alt-F4.** In Windows terminology, this keystroke combination closes the application window. But in plain English, it quits Microsoft Excel.
Range, deleting	**1. Choose Formula Define Name.** **2. Select the name you want to delete.** **3. Choose the Delete button or press Alt-D.** Deletes specified range names.
Range, naming	**Choose Formula Define Name.** Defines a name for a single cell range, value, or formula.
Range, naming (shortcut)	**Press Ctrl-F3.** A shortcut to choosing Formula Define Name.
Ranges, naming	**Choose Formula Create Names.** Names areas of a spreadsheet using text at the edge of the area as names for the ranges.
Ranges, naming (shortcut)	**Press Ctrl-Shift-F3.** A shortcut to choosing Formula Create Names.
Repeating characters	**Choose Format Alignment and select Fill.** Repeats the contents of a cell until it's filled. To create a true underline, as opposed to a border, enter a single hyphen (minus sign) in a cell and then choose this command.
Retrieving a file	(See: File, opening.)
Right justification	(See: Aligning data.)
Row headings	(See Headings, displayed; Headings, printed.)
Row height, changing	**Choose Format Row Height.** Sets height of selected rows, in points.
Rows, deleting	(See: Deleting cells.)
Rows, hiding	(See: Hiding rows or columns.)
Rows, selecting	(See: Moving the selection.)
Shade	**Choose Format Border and select Shade.** Shades the selected area of the spreadsheet.

Operation	*Action and Explanation*
Sorting	**Choose Data Sort.** Sorts the selected area by either row or column, using up to three sort keys.
Titles, in the worksheet	(See: Window panes.)
Underline	(See: Borders; Repeating characters.)
Values, in a range	**1. Select the range of formulas you want to change into values.** **2. Press Ctrl-Ins to copy this range to the clipboard.** **3. Choose Edit Paste Special, select Values, and choose OK.** This method changes a range of formulas into values.
Values, in a single cell	**1. Select the single cell you want to change into a value.** **2. Press F2 (Edit) and then F9 (Calc) to convert the formula in the formula bar into a value.** **3. To enter this value, press Enter; or to leave the formula as it was, press Esc.** This procedure changes a single formula into its value.
Window panes	**1. Press Alt-- (hyphen) and select Split.** **2. Use the Right or Left direction key to move the gray lines to where you want to divide your window.** **3. Press Enter.** **4. Press F6 to move between panes.** **5. Use the same approach to reset the windows, moving the gray lines back to the top and left borders of the sheet.** Lets you open multiple windows in one spreadsheet. (Page 217 of the *Microsoft Excel Reference Guide* explains how to open window panes with a mouse.)
Worksheet, new	(See: File, new.)
Zeros, hiding globally	**Choose Options Display and select Zero Values.** Switches the display of 0 values off or on throughout the document.

Operation	*Action and Explanation*
Zeros, hiding locally	**1. Choose Format Number and then select a format.** **2. In the text box, type a semicolon immediately after the format characters for the negative value, and then choose OK.** This approach uses custom formats to hide zeros. For example, these formats hide 0 values and display positive and negative values, as well as text: 0.00 ;(0.00); 0%;–0%; If the format you choose does not include format characters for negative values, you must add these characters; otherwise, you will hide negative values. For example, these formats hide negative values and display positive values, zeros, and text: 0.00; 0%; Refer to the entry "Hiding cells" in this appendix for information about creating a custom format that hides all data.

Appendix C

Defining Range Names Dynamically

It's a good idea to include a blank cell at the top and bottom of a SUM range. In this way, you can insert rows of data above the first value in a column and below the last value, while keeping all data within the SUM range. This is an example of a simple dynamic range definition; it expands and contracts as you insert or delete rows of data in your spreadsheet. This common approach works well because the SUM function assigns the value 0 to the blank cells when it adds a column.

But array formulas aren't as forgiving as SUM formulas. Array formulas will not assign the value 0 to blank cells; instead, blank cells included in an array often generate the #VALUE! error value shown for Formula 1 in Figure C-1. The error value is a safety feature because if array formulas were to treat blank cells at the top and bottom as 0 values, they would return incorrect results. Array formulas, therefore, must refer to ranges that contain only data.

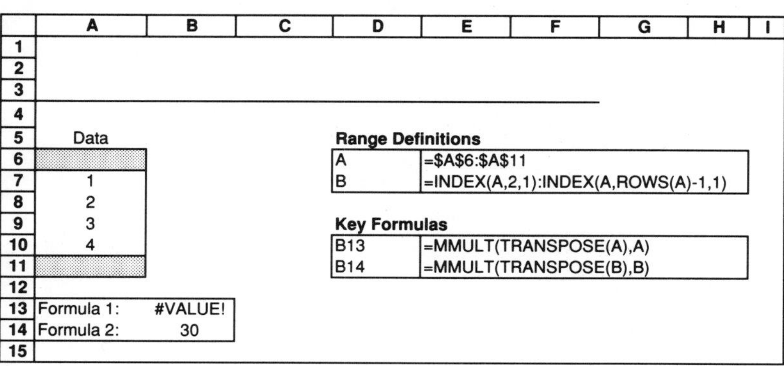

	A	B
5	Data	
6		
7	1	
8	2	
9	3	
10	4	
11		
12		
13	Formula 1:	#VALUE!
14	Formula 2:	30

Range Definitions

A	=$A$6:$A$11
B	=INDEX(A,2,1):INDEX(A,ROWS(A)-1,1)

Key Formulas

B13	=MMULT(TRANSPOSE(A),A)
B14	=MMULT(TRANSPOSE(B),B)

Figure C-1. *How to define range names dynamically.*

Solve this problem by using dynamic array definitions. To do so, define two ranges. Define one range to include the top and bottom blank cells, as you normally would; range A illustrates this method. Define the second range to be one cell down from the top border and one cell up from the bottom border, as in range B. Therefore, as you insert rows anywhere between the shaded borders, range A adjusts as you expect. But range B, which uses A as a reference, automatically adjusts as well. Range B adjusts, in other words, to the correct dimensions of your actual data. Formula 2 illustrates the result, correctly returning the sum of the squared values in the column.

When you enter a dynamic range definition, it's always a good idea to check that you've defined the range you intend. To do so, first press the F5 (Goto) key. When the Goto dialog box appears, you will *not* see any dynamic range names listed; Microsoft Excel doesn't display any ranges defined by formulas. Even so, when you type the name of the range and then press Enter, Microsoft Excel highlights the range you've defined.

As you use dynamic range definitions, other applications will occur to you. Figure 7-10 on page 342, for example, ties the definitions of dynamic arrays to the date value in a cell. As the date increases, each dynamic array expands in size, which automatically increases the data available to hundreds of formulas within the spreadsheet.

Appendix D

A Guide to Linear Regression Formulas

This appendix presents an updated version of a guide that I've used for more than ten years. I first created it when, as an MBA student, I was frustrated because each textbook seemed to use different symbols and formulas to calculate linear regression statistics. Finally, I put together this guide, which ignores academic foolishness and simply shows how to calculate these statistics using the few building blocks shown.

Notice that the guide offers a number of alternative formulas. I've included these for two reasons. First, an alternative formula often provides a more intuitive sense of the calculation than does the preferred formula. For example, the preferred formula for "the sum of the squared deviations from the mean of X" is =VARP(X)*n. Although this formula calculates quickly, the alternative array formula =SUM((X–AvgX)^2) expresses more clearly what you want, even though it takes slightly longer to calculate.

Second, if possible, you'll want to produce a statistic in terms of the other statistics you've already calculated in a spreadsheet. Figure 7-5, for example, uses the last alternative shown in this guide to calculate the t statistic in terms of Sxx, Syy, and Sxy. The other two formulas for the t statistic in this guide use values that weren't readily available in that particular spreadsheet.

Notice also in the guide that the symbol for the correlation coefficient is "r." (with a period), not "r". Microsoft Excel won't allow the range names R, r, C, or c because in R1C1 mode, the program interprets these letters as specifying rows or columns. This presents a problem because r and r^2 are well-known symbols used in statistics. Therefore, to get around the difficulty, I used the name "r." for the correlation coefficient.

BUILDING BLOCKS			
Independent Variable	X		
Dependent Variable	Y		
Mean Value of X	AvgX	=AVERAGE(X)	
Mean Value of Y	AvgY	=AVERAGE(Y)	
Number of Observations	n	=COUNT(X)	
Sum of Squared Deviations from AvgX	Sxx	=VARP(X)*n	
Alternative Formula	Sxx	=SUM((X-AvgX)^2)	{array formula}
Sum of Squared Deviations from AvgY	Syy	=VARP(Y)*n	
Alternative Formula	Syy	=SUM((Y-AvgY)^2)	{array formula}
Sum of X Deviations Times Y Deviations	Sxy	=Sxx*LINEST(Y,X)	
Alternative Formula	Sxy	=SUM((X-AvgX)*(Y-AvgY))	{array formula}

CORRELATION		
Correlation Coefficient	r.	=Sxy/(Sxx*Syy)^0.5
Coefficient of Determination		=r.^2
Standard Deviation of Y Given X	s	=((Syy*(1-r.^2))/(n-2))^0.5
(Also called the Std Error of Estimate)		
Variance of Y Given X		=s^2

REGRESSION COEFFICIENTS		
Slope	b	=LINEST(Y,X)
Alternative Formula	b	=Sxy/Sxx
Constant	a	=INDEX(LINEST(Y,X),1,2)
Alternative Formula	a	=AvgY-b*AvgX
Standard Deviation of Slope (b)	sb	=s/Sxx^0.5
Standard Deviation of Constant (a)	sa	=s*(1/n+AvgX^2/Sxx))^0.5

ANALYSIS OF VARIANCE (ANOVA)		
Sum of Squares:		
Regression	SSR	=Syy*r.^2
Errors	SSE	=Syy*(1−r.^2)
Total	SST	=Syy
Alternative Formula	SST	=SSR+SSE
Degrees of Freedom (df):		
Regression		=1
Errors		=n−2
Total		=n−1
Mean Sum of Squares:		
Regression	MSR	=SSR
Errors	MSE	=SSE/(n−2)

TEST OF SIGNIFICANCE		
F Statistic with df = (1, n−2)	F	=SSR/s^2
Alternative Formula	F	=MSR/MSE
t Statistic with df = (n−2)	t	=F^0.5
Alternative Formula	t	=b/sb
Alternative Formula	t	=((Sxy^2*(n−2))/(Sxx*Syy−Sxy^2))^0.5

Appendix E

Speeding Up Calculations When Using Name Definitions

The formulas in ranges A and B of the spreadsheet in Figure E-1 both calculate the sum of the squares of the values 1 through 1,000. Even though the formulas are identical, each reference to range A calculates immediately, while each reference to range B takes roughly four seconds to calculate, depending on your computer.

	A	B	C	D	E	F	G	H
1								
2								
3								
4								
5				**Range Definitions**				
6	Range A			A	=$A$7			
7	333833500			B	=SUM(ROW($1:$1000)^2)			
8								
9	Formula			**Formulas**				
10	References			A7	=SUM(ROW($1:$1000)^2)			
11	333833500			A11	=A			
12	333833500			A12	=B			
13								
14								

Figure E-1. *How to speed up calculations when using name definitions.*

The difference between these ranges is that range name A refers to the formula contained in cell A7; range name B contains the formula itself. Each time range name B appears in a formula, the program recalculates the value of B. But each time range name A appears in a formula, the program merely takes the value contained in cell A7.

Therefore, to speed spreadsheet calculations, put into your spreadsheet the range formulas that don't have to be recalculated for each reference. Doing so, however, frequently creates the clutter of side calculations in your spreadsheet. You must therefore make a trade-off: increased speed *vs* increased clutter.

INDEX

References to illustrations are in italics.

Special Characters

A

E

J–K

L

M

N

O

P

Q

R

S

Y–Z

Charles W. Kyd

Spreadsheet expert Charles W. Kyd spent 10 years as chief financial officer for several fast-growing manufacturers and start-up and turn-around companies. He has also worked to develop accounting systems for companies such as Arthur Young and Hewlett-Packard. Kyd left Arthur Young in 1987 to devote his time to writing, teaching, and consulting. He is a regular columnist for both *Inc.* and *LOTUS* magazines. In addition, he is the author of *Financial Modeling Using Lotus 1-2-3*, published by Osborne/McGraw-Hill. Kyd lives with his family in Seattle, Washington.

The manuscript for this book was prepared and submitted to Microsoft Press in electronic form. Text files were processed and formatted using Microsoft Word.

Cover design by Ted Mader and Associates
Interior text design by Darcie S. Furlan
Principal typography by Carol Luke

Text composition by Microsoft Press in Garamond with display in Helvetica Black, using the Magna composition system and the Linotronic 300 laser imagesetter.

Disk Order Form

For all spreadsheets, macros, and graphs presented in this book

Disk	Chapters	Description	Quantity
1	Chapters 1 & 2 & Appendixes	(Basic Statements, General Ledger, Checkbook, Reference Guide, Templates for Loading Reports....).............	________
2	Chapters 3 & 4	(Currency Translation, Cash to Accrual, Consolidations, A/R Analysis, A/R Collections Forecast....)............	________
3	Chapters 5 & 6	(Financial Calculator, Amortization Schedules, Notes Payable Schedule, Sales Reporting & Analysis....)	________
4	Chapters 7 & 8	(Single & Multiple Regression, Time-Series Analysis, Budget Reporting, Forecasting Labor & Materials....).....	________
5	Chapters 9 & 10	(Cash Flow Reporting, Forecasting, & Analysis; ROI Analysis; Break-Even Analysis; Variance Reporting....) ...	________

Disk format desired:

☐ 5.25-inch ☐ 3.5-inch

☐ Send me information on other books and templates by Charley Kyd. My special interests are:

____

____

____

____

Total quantity ordered .... ________

Price per disk $20.00

Subtotal .... ________

Washington residents add 8.1% sales tax ($1.62 per disk)... ________

Plus first-class shipping and handling within U.S. and Canada.................................... $ 5.00

For other foreign orders add $4.00. For overnight orders in U.S., add $10.00; in Canada, add $18.00. .... ________

Grand total (U.S. dollars) .... ________

Order Information

Method of payment: ☐ Check ☐ Visa ☐ MasterCard ☐ Money Order

CARD NUMBER ________ EXP. DATE ________

CARDHOLDER'S NAME ________

SHIP-TO NAME ________ TITLE ________

COMPANY ________

SHIP-TO ADDRESS ________ (Business? ☐ Home? ☐)

CITY ________ STATE ________ ZIP ________

BUSINESS TELEPHONE NUMBER ________ HOME TELEPHONE NUMBER ________

Mail orders to:

CashMaster Business Systems, I
12345 Lake City Way NE
Suite 220
Seattle, WA 98125

Or call:

800-999-4KYD
206-367-8808
(Staffed during normal business hours, Pacifi